THE CHILD WELFARE CHALLENGE

MODERN APPLICATIONS OF SOCIAL WORK
An Aldine de Gruyter Series of Texts and Monographs

SERIES EDITOR
James K. Whittaker, *University of Washington*

Paul Adams and Kristine E. Nelson (eds.), **Reinventing Human Services: Community- and Family-Centred Practice**

Ralph E. Anderson and Irl Carter, with Gary Lowe, **Human Behavior in the Social Environment: A Social Systems Approach** (Fifth Edition)

Richard P. Barth, Mark Courtney, Jill Duerr Berrick, and Vicky Albert, **From Child Abuse to Permanency Planning: Child Welfare Services Pathways and Placements**

Gale Burford and Joe Hudson, **Family Group Conferencing: New Directions in Community-Centred Child and Family Practice**

Dana Christensen, Jeffrey Todahl, and William C. Barrett, **Solution-Based Casework: An Introduction to Clinical and Case Management Skills in Casework Practice**

Marie Connolly with Margaret McKenzie, **Effective Participatory Practice: Family Group Conferencing in Child Protection**

Kathleen Ell and Helen Northen, **Families and Health Care: Psychosocial Practice**

Marian F. Fatout, **Models for Change in Social Group Work**

Mark W. Fraser, Peter J. Pecora, and David A. Haapala, **Families in Crisis: The Impact of Intensive Family Preservation Services**

James Garbarino, **Children and Families in the Social Environment** (Second Edition)

James Garbarino and Associates, **Special Children—Special Risks: The Maltreatment of Children with Disabilities**

James Garbarino and Associates, **Troubled Youth, Troubled Families: Understanding Families At-Risk for Adolescent Maltreatment**

Roberta R. Greene, **Human Behavior Theory: A Diversity Framework**

Roberta R. Greene, **Human Behavior Theory and Social Work Practice** (Second Edition)

Roberta R. Greene, **Social Work with the Aged and Their Families** (Second Edition)

André Ivanoff, Betty J. Blythe, and Tony Tripodi, **Involuntary Clients in Social Work Practice: A Research-Based Approach**

Susan P. Kemp, James K. Whittaker, and Elizabeth M. Tracy, **Person-Environment Practice: The Social Ecology of Interpersonal Helping**

Jill Kinney, David A. Haapala, and Charlotte Booth, **Keeping Families Together: The Homebuilders™ Model**

Gary R. Lowe and P. Nelson Reid, **The Professionalization of Poverty: Social Work and the Poor in the Twentieth Century**

Robert M. Moroney and Judy Krysik, **Social Policy and Social Work: Critical Essays on the Welfare State** (Second Edition)

Peter J. Pecora, Mark W. Fraser, Kristine Nelson, Jacqueline McCroskey, and William Meezan, **Evaluating Family-Based Services**

Peter J. Pecora, James K. Whittaker, Anthony N. Maluccio, and Richard P. Barth, with Robert D. Plotnick, **The Child Welfare Challenge: Policy, Practice, and Research** (Second Edition)

Norman A. Polansky, **Integrated Ego Psychology**

John R. Schuerman, Tina L. Rzepnicki, and Julia H. Littell, **Putting Families First: An Experience in Family Preservation**

Madeleine R. Stoner, **The Civil Rights of Homeless People: Law, Social Policy, and Social Work Practice**

Albert E. Trieschman, James K. Whittaker, and Larry K. Brendtro, **The Other 23 Hours: Child-Care Work with Emotionally Disturbed Children in a Therapeutic Milieu**

Harry H. Vorrath and Larry K. Brendtro, **Positive Peer Culture** (Second Edition)

Betsy S. Vourlekis and Roberta R. Greene (eds.), **Social Work Case Management**

James K. Whittaker and Associates, **Reaching High-Risk Families: Intensive Family Preservation in Human Services**

THE CHILD WELFARE CHALLENGE
Policy, Practice, and Research

SECOND EDITION

Peter J. Pecora, James K. Whittaker,
Anthony N. Maluccio, and Richard P. Barth,
with Robert D. Plotnick

ALDINE DE GRUYTER
New York

About the Authors

Peter J. Pecora Manager of Research for the Casey Family Programs, and Professor, School of Social Work, University of Washington.

James K. Whittaker Professor, School of Social Work, University of Washington.

Anthony N. Maluccio Professor, Graduate School of Social Work, Boston College.

Richard P. Barth Frank Daniels Distinguished Professor, School of Social Work, North Carolina, Chapel Hill.

Robert D. Plotnick Professor, Daniel J. Evans School of Public Affairs and Adjunct Professor, School of Social Work, University of Washington.

ALDINE DE GRUYTER
A division of Walter de Gruyter, Inc.
200 Saw Mill River Road
Hawthorne, New York 10532

The paper used in this publication meets the minimum requirements of American National Standard for Information Sciences—Permanence of Paper Printed Library Material, ANSI Z 39.48-1984. ∞

Library of Congress Cataloging-in-Publication Data

The child welfare challenge : policy, practice, and research / Peter J. Pecora ... [et al.].— 2nd ed.
    p.   cm. — (Modern applications of social work)
  Rev. ed. of: The child welfare challenge / Peter J. Pecora, James K. Whittaker, Anthony N. Maluccio, with Richard P. Barth and Robert D. Plotnick. c1992.
    Includes bibliographical references and index.
    ISBN 0-202-36125-X (cloth : alk. paper) — ISBN 0-202-36126-8 (paper: alk. paper)
    1. Child welfare—United States. I. Pecora, Peter J. II. Series

HV741 .C512 2000
362.7—dc21

                                         00-035534

Manufactured in the United States of America

Contents

Preface   xi
Acknowledgments   xv

1   The Purpose and Goals of Child Welfare Services

Child Welfare Services as a Critical and Changing Resource
    for Families in America   1
Philosophical Underpinnings of Child Welfare Services   4
Mission and Goals of Child Welfare Services   8
Key Goals and Outcomes for Child Welfare Services   9
Significant Costs and Complex Family Situations:
    Crucial System Challenges   13
Practice Transformations   14
Conclusion   20
Notes   20
For Further Information   20

2   Understanding the Policy Context for Child Welfare

Introduction   21
What Is Policy?   22
Some Population Statistics from the 1990 Decennial Census   25
Family Issues and Trends   26
Major National Legislation That Has Helped Shape
    Child Welfare Services   29
Substance Abuse, Imprisonment of Women, and HIV:
    Policy Implications   52
Opportunities for Policy Practice   57
Conclusion   60
Notes   61
For Further Information   62

3   **Child and Family-Centered Services**

Conceptual Framework for Family-Centered Practice   65
Applying a Family-Centered Practice   78
Establishing a Continuum of Services   81
Conclusion   88
Notes   92
For Further Information   93

4   **Economic Security for Families with Children**

The Economic Status of Families with Children   96
Child Maltreatment and Other Consequences of Poverty   102
Policies to Reduce Child Poverty   104
Program Challenge: Doing a Better Job of Reducing Poverty
    and Increasing Economic Security among Children   121
Conclusion   124
Notes   125
For Further Information   126

5   **Child Maltreatment Incidence, the Casework Process,
     and Services for Physically Abused Children**

Introduction   128
Conceptualizing Child Maltreatment   128
Definition and Incidence of Child Maltreatment
    in the United States   131
Who Is Served? Current Statistical Data on Child Abuse
    and Neglect   134
Child Maltreatment Severity and Reporting   140
Child Protective Services as a Major Program Area
    in Child Welfare   141
Intake in Child Welfare and Child Protective Services   143
Theoretical Perspectives Regarding the Contributing Factors
    to Child Maltreatment   147
Physical Abuse   151
Treatment of Physical Abuse   157
Program Challenges   160
Recommendations for CPS Program Improvement   163
Conclusion   168
Notes   168
For Further Information   169

6   Sexual Abuse: Prevention and Treatment

Introduction   171
Treatment of Sexual Abuse   183
Current Program Challenges   191
Conclusion   193
Notes   193
For Further Information   194

7   Child Neglect and Psychological Maltreatment

Physical Neglect   196
Nonorganic Failure to Thrive as a Special Case of Neglect   209
Psychological Maltreatment   215
Current Policy, Practice, and Research Issues in Neglect
    and Psychological Maltreatment   226
Conclusion   227
Notes   228
For Further Information   228

**8   Family Support and Other Preventive Services
       Related to Child Welfare**

Introduction   229
A Framework for Prevention   230
A Program Typology of Family Support and
    Family-Based Services   231
Family Resource, Support, and Education Services   239
Conclusion   258
Notes   261
For Further Information   261

9   Family-Based and Intensive Family Preservation Services

Introduction   262
Family-Based Services   264
History of Family-Based Services   265
Intervention Components   275
Selected Program Implementation Challenges
    in Family-Based and Intensive Family
    Preservation Services   291

Conclusion   294
Notes   295
For Further Information   296

10   **Family Foster Care**

Evolution of Family Foster Care   298
Definition and Purpose of Family Foster Care   303
Children and Youth in Family Foster Care and Their Families   305
Professionalization of Foster Parents   314
Training of Social Workers and Foster Parents   318
Effectiveness of Services   319
Current Status of Family Foster Care   324
Conclusion   326
Notes   327
For Further Information   328

11   **Family Reunification**

An Expanded Definition of Family Reunification   330
Underlying Principles and Guidelines   332
Family Reunification Competencies   335
Effectiveness of Family Reunification Services   338
Kinship Care   347
The Reunification of Very Young Children from Foster Care   355
Recurring Issues and Dilemmas   359
Conclusion   360
Notes   361
For Further Information   361

12   **Adoption**

Introduction   363
Major Adoption Legislation   369
Current Adoption Practice   378
Model Practices and Programs   391
Current Program Challenges   402
Conclusion   403
For Further Information   404

13   Residential Group Care Services

The Ambivalence Toward Group Child Care
    as a Helping Service   406
The Research Base for Group Child Care   411
Varieties of Residential Services   419
Future Challenges for Residential Child and Youth
    Care Services   426
Conclusion   429

14   Organizational Requisites for Child Welfare Services

Introduction   431
Establishing a Clear Agency Mission, Philosophy,
    and Program Objectives   433
Recruitment, Selection, and Training of Child
    Welfare Personnel   437
Challenges to Professionalizing Child Welfare Staff   439
Specifying Measurable Performance Criteria
    and Appraisal Methods   447
Evaluation of Services   448
Providing Quality Supervision   450
Addressing Organizational and Worker Liability   454
Conclusion   456
Notes   456
For Further Information   457

Appendix A: Special Issues in Child Abuse and Neglect

Historical Overview of CPS in the United States   458
Child Abuse and Neglect   461
Special Groups and Child Maltreatment   467
CPS Intake Challenges   469
Risk Assessment Concepts and Issues   476
Cultural Issues in Child Protective Services   480
Conclusion   482

References   485
Subject Index   569
Author Index   585

Preface

PURPOSE

Within a historical and contemporary context, this book examines major policy, practice, and research issues as they jointly shape current child welfare practice and possible future directions. In addition to describing the major challenges facing the child welfare field, the book highlights some of the service innovations that have been developed, as these could be used to help address some of these challenges.

In "child welfare," our primary focus is on families and children whose primary recourse to services has been through publicly funded agencies. In particular, we will consider those historical areas of service—foster care and adoptions, in-home family-centered services, child-protective services, and residential services—in which social work has a legitimate, long-standing, and important role and mission. We lay no claim to comprehensiveness, and many areas of practice such as day care, and early intervention invite further exploration. Readers also should be conscious of the many other fields of practice in which child and family services are provided or that involve substantial numbers of social work programs, such as services to adolescent parents, child mental health, and juvenile justice agencies.

ORGANIZATION OF CONTENT

The book discusses the major policy, practice, and research issues as they jointly shape current child welfare practice and possible future directions. Each chapter describes how policy initiatives and research data can or should influence program design and implementation. In general, each chapter will follow the same format, with an attempt to highlight historical milestones while describing some of the central policy and program issues within a context of the major research findings in that area. Program challenges and future directions are discussed, along with suggested readings for further information. In each area, we hope to show how practice *has* changed in response to policy initiatives and empirical findings and what challenges lie ahead. After describing the mission, goals, and key outcomes of child welfare in Chapter 1, key demographic trends, laws, and other policies that shape child welfare services are discussed in Chapter 2.

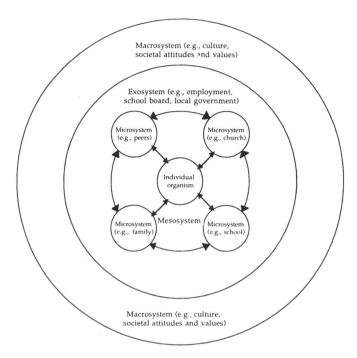

Figure 1. The levels of the Ecological System. Adapted by Hefferman, J., Shuttlesworth. J., & Ambroseno, R. (1988). From Garbarino J. (1982), *Children & Families in the Social Environment,* NY: Aldine Publishing Company.

A number of important perspectives are being synthesized to move the field to a more effective service paradigm—one of "family-centered child welfare practice" that builds on ecological, competence, developmental, and permanency planning perspectives. Discussed more fully in Chapter 3, this paradigm illustrates how children and families influence and are influenced by the multiple environments of family, neighborhood, school, and workplace—as well as society. Presented in Figure 1 is one example of an ecological diagram, which portrays the complex family—environment relationships to which child welfare practitioners must be sensitive. Thus, competence-based, developmental, and permanency perspectives that shape practice in turn are influenced in part by the ecology of the family's living situation. These perspectives are part of an ever-evolving knowledge base in which theory, research, and "practice wisdom" all inform program design and practice.

As illustrated in Figure 1, child welfare practitioners and the families they serve are affected by the larger social contexts in which they interact. In America, this social context includes values that sometimes encourage parents to view children as property, without rights as individuals. In addition, family services and client self-improvements are often hindered by oppression in its various forms: institutional racism, sexism, and discrimination against individuals according to their religious beliefs, sexual orientation, and handicapping conditions (for example, see Bricker-Jenkins, Hooyman, & Gottlieb, 1991; Brissett-Chapman & Issacs-Shockley, 1997; Pinderhughes, 1989). Child welfare practitioners must be cognizant of these conditions and incorporate strategies for helping clients overcome discrimination into their case plans if long-term success is to be achieved. One of the requisites for developing such case plans is a knowledge of the cultural issues related to that family, i.e., staff members must be "culturally competent" (Cross, Bazron, Dennis, & Isaacs, 1989). These practice competencies require specialized training and practice skills. How some of these contextual issues affect service delivery in various program areas will also be highlighted throughout the book.

Child and family well-being are inextricably linked with family income. In Chapter 4 Robert Plotnick outlines the major economic security issues facing the United States today, and provides some contrasting data from other countries. Readers will note the considerable amount of attention paid to child abuse and neglect (Chapters 5 through 7 and Appendix A). Many social work professionals feel that child-protective service issues have dominated the child welfare service delivery system at the cost of more preventive or rehabilitative services. Although we agree with many of these concerns, we have included considerable material on child maltreatment for a number of reasons:

- the seriousness of this enduring social problem and the consequent importance attached to it in the field—nowhere in child welfare is the fundamental tension between child protection and family preservation more clearly highlighted than in the area of child maltreatment;
- the need for social workers—in a range of practice settings beyond public child welfare—to be knowledgeable about the phenomenon of child maltreatment and its consequences;
- the rapidly changing nature of our knowledge base regarding this phenomenon, and therefore the importance of addressing the latest policy, research, and practice issues.

In Chapters 8 and 9, we describe the policy, research findings, and program design issues for family support and family-based services; subsequent chapters present a similar scope of issues for family foster care (10); reunification services (11); adoption (12); and group child care services (13). The book ends with Chapter 14, which takes a close look at what organizational requisites are necessary for effective services such as staffing, supervision, program quality improvement, and information technology.

We are in debt to many child welfare scholars who preceded us and on whose works we drew freely. Their many excellent texts are ones that readers are referred to throughout this volume. We believe this book will serve as an introduction for new practitioners, as well as a summary of recent developments for experienced practitioners. One of the goals is to convey some of the substantial contributions that social work has made to meeting the needs of families and children, and the value of research from allied disciplines such as psychology, sociology, nursing, public health, and medicine, as well as detailing the considerable work that remains.

Acknowledgments

A large number of colleagues, students, and others have contributed to the development of this second edition. We have benefited greatly by their advice and encouragement and, of course, take full responsibility for any errors or omissions contained within this volume. Our students have taught us much of what should be addressed in a child welfare course through their questions and reactions to some of the material. It is they who are the future of child welfare, and we hope this textbook may help contribute to their preparation for the field.

John Fluke provided important materials and advice regarding reporting rates for child maltreatment. James Gaudin, Susan Zuravin, and Fredi Rector generously shared their thoughts about child neglect. Diana English and Wayne Holder were valued consultants concerning risk assessment. Mark Courtney, Jill Duerr Berrick, Bob Goerge, Melissa Jonson-Reid, Penny Maza, Barbara Needell, Robin Warsh, and Fred Wulczyn offered stimulating and instructive interpretations of data cited in these pages.

Kellie Reed-Ashcraft, Charlotte Booth, Mark Fraser, David Haapala, Jill Kinney, Ray Kirk, Jacquelyn McCroskey, and Bill Meezan were a source of new ideas and critical questions regarding family-based services. The staff members at Boysville of Michigan, Casey Family Programs, Casey Family Services, Father Flanagan's Boystown, PATH, Pressley Ridge, and many other public and private child welfare agencies taught us much about the realities of the practice world. We express our gratitude to Edith Fein for her valuable suggestions for revision of earlier versions of the family foster care and family reunification chapters.

We appreciate the dedication of Candace Grossman, Pamela Harrison, Ben Warren, Cecily Novak, and Christine Guiao for their patience and skill in designing and revising these chapters. Finally, we thank Ruth Massinga, Jean McIntosh, and James Marquart (of the Casey Family Programs), whose support helped make the completion of this second edition possible.

1

The Purpose and Goals of Child
Welfare Services

CHILD WELFARE SERVICES AS A CRITICAL AND CHANGING
RESOURCE FOR FAMILIES IN AMERICA

As we complete this new edition of *The Child Welfare Challenge,* the child and family social services delivery system in many areas of the country remains stressed. For example, in 1997, nearly 3 million children were reported as abused and neglected—an increase of 18% since 1990 (U.S. Department of Health and Human Services, 1998, pp. 2–5; 1999, pp. 2–4). As of March 31, 1998, 520,000 children were residing in foster placements of various types in the United States (U.S. Department of Health and Human Services, Administration for Children and Families, Administration on Children, Youth and Families, Children's Bureau, 1999, p. 1). Although about 200,000 children each year eventually enter out-of-home care under child welfare supervision, the volume of child entries, exits, and return to care is huge—the system was estimated to have served an annual total of 710,000 children and adolescents in 1995 alone (Tatara, 1997, pp. 1–2).[1] In the major states, about 1 in 25 infants born each year will enter foster care that year (Wulczyn, Harden, & Goerge, 1997) (see Table 1.1). Furthermore, people of color are underrepresented among child welfare staff, and there are insufficient services to ensure that children achieve permanency by returning home or getting adopted.

Major societal and program reforms need to be implemented and agencies must concentrate the resources that they have in a focused, strategic manner (see Geen & Tumlin, 1999). There are, however, new resources and ideas reshaping child welfare practices in many locales. Agencies are making successful efforts to reduce the length of stay of children in out-of-home care, are reducing the level of restrictiveness of child placements in some areas, and are increasing the proportion of children placed with relatives or clan members (i.e., kinship care). In addition, the number of children being adopted or securing a form of permanence through guardianship has increased over the past two decades and the time to adoption has been halved in some states (Avery, 1998). These innovations may increase further with new initiatives underway such as child welfare demonstration waivers (see Table 1.2), expedited adoptive parent assessments, expedited approvals of subsidy applications, increases in judicial personnel, and heightened attention by the agen-

1

Table 1.1. Children in Foster or Group Care in the United States, 1977 vs. 1994[a]

Statistic	1977	1994
Number in care	538,424[b]	501,611
Median length of stay	29 months	20 months
Mean length of stay	47 months	31 months
Percentage in care more than 18 months	54%	52%
Number in care more than 18 months	291,690	240,520
Males in care	57%	55%
Age distribution		
Less than 2	1%	1%
2–5	11%	22%
6–12	39%	46%
More than 13	49%	31%
Type of placement		
Foster family	84%	88%[c]
Group home	5%	5%
Institution	11%	7%
Preadopt home	N/A	N/A
Race/ethnicity		
White	59%	26%
Black	34%	56%
Hispanic	5%	13%
Asian/American Indian	2%	3%
Other	0%	2%
Principal child caring person		
Employed full-time	25%	10%
Employed part-time	5%	3%
AFDC	22%	41%
Adoption services recommended	17%	
Goal—adoption		29%

[a]The 1977 data are a reanalysis of data from the *National Study of Social Services to Children and Their Families.* The 1994 data are from the *National Study of Social Services Delivered to Children and Their Families* conducted in 1994. The major reason the total figures for the number of children in care differ from those reported from the Voluntary Cooperative Information System (VCIS) is that these studies are based on national random samples of children receiving all types of services from child welfare agencies in the respective years. Information from these studies is not available on a state-specific basis. (See Appendix A for additional cautionary notes.)

[b]This number was originally reported at 502,000. Reanalysis of data indicated that the number was higher, as reported here.

[c]About one-third of these children are in kinship care.

Source: Maza, P.O. (May 10, 1996). *Children in care: 1977 vs. 1994* (mimeograph), Washington, DC: U.S. Children's Bureau.

Table 1.2. Examples of Early State Child Welfare Demonstration Waivers

WASHINGTON, Sept. 29, 1998 /U.S. Newswire/—Health and Human Services (HHS) Secretary Donna E. Shalala today announced approval of child welfare demonstration projects for Montana and Washington state. " In the past two weeks, the Clinton administration approved six innovative state demonstrations with projects to increase adoptions, overcome the problems of substance abuse, and better coordinate services to meet the individual needs of children—an impressive effort for America's most vulnerable children," said Secretary Shalala. "Today, we add Montana with its promising efforts to give children more permanent homes more quickly and Washington state with its new local approach to ensure children get the most appropriate services."

These demonstrations are among the first to be approved through the expanded authority provided under the Adoption and Safe Families Act signed by President Clinton in 1997. The new authority enables HHS to give states more flexibility in trying innovative child welfare projects.

Montana will offer subsidized guardianships as an option for children over 12 years of age in state or tribal custody for whom reunification and adoption are not viable options. The state will use federal foster care and adoption funds to establish legal guardianships, provide subsidies to families, train staff, and pay administrative expenses. Guardianship is expected to provide the child and family a legally recognized relationship and increase the sense of family by granting caretakers the right and responsibility to make important decisions regarding the child. It will also provide a more stable alternative to terminating parents' rights when children cannot return home.

The state of Washington will use federal foster care funds to provide comprehensive, individualized services to children 8 to 17 who are in need of mental health or special education services and are likely to be referred to group care. To avoid group care assignments, the state will contract with local service providers to create and implement individualized treatment plans. The state will gauge the impact of the fixed case rate approach, which allows services to be tailored to meet the complex needs of these children and their families at a reasonable cost.

Washington will begin the project in Spokane County and phase in up to nine more counties during the project. "We're very pleased that Montana is the first state to receive approval for a demonstration to work with both Native American and general state population children, a goal for this round of innovations in child protective services," said Olivia A. Golden, HHS assistant secretary for children and families. "Washington will test two important goals for new services to children, better coordination with health and education needs, and achieving the most effective use of government funds."

Prior to the Adoption and Safe Families Act, Congress had given authority to HHS to grant up to 10 demonstration projects to states. Ten states were approved, though many more were interested. The new law allows HHS to approve up to 10 more demonstrations each year for the next five years. HHS has encouraged states to develop projects in several key areas: increasing adoptions of special needs children; promoting community-based services to prevent child abuse and neglect; improving the access to needed health and mental health services; and projects to meet the unique needs of American Indian children. Both Montana's and Washington's projects are for five years, will be cost-neutral, and include a rigorous evaluation.

cies and courts to the need for more timely permanency planning.[2] In this introductory chapter we will outline the mission, goals or outcomes, philosophical underpinnings, and selected areas of practice transformation.

PHILOSOPHICAL UNDERPINNINGS OF CHILD WELFARE SERVICES

We believe that a core set of philosophical principles can be used to inform the selection of key outcomes for child welfare and the strategies for achieving them. The principles can also provide useful guideposts for agencies as they design performance-based contracts, implement managed care approaches to service delivery, or design staff development programs.

The following section is reprinted with slight adaptations from part of a summary of philosophical principles and recommended performance indicators that was developed by a consortium of private foundations, national professional associations, researchers, agency administrators, foster care alumni, a state legislator, a juvenile court judge, and a parent representative (American Humane Association, Children's Division; American Bar Association, Center on Children and the Law; Annie E. Casey Foundation; Casey Family Services; Institute for Human Services Management; and The Casey Family Programs, 1998, pp. 3–8). This list is not intended to be exhaustive or definitive, but proposes seven key principles for the child welfare field to consider. Note that this set of principles reflects the position of some family advocates and researchers that both child safety and family support need to be emphasized simultaneously. Again, there are differing perspectives on this issue, and it can be argued that child safety should be listed first and by itself as an overarching goal and principle of child welfare. The seven key philosophical principles are as follows:

1. Child Safety and Family Support. A safe and permanent home with family members is the best place for children to grow up. All children have the right to be free from physical, sexual, emotional, and other forms of harm by their parents or caregivers. Parents have a responsibility to meet children's needs for adequate food, shelter, clothing, and a safe environment.

Most parents want to be good parents and have the capacity, when adequately supported by the community, to care for their children and keep them safe from harm. Child welfare agencies can often accomplish their overriding goal of ensuring child safety by keeping families together and actively reaching out to parents to support their strengths as caregivers. When a child or youth is at risk of harm, the child's parents, extended family or kin, substitute caregivers, and community members who are already known to and trusted by the child (e.g., teachers, health care providers, clergy) all have a role to play in the development and implementation of a safety plan. Supporting and strengthening families often promotes child safety. However, if parents or caretakers cannot provide a safe home for children, agency intervention to provide an alternate permanent home is warranted, including, if appropriate, independent living for youths in out-of-home care (see, for example, American Humane Association and National Association of Public Child Welfare Administrators, 1996).

2. Child and Family Well-Being. Child well-being means that a child's basic needs are met and the child has the opportunity to grow and develop in an environment that provides consistent nurture, support, and stimulation. Practice and research in child development have documented that families can usually best provide the consistent, nurturing environment, and secure, uninterrupted relationships with caring adults that are necessary to achieve child well-being.

Family well-being means that a family has the capacity to care for its children and fulfill their basic developmental, health, educational, social, cultural, spiritual, and housing needs. Providing families with community-based formal and informal supports, resources, or treatment that will enable them to maintain a secure, stable environment for their children, often results in achieving child well-being.

Supporting family efforts to care for children (when consistent with child safety) is therefore an important goal of child welfare services agencies. By reinforcing effective family functioning, agencies maximize the opportunity for children or youths who are at risk for maltreatment to remain safely with their families. Providing services needed to support family reunification or kinship care, when these alternatives are appropriate, is also essential (see, for example, American Humane Association and National Association of Public Child Welfare Administrators, an affiliate of the American Public Welfare Association, 1996).

3. Community Supports for Families. Families raise children within communities. Family efforts are affected by the community's social and economic health. Communities therefore need to support families in providing a safe and nurturing childrearing environment. Healthy communities offer both formal and informal supports to families that clearly help to prevent harm to children; prevention efforts are key component of the child welfare system.

Sound social, economic, and moral reasons compel equal attention and resources to preventive programs and to services that support child well-being and effective family functioning. Basic supports such as jobs, housing, and community economic development are needed so that the child welfare system can stem the causes of child maltreatment, rather than simply responding after children have suffered abuse or neglect.

Preventive and family supportive services that are easily accessible to all children and families in their own communities and integrated with other community support systems (such as housing, health care, education, and early child development) are critical underpinnings for a responsive child welfare system. No single model or system will fit all communities. But all communities need to offer a full range of prevention, intervention, and treatment resources to respond to the needs of children and families and to ensure that resources are not disproportionately directed to more intensive, expensive services (see, for example, American Humane Association, 1996; Harvard Executive Session on Child Protection, 1997; Schorr, 1997).

4. Family-Centered Services. Responsive child welfare approaches offer family-centered services that directly address the needs and interests of individual children and families (see Chapters 2 and 3). When families are actively involved in making key decisions about the family's children and in designing services to meet the family's needs, it is more likely that the family's capacity to parent its children safely will be increased.

Effective child welfare agencies work to create an atmosphere in which families feel comfortable in speaking honestly and openly about their strengths and needs. In partnership with families, these agencies strive to construct service responses that support effective family functioning and allow children to remain safely with their families. Help is family driven; the availability of a particular funding stream should not be allowed to drive the provision of services that do not address the needs of a specific child and family.

Most families have the motivation and capacity to be actively involved in providing or creating provisions for their children's safety and well-being, as long as they are properly supported. Even when a child's parents cannot be her or his primary caregivers, family members and extended family are a vital part of the caring circle for children, and can contribute to the child's growth and development.

When a child has been placed outside of his or her own home, agency workers should strive to maintain relationships of continuity for the child, ideally with birth parents and with kin or previous caregivers. If other out-of-home care is required, the least restrictive, most family-like setting possible, which is responsive to a child's cultural background and any special needs, is the preferred setting for this care (see, for example, American Humane Association, 1994, 1996). It should be noted, however, that *routinely* making same-race foster care or adoption placements is not allowable under the Multi-Ethnic Placement Act of 1994 and Inter-Ethnic Adoption Provisions, Act 2, 1996, unless the child has unique cultural needs (e.g., speaks only Spanish).

5. *Cultural Competence.* A culturally competent child welfare system is one that develops behaviors, attitudes, and policies to promote effective cross-cultural work. By engaging in a cultural self-assessment process to help both the organization and individual workers to clarify their basic cultural values, agencies can (1) address how agency and worker values may affect serving clients with cultural orientations different than those of the agency and its workers; and (2) improve the access, availability, acceptance, and quality of services to all cultural groups being served. Providing workers, and the agency or organization as a whole, with a flexible context for gaining and expanding cultural knowledge, understanding the dynamics arising from cultural differences, and promoting the successful adaptation of services to meet unique cultural needs in partnership with community members are the most effective ways for agencies to improve their cultural competence (see, for example, American Humane Association, Children's Division, Policy Statement on Cultural competence of child protective services agencies, May 15, 1994; Bricker-Jenkins, Hooyman, & Gottlieb, 1991; Brissett-Chapman & Isaacs-Shockley, 1997; Cross, 1989; Isaacs-Shockley, 1998).

Some program approaches or service innovations worth monitoring for their ability to support more culturally competent practice in child welfare include the following:

- Materials to support more culturally competent risk assessment systems have been produced in California (Walker & Tabbert, undated), Washington (Pecora & English, 1994), and elsewhere (Stevenson, Cheung, & Leung, 1992).
- The "Family Group Conferencing" models that have been adapted from New Zealand and elsewhere may help to support more family-centered services (Merkel-Holguin, Winterfeld, Harper, Coburn, & Fluke, 1997) (although evaluation data are just beginning to be collected for these programs).
- Wraparound service programs such as those pioneered by Karl Dennis and his Chicago Kaleidescope project staff appear to be operating successfully.
- In some communities such as Portland and in the Annie E. Casey "Family-to-Family" demonstration sites, there are efforts underway to provide more neighborhood-based and family-centered foster care.
- Agencies are trying to keep siblings together.
- Kinship care has been increasing in many states, with much of that out-of-home care acting as a form of "family preservation services."

These are just a few of the service reform efforts underway. There are many barriers to more effective services in the United States, not the least of which is continuing institutional racism and major inequities in income distribution. However, with clear priorities, adequate funding, and systematic attention paid to organization and community barriers, culturally competent service delivery systems can be developed and succeed.

6. System Accountability and Timeliness. A well-organized service delivery system, accountable to specific performance standards and time frames for service provision, is essential to effectively protect children and strengthen families. The child welfare system's effectiveness is being measured in terms of its ability to produce defined and visible outcomes for children and families through a continuum of resources. Multiple perspectives on these outcomes are considered in the continuous process of improving services that can be shown to

- prevent family problems from occurring in the first place;
- increase and maintain children's safety and families' emotional health and ability to care for their children during a stressful time or transition; and
- prevent revictimization or another family problem, or slow progressively deteriorating conditions.

Responses from surveys of youth and families and from organizations of foster parents and current and former foster youth are increasingly sought out. Effective services are those that are timely from a child's perspective, that is, services are provided quickly enough to respond to a child's or youth's developmental and emotional needs. For example, one year may seem a short time frame for adults, but for young children it is a major period in terms of growth and development. For youth, the teen years can be a critical time period as they prepare for adulthood. Service providers and the system as a whole can recognize the imperative of children's developmental time frames and ensure that services are organized to coincide with them. Service provision that is sensitive to a child's sense of time helps (1) children to remain in or be placed in safe and permanent homes; (2) caseworkers to more effectively perform their jobs; and (3) workers and the courts to make critical decisions with greater wisdom and competence (see Hardin, 1992; Pecora, 1997; Young, Gardner, Coley, Schorr, & Bruner, 1994).

7. *Coordination of System Resources.* A cohesive system of family-centered, community-based, culturally competent, timely, and accountable services and supports for children and families is what we are striving for in child welfare. Organizing system resources to ensure consistent, reliable coordinated service delivery, along with the availability of informal supports for families in their own communities, will maximize the effectiveness of the child welfare system.

At the individual family level, formal efforts to coordinate services and supports are necessary among different providers serving the same family. The child welfare system and its workers have a responsibility to act as coordinators by ensuring that all family needs are identified, assessed, and met with a coordinated plan to provide resources that will achieve specific outcomes for children and their families.

At the systems level, formal cooperative agreements or protocols can increase the cohesiveness of related services provided by different agencies. Funding that is not limited to specific service categories, or that allows for the provision of a combination of resources to meet individual child and family needs, also strengthens a coordinated response to families. Resource allocation at the system level should allow communities the flexibility to meet local needs and to provide a holistic array of services, resources, and informal supports for children and families (see, for example American Humane Association, 1991; Kamerman & Kahn, 1989; United States General Accounting Office, 1992, 1995, 1997).

MISSION AND GOALS OF CHILD WELFARE SERVICES

The mission of child welfare has long been to respond specifically to the needs of children reported to public child protection agencies as abused or neglected, or at risk of child maltreatment. Recently, there has been more emphasis on looking beyond public and private child welfare agencies to involve communities as a whole in the protection and nurturing of children, and to formulate collaborative community efforts to prevent and respond to child abuse and neglect. This new direction is well taken, for although all children have highly individual needs and characteristics they live "in the context of their families, families in the context of their cultures and communities, and communities in the context of their social, economic, cultural and political environments" (Child Welfare League of America, 1996). A child welfare system that fails to incorporate and draw on the richness and strength embodied in this context of family life is a system that cannot effectively respond to the needs of vulnerable children and troubled families. Although agency mission statements provide the overall context for service, it is essential that key goals or outcomes are specified to help guide such key functions as establishing agency strategic plans, policy formulation, funding decisions, and worker practice (American Humane Association, 1998). These are discussed in the next section.

KEY GOALS AND OUTCOMES FOR CHILD WELFARE SERVICES

Child welfare services is gaining more clarity and consensus about its primary mission. We propose one primary goal and two secondary goals for child welfare services: The primary goal is to protect children from harm and is above all other goals. The second goal is to preserve existing family units, which we understand to include both birth-family or relative families as appropriate. The third goal is to promote children's development into adults who can live independently and contribute to their community, which may require a variety of permanency planning alternatives such as family reunification, placement with relatives, different forms of guardianship (depending on local law), adoption, and *planned* long-term foster care or kinship care with some kind of legal safeguards such as guardianship.

Readers should note that there is some debate in the field about placing child safety as a superior goal to family support—many family advocates and some researchers will argue that without an emphasis on both child safety and family support simultaneously, neither will happen in an equitable manner. For families in which there are no significant safety concerns, the personal price of removal may be higher than what they would experience were they to receive in-home services. Throughout this text we will attempt to provide a full range of information so that readers can decide for themselves where their position lies. We now describe in more detail the key components of each of these major goals (also called "outcome domains").

Safety

A core goal for child welfare services is keeping children safe from child abuse and neglect. This includes children living with their birth families, returned home to their families, and children placed in out-of-home care. In terms of concrete outcomes, citizens should be looking to child welfare services to *prevent children from being maltreated* and to *keep families safely together* that are functioning at least at a minimum standard of parenting. Child welfare workers operate on the philosophical basis that all children have a right to live in a safe environment and receive protection from abuse and neglect. For example, the focus of child protective services (CPS) should be to deliver services that are preventive and nonpunitive and that are geared toward parent rehabilitation through identification and treatment of the factors that underlie the problem.

At the most general level there is a firm consensus regarding the mission of child protective services: it is designed to protect children from child maltreatment committed by their parents or other caretakers. But in translating this broad mandate into practice, the consensus breaks down in a variety of areas such as defining what is child abuse or neglect, establishing standards for agency intervention, and specifying what constitutes a minimum standard of parenting (popularized recently by the question "what is a good enough parent?").

Standards used in case decision making seriously affect provision of services. Historically, the standard used for CPS intervention was based on the "best interests of the child." Such a broad and subjective standard skewed social workers' actions toward frequent removal of children. This approach to practice resulted in an emphasis (and a public expectation) that child welfare services should be used to improve all areas of family functioning. In addition, child placement was also justified because it was the "best" plan for the child. The public and certain community agencies expected that family functioning had to be improved from an "F" level to an "A" level before the case was closed.

That expectation is no longer feasible or ethical. It is not feasible because high caseloads and a shortage of services have forced agencies to target their services to clients most in need. From an ethical standpoint, laws protecting parent rights and family privacy prohibit forcing services on families whose functioning does not fall below a certain minimum standard of parenting. These families are best served by other community agencies. It is currently recognized that the emotional price of removal is often much more damaging to children than allowing them to remain in the home while family treatment and other services are provided. Finally, we lack the research data that allow us to predict what is in the child's best interest, beyond protecting children in severe situations. In other words, the social sciences are not yet able to predict outcomes for children in relation to determining whether child placement would be superior for many cases (Stein & Rzepnicki, 1983). Child protective services and child welfare staff are instead focusing on *minimum standards of parenting,* with a requirement that involuntary CPS intervention proceed only if there is evidence that children have been harmed or will be at risk of maltreatment in the near future. Consider these observations from Stein and Rzepnicki (1983):

> Moreover, a focus on minimum standards reinforces the value that our society places on family privacy—on the rights of parents to raise their children free of outside intervention—while simultaneously protecting a child's right to be safeguarded from

undue harm as well as the right to be raised by the family of origin. The best interest standard leaves a wide margin for subjectivity and individual biases to influence decisions as to when intervention should occur, thereby undermining these values.

A focus on minimum standards facilitates describing the data base for decision making and the establishment of decision-making rules. For example, rather than being concerned with a parent's use of drugs or alcohol, one would ask the question, How is the child being harmed by such behaviors or what harm might be expected to occur if substance abuse continues? Assessment would focus on the child's needs for supervision, medical care, and other areas noted above.

In most states, CPS workers are therefore encouraged to focus on minimally adequate care and levels of risk to the child, rather than requiring that all parents provide some "optimal" level of nurturing. The types of services available to help parents meet a minimal standard of parenting heavily influence CPS decision making and the case plan to be implemented. No agency has a completely adequate range of services, but within most communities there should be a variety of resources to supplement and support what CPS staff can provide, such as crisis nurseries, treatment day care, home-based services, and parenting support groups. Finally, perhaps one of the most pivotal determinants is client ability or willingness to use the services. Regardless of what a worker can do for or plan with a family, a successful outcome is dependent on the ability of family members to benefit from the service and their willingness to work with child welfare staff.

Permanence[3]

When the state steps in to protect an abused or neglected child, it is not enough for the state to make the child safe; the state must also consider the child's needs for permanent and stable family ties. In addition to protecting a child, the state should ensure that the children will be brought up by stable and legally secure permanent families, rather than in temporary foster care under the supervision of the state. As considered further in Chapter 3, this principle has been well established in federal law, first by the Adoption Assistance and Child Welfare Act of 1980 and then by the Adoption and Safe Families Act of 1997.

Although permanency alone does not guarantee a normal healthy childhood, it is a key factor in the successful upbringing of children for a number of reasons. First, many mental health experts have concluded that stable and continuous care givers are important to normal child development[4] (see, for example, Goldstein, Freud, & Solnit,1973; Rosenberg,1983, pp. 550–574; Rutter, 1981, pp. 179–197). Children need secure and uninterrupted emotional relationships with adults who are responsible for their care in order to learn how to form healthy relationships later on.

Second, children need parents who are fully committed to caring for them, and it is easier for parents (whether biological, foster, or adoptive) to maintain a strong commitment to the child when their role is secure. Not having parents who provide consistent love and care can represent a profound insult to a child's self-image.[5] Children are likely to feel more secure under the control of parents than of child welfare agencies. In addition, fully committed parents are more likely to provide conscientiously for the child's needs.

Third, having a permanent family adds a critical element of predictability to a child's life, thereby promoting their sense of belonging. Being in foster care and never knowing when and where one might be moved can impose great stress on a child. With a permanent family, a child can form a more secure sense of the future and can better weather other difficulties and changes in childhood and adolescence (see, for example, Maluccio, Fein, & Olmstead, 1986; Pike et al., 1977, pp. 1–2; Allen & Knitzer, 1978, p. 41).[6]

Fourth, autonomous families generally are more capable of raising children than is the state.[7] Decision making for children in state-supervised foster care tends to be fragmented and diffuse because it is shared by social workers, professional therapists and evaluators, foster parents, court personnel, and biological parents. Full-time permanent parents, who concentrate far more personal commitment and time on the child than any professional, are best able to make fully informed and timely decisions for a child.

In terms of concrete outcomes, citizens should be looking to child welfare services for a number of permanency-related outcomes, including *purposeful case plans* that explicitly address the child's legal status and need for permanency planning. If permanent placement is an important goal for an abused and neglected children, it follows that service plans for such children should be designed, in part, for that purpose. Whether a service plan has been logically designed to achieve a safe and permanent home for the child is a key indicator by which to measure the appropriateness of the plan and, ultimately, to measure the plan's success, and that of the child welfare agency (Hardin, 1992).

Other outcomes (framed in italics to help distinguish them from one another) include children being *placed in the least restrictive placement* possible, *with siblings* whenever possible, with *minimal placement moves or disruptions,* and with a *timely resolution of their legal status* so that they can be adopted by a caring adult if a birth parent is unable to care for them.

Child Well-Being

Achieving child well-being means, foremost, that a child *is safe from child abuse or neglect.* This requires that a *child's basic needs are met* and the child has the *opportunity to grow and develop* in an environment that provides consistent nurture, support, and stimulation. In this outcome domain we include the need for children to develop *a healthy sense of identity,* an *understanding of their ethnic heritage,* and *skills for coping with racism, sexism, and other forms of discrimination* that remain prevalent in our society. Although there are limits to what child welfare services can provide, the system should be promoting at least minimal standards of parenting that will provide a child with the developmental opportunities and emotional nurturance needed to grow into an adult who can live as independently as possible.

Family Well-Being

As noted in the preceding section, family well-being means that a family has the capacity to *care for its children* and *fulfill their basic developmental, health, educational, social, cultural, spiritual, and housing needs.* It implies that child welfare staff members have some responsibility for locating these essential services and supports, and helping sustain or promote the parents in their child-rearing roles.

SIGNIFICANT COSTS AND COMPLEX FAMILY SITUATIONS: CRUCIAL SYSTEM CHALLENGES

It was projected that America would spend close to $12 billion on public agency child welfare services in 1997 (Committee on Ways and Means, U.S. House of Representatives, 1996; Lipner & Goertz, 1996, p. 3). The majority of these funds paid for the provision of out-of-home care for children supervised in some way by public child welfare agencies. Children who are receiving child welfare services are more likely than the general population to be younger than six; to experience high levels of health, mental health, and educational problems; and to have parents who also experience high levels of involvement with substance abuse, mental illness, and/or corrections (Berrick et al., 1998). Consequently, child welfare agencies need a readily available array of supplemental services, well-trained and supervised staff members, and low staff turnover to be effective.

Foster care is a system under strain in many parts of the country, with many workers undertrained and overloaded. State-by-state analyses reveal a huge variation in placement rates, length of stay in foster care, and other key indicators (Goerge, 1990; Wulczyn, Harden, & Goerge, 1997), which indicates that there are cities, counties, or other areas (e.g., Grand Rapids, Michigan) that are experiencing good to excellent system performance in key areas. So good service delivery systems succeed despite (and in some cases *because of*) local community conditions.

We have listed what we view as some of the most crucial challenges in Table 1.3. So to some degree the field is addressing the "Child Welfare Challenges" successfully in some areas—we have new evidence that foster care length of stay in many states is at an all time low, the field has developed more options for children (e.g., kin care, treatment foster care, wraparound services, family preservation, shared family care), adoptions are increasing, the research (although still in need

Table 1.3. The Top 10 Child Welfare Challenges

---

1. Ensuring that child welfare services work collaboratively with community resources and agencies to strengthen families that without special support would otherwise need child welfare services.
2. Ensuring that children do not become involved with child welfare services when income assistance, job training, and other social service programs could have prevented abuse and neglect.
3. Ensuring that children and families receive the preventive services that are effective and result in high levels of child safety and child well-being.
4. Ensuring that the safety needs of children and the rights and responsibilities of parents to care for their own children are balanced so that children are not removed unnecessarily from their parent(s) care when the children have been abused or neglected.
5. Ensuring that families of children placed in foster care are given the opportunity to experience timely and effective family reunification services so they do not remain in care an undue time or return home prematurely.
6. Ensuring that children placed into foster care who cannot otherwise go home are given a substantial opportunity for adoption.
7. Ensuring that services are financed and organized so that higher cost programs provide more benefit to children than lower cost programs and are focused on the children most in need of them.
8. Ensuring that child welfare services are delivered fairly and not based on the race, ethnicity, geographic location, or sexual orientation of the child or family.
9. Ensuring that child welfare services experience continuous improvement as a result of routine monitoring of the delivery of the services and the outcomes.
10. Ensuring that child welfare services allow scrutiny by researchers and the media in ways that maximize public understanding but minimize threats to the confidentiality of clients.

---

of improvement) is the most robust it has ever been, and new Federal Title IV-E programs are providing stipends and helping to professionalize the field.

PRACTICE TRANSFORMATIONS

The field of child welfare has undergone a transformation in the past 20 years—a process that has reaffirmed the importance of strengthening families and providing services in the "least restrictive environment." From an ecological perspective, this means "that environment which is most free from bureaucratic and institutional features such as lack of intimacy and depersonalization, that environment closest to the natural caring system, the biological family" (Laird & Hartman, 1985, p. xxiii).

The field, more than ever, struggles to fulfill its twin mandates: to protect the child while preserving the family and promoting the future of children whenever possible. Thus, staff members are attempting to build on family strengths and resources rather then focusing exclusively on individual deficits. Yet, helping families to take care of their basic needs has been difficult because of continuing high rates of poverty and a lack of basic supports such as housing, medical insurance, and food assistance. When the provision of these and other services is insufficient and children must be placed, a growing emphasis has been to place the children with relatives, kinship members, or in a foster home arrangement as geographi-cally near the family as possible to facilitate contact between the children and their families.

Although child welfare agencies in some parts of the country continue to suffer from inconsistent political leadership and underfunding, there is also a growing re-alization that "business as usual" in many areas of child welfare is not adequate for strengthening families and protecting children. Consequently, a number of service reforms are being implemented:

Reemphasis on Safety Planning and Permanency Planning

Even with the increase in efforts devoted to keeping families together, develop-ments in risk assessment and recognition of the need to remove some children per-manently from their birth parents have advanced the practice of "safety planning" for children. (e.g., Holder & Corey, 1987). With the promotion of "permanency planning" in the 1970s, social workers have focused on family preservation, re-unification, termination of parental rights and adoption, or long-term foster care with guardianship—in that order of priority. As discussed in Chapter 3, the objec-tive is to keep families together whenever possible, and if placement is necessary, to minimize "foster care drift," where children languish in family foster care with-out a sense of permanence or are moved from home to home without a compre-hensive case plan. The ultimate goal is to ensure that every child has a "forever home," despite the reality that a small but significant percentage of children "grow up" in family foster care or group care, and are never reunified with family mem-bers or adopted.

Innovative Service Delivery Models

The use of more community-based and neighborhood-based programs, school-based services, wraparound services, youth employment programs, certain man-aged care techniques, and a variety of community-based initiatives is broadening the mix of service options. As important, these innovations are enabling child wel-fare agencies to become more integrated into the community and better positioned to call on the economic development, educational, mental health, housing, voca-tional education, and other community resources for assistance in achieving the shared outcomes they have for children and parents. Strides are also being made in developing new cost-effective treatment strategies.

System of Care Approaches

Arising from innovations in mental health services, Systems of Care approaches seek to operationalize a philosophy about the way in which services should be organized for children and their families, with three core values: (1) child and family centered, (2) community based, and (3) culturally competent (Stroul & Friedman, 1996). These service delivery systems, by implementing these core values, are attempting to reduce barriers to service, more extensively involve parents and children, and increase the coordination of services. More recently, these approaches are being reformulated to include better integration with child welfare services.

Partnerships with Public Health and Substance Abuse
Treatment Providers

A number of "home visiting" models of child abuse prevention and family support are being pilot tested using public health nurses, social workers and/or other types of staffing designs (e.g., Olds & Kitzman, 1995). These program hold promise of more extensive partnerships between child welfare and public health agencies, as well as the potential to strengthen universal and selective preventive services in nonstigmatizing ways.

Similarly, with the increase in substance abuse-involved families, the need for prevention and treatment programs becomes critical and partnerships between child welfare, early childhood, education, mental health, primary health care, and substance abuse treatment facilities are crucial (see, for example, Office of Early Childhood, Substance Abuse and Mental Health Administration, 1998); and alignment of the timelines from public assistance [Temporary Assistance to Needy Families (TANF)] and social service program guidelines [Adoption and Safe Families Act (AFSA)] with the realities of relapse prediction and treatment is crucial for family preservation. (See Table 1.4.)

Increased Accountability

Programs are trying to achieve a better balance of accountability with respect to service delivery process and outcomes. Administrators and practitioners are reexamining and then refining their intervention models to better achieve the short-term and intermediate results for which they should be held accountable. Funders such as the United Way and state and county governments are reinforcing this approach through a focus on achieving key results and performance-based contracts (see, for example, Center for the Study of Social Policy, 1994; Friedman, 1997).

Table 1.4. The Impact of Substance Abuse on a Young Child's Life

The most recent data from the National Institute on Drug Abuse suggest that more than 1 million children per year are exposed to alcohol and/or illicit substances during gestation. Across a wide array of studies, most researchers now agree that neonates prenatally exposed to alcohol or illicit drugs exhibit high rates of intrauterine growth impairment, prematurity and impaired neurobehavioral functioning. Recent long-term studies have revealed that prenatal drug exposure has a direct impact on the child's behavior at 4 to 6 years of age, with prenatally exposed children sowing significantly high rates of depression and anxiety, aggressive behavior, thought problems, impulsivity, and distractibility. In addition, the mother's continuing drug use during the early childhood years is a major factor that predicts the child's level of cognitive functioning at school age.

Infants removed from their homes because of substance abuse problems in the family are a huge proportion of this growth. In fact, nearly half the states report that substance abuse is the dominant characteristic in Child Protective Services (CPS) caseloads. In 1991, it was estimated that 55% of the very young children placed in substitute care had been prenatally exposed to cocaine or cocaine derivatives, and another 11% had been exposed to alcohol and other drugs. In 1992, it was reported that up to 80% of the children in substitute care were placed there because of substance abuse-related reasons.

In studies of the association between substance abuse and child abuse, researchers have found that children born to substance-abusing women have a rate of physical abuse two to five time higher than matched children from similar backgrounds but with no history of prenatal drug exposure. The National Committee for Prevention of Child Abuse has estimated that 675,000 children are seriously mistreated annually by an alcoholic or drug-abusing caretaker. Using data from the National Institute for Mental Health's Epidemiologic Catchment Area survey, researchers recently found that about half of abusive or neglectful parents have "a lifetime prevalence substance abuse disorder." When other factors were taken into account, substance-abusing parents were approximately three times more likely to abuse or neglect their children than nonsubstance abusers.

Source: Reprinted from Chasnoff, I.J. (1998). Silent violence: Is prevention a moral obligation? *Pediatrics, 102,* 145–148. Used with permission of the American Academy of Pediatrics.

Restructured Funding Mechanisms

The field has been hampered by federal and state funding policies that have rewarded the wrong program emphases such as completing child abuse investigations (rather than preventing the need for new ones) and keeping children in foster care (instead of securing a more permanent home for them). So agencies are now striving to align funding priorities and performance incentive mechanisms to support preventive services and more program flexibility. Witness the original Title IV-E waivers for pilot programs summarized in Table 1.5, the more recent Title IV-E waivers for experimental services that were cited earlier in Table 1.3, and the recent proposal by the American Public Human Services Association to reform federal legislation related to performance measurement, funding methods, and performance incentives (APHSA Finance Work Group, 1998).

Table 1.5. Waiver States by Start Date, Intervention, and Evaluation Design

State	Start Date	Intervention	Evaluation Design
Delaware	7/1/96	1. *Services to Substance-Abusing Caretakers.* Provide substance abuse counselors to work with CPS staff and identified families to link to treatment and other services. 2. *Assisted Guardianship.* Obtain legal guardianship for children in stable foster care placements for whom adoption and reunification are not possible. Subsidy payment will not exceed current foster care payment.	1. Random assignment of cases to units with substance counselors (treatment) and without (control). 2. Track costs and outcomes of cases with guardianship—anticipate 20 cases per year.
Illinois	5/1/97	*Assisted Guardianship.* Obtain legal guardianship and provide subsidy payments for foster parents and kin who provide stable placements. Payments will range from $343 to $415 per month. Expect to place 8,000 children statewide	Random assignment of eligible cases to control and experimental groups.
North Carolina	7/1/97	1. *System Reform.* Counties will have flexibility to develop programs that will reduce foster placements and length of stay in care. Counties will not receive any new or additional money, but will have the flexibility offered under the waiver for IV-E funding. 2. *Assisted Guardianship.* Obtain legal guardianship and provide subsidy payments for relatives and other care givers approved by the juvenile court, and who have provided a stable placement for the child for at least six months. Assisted guardianship will be an option for children whom adoption and reunification are not possible.	1. Nineteen counties each involved in experimental and comparison group. 2. Not designed yet.
Oregon	7/1/97	*Systems Reform/Managed Care.* To provide a flexible service system to prevent family breakup specifically tailored for particular children and their families. Counties will have flexibility to develop programs and services that will reduce foster care placements and length of stay in care.	Comparison groups
Ohio	10/1/97	*Systems Reform/Managed Care.* Managed care demonstration counties will receive fixed amount of funds to serve child welfare families; counties will have flexibility to develop programs and services that will reduce foster care placements, costs, and length of stay in care.	Comparison groups
California	Summer 1998	1. *Extended Voluntary Placement (10 counties).* Will extend voluntary placement agreements from 180 to 365 days to reduce court costs and conflicts with families.	1. Comparison counties

State	Start date	Intervention	Evaluation design
		2. *Kinship Performance (4–10 counties)*. Obtain legal guardianship for relatives of children over 13 who receive Federal foster care payments, who are in stable placements, and for whom reunification and adoption are not options. Subsidy payments will not be greater than foster care payment. 3. *Intensive Services (12 counties)*. Counties to develop own intensive service plans and specify outcomes.	2. Random assignment of cases 3. Random assignment.
Indiana	1/1/98–6/30/98	*Intensive Home- and Community-Based Services*. Increase capacity for in home services and community foster family homes as alternative to group and institutional care, especially out-of-state care. Demonstration will be operational in all 92 counties within 18 months. A total of 4,000 children at any given time will receive services under the demonstration. Estimated stay in project = 20 months per child.	Retrospectively matched sample of children receiving traditional IV-E placements/services compared with experimental group.
Maryland	2/28/98	*Assisted Guardianship*. Obtain legal guardianship and provide subsidy payments and services to foster parents and kin who receive AFDC/TANF child-only payments. Payments will be $300 per month. Children must be in stable placement, and adoption and reunification have been ruled out as options.	Random assignment of children to experimental and control groups.
Michigan	10/1/98	1. *Managed Care Component*. Up to six counties will establish a capitated payment program to provide wraparound services for high-risk children in foster care or at imminent risk of placement. 2. *Community Services for Delinquent Youth*. Children aged 10 or older in contact with the juvenile justice system who are adjudicated, or at risk of being adjudicated, will be provided a range of preventive and reunification services.	1. In at least two counties, random assignment to treatment and control groups. 2. Comparison counties in terms of child poverty, public assistance, and abuse/neglect rates.
New York	4/1/98–12/31/98	*Managed care*. Up to 10 districts will test approaches to managed care. Each district may design its own service delivery system and prospective payment system including capitated payment systems and contract-based payment arrangements	Random assignment or comparison groups, determined by each district.

Source: U.S. Children's Bureau, Administration of Children, Youth, and Families. (1998). *Waiver states by start date, intervention, and evaluation design* (Mimeograph). Washington, DC: Author.

CONCLUSION

We hope that this chapter has established a foundation for the chapters that follow. The emphasis on achieving a number of key outcomes as the most important criterion on which to judge the effectiveness of child welfare agencies is important for practice as well as policy. Key demographic trends, laws, and other policies that shape child welfare services are discussed in Chapter 2.

NOTES

1. Estimating the number of children served in out-of-home care is complex in that different data bases have used partial groups of states or sampling methods to arrive at the statistics. For example, in contrast to the AFCARS data cited in this section, 483,000 children were in foster care on the last fiscal day in 1995 according to Tatara (1997, p. 1). Furthermore, some statistics are not clear about whether they have included children in family foster care, group care, and/or juvenile justice facilities. Wherever possible, we will try to be explicit about which children are being counted where.

2. For example, in New York City, 4,117 children placed in out-of-home care were adopted in 1997 as compared to 3,996 in calendar year 1995 and 3,238 in calendar year 1996 (Festinger, 1998, p. 1).

3. Adapted from Mark Hardin (1992, pp. 11–12).

4. See, for example, Goldstein, Freud, and Solnit (1973) Rosenberg (1983, pp. 550–574), and Rutter (1981, pp. 179–197).

5. See Fanshel and Shinn (1978, pp. 479–482), Wald (1976, pp. 623, 645), and Weinstein (1960).

6. See Chapter 3; Pike et al. (1977, pp. 1–2) and Allen and Knitzer (1978, p. 41).

7. See Goldstein, Freud, and Solnit (1973, pp. 51–52), Rosenberg (1983, pp. 550–574), and Wald (1975, pp. 985, 989–1000).

FOR FURTHER INFORMATION

Friedman, M. (1997). *A guide to developing and using performance measures in results-based budgeting.* Washington, D.C.: The Finance Project. Presents a conceptual framework for how to measure agency performance that emphasizes quality and results.

Stroul, B.A., & Friedman, R.M. (1996). The system of care concept and philosophy. In B. A. Stroul (Ed.), *Children's mental health: Creating systems of care in a changing society.* Baltimore: Paul H. Brookes Publishing. A rich resource of readings on the nature and current status of systems of care models across the country.

2

Understanding the Policy Context
for Child Welfare

INTRODUCTION

Most social workers are engaged in what the late Bertha Reynolds called "retail" as opposed to "wholesale" aspects of social reform. Their focus is on the individual, family, or group in need of advocacy, information, support, counseling, or treatment. Indeed, the chapters to follow are replete with examples of the challenges, dilemmas, and strains involved in many arenas of direct service in child welfare: family foster care, family-based or family preservation services, residential services, special-needs adoption, and services to abused and neglected children and their families. Yet increasingly, the effects of public policy are being felt in the most intimate aspects of direct practice. For example, public policy can and often does prescribe the duration, length, and focus of family counseling efforts (in family preservation services); the degree of confidentiality between parent and worker (in child abuse and neglect cases); the conditions under which certain services (out-of-home placement) may be used; and the criteria against which the performance of the individual worker will be measured.

Like it or not, each practitioner is involved in the policy process, at least insofar as implementation is concerned. Fundamentally then, child and family social work practitioners have a stake in public policy to the extent it is increasingly determinative of professional activities. Beyond that, the profession of social work has a long and impressive record of policy contributions affecting the lives of children and families whose only recourse to help was to public sector provision. The distinguished social welfare historian, Clarke Chambers, notes that "no segment of the progressive crusade engaged more fully the moral energies of reformers than the battle against the exploitation of children in mine, factory, street and field" (Chambers, 1963, p. 29). Pioneers like Jane Addams, Julia Lathrop, and Grace Abbott labored tirelessly for the creation and expansion of child welfare services, while at the same time pointing out their limits in redressing basic systemic problems like family poverty. "The power to maintain a decent family living standard is a primary essential in child welfare," said Julia Lathrop in 1919 (quoted in Chambers, 1963, p. 56). In so saying, she laid out the dimensions of what continues to be a delicate balance within the profession between efforts to improve, expand, and make more accessible needed case services, while at the same time recognizing their limits, absent a policy that attends to more basic needs of families for adequate income, jobs, health care, and a safe and nurturing community environment. This remains a critical issue, as discussed in Chapter 4.

This argues for an informed and active participation in the policy process by all social workers: first and foremost, as citizens helping to shape difficult choices, and second, as members of a profession intimately involved in the lives of children and families who are the objects of public policy's concern—the abused and neglected child, the teen parent, the family in crisis, the child with special needs awaiting adoption, and the youth in out-of-home care. As individual practitioners and as a profession, social work has much to contribute to the policy discourse; indeed, involvement in policy formation is an ethical responsibility.

WHAT IS POLICY?

Policy is described by MacRae and Wilde (1979) as a chosen course of action affecting large numbers of people. If chosen by government, we refer to this as public policy. Policy analysis, according to Haskins and Gallagher (1981, p. 2), refers to the application of reason, evidence, and an evaluative framework to public decisions. What do these terms mean? The "application of reason" typically involves a prolonged period of debate and discussion in legislative and citizen committees, as well as in popular and professional journals, on the nature of the problem and the relative merits of various solutions. For example, the landmark child welfare reform legislation enacted by Congress in 1980, Public Law (PL) 96-272, was preceded by many years of debate and discussion on the plight of children "adrift" in the foster care system. Sometimes a consensus is formed by the careful building of arguments—one on another—and at other times is galvanized through the dramatic single example, often of governmental or societal inaction. The latter occurred near the turn of the century when muckraking writers in the popular press pointed out that the government spent more time and money advising American farmers on the care and feeding of swine than advising American parents on the care and feeding of children. Another example comes from congressional testimony leading up to PL 96-272, when one witness noted (only partly in jest) that the government kept a better count of benches in our national parks than children in the foster care system! A more recent example was the passage of the Promoting Safe and Stable Families Program in 1997 (under PL 105-89), where the concerns of some advocates, researchers, the media, and others resulted in an emphasis on child safety over family preservation or reunification.

The "evidence" or research base for public policy in child welfare varies by area, but is by now substantial as will be obvious in the chapters to follow. In their timing and impact, some studies have achieved a kind of landmark status in policy formulation, such as the classic study *Children in Need of Parents* by Maas and Engler (1959) and of status changes of children in foster care in New York City by Fanshel and Shinn (1978). At other times, significant research follows rather than precedes the policy and helps to clarify what we can reasonably expect from certain policy initiatives. Here the very fruitful analyses following the passage of Head Start and a group of studies in family preservation practice are germane (e.g., Schuerman, Rzepnicki, & Little 1994; Maluccio, 1991b; McCroskey & Meezan, 1997).

At its heart, however, the policy debate involves questions of value: What are basic rights and entitlements of individual children and their families in a complex society such as ours? Which problems are best viewed as private troubles of individual citizens and which should we elevate to public social concern? How blind should policy be to questions of race, ethnicity, and disadvantage? How active a role should government play in seeking out and remedying individual dysfunction? Can policy take into account that although men primarily hold power, those with the greatest stake in the child welfare system are women and children (Miller, 1991, p. 592)? Child welfare policy, as all other areas of social policy, has occasioned much spirited discussion over the past decade on the proper role of government in fulfilling its historical role as "parents patriae"—the ultimate parental authority (Downs, Costin, & McFadden, 1996), and the balance between acting "in the best interests of the child" versus family preservation (e.g., Goldstein, Solnit, Goldstein, & Freud, 1996; Goldstein, Freud, & Solnit 1979a,b).

In many different areas of child welfare, the debate over parental and guardianship responsibilities (wherein do they lie? how are they best exercised? who decides what is "good enough" parenting?) is evidenced daily and is woven through many of the chapters to follow. Some examples include the following:

Balancing Child Protection and Family Preservation

Some critics argue that in the rush to reintroduce a family focus in child welfare, agencies may be going too fast with unproven interventions, thereby placing individual children at risk by allowing them to remain in families where the potential for abuse remains high (Gelles, 1996; Wald, 1988). Others argue that the state itself put children at risk in nonparental caregiving arrangements and that, in any case, the best means we have for protecting individual children is through preventive efforts that provide much needed support to families (Nelson, 1990). Balancing the rights of children and parents is no easy matter (Besharov, 1985a).

Providing "Universal" Services/Benefits versus
Those That Are "Categorical" and Targeted

Although targeting a specific problem, group, or condition can have the effect of making the best use of scarce resources, it can also result in a failure to consider a more comprehensive response to meeting the needs of children and families. Kahn and Kamerman, two of the country's leading policy scholars in family and child services, illustrate this in their analysis of the limitations of current targeted efforts to address the problems of child maltreatment in lieu of more universal solutions, such as employment programs, pre- and postnatal services, housing, or other basic supports that should be available to all families, similar to fire and police protection (Kamerman & Kahn, 1990, 1995).

In-Home, Family-Centered versus Out-of-Home,
Substitute-Care Approaches

As the following chapters on family-based services, foster family care, and group care services will illustrate, much debate has tended to polarize placement and nonplacement services, sometimes at the expense of the substitute-care sector (Kamerman & Kahn, 1990). A challenge for the future remains to identify under what circumstances and for which types of children and families each service should be used. A related challenge involves specifying how a policy of family support can be realized even when the child is temporarily placed out of the home.

Employing the Right Mix of Professional
versus Lay Staff Members

Some have argued for the necessity of bolstering child welfare services with additional professional expertise (see Chapter 14). Others have countered that there is a greater danger in overprofessionalization and the resulting "problematization" that inevitably follows. Critical questions await study on the potential strengths and limits of volunteers, self-help groups, and other informal efforts in an overall societal response to a problem, such as child maltreatment. In each of the subareas of child welfare described in the chapters to follow, professionals and lay helpers are forging relationships for working together. And empirical research in many areas is establishing the importance of paraprofessional services and informal self-help groups.

Prevention versus Treatment

By one calculation, child welfare services have been offering too little too late. Efforts must be redirected at those children and families at risk but as yet unaffected by major problems and still outside the categorical service net. Much of the argument for "family support" (through employment programs, family leave policies, income supports, housing prenatal care, and other services) and early intervention proceeds from this basis (Gil, 1970; Pelton, 1989). This approach, however, is not without complications:

• many at-risk families ultimately do not require treatment (remedial) services and it is hard to predict which specific families will actually require assistance;

- thus, depending on the nature of the service, a significant proportion of preventive services may be provided to families who do not really need them;
- however, there are limited resources available for both kinds of services;
- thus, we have to strike a balance between preventive and treatment (remedial) services.

Yet many families and children are already caught up in the system and surely have some claim on resources, particularly given the fact that intervention may have a secondary preventive effect in keeping them from sliding further into the system.

Balancing Short-Term Expense and Long-Term Gain

A child welfare advocate pointed out that all too frequently we ask politicians for the exact reverse of what they are proposing: We say, "Pay now, see results later"; they say, "Show results now and defer the bills to the future" (B. Cahill, personal communication, May 18, 1990). What arguments can be mustered for acting and paying now? Less crime? Reduced costs for subsequent hospitalization and incarceration? A broader tax base? A more productive work force? In a world of limited resources, there are some trade-offs that must be made.

In 1997, there were 76.9 million children under age 18 in the United States, increasing significantly since 1950. This number is expected to increase to 77.6 million by 2020. In 1997, there were approximately equal numbers of children, about 19 million, in each age group (0–4, 5–9, 10–14, 15–19) (U.S. Bureau of the Census, Population Reports, P25-1095, and Population Paper Listings 91, p.15) *www.census.gov/prod/3/98pubs/98statab/sasec1.pdf).* These data from the most recent (1997) census show that as a percentage of the total population, children (ages 0–18) are over double those 65 and older (U.S. Bureau of the Census, 1999, p. 15). Yet any assessment of political clout would surely show exactly the opposite. The task of translating what Steiner (1976) has called "the Children's Cause" into mainstream political power remains one of the most daunting and critical of tasks awaiting child welfare advocates. To better understand the current policy context for children and families, the following section describes some salient characteristics and trends from the present population and briefly reviews the key legislation related to child welfare services affecting the lives of children and families.

SOME POPULATION STATISTICS FROM THE 1990 DECENNIAL CENSUS

The population of the United States is changing in ways that will shape child welfare services delivery. In 1997, children made up 29% of the population, down from a peak of 36% in 1960 (U.S. Bureau of the Census, 1999, p. 15). It should be noted that the Census Bureau figures have been criticized as undercounting the number of ethnic-minority, homeless, migrant-farm-worker, and illegal-alien populations in this country. The current approaches to categorizing and estimating the proportion of various ethnic groups in the United States also have limitations (see, for example, Lieberson & Waters, 1988; U.S. Bureau of the Census, 1999, p. 1). The census data, however, are enormously valuable for tracking trends in population and other socioeconomic conditions that have significant implications for families in this country.

Although the national census figures do not reflect how diverse many individual cities in the United States have become, they do reflect that as of 2010 a growing proportion of the total population of children is African-American (12.6%), Hispanic origin of any race (13.8%), Asian or Pacific Islander (4.8%), and Native American or Alaskan Native (0.8%), including 71.8% who were white (U.S. Bureau of the Census, 1999, p. 19). Most of these children are well cared for, and their parents and other family members have been able to fulfill the various caregiving roles. Other children are not so fortunate, as indicated by the statistics gathered by the Children's Defense Fund (1998, p. xviii). Part of the reason for these events is a combination of economic stresses and the fact that current provision of basic societal supports is inadequate. One result is an expansion of fragile families, which are more vulnerable to these social problems.

FAMILY ISSUES AND TRENDS

Although many advocates are working toward the provision of more universal primary prevention types of services, most child welfare services (narrowly defined) are being delivered because parents and children are experiencing difficulty in various areas of social functioning (e.g., parenting skills, provision of basic necessities, household management).

These difficulties have many causes, some of which interact in complex ways, but major factors that often strain families are unemployment and underemployment, family breakup through divorce or desertion, poverty, the imbalance of power between men and women (Abramovitz, 1991; Miller, 1991), and a lack of social supports available from other family members (Bumpass, 1990). These next sections highlight some of these trends.

Family Composition

If the family situations presented on certain television reruns such as "Leave it to Beaver" or the "Cosby Show," seem less representative than they once were, it is because the living arrangements of children in the United States have shifted so dramatically. Children and their parents are vulnerable today to the stresses and dangers of poverty, homelessness, substance abuse, spouse abuse, and child maltreatment. Consider some of these facts:

- Just over one-third of first marriages now remain intact for life.
- Today more than half of all women with a child under age 6 are in the paid labor force.
- Over 6 million households with young children are headed by a single parent, and this number could increase to 7.5 million by the year 2000 under current trends (De Vita & O'Hare, 1990, p. 3).
- Of the almost 500,000 births to those 15–19 years of age, 78% are out of wedlock (Center for Disease Control, 1999).

Approximately 30–40% of teens who become pregnant will conceive again within 2 years. Nearly half of teenage mothers receive public assistance within 4 years of giving birth, although the majority (76%) stop receiving public assistance within 4 years. Contrary to public belief, teenage childbearing is not just a problem for ethnic minority children. About two-thirds of teenage births are to white teens. But adolescents of color are at greater risk of early parenthood and particularly of being unmarried parents (De Vita & O'Hare, 1990, p. 8). Overall, the teen birth rate declined by 16% from 1991 to 1997, with all states recording a decline in teens 15–19 years old (National Center for Health Statistics, Center for Disease Control, 1999). Although the rates of teenage childbearing have decreased slightly, they remain at a significantly high level.

In too many cases children are left without adequate support. According to the U.S. Census Bureau, nearly 9 million families have children with absent fathers. In 1987, 4.8 million mothers had either voluntary or court-ordered child support awards. But 1.2 million (24%) of them did not receive any payment whatsoever, and only 25% received partial payment. As might be expected, the women receiving full payment tended to be in the higher income categories (Committee on Ways and Means, 1991, p. 666).

One of the factors contributing to this problem may be the more tenuous bonds between the noncustodial spouse and his or her children. The proportion of children living with one parent who was never married rose from 4.2% in 1960 to 30.5% in 1987 (U.S. Bureau of Census, 1989, p. 15). Furthermore, in 1996, 68% of U.S. children lived with two parents, down from 85% in 1970. White children are much more likely than black children and somewhat more likely than Hispanic children to live with two parents. In 1995, 32% of all births were to unmarried women, up from 5% in 1960. Almost two-thirds of the children living with only their mothers in 1995, however, were living with formerly married mothers (Federal Interagency Forum on Child and Family Statistics, 1997).

Complexities of patterns in living arrangements, parent decision making regarding paternity, economics, and other factors need to be carefully considered. Although this situation is not a simple one, serious attempts at developing strategies for addressing child support enforcement, as well as support of married and unmarried fathers, could bring substantial benefits to the children involved and therefore to the larger society (see, for example, Wattenberg, Brewer, & Resnick, 1991).

Certain positive trends can place greater demands on society as well. The rising life expectancy (from just below 62 years in 1935 to about 75 years in 1990) ironically, may place an ever greater strain on delivery of social and health services because of the greater numbers of elderly competing with families for funding resources (De Vita & O'Hare, 1990, p. 3).

Family Income Trends

In 1996, almost 14.5 million U.S. children (one in five) were poor. That's almost twice the adult poverty rate of 11.4% (see Chapter 4). Full-time, year-work at the 1997 minimum wage of $5.15 per hour equals only 82% of the poverty line for a three-person family (Children's Defense Fund, 1998, p. 5).

An issue that is beginning to concern many Americans is the widening gap in income between the rich and the poor. As discussed more thoroughly in Chapter 4, the poorest one-fifth of families (with or without children) in 1996 had incomes of 9% or lower than in 1973, while family income in the wealthiest fifth increased 35% (Children's Defense Fund, 1998, p. 2). Economic polarization is affecting the number and composition of people who are poor, and raising questions about the vitality of America's middle class, as well as social and economic prospects for our youth (De Vita and O'Hare, 1990, p. 4). Consider these other indicators:

America's ongoing economic recovery has benefited the wealthiest one-fifth of households while others have lost income between 1989 and 1996, leaving the gap between rich and poor at historically high levels. The effects of the growth in the economy over the past two decades have been uneven, and tens of millions of American parents continue to find it hard to get stable jobs with wages and benefits that are adequate to support their families (Children's Defense Fund, 1998).

Despite some of the successes of our income maintenance programs (Dear, 1989), a significant proportion of these children are living in poverty and are in danger of not receiving the kind of nurturing, health care, education, and other basic supports that they need to grow and develop to be productive citizens in this country (see Chapter 4). Nowhere is this more starkly presented than in Table 2.2, a summary of some of the issues in health care provided for pregnant mothers and young children.

But the struggle to obtain decent health care is, unfortunately, accompanied by equally difficult struggles for some families to locate affordable housing and jobs that pay a "living wage" and basic benefits. This is a serious issue, even for two-parent families (see Chapter 4). The rise of part-time positions has become problematic for many persons and families who need steady, full-time employment with benefits to stay above the poverty line and to afford basic health care (see

Levitan & Shapiro, 1987). Employment, therefore, is one of the cornerstones for supporting families. Unfortunately, the United States Congress has been more willing to pass legislation authorizing the provision of remedial services than in establishing programs to help promote a higher level of employment. Selected child welfare legislation is discussed in the next section.

Health Care and Insurance

The number of uninsured children has risen from 8.2 million in 1987 to 11.3 million in 1996 (Children's Defense Fund, 1998, p. 22). Ninety-two percent of uninsured children have a working parent; 66% have a parent who works full-time, year-round (Children's Defense Fund, 1998, p. 22). The Children's Health Insurance Program (CHIP) is also helping to extend medical insurance to more children. (See Table 2.1 for additional health statistics.)

MAJOR NATIONAL LEGISLATION THAT HAS HELPED SHAPE CHILD WELFARE SERVICES

Child welfare programs are supported financially and shaped, in large part, by national, state, and local laws and regulations. Some of the major pieces of national legislation that have shaped child welfare services are listed in Table 2.2 and summarized in the sections that follow. (See also Table 2.3 for a summary of major child welfare programs and the FY 2000 appropriations for them, with reference to the authorizing legislation.)

Child Abuse Prevention and Treatment Act of 1974
(PL 93-247)

This legislation was passed in response to public concern about the abuse of children—concern that was stimulated, in part, by the publicizing of "battered child syndrome" in the early 1960s based on the earlier work of pediatric radiologists (see Chapter 8 in this text; Anderson, 1989). The purpose of the Act was to "provide financial assistance for demonstration programs for the prevention, identification, and treatment of child abuse and neglect, and to establish a National Center on Child Abuse and Neglect" (Child Abuse Prevention and Treatment Act Report, 1973, as cited in Light, 1973, p. 238).[1]

Not only did the Act provide a means of funding more programs in this area, it mandated that states "must provide for the reporting of known or suspected instances of child abuse and neglect" [American Civil Liberties Union (ACLU), 1977, as cited in Stein, 1984, p. 303]. Although the program supports authorized

Table 2.1. Health Care in the Early Years

Demographic statistics show that many children in the United States begin life on relative-ly shaky ground. Over 7% of all children born in 1988 were considered low birth weight—that is, they weighed less than 5.5 pounds—and black infants were twice as likely as white infants to be low birth weight (Children's Defense Fund, 1998, p. 23). Because birth weight is the best predictor of a child's chances of survival in the first few weeks of life, the prevalence of low-birth-weight infants is one of the earliest and most critical indicators of a child's well-being. Low-birth-weight infants, for example, if they survive, are at greater risk of long-term health problems ranging from neurodevelopmental disabilities to lower respiratory tract conditions such as asthma. About one-quarter of all low-birth-weight infants born in 1988 (or 67,000 chil-dren) will enter the next century with a permanent disabling condition (De Vita & O'Hare, 1990, pp. 5–6).

Despite advances in medical technology that can increase an infant's chances of survival, the United States ranks below many other developed nations in terms of infant mortality—Southern states tend to have the highest rates of infant deaths. But even among states with the lowest infant mortality rates, there are wide differences by mother's race or ethnicity and by geographic regions within a state (De Vita & O'Hare, 1990, p. 5). The good news is that the infant mortality rate dropped to 7.6 deaths per 1,000 live births in 1995—the lowest level ever (Children's Defense Fund, 1998, p. 22).

The risks of low birth weight and infant deaths are closely linked to the socioeconomic and demographic characteristics of the mother and her access to health care. Babies born to women who are younger than age 20 or older than 34, who are minority, unmarried, poorly educated, or living in poverty are at greatest risk of being low birth weight or of dying. Indeed, the problem is particularly acute in the black community. In 1995, for example:

- Infant mortality rates among blacks were more than twice as high as among whites (15.1 per 1,000 births versus 6.3 per 1,000 births, respectively). Infant mortality for Hispanics was 6.1 per 1,000, but this figure may understate actual rates because of reporting prob-lems.
- Proportionately twice as many black babies (13%) as white or Hispanic babies (6%, each) were low birth weight.
- The percentage of mothers who received late or no prenatal care was twice as high for Hispanics (7.4%) and blacks (7.6%) as for whites (3.5%).
- The percentage of infants born to unmarried mothers was more than twice the rate for black women (69.9%) as for whites (25.3%) and almost double the rate for Hispanics (40.8%) (Children's Defense Fund, 1998, p. 23).

A key element to addressing these problems is improving access to medical care for preg-nant women and young children. Research has shown that for every $1.00 spent on prenatal care for low-income and poorly educated women, $4.40 could be saved during the first year of an infant's life in child health services. Some experts estimate that as many as 1 in 10 in-fant deaths could be prevented by early medical intervention and better prenatal care. New federal regulations extending Medicaid coverage to all pregnant women who meet AFDC in-come and resource requirements and all children under age 18 may help to ease the prob-lem, but states question how they will pay for these additional services without additional federal funds.

Table 2.2. A Select List of Child Welfare-Related Federal Legislation[a]

Legislation	Purpose	References
Child Abuse Prevention and Treatment Act of 1974 (P.L. 93-247)	Provides some financial assistance for demonstration programs for the prevention, identification, and treatment of child abuse and neglect; mandates that states must provide for the reporting of known or suspected instances of child abuse and neglect.	Light (1973), Stein (1984)
Juvenile Justice and Delinquency Prevention Act of 1974 (P.L. 93-415)	Provides funds to reduce the unnecessary and inappropriate detention of juveniles and to encourage state program initiatives in the prevention and treatment of juvenile delinquency and other status offenses.	Costin, Bell, and Downs (1991, pp. 71–72)
Title XIX of the Social Security Act	Mainly provides health care to income-eligible persons and families. One of the sections of this act established the Early and Periodic Screening, Diagnosis, and Treatment program, which provides cost-effective health care to pregnant women and young children.	
The Education of all Handicapped Children Act of 1975 (P.L. 94-142)	Act requiring and supporting education and social services to handicapped children. The Act requires states to (1) offer programs for the full education of handicapped children between the ages of 3 and 18, (2) develop strategies for locating such children, (3) use intelligence testing that does not discriminate against the child racially or culturally, (4) develop an IEP for each child, and (5) offer learning opportunities in *the least restrictive educational environment* possible, with an emphasis on mainstreaming—integrating handicapped children into regular classrooms.	Costin, Bell, and Downs (1991, pp. 300–303); Singer and Butler (1987)
Individuals with Disabilities Education Act (IDEA) (P.L. 101-476)	Act modifying services for special education students.	
Title XX of the Social Security Act (as amended by the Omnibus Reconciliation Act of 1981)	Through a block grant arrangement, provides states with federal funds for a variety of social service programs.	Mott (1976)
The Indian Child Welfare Act of 1978 (P.L. 95-608)	Strengthens the standards governing removal of Native American children from their families. Provides for a variety of requirements and mechanisms for tribal government overseeing and services for children.	Miller, Hoffman, and Turner (1980); Plantz, Hubbell, Barrett, and Dobrec (1989)

(continued)

Table 2.2. (Continued)

Legislation	Purpose	References
The Adoption Assistance and Child Welfare Act of 1980 (P.L. 96-272)	A child welfare reform legislation that uses funding incentives and procedural requirements to promote placement prevention and permanency planning.	Pine (1986)
Independent Living Initiative (P.L. 99-272)	Provides funding for services to prepare adolescents in foster care for living in the community on an independent basis.	Mech (1988)
Preschool Amendments to the Education of the Handicapped Act of 1986 (P.L. 99-457)	Mandates health, rehabilitation, education, and social services to children who have special needs from birth.	
Family Support Act of 1990	Establishes new initiatives for financial assistance for low income families.	
1990 Farm Act (P.L. 101-624)	The Food Stamp Program was reauthorized until 1995 as part of this bill.	American Public Welfare Association (1991)
Foster Care Independence Act (HR 3443) of 1999	It doubles funding to $140 million for the John H. Chafee Foster Care Independence Program, and allows states to use up to 30% of these funds for room and board for youths ages 18 to 21, transitioning from foster care. It also gives states the option of extending Medicaid to these older youths transitioning from foster care.	http://thomas.loc.gov; http://www.connectforkids.org

[a]A number of other pieces of legislation are important to child welfare services but are not summarized in this table, including the Social Security Act of 1935, amendments to the Act passed in 1939, 1950, 1962, 1965, 1967, 1974, and 1983, some of which are also known as the Title amendments of Title IV, IV-A, IV-B, IV-E, IV-F, and V. These title amendments established, terminated, or altered a wide range of income assistance, medical, social service, and other programs. For more information, see Costin et al (1991), DiNitto and Dye (1989), and Stein (1991).

by the Act were badly needed, the inclusion of mandatory reporting clauses and the imprecise definitions of what constitutes child maltreatment have been cause for much concern and criticism:

> The law fails to specify the conditions that should be defined as child abuse or neglect or the evidential standards for reporting. Moreover, although the intent of the legislation is conveyed clearly in its title, the implementing regulations focused attention on mandatory reporting and investigation, not prevention and treatment. Consequently, this law has had the effect of greatly enlarging the pool of children coming to the attention of public authorities as potentially in need of care and protection, without providing the resources or guidelines necessary to enable states to deal more effectively with this population. (McGowan, 1990, p. 72)

Thus, the implementation of the Child Abuse Prevention and Treatment Act has been problematic because of problems in reporting laws, underdeveloped risk assessment technology, too broad a scope of intervention, insufficient funding, lack of worker training, poor program design, lack of adequate intervention research, and other issues.

Title XX Amendments to the Social Security Act of 1975

Title XX was an important piece of legislation in that it authorized payment to the states for a broad array of social services. This legislation amended the Social Security Act by creating a new section, Title XX, that authorized the spending of funds to persons who were receiving cash payments as part of the Aid to Families with Dependent Children (AFDC) or Supplemental Security Income (SSI), and for specially defined low income families (Downs, Costin, & McFadden, 1996, pp. 18–22). This law gave states and their local governments much more power and discretion regarding how to allocate these federal dollars for programs (see Mott, 1976). In 1981, as part of the Omnibus Reconciliation Act (PL 97-35), the Act was converted into a social services "block grant," where the amount provided to each state had fewer restrictions on what it must be spent on. In effect, states were no longer required to target specific goals or to provide free services to public assistance recipients:

> Under the Act's original mandate, each state was required to provide at least one service directed toward meeting each of five goals: self-support, self-sufficiency; preventing abuse and neglect and preserving and reuniting families; preventing inappropriate institutional care; and securing appropriate institutional care and services. Although Congress provided only minimal direction to the states as to how the funds were to be used, it provided clear instructions on funding levels, incorporating the $2.5 billion ceiling on the program that had been imposed on the predecessor social services program three years earlier (the Title XX program replaced the social

services programs previously authorized under Titles IV-A and VI of the Social Security Act). Generally the legislation also required states to provide a 25% match for federal dollars received. Although one-half of the funds had to be targeted to low-income persons and eligibility for most services was income-related, some services such as protective services for children, could be provided to anyone regardless of income. (Allen & Knitzer, 1983, pp. 97–98)

For 1999, Title XX appropriations were funded at 1.9 billion (see Table 2.3). But because of the breadth of services that this legislation supports and the lack of specific state requirements, primary prevention and placement prevention services remain inadequately funded, and the general child welfare caseloads remain inordinately high (see Chapter 14).

The Indian Child Welfare Act of 1978 (PL 95-608)

Congress enacted the Indian Child Welfare Act (ICWA) of 1978, finding that "there is no resource more vital to the continued existence and integrity of the Indian Tribe than their children" and "an alarmingly high percentage of Indian families are broken up by the removal, often unwarranted, of their children . . . by nontribal public and private agencies." The Act creates procedural safeguards in matters pertaining to the custody and placement of Indian children. It was an important first step in strengthening federal and state policy toward Indian families. Briefly stated, the major provisions of the Act are as follows:

Tribes are given exclusive jurisdiction over reservation Indian children. An exception is made for reservations in those states that have assumed jurisdiction over reservations under the authority of PL 83-280 (1953). Tribes in such states can petition the secretary of the interior to reassume their jurisdiction over child welfare matters. According to the Act, "full faith and credit" must be given to the judgments of tribal courts over child welfare cases.[2]

State jurisdiction over child custody hearings can be transferred to the tribe. Cases of Indian children not residing or domiciled on the reservation can be transferred to the tribal court at the request of the tribe, parents, or Indian custodian unless either of these parties objects or the court finds "good cause" to the contrary.

Both tribes and parents of Indian custodians have the right to be notified of and to intervene in state court proceedings. The party seeking custody of an Indian child is required to notify the parents and the tribe. All tribes that might be the Indian child's tribe should be notified. If either of these parties cannot be located, the Secretary of the Interior also must be notified. Emergency removals can be made without notification, but subsequent hearings must follow notification procedures.

Higher standards of proof are applied to state custody proceedings involving Indian children. A foster care placement may be ordered only if it is proved by "clear and convincing" evidence, including the testimony of a qualified expert witness, that continued custody by the parent or custodian is likely to result in serious

Table 2.3. Appropriations for Selected Child Welfare Programs (in Millions)

Program	FY 1999	FY 2000
Protective and Preventive Services		
Child Welfare Services Program (Title IV-B)	$292.0	292.0
Promoting Safe and Stable Families (Title IV-B, Subpart 2)[a]	275.0	295.0
Child Welfare Training (Title IV-B)	7.0	7.0
CAPTA Child Protective Services State Grant Program	21.0	21.0
CAPTA Discretionary Grants Program	14.2	18.6
CAPTA Community Based Family Resource Centers	32.8	32.8
Family Violence Prevention and Services Act[b]		
Social Services Block Grant Program (Title XX)	2,380.0	1,775.0
Indian Child Welfare Grant Program	13.6	13.6
Out-of-Home Care Services		
Foster Care Program (Title IV-E)[c]	3,982.7	4,537.2
Adoption Services		
Adoption Assistance Program (Title IV-E)[c]	868.8	1,020.1
Adoption Opportunities Act	25.0	27.5
Adoption Incentives Payments[d]	20.0	43.0
Child Day Care Services		
Child Care and Development Block Grant (discretionary)	1,182.7	1182.7
Child Care and Development Block Grant (mandatory)[e]	2167.0[e]	2,367.0[e]
Head Start	4,660.0	5267.0
Health Care Services		
Children's Mental Health Services Program	78.0	83.0
Community Mental Health Performance Partnership Block Grant	288.8	356.0
Ryan White AIDS Resources Act (Title IV)	46.0	51.0
Individuals with Disabilities Education Act: Early Intervention Services Program (Part H)	370.0	375.0
Family Planning Program	214.9	238.9
Substance Abuse Services		
Abandoned Infants Assistance Act	12.3	12.3
Substance Abuse Prevention Partnership Block Grant	1,585.0	1,600.0
Consolidated Men. Hlth. and Sub. Abuse Demo. Program		
Housing and Homelessness Assistance		
Family Unification Program[f]	[f]	
Welfare to Work Housing Vouchers[g]	283.0[g]	
Youth Services		
Independent Living Program (Title IV-E)	70.0	105.0
Juvenile Justice and Delinquency Prevention Act (State Formula)	89.0[h]	89.0[h]
Juvenile Justice Discretionary Prevention and Treatment Programs	42.8	42.8
Youth Gangs	12.0	12.0
Juvenile Justice State Challenge Activities	10.0	10.0
Juvenile Mentoring	12.0	13.5
Delinquency Prevention Act (Grants)	95.0	95.0[i]

(*continued*)

Table 2.3. (Continued)

Program	FY 1999	FY 2000
Youth Services (continued)		
Juvenile Accountability Incentive Block Grant Program	250.0	250.0
Runaway and Homeless Youth Act (Basic Centers)	43.7	43.7
Transitional Living Program for Homeless Youth	14.9	20.8
Grants to Reduce Sexual Abuse and Exploitation of Runaway, Homeless and Street Youth (Street-based Service)	15.0	15.0
National and Community Service Activities	434.5	434.5
Public Assistance (Welfare)		
Temporary Assistance for Needy Families (TANF) [j]		

Note: The final budget agreement triggers a 0.38% across-the board cut in discretionary spending throughout the federal government. Federal agencies have the discretion to determine the reduction. Of the 0.38% cut federal agencies may cut unly up to 15% from any individual program.

[a]Adoption and Safe Families Act of 1997 (P.L. 105-89) retitled this program from Family Preservation and Family Support Program.

[b]Combines funding for this program with funding for grants authorized under the Violence Against Women Act.

[c]Because this is an entitlement program its annual funding is automatically set at the level required to fund the services authorized for eligible persons. Statutory changes in eligibility or benefit levels, as well as changes in the number of eligible persons actually participating, affect federal outlays.

[d]These payments were authorized in the Adoption and Safe Families Act of 1997 (P.L. 105-89).

[e]The Personal Responsibility and Work Opportunity Reconciliation Act of 1996 (P.L. 104-193) preappointed mandatory entitlement funding for this program. This new block grant combines child care for AFDC recipients in work or training, "transitional child care" for those who have just left work, and assistance for families who need help to remain employed into one block grant with capped funding.

[f]Funds for this program are to be drawn from the overall appropriation for Section 8 low-income rental assistance.

[g]Funds 50,000 new housing vouchers for families searching for apartments as they move form welfare to work.

[h]Funding for this program is included in a proposed local youth crime intervention program. In 1999, a portion ($26.5 million) of the state formula grants is reserved for states that have adopted (or will have in effect not later than one year after date of application) policies and programs that ensure that juveniles are subject to accountability-based sanctions for every act for which they are adjudicated delinquent.

[i]$52.5 million of this program is reserved for a safe school initiative, tribal youth programs, and enforcement of enforce underage drinking laws.

[j]This program replaced Aid to Families with Dependent Children (AFDC) as the nation's primary welfare program, as a result of enactment of the Personal Responsibility and Work Opportunity Reconciliation Act of 1996 (P.L.104-193) on August 22, 1996.

Sources: Adapted from Child Welfare League of America (1999). Funding for selected children's programs. *Children's Monitor, 12*(9), 2–3.

emotional or physical damage to the child. Termination of parental rights and responsibilities can be ordered only if evidence to this effect is "beyond a reasonable doubt," which is a more stringent level of evidence. Expert testimony is required here as well. In both cases it must be shown that active efforts have been made to prevent family breakup. The Act also authorizes the secretary to pay for legal services to parents if not provided by the state.

The Act specifies placement preferences for states in placing Indian children in foster and adoptive homes. First preference is to be given to the child's extended family, then to foster homes licensed or approved by the tribe, then to other Indian foster homes or appropriate Indian institutions. Tribal governments may legislate their own preferences and state courts ordinarily must follow them. Standards for the selection of Indian homes are to be the prevailing social and cultural standards of the Indian community.

Voluntary placements of Indian children for foster care or adoption must be well informed and are revocable in certain cases. Any parent of an Indian child must execute consent in writing before a judge who certifies that the consent was explained in a language that the parent understood. Consent cannot be given prior to 10 days after the birth of a child. The parent may withdraw consent to a foster care placement at any time. He or she may withdraw consent to adoption up until the entry of the final decree of termination or adoption. If the parent can show that consent was obtained under duress, an adoption may be overturned up to 2 years after finalization.

Grants to Indian tribes and organizations to establish Indian child and family services are authorized. Many considered this the most important section of the act, providing some mechanism for Indian-delivered preventive services. Unfortunately, to date insufficient funds have been allocated to implement this section. Placements can be overturned if it can be shown that the Act was not followed with respect to notification, rights to intervention and transfer, counsel for parents, standards of evidence and testimony, and consent procedures.

Those involved in the implementation of the Act have noted numerous inconsistencies in language and confusion in interpretation in several key areas, in major part stemming from the problems encountered in trying to pass the legislation (Gross, 1989). Among these inconsistencies are definition of "Indian child," particularly Alaskan Native children, lack of clarity over notification procedures, and definitions of "expert witness" and "good cause." Although guidelines for state courts were published in the *Federal Register,* each state has developed court rules for its judges. Judges and child welfare agencies are responsible for following the Act in the face of difficulties in interpretation and confusion over procedure. They must determine tribal affiliations in order to notify parents and tribes and be fully aware of court and service requirements. If the Act is not followed, it will be Indian children who suffer from the disruption of homes and placements. Accordingly, child welfare professionals must have expertise in several of the following areas:

- how to establish links with local tribes and Indian organizations (although the act mandates Indian involvement only at the point of judicial proceedings, prior working relationships are imperative);
- working knowledge of the Act itself and legal pitfalls associated with it;
- awareness of the state's policies on jurisdiction and the status of state court rules developed to implement the Act;
- access to a listing of American tribes and contact persons for each tribe;
- actively seeking out and developing training on the Act and in work with American Indian families.

Although the Indian Child Welfare Act has improved services to many Native American families, serious problems remain. For example, the act applies only to tribes recognized by the U.S. Bureau of Indian Affairs (BIA), so some Native Americans may need these protections but will not be covered. Furthermore, in one study involving a national mail survey and case record reviews in four states, proactive efforts were documented in only 41% of the records of cases under state jurisdiction. A case record review in the four states revealed that 53% of the Native American children were placed in non-Indian homes (Plantz, Hubbel, Barrett, & Dobrec, 1989, p. 25):

> Factors that respondents believe deter or undermine implementation of the ICWA include unfamiliarity with or resistance to the Act; lack of public agency experience in working with tribes; staff turnover; lack of funding; concern about tribal accountability for providing services and caring for children; and absence of tribal courts with the authority to assume jurisdiction over proceedings involving tribe members. (p. 26)

What is helping to improve implementation of the law is the passage of more specific state Indian child welfare laws that promote specific reforms and compliance mechanisms by state and local agencies. The employment and retention of more Native American staff are improving service, along with the training of existing staff members in the provisions of the federal and state laws. In other areas, helpful strategies include "state/tribal agreements that provide formal support for substitute care placements and for child welfare services; training and technical assistance to help develop tribal welfare services" (Plantz et al., 1989, p. 26).

The Adoption Assistance and Child Welfare Act (AACWA) of 1980 (PL 96-272)

Public Law 96-272 and its successor, the Adoption and Safe Families Act of 1997, are in many ways the most important pieces of child welfare legislation in the past 20 years. The AACWA recognized the major problems in the child welfare, service delivery system and attempts to promote a number of empirically validated practice approaches and service delivery guidelines. The Act amends Title IV-A and Title IV-B of the Social Security Act and created a new Act, Title IV-E. Thus, PL 96-272 essentially established a two-tier funding framework, with additional procedural and practice requirements for higher levels of funding.

Through the funding regulations, the Act discouraged state use of custodial foster care. Instead, Title IV-B supported more funding for preplacement preventive services for families in crisis and IV-E supported permanency planning for children unable to remain with their own families. A new adoption subsidy program is created as well. Finally, the Act requires the maintenance or institution of a number of "best practice" requirements by state child welfare programs.

Title IV-E, PL 96-272 set up essentially a two-tier system for funding child welfare services. Each state, based on the history of its foster care program costs, was given an allotment with a ceiling to minimize foster care maintenance costs.[3] If the state stayed under the ceiling, Title IV-E funds could be transferred to the Title IV-B funding allocation, which allowed more flexible use of funds. These federal limitations on foster care maintenance payments represent an important reform but has not been used much.

To receive IV-E funds states have to institute or document a number of program or procedural reforms. Some of these reforms and other significant aspects of the Act are presented below. To receive maximum federal financial participation in their child welfare programs, states must implement or use the following programs or procedural reforms:

- state inventory of children in care (requires a one-time listing of all children who have been in foster care for 6 months or more by case number, date of birth, date of initial and current placement, date of last administrative or judicial review, and other information);
- statewide information system (provides data so that the legal status, demographic characteristics, location, and goals for placement of every child currently receiving foster care services or who has been in foster care within the preceding 12 months are known);
- preplacement preventive services [includes 24-hour emergency caretaker and homemaker services, day care, crisis counseling, individual and family counseling, emergency shelters, access to emergency financial assistance, and temporary child care; agencies must demonstrate they have provided "reasonable efforts" in terms of their services to prevent child placement (Allen, 1991; National Council of Family and Juvenile Court Judges et al., N.D.)];
- reunification or permanent planning services (a core of reunification services must be provided such as day care, homemaker or caretaker services, and family and individual counseling for parents and children; other services appropriate for reunification may also be provided such as respite care and parent education; further services to facilitate adoption or legal guardianship are included such as legal, adoptive services, staff training, and adoption follow-up);

- detailed case plan (must incorporate goals for reunification or other permanent placement, documentation of caseworker's actions);
- periodic case review (must occur and includes judicial or administrative review every 6 months and dispositional hearing by a court or court-appointed administrative body within 18 months of the child's placement);
- standards for care (placement must be in the least restrictive setting available, with close proximity to parents and with relatives where possible);
- procedural safeguards regarding removal and placement agreements; parents and child (if appropriate age and circumstance) must participate in the development and approval of case plans; child removal without judicial determination is allowed only in emergency situations; there must be an availability of fair hearings for child, parent, or foster parent who feel they have been aggrieved by a child welfare agency;
- standards for payment (federal payments are allowed for group care non-detention services where such facilities do not exceed a certain number in a state);
- Indian child welfare (tribes can be reimbursed directly for Title IV-B child welfare services);
- voluntary placement guidelines (federal reimbursement is available for the first 180 days if the state meets the above requirements);
- adoption subsidies for children with special needs (adoption subsidies for special-needs or low-income children).

One of the most important components of the Act was the availability of federal funds for subsidized adoption for children who are classified as having special needs and who are income eligible. Children with special needs or those described as hard to place are generally children available for adoption who are over 12 years of age, are handicapped, belong to a minority group, or are part of a sibling group to be placed together. For children to receive subsidized adoption funds, they must be eligible for AFDC or SSI. Finally, a key provision of the Act stipulated that adoptive families did not have to pass a "means test" in order to receive subsidized adoption payments.

The Adoption Assistance and Child Welfare Act of 1980 (PL 96-272) represents a landmark piece of legislation in that it provided a federal policy framework and a set of fiscal incentives were consistent with what research showed were "best practice" standards and procedures. Unfortunately, the growth of prevention services has not occurred.

In summary, PL 96-272 used a "carrot and stick" approach to promoting reform in substitute care by attempting to make additional funds available to states that implement services and procedures geared to keeping families intact. Where family preservation is not possible, the Act emphasized providing children with continuity of care and a respected social status through time-limited case plans and use of a range of permanent placements such as guardianship, adoption, or long-term family foster care.

Multi-Ethnic Placement Act of 1994 (PL 103-382)

At least one-third of the children placed in foster care will never return to their birth parents, leaving those children in need of permanent homes. And certain groups of children wait longer than others to belong to a new family. For example, minority children—who made up over 60% of those in foster care nationwide in 1994—wait about twice as long as other children (Government Accounting Office, 1998, p. 1) Berrick, Needell, Barth, and Jonson-Reid (1998) and Barth (1997) have also documented that African-American children have much lower likelihood of adoption than other children.

In 1994, the Multi-Ethnic Placement Act (MEPA) was signed into law by President Clinton eliminating policies that favor same-race placements. The law is intended to prevent discrimination in the placement of children in foster care and adoption on the basis of race, color, or national origin, to decrease the time children wait to be adopted, and to ensure agency recruitment of a pool of foster and adoptive parents that reflects the racial and ethnic diversity of the children available for adoption. MEPA prohibits states or any agencies that receive Federal funds from delaying or denying the placement of any child solely on the basis of race, color, or national origin. In 1996, MEPA was amended by the Inter-Ethnic Adoption Provisions Act. This revision removed language explicitly permitting the consideration of race and ethnicity as one of a number of factors used to determine the best interests of the child and adds penalties for states not in compliance with the law. Through this amendment, Congress intends to eliminate any delays in placement that can be avoided. More specifically, race, culture, or ethnicity may not be used as the basis for denial of placement, nor may such factors be used as a reason to delay any foster or adoptive placement.

Any child welfare agency that receives federal funds is affected by the Inter-Ethnic Adoption Provisions Act of 1996 (IAP). The law does not affect the Indian Child Welfare Act, or the responsibilities of the states to be in compliance with ICWA standards for eligible Indian children in their care.

In the past, many children of color have experienced significant delays before being placed with a foster family or for adoption because of the reluctance of caseworkers to make transracial placements. According to the data, lower reunification with the biological family is a contributing factor of African-American children staying in the system for longer periods (Barth, 1997). One of the reasons for the large number of African-American children in the system is the high incidence of substance abuse among African-American parents (Courtney, 1998). It is strongly correlated with higher rates of poverty because of discrimination and single motherhood. A lack of effective drug treatment and the lack of resources for the families may also be contributing to this trend. Some states and agencies have policies that discourage transracial placements or that allow lengthy searches for same-race families before authorizing transracial placements. Some families are informally discouraged from ever applying to adopt children of a different race or ethnicity. It is too early to determine the full effects of these changes in statute. Although MEPA requires states to make diligent efforts to recruit families that reflect the ethnic and racial diversity of children needing homes, IAP prohibits states and agencies from denying anyone the opportunity to adopt on the basis of race. The lack of federal funding may hinder diligent recruitment of families of color as most state child welfare agencies may rush to process interracial adoption, rather than allocating enough money for recruitment of families of color. (See Chapter 13 for more information.)

Because of the large number of multiethnic children awaiting a more permanent home, major service reforms were needed and MEPA was one attempt to address these problems. Among the challenges in fully implementing this act is the very real dilemma that ethnic minority administered and staffed child welfare agencies are rare; and that, where adequately funded and staffed, these agencies appear to be able to place children of color in same/similar race homes. (Better research is clearly needed in this vital area.)

In terms of specific implementation barriers to adoption placement that fit the intent of these laws, the Government Accounting Office in a recent review of MEPA identified the following three barriers: (1) translating legal principles into practical guidelines and strategies for caseworkers where much confusion exists about the Act; (2) changing long-standing casework beliefs and practices, such as placement of children in same-race homes is in the best interests of children; and (3) developing compliance-monitoring systems (General Accounting Office, 1998, p. 3).

Adoption and Safe Families Act (PL 105-89)[4]

On November 19, 1997, the President signed into law (PL 105-89) the Adoption and Safe Families Act of 1997, to improve the safety of children, to promote adoption and other permanent homes for children who need them, and to support families. This law makes changes and clarifications in a wide range of policies established under the Adoption Assistance and Child Welfare Act (PL 96-272), the major federal law enacted in 1980 to assist the states in protecting and caring for abused and neglected children. Because of the impact this law is having on the delivery of child welfare services, a comprehensive summary from the Child Welfare League of America (1997) is reprinted below. The new law does the following:

Continues and Expands the Family Preservation and Support Services Program. The Family Preservation and Support Services Program, renamed the Promoting Safe and Stable Families Program, is reauthorized through FY 2001 at the following levels: FY 1999 at $275 million; FY 2000 at $295 million; and FY 2001 at $305 million. The set-asides are maintained for the Court Improvement Program, evaluation, research, training, technical assistance, and Indian tribes.

State plans are now also required to contain assurances that in administering and conducting service programs, the safety of the children to be served will be of paramount concern.

The new law further clarifies that for the purposes of the maintenance of effort requirement in the program, "non-federal funds" may be defined as either state or state and local funds. This change is made retroactive to the enactment of the Family Preservation and Support Services Program (PL 103-66) on August 10, 1993.

In addition to the funds to prevent child abuse and neglect and to assist families in crisis, the program's funds specifically include time-limited reunification services such as counseling, substance abuse treatment services, mental health services, assistance for domestic violence, temporary child care and crisis nurseries, and transportation to and from these services. Adoption promotion and support services are also included and are defined as pre- and postadoptive services and activities designed to expedite the adoption process and support families.

Continues Eligibility for the Federal Title IV-E Adoption Assistance Subsidy to Children Whose Adoption Is Disrupted.   Any child who was receiving a federal adoption subsidy on or after October 1, 1997, shall continue to remain eligible for the subsidy if the adoption is disrupted or if the adoptive parents die.

Authorizes Adoption Incentive Payments for States.   The Act authorizes $20 million for each of FY 1999–2003 for payments to eligible states that exceed the average number of adoptions the state completed during FY 1995–FY 1997, or in FY 1999 and subsequent years, in which adoptions of foster children are higher than in any previous fiscal year after FY 1996. The amount of the bonus is $4,000 for each foster child adopted and $6,000 for each adoption of a child with special needs previously in foster care. To be eligible to receive these payments for FY 2001 or FY 2002, states are required to provide health insurance coverage to any special needs child for whom there is an adoption assistance agreement between the state and the child's adoptive parents.

Requires States to Document Efforts to Adopt.   States are required to make reasonable efforts and document child specific efforts to place a child for adoption, with a relative or guardian, or in another planned permanent living arrangement when adoption is the goal. The law also clarifies that reasonable efforts to place a child for adoption or with a legal guardian may be made concurrently with reasonable efforts to reunify a child with his or her family.

Expands Health Care Coverage to Non-IV-E Eligible Adopted Children with Special Health Care Needs.   States are required to provide health insurance coverage for any child with special needs for whom there is an adoption assistance agreement between the state and the adoptive parents and whom the state has determined could not be placed for adoption without medical assistance because the child has special needs for medical, mental health, or rehabilitative care.

The health insurance coverage can be provided through one or more state medical assistance programs including Medicaid and must include benefits of the same type and kind as provided under Medicaid. The state may determine cost sharing requirements.

Authorizes New Funding for Technical Assistance to Promote Adoption. The U.S. Department of Health and Human Services (HHS) may provide technical assistance to states to promote the adoption, or other alternative permanent placement, of foster children. The technical assistance may include guidelines for expediting termination of parental rights; encouraged use of concurrent planning; specialized units and expertise in moving children toward adoption; risk assessment tools for early identification of children at risk of harm if returned home; encouraged use of fast tracking for children under age one into preadoptive placements; and programs to place children into preadoptive placements prior to termination of parental rights. At least half of the appropriated funds are reserved for providing technical assistance to the courts.

Addresses Geographic Barriers to Adoption.   States are required to ensure that the state will develop plans for the effective use of cross-jurisdictional resources to facilitate timely permanent placements for children awaiting adoption. The state's Title IV-E foster care and adoption assistance funding is conditioned on the state not denying or delaying a child's adoptive placement, when an approved family is available outside of the jurisdiction with responsibility for the child. Funding is also conditioned on the state granting opportunities for fair hearings for allegations of violations of the requirements. The U.S. General Accounting Office must study and report to Congress on how to improve procedures and policies to facilitate timely adoptions across state and county lines.

Establishes Kinship Care Advisory Panel.   HHS was required to prepare and submit, by June 1, 1999, a report for Congress on the extent of the placement of children in foster care with relatives and to convene an advisory panel on kinship care to review and comment on the report before it is submitted.

Issues Sense of Congress on Standby Guardianship.   It is the Sense of Congress that states should have laws and procedures to permit a parent who is chronically ill or near death to designate a standby guardian for their child, without surrendering their own parental rights. The standby guardian's authority would take effect on the parent's death, mental incapacity, or physical debilitation and consent.

Establishes New Time Line and Conditions for Filing Termination of Parental Rights.   Federal law did not require states to initiate termination of parental rights proceedings based on a child's length of stay in foster care. Under the new law, states must file a petition to terminate parental rights and concurrently, identify, recruit, process, and approve a qualified adoptive family on behalf of any child, regardless of age, that has been in foster care for *15 out of the most recent 22 months*. A child would be considered as having entered foster care on the earlier of either the date of the first judicial finding of abuse or neglect, or 60 days after the child is removed from the home.

This new requirement applies to children entering foster care in the future and to children already in care. For children already in care, states are required to phase in the filing of termination petitions beginning with children for whom the permanency plan is adoption or who have been in care the longest. One-third must be filed within 6 months of the end of the state's first legislative session following enactment of this law, two-thirds within 12 months, and all of them within 18 months. A state must also file such a petition if a court has determined that an infant has been abandoned (as defined in state law) or if a court has determined that a parent of a child has assaulted the child, or killed or assaulted another one of their children. Exceptions can be made to these requirements if (1) at the state's option, a child is being cared for by a relative; (2) the state agency documents in the case plan that is available for court review a compelling reason why filing is not in the best interest of the child; or (3) the state agency has not provided to the child's family, consistent with the time period in the case plan, the services deemed necessary to return the child to a safe home.

Sets New Time Frame for Permanency Hearings.   Former federal law required a dispositional hearing within 18 months of a child's placement into out-of-home care. The new law establishes a permanency planning hearing for children in care that occurs within 12 months of a child's entry into care. At the hearing, there must be a determination of whether and when a child will be returned home, placed for adoption and a termination of parental rights petition filed, referred for legal guardianship, or another planned permanent living arrangement if the other options are not appropriate.

Modifies Reasonable Efforts Provision in PL 96-272.   States continue to be required to make reasonable efforts to preserve and reunify families. In making decisions about the removal of a child from, and the child's return to, his or her home, the child's health and safety shall be the paramount concern. The *reasonable efforts requirement does not apply in cases in which a court has found that*

- the parent has subjected the child to "aggravated circumstances" as defined in state law (including but not limited to abandonment, torture, chronic abuse, and sexual abuse);
- the parent has committed murder or voluntary manslaughter or aided or abetted, attempted, conspired, or solicited to commit such a murder or manslaughter of another child of the parent;
- the parent has committed a felony assault that results in serious bodily injury to the child or another one of their children; or
- the parental rights of the parent to a sibling have been involuntarily terminated.

In these cases, states would *not* be required to make reasonable efforts to pre-serve or reunify the family but are required to hold a permanency hearing within 30 days and to make reasonable efforts to place the child for adoption, with a legal guardian, or in another permanent placement.

Requires States to Check Prospective Foster and Adoptive Parents for Criminal Backgrounds. States are required to provide procedures for criminal record checks for any prospective foster or adoptive parents, before the parents are approved for placement of a child eligible for federal subsidies. When a criminal record check reveals a felony conviction for child abuse or neglect, spousal abuse, another crime against a child (including child pornography), rape, sexual assault, or homicide, final approval of foster or adoptive parent status shall not be granted. In a case of a felony conviction for physical assault, battery, or a drug-related of-fense that was committed in the past 5 years, approval could not be granted. States can opt out of this provision either through a written notice from the Governor to HHS, or through state law enacted by the state legislature.

Requires Notice of Court Reviews and Opportunity to be Heard to Foster Parents, Preadoptive Parents, and Relatives. A foster parent, any preadoptive parent, or relative caring for a child must be given notice of, and an opportunity to be heard in, any review or hearing involving the child. This provision does not require that any foster or preadoptive parent or relative be made a party to such a review or hearing.

Directs States to Establish Standards to Ensure Quality Services. By Jan-uary 1, 1999, states are required to develop and implement standards to ensure that children in foster care placements in public and private agencies are provided qual-ity services that protect the safety and health of the children.

Requires Assessment of State Performance in Protecting Children. HHS will develop, in consultation with governors, state legislatures, state and local pub-lic officials, and child welfare advocates, a set of outcome measures to be used to assess the performance of states in operating child protection and child welfare programs to ensure the safety of children and a system for rating the performance of states with respect to the outcome measures. HHS must submit an annual report to Congress on state performance including recommendations for improvement. The first report was due May 1, 1999. Outcome measures include length of stay in foster care and number of foster placement adoptions, and, to the extent possible, are to be developed from data available from the Adoption and Foster Care Analy-sis and Reporting System (AFCARS).

Directs Development of Performance-Based Incentive Funding System. HHS, in consultation with public officials and child welfare advocates, was required to develop and recommend to Congress a performance-based incentive system for providing payments under Title IV-B and Title IV-E of the Social Security Act by February 1999, and to submit a progress report on the feasibility, timetable, and consultation process for conducting such a study by May 1998.

Expands Child Welfare Demonstration Waivers.   Under previous law, HHS had the authority to approve up to 10 child welfare demonstration waivers. Eight states (CA, DE, IL, IN, MD, NC, OH, OR) have received approval to date. This new law authorizes HHS to conduct up to 10 demonstration projects per year from FY 1998 through 2002. Specific types of demonstrations to be considered include projects designed to identify and address reasons for delay in adoptive placements for foster children; projects designed to address parental substance abuse problems that endanger children and result in placement of a child in foster care; and projects designed to address kinship care. Eligibility for these waivers is not available if a state fails to provide health insurance coverage to any child with special needs for whom there is in effect an adoption assistance agreement.

Requires Study on the Coordination of Substance Abuse and Child Protection.   HHS will prepare a report that describes the extent and scope of the problem of substance abuse in the child welfare population, the types of services provided to this population, and the outcomes resulting from the provision of such services, including recommendations for legislation needed to improve coordination in providing such services.

Authorizes the Use of the Federal Parent Locator Service.   Child welfare agencies can now use the Federal Parent Locator Service to assist in locating absent parents.

Extends Independent Living Services.   Young people who are no longer eligible for federal foster care assistance because their savings and assets exceed $1,000 will still be eligible for independent living services, provided their assets do not exceed $5,000.

Funding Source.   The provisions of this law are partially funded ($40 million over 4 years) from an adjustment to the $2 billion Federal Contingency Fund for State Welfare Programs, created by the 1996 welfare law (PL 104-193). HHS is also required to make recommendations to Congress by March 1, 1998, for improving the operation of the Contingency Fund for State Welfare Programs (Child Welfare League of America, 1997).

In reviewing the various provisions of this Act, it is clear that child safety is being placed as a paramount concern, along with the more timely achievement of a permanent living situation and parenting arrangement for children. Birthparent rights are circumscribed by stringent time frames within which demonstration of the ability to raise their children must be demonstrated. A number of child welfare experts are concerned about the combined impact of welfare reform (e.g., TANF), AFSA the law described here, and the customary course of treatment (and relapse) for substance abuse. Some families may find themselves caught unfortunately in the intersection of two "time clocks" in which time limits for both public assistance (5 years lifetime) and reunification (18 months) intersect with the time during which relapses that are viewed as part of the normal course of substance abuse treatment generally occur (15–20 months).

In contrast, there are a number of positive features of this act including better coordination with substance abuse treatment, additional demonstration waivers, and clarification of when expedited termination of parental rights and responsibilities can occur.[5] In addition, HHS, in consultation with public officials and child welfare advocates, is required to develop and recommend to Congress a performance-based incentive system. During the Spring of 1999 a set of performance indicators was chosen, virtually all of them able to be obtained from the AFCARS state–federal data-reporting system to make the implementation of the system feasible by the deadline imposed by Congress (May 1999). Although this set of indicators is largely devoid of measures directly related to child and family well being, the set does contain a number of measures addressing child safety and permanence. At a time when agencies are struggling with managing to outcomes instead of exclusively to service delivery process, these efforts should provide some data and incentives for system improvements.

Family Preservation and Support Services Act of 1993 (PL 103-66)

The Family Preservation and Support Services Act of 1993 (PL 103-66) was reauthorized, expanded, and renamed the Promoting Safe and Stable Families Program (under PL 105-89). The reauthorized family preservation program continues through FY 2001 at the following levels: FY 1999 at $275 million, FY 2000 at $295 million, and FY 2001 at $305 million. States are now expected to commit a substantial portion of funds (conventionally thought to be at least 10%) to cover family support, family preservation, family reunification, and postadoptive services. State plans are now required to contain assurances that in administering and conducting service programs, the safety of the children to be served will be of paramount concern.

Independent Living Initiative (PL 99-272)

This law provides funding for services to prepare adolescents in foster care for independent living. Insufficient funding and limited implementation of the full-service program necessary to support children effectively are hampering the effectiveness of this measure. In addition, many agencies wait until the last minute to provide services to the children and are constrained from continuing the support necessary when a youth reaches age 21 or 22. This is counterproductive, since many youths in foster care are developmentally delayed because of previous maltreatment and disruptions in living situation. These youths need special support into young adulthood.[6]

The Foster Care Independence Act (H.R. 3443)

To address some of the issues mentioned above, The Foster Care Independence Act (H.R. 3443) was approved in November of 1999. It doubles funding to $140 million for the John H. Chafee Foster Care Independence Program, and allows states to use up to 30% of these funds for room and board for youths ages 18 to 21, transitioning from foster care. It also gives states the option of to extend Medicaid to these older youths transitioning from foster care. H.R. 3443 also includes several new provisions, most added from the Senate bill. They include the following:

- changing the name of the program to the John H. Chafee Foster Care Independence Program as a testimonial to Senator Chafee's longstanding leadership for children in foster care;
- clarifying in the findings that independent living activities should not be seen as an alternative to adoption for children, and can occur concurrently with efforts to find adoptive families for these children;
- adding adoptive parents to the groups to receive training with IV-E funds to help them understand and address the issues confronting adolescents preparing for independent living;
- adding achievement of a high school diploma and incarceration to the list of outcomes to be developed by the Secretary of HHS to assess the performance of states in operating independent living programs, and requiring the Secretary to submit to Congress with its report on outcomes and data a plan for imposing penalties on states that do not report data; and
- establishing a $500,000 minimum allotment for states under the John H. Chafee Foster Care Independence Program (*http://thomas.loc.gov*, www. childrensdefense.org , and *www.cwla.org*).

Survivor's Insurance, Aid to Families with Dependent Children (AFDC), and the Temporary Assistance to Needy Families (TANF)[7]

Survivors Insurance, established in 1939, provides benefits to surviving dependents of a deceased worker who has paid Social Security taxes. Children under age 18 are entitled to benefits based on the deceased parent's earnings record, as is the surviving parent until the youngest child reaches age 16. Most single-parent families now arise through divorce or nonmarital childbearing and do not qualify for Survivors Insurance. If their private incomes are low, as is often the case, they must rely on AFDC's recent successor, TANF, for income support (see Chapter 4 for further information).

The Personal Responsibility and Work Opportunity Reconciliation Act of 1996 (PRWORA) replaced AFDC and the welfare-to-work programs authorized by the Family Support Act with the TANF block grant. TANF ends entitlement to welfare and leaves it up to each state whether to aid all qualifying families. TANF benefits cannot be received by any family with a member who has received aid as an adult for 5 years. A state can exempt up to 20% of its cases from this time limit, but can also impose tighter limits. TANF also requires recipients to work after 2 years, requires unmarried parents under age 18 to live with an adult and stay in school to be eligible for benefits, gives states much greater control over all eligibility and administrative rules (including permission to deny aid to two-parent families), makes most poor immigrants ineligible for most forms of income assistance, and makes other major changes in cash and noncash programs of the safety net[8] (See Chapter 4).

The National School Lunch Program (NSLP) [PL.101-147] was officially instituted as a United States federal policy with the passage of the National School Lunch Act in 1946. The program is intended to provide children in public and non-profit schools and residential child care institutions with a nutritionally balanced lunch each school day. The program also offers free and reduced priced lunches for eligible children from low-income families. (United States Code, 1995). During fiscal year 1997, more than 26 million children—14.6 million of whom were from low-income families and received a free or reduced-priced lunch—consumed a lunch from the national program each day (FRAC, 1998; United States Code, 1995). Those children whose family's income is at or below 130% and 185% of the poverty line may eat lunch at a reduced price, which is not to exceed 40 cents. Children from families with incomes over 185% of the poverty line pay a full price for lunch, although their meals are still subsidized to some extent (United States Code, 1995).

The NSLP is administered by the Secretary of Agriculture. However, the program is still considered a Health and Human Services function, not an Agriculture function. Based on the number of lunches served and the current value of food, the Secretary distributes money and commodities to state educational agencies. The state educational agencies then allocate resources to the schools based on need and attendance. In addition, the Secretary is responsible for providing technical assistance and training in food preparation to food service providers and schools (United States Code, 1995).

Juvenile Justice and Delinquency Prevention Act
of 1974 (PL 93-415)

The 1970s were a time of growing concern that the rights of children and adolescents were being violated "in their best interests" (Rothman, 1980). For example, adolescents who were truant or had run away from home were being kept in adult jails and detention centers while awaiting the necessary court hearings. The act was designed both to reduce the unnecessary and inappropriate detention of juveniles and to encourage state program initiatives in the prevention and treatment of juvenile delinquency and other status offenses.[9] However, this law too has not been fully funded or implemented.

The Juvenile Justice and Delinquency Prevention Act (JJDPA) is intended to benefit the approximately 70,000 juveniles currently held in detention facilities (Moone, 1997), status offenders and neglected youth that are no longer in the juvenile system, and all minority youth who are unfortunately more likely to come into contact with the juvenile justice system. The program is administered by the federal government with a grant to states. To be eligible for the grant, states must follow the mandates of the JJDPA—deinstitutionalization of status offenders, removal of juveniles from adult jails and institutions, and reduction of the disproportionate representation of minority youth in confinement.

The JJDPA has had mixed results. Recent data show that an overwhelming majority of states and territories are in full compliance with the first two major JJDPA mandates. Forty-five of 50 states have removed juveniles from their jails, and only two states do not adequately separate juveniles from adult inmates in their jails (Schiraldi & Soler, 1998). Another positive result is that most status offenders are not being held in jails or detention centers—54 states and territories are in full compliance with this mandate (Howell, 1998). In 1995, 249,500 juveniles were arrested as runaways and another 149,800 for curfew violations (Schiraldi & Soler, 1998). If these youth were sent to detention centers or jails, overcrowding would be much more of a problem than it is today. A majority of states (28) are also complying with the mandate to reduce disproportionate minority confinement. Studies have shown that in areas in which alternative programs to incarceration have been developed and treatment is tailored to individuals, the recidivism rates have dropped (Schwartz, 1984). These improvements have come about because of the JJDPA.

However, results have been less that what was hoped and expected. Schwartz (1984) states that "one is hard-pressed to find many jurisdictions with sensible and cost-effective juvenile crime control policies" and that juvenile justice programs " have been disappointing and unimaginative." Some argue that alternatives to incarceration are not working and that many youth, particularly status offenders, are left without services and protection they might otherwise receive (Krisberg et al., 1986). As previously stated, the minority population in detention centers is still critically high, and only 28 of 50 states are undertaking programs to correct this problem. More juveniles are being held in secure detention and correctional facilities than ever before, and they are also being incarcerated for longer periods of time.

Thus, the JJDPA has reformed the juvenile justice system and helped to better protect the rights of young people. It has resulted in the removal of juveniles from adult jails and prisons, the deinstitutionalization of status offenses, and the recognition of the disproportionate number of minority youth in detention. However, the lack of funding and the "get tough" attitudes of policymakers and citizens have reduced the effectiveness of the JJDPA.

SUBSTANCE ABUSE, IMPRISONMENT OF WOMEN, AND HIV: POLICY IMPLICATIONS

Substance Abuse

Some of the continued high rates of child placement presented in Chapters 1 and 11 are no doubt due to increased substance abuse among parents. A number of studies have found that various forms of child maltreatment are associated with alcohol or other drug abuse (see Chapters 5, 6, and 7; Murphy et al., 1991).

> The exact number of substance abusing parents is an impossible number to calculate. However, with over six million children of alcoholics under the age of 18 and an additional number of children of cocaine or other drug abusers, the total number of children under 18 directly affected by substance abusing parents is estimated to be nine to ten million. Further, both alcohol and other drug abuse are increasingly being cited as a major presenting problem for those being reported for child abuse. At a minimum, as many as 675,000 children are seriously mistreated annually by a substance abusing caretaker. (Mitchell & Savage, 1991, p. 1)

Equally disturbing is a set of research findings documenting that children of substance-abusing parents, once placed, are reunified in lower numbers and after a longer time than other children (Tracy, 1992). Substance abuse has been reported as a major factor driving the increase in CPS reports, according to child welfare agency managers (Tatara, 1989). It appears that considerable numbers of drug-exposed newborns are being placed in substitute care. During fiscal year 1988, 59.9% (1,438) of the 2,402 newborns placed in care in New York State had been drug exposed. One problem, however, is a lack of reliable data on a national basis because of inadequate state data collection and differences in definitions used (Besharov & Hanson, 1994; Tatara, 1989–1990). The National Institute on Drug Abuse suggests that over one million children per year are exposed to alcohol and/or illicit substances during gestation (National Institute on Drug Abuse, 1994). Why should we be concerned about maternal substance abuse and drug-exposed infants? For one, miscarriages and stillbirths are higher for cocaine-using mothers. Many fetuses exposed to crack cocaine sustain neurological damage or physical malformations such as deformed hearts, digestive systems, or limbs.

Imprisonment of Women

Many women who are imprisoned have substance abuse problems that contributed to their crimes. Since many of these women have children who are placed by child

Female prisoners

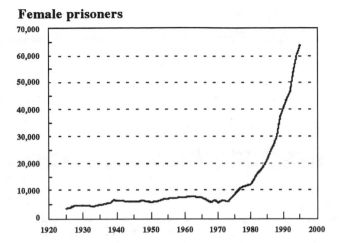

Figure 2.1. Sentenced female prisoners in state and federal institution on December 31: United States, 1925–1995. Reprinted from *Sourcebook of Criminal Justice Statistics* (1996, Figure 6.2), http://www.albany.edu/sourcebook/1995/tost_6.html#6_l, 5/30/98).

welfare agencies, substance abuse and the resulting incarceration of mothers (and fathers) have a number of policy implications. For example, the types of substance abuse prosecution, treatment, and child custody/placement policies that are adopted by this country have significant implications for these parents and their children (see Table 2.4 and Figure 2.1; also see Beatty, 1997; Caulkins & Reuter, 1997; Gabel & Johnston, 1995; Humphreys, 1993).

HIV and Children

In addition, the rate of HIV and AIDS infections among children continues to rise dramatically. According to the Centers for Disease Control and Prevention's HIV/AIDS Surveillance report for year-end 1998, 8,461 children under the age of 13 had been infected with AIDS and 1,875 were HIV positive. Seventy-nine percent were children under the age of five. Of those children with AIDS, 91% were exposed by mothers with or at risk for HIV infection. Black children comprised the highest number of pediatric AIDS (58%) and HIV-positive cases (63%). As of December, 1998, 4,984 children had died from AIDS.

Among the more than 109,000 adult and adolescent females with AIDS (excludes HIV-positive cases), 38% reported exposure to the virus through heterosexual contact. Twenty-nine percent were infected through intravenous drug use. The increase in HIV infection among women has been particularly dramatic in communities of color. Although African-American and Hispanic women comprise

Table 2.4. Substance Abuse and the Imprisonment of Women:
An Issue for Child Welfare

Seana Golder
(University of Washington)

Although women comprise a relatively small percentage of the adults incarcerated in state and federal prisons (6.4% as of June, 1997), women represent the fastest growing segment of those involved in the criminal justice system and have unique needs—particularly when they have children (Bureau of Justice Statistics, 1997; Gabel & Johnston, 1995). The number of women incarcerated in state or federal prisons has skyrocketed since the 1980s: Figure 2.1 illustrates the magnitude of this trend. As numerous researchers have argued, this is a direct result of the War on Drugs and policies of mandatory sentencing for drug possession (Belknap, 1996; Covington, 1997; Ferguson & Kaplan, 1994; Harm, 1992; Kaplan & Sasser, 1996; Phillips & Harm,1997). Between 1986 and 1991, there was a 432% increase in women serving time on drug offenses in state prisons. This is compared to a 281% increase for men during the same time period (Bureau of Justice Statistics, 1994). Furthermore, the Federal Bureau of Prisons reports over 60% of women in their custody are serving time on drug offenses (Covington, 1997). Today, the number of women being incarcerated continues to rise and the predominant cause remains convictions for drug offenses.

A simple gender analysis of this increase, however, does not comprise a complete analysis. The War on Drugs and the social control policies it generated, disproportionately affect people of color (Belknap, 1996; Tonry, 1994). For adults, regardless of gender, there was a 707% increase in the number of African-Americans sentenced to State prison for drug offenses between 1985 and 1995. During the same time, the number of white people sentenced to State prison for drug offenses rose a comparably small 306% (Bureau of Justice Statistics, 1997). (The rise in people sentenced for drug offenses regardless of race represented the category of offense with the greatest increase. This is a further indication of the "success" of the War on Drugs and mandatory sentencing as social control policies.) Similarly, women of color constitute the largest proportion of the women being incarcerated (Belknap, 1996).

Approximately 78% of incarcerated women in 1992 were mothers. Of these woman 71.7% lived with their minor child(ren) prior to incarceration. After incarceration, approximately 70% of children went to live with grandparents or other relatives; only 25% went to live with their father. In comparison, 63.9% of incarcerated men were fathers, although only 52.9% had lived with their children prior to incarceration. More importantly, 89.7% of their children resided with their mothers after the father's incarceration (Bureau of Justice Statistics, 1994a). What does this mean? Simply, most women who are incarcerated are mothers and they are the primary financial and emotional caretakers of their children (Belknap, 1996). For female inmates this separation from the maternal role and their children is a particularly harsh and potent "pain of imprisonment" (Enos, 1997).

A closely related issue with significant policy implications is the effect of incarceration on the woman's children. Phillips and Harm (1997) argue that children of incarcerated women may be particularly susceptible to "enduring trauma." They define enduring trauma as referring to "recurrent episodes of multiple types of trauma throughout at least one stage of a child's development" (Phillips & Harm, 1997, p. 5). These traumas may include abuse, neglect, molestation, witnessing violence, grief, parent–child separation, and multiple placements involving changes in caregiver.

Source: Seana Golder, School of Social Work, University of Washington.

less than 25% of all women in the United States, they account for 77% of AIDS cases reported to date among women in the United States. Of the 10,998 women reported with AIDS in 1998, 62% were African American, 19% were Hispanic, and 18% were white. In addition, African-American and Hispanic women represent more than 75% of HIV infections reported among females between the ages of 13 and 24 for all years combined (Centers for Disease Control and Prevention, 1998)

The available statistics indicate that child welfare service agencies need to strengthen their intervention knowledge base regarding substance abuse if placement prevention is to be achieved or children are to be returned home. For example, of the 24,786 children entering substitute care in 1988 in New York, 43.2% were placed, in part, because drug abuse in the home was one of the problems present. In Indiana, it was 7%, in Nebraska it was 22.1%, in Ohio it was 42.2%, and in Utah it was 19.6% (Tatara, 1991, p. 3). These states were among the few collecting such data. And the placement statistics reflect the kinds of abuse or neglect that often accompany substance abuse, particularly crack cocaine, which appears to affect users more adversely in terms of addiction and behavior while high on the drug (Besharov & Hanson, 1994). More recent reviews have only reinforced the impact of substance abuse on parenting and the need for child placement (e.g., Chasnoff, 1998).

States have been facing the complex questions surrounding balancing parental rights and a duty to protect the unborn or young child from the effects of the mother's drug abuse. At least 17 American cities are reporting higher enrollments of preschool children in special education since the onset of the crack cocaine problem in their neighborhoods, as documented in a new study by the Senate Judiciary Committee. In two of the cities hit first by crack—Miami and Los Angeles— the number of 3 to 5 year olds in special education has doubled since 1986. Columbus, Ohio, Nashville, Tennessee, and Jacksonville, Florida, also have experienced large increases, and in 1990 New York City had a 26% increase in preschool special education enrollments (Child Protection Report, 1991, p. 2). So, national and local legislative initiatives will need to promote more effective ways of preventing some of the root causes of substance abuse (e.g., unemployment, child maltreatment) if the country is to be able to minimize the increase of this problem.

Continuing Policy Challenges

With the recent welfare reform legislation, we are at a crossroads in terms of whether states and counties will adequately fund the quality day care, health care, training, and other supports necessary for birthparents to work and provide adequate child care for their children. TANF advocates assumed that there was only one pathway to growth and self-sufficiency—working—with a 5 year maximum lifetime use limit to help ensure recipient progress in this area. Thus there is an inherent tension between the more time-oriented TANF programs and relationship-based child and family support programs; and it appears that the first year work exemption period is a crucial opportunity to work intensively with these adults. Child welfare and other staff members would be wise to know how their local agencies are interpreting and trying to succeed within the constraints of TANF and other related legislation (Knitzer, 1999).

In addition, many child advocates and researchers are concerned that a continued low level of funding for Title IV-B ($292 million was appropriated for 1999 for the child services program category) and problems in service delivery will continue to interfere with the important objectives for this legislation to prevent unnecessary foster care placement and achieve permanency for children through family strengthening and more focused services:

> Whether workers are developing case plans in accordance with the guidelines described in the law, whether case reviews are substantive or whether reviewers are merely rubber-stamping plans made, whether administrators are utilizing the data from information management systems to facilitate planning for children are only some of the issues that should be addressed if the intent of the law is to be realized. Unless implementation is monitored, the framework created by the Act may be little more than a house of cards. (Stein & Gambrill, 1985, pp. 91–92)

In fact, many would argue that the focus on permanency planning, creative service alternatives, and child stability has not been maintained through staff training, supervision, and providing the necessary resources. And although substance abuse is an issue, part of the increase in child placements in some areas is due to the case overloads in the system and a lack of effective program design (see Chapter 15; General Accounting Office, 1990). Many advocates would argue that a small but significant number of children would be prevented from being placed if sufficient resources were available for family income assistance, housing, health care, and crisis intervention support.[10] For example, one small but significant recent accomplishment was funding the Family Unification Program of the Housing and Urban Development (HUD) Department. This legislation provides Section 8 housing certificates to families (allowing them to rent federally subsidized housing) whose children are at risk of being placed in foster care because of homelessness or substandard housing, and to families that are unable to have their children return home from foster care because of lack of adequate housing (Allen, 1991; Child Welfare League of America, 1991, p. 9). And yet, the fact that it took this long to pass such legislation says much about the problems being encountered in more fully implementing PL 96-272, let alone the significant deterioration of our federal housing programs (see Moroney, 1991, pp. 77–104).

Part of the problem—besides poor program design—is inadequate funding. Although funding levels for Titles IV-B, IV-E, and other areas are significant, these appropriations represent in most cases only small increases after almost two decades of steady erosion in funding. The nation's social services and public assistance programs have been battered by federal, state, and local budget cuts, while there have been increases in real need on the part of families and children. We have a continuing high rate of foster care placement in this country, a rate that is not entirely due to the problem of drug abuse and homelessness, but is caused in part by the lack of service alternatives and the resources to support creative interventions to meet the unique needs of individual families. For example, funding for PL 96-272, some of which is used for placement prevention, has steadily but modestly increased, while funding for family foster care has increased dramatically to over $3.9 billion for 1999 (see Table 2.3). The following observation by Leroy Pelton raises some important policy and practice issues for the field:

> In the absence of prevention-of-placement services, the foster care population varies with the amount of resources available for child removal, more than any other factor. . . . The pool of potential candidates for foster care is always quite large and consists mainly of children from families most deeply submerged in poverty [Pelton, 1989, pp. 108–109]. It is the "reasons" we find to remove such children that change and, with them, the amount of resources that become available to do so.
> This is not to deny that some of these reasons are not merely re-characterizations of the same old poverty-related child care issues, but represent the real new growth of some poverty-related problems such as substance abuse or homelessness. But the crucial factor affecting the size of the foster care population is the nature of the social interventions we choose to utilize, and the changes in the resources we devote to them, not the fluctuating size of the poverty population. Homelessness, for example, which is another factor to which the select committee attributes the new rise in the foster care population, is not a sufficient reason for placement since we can intervene in other ways—such as helping the family to obtain housing or shelter—that would ameliorate the child welfare concerns involved. Even alleged child abuse or neglect is not sufficient reason for placement since many children who have been abused or neglected can be served and protected in their own homes. (Pelton, 1990, p. 20)

One of the key policy dilemmas facing child welfare, therefore, is how to increase the provision of preventive services while offering children adequate protection from serious child maltreatment. It is at this juncture that the recommendations offered by the National Association of Public Child Welfare Administrators (1999), Kamerman and Kahn (1990), Pelton (1990, 1991), Schorr (1988, 1997), and Thomas (1990) begin to diverge over such issues as how best to handle child abuse and neglect cases, what family circumstances merit involuntary investigation and service, and how to protect children while increasing funding for prevention.

OPPORTUNITIES FOR POLICY PRACTICE

It is important to note that none of these laws is static. They are constantly changing through a process of regulatory review at the federal and state levels. Moreover, their actual implementation depends in many cases on the efforts of trained social workers who interpret, enforce, and carry out the legislative or judicial intent. It is in this fundamental, grass roots sense that we see social workers as intimately involved in the policy process: not merely as passive purveyors of services and benefits, but as policy practitioners (Jansson, 1994), promoters of strength-based social policy, and active agents of change.

A caseload of publicly funded client families and children in foster care, child-protective services, or family-based services represents not just a discrete number of individuals in need, but a "window" into the needs of many other families who lack information or access to help. It is a fundamental child welfare task to convey what is seen in that window to the appropriate legislative, administrative, judicial, and professional bodies for purposes of redress. In short, we believe that the raising of private troubles to public social concerns is at the heart of what social work should be about in child welfare. It is in that sense that all child welfare practitioners are intimately connected to the policy process with the overarching goal of improving society's response to families and children in need. We find it useful to think less in "us" and "them" terms and more in terms of what the social work great, Charlotte Towles (1948), referred to as *common human needs*. A "family-centered" approach to public policy rests squarely on the notion of partnership between professionals and families, as well as on the realization that each of us, save for the accident of life circumstances, remains but a half-step away from the service system we will describe in the chapters to follow. As readers review the policies connected with the program areas addressed by the remainder of the book, a policy analysis framework that we have used with students and practitioners may be useful (see Table 2.5).

Table 2.5. One Example of a Policy Analysis Framework

A. The Issue or Problem Constituting the Focus of the Policy
  1. Nature and scope of the issue or problem
    • Who is affected?
    • In what historical context (social, cultural, legal) has the problem evolved? (Consider various dimensions of the problem as applicable e.g., political, economic, race, class, gender)
    • What are the major contributing factors and, if relevant, causal theories or hypotheses?

B. Policy Outcome Objectives and Rationale
  1. Policy objectives: what specific outcomes is the policy attempting to accomplish? (e.g., ensuring greater access, providing better job training, protecting children from abuse or neglect)
  2. What is to be provided? (e.g., opportunities, services, goods)
  3. Empirical rationale for the policy and program(s) (i.e., what research data support this policy?)
  4. Other driving forces? (e.g., values, politics, economics, mass media, legal, religion, technology)

(continued)

Table 2.5. (Continued)

C. Policy Implementation

1. Bases of social allocation
   - How many people each year are intended to benefit from this policy? (e.g., receive a service, goods, or income)
   - What eligibility criteria are used to select who is eligible to benefit from the policy? (e.g., attributed need, compensation, diagnosis, means test)
2. Under what auspices will the program be administered (local, state, federal, private, public, etc.)? How do the different auspices relate to one another?
3. Financing methods: how is the policy and its related programs funded?

D. Policy Evaluation

1. What criteria/indicators do the policy or program staff use to evaluate whether the policy (and its related programs) are accomplishing the goals and objectives?
   - To date, what proportion of the target population has the policy/program actually reached?
   - What are the general outcomes or effects? (e.g., consumer outcomes, distribution of rights, power allocated, rewards, assignment of status's, aspects of quality of life)
   - What do the data regarding overall costs in relation to outcomes/benefits demonstrate?
2. What factors are affecting implementation effectiveness?
   - What are the major barriers to implementing the policy? (e.g., value conflicts, regulatory constraints, politics)
   - What is the extent of the discrepancy between services actually offered and services that were stated to be the goals of the program? If the discrepancy is significant, why did it occur?

E. Policy Revisions

1. What specific changes or alternative policies could be used to meet the policy objectives? Provide a rationale (e.g., research data, values).

F. Proposed Implementation Plan for the Revised Policy

1. How should the revised policy be implemented differently?
2. How will the financing methods be altered?
3. What effects or outcomes do you anticipate would be *different from* the current policy? (e.g., resources, values, distribution of rights, power, new roles, relationships between people or organizations, rewards, client outcomes, assignment of statuses, aspects of quality of life)
4. What problems might be encountered in implementing the proposed policy refinements and how would you address them?

Source: Pecora, P.J., & Nollan, K. (2000). *One example of a policy analysis framework.* Seattle, WA: University of Washington, School of Social Work (mimeograph). References: Gil, D.G. (1974). A systematic approach to social policy analysis. *Social Service Review, 44* (4), 421–425. Haskins, R., & Gallagher, J.J. (Eds.) (1981). *Models for analysis of social policy— An introduction.* Norwood, NJ: ABLEX. Haas, P. J., & Springer, J. F. (1998). A*pplied policy research—Concepts and cases.* New York: Garland.

CONCLUSION

As child maltreatment continues to be a major social problem, the foster care population remains at high levels in many geographic areas, clear pathways for system reform remain unclear, and child welfare agencies close their doors to all but the seriously abused or neglected, the need for new federal legislation has been recognized (Halpern, 1999; Kamerman & Kahn, 1989). A growing coalition of public and private agency officials and legislators is backing a three-tiered approach to reform: The first tier consists of a universal system of family support services in order to promote family well-being and prevent problems from occurring. The second tier involves a wide range of family-focused community services—from mental health, health, juvenile justice, education, economic, and other agencies—to provide services designed to strengthen and preserve families before those problems become too severe. The third tier involves the current child welfare system but would support more family-focused approaches to child protection to preserve families and achieve permanency planning wherever possible (Allen, 1991).[11]

A broad coalition of commissions (e.g., the National Commission on Child Welfare and Family Preservation) and national organizations—including the American Public Welfare Association, National Association of Social Workers, Child Welfare League of America, American Association for Protecting Children, and Children's Defense Fund—is developing a set of legislative initiations that reflects "the growing consensus around the need for greater focus on prevention, improvements in the quality of out-of-home care, and enhancements in service delivery that encourage interagency coordination" (Allen, 1991, p. 620). Many of these legislative initiatives seeks to incorporate innovative ways of adequately funding preventive family support services while addressing other gaps in the service delivery system. Proposals for health care reforms are also constantly being put forward for consideration by Congress, including ways to better provide insurance coverage to the thousands of adults and children in the United States who lack such a basic social benefit.

After describing the central principles of a child and family-centered approach to child welfare services in the next chapter, the authors will discuss some of the major policy, research, and practice issues currently facing practitioners and administrators. Practice principles that are supported by empirical literature will be highlighted, and current program challenges will be discussed. But we caution readers that high-quality child welfare services in the traditional sense are insufficient for meeting the needs of families in America. The following comment by Halpern (1990) in his essay reviewing Lisbeth Schorr's book, *Within Our Reach,* illustrates the importance of some of the observations made in this chapter; why an entire chapter (Chapter 4) has been devoted to the issues of income support; and why the value dilemmas that affect the design of child welfare services are noted throughout this text.

There is . . . a real danger that we will continue to rely too much on services to resolve basic societal issues that should be, but are not being, addressed in the political and civic arenas. Even the best services can hardly affect the contextual reality from which a child constructs a sense of what the world is like and what he or she will become. Services cannot alter the social conditions that produce or exacerbate, and ultimately reproduce, individual and family problems. Services cannot bridge the huge social and racial divisions that persist in American society, nor can they be the catalyst that causes self-sufficient Americans to see that they share common needs and a common world with vulnerable and dependent Americans. (Halpern, 1990, p. 647)

Halpern (1990, p. 647) goes on to observe that "good services are not everything. But, given our continuing reluctance to alter basic social arrangements and priorities that cause damage to so many children and families, we should at least commit ourselves to the objective of assuring them good quality services."

Many serious policy issues remain to be addressed. How can the "reasonable efforts" provisions in PL 96-272 and more recently enacted by AFSA be enforced and strengthened?[12] How can advocates secure the financial opportunities and housing, medical insurance and other basic service supports needed by all families in America? To what degree can the controversy surrounding development of a comprehensive family policy in the United States be addressed while addressing the issues associated more closely with child welfare policy? What social policies will help social service and other agencies to refocus their efforts on clients as individuals with unique needs and to view services as means to achieve certain client outcomes rather than as ends in themselves?

How can programs in child welfare rise to these challenges, all the while balancing parent rights with a duty to help protect and nurture children? These are just a few of the questions the following chapters will attempt to address. The issues highlighted here illustrate some of the reasons why working in child welfare is so difficult and yet so important. Daniel Patrick Moynihan, no stranger to the family policy debate, in a sobering analysis of prospects of major improvement for the family agenda in modern American society, sums up precisely what is at stake:

A commonplace of political rhetoric has it that the quality of a civilization may be measured by how it cares for its elderly. Just as surely, the future of a society may be forecast by how it cares for its young. (Moynihan, 1986, p. 194)

The next chapter describes a family-centered approach to care for children by strengthening families and improving their living environments, an approach that is being increasingly adopted by child welfare agencies.

NOTES

1.   For more information regarding the problems associated with The Child Abuse Prevention and Treatment Act, see Light (1973), Stein (1984), and American Civil Liberties Union (1977).

2. This description of the Indian Child Welfare Act is based on the following sources:

American Indian Lawyer Training Program (1979), Federal Register (1979a,b), Unger (1978), and Wright (1980). Basic definitions for the Indian Child Welfare Act are as follows: An "Indian" is defined as any person who is a member of a federally recognized tribe or who is an Alaskan Native and a member of a Regional Corporation. An "Indian child" is any unmarried person who is under age 18 and is a member of an Indian tribe or the child of an Indian and eligible for enrollment in a tribe. This is a restrictive definition since it excludes children who are not eligible for enrollment but who are Indian by culture, children of terminated tribes, and Canadian Indian children. An "Indian parent" is any biological or adoptive parent of an Indian child including the non-Indian parent of an Indian child. An "Indian custodian" is any Indian person who has legal custody of a child under tribal law or custom or state law, or to whom temporary custody has been given by the parent. The "Indian child's tribe" is the one in which she or he is eligible for enrollment. In the case of a multi-tribe child, it is the tribe with which he or she has the most significant contacts. The determination of "significant contacts" is done by the court and may become a difficult issue. A "child custody hearing" is one which involves a foster care placement, termination of parental rights, preadoptive placement, or adoptive placement. The Act does not require tribal involvement in the prejudicial phases of service to an Indian family. (Potter, 1980, p. 1)

3. "Foster care maintenance" is defined as payments to cover the cost of/or to provide food, clothing, shelter, daily supervision, school supplies, personal incidentals, and liability insurance for a child, and reasonable travel to the home for child visits. In the case of institutional care, the term includes reasonable costs of administration and operation of an institution.

4. This section is adapted from Child Welfare League of America, public policy department (November 25, 1997). *Summary Of The Adoption And Safe Families Act of 1997* (PL 105-89) (mimeograph). Washington, D.C.: Author. Reprinted with permission.

5. In using the term "parental rights termination" we neglect the important implication that the parent's responsibilities are also terminated. There is a balance of rights and responsibilities that the government, parents, and children have; and these rights are almost always balanced by responsibilities. Indeed, in some work underway to understand the path to voluntary relinquishments of children involved in the foster care system, biological parents indicate that not having to fulfill all responsibilities of parenting can be a great relief to them. So we will generally use the term "termination of parental rights and responsibilities" instead of termination of parental rights.

6. See Chapter 11 in this text and Maluccio et al. (1990), Mech (1988), Nollan et al. (2000), and Wedeven and Mauzerall (1990).

7. This section is adapted from Chapter 4, authored by Robert Plotnick.

8. Legislation in 1998 restored federal food stamp eligibility for about 250,000 legal immigrants—including most children—who had lost eligibility under the PRWORA. The law restores eligibility to slightly fewer than one of every three legal immigrants who lost it. Most legal immigrant adults who are neither elderly nor disabled remain ineligible. Most immigrants who arrived in the United States after the PRWORA was signed—August 22, 1996—also continue to be ineligible.

9. For more information regarding the gender bias issues or other implementation problems associated with implementing the Juvenile Justice and Delinquency Prevention Act of 1974, see Costin, Bell, and Downs (1991, pp. 66–99) and Coates, Miller, and Ohlin (1978).

10.   See, for example, Edna McConnell Clark Foundation (1985), Kamerman and Kahn (1989), Pelton (1990), and Schorr (1988, 1997).

11.   For more information about child welfare services delivery reform, also see Briar (1990), Bruner (1991), Harris and Warner (1988), Jencks and Peterson (1991), and Sherraden (1991).

12.   See, for example, National Council of Juvenile and Family Court Judges et al. (N.D.) and American Association for Protecting Children (1989).

FOR FURTHER INFORMATION

Kamerman, S., & Kahn, A. (1990). Social services for children, youth, and families in the United States. *Children and Youth Services Review, 12,* 1–185. An excellent analysis of child and family policy and services in the United States.

McGowan, B. (1990). Family-based services and public policy: Context and implications. In J. Whittaker, J. Kinney, E. Tracy, & C. Booth (Eds.), *Reaching high-risk families.* Hawthorne, NY: Aldine de Gruyter. Presents a concise but cogent overview of major child welfare legislation as these policies relate to family preservation services.

Nollan, K.A., & Downs, A.C. (2000). Independent living in America: Proceedings of the Independent Living Forum. Washington, DC: Child Welfare League of America.

Pelton, L.H. (1989). *For reasons of poverty: A critical analysis of the public child welfare system in the United States.* New York: Praeger. Discusses major problems in the child welfare service delivery system and possible solutions.

Schorr, L.B. (1988). *Within our reach: Breaking the cycle of disadvantage.* New York: Doubleday.

Schorr, L.B. (1997). *Common purpose: Strengthening families and neighborhoods to rebuild America.* New York: Doubleday. These two books review major policy and program innovations in child and family services.

3

Child and Family-Centered Services

In accordance with the policy issues highlighted in the previous chapter, in recent years there has been increasing emphasis on family-centered social work services. This is an approach that focuses on the family as the unit of attention. It is built on the premise that "human beings can be understood and helped only in the context of the intimate and powerful human systems of which they are a part," of which the family is one of the most important (Hartman & Laird, 1983, p. 4). How the family is defined has important implications for practice, including eligibility for service, distribution of resources, and helping approaches. By family we mean "two or more people in a committed relationship from which they derive a sense of identity as a family," thus including "nontraditional family forms that are outside the traditional legal perspective, . . . families not related by blood, marriage, or adoption" (Nunnally, Chilman, & Cox, 1988, p. 11).

As Gambrill (1997, p. 571) observes:

> Families may be defined by biological relatedness and/or living arrangements. There are many kinds of families including step-families, nuclear families, extended families, gay/lesbian families, single-parent families, families without children, families with grown children, and bicultural families.

In line with the above, "respect for diversity requires that *family* be defined openly and broadly so as to include whomever the family itself—with its unique culture, circumstances, and history—designates" (Allen & Petr, 1998, p. 8).

Family-centered social work services, of course, are consonant with the longstanding concern of social workers with families, particularly in the field of child welfare. Accordingly, this chapter presents an integrative, child/family-centered conceptual framework for child welfare, along with selected implications for policy and practice (see Figure 3.1). The framework builds on four major components:

> an ecological perspective, which offers a broad conceptual lens for analyzing human behavior and social functioning within an environmental context; a competence-centered perspective, which highlights practice methods and strategies that promote the effective functioning of children, parents, and families; a developmental perspective, which provides a frame of reference for understanding the growth and functioning of human beings in the context of their families and their families' transactions with their environments; and a permanency planning orientation to child welfare, which embodies a mandate to maintain children in their own homes or, if necessary, place them permanently with other families.

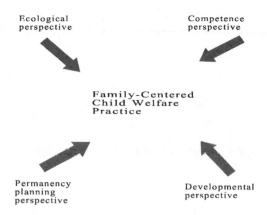

Figure 3.1. An integrative framework for family-centered child welfare practice. Reprinted from Maluccio (1990).

CONCEPTUAL FRAMEWORK FOR FAMILY-CENTERED PRACTICE

Ecological Perspective

The ecological perspective draws from fields such as ecology, systems theory, anthropology, and organizational theory. In particular, it builds on ecology as a metaphor and thus on the study of the interactions between living organisms and their environments (Bronfenbrenner, 1979, 1986; Garbarino, 1992; Moen, Elder, & Luscher, 1995).

As Germain and Gitterman (1996, p. 6) indicate, "ecology also rests on an evolutionary, adaptive view of the development of human beings and the characteristics of the species." As an orientation to practice, ecology helps us to appreciate that human beings are engaged in continuous transaction with their environment; furthermore, the ecological perspective provides insight into the nature and consequence of such transactions both for human beings and for the physical and social environments in which they function (Germain & Gitterman, 1996, pp. 5–19).

By offering a broad conceptual lens for viewing human functioning and needs, the ecological approach underscores that social work intervention should address the interface between human beings and their impinging environments: practitioners focus on improving the transactions between people and environments in order to enhance adaptive capacities as well as enrich environments for all who function within them (Germain & Gitterman, 1996). In particular, they seek to influence the trajectory of change in both the person and the environment toward a positive direction.

Consider, as an example, the ecology of a family in the following situation of a young couple referred to an agency because of their neighbors' concern about possible maltreatment of their child:

> This is the case of a young couple with a three-year-old son who is developmentally delayed. Both parents have unmet needs for affection, and they have not yet developed a sense of mutuality as a couple. In addition, it has been difficult for them to manage financially, as neither has had regular employment. The family has been moving from community to community in the past few years, in search of employment. (Adapted from Kirsh & Maidman, 1984, p. 11)

From this brief sketch, one can begin to see how and why the family is functioning poorly. There are numerous stresses in their environment. Their skills do not match the employment opportunities in their community; the couple has not been in one community long enough to develop adequate support systems; and they are not yet capable of giving each other much-needed support. At the same time, their son demands a great deal of attention. Under these circumstances, it is easy to see how the child might have become the target of his parents' frustrations and anger, particularly in light of their own unmet needs.

As this example suggests, many personal, family, and environmental factors converge and interact with each other to influence the family. In other words, human behavior is not solely a function of the person or the environment, but of the complex interaction between them. As Kurt Lewin (1935) captured it decades ago, $B = f(P + E)$, that is, behavior is a function of person and environment in continuous interaction. When viewed from the perspective of ecology, the above case example suggests various principles useful in child welfare practice.

First, utilizing a health/growth orientation, practitioners can help mobilize the actual and potential strengths and resources of individuals, families, and groups, while simultaneously seeking to render environments more responsive to the adaptive and coping needs of human organisms (Kemp, Whittaker, & Tracy, 1997; Maluccio, 1981, 1999). Second, workers must understand the relationships between families and their environments and identify the significant sources of support as well as stress and conflict.[1] Workers can then assess more objectively the complex personal and environmental factors affecting parents and children and arrive at more appropriate treatment plans and recommendations.

Third, effective practice requires that practitioners appreciate the unique qualities, styles, and needs of different ethnic, racial, and cultural groups and thus facilitate the provision of services that are culturally relevant, particularly for children and families of color, who are not only disproportionately represented but also appear to receive less than their fair share of child welfare services.[2] Fourth, directing professional help to the interaction between the family and its environment is also important. Practitioners should seek to partner with family members to make positive changes not only in the parents or other family members but also in their environment, so that it may become more nutritive and supportive. For instance, in the illustration given above, it would be particularly urgent to relieve the stresses of unemployment and frequent moves and to help the family establish more adequate social supports.

Finally, it is useful to conceptualize child welfare as a comprehensive continuum of services with a strong preventive component. Each child welfare service tries to prevent the use of a more intensive and intrusive service, and child welfare services in the aggregate endeavor to prevent the transition of children into more restrictive services such as juvenile justice. The ecological perspective stimulates a marked shift from a narrow orientation of inadequate parenting to a broad view of child welfare that emphasizes a multifaceted practice approach to children and their families in the context of their life situation and environment (Germain & Gitterman, 1996; Pelton, 1991). Scholars from diverse disciplines have applied the ecological perspective to policy and practice in child welfare. In particular, various authors have called attention to the impact of the environment on the child's development and functioning.[3] For example, Kamerman and Kahn (1995) and Berrick, Needell, Barth, and Jonson-Reid (1998) have noted the importance of social policies that respond to the unique needs of young children and families. Additionally, Garbarino (1992) has emphasized the influence of "sociocultural risks," that is, the impoverishment of the child's world:

> Children who grow up wanting for food, for affection, for caring teachers, for good medical care, and for values consistent with intellectual progress and social competence grow up less well than those children who do not lack these things. Their absence places a child "at risk" for impaired development. (Garbarino, 1992, pp. 35–36)

To counteract the adverse impact of sociocultural risks, Garbarino and other authors call for active professional intervention in the social environment and for designing service programs that are guided by the ecological perspective. Holohan, Wilcox, Spearly, and Campbell (1979) identify two fundamental implications of this perspective:

> The environmental emphasis of the ecological view supports environmentally oriented interventions directed towards strengthening or establishing methods of social support, [whereas] the transactional emphasis of the ecological perspective fosters individually oriented interventions directed towards promoting personal competencies for dealing with environmental blocks to achieving personal objectives. (Holohan et al., 1979, as quoted in Whittaker & Tracy, 1989, p. 26)

Following these implications, Whittaker, Schinke, and Gilchrist (1986, p. 492) argue for (1) building more supportive, nurturant environments for clients through various forms of environmental helping that are designed to increase social support and (2) improving clients' competence in dealing with both proximate and distal environments through the teaching of specific life skills. Andrews (1997) reviews a range of studies that identify ways of enhancing child developmental outcomes and quality of life by improving neighborhood and community conditions.

Other authors offer additional suggestions. Fraser (1997), Kaplan and Girard (1994), and Pelton (1989), among others, underscore the role of preventive services in ameliorating the effects of poverty and other stressful environmental factors. Garbarino (1992, p. 66) advocates "weaving a strong social fabric around child and parent"; he further observes that "this wondrous human child can and will become a competent person, if we only give it a chance" (p. 67). Whittaker (1979, pp. 137–154) urges the involvement of parents as full and equal partners in the helping process; he also advocates forming a "service net" by establishing linkages among child welfare agency, family, school, peer group, juvenile justice systems, and other community services. Cameron and Vanderwoerd (1997) describe a variety of programs for supporting families. Melton and Barry (1994) and their contributors offer a multifaceted national strategy for protecting children from abuse and neglect. Kamerman and Kahn (1995) propose a range of options for policies and programs on behalf of young children, as informed by extensive experiences in several European countries. Greene and Watkins (1998) apply the ecological perspective to work with diverse groups, offering models for practice principles across cultures.

Competence-Centered Perspective

Although its usefulness in clinical practice has been questioned (Wakefield, 1996a, 1996b), we believe that the ecological view is most promising for human services, since it heightens our awareness of the importance of an ecological person–environment perspective in understanding human beings and intervening in human problems (Gitterman, 1996; Kemp, Whittaker, & Tracy, 1997). Also crucial is a related perspective about which there is a growing consensus in the human services, namely, a competence-centered or strength-oriented approach to practice that contrasts with the more traditional pathology or deficit model (Hodges & Pecora, 2000; Maluccio, 1981, 1999; Rapp, 1998; Saleebey, 1997). While the metaphor of ecology provides a way of perceiving and understanding human beings and their functioning within the context of their environment, knowledge about competence development offers specific guidelines for professional practice and service delivery.

The competence perspective draws from ego psychology; psychodynamic psychology; and learning, developmental, and family systems theories. In social work as in other fields, competence is generally defined as the repertoire of skills that enables the person to function effectively. However, a distinction should be made between the notion of discrete competencies or skills and the broader, ecological or transactional concept of competence. The latter may be defined as the outcome of the interplay among

- a person's capacities, skills, potentialities, limitations, and other characteristics;
- a person's motivation—that is, her or his interests, hopes, beliefs, and aspirations; and
- the qualities of the person's impinging environment—such as social networks, environmental demands, and opportunities (Maluccio, 1981).

The ecological concept of competence leads to competence-centered social work practice, a perspective that explicitly holds that the promotion of competence in human beings is a central function of social work intervention (Maluccio, 1981, 1999). Competence-centered social work practice embodies a set of attitudes, principles, and strategies designed to promote effective functioning in human beings by focusing on their unique coping and adaptive patterns, mobilizing their actual or potential strengths, emphasizing the role of natural helping networks, building on their life experiences in a planful way, and using environmental resources as major instruments of help. In conjunction with the ecological perspective, the competence orientation suggests several interrelated themes useful in guiding social work practice with children and families:

- Parents and children are viewed as engaged in ongoing, dynamic transactions with their environment and in a continuous process of growth and adaptation.
- Parents and children are regarded as "open systems" that are spontaneously active and essentially motivated to achieve competence in their coping with life demands and environmental challenges.
- The emphasis shifts away from "treating" clients toward teaching them coping and mastery skills as well as ways of using their life experiences in a planful way.
- Each person's efforts to grow, achieve self-fulfillment, and contribute to others is sustained and promoted by varied environmental opportunities and social supports.
- Appropriate supports are matched to the person's changing qualities and needs in order to maximize the development of her or his competence, identity, autonomy, and self-fulfillment.

As an example, consider the situation of a single mother of young children who is employed and must rely on day care for her children. Due to the inadequacy of available resources, she is forced to leave her children in a poor arrangement. She then becomes so anxious and withdrawn at work that her performance suffers, and she is threatened with losing her job. At times she becomes quite depressed. If she were to go for help at a mental health clinic, she would most likely be diagnosed as being depressed and would be provided only with counseling, thus further lowering her already low self-image and diminishing her sense of competence. In contrast, she would become more self-confident and function more effectively if her therapist helped her to understand that her feelings were natural, given her circumstances; to cope with and decrease her feelings of depression; and to find and mobilize adequate day care resources or her children. Again, the perspective emphasized here focuses on helping clients learn or relearn skills so as to improve their competence through teaching, counseling, advocacy, and resource mobilization. Although some persons need more intensive or long-term mental health services, most could benefit from the type of focused skills-based intervention outlined above.

Developmental Perspective

By the developmental perspective we mean a certain frame of reference for understanding the growth and functioning of human beings in the context of their families and their families' transactions with their environments. The developmental perspective is akin to the ecological perspective in that it views human behavior and social functioning within an environmental context. It goes beyond ecology, however, by bringing in other aspects such as the stages and tasks of the family's life cycle; the biopsychosocial principles of individual growth and development; the goals and needs that are common to all human beings and families; and the particular aspirations, needs, and qualities of each person and each family, in light of diversity in areas such as culture, ethnicity, race, class, and sexual orientation. Also, this highlighting of developmental theory should not be construed as minimizing the importance of attachment, trauma, social control, strain, and social learning theories.

There is an extensive body of knowledge from a variety of disciplines that is related to the developmental perspective. For example, various texts delineate the developmental stages of human beings through the life cycle, from infancy to adulthood, and the tasks associated with each stage (cf. Bloom, 1985; Germain, 1991; Newman & Newman, 1995; Zastrow & Kirst-Ashman, 1997). Other authors focus on the life cycle of the family (cf. Carter & McGoldrick, 1999; Falicov, 1988; Farley, 1990); the linkages among developmental, family, and life cycle theories (cf. Freed, 1985); and comparative analysis of traditional and alternative perspectives on human behavior and development (cf. Schriver, 1995).

The above texts may be consulted for details regarding such prominent aspects as the tasks and challenges associated with different individual and family developmental cycles; the repetition of the family life cycle in blended families; the role of family routines and rituals; the significance of cultural, ethnic, racial, and gender relativity; and the ways in which family functioning (cohesion, adaptability, communication, and role fulfillment) is in part dependent on the developmental levels of individual family members. For purposes of this chapter, a number of themes flowing from the developmental perspective are highlighted:

- Family-centered services and practice need to take into account the concept of development, through explicitly considering this question: Which interventions are effective, with which specific child/family problems, in which environmental settings, and at what particular developmental stages? The stage of development seems to be increasingly important in the individual's as well as the family's ability to enter into and use help in the field of human services.

- Policies, services, and practice should reflect current knowledge about the development of women, minorities, and other special populations, rather than rely primarily on traditional models such as those derived from psychoanalysis. For example, Erikson's (1963) contribution has been criticized in recent years as inadequately portraying female development, although it has much to offer the field to help guide child assessment and clinical interventions (see Marcia, 1980). Gilligan (1993) has questioned the popular "ages and stages" model as being unrepresentative of female development. Okun (1996) and Devore and Schlesinger (1996), among others, have focused on human diversity and its significance for ethnic-sensitive social work practice.

- Individual as well as family development is multiply determined and always occurring (Freud, 1988; Kreilkamp, 1989). Indeed, implicit in the developmental perspective "is a thoroughgoing belief in the inevitability of change, in the dynamic tendencies inherent in human existence" (Kreilkamp, 1989, p. 89). At the same time, there may be some underlying individual characteristics that may be difficult to change, particularly in troubled families (Cadoret et al.,1995).

- Peer groups play an important role in a child's development and should be accorded adequate attention in child welfare practice (Harris, 1995).[4]

- Caution should be exercised in applying to human beings or families any developmental scheme said to be normative. In this regard, Germain and Bloom (1999) and Kagan (1984) have challenged the very notion of an orderly, well-connected sequence of developmental stages, each building on the former and containing within it building blocks of the next:

[The] discussion of connectedness challenges two favorite assumptions in Western views on human development. Many observers want the past to seriously constrain the present through material links that join the universal milestones of growth into a forged chain. Each child must step on every link—no skipping permitted—as he or she journeys into maturity . . . . The second popular assumption . . . holds that qualities acquired first will be the last to go. Hence, by looking at an infant, we not only obtain a preview of what is to come, but we are also justified in explaining a particular adult's personality as a necessary product of the distant past. These two suppositions ignore the power of the many social forces and maturing abilities that appear later in life. (Kagan, 1984, pp. 110–111)

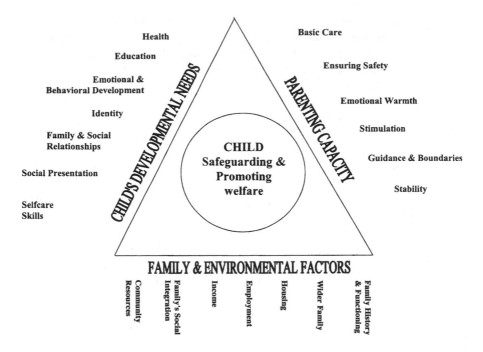

Figure 3.2. Assessment framework. *Source:* Social Care Group, Department of Health. (1999). *Framework for the assessment of children in need and their families.* London, United Kingdom: Department of Health.

As suggested by the above quotation, family-centered practice should be guided by an optimistic view of the capacity of children—and adults—to overcome early deprivation and other adverse early life experiences through nurturing and supportive experiences throughout the life cycle (see, for example, Anthony & Cohler, 1987; Rhodes & Brown, 1991; Weissbourd, 1996). In short, human development is a dynamic process that involves complex and interdependent connections among human beings, their families, and their social and physical environments (Germain & Bloom, 1999). Human beings actively shape—and are also shaped by—their social contexts (Garbarino, 1992).

A child and family-centered perspective with these components seems applicable to many countries as well. This perspective has been further elaborated in the assessment framework recently adopted in Great Britain by the Department of Health (see Figure 3.2).

Permanency Planning Orientation

Another perspective that since the 1970s has influenced child welfare services and practice even more directly than either the ecological model or the competence orientation is that of *permanency planning*. Since most children coming to the attention of the child welfare system are at risk of placement out of their homes, a comprehensive framework for child welfare practice must incorporate the values, goals, and principles of permanency planning.

Definition. Permanency planning is the systematic process of carrying out, within proscribed time frames, a set of goal-directed activities designed to help children live in safe families that offer them a sense of belonging and legal, lifetime family ties (Maluccio et al., 1986).

Permanency planning thus refers to the process of taking prompt, decisive action to maintain children in their own homes or place them in legally permanent families. Above all, it addresses a single—but crucial—question: What will be this child's family when he or she grows up? It embodies a family-focused paradigm for child welfare services, with emphasis on providing a permanent legal family and sensitivity to ensuring family continuity for children across the life span (McFadden & Downs, 1995).

Emergence. Permanency planning has been hailed as a popular movement representing a revolution in child care comparable to the earlier closing down of mass congregate institutions (Fanshel & Shinn, 1978, p. 478). It formally emerged over two decades ago as an antidote to long standing abuses in the child welfare system, particularly the inappropriate removal of children from their families and the recurring drift of children in care. Permanency planning complemented the deinstitutionalization movement occurring in mental retardation and mental health, and it was soon adopted as a vital means of dealing with the needs of children and youths living away from their own families with little sense of stability or continuity in their living arrangements.

Permanency planning incorporates a basic and nonrevolutionary idea: namely, that every child is entitled to live in a family—preferably her or his own biological family—to have the maximum opportunity for growth and development. It is an idea that has ancient origins, and it has been restated over and over throughout the history of child welfare. During the 1970s, it was promoted through the Oregon Project, a landmark, federally funded demonstration project carried out by the Oregon State Department of Human Resources in collaboration with the Regional Research Institute for Human Services at the Portland State University School of Social Work (Pike, 1976).

The project, entitled Freeing Children for Permanent Placement, "sought to achieve permanent homes for children . . . who were adrift in long-term foster care" (Pike, 1976, p. 22). It was so effective that it contributed to the promotion of permanency planning as a large scale national movement. In particular, it eventually demonstrated that many of these children could be returned to their families of origin or placed in adoption, through intensive agency services emphasizing systematic decision making, deliberate planning, and aggressive outreach efforts (Pike, 1976; Pike, Downs, Emlen, Downs, & Case, 1977). These strategies and principles were disseminated widely throughout the country. The philosophy and practice of permanency planning then gradually expanded to include not only adoption and reunification of children in placement with their families, but also prevention through attention to families with children at risk of out-of-home placement.

As a result in large measure of the dissemination efforts of the Oregon Project and other programs such as the Alameda Project (Stein, Gambrill, & Wiltse, 1978), the goal of permanency planning for every child or youth came to shape the philosophy and practice of many child welfare agencies. As suggested above, there ensued considerable emphasis on a child's entitlement to a family *intended* to last indefinitely, although it was recognized that such an outcome could not be guaranteed (cf. Pike et al., 1977; Wiltse, 1980). Moreover, the adequacy of an agency's performance began to be increasingly assessed on the basis of its success in ensuring permanency in living arrangements and continuity of relationships for children in its care.

Federal Legislation.   The goal of permanency for each child is also reflected in federal legislation, namely, the Adoption Assistance and Child Welfare Act (AACWA) of 1980 (PL 96-272), which was enacted following over a decade of advocacy on behalf of children in out-of-home care and pressures by various groups for child welfare reform. As summarized in Chapter 2, federal policy mandates the states to promote permanency planning for children and youths coming to their attention through means such as subsidized adoption, procedural reforms, time limits, and, above all, preventive and supportive services to families. Each state has enacted legislation or policies designed to implement PL 96-272, resulting in major changes in service delivery and outcomes for children in foster care and their families (see Chapter 2; Anderson, Ryan, & Leashore, 1997; Barth & Berry, 1994).

Specifically built into PL 96-272 are the following priorities:

- providing supports to families in order to prevent separation of children from their families;
- where separation is necessary, providing support services to enable children to be reunited with their families; and
- where reunification with the own families is not possible or appropriate, providing services that enable children to be adopted or placed in permanent foster homes with some form of legal protection.

To accomplish these purposes and priorities, the above law incorporates a number of procedural reforms and fiscal incentives:

- provision of preplacement services to keep children in their own homes or reunite them with their families as soon as possible;
- requirement of case plans, periodic reviews, management information systems, and other procedures to ensure that children are removed from their homes only when necessary and are placed in permanent families in a timely fashion;

- redirecting federal funds away from inappropriate foster care placement and toward permanent alternatives, particularly adoption; and
- establishment of adoption assistance programs, specifically federally funded subsidies for adoption of children with special needs, such as older, disabled, and minority children.

As discussed in Chapters 2 and 10, the delivery of permanency planning services continues to evolve under new federal legislation, particularly the Adoption and Safe Families Act of 1997 (ASFA) (PL 105-89), which builds on the principles of AACWA. This law changes and clarifies a range of federal policies established in 1980; in particular, it seeks to improve the safety of children exposed to abuse and neglect, promote adoption, and support birth families. In addition, permanency planning policy and practice are affected by other federal legislation, including the Family Preservation and Support Services Act of 1993 (PL 103-66), which was reauthorized, expanded, and renamed the Promoting Safe and Stable Families Program (under PL 105-89). The reauthorized family preservation program continues through FY 2001 at the following levels: FY 1999 at $275 million, FY 2000 at $295 million, and FY 2001 at $305 million. States are expected to commit a substantial portion of funds (conventionally thought to be at least 10%) to cover family support, family preservation, family reunification, and postadoptive services. In addition, state plans are required to contain assurances that in administering and conducting service programs, the safety of the children to be served will be of paramount concern.

As the meaning of permanency planning is considered, one should note that there are different options or routes to it (Thoburn, Murdoch, & O'Brien, 1986). These include maintaining the child in her or his own home, reunification of placed children with their biological families, adoption, and permanent or long-term foster family care in special situations, such as those of older children with ongoing relationships with their birth parents. This hierarchy of options is generally accepted in the field of child welfare. This does not mean, however, that any one of these options is inherently good or bad for every child, although the top preference is for maintaining or reuniting the child with the biological family. It does mean that in each case there should be careful assessment and extensive work to maintain children with their own families or to make other permanent plans when it has been demonstrated that the parents cannot care for the child. In short, permanency planning encompasses both prevention and rehabilitation and can serve as a framework for child welfare practice in general. It involves attention not only to children in care but also to those who are at risk of out-of-home placement.

Permanency planning embodies a number of key features:

- a philosophy highlighting the importance of the biological family and the value of rearing children in a family setting;
- a theoretical perspective stressing that opportunities for stability and continuity of relationships should be thoroughly explored because they can promote a child's growth and functioning;[5]

- a program focusing on systematic planning within specified time frames for children who are in foster care or at risk of placement out of their home;
- a case management method emphasizing practice strategies such as case reviews, contracting, and decision making, along with participation of parents in the helping process; and
- active collaboration among various community agencies, child care personnel, lawyers, judges, and others working with children and their parents (Maluccio et al., 1986, p. 5–15).

Current Status.   In conjunction with the other perspectives that have been described, permanency planning can be a powerful tool in our efforts to meet the needs of children, parents, and families through an approach that is consonant with a developmental rather than a remedial conception of services. Permanency planning has achieved a permanency of its own in the landscape of child welfare and has had a marked impact on service delivery.

Since the beginning of the 1990s, however, permanency planning has been questioned and perhaps seen as an outmoded response to a complex problem.[6] In our view, however, it is not outmoded. Indeed, it should endure, both as a philosophy and as a method or program, because it incorporates a basic value—namely, that every child is entitled to live in a family, preferably her or his own biological family, so as to have the maximum opportunity for growth and development. In today's context, it means serving children at risk of out-of-home care and their families through policies and programs that

- emphasize the safety of the child;
- balance concern regarding the parents' or children's problems with greater attention to the conditions that create or sustain family dysfunctioning;
- give serious attention to family preservation, through an array of services including intensive, home-based preventive and supportive services;
- promote collaboration among the various helping systems, particularly child welfare, courts, education, housing, health, and income maintenance;
- provide supports to child welfare workers, foster parents, and other child care personnel and empower them to do their job—rather than burn out in an unrewarding and unsupportive work environment;
- establish a continuum of services—from day care to residential treatment;
- strengthen the roles of mental health practitioners with children and youths in settings such as child guidance clinics, psychiatric programs, and the juvenile justice system;
- address juvenile court and other legal and procedural issues that inhibit the timely decision making required in permanency planning; and
- provide after-care services to maintain the child in the biological or other permanent family following discharge from foster care.

Recent legislation has also clarified the "reasonable efforts" clause of PL 96-272. The latter law indicated that "reasonable efforts" must be made to prevent out-of-home placement or return the child to the biological home following placement; however, it did not clearly define what would constitute reasonable efforts, leading to considerable confusion and controversy in the field. Critics complained that "unreasonable efforts" were being used to keep children at home or return them inappropriately home. As a result, this provision has been substantially revised under ASFA to indicate the grounds under which no "reasonable efforts" need to be made prior to the placement of a child in foster care or to achieve reunification. These exceptions include findings by a court that (1) the parent has subjected the child *to aggravated circumstances* (as defined by each state and possibly including abandonment, torture, chronic abuse, and sexual abuse), (2) the parent has committed or aided or abetted murder or voluntary manslaughter of another child of the parent; (3) the parent has committed a felony assault that results in serious bodily injury to the child or another child of the parent; or (4) the parental rights of the parent to a sibling have been terminated involuntarily. If reasonable efforts are not judged appropriate, then a permanency hearing shall be held for the child within 30 days after the determination; reasonable efforts to achieve adoption or guardianship shall be completed. Further, even when reasonable efforts are provided to keep the child at home or return to the home, ASFA allows that efforts to place a child for adoption or with a legal guardian can begin concurrently with efforts to keep the child at home.

Concurrent Planning.   A recent innovation in child and family welfare is concurrent planning, that is, working "towards family reunification while, at the same time, developing an alternative permanent plan" (Katz, 1999, p. 72). The concurrent planning model, pioneered in Washington state in the early 1980s, was specifically designed for very young children who were drifting in foster care due to their family's chronic pathology. As explained by Katz (1999, p. 72), one of its originators, the model "addresses this difficult-to-treat family constellation by combining vigorous family outreach, expedited timelines, and potentially permanent family foster care placements to improve the odds of timely permanency for very young children."

At its best, concurrent planning represents team decision making involving professionals as well as the child, the child's caregivers, birth parents, and extended family members. Its central purpose is accomplished through comprehensive assessment of the parent–child relationship, parental functioning, and support systems; front loading of services in areas such as financial assistance, parenting skills, health and mental health, substance abuse, and domestic violence; and frequent staffings including child, family, caregivers, and service providers. Katz (1999) delineates strategies for implementing this model, particularly by completing an early assessment of the family's likelihood of being reunited, establishing with the family clear timelines for timely permanency, vigorously promoting frequent parental visiting, and using written agreements. Katz also calls attention to a number of pitfalls in implementation, including failing to consider cultural differences; equating concurrent planning with adoption while minimizing reunifi-

cation efforts; designing case plans that are not family centered; providing insufficient training to social workers, foster parents, and family members; and not collaborating adequately with other community agencies.

APPLYING A FAMILY-CENTERED PERSPECTIVE

This chapter has thus far presented a comprehensive conceptual framework for
child-focused and family-centered practice consisting of ecological, competence,
and developmental perspectives along with a permanency planning orientation.
The framework leads to a range of implications for policy and practice, which will
be highlighted here and integrated in subsequent chapters.[7]

Focus on the Family

The ecological approach requires, first, that we maintain a principal focus on the
child's well-being and safety within a family-centered context in child welfare.
Among other aspects, this involves two major directions: (1) emphasis on the family as the central unit of attention and (2) emphasis on preservation of family ties
or creation of a new legal family.

The Family as Central Unit of Attention.   Focus on the family does not imply that the child's safety, needs, and interests are of secondary importance. It
means that, in most cases, the child can best be helped through regarding the family as the central unit of service or focus of attention, whenever and as much as
possible. Human beings can best be understood and helped within their significant
environment, and the family is the most intimate environment of all. It is here that
the child develops and forms her or his identity and basic competence. The family has the potential for providing resources throughout the life cycle, particularly
as its members are sustained and supported by various services (Germain &
Bloom, 1999; Hartman & Laird, 1983). The family's own environment can be employed as the arena in which practitioners intervene to help strengthen communication, parenting skills, and parent–child relationships. As Laird (1995: p. 153)
has observed, "Family clinicians view the family as the most salient context for
understanding and changing many individually defined problems."
     The concept of the family as the central unit of attention has often been difficult
to implement, even though professionals generally agree with it. The tendency has
been to fragment helping efforts by concentrating variously on the children, the
parents, the relatives, or the foster parents rather than working with the children,
parents, and kin as interacting components of one family system. Obstacles such
as heavy caseloads, emergency situations, and complex family problems have often prevented us from fully incorporating into practice new knowledge about families and new approaches to intervention with family systems. Other factors, such

as bias against parents, have complicated efforts to provide adequate services to families.

Various authors have described programs and methods demonstrating what can be accomplished through a concentrated focus on the family (e.g., Dunst, Trivette, & Deal, 1988; Schorr, 1988, 1997) and the provision of family support services (Kagan & Weissbourd, 1994). These authors argue that many parents can be rehabilitated or helped to plan responsibly for their children so that they can avoid substantial problems in parenting. In particular, the growth of the family-based therapy movement has led to the application of family treatment approaches as alternatives to placement of children out of their homes or as methods of speeding up the reunification of these children with their families.[8]

To be effective with families coming to the attention of the child welfare system, these treatment approaches need to view the family from an ecological perspective. Assessment and intervention thus focus on the family's transactions with its kinship system, school, community institutions, and other social networks that impact its functioning. Intervention strategies are directed not only toward engaging the family in treatment but also toward changing the social systems that influence it. Family preservation programs, such as the HOMEBUILDERS™ model, reflect such a focus on the family unit and the range of strategies that have been found to be useful.[9] Yet these programs recognize that some staff time should also be committed to work with social supports and community networks (cf. Tracy, 1995).

As delineated further in Chapter 10, the focus on the family should be maintained even when a child must be placed out of the home. To do so, foster family or group care placement of a child should be seen as a part of the overall service rather than as *the* service—as a tool, rather than as an end in itself. At the same time, as noted throughout this volume, it should be stressed that the child's safety is a paramount concern, and that there should be vigorous efforts to engage and support the family's capacity to provide a safe environment for the children.

Preservation of Family Ties.   When children must go into out-of-home placement, there is the challenge of preserving family ties between them and their families as much as possible. The natural bonds between children in care and their parents may continue to be important for parents as well as children long after they are physically separated. In such instances, finding ways to preserve contact among children, siblings, kin, parents, and former caregivers will benefit children.

A key means of accomplishing the preservation of family ties is consistent parent visiting of children in substitute care. The findings of various studies have highlighted the crucial role played by parental visiting or other parent–child contact in the outcome of the placement as well as the child's functioning and development. For instance, research has demonstrated the importance of parental visiting of children in foster care as the best single predictor of the outcome of placement. In their longitudinal study of foster care in New York City, Fanshel and Shinn (1978) observed that children who were visited frequently by their parents during the first year of placement "were almost twice as likely to be discharged eventually as those not visited at all or only minimally" (p. 96). In another study, Whittaker, Fine, Grasso, and Mooradian (1990) provided additional empirical evidence for the positive association between early establishment and maintenance of family contact and successful outcomes for youths in residential treatment. More recently, in an extensive investigation of children leaving out-of-home care, Davis, Landsverk, Newton, and Ganger (1996) found that the majority of children with parental visits at the level recommended by the courts were ultimately reunified.

Of course, the above studies are only correlations, and it may be that those children whose families seem most promising are the ones whose parents are encouraged most by professionals to be involved with the child. Experimental research is needed to demonstrate convincingly that visiting plays a causal role in the outcome of the placement; but, in the meantime, we should assume that it plays at least some such role and proceed to facilitate visiting. In addition to promoting family reunification, parent–child contact can enhance social functioning by assuring the child that he or she has not been rejected, helping the child and parents to understand why he or she cannot live at home, preventing the child's idealization or villainization of the parent, and helping parents maintain their relationships with their children (Aldgate, 1980). Practice principles and issues regarding parent–child visiting are considered further by Hess and Proch (1988, 1993), Palmer (1995), and Warsh, Maluccio, and Pine (1994), and in Chapter 11.

Children's Interests and Parental Rights and Responsibilities.   One of the central dilemmas of family-focused practice is to understand the relationship between children and their families in a way that protects the child's interests in living in a safe and loving family and supports the parents' rights and responsibilities as the leaders of their family. Houlgate (1988) has described three conceptualizations of the family that are useful for thinking about the relationship between children and families and society. In the *organic* family model, each family member is subject to the family's overall survival—in essence each part of the family exists to serve the needs of the whole. In the *individualistic* model, the family is conceived as composed of individuals who are basically competent outside of the family but reside in the family as a result of a de facto partnership agreement to be part of the family; the reason for fulfilling family roles is that members of the family have agreed to do so. In the *communal model,* the family is viewed as the most successful contributor to the well-being of all family members and all family members are regarded as moral equals in that each is deserving of the other's benevolence and care. The family has goals that are independent of each member's individualistic desires and, yet, no family member's well-being is structurally subjugated to support the overall goals of the family.

Family-focused child welfare work operates under the principle that the individual needs of children must be acknowledged and protected and the institution of the family respected, yet the well-being of children cannot be subjugated to overall family goals and the obligations of family members (particularly parents) transcend the limits of casual partnerships that can be dismissed when parenting becomes more complicated than parents thought they had bargained for. Family membership is not to be used to subjugate family members nor can it be thought of as a convenient partnership that can be casually abrogated by family members or by civil procedures. Policies and practices that promote the communal model of families would appear to have the greatest potential to benefit children.

ESTABLISHING A CONTINUUM OF SERVICES

The ecological perspective ultimately requires a shift to a society-centered approach to child and family welfare that focuses particularly on economics, employment, public health, and education. In the meantime, in response to the multiple needs of families in basic areas of living, there must also be comprehensive as well as intensive services. These include both "soft" services, such as counseling, and "hard" services, such as financial assistance. Various studies have shown that troubled families require a range of services to prevent out-of-home placement or to reunite children with their families.[10] In other words, as discussed further in Chapter 8 and 9, a continuum of services is often required to preserve families, including early intervention programs, concrete services such as housing and transportation, counseling, day care, and emergency foster care.

There should be an emphasis on a continuum of services providing both therapeutic help and environmental supports to the family before, during, and after the child's placement in care. Moreover, services should concentrate on strengthening the parents' coping and adaptive capacities. A family often may require services on an ongoing basis, even after the immediate crisis is resolved (Kagan & Schlosberg, 1989; Kaplan & Girard, 1994). In this regard, practitioners should challenge current state and federal policies that fund primarily programs providing time-limited help, with insufficient assessment of the need for follow-up services. What results is that families often fail when left unsupported after the time-limited service has ended. Through advocacy efforts, backed by research data, this trend must be reversed. Policymakers must acknowledge that many vulnerable families continue to need help, sometimes indefinitely, given their chronic problems and lack of support in their environment. Society cannot expect such families to be "cured," even with intensive and excellent short-term help.

Emphasizing Neighborhood-
or Community-Based Services

Research has also shown that services are most effective if they are not only comprehensive but also located at the neighborhood or community level. Neighborhood- or community-based services appear to facilitate maximum responsiveness to the needs and qualities of each child or family (Brown & Weil, 1992; Leon, 1999). The community orientation is seen in such practices as continuity between group care settings and community-based services, integrating services for "troubled" and "normal" youths, and expanding various types of family resource centers.

Community-based centers make a lot of sense, particularly since they provide help to families in their own natural surroundings and in nonstigmatizing or less stigmatizing ways. In addition to the continuum of services noted earlier, the community orientation requires flexible access, creation of new resources as gaps are identified, interagency and intraagency collaboration, and monitoring of the delivery and effectiveness of services for particular families. Leon (1999) describes a "family support model" that reflects such a community orientation and that has been successfully implemented in Florida by means of Neighborhood Centers for Families. The model provides integrated services that incorporate the following features:

- neighborhood base;
- coordination with other community agencies;
- measurement of service effectiveness; and
- involvement of the community in collaborative efforts.

Restructuring the Family's Environment

Through the provision of comprehensive, community-based services, professionals have an opportunity to help families to restructure their environment, that is, to modify or enrich it so that it is more suited to their needs and qualities and more conducive to their positive functioning. Social workers have a major responsibility in this area, to help counteract the impact of the "sociocultural risks" noted earlier in this chapter. Although there is consensus about the need to improve a family's social and physical environment, it is often difficult to do so. But it is not impossible, and various guidelines are available, as considered below.

Developing Partnerships between Professional Helpers and Informal Helpers. First, it is important to develop a close working relationship between professional helpers and informal helpers in a family's social networks. In many cases, much can be accomplished by helping parents to identify and use actual or potential resources in their social networks, e.g., relatives, neighbors, friends, volunteers, and other informal helpers. Studies have shown the value of complementing professional help with the services of paraprofessionals, such as homemakers or older persons who model effective parental behavior and coping skills. These aides help to meet the basic needs of parents, enrich the family's environment, and prevent placement or replacement. They provide parents with opportunities to learn skills, fulfill needs, and develop competence. The introduction of a new, supportive person such as a grandparent figure or a homemaker helps meet the needs of parents themselves and enhances their capacity to give to their children.[11]

Involving the Extended Family. In addition, a major source of help often can be the family's own extended kinship system (Danzy & Jackson, 1997; Everett, Chipungu, & Leashore, 1991). For example, Boyd-Franklin (1989) underscores the crucial role of informal adoption among black families. She further notes: "For many Black extended families, reciprocity—or the process of helping each other and exchanging and sharing support as well as goods and services—is a very central part of their lives" (p. 43). There should be an emphasis on strengthening and preserving cultural resources through means such as providing support for placements with relatives.

Although the use of relative foster placements has increased dramatically, research has shown that there is insufficient involvement of relatives or broader kinship networks in terms of preventive child welfare services. More could be done to try to mobilize the resources of relatives themselves. There are many cases in which the extended family, with agency support, can help a parent care for a child so as to avert placement in an unfamiliar institution or foster home or to reduce the duration of placement. Furthermore, family group conferences can be used to involve relatives and others significant persons in the family's environment to develop and implement permanency plans for a child. This innovative model of family decision making in child welfare originated in New Zealand, based on indigenous decision making practices. In that country, national law requires child welfare agencies to refer for family group conferences every substantiated case of child abuse and neglect. The conference, which is led by a court-appointed "care and protection coordinator," involves family members and kin, friends, professionals, and others who are in one way or another connected to the family. Its purpose is to help the extended family to reach a decision regarding care of the child in question, following extensive deliberations (cf. Burford & Pennell, 1995; Lupton, 1998; Pennell & Burford, 2000).

The New Zealand model is increasingly being adopted in private and public child welfare agencies in the United States and Canada, as a means of promoting involvement of the extended family in the care and protection of children at risk of child abuse and neglect and out-of-home placement (Burford & Hudson, 2000). Connolly and McKenzie (1999) delineate the application of family group conference concepts in the United States, focusing on a model of decision making that they call *Effective Participatory Practice.* Hardin (1996) describes in concrete terms how family group conferences work, explains their advantages and pitfalls, and identifies issues regarding their application in the United States. He encourages proper evaluation of their effectiveness within the United States context, particularly in light of the belief in "confidentiality of private information obtained by government entities and/or personnel" (p. 170). He then concludes as follows:

> family group conferences in various formats do have a place in this country and, at present, are beginning to be piloted or otherwise explored in various jurisdictions. Before they are likely to be more widely implemented, however, many states will have to expand their child welfare confidentiality statutes to permit agencies and families to actually talk with one another. (Hardin, 1996, p. 171)

At the same time, we should not romanticize the extended family—or other informal helpers. As noted years ago by Stack (1974), some families feel trapped by aversive social networks and kin. In addition, extended family members often are already overburdened by many demands and pressures, and we should assess carefully whether they can take on any additional burden as well as determine the help that they themselves will need from the agency.

Using Advocacy and Social Action.   Above all, restructuring the family's environment means that agencies and social workers must become involved in advocacy and social action, to help resolve the systemic or societal problems that lead to out-of-home care in the first place. There is ample evidence of a high correlation between entry into out-of-home care and social problems such as poverty, deprivation, and racism.[12] In particular, attention must be paid to establishing a living wage and decent employment opportunities for all families, with adequate income maintenance and day care services to support families struggling in the work force (see Chapter 4). From an ethical standpoint, child welfare staff should at times serve not only as clinical and administrative practitioners but as policy advocates and practitioners as well (Jansson, 1994).

The ecological perspective directs our attention to these larger social and economic forces and the environmental context in which families function. Permanency planning cannot substitute for preventive services; increased investment in our children and their families long before symptoms emerge is essential and— in the long run—more cost effective.

Adopting a Competence Perspective

Adopting a competence perspective, as described earlier in this chapter, leads to the following implications for practice.

Focus on Strengths of Child and Family.   Parents and children are regarded as active and striving human organisms who are basically motivated to grow and achieve competence. Pathology is deemphasized, along with acknowledgment that the problems faced by troubled families reflect the societal conditions that limit the power of parents and interfere with their coping efforts. Professional practices and policies should strive to promote family involvement, including

> family-organized service systems, policies, . . . and programs that are developed by families to meet needs and to address aspirations. (Briar-Lawson, 1998, p. 544)

In addition, human problems, needs, and conflicts are translated into adaptive tasks providing the client with opportunities for growth, mastery, and competence development. For example, a parent who is labeled as abusing or neglectful can be helped to learn or relearn skills in child care. To accomplish this, the problem has to be redefined or reframed as a condition involving lack of knowledge or inadequate parenting skills, rather than a situation of parental neglect. In short, the focus is on identifying and removing obstacles that interfere with the parents' cop-ing capacities and on practice strategies that help empower children, parents, and families by mobilizing their strengths and potentialities (Hegar, 1989; Hegar & Hunzeker, 1988; Hodges & Pecora, 2000; Russo, 1999; Saleebey, 1997).

Viewing Parents as Resources. The emphasis on human strengths also leads to the view of parents as resources on their own behalf—as partners in the help-ing process—rather than as carriers of pathology. As we shift from a pathological view of parents to a competence orientation, we are more likely to identify strengths in parents themselves and involve them in growth-producing activities. As they are given adequate opportunities, parents and other family members are better able to mobilize their own potentialities and natural adaptive strivings. They are thus empowered to act on their behalf (Maluccio & Whittaker, 1988; Pinder-hughes, 1989, 1995). For example, substance-abusing families and their conse-quent child neglect represent a huge current issue; empowering parents requires that we confront the lack of treatment facilities, housing, and employment train-ing programs, among many needs.

To support the efforts of parents to be resources for themselves and their fami-lies, agencies need to stress educational approaches, such as teaching skills in social interaction, communication, advocacy, problem solving, and parenting. Practitioners also need to emphasize the participation of parents and children in processes such as case contracting and decision making. These principles are be-ing implemented in the more effective child abuse treatment, family-based, and permanency planning programs.

In regard to the use of educational approaches, the potential value of parent training programs is often underestimated. Many of the parents who come to the attention of child welfare agencies lack basic information and basic skills, even in seemingly simple areas such as personal hygiene or nutrition. Although we are in-creasingly providing training for foster parents, little in the way of training is of-fered to the biological parents. This has to do in part with the typical view of parents as people who are sick and need to be treated rather than educated. Yet, parent train-ing has been proposed as an effective means of helping parents become more com-petent, particularly when it is offered in a nonstigmatizing setting such as at home or in a family center, and with due regard to the parents' personal needs, life-styles, and cultural values. This principle is often difficult to operationalize fully, and ten-sion still exists between balancing parents' rights and family preservation with child protection. The benefits, however, often outweigh the risks involved. For ex-ample, as discussed by Berry and Cash (1998), psychoeducational support groups can be effective in helping families to remain together and safe.

Using Self-Help Groups. Adopting a competence perspective also means helping parents to become involved in self-help groups. Indeed, as demonstrated in recent years by the success of self-help groups such as Parents Anonymous, par-ents can be regarded as resources who can help each other. Practitioners should aim toward encouraging clients to accomplish their purposes and meet their needs through individual and collective efforts, as Solomon (1976) has argued in her book on empowerment in black communities. For parents of children in foster care, for instance, working together to obtain needed resources for a better life for themselves and their children is an excellent way to counteract feelings of powerlessness and promote competence and self-esteem (Carbino, 1981). By participating as citizens in efforts to influence policies and programs, they "can develop personal, interpersonal, and intergroup knowledge and skills that improve both their self-concepts and their day-to-day functioning" (Gamble & Weil, 1995, p. 484).

Self-help groups have proven effective with parents from varied socioeconomic and ethnic backgrounds (Gitterman & Shulman, 1994; Whittaker & Garbarino, 1983). For example, Leon, Mazur, Montalvo, and Rodrieguez (1984) describe a self-help group for Hispanic mothers that benefited the mothers in a number of ways: building personal relationships and mutual support systems with others sharing similar concerns and interests, feeling free to express their problems and anxieties as parents, strengthening their self-esteem and increasing their self-confidence in parenting, and learning how to negotiate the intricacies of the service delivery system. Child welfare practitioners need to be able to organize and maintain such groups as important methods of intervention.

Roles of Practitioners and Clients

From the family-centered perspective also flow various implications regarding the roles of social workers working with families, as well as the roles of biological parents and children, foster parents, and other child care staff members. The primary role of the social worker is that of a catalyst or enabling agent—someone who actively and systematically helps the family to identify or create and use necessary resources. The worker uses flexible approaches and calls on a variety of resources to help provide the conditions necessary for parents to achieve their purposes, meet life's challenges, and engage in their developmental processes. Above all, practitioners should become experts in methods of environmental modification, use of existing community resources and natural helping networks, creation of new resources that may be needed by their clients, and mobilization of family members' own resources.

To carry out such roles, workers need to be skilled in a variety of interrelated functions. As discussed in more detail elsewhere (Maluccio et al., 1986, pp. 65–76), these include the following:

- Case planning: developing and maintaining the overall plan of service in each case. For example, child welfare workers are generally responsible for assessing child, parent, and family functioning so that time-limited, behaviorally specific, goal-oriented case plans can be developed.
- Case management: facilitating and monitoring the delivery of services to the family by multiple service providers and mediating between clients and

agencies in case of conflict. For example, foster care workers are typically responsible for assisting parents with developing new child management skills, often by referring them to another service provider.

- Therapy: providing necessary clinical services to children and families. This frequently involves helping families to alter family dynamics and promote positive parent–child relationships.
- Advocacy: ensuring that the rights of parents and children are maintained and that they receive services to which they are entitled. Thus, often there needs to be pressure on community resources to provide culturally responsive services.
- Court witness: providing testimony in court. Increasingly, social workers are called on to testify in court in relation to issues such as termination of parental rights.

These roles interweave and overlap, each taking priority over other aspects at different times, depending on the evolution and developments in each case. In many agencies, particularly smaller ones, one social worker may play all roles, whereas in larger agencies workers specialize in one or more roles. There are advantages and disadvantages in either approach. For example, being required to play all of these roles can create conflicts for the worker, such as having to choose between the needs and interests of different members of the client system. On the other hand, specialization can lead to greater client satisfaction and more efficient service delivery.

Roles of Biological and Foster Parents

In line with the emphasis on collaboration that is inherent in permanency planning, efforts should be made to have parents, foster parents, and other child care personnel regard themselves as partners in a shared undertaking, with common goals and mutually supportive and complementary roles. This can lead to new helping systems that are ultimately more effective and rewarding for everyone concerned. For instance, as considered further in Chapter 10, foster parents can be involved as resources for parents through means such as role modeling or serving as parent aides (Ryan, McFadden, & Warren, 1981; Warsh, Maluccio, & Pine, 1994).

As suggested by these authors, foster parents can become allies of biological parents and be more actively involved in the treatment plan in behalf of each family, as long as their roles are clarified and they are provided with adequate supports and rewards. For example, ways can be found in at least some cases to enable a foster family or residential treatment center to become an extension of the biological family, rather than its substitute, as is often the case (Watson, 1982). Further, in many cases the foster family could become an integral part of the overall treatment program and help promote the adaptive functioning of the biological parents (see Chapter 10, and Kufeldt, 1994). One emerging approach, known as *shared family care,* involves having parents with weak parenting skills live together with their children in foster or group care so they can observe and practice parenting in a protective environment (Barth, 1994; Barth & Price, 1999).

In a related program described as "whole-family foster care," the foster family becomes an "extended family" that can "direct parents in crisis to community resources as well as offer emotional supports while the family re-establishes itself" (Nelson, 1992, p. 576).

Roles of Children and Youths

Engaging children and adolescents is also important. Children and youths themselves can also be actively involved in the helping process, including reaching decisions regarding the best permanent plan for them. As practitioners become more comfortable in asking about their views, they find that children and youths have a lot to say that should be taken into account in planning services on their behalf.[13] For example, some older children make it clear that they prefer to be in a long-term foster home with continuing contacts with their parents rather than being adopted or placed in an institution (Barth & Berry, 1994). Other young people vividly express their views about their experiences in foster care through poems, essays, and stories (Desetta, 1996; Fay, 1989). Foster youth members of the California Youth Connection offer thoughtful ideas for improving the child welfare system (Knipe & Warren, 1999).

Appreciating the young person's perspective of course is critical in child and family welfare services, as illustrated in the story in Table 3.1, which reflects a child's experiences in moving into foster care. In addition to understanding the child's perspective, we should consider that the contract or written agreement can be profitably used as a means of helping children to make decisions, assume responsibility for their behavior, and take some control over their lives. For example, with adolescents in foster care, agreements can be used to clarify the tasks to be performed by the young person, the foster parents, and the social worker so as to facilitate the process of preparation for emancipation and independent living (Maluccio, Krieger, & Pine, 1990).

CONCLUSION

This chapter has presented a conceptual framework for family-centered child welfare practice, based on the interrelated perspectives of ecology, competence, human development, and permanency planning. For such an integrative framework to become fully implemented in the reality of practice, a number of issues and challenges will have to be confronted in the years ahead.

First, it will be necessary to adopt an institutional/preventive/developmental orientation to service delivery with children and families. This will involve, among other aspects, a shift away from the traditional remedial or "pick-up-the-pieces" approach, reallocation of more resources into community-focused early intervention activities, recycling of existing facilities from solely crisis services to a continuum of care, an explicit focus on policy issues and structural reform, willingness to change the substance as well as the form of services, and greater attention to issues of human diversity in service delivery.

Second, there will need to be much more in the way of (1) collaboration within the field of human services, particularly linkages of child welfare with related systems such as education, income maintenance, juvenile justice, law, and mental health; (2) multidisciplinary collaboration, with clarification of respective contributions and working relationships; and (3) multiagency collaboration, with special attention to clarification of respective roles and purposes, issues of territoriality, competition for funds, fragmentation in service delivery, and a more effective public-private–partnership.

Third, there will be a variety of challenges in the area of personnel, including meeting the need for highly skilled staff, offering a range of educational opportunities, providing rewards and career ladders, retraining existing personnel as programs and practices change, and clarifying the roles and functions of different kinds of personnel (see Chapter 14 for further discussion).

Last, but not least, it will be necessary, perhaps more than ever before, to avoid theoretical or ideological rigidities and provincialism. The future of child welfare demands that diverse disciplines, agencies, and professionals be ready to develop new theories, try new methods and approaches, and test their effectiveness in the provision of services to vulnerable families and children. The resulting integrative framework will thus be an open and evolving one, and the promise of a more effective continuum of services in child welfare will be more than an illusion.

Table 3.1. A Foster Child's Story
By Francisco Maltos[a]

Preface

The following story of a child placed in family foster care is based on a true event, which is described with additional information from the experiences of other youths. It is intended to help readers imagine what it would be like to be a young person in this situation. The story reflects one child's lived experience and is presented here to underscore the importance of considering a child's background and perspectives in the provision of child welfare services. It should also be noted that foster care will continue to be a reality for many children despite the best efforts at prevention. When provided effectively, foster care can be a caring and culturally sensitive option for at least some children.

The Story

The time of year is early summer. You are 10 years old. You live in a small house about 10 miles from town. You are of Mexican descent. You have brown skin and black hair. You are

(continued)

Table 3.1. A Foster Child's Story (continued)

healthy, and at this time in your life, you have no reason to have any fears. On the radio, Jose Alfredo is singing, a voice you are very familiar with.

Your mom calls for you to come and eat and says, "Lavate sus manos y vengase a comer hijo" (wash your hands and come to eat, son). Your mother was American born near the border, your father is a Mexican immigrant. You and your family have been living in Washington State now for 8 years. Both of your parents are farm workers.

Your culture is Mexican. At home, your parents speak only Spanish. You speak English, but only at school. Your English is not as fluent as the other students and sometimes you are embarrassed by that because sometimes you are laughed at. At home, you watch mostly Spanish TV shows. You listen to Mexican music on the radio, and about the only American culture you are exposed to at home are the English TV shows you occasionally watch. On the walls of your home hangs a picture of the Virgin de Guadalupe and a brown Jesus Cristo (Jesus Christ). In the corner sits a colorful pinata that will be broken next week at a friend's birthday party.

Your mom calls you again to eat. Before you begin to eat, you bless yourself. Your plate is already served. You reach for a hot tortilla and use it to eat your food, which is arroz, picadillo, chopped papas (potatoes), and asparagus that your mom makes in a special sauce. You use silverware to eat some foods, but most of the time, you prefer using a tortilla. At the table, your parents are talking about El Cinco de Mayo festivities that are going on in town and you look forward to attending. Your father also talks about attending Spanish Mass where one of his compadres is going to baptize his newest born. Then after the baptism there will be a barbacoa (barbecue), where a goat will be killed and prepared to eat. Those are always fun because there is music, food, and kids your age.

Next month, your parents are invited to a Quincienera. There will be a big dance and a lot of children, and you always have a good time chasing one another on the dance floor, around and through the people as they are dancing. Besides the Quincieneras, you are familiar with the other traditions of breaking pinatas on birthdays, making cascarones for Easter, having tamales around Christmas, and bunuelos around New Year's.

Respect toward your parents is important. You risk getting slapped if you are smart with them. No drinking or smoking is allowed in the home. You are forbidden to use bad words. You never raise your voice at your parents and you notice your parents don't do that with other people.

The only contact you have at home with Anglos is when they come to your home to sell things, or when they are looking for your parents to ask about the bills they owe. At school you hang around mostly Mexican kids. You have white friends too, but not as many. You feel content at home, and you have no reason to question who you are. Your identity as an individual is forming, and although you are still too young to conceptualize this into words, your identity as Mexican is important to you.

Then a traumatic event changes everything. Both of your parents have been arrested by federal agents as they are working that morning cutting asparagus. They are taken to the local jail and are charged with defrauding the government of food stamps and public assistance. Unknown to you, your parents have been engaged in this illegal activity for 3 years, and will now face an indefinite amount of time in jail or prison. Your parents fear what will happen to you.

That afternoon at school, you are called to the office to meet with a social worker from child protective services. The social worker is white. He talks to you, using words that you don't understand. There are no interpreters available to help. You have no other family or relatives that can take you, so the decision is made to place you in foster care.

(continued)

Table 3.1. A Foster Child's Story (continued)

When you arrive at the foster home in town, the home seems so big compared to yours. You ask the social worker how long you will be here and he says: "Not too long." A large, white woman answers the door. She smiles and walks you into the home. It smells strange; you don't like it. You hear English music, you see pictures of a white Jesus Christ. There is a dog in the home and you think that this is unclean. The odor of cigarettes is in the air, and it smells bad. You feel afraid—not just because you are not at home, but because you are in a strange home, you are in an Americano home. "Will they treat me bad because I am Mexican? What if I can't understand what they say? Will they make fun of me when I talk?" The foster mom tries to comfort you, but she frightens you because her voice is so loud, and you are not used to that. Some older boys and girls come in the home now and they look at you. "Are they staring at me because I'm not white, or are they just wondering who I am, like I am wondering who they are?"

That evening, you meet the foster father. He is loud too, and you think he must be angry. He shakes your hand and he grabs you tight. It hurts. You're not used to that either. After a while, you are called to eat. After the blessing, you look at your food and recognize nothing you eat at home except what looks like rice. You automatically reach for a tortilla that's not there. Instead you grab a piece of bread and use that. You quickly hear: "Use your fork, not your hands." The other children stare. It's hard to swallow your food. You feel so out of place. When you try to answer their questions, they tell you, "Speak up, I can't hear you." You try to speak louder, but it's too hard because something inside of you says you're not supposed to.

After a few weeks go by, you are a little more comfortable. The other children have asked you to teach them Spanish. The foster mom hears you and tells you "Stop that, speak English in this home." It hurts you to hear that. You want to tell her something but you don't. After awhile, you decide it's best to do as she says.

It's now been about 3 months and legal entanglements keep your parents in jail. In fact, they will both be sent to a federal prison in California for 2 more years.

At your foster home, you are becoming much more fluent in English and you like that. You have learned to like English music a lot, and you almost never listen to Mexican music. You never speak Spanish at home and you never eat any authentic Mexican food. Even the way you dress now is different. You like the baggy pants and T-shirts, as long as they have the brand names. You are starting to try some of the cuss words now, but you're not quite brave enough to use them in the house.

Months continue to go by, and the social worker has no luck locating any relatives, and there are no Hispanic families locally to take you.

Time passes, and now it has been about 12 months and unnoticed by you, you are becoming quite acculturated. You only watch English TV shows, you never go to Mexican celebrations like Quincieneras or Cinco de Mayo, and English church is not quite the same as Spanish Mass. The only socializing you do is with the foster parent's friends and relatives, and it's very obvious to them that you are not a blood relative.

The social worker needs to decide on a permanent placement for you and because you have adjusted so well, he is going to recommend that you stay in the home under a guardianship approved by the juvenile court. The foster parents agree to this because they consider you to be like one of their own now.

It's been a quick year in foster care, and you don't even realize all that has happened to you. There is no telling how long you will be living in your new home.

[a]Francisco Maltos, M.S.W., is a social worker in the Yakima (Washington) Division of The Casey Family Programs.

NOTES

1. For more information about social supports, see Garbarino (1992), Gitterman and Shulman (1994), Kemp, Whittaker and Tracy (1997), Thompson (1995); Whittaker and Garbarino (1983), and Whittaker and Tracy (1989).

2. For more information on multicultural dimensions and human diversity, see Anderson, Ryan, and Leashore (1997), Cohen (1992), Courtney et al. (1996), Denby, Curtis, and Alford, (1998), Fong (1994), Hogan and Siu (1988), Ingoldsby and Smith (1995), Lynch and Hanson (1998), Pinderhughes (1989), Pinderhughes (1991), and Whittaker and Tracy (1989).

3. The impact of the environment on child development and functioning has been discussed, among others, by Fraser (1997), Garbarino (1992), Haggerty, Sherrod, Garmezy, and Rutter (1994), and Kemp, Whittaker, and Tracy (1997).

4. Harris (1995) argues that peer groups of childhood and adolescence are more important in socialization than parents.

5. It should also be noted that in some cases discontinuity can be beneficial. Maintaining continuous ties with families and communities may not, under many circumstances, have the advantages of discontinuity. Many parents, every year, make decisions to move their children to other schools in order to help them to improve educational attainment, even though it might involve disrupting children's friendships and possibly moving the entire household. In some child welfare cases, planned discontinuity can also benefit children. In one of the authors' cases, a judge seeking to maintain continuity between a mother incarcerated for murder and her three children (ages 2, 3, and 7) refused to free any of them for adoption because the older child had expressed interest in continuing relationships with the biological mother and younger children. By not having the option to discontinue their legal ties to their mother (while encouraging some continuous ongoing contact with her and each other), these children were exposed to long-term foster care that is likely to have many placement moves and much discontinuity in store for them (Berrick, Needell, Barth, & Jonson-Reid, 1998).

6. In a provocative essay, Gilligan (1997) proposes a shift from permanence to *resilience* as an organizing concept for child placement planning and practice. He defines resilience as "the capacity to transcend adversity" (p. 14). Although continuing to embrace the positive aspects of the permanency planning perspective, he argues that it may be more helpful to strive to foster resilience in children as a major imperative in child welfare.

7. For further discussion of family-centered practice, see the special issue of *Families in Society: The Journal of Contemporary Human Services,* Vol. 76 (March 1995). For examples of application of the family-centered framework to specific cases, see Maluccio et al. (1986, pp. 86–89) and Warsh, Maluccio, and Pine (1994).

8. For extensive consideration of programs and practices focused on helping multi-problem families coming to the attention of the child welfare system, see Cole (1995), Kagan and Schlosberg (1989), Kaplan and Girard (1994), Maluccio and Whittaker (1988), and Schwartz and AuClaire (1995).

9. For description of family preservation programs and related issues, see Chapter 9 and Berry (1997), Fraser, Pecora, and Haapala (1991), Kinney, Haapala, and Booth (1991), McCroskey and Meezan (1997), Pecora, Fraser, Nelson, McCroskey, and Meezan (1995), Schuerman, Rzepnicki, and Littell (1994), Whittaker (1991), and Whittaker, Kinney, Tracy, and Booth (1990).

10. See, for example, Fein, Maluccio, and Kluger (1990), Jones (1985), Stein (1985), and Webb and Aldgate (1991).

11. See Burnette (1997), Everett, Chipungu, and Leashore (1991), Miller, Fein, Howe, Gaudio, and Bishop (1984), and Whittaker and Garbarino (1983).

12. For a discussion of the connection between social problems and child placement, see Berrick et al. (1998), Halpern (1990), Kamerman and Kahn (1990), and Pelton (1989, 1994).

13. For studies that gathered information directly from children and youths, see Aldgate, Maluccio, and Reeves (1989), Biehal, Clayden, Stein, and Wade (1995), Garbarino, Stott, and associates (1989), Johnson, Yoken, and Voss (1995), Martin and Palmer (1997), McMillen, Rideout, Fisher, and Tucker (1997), Mech and Rycraft (1995), and Wedeven, Pecora, Hurwitz, Howell, and Newell (1997).

FOR FURTHER INFORMATION

Anderson, G.R., Ryan, A.S., & Leashore, B.R. (Eds.) (1997). *The challenge of permanency planning in a multicultural society.* New York: The Haworth Press. Thorough discussion of issues, concepts, and strategies in achieving permanency planning, particularly for African-American, Latino, and native American children, gay and lesbian adolescents, and unaccompanied refugee minors.

Bronfenbrenner, U. (1979). *The ecology of human development.* Cambridge, MA: Harvard University Press. A classic book that presents a useful conceptual framework for analyzing the various layers of the environment and their dynamic influence on the development of human beings.

Brown, J., and Weil, M. (Eds.) (1992). *Family practice: A curriculum plan for social service.* Washington, DC: Child Welfare League of America. Outlines a comprehensive model for delivery of family-centered child welfare services, with emphasis on the transition from child-centered to family-centered practice.

Germain, C., & Gitterman, A. (1996). *The life model of social work practice—Advances in theory and practice.* New York: Columbia University Press. Delineates the application of the ecological perspective to social work practice with individuals, families, and groups, following a "life model" of social work developed by the authors. Also examines "life-model" practice aimed at improving community life, advocating for policy and program changes, and using political strategies to promote social justice.

Hartman, A., & Laird, J. (1983). *Family-centered social work practice.* New York: Free Press. Comprehensive integration of concepts, theories, and techniques useful in family-centered practice, with numerous case illustrations.

Kaplan, L., & Girard, J.L. (1994). *Strengthening high-risk families—A handbook for practitioners.* New York: Lexington Books. In-depth discussion of principles and strategies of practical use for child welfare workers working with vulnerable families experiencing chronic and severe problems.

Lynch, E.W., & Hanson, M.J. (Eds.) (1998). *Developing cross-cultural competence,* 2nd ed. Baltimore, MD: Paul H. Brookes Publishing. Detailed guide for working with children and families from a range of ethnic, cultural, and racial groups.

Maluccio, A.N. (Ed.) (1981). *Promoting competence in clients: A new/old approach to social work practice.* New York: Free Press. Describes competence-centered social work practice and its application to various client groups, including children and youths.

Maluccio, A.N., Fein, E., & Olmstead, K. A. (1986). *Permanency planning for children: Concepts and methods.* London and New York: Routledge, Chapman and Hall. Presents an integrative, in-depth discussion of the philosophy, theory, and practice of permanency planning for children and youths within a family-centered orientation.

Pecora, P.J., Fraser, M.W., Nelson, K.E., McCroskey, J., & Meezan, W. (1995). *Evaluating family-based services.* New York: Aldine de Gruyter. Review of the basic features of evaluation of family-based programs in light of current knowledge, including design and measurement issues and research instruments for measuring changes in child and family functioning.

Pike, V. (1976). Permanent families for foster children: The Oregon project. *Children Today, 5,* 22–25. Includes a concise, early formulation of permanency planning for children in foster care, by the originator of the landmark project that helped promote the philosophy and practice of permanency planning.

Sotomayor, M. (Ed.) (1991). *Empowering Hispanic families: A critical issue for the '90s.* Milwaukee, WI: Family Service America. Examines the delivery of human services from the perspectives of Hispanic-American groups and offers recommendations for strengthening services to children and families.

Whittaker, J.K., Kinney, J., Tracy, E.M., & Booth, C. (Eds.) (1990). *Reaching high-risk families: Intensive family preservation in human services.* New York: Aldine de Gruyter. Systematic description and evaluation of the critical features of Homebuilders™, an exemplary program for working with families in crisis. Exploration of implications for traditional practice with families and children.

4

Economic Security for Families with Children

Robert Plotnick

Most of this text deals with child welfare and family services—the key programs, the important service delivery issues, the challenges facing such services, and the practice principles gleaned from careful research. Delivering and improving these services contribute to children's well-being and are central tasks of social workers.

But these services do not, by themselves, guarantee the well-being of children. For healthy growth and development, children need adequate income from their parents to provide the material supports of life—food, clothing, shelter, medical care, etc. If parental income is low or absent, children need to rely on income maintenance programs.

This chapter examines the economic situation of children under age 18, with particular emphasis on the problem of child poverty in the United States. It looks at the development and current status of American antipoverty policies for children (Table 4.1). It evaluates these policies, discusses alternative strategies for reducing child poverty, and compares the situation in the United States with that in other affluent countries.

A chapter on poverty and antipoverty policy may seem out of place in a child welfare text, but it really is not. Unemployment and low family income are associated with family problems requiring child welfare services. Raising family income, then, may be an effective way to reduce the number of families needing child welfare services and, thereby, ease the caseload burden on child welfare workers and reduce the budgetary pressures on child welfare agencies. To improve children's lives, we need both an "incomes" strategy and the "services" strategy with which social workers are more familiar. Understanding the role of labor market and income maintenance policies in enhancing families' economic security can help social workers develop a more integrated approach to child welfare policy issues and, more generally, to improving the lives of children.

Table 4.1. Significant Events Related to Child Poverty and Antipoverty Policy

Year	Event
1911–1935	Mothers' pensions laws adopted in 46 states.
1935	Aid to Dependent Children (ADC) established as Title IV-A of the Social Security Act.
1939	Survivors Insurance established.
1950	ADC expanded to aid a caretaker relative (usually the mother) as well as child.
1962	ADC's name changed to Aid to Families with Dependent Children (AFDC). States given option to extend AFDC to two-parent families with an unemployed father, later changed to unemployment of either parent (AFDC-UP).
1964	War on Poverty begins with passage of Economic Opportunity Act, ushering in 15 years of rapid growth in income support and related social welfare programs. Food Stamp Act passed.
1965	Medicaid established as Title XIX of the Social Security Act.
1967	Work Incentive Program (WIN) enacted, introducing work and training requirements for many AFDC recipients.
1969	Federal government adopts an official definition of poverty based on a poverty measure developed in 1963 and 1964.
1975	Earned Income Credit enacted. Child Support Enforcement program established as Title IV-D of Social Security Act.
1981	Omnibus Budget Reconciliation Act reduces generosity of AFDC and other needs tested programs, strengthens work requirements in AFDC.
1984	Amendments to Title IV-D strengthen federal role in child support policy.
1986	Tax Reform Act eliminates federal income tax liability for poor families, expands Earned Income Credit.
1986–1991	A series of laws broadens Medicaid eligibility to many more poor and near-poor children and pregnant women, even if they are not receiving AFDC.
1988	Family Support Act broadens employment and training requirements for AFDC recipients, mandates AFDC-UP, and strengthens child support enforcement.
1993	Earned Income Credit benefits are expanded again.
1996	Personal Responsibility and Work Opportunity Reconciliation Act replaces AFDC with Temporary Assistance for Needy Families, further strengthens child support enforcement, and makes major changes in other major cash and noncash assistance programs.
1997	Taxpayer Relief Act provides $500 tax credit for most children.

THE ECONOMIC STATUS OF FAMILIES WITH CHILDREN

Recent Trends in Incomes of Families with Children

Table 4.2 shows median family income for three selected years for all families with children, and separately for those with either one or two parents present.[1] All the

Table 4.2. Median Real Income and Distribution of Family Types for Families with Children. Selected Years, 1979–1996 (1997 dollars)

	1979	*1989*	*1994*	*1997*	*Percentage Change 1979–1997*
All families	$43,810	$43,307	$41,073	$43,545	−0.6
with children	100%	100%	100%	100%	
Married-couple families	$49,054	$51,768	$51,165	$54,395	+10.9
with children	80.4%	74.3%	71.6%	70.6%	
Female-headed families,	$17,779	$16,799	$16,139	$17,256	−2.9
no husband present,	17.6%	21.7%	23.6	23.5%	
with children					
Male-headed families,	$34,773[a]	$32,043	$26,092	$28,668	−17.6
no wife present,	2.0%	4.0%	4.8%	5.8%	
with children					

Source: U.S. Census Bureau, "Presence of Children Under 18 Years Old by Type of Family—Families (All Races) by Median and Mean Income: 1974 to 1997," <http://www.census.gov/hhes/income/histinc/f010.html>; revised May 25, 1999.
[a]Figure is for 1978.

income figures are adjusted to the 1997 price level so we can directly compare the real purchasing power of incomes received in different years.

Median family income was nearly stagnant between 1979 and 1989. Between 1989 and 1994 families with children did not fare well economically and the typical income dropped more than 6%. In the prosperity of the mid-1990s incomes recovered so that by the end of the entire 18-year period, median real income was virtually unchanged. The trends are similar for white, black, and Hispanic families, but the two minority groups have always had much lower median incomes than the white group.

When we compare two-parent to single-parent families, important differences appear. Between 1979 and 1997, the median income of two-parent families increased by 10.9%. In contrast, the median for families with a female parent and no husband fell 2.9%, and the median for families with a male parent and no wife fell more than 17%. The proportion of families with just one parent grew from 19.6% of all families with children in 1979 to 29.4% in 1997. An interesting social development is that families with a male parent and no wife are the most rapidly growing family type and now account for almost 6% of all families with children. Since a growing proportion of children are likely to live in single-parent families, the falling incomes of such families and growing income gaps between these family types and married-couple families is a serious concern.

Changes in median income do not show how families in different positions in the income distribution have fared. To see this, researchers rank families by income, divide them into quintiles (five equal sized groups), and compute each quintile's share of the income received by all families with children. This has been done in Table 4.3.

Table 4.3. Share of Total Cash Income Received by Each Quintile of Families with Children, 1979–1994

| | Quintile Percentage Share of Income | | | | |
Year	Poorest	Lower Middle	Middle	Upper Middle	Richest
1979	5.1	12.2	18.2	24.6	39.9
1989	4.0	10.8	17.3	24.8	43.0
1994	3.7	10.2	16.9	25.1	44.1

Source: Committee on Ways and Means (1998), p. 1335.

Two points stand out. In every year the degree of inequality is large. In 1994, for example, the poorest fifth received 3.7% of total income while the richest fifth received more than 11 times that amount, 44.1%. Also, inequality has increased since 1979 (in fact, the increase began in the mid-1970s). The ratio of the top fifth's share to the poorest fifth's was 7.8 in 1979, 10.8 in 1989, and 11.9 in 1994.

Table 4.4 shows the real average income of a family in the poorest quintile fell from $12,127 in 1979 to $8,857 in 1994, a drop of 27%. There were also significant declines in the real average income of the second and third quintiles. Families in the top quintile increased their average income over the same period.

On average, then, the economic resources available to families with children have declined in the past 15 to 20 years. More troubling is that children from less affluent families have faced a large decline in real income. There have been signs since 1995 that the trends of rising inequality and declining real incomes at the bottom may finally have reversed. Even if the new trends continue, it will take a number of years to regain the economic ground lost by families with children since the 1970s.

Table 4.4. Average Cash Income of Families with Children by Income Quintile in Constant 1997 Dollars, 1979–1994

| | Mean Income of Quintile | | | | | |
	Poorest	Lower Middle	Middle	Upper Middle	Richest	Mean of All Families
All families with children						
1979	12,127	28,948	43,124	58,168	94,450	44,973
1989	9,985	26,747	42,800	61,116	106,093	46,859
1994	8,857	24,321	40,533	60,074	105,399	45,424
Percentage change						
1979–1994	−27.0	−16.0	−6.0	+3.3	+11.6	+1.0

Source: Committee on Ways and Means (1998), p. 1332. Inflation adjustments by author.

Poverty among Children

Measuring Poverty.   Mollie Orshansky, an economist at the Social Security Administration, developed a definition of poverty in 1963. With a few modifications, the federal government adopted Orshansky's measure as the official definition of poverty in 1969, and has further modified it in small ways since then. It provides a set of "poverty lines" that vary by household size, the age of the head of the household, and the number of children under 18. The lines are updated yearly to match the change in the Consumer Price Index, so they represent the same purchasing power each year. For 1998 the poverty line ranged from $7,818 for a single person over age 65 to $33,339 for a family of nine or more. For a family of four with two children it was $16,530, or $318 per week. If a family's annual income falls below its poverty line, its members are counted as poor.

The official poverty definition measures income by counting cash income from all public and private sources, except capital gains. It does not take into account public or private noncash benefits such as food stamps, subsidized public housing, Medicaid, or employer-provided health insurance, nor does it subtract taxes. Yet both noncash benefits and taxes affect a family's standard of living.

The official poverty lines and income concept have been criticized on a number of grounds (Citro & Michael, 1995; Jencks & Mayer, 1996). Some critics think the lines are too low. Some argue for different methods of adjusting the lines over time or for differences in family size or the local cost of living. Some want to include noncash benefits, subtract taxes, or make other adjustments to the income measure. Despite these debates, the official measure remains an important social indicator and symbolizes the nation's concern with the standard of living of its poorest citizens.

Trends in Poverty among Children.   Children are now the poorest age group in the United States. Table 4.5 shows that in 1998, 18.9% of American children, or 13.5 million, were poor according to the official definition. Among children under age 6 the poverty rate was even higher: 22.0%. The rates of poverty among adults age 18 to 64 and age 65 or more were both 10.5%. In 1998, then, children were 1.8 times as likely to be poor as adults.

Children have been the poorest age group since 1974. Before then, the aged were the poorest. Because of better Social Security benefits and larger private pensions, poverty among the aged has gradually declined for the past 30 years. Poverty among children has not. It fell throughout the 1960s, inched slowly upward during the 1970s, and sharply increased in the early 1980s. Since 1980 the child poverty rate has fluctuated between 18.3 and 22.7%. The rate of poverty among children in 1998 was 1.3 percentage points *greater* than in 1966, and 4.9 percentage points greater than in 1969, the year when child poverty was lowest.

Jencks and Mayer (1996) offer strong evidence that the official estimates of the trend in child poverty are biased upward. Although official statistics suggest the

Table 4.5. Poverty among Children and Adults, Official Measure 1959–1998

	Percentage in Poverty		
Year	Children under 18	Adults 18–64	Adults 65+
1959	27.3%	17.0%	35.2%
1966	17.6	10.5	28.5
1970	15.1	9.0	24.6
1975	17.1	9.2	15.3
1980	18.3	10.1	15.7
1985	20.7	11.3	12.6
1990	20.6	10.7	12.2
1992	22.3	11.9	12.9
1994	21.8	11.9	11.7
1996	20.5	11.4	10.8
1997	19.9	10.9	10.5
1998	18.9	10.5	10.5

Source: U.S. Census Bureau, Current population reports, series P-60, No. 207, Poverty in the United States: 1998. Washington, DC: U.S. Government Printing Office, 1999, Table B-2.

level of child poverty rose by a sixth in the 1970s, and another fifth in the 1980s, Jencks and Mayer's adjustments show child poverty declined a quarter in the 1970s and hardly changed over the 1980s. Direct measures of children's material well-being, such as housing quality, access to medical care, and availability of common household appliances and motor vehicles, were largely consistent with these revised trends in income poverty.

Jencks and Mayer's evidence suggests that the off-heard claim that the War on Poverty was a total failure is exaggerated, at least for children. Despite a number of adverse social and economic trends in the 1970s and 1980s, they argue that child poverty as commonly understood—inadequate income and material deprivation—has probably fallen. At the same time, even with their adjustments the child poverty rate was between 14 and 15% in 1989. This exceeded the unadjusted poverty rate for adults of any age, so the adjustments do not change the fact that children are the poorest age group. And a poverty rate of 14% still means one of every seven children, 10 million in 1999, must get by on income below the official minimally decent level. Child poverty remains a serious problem, however we measure it.

Child Poverty, Race and Type of Family.   Children's chances of being poor strongly depend on their race and ethnicity. In 1998 black and Hispanic child poverty levels were more than three times higher than the non-Hispanic white level (see Table 4.6). Poverty among children of Asian and Pacific Islander descent was 70% higher than among non-Hispanic whites. Between 1976 and 1985 child poverty increased about 33% for whites and Hispanics, but only 7% for blacks. Since 1985, the trends have been similar for these three groups.

Table 4.6. Poverty Among Children Under 18, by Race and Ethnicity 1976–1998

Year	White, Not Hispanic	Black	Hispanic[a]	Asian/Pacific Islander
1976	9.8	40.6	30.2	NA
1980	11.8	42.3	33.2	NA
1985	12.8	43.6	40.3	NA
1987[b]	11.8	45.1	39.3	23.5
1990	15.9	44.8	38.4	17.6
1992	13.2	46.6	40.0	16.4
1994	12.5	43.8	41.5	18.3
1996	11.1	39.9	40.3	19.5
1997	11.4	37.2	36.8	20.3
1998	10.6	36.7	34.4	18.0

Source: U.S. Census Bureau, Current population reports, series P-60, No. 207, Poverty in the United States: 1996. Washington, DC: U.S. Government Printing Office, 1999, Table B-2.
[a]Persons of Hispanic origin may be of any race.
[b]1987 is the first year with data on Asian/Pacific Islanders.

Family structure is also a key determinant of poverty status, as the income differences in Table 4.2 suggest. In 1998 children in families with a female parent and no spouse present suffered a poverty rate of 46.1%. Children in married couple families had a rate of only 9.0%; children in other family structures (mainly families with an adult male but no spouse present) had a rate of 20.0% (U.S. Census Bureau, 1999, Table 2).

Families with a female householder and no male present contain 60% of all poor children. Families with a nonwhite male householder contain another 9%. Families with a white male householder contain the remaining 32%. Though child poverty is concentrated in families with minority and female heads, we must recognize that poor children come from all types of families.[2]

Causes of Continuing High Levels of Child Poverty.   There are three main reasons why child poverty has remained high. First, during the past 20 years an increasing proportion of heads of families have been unable to earn enough income to keep their dependents out of poverty. Real earnings and wage rates among men with 12 or fewer years of schooling have fallen in absolute terms over the past 2 decades, while they have at best been stagnant for similarly educated women. Even many workers with some postsecondary schooling have had problems earning more than the poverty line in the more difficult economic environment of the 1980s and 1990s.

Though a full understanding of the causes of the losses at the bottom of the earnings distribution eludes researchers, major factors likely include technological change and increasing international competition, both of which reduced the demand for less skilled workers, and heavy immigration flows that increased the supply of domestic less skilled workers (Danziger & Gottschalk, 1995). These market forces placed downward pressure on the wages such workers can command. Erosion of the real value of the minimum wage and the rapid decline since 1975 in trade unionization are changes in wage-setting institutions that have played more minor roles in depressing the wages of less skilled workers. In addition, less skilled men have increasingly been likely to drop out of the labor force or had to settle for part-time work. These developments reinforced their declining real wages to produce substantial declines in real earnings (Blank, 1995).

Second, because of increases in divorce and out-of-wedlock childbearing, a larger proportion of children live only with one parent (recall Table 4.2). Mother-only families are much more likely to be poor than two-parent families because the earning power of single mothers tends to be low, absent fathers often fail to contribute child support, and public assistance benefits are low. Even when the single parent is the father, having at most one earner instead of two makes it more likely the family will be poor. This shift toward one parent families accounts for at least a third and perhaps more than half of the increase in officially measured poverty among children (Bianchi, 1993; Lerman, 1996).

Third, real government income support benefits for children declined from the early 1970s to the early 1980s and have not recovered in the past decade. We return to income support policy issues later.

Other social changes worked to counteract these poverty-increasing forces (Bianchi, 1993). The average number of children per family declined. Since smaller families have lower poverty lines, this made it more likely that a given income would keep a family out of poverty. Parents' educational levels have risen and a higher proportion of mothers are in the paid workforce. These changes helped improve the earnings opportunities of families with children. These positive developments were, however, too weak to overcome the adverse factors.

International Comparisons. Bradbury and Jantti (1998) measured child poverty in 17 affluent societies. Most of their data are from the 1991 to 1995 period. The U.S. child poverty rate of 27.2% was by far the highest (Table 4.7). Italy, at 21.5%, and the United Kingdom, at 20.5%, were next highest, followed by Australia, Ireland, and Canada, all between 16% and 17%. Eight countries had a child poverty rate less than 10%. We discuss the reasons for these dramatic differences later.

CHILD MALTREATMENT AND OTHER CONSEQUENCES OF POVERTY

Being economically poor in the United States means enduring a low standard of living. Poor children are more likely to be hungry, threadbare, cold, crowded into poor quality housing, and without adequate medical care. Poor neighborhoods tend to be more crime ridden, dangerous places to live and receive subpar public

Table 4.7. Poverty among Children
in 17 Affluent Nations

Nation (Year of Measurement)	Child Poverty Rate (%)
Australia (1994)	16.7
Belgium (1992)	6.1
Canada (1994)	16.1
Denmark (1992)	5.9
Finland (1991)	3.0
France (1989)	13.2
Germany (1994)	11.6
Ireland (1987)	16.3
Israel (1992)	14.7
Italy (1995)	21.5
Luxembourg (1994)	6.4
The Netherlands (1991)	8.4
Norway (1995)	4.4
Sweden (1992)	3.7
Switzerland (1982)	7.6
United Kingdom (1991)	20.5
United States (1994)	27.2

Source: Bradbury, B., and Jantti, M. 1998. Child poverty across indus-trialized nations. Paper presented at the 25th General Conference of the International Conference for Research on Income and Wealth, Cambridge, England, August 1998, table 2.3. Poverty is defined as the percentage of children living in households with disposable cash income, adjusted for needs, less than 50% of median adjusted dis-posable cash income. This "relative" approach is often used in inter-national comparisons, but since it differs from the procedure for determining the official U.S. poverty lines, U.S. poverty statistics in this table cannot be directly compared with those in the rest of the chapter. Income includes all cash transfer and tax benefits.

services. Poor children are more likely to attend worse schools, do worse on tests of cognitive ability and educational achievement, complete fewer years of school-ing, and do worse in the labor market as young adults (Duncan, Yeung, Brooks-Gunn, & Smith, 1998). Children born to low income women have higher chances of infant and child mortality, poor health, and developmental disabilities (Starfield & Budetti, 1985).[3]

Besides these distressing consequences, children living in poor families are more likely to suffer maltreatment. Though child maltreatment occurs among all economic classes, it is disproportionately reported among poor families, particu-larly among the poorest of the poor (Panel on Research on Child Abuse and Ne-glect, 1993). Chapters 5, 6, and 7 discuss the many factors, including poverty, associated with child maltreatment. No one of them provides a complete explana-tion for this behavior. Certainly, most poor parents do not maltreat their children.

There is disagreement over how to interpret the association between low income and reports of maltreatment. One plausible explanation is that low income creates family stress that leads to a higher chance of abuse or neglect. A related explanation is that parents with minimal incomes may, despite the best intentions, be forced to provide inadequate physical care to their children. To the extent these explanations are correct, reducing the number of families with low incomes would reduce child abuse and neglect.

A second possibility is that some parents' characteristics make them more likely to be both poor and abusive. For example, poor interpersonal skills, a short temper, or a drinking problem may cause an adult to lose jobs and have low earnings, and make it more likely that he or she will be abusive. For families where poverty and abuse are jointly caused by some third factor, that factor must be directly addressed to curtail the abuse. Simply increasing income will not eliminate the root cause of abusive behavior (the temper, heavy drinking, or whatever). Such individuals may benefit more from the service interventions discussed in Chapters 5, 6, and 7.

In some cases, of course, parents both suffer from the stresses caused by inadequate incomes and have characteristics that make them more likely to maltreat their children. For them, income and service strategies would both be in order.

Some argue that being poor makes a family more at risk of being reported to a child protective agency. Poor families have more contact with persons who have responsibilities to report possible cases of abuse (e.g., in welfare offices, public health clinics, emergency rooms). If this is the main reason for the observed association between poverty and abuse, policies that reduce poverty might reduce *reported* cases of abuse, but might not affect the *actual* level of abuse.

There is probably some truth in each interpretation. With the current level of knowledge, researchers do not know how much of the association between poverty and child maltreatment is due to each. Still, reducing poverty will in no way increase child maltreatment, will mean fewer children will suffer from lack of basic material necessities, and will improve children's life chances. If the first interpretation is most applicable, policies to reduce poverty have real potential to reduce the physical and emotional damages from child maltreatment.

POLICIES TO REDUCE CHILD POVERTY

Public policies that deal with child poverty have several broad objectives. One is to shield children from the adverse effects that poverty has on their physical, mental, and emotional development. Child welfare and related social services aim, in part, at meeting this objective. The key policy and practice issues for these services are discussed elsewhere in this text.

A second important objective is to help able-bodied parents with low market skills earn their way above the poverty line and achieve self-reliance, which is so highly valued in the United States. Public policies to raise the earnings of poor parents with children are a subset of more general policies to improve the earnings of all low wage workers, most of whom either are now parents or will soon be. A third is to ensure that a minimum level of resources is available to meet children's needs for food, shelter, health care, and other necessities if parents cannot provide them out of private earnings. This requires supplementing low private market incomes with public cash transfers and tax credits, noncash benefits such as housing, health care, or nutritional aid, and private cash child support payments from absent parents. Supplements to a family's market (or "pretransfer") income either bring its total posttax, posttransfer income above the poverty line, or reduce the gap between its total income and poverty line.

This section describes America's major programs for fighting child poverty, assesses their success, and compares them to other nations' policies. Since the high levels of child poverty in Tables 4.5 and 4.7 suggest that American policies have not performed as well as we would like, the next section discusses alternative policy options.

Policies for Increasing Market Incomes to Prevent Poverty

Increasing demand for low wage workers and, hence, their employment and earnings can, in principle, be achieved by subsidizing firms that hire them. The 1993 federal enterprise zone program, which offers tax benefits to firms that locate in and hire a certain percentage of their workers from economically distressed neighborhoods, takes this approach. So does the Work Opportunity Tax Credit, which provides tax savings to firms that hire low wage workers from certain disadvantaged groups, and its precursor, the Targeted Jobs Tax Credit (TJTC), which operated in most years from 1979 to 1995.

In practice the TJTC had a limited impact that mainly helped disadvantaged youth rather than adults with children (Katz, 1998; Lehman, 1994). Many firms eligible for the credit do not claim it and most credits go to firms that would have hired the targeted workers even without the TJTC. Perhaps more troubling is that being explicitly identified as belonging to a targeted, needy group appears to stigmatize intended beneficiaries in the eyes of employers, who then regard them as less qualified. The enterprise zone program has not yet been evaluated. Experience with analogous state-level programs suggests, at best, limited impact (Lehman, 1994).

Improving job readiness and occupational skills of low wage workers to help them enter the labor market and get better paying jobs has been and remains the mainstay of efforts to reduce pretransfer poverty. Though outlays for such activities are a small fraction of spending on income supplements, the primacy that Americans accord to work and self-reliance and their endorsement of efforts to help persons become self-supporting ensure continued attention to such policies (Heclo, 1994).

This "human capital" approach includes welfare-to-work and related programs for welfare recipients as well as a variety of programs for other groups facing serious labor market disadvantages. Most poor children live in households that can benefit from these programs.

Federal guidelines allow states broad latitude in designing welfare-to-work programs. Although the programs differ in many specifics, there have been some common features (Blank, 1994; Burtless & Friedlander, 1995). Adult welfare recipients are initially assessed to determine if they are ready for work. If so, participation in some work-related activity is mandatory; failure to do so risks a cut in benefits ("sanctions"). They receive counseling to improve their job search skills and, in some states, skills training or remedial schooling, then help in finding work. Subsidized child care, help with transportation costs, and, if a participant leaves welfare, temporary continuation of child care assistance and Medicaid, may be offered to facilitate participants' training, search, and work efforts.

Young (16–21 years old) single mothers on welfare and their children face particularly high risks of long-term poverty and need for welfare. The Teenage Parent Demonstration (TPD) and Ohio's Learning, Earnings and Parenting (LEAP) program are examples of mandatory welfare-to-work programs aimed at helping these women. LEAP focuses on getting mothers to regularly attend classes and complete high school or, if they have dropped out, to return or seek a GED. TPD requires teens to enroll in education, job search, or training programs, or to work.

Evaluations of welfare-to-work programs indicate that they usually increase work and earnings, lead to small declines in welfare use, and produce savings to public agencies that exceed the costs of operation (U.S. Department of Labor, 1999; Blank, 1995). Programs focused on rapid job placement appear to have better results than those that emphasize classroom education.

The disappointing news is that the favorable impacts are very small in practical terms. For example, in four major welfare-to-work programs operated in the early 1980s, the largest increase in income was merely about 3% of the poverty line for a three-person family (Burtless & Friedlander, 1995). In 1999, this would only have been $400 a year. Similarly, although TPD participants earned 20% more than similar teens who did not receive the services, the absolute increase was merely $340 (1999 dollars). These findings underscore the challenges facing the welfare-to-work programs if they are to achieve reductions in both welfare use and poverty.

Along with mandatory welfare-to-work programs are programs that allow welfare recipients to voluntarily enroll in job training and placement activities. Two small experimental programs produced annual initial earnings increases in the $1,700–2,200 range (1999 dollars). The gains were sustained at lower levels for at least 5 years after leaving the programs (U.S. Department of Labor, 1995). Welfare recipients also experience comparable earnings gains from the Job Training Partnership Act's (JTPA) less intensive on-the-job training program, which offers private employers temporary subsidies to hire and train disadvantaged persons.

Three other voluntary training programs generally failed to increase earnings (Leigh, 1995; U.S. Department of Labor, 1995).

Even for successful voluntary programs, the net effects on poverty were small. As in the mandatory welfare-to-work programs, welfare benefits were reduced as earnings rose and clients had very low earnings to start with, so the increases in earnings still left most participants well below the poverty line.

Some of JTPA's programs serve disadvantaged adults in general. Participants receive a combination of classroom instruction, job search assistance, and subsidized on-the-job training. A rigorous evaluation of JTPA reports significant earnings increases of about $1,000 for both men and women. Again, in practical terms gains of $1,000 are too small to have much impact on poverty (Blank, 1995; U.S. Department of Labor, 1995).

We conclude that many human capital programs improve parents' abilities to compete in the labor market. However, given that most programs try to help high school dropouts earn a GED or provide modest additional training to high school graduates, and given the declining demand for less-skilled workers, it is not surprising that the programs fail to deliver dramatic increases in earnings. Improving the labor market prospects of low-skill, disadvantaged parents is a costly, slow process. Larger gains will require commensurably larger public investments. Yet, reflecting political realities when the Personal Responsibility and Work Opportunity Reconciliation Act of 1996 (PRWORA) was enacted, funding for programs to meet the work requirements imposed on welfare recipients by PRWORA falls $12 billion short of what is likely to be needed (Super et al., 1996).

Increasing the minimum wage is one of the most popular proposals for reducing poverty. The federal minimum rose to $5.15 in 1997. Though this is $0.90 higher than from 1991 through 1996, its real purchasing power is still 14% below its 1979 level. Automatically adjusting the minimum for inflation would protect against future declines in its real value, but Congress has never taken this step. As a result of the increase, a full-time minimum wage worker earns $1,800 more and receives as much as $720 in additional Earned Income Credits (discussed below), for a total income gain of about 16% of the poverty line for a four-person family. Workers earning slightly above $5.15 will probably also gain as employers restore part of wage differentials eroded by the higher minimum.

The common concern that a higher minimum wage discourages new job creation and leads to layoffs or fewer work hours among low wage workers carries little weight if we are mainly interested in helping poor adults with children. Job losses among adults due to the minimum wage are negligible (Card & Krueger, 1995). Even if some jobs or work hours are lost, the higher wage per hour of remaining employment far offsets such losses and increases total earnings among low-skill parents affected by a rise in the minimum wage.

A more serious limitation of using the minimum wage to fight poverty is that relatively few poor households actually benefit from an increase. The wage rates of more than 80% of workers in poor households already exceed the minimum. Their poverty results from working too few hours because of either the difficulty of finding full-time work or family responsibilities. A higher minimum wage will do little for them and their children, nor will it help children in families where no one is employed or the parents are self-employed. Poor families containing persons earning at or below the minimum wage will gain from an increase, but the antipoverty impact is small. Counterintuitive though it may seem, most minimum wage workers live in families with incomes more than double the poverty line because they are teens living at home or adults living with other workers so that total family income comfortably exceeds the poverty level. Less than 20% of the earnings gains generated by raising the minimum goes to workers in poor families (Burkhauser, Couch, & Wittenburg, 1996).

Other employment-related policies can play a valuable supporting role in helping poor families earn more. Policies to improve the accessibility, affordability, and quality of child care can facilitate entry into the labor force by the principal caregivers in poor families with young children (Bergmann, 1996). Ensuring continued coverage by Medicaid, or some other source of health insurance, for all members of families that leave welfare will make work more attractive to current welfare recipients. Improved routing of public transportation systems, changes in the location of low-income and subsidized housing, and more rigorous enforcement of fair housing laws can help inner city parents gain better access to job opportunities and break down spatial barriers to employment created by housing segregation (Rosenbaum & Popkin, 1991; Yinger, 1995). Last, better enforcement of policies to prevent labor market discrimination can improve earnings opportunities for poor minority parents (Holzer, 1994). The effect on child poverty of these kinds of interventions will depend on their size and specific design.

The success of programs to increase earnings critically depends on having a healthy economy. Such programs will be largely ineffective when unemployment rises. Employers will be reluctant to expand hiring or training even with tax incentives to do so, and low wage workers who have upgraded their skills will find it hard to realize a return on their human capital investments as job openings and promotion opportunities disappear. Unfortunately, economic knowledge about how to prevent recessions is incomplete and political circumstances sometimes prevent action that would minimize economic downturns.

Economic downturns are inevitable. There are powerful long-term forces that have been eroding job opportunities for the less skilled. We have no evidence that human capital programs and the other interventions discussed above can produce large increases in earnings leading to a substantial decline in pretransfer poverty. And labor market policies do not deal with families' short-term income needs produced by the temporary unemployment that many workers experience even when the overall economy is doing well, nor can they help children in families in which the adults cannot be expected to work. It follows that efforts to reduce pretransfer poverty among families with children must be accompanied by effective income support policies that supplement market earnings.

Supplementing Market Incomes to Reduce Poverty

Overview of U.S. Income Support Programs.   In 1994, federal, state, and local government spending on cash and in-kind income support programs totaled $974 billion, or about 36% of all government spending (U.S. Census Bureau, 1998, Tables 499 and 601). Public income support programs can be divided into *social insurance* and *income assistance.* Social insurance programs are financed by special taxes from workers, employers, or both. Contributors and their dependents have a right to receive benefits if earnings are reduced or eliminated by events such as unemployment, retirement, or death. The size of the benefit depends on the amount of prior "covered" earnings, though the link between benefits and earnings is rather loose in some programs. Benefits do not depend on the family's current income or assets. An unemployed husband can collect benefits even if his wife is earning $50,000 a year. The major social insurance programs include Social Security (which insures against old age, death of a family breadwinner, and long-term disability), Medicare, unemployment insurance, and workers compensation for job-related injury. Social insurance accounts for about 70% of government spending on income support.

Income assistance programs are financed out of general tax revenues. Eligibility depends on having a low current income (and few assets) and, usually, on meeting another condition such as being blind or having children. Benefits decline as other sources of income increase and are independent of the amount of past earnings or taxes paid. Other labels for "income assistance" include "income tested," "income conditioned," "means tested," "public assistance," "social assistance," and "welfare."

There are more than 40 income-tested programs that provide cash, food, housing, medical, or energy assistance. The major ones are Temporary Assistance for Needy Families (TANF), Supplemental Security Income (SSI), the Earned Income Credit, food stamps, and Medicaid. The familiar Aid to Families with Dependent Children program, or AFDC, which has been the most controversial income-tested program, was replaced in 1996 by TANF as part of the PRWORA. Though many considered AFDC to be synonymous with "welfare," it accounted for only one-twelfth of all income assistance in 1994. TANF's share is likely to be smaller. Almost three-quarters of income assistance is provided in-kind rather than as cash, most of it through Medicaid.

Income Support Programs for Children.   The United States uses three approaches to supplement the private incomes of poor families with children: government income support programs, tax policy, and private child support payments from the absent parent to the custodial parent. This section describes the main elements of each approach, discusses some of the important recent developments and controversies surrounding these policies, and reports on the extent to which they reduce child poverty.

Approximately 25% of government spending on cash, medical care, nutrition, and housing transfers goes to families with children (Garfinkel, 1996). Most of the balance flows to the elderly. The major cash programs that focus on maintaining or improving the economic status of dependent children are the Social Security program through its provisions for dependents benefits, TANF, the Earned Income Credit, and SSI for disabled children. The major noncash programs that we also discuss are food stamps, Medicaid, and the child nutrition programs.[4]

Survivors Insurance. Survivors Insurance, established in 1939, provides benefits to surviving dependents of a deceased worker who has paid Social Security taxes. Children under age 18 are entitled to benefits based on the deceased parent's earnings record, as is the surviving parent until the youngest child reaches age 16. Benefits increase with the rate of inflation. In 1996, 1.9 million minor children received Survivors Insurance benefits. The average monthly benefit was $487.[5]

In accord with social insurance principles, benefits are higher for survivors of workers with higher earnings. However, the "replacement rate"—benefits as a percentage of the worker's earnings—is larger for survivors of workers with low earnings. Thus, survivors of low earners do not suffer as large a fall in their standard of living as survivors of high earners. Survivors Insurance and the other Social Security programs are financed by a tax on earnings.

AFDC and TANF. Congress instituted Survivors Insurance when most single mothers were widows. Its intent was to provide financial support to widows and their children without forcing them onto welfare. Congress expected that the need for Aid to Families with Dependent Children, established in 1935, would gradually decline as all families became covered by Survivors Insurance. Times have changed. Most single-parent families now arise through divorce or nonmarital childbearing and do not qualify for Survivors Insurance. If their private incomes are low, as is often the case, they must rely on AFDC's recent successor, TANF, for income support.

Until replaced by TANF, AFDC was the main cash assistance program for children under age 18 and their parents or caretaker relatives who need financial support because one parent is absent from home, unemployed, deceased, or incapacitated.[6] Initially, AFDC was restricted to children in single-parent families. Between 1962 and 1990, Congress gave states the option to provide benefits to two-parent families who were needy because one parent was unemployed. Between 1990 and 1996 federal law required all states to have a two-parent program to help reduce poverty and eliminate any incentive for one parent to leave so the spouse and children could receive AFDC. In 1996 only 7% of families on welfare received aid from the two-parent program (Committee on Ways and Means, 1998, p. 423).

In 1996, AFDC benefits totaled $20.4 billion and, in an average month, served 4.6 million families containing 8.7 million children. AFDC has been a far more important source of support to children than Survivors Insurance. The average cash benefit per family was $374 (Committee on Ways and Means, 1998, p. 413).

AFDC was an entitlement—all families who satisfied the eligibility rules were assisted. During most of its existence AFDC largely concentrated on providing income support without expecting recipients to make much effort to become self-sufficient, and did little to help those who wanted to work. Although this approach attracted support from some of those reluctant to impose obligations on recipients, any consensus it once commanded had broken down by the early 1980s. Emphasis shifted to viewing welfare as a reciprocal obligation: receiving a welfare check and help with child care and other work-related support services from society carries with it the expectation that a recipient look for and accept a job, or participate in publicly funded education, training, or work experience activities to prepare for work. This approach, in which conservatives agreed to support training, child care, and other services, while liberals gave up the policy that welfare mothers had a right not to work, became known as the "welfare-to-work" strategy or, sometimes, "workfare." It became the centerpiece of the Family Support Act of 1988, the major welfare reform enacted during Ronald Reagan's presidency.

The Personal Responsibility and Work Opportunity Reconciliation Act of 1996 replaced AFDC and the welfare-to-work programs authorized by the Family Support Act with the TANF block grant. TANF ends entitlement to welfare and leaves it up to each state whether to aid all qualifying families. TANF benefits cannot be received by any family with a member who has received aid as an adult for 5 years. A state can exempt up to 20% of its cases from this time limit, but can also impose tighter limits. TANF also requires recipients to work after 2 years, requires unmarried parents under age 18 to live with an adult and stay in school to be eligible for benefits, gives states much greater control over all eligibility and administrative rules (including permission to deny aid to two-parent families), makes most poor immigrants ineligible for most forms of income assistance, and makes other major changes in cash and noncash programs of the safety net.[7] Total federal funds allocated for fiscal years 1997–2002 for the large set of programs covered by PRWORA are estimated to be $55 billion less than what would have been spent if the programs had not been changed.[8] In place of the Family Support Act's commitment to reciprocal obligations, PRWORA shifted national welfare policy toward imposing tougher obligations on welfare recipients, while cutting back support for work or training.

Assigning states the major responsibility to provide aid, and under what conditions, represents another big change in the philosophy underlying the nation's safety net. Advocates of "devolution" argued that state and local offices can better identify the needy, the type of aid that makes most sense, and the most effective way to deliver it. Others, concerned about differences in the willingness and fiscal ability of states and localities to help the poor and ensure fair administrative processes, hold the central government primarily responsible for funding and overseeing income assistance, as it had been during the 60 years of AFDC. The debate about which level of government is best suited to provide aid is an enduring one in our federal system.

In a typical year about half of single mothers with children received AFDC. About 42% of single mothers who did receive AFDC spent no more than 2 years on it. Another 23% received AFDC for 3 to 5 years, while 35% received it for more than 5 years (Committee on Ways and Means, 1998, p. 531). Because long-term recipients were more likely to be on AFDC in any particular month, at each point in time they represented a large share of the caseload. Currently, it is estimated that in any given month about 76% of the women on the welfare rolls are in the midst of a spell of welfare that will last more than 5 years. These data imply that TANF's 5-year time limit is likely to drastically reduce the incomes of millions of needy families, unless its welfare-to-work programs are far more effective than earlier ones. In view of the limited funding for such efforts, there is little reason to think that they will be.

Benefit levels vary widely across states under TANF, just as they did under AFDC. In January 1997, the maximum monthly benefit for a family of three ranged from $120 in Mississippi to $923 in Alaska. The median was $377, or 34% of the poverty line. Since 1970, the median real benefit has fallen 50% (Committee on Ways and Means, 1998, pp. 416–418, 430–431).

Most TANF recipients qualify for food stamps, as did most AFDC recipients. The food stamp program is federally funded with uniform benefits across all states. A family's food stamps are reduced as its cash income, including any TANF, increases. Since families in high TANF states receive fewer food stamps than those in low TANF states, food stamps reduce state disparities in benefit levels. In January 1997, a family of three receiving the maximum combined food stamp and AFDC benefit was still poor in every state. In the median state, the combined monthly AFDC and food stamp benefit of $692 equaled 62% of the poverty line (Committee on Ways and Means, 1998, pp. 416–418).

TANF may create further downward pressure on benefits for several reasons. Under AFDC, the federal government paid from 50 to 78% of the benefit authorized by a state. Thus, if a state lowered benefits, most savings went to the federal treasury; if it raised benefits, most of the cost was borne federally. As a block grant, TANF funds allocated to a state will not change in response to benefit changes. So if a state lowers benefits, all the savings accrue to it, and if it raises benefits, it pays all the costs. This change in fiscal incentives, as well as other provisions of the Act that allow states to divert funds from income support and welfare-to-work programs, will encourage states to cut benefits. Also, TANF funds will probably grow more slowly than what prior law would have provided, particularly when a recession hits, so states will have fewer federal dollars to support welfare spending. And TANF reduced food stamp benefits, which will directly lower combined cash and food benefits even if states do not cut cash benefits. The end of cost sharing may also increase disparities among states since the net cost of benefits will rise most sharply in lower income states, which received the highest federal cost sharing rates and already tend to have lower benefits (Chernick & Reschovsky, 1996).

AFDC families qualified for Medicaid, which covers many health care expenses. Covered services vary among the states. Medicaid is very important to most families on welfare. Among AFDC families Medicaid spent an average of $1,046 dollars per child and $1,708 per adult in 1995 (Committee on Ways and Means, 1998, p. 976). Although it is hard to argue that a dollar of Medicaid benefit is just like a dollar of cash or food aid, the availability of Medicaid helps improve the overall "package" of welfare benefits.

Many needy children and pregnant women who have not been eligible for AFDC and who may not qualify for TANF receive Medicaid benefits because their families meet certain other eligibility conditions. In addition, under the PRWORA, families that would have qualified for AFDC as of July 1996 will remain eligible for Medicaid even if they do not qualify for aid based on state rules enacted under TANF, have lost cash aid because of the 5-year limit or other restrictions, or are qualified but do not receive TANF benefits because of the loss-of-entitlement provision. Thus, this important piece of the safety net has remained largely intact.

Collecting AFDC involved more than receiving a monthly check and facing rules that discourage work. Recipients have faced a system that often frustrated, confused, and stigmatized them. Eligibility rules have been complex and required checking an applicant's income, assets, and living situations. Long waits, visits to several offices, dealing with a variety of bureaucrats, and complying with complicated regulations have been routine.

It is still too early to fully assess how the complex PRWORA will affect poor families, low wage labor markets, operation of welfare offices, and other social services agencies. Early evidence suggests, however, that many women who left welfare soon after TANF was implemented were not working or otherwise were encountering serious economic struggles (Loprest, 1999). Another report finds that since PRWORA, incomes among the poorest single-mother families declined, despite the robust economy. The decline was largely due to decreases in assistance from means-tested programs (Primus et al., 1999). The report correctly observes that the ultimate test of welfare reform should include whether the well-being of poor children and families has improved, not simply how much welfare caseloads fall. How states redesign and fund their income assistance programs and welfare-to-work initiatives in response to the broad latitude they now have, how effectively they implement changes, and how the economy performs together will determine how well the welfare system assists poor families with children in the years ahead.[9]

Supplemental Security Income. Supplemental Security Income provides monthly cash payments to needy aged, blind, and disabled persons, including children under age 18. Children are eligible if they have a physical or mental disability similar to one that would prevent an adult working. Unlike TANF, the federal government establishes eligibility rules and provides a uniform minimum benefit across all states. States may supplement federal payments. Children also benefit indirectly if another family member receives SSI.

Prior to 1990, eligibility was based on whether a child had one of a list of severe medical impairments. In 1990, the Supreme Court ruled that eligibility must be determined via an assessment of a child's "functional limitations." As a result, the number of child SSI recipients rose from 332,000 in 1990 to 1,018,000 by December 1996. The PRWORA has done away with the functional limitation assessment and restricted eligibility in other ways. The Congressional Budget Office estimates that by 2002 about 315,000 children who would have qualified under past law will be denied SSI (Super et al., 1996).

Child Nutrition Programs. Aside from food stamps, federal food assistance has concentrated on improving child nutrition. Through the school lunch and breakfast programs children in families receiving TANF or food stamps and from families with incomes at or below 130% of the poverty line may receive free meals. Children from other near-poor families receive smaller subsidies. In 1996, at a federal cost of $5.4 billion, 25.9 million children received subsidized lunches each school day, of which 12.6 million were free. The smaller breakfast program cost $1.1 billion and assisted 6.6 million children a day, of which 5.3 million received a free breakfast (Committee on Ways and Means, 1998, pp. 999–1000).

The Special Supplemental Food Program for Women, Infants and Children (WIC) provides food assistance to low income pregnant and postpartum women and their infants, as well as to low income children up to age 5. Participants must have incomes at or below 185% of the poverty line and be nutritionally at risk. WIC cost $3.7 billion in 1996 and served a monthly average of 7.2 million persons, 77% of them children (Committee on Ways and Means, 1998, pp. 1000–1002).

Tax Policies and Poor Children. Tax policy alters the net incomes low income families have available for consumption and, hence, affects their living standards. One of the more encouraging developments in antipoverty policy since the mid-1980s has been the sharp decline in the federal tax burden on poor families. In 1984, a two-parent family of four with earnings equal to the poverty line paid 10.1% of its gross income in federal income and payroll taxes. Because of the Tax Reform Act of 1986, the combined tax rate on the same family had fallen to only 0.3% by 1992. By 1997, expansion of the Earned Income Credit (see below) further lowered the combined tax rate to minus 8.7%, which provided the family with a tax refund of $1,437 (Committee on Ways and Means, 1998, p. 901). The tax burden on single-parent families declined in a similar fashion over this period.

The steady expansion of the Earned Income Credit (EIC) is the major reason for the decline. Enacted in 1975, the EIC supplements earnings of low-income families with children.[10] Families with low earnings receive credits against their federal income tax. If they owe no income tax, they get a cash refund. In 1999 a family with one child (two children) received a credit of 34 (40) percent of its first $6,800 ($9,540) of earnings. The maximum credit was $2,312 ($3,816). Families with incomes between $6,800 and $12,460 ($9,540 and $12,460) received the maximum credit. For each dollar of income above $12,460, the credit declined by 16 (21) cents, until it vanished at an income of $26,928 ($30,580). All the income thresholds are adjusted for inflation yearly. For persons not working or earning very little, the EIC encourages work by raising its net return, in contrast to assistance programs such as TANF or food stamps. The phase-out rule ensures that benefits go only to poor and near-poor families.

In 1997 the EIC provided an estimated $27 billion of assistance to 18.6 million low income families (Committee on Ways and Means, 1998, p. 872). The program has become the largest cash assistance program for families with children. Four states have similar refundable EICs, and three have nonrefundable ones. These lower the burden of their own income taxes on low income families and partly offset the regressive aspects of state and local taxes (Lav & Lazere, 1996). More widespread use of state EICs would, of course, produce greater poverty relief.

Antipoverty Impacts of Government Income Support Programs and Taxes

Table 4.5 showed that much child poverty remains despite the EIC and existing income support programs. But the situation would be much worse without these programs.

The pretransfer poverty statistics in row 1 of Table 4.8 show the percentage of children living in families whose incomes from private sources fall below the poverty line. Many, but not all of these families receive income support benefits. The second row shows the child poverty rate after all cash transfer benefits are included in family incomes. This is the official measure of child poverty. By comparing row 1 with row 2, we can gauge the antipoverty impact of cash benefits. The fourth row shows the poverty rate after food, housing, and medical transfer benefits and the net balance of taxes and tax credits are also included in family incomes. A comparison of rows 1 and 4 gauges the antipoverty impact of a wider array of government income support policies.

Table 4.8 assumes for simplicity that pretransfer incomes are not affected by transfers and taxes. Since such policies reduce work and may lead to other behaviors that increase the level of pretransfer poverty, Table 4.8 overstates the antipoverty impact of government programs. However, the trend in antipoverty impact is probably captured reasonably well. We discuss the incentive issue in more depth later.

Table 4.8. Impact on Child Poverty of Government Cash, Food, Housing, and Medical Transfers and Taxes, 1979–1997

	1979	*1985*	*1990*	*1997*
Pretransfer poverty rate	20.1%	23.7%	23.5%	22.9%
Postcash transfer rate	16.4%	20.7%	20.6%	19.9%
Percentage reduction in poverty due to cash transfers	18.4	12.7	12.3	13.1
Posttransfer, posttax poverty rate	11.4%	16.8%	15.8%	13.8%
Percentage reduction in poverty due to all transfers and taxes	43.3	29.1	32.8	39.7

Source: For 1979, 1985, and 1990, U.S. Census Bureau. Measuring the Effect of Benefits and Taxes on Income and Poverty: 1979 to 1991, Current Population Reports, Series P-60, No. 182RD. Washington, DC: U.S. Government Printing Office, 1992, p. 98. For 1997, U.S. Census Bureau. Poverty in the United States: 1997, Current Population Reports, Series P-60, No. 201. Washington, DC: U.S. Government Printing Office, 1998, pp. 24, 25. Pretransfer income is measured as all cash income from private sources, excluding capital gains. Postcash transfer income is pretransfer income plus all cash government transfers. Posttransfer, posttax income is postcash transfer income minus social security taxes and federal and state income taxes, plus Earned Income Tax Credits, food stamp benefits, and the estimated value of Medicare, Medicaid, school lunch, and housing benefits.

We see that in 1979, 20.1% of all children were pretransfer poor. After counting cash transfers, the poverty rate was 16.4%. Thus, as shown in row 3, cash transfers lifted 18.4% of pretransfer poor children over the poverty line. (This is the percentage difference between 20.1 and 16.4%.) When noncash benefits, taxes, and tax credits are counted in incomes, the antipoverty impact increases to 43.3% (row 5) and the poverty rate shrinks to 11.4%. Six years later, after severe cuts in means-tested benefits and inflation-induced "bracket creep" that created income tax liabilities for poor families, public programs pulled only 29.1% of pretransfer poor children out of poverty. By 1990, the antipoverty impact had modestly rebounded to 32.8% due to restoration of some program cuts and, more importantly, tax reform. By 1997, as the 1993 legislation that expanded the EIC took effect, the antipoverty impact had risen sharply to 39.7%, slightly less than in 1979.

When single and two-parent families with children are examined separately, the time patterns are similar in many regards but with one important exception. For two-parent families, tax and transfer policy was more effective against poverty in 1997 than in 1979. For single-parent families, it was still significantly less effective. The retrenchment in income-tested benefits for this group has not been restored.

Although the complete phase-in of the more generous provisions of the 1993 EIC has improved the antipoverty impact, cutbacks either directly mandated by the PRWORA or enacted in response to it will have the opposite effect and may be stronger. A major study projects that the Act will push 1.1 million children into poverty and worsen the poverty of children already poor, even after accounting for full phase-in of the EIC (The Urban Institute, 1996). Another analysis reports that since PRWORA, incomes among the poorest single-mother families declined, despite the robust economy. The decline was largely due to decreases in assistance from means-tested programs (Primus et al., 1999). The antipoverty impact of transfers and taxes for families with children is likely to be no higher in the late 1990s and early 2000s than it was through much of the 1970s. If states respond to the fiscal incentives of block grants and reduce family benefit levels, it may well be lower. Only significant expansion of benefit levels and eligibility in existing income support programs, or adoption of a large new one would appreciably improve the antipoverty impact.

Behavioral Side Effects of Income Support Programs and Taxes.   There is widespread concern that the EIC and income transfer programs provide incentives for socially undesirable behaviors as an unavoidable side effect of reducing poverty. Because AFDC provided income support if the parent did not work and, if there were earnings, offset a large portion of any earnings increase with benefit cuts, it tended to discourage work.[11] The eligibility rules of AFDC also created incentives to become an unmarried mother, divorce, delay remarriage, and make other demographic choices that were likely to result in more poor single-parent families. Similarly, the EIC embodies a complex set of incentives that may affect work and marriage decisions, of which some would help reduce pretransfer poverty and some increase it.[12] There is less concern about work disincentives from Social Security received by survivors or disabled workers and their dependents, or from SSI received by children, since few of these recipients are able or expected to work.

The policy implications of these incentives depend crucially on how strongly individuals react to them. For example, if a transfer program has small effects on earnings, nearly all the money received by recipients raises their families' standards of living, the transfer achieves its intended redistributive purpose, and American values about the importance of work are upheld. But if it leads to large earnings reductions that offset much of the income it provides, then its net antipoverty impact would be small. Taxpayers would largely be subsidizing less work effort by recipients, though parents would be spending more time with their children. Similarly, if transfers have little effect on family structure, they accomplish their intended purpose, but if they have large adverse effects, they help create some of the poverty they then relieve and will raise moral questions among some citizens. Yet, if the availability of public income support helps some mothers leave abusive husbands, such an impact on family structure might be considered a benefit.

Although people have different opinions on when transfers' undesired side effects outweigh their beneficial impact on poverty, the larger the adverse responses, the stronger the case for reforms to improve the tradeoff. The dilemma posed by this trade-off is clear. Most people want to help poor *children,* who can hardly be held responsible for their poverty. But some people are concerned that too much help or the wrong kind of help will lead the *parents* to act irresponsibly and unduly increase program costs. Yet rules that curtail irresponsible behavior or at least curtail public subsidies to such behavior risk hurting the children by undercutting the basic missions of income support programs: providing a minimally decent standard of living, cushioning unexpected income losses, and helping families obtain essentials such as food, housing, and medical care. People differ on how much weight to give these competing concerns. The dilemma strikes at strongly held values and makes for sharp debates about the appropriate role of government in relieving poverty.

Many advocates of PRWORA believed the incentive effects of the old welfare system were so adverse that they had actually helped create a class that became dependent on public aid. In this view, only drastic reform that scaled back the government's role and imposed strong requirements could counteract the incentives and induce the poor to move themselves out of poverty and dependence on public aid. Many critics of PRWORA argued that the incentive effects were modest and contributed very little to the problem, the cutbacks in benefits will do far more harm than good, and the funding to help recipients obtain and keep jobs and escape welfare is far too little. They contend that only government can mobilize the resources necessary to help the poor and that more aid is needed in light of the large number of poor children.

Empirical evidence suggests that for every dollar transferred to single mothers via AFDC, about 37 cents was offset by reduced earnings. For two-parent families the offset was higher—60 to 80 cents less earnings for every dollar of AFDC transferred. Noncash income assistance programs such as food stamps, Medicaid, and housing benefits also tend to reduce work. The EIC, in contrast, has either a neutral or small positive effect on work effort even as it transfers substantial income to low income families.[13]

Higher AFDC benefits for single parents have been associated with greater rates of female headship and divorce, lower rates of remarriage, and a greater likelihood that a single mother will live independently rather than with her parents. Although these behavioral responses tend to increase the number of low income mother-only families, the estimated effects are generally small and, in some well done studies, are not statistically significant. Surprisingly, extension of AFDC to two-parent families does not appear to have affected family structure. A reasonable reading of the evidence on the relationship between welfare and nonmarital childbearing is that higher welfare benefits are associated with small increases in the likelihood of becoming an unwed mother, but only among whites. Among blacks there is no relationship. There is no evidence that welfare affects subsequent childbearing by women who already are mothers. Based on limited research, there also is no evidence that the EIC affects marriage and other demographic choices.

The weight of the current evidence implies that demographic responses to welfare account for only a small portion of the increases in female headship and nonmarital childbearing since the 1960s. The main reasons for the increases almost certainly lie outside the welfare system and probably reflect the growing social acceptability of single parenthood, the declining stigma of unwed motherhood, improvements in the earning power of women, and declines in the earning power of men. It follows that welfare reforms aimed at reducing female headship and non-marital childbearing (e.g., "family caps," which deny higher benefits to welfare recipients if they have more children) are unlikely to have large effects.

The Child Support System for Single-Parent Families

The child support system provides another source of nonlabor market income to single-parent families besides public income support benefits. Under the family court systems administered by the states, the noncustodial parent (almost always the father) may be ordered to contribute monthly payments to help finance his children's material needs. The father then pays support directly to the mother.[14]

Congress has enacted four major laws in recent decades to help custodial parents secure and enforce child support awards, and to force absent parents to honor their financial obligations to their children. In 1975 it approved Title IV-D of the Social Security Act. This law created the Child Support Enforcement program, a public bureaucracy to improve enforcement of private child support obligations. The Child Support Enforcement Amendments of 1984, and provisions in the Family Support Act of 1988 and the PRWORA of 1996, build on this foundation. To increase the percentage of single parents with child support awards, the laws mandate that states operate programs to locate absent parents, cooperate to track them across state lines, and establish paternity for children born out-of-wedlock. States must standardize child support awards across families by adopting uniform guidelines (with written justifications for exceptions), and review individual awards every 3 years and the guidelines every 4 years. Compared with earlier procedures that relied on a case-by-case approach to set awards, these rules are intended to reduce unequal treatment of absent parents in similar economic circumstances and to help awards keep pace with inflation. To ensure that caretakers receive the mandated payments, states must automatically withhold child support from paychecks of all absent parents, instead, as for years, of doing so only for those who are in arrears. Other penalties on absent parents who do not pay support have expanded as well (Committee on Ways and Means, 1998, Section 8). These reforms are consistent with strongly held values that parents should provide for their children, whether they live together or not.

In 1987, states established paternity for 29% of out-of-wedlock births; in 1994, for 46%. Support collected through government-funded child support services rose 235% in real terms between 1984 and 1996. Thus, reforms appear to have brought some progress. Yet only 55 to 60% of all custodial parents have child support agreements and, of those entitled to payments, about 50% received full payment, 25% received partial payment, and 25% received nothing. This payment pattern has not appreciably changed since 1978. The average annual amount for families who do receive payments is low (about $3,150 in 1993).[15] Practical problems such as the difficulty of tracking absent parents and their earnings, and reluctance of some mothers to cooperate with enforcement authorities for fear of alienating the fathers, have hampered enforcement. So, although the child support system has the potential to increase support payments by billions of dollars and its performance now receives careful attention from policymakers, ample room for improvement remains.

Lessons from Abroad for Child Antipoverty Policy

Table 4.7 showed that the United States had by far the highest child poverty rate of 17 affluent societies. What distinguishes the United States from most of these societies is the set of income redistribution policies each has used to respond to the poverty produced by private markets (Rainwater & Smeeding, 1995). American policies took only 17% of pretransfer poor children out of poverty.[16] This tied Italy for the smallest reduction. It is the reason why America's posttransfer child poverty rate was highest, even though its pretransfer poverty rate was not.

Several features of America's policy explain its relatively high rate of pretransfer poverty and the low antipoverty impact of its taxes and transfers. American social values are relatively skeptical about the wisdom of government intervention to alter free market outcomes. As a result, the United States has consistently devoted a smaller portion of its economic output to government social welfare spending than other western societies. Although there is high value placed on families earning their way out of poverty, public commitment is tepid for government programs to foster more work and earnings, such as adult education, job training, job creation subsidies, subsidized child care, and paid parental leaves. The EIC, unique to this country, is an important exception. There is also less public income support available for low income families with both working and nonworking parents. Of the 17 societies, the United States is the only one without a child allowance that guarantees modest support for all children regardless of family income. Nor, in contrast to several European nations, does it guarantee child support for families with absent parents.

American employment and income support policies do little to reduce pretransfer poverty, little to supplement pretransfer incomes, and so result in a high level of child poverty. Other affluent countries do not all rely on an identical mix of employment and income support policies, but all achieve much lower levels of child poverty. Their records demonstrate that more effective mixes than those in the United States are feasible.

At the same time, other nations have cut back their social safety nets in response to concerns about burgeoning costs, high taxes needed to finance them, and the negative economic consequences that may result, such as declining labor flexibility and slow job growth. If such developments continue, the antipoverty impact of other nations' policies will erode.

PROGRAM CHALLENGE: DOING A BETTER JOB OF REDUCING
POVERTY AND INCREASING ECONOMIC SECURITY
AMONG CHILDREN

When judging how well America's labor market and income support policies fight
child poverty, both their successes and shortcomings should be recognized. As we
saw earlier, labor market policies have helped low-skill workers earn more, but
these policies have not had a large impact. Indeed, the powerful economic forces
eroding the earnings of low skill workers have more than offset the modest successes, for, as shown in the first row of Table 4.8, pretransfer poverty increased by
2.8 percentage points between 1979 and 1997. Similarly, the last row in the table
shows that income support policies now eliminate about 40% of the pretransfer
poverty generated by markets. But it also shows these policies have not become
more effective at reducing child poverty since 1979, and only recently returned to
their earlier effectiveness. Child support policy has also become more effective in
recent years, but billions of potential child support payments remain uncollected.

   Clearly there is room to improve the performance against child poverty of America's labor market, income support, and child support policies. This section discusses possible strategies for doing so. Given the diverse sources of child poverty,
focusing on a single approach is unlikely to be a cure-all. Rather, a sound strategy
would combine elements from all three, while retaining the successful elements of
the current set of policies.

Improving Earnings

Government assistance with child care can help poor families with children not on
welfare, as well as welfare families. A modest child care tax credit is available.
Since it is not refundable it does not help the poor, who pay no income taxes. Making this credit refundable, like the EIC, would improve matters. Still, we should
recognize that a policy on child care, although addressing an important social issue, is not primarily an antipoverty policy. The majority of its benefits help the nonpoor, making it expensive relative to the amount of help going to the poor (Ellwood,
1988).

   Although the Work Opportunity Tax Credit and its precursor, the Targeted Jobs
Tax Credit, have been the major policies for increasing demand for low wage workers, a better alternative may be an expanded version of the New Jobs Tax Credit,
which was tried only in 1977–1978 and created jobs for less-skilled workers
(Haveman & Scholz, 1994). If reenacted, a program like this could provide, for example, a tax credit of 50% of the first $10,000 paid to each worker hired beyond
102% of the firm's previous year's employment level. Because the subsidy is a larger proportion of total wages for the less skilled, it tilts incentives toward hiring such
workers without stigmatizing them by requiring membership in a targeted group.

The subsidy rate, earnings limit, and incremental threshold can be varied depending on how enticing a program one wants.

Public service employment directly raises demand for disadvantaged workers. Two recent proposals are guaranteed minimum wage jobs for persons who have reached their time limit on welfare, and subminimum wage public sector jobs for any applicant, starting with a small effort and expanding it if successful (Ellwood, 1988; Danziger & Gottschalk, 1995). Public service jobs can provide persons with experience that may help them get private sector jobs and, combined with earnings supplements such as the EIC, can raise families with full-time workers close to the poverty line.

Large public sector jobs programs must contend with criticisms that they provide poor jobs that largely substitute for jobs that otherwise would exist, may displace traditional public employees and weaken public employee unions, and cost too much. There is concern that to hold down costs, not enough jobs will be funded and some families unable to receive TANF benefits will be left with no source of support. They also face political resistance grounded in the real and perceived failures during the 1970s of the public sector jobs component of the Comprehensive Employment and Training Act and in American skepticism about "big government" efforts (Lehman, 1994). Experimenting with this approach on a small scale and carefully evaluating it might make sense.

Overall, noncategorical jobs tax credits and wage subsidies may be the most promising of the demand-side options. They appear to be modestly successful at creating jobs and, in combination with job search assistance and skills training programs discussed earlier, and bolstered by the EIC, help raise incomes of low-skill adults. Unlike direct job creation efforts, their implementation has not been strongly criticized.

Improving Nonwelfare Income Support

Income support delivered outside the welfare system has important advantages. It does not stigmatize its recipients nor involve them in a complex, dehumanizing system the way welfare does. Because nonwelfare benefits do not decline as earnings increase, they discourage work less and promote self-reliance. Three options along this line are (1) ensuring medical care coverage to all persons, (2) improving the child support system, and (3) instituting a child allowance.[17]

Ensuring Medical Care Coverage to All Persons. Policy analysts from across the political spectrum tend to agree that all poor people ought to have medical coverage. Medicaid provides coverage to a broad group of poor children as a result of expansions in eligibility beginning the late 1980s. The Balanced Budget Act of 1997 provides funds for states to expand Medicaid coverage to more children. Still, even before the 1997 expansion, about 20% of children eligible for Medicaid were neither enrolled in it nor covered by other health insurance (Summer et al., 1996). Stronger outreach by states to inform poor families of their potential eligibility would improve the situation. The PRWORA offers states an opportunity to broaden health care coverage to low income working parents (Guyer & Mann, 1998). It remains to be seen if states will do so.

Another approach would require employers to provide medical insurance (employers with very few workers might be exempt). By raising employment costs, this might cause job losses among the working poor. It would not help those who are unemployed or unable to work. It does avoid the need to increase government spending and taxes, an important consideration in a political climate emphasizing federal debt reduction. A third approach would be a government-sponsored residual insurance plan. Persons not covered by an approved private plan would be able to buy into the government one. The price would be scaled to the family's income (say 10%). That way, no family would have to devote a huge fraction of its income to medical insurance. At present, federal health care legislation that might include these latter two approaches appears unlikely.

Improving the Child Support System.   Irwin Garfinkel, professor of social work at Columbia University and an early advocate of reforming child support law, has proposed the "assured child support benefit" to further improve the child support system (Garfinkel, 1992). This reform would have state governments guarantee custodial parents a minimum annual child support payment, for example, $2,000 per child. The minimum could be indexed. If an absent parent's payment was less than the minimum, the state would make up the difference.

An assured minimum provides a kind of unemployment insurance for children that shields them from the full effects of an absent parent's decline in earnings. Equally important, the assured minimum becomes a stable foundation of *nonwelfare* income on which the caretaker parent can build. Alone, it would not have much impact on poverty since it would mostly be offset by lower TANF payments. But unlike TANF, it would not be reduced as earnings rise. Part-time work combined with the minimum benefit (or more if the absent parent's payments are high enough) and the EIC would often suffice to move the family off welfare and over the poverty line. By ensuring custodial parents a stable source of income, an assured benefit could also reduce financial instability and its accompanying stress. Because the program would apply to poor and nonpoor alike, benefits would not be seen as welfare for the poor, with the attendant stigma, hostility, weak political support, and bureaucratic indignities of that program.

An assured benefit, however, establishes a new, possibly costly, entitlement program, increases incentives for potential custodial parents to leave their spouses, and reduces incentives for a poor absent parent to contribute because his payment would only reduce the assured benefit rather than increase income available for the child.

Research suggests that if all legislated child support reforms were fully implemented and enforced, and an assured benefit enacted, single-parent families would have much greater child support income. A fourth to a third of their poverty would be eliminated (Garfinkel et al., 1992). Continuing efforts to establish paternity, obtain support orders and enforce support obligations, and further child support reforms are a key to reducing poverty and welfare use among single-parent families, but will not eliminate the need for other interventions.

Instituting a Child Allowance.   Many industrialized countries provide small yearly child allowances that benefit all families with children, not just those with an absent parent. The appeal is their universality and simplicity. Because all children receive one regardless of family income, the stigma, isolation, and administrative hassles of welfare are avoided.

The federal tax code reduces taxable income by $2,750 per child (as of 1998). Income taxes are lowered by $2,750 times the tax rate. The exemption is thus worth $413 per child for families in the 15% tax bracket and $770 for more affluent families in the 28% bracket. The poorest families, who have no income tax liability, receive no benefit from the child exemption. The Taxpayer Relief Act of 1997 provides an additional tax credit for most children under age 17 that is worth up to $500. Again, because the credit is payable only to families who owe federal taxes, the poorest families do not benefit.

A *refundable* child tax credit is an alternative. Subtract the credit from taxes owed and refund any excess to the family. Families with no income tax liability would receive the entire credit. This would mimic a child allowance without setting up new administrative arrangements. If Congress enacted a uniform credit that cost as much in terms of foregone taxes as the current exemption, poorer families would gain and richer ones lose compared to the exemption. Raising the credit would have a greater antipoverty impact, of course. But doing so would be very costly because so many nonpoor families also receive benefits.

CONCLUSION

Currently, approximately one in five American children lacks minimally decent levels of food, shelter, medical care, and other necessities. They are poor because their parents earn too little and their families receive inadequate income support benefits. To reduce poverty among children, public policy must help families earn more in the labor market, and improve public income support programs and child support collections.

The information and analysis in this chapter can help social workers more effectively provide child welfare services. Labor market, income support, and child support programs form part of the social environment of families who need services. The nature of the welfare system and the demands it often imposes on recipients, such as participating in a training program or moving into work more rapidly, are likely to affect family dynamics, the amount of time parents spend with their children, and child well-being. The financial pressures faced by all poor families, and financial emergencies that may arise if administrative errors or other snafus delay or deny income support and child support benefits, stress families and place children at greater risk. Social workers need to consider how to take account of these circumstances when planning intervention services.

Social workers are well positioned to observe and document the links between poverty and problems that bring families to the attention of child welfare agencies. They should also recognize that a minimally adequate standard of living is an essential requisite for promoting competence and later success. Attempts to teach coping and mastery skills and to foster personal growth may be undermined by the financial pressure and psychological stress generated by low and unstable income. To improve the effectiveness of child welfare services, social workers committed to competence-centered practice have a professional responsibility to advocate for more effective antipoverty policies.

ACKNOWLEDGMENT

I thank Inhoe Ku for outstanding research assistance.

NOTES

1.   Throughout this chapter, a "child" is any person under age 18. By definition, half the families have incomes below the median, and half have incomes above.

2.   All figures from Committee on Ways and Means (1998, p. 1290–1291). When we look at the chances that a member of a demographic group is poor, we are concerned with the level or *incidence* of poverty within that group. When we look at the make-up of just the poor, we are concerned with the *composition* of the poor. Students should recognize that the two concepts differ and avoid confusion between them.

3.   Although poor children have worse outcomes, is it their low incomes that lead to these problems, or are others factors, correlated with income, more important reasons for the problems? Many believe income is the key variable; for a thoughtful contrary view see Mayer (1997).

4.   Unemployment insurance and workers compensation also help families with children. That children gain from such programs is largely incidental to their main purpose of insuring workers against unanticipated earnings losses, so they will not be discussed.

5.   If a minor child's parents receive Old Age Insurance or Disability Insurance benefits paid by other Social Security programs, the child is also entitled to benefits. About 1.9 million children received these forms of Social Security in 1996. The average benefit of $227 was much less than that paid under Survivors Insurance. Committee on Ways and Means (1998) describes Survivors Insurance and the related Social Security programs and provides the recipient and benefit figures (p. 17).

6.   For descriptions of AFDC and TANF, see Committee on Ways and Means (1998).

7.   Legislation in 1998 restored federal food stamp eligibility for about 250,000 legal

immigrants—including most children—who had lost eligibility under the PRWORA. The law restores eligibility to slightly fewer than one of every three legal immigrants who lost it. Most legal immigrant adults who are neither elderly nor disabled remain ineligible. Most immigrants who arrived in the United States after the PRWORA was signed—August 22, 1996—also continue to be ineligible.

8.   The wide variety of state-level reforms approved in recent years under the federal "waiver" process will be permitted to continue and need not conform with all the new aspects of the Act if the waivers already address those aspects.

9.   Major provisions of states' TANF plans as of late 1997 are summarized in Committee on Ways and Means (1998) and Gallagher et al. (1998).

10.   In 1993 eligibility was expanded to childless workers. For further discussion of the EIC, see Lav and Lazere (1996), Blank (1995), and Committee on Ways and Means (1998, pp. 866–870).

11.   Under TANF states are free to set whatever benefit reduction rates they desire.

12.   Since the EIC subsidizes earnings until they hit a specified limit, it provides incentives to start working and increase earnings up to the limit. However, for persons who would earn above the limit in the absence of the EIC, the extra income from the EIC and the phase-out of benefits, which creates an implicit tax on earnings, both exert work disincentives. The EIC can also lead to financial rewards or penalties for marriage versus living apart or cohabiting, depending on the earnings of the two partners.

13.   Evidence summarized in this and the following paragraph is from Moffitt (1992, 1998) and Hoynes (1995, 1996a, 1996b).

14.   See Garfinkel (1992) and Garfinkel et al. (1994) for an extended discussion of child support issues.

15.   Figures in this paragraph are from Committee on Ways and Means (1998, pp. 549, 605, 608, 650, 651).

16.   For reasons explained in Table 4.7, we cannot compare this antipoverty impact with those in Table 4.8.

17.   Parts of this discussion are drawn from Ellwood (1988).

FOR FURTHER INFORMATION

Children and Youth Services Review. (1995). Vol. 17, No.1/2. Special issue on child poverty with articles by leading experts from a range of backgrounds.

The Future of Children. (1997). Vol. 7, Summer/Fall. Another special issue on child poverty with articles by leading experts. Each issue of this free journal focuses on a specific topic concerning the social conditions and problems of children. The journal is on-line at http://www.futureofchildren.org.

Chase-Lansdale, P.L., & Brooks-Gunn, J. (Eds.) (1995). *Escape from poverty: What makes a difference for children?* New York: Cambridge University Press. Provides current and historical overview of child poverty in the United States. It examines policies to reduce it, with a particular focus on mothers' employment, child care, fathers' involvement, and health care.

Center on Budget and Policy Priorities. A major nonpartisan research organization and policy institute that addresses a range of government policies and programs, with an emphasis on those affecting low and moderate income people. A highly respected source of information and analysis as well as policy ideas and strategies and other forms of assistance for organizations working to reduce poverty. The web site with its publications and other information is ⟨http://www.cbpp.org⟩.

Children's Defense Fund. (1998). *Poverty Matters: The Cost of Child Poverty in America.* This report from the nation's premier advocacy organization for children indicates the costs of child poverty and explores why poor children fare worse than nonpoor children. It calls for a work- and family-based strategy for ending child poverty. On-line at ⟨http://www.childrensdefense.org/fairstart_povmat.html⟩.

Committee on Ways and Means, U.S. House of Representatives. (1998). *1998 Green book: Background material and data on programs within the jurisdiction of the Committee on Ways and Means.* Washington DC: U.S. Government Printing Office. Provides a wealth of information on federal income support and social services programs, poverty, income inequality, and related social conditions for all population groups, not just children. It is an excellent reference for up-to-date facts in these areas. Updates are published every other year. It is available on a federal government web site.

Duncan, G., & Brooks-Gunn, J. (Eds.) (1997). *Consequences of growing up poor.* New York: Russell Sage Foundation. Discusses the ways economic deprivation damages children during their development. Chapters have been contributed by economists, psychologists, and sociologists.

Ellwood, D.T. (1988). *Poor support: Poverty in the American family.* New York: Basic Books. Thought provoking analysis of the causes of poverty, which also lays out a clear policy agenda for reducing the problem. Ellwood was one of President Clinton's top social policy advisors. It combines sound analysis with an appreciation of the social values that underlie the policy debates. Though the data are now dated, the broader issues and policy framework that are presented by Ellwood remain relevant.

Garfinkel, I., Hochschild, J., & McLanahan, S. (Eds.) (1996). *Social policies for children.* Washington DC: The Brookings Institution. Leading experts discuss the case for new social policies for children. It covers income support, education and training, child care, health care, crime, and child abuse policies.

The Urban Institute. Another major nonpartisan policy research organization that studies a range of government policies and programs affecting poor children and families. It is conducting a major analysis of the effects of the 1996 welfare reform. The web site with its publications and other information is ⟨http://www.urban.org⟩.

5

Child Maltreatment Incidence, Casework Process, and Services for Physically Abused Children

INTRODUCTION

Child maltreatment represents one of the primary reasons that parents and children are referred or reported to child welfare agencies for service. These staff persons provide families with a range of services to address family needs or problems as a way of preventing or treating child maltreatment. This chapter will present (1) current data on the definitions, incidence, and reporting of broadly defined categories of child abuse and neglect; (2) theoretical perspectives regarding contributing factors; (3) an overview of the casework processes involved in assessing a report of child maltreatment; and (4) treatment of physical abuse. Chapters 6 and 7 will focus on sexual abuse, physical neglect, and psychological maltreatment.

CONCEPTUALIZING CHILD MALTREATMENT

Individual, Familial, Community, and Societal
Perspectives

Child abuse is typically thought of as a family-related event, occurring when a parent or caretaker physically injures, neglects, or sexually abuses his or her child. Child maltreatment, however, should more properly be conceptualized as occurring on a variety of levels: individual (ontogenetic development), family (microsystem), community environment (exosystem), and culture [or society] (macrosystem). For example, individual factors could be those characteristics in a child (e.g., colicky, unresponsive to caregiver nurturing) or adult (e.g., low self-esteem, low impulse control) that influence their behavior and may contribute to child maltreatment. Familial factors may include low income, an intergenerational pattern of abuse or neglect, poor communication, and a lack of household routine with respect to meals and bedtime, among others (Belsky, 1980; Panel on Child Abuse and Neglect, National Research Council, 1993, pp. 110, 126–136)

The community environment (exosystem) can contribute much or little to a family's ability to raise their children in terms of safe housing, neighbors that are willing to help care for children, and other basic supports or conditions. The existence of inadequate educational programs and unequal employment opportunities places families and children at risk. But the set of cultural and social values that promotes certain kinds of behaviors and life styles cannot be overlooked either—as embodied in a culture or society (macrosystem). For example, does an emphasis on family privacy or a preoccupation with violence in the media contribute to child maltreatment? (Panel on Child Abuse and Neglect, National Research Council, 1993, p. 136).

Societal abuse can also be conceived as "the sum of that society's actions, beliefs, and values that impede the healthy development of its children" (Giovannoni, 1985, p. 194). Risk of abuse is also increased when our society permits a relatively high degree of violence to be employed in child rearing, and when the victimization of women is overlooked because of sexual mores and values (Gil, 1970; Giovannoni, 1985). In fact, some child advocates emphasize that the allowance of any form of corporal (physical) punishment by parents, schoolteachers, or anyone else provides a societal context in which violence against children is more likely to occur (Moelis, 1989). This is why a number of Scandinavian countries have outlawed all forms of corporal punishment (Haeuser, 1989).

"Institutional maltreatment" (what one might view as a blending of culture and community systems) occurs when major societal institutions such as school, legal authorities, and medical care organizations operate in ways that discriminate against the fair and adequate treatment of children. For example, state laws regarding the rights of children in an abuse or neglect court proceeding vary in ways that promote unequal treatment of children. Until the passage of the Indian Child Welfare Act (PL 95-608), Native American children were being placed in substitute care at an alarming rate (see Chapters 2 and 10). Recent studies of the U.S. educational system have documented that low income and ethnic minority children are dropping out of school in unacceptably high numbers. Furthermore, children are not totally safe from maltreatment, even when they are removed from their homes and placed in child welfare institutions such as foster family homes or residential treatment centers (see, for example, Poertner, Bussey, & Fluke, 1999; Rindfleisch & Rabb, 1984).

In contrast to societal or institutional maltreatment, familial abuse or neglect generally refers to "the mistreatment of children by their own families, particularly by those entrusted as primary caretakers—parents or parent substitutes" (Giovannoni, 1985, p. 198). This type of maltreatment is the form most commonly recognized, and it represents a focal point for intervention by the child welfare service delivery system. Another commonly cited definition, which has formed the foundation for many state child abuse laws throughout the country, was developed for inclusion in the Federal Child Abuse Prevention and Treatment Act of 1974 (PL 93-237):

the physical or mental injury, sexual abuse, negligent treatment, or maltreatment of
a child under the age of eighteen by a person who is responsible for the child's welfare under circumstances which would indicate that the child's health or welfare is
harmed or threatened thereby. (as cited in Giovannoni & Becerra, 1979, p. 13)

Giovannoni and others have emphasized the problems in delineating more precise definitions of child abuse and neglect because the definitions are dependent
on the "seriousness of the maltreatment in relation to societal willingness to in-
trude on the family's autonomy" (Giovannoni, 1985, p. 199), lack of precise definitions, and disagreement among professional groups. Our lack of knowledge
with respect to how child development is precisely affected by various forms of
maltreatment also complicates defining what constitutes child maltreatment and
state standards for intervention. So whether a particular type of parental behavior constitutes "abuse" or "neglect" will depend on a number of factors, including societal willingness to deliver voluntary and involuntary services, our current
knowledge of child development regarding what is harmful to children, the values held by the dominant culture in relation to various subcultures, and societal
capability to provide adequate services (Rodwell, 1988; Youssef, Attia, & Kamel,
1998).

In other words, there is no universal standard for childrearing. This can be most
clearly illustrated by examining the cross-cultural research in child abuse:

Those who seek to develop a cross-cultural definition of abuse face the dilemma of
choosing between a culturally relevant standard in which any behavior can be abusive or nonabusive depending upon the cultural context or an idiosyncratic standard
whereby abusive acts are those behaviors at variance with the normal cultural standards for raising children. (Gelles, 1987, p. 23)

Definitions of child maltreatment are likely to change in relation to cultural developments as well as other factors. Another example of how these factors interact can be found in the recent emphasis among researchers and clinicians in
defining and documenting more precisely the nature, prevalence, and causes of
psychological or emotional maltreatment of children (see Chapter 7). With these
definitional limitations in mind, the next section will present an overview of the incidence of child maltreatment in the United States and discuss some of the difficulties in estimating the prevalence of various forms of child abuse and neglect.
The focus will be on child abuse and neglect committed or allowed by a parent or
child caretaker. (Maltreatment by nonrelated adults will not be presented because
of limitations in the existing databases and because child welfare workers typically refer those cases to law enforcement personnel after ensuring that the child is
safe.) Following those sections, we present an overview of the casework processes
involved in assessing a report of child maltreatment.

DEFINITION AND INCIDENCE OF CHILD MALTREATMENT
IN THE UNITED STATES

Some Approaches to Estimating the Incidence
of Child Maltreatment

There are three basic approaches to estimating the incidence of child maltreatment (i.e., child abuse or neglect, abbreviated "CAN" in this section). One approach is to just rely on official reports, with a focus on suspected and substantiated/confirmed/founded reports. Some drawbacks with this approach are that definitions vary across jurisdictions about what these determinations mean, and, most important, this approach does not include all of the incidents that were never officially reported.

A second approach is called a "sentinel study" in that it surveys people who are designated as the official reporters of CAN—social services, educational, medical, day care, law enforcement, and other mandated or thought to be the most suitable reporters. This approach is essential in that it attempts to include all the cases known to these people that were both reported and unreported.

A third approach is to survey the general population of adults (and possibly) even older children directly to determine if they have been maltreated. The advantage of this approach is that it collects data directly from those who might have experienced the problem and, depending on any response bias or hesitancy to identify themselves as a victim, may provide the most accurate data.

In recent evaluations of the effect of new approaches to community-based child protective services, it was thought that a combination of all three approaches, although expensive, is necessary to truly estimate the incidence of CAN in a community and how it changes over time (Personal Communication, Steve Budde, October 28, 1998). In the sections that follow, child maltreatment data from each of these approaches will be presented.

Incidence Versus Prevalence—A Statistical Note

As one examines data regarding child maltreatment and other statistics on child welfare, it is important to distinguish two major types:

- *Incidence* refers to the number of new cases reported within a specific time period, e.g., 42 children out of 1,000 were reported for child maltreatment in 1997 (U.S. Department of Health and Human Services, 1999, p. 3-2).
- *Prevalence* with respect to many types of child welfare statistics can refer to all the living persons at that time who had experienced the event at any time up to the present (e.g., it is likely that a much larger number of children in the

United States would have reported having been physically abused during some point in their childhood if they had been surveyed in 1997).

For example, when Straus and Gelles (1986) conducted their national surveys on family violence, they were able to capture both kinds of information: events just during that year (incidence) and how many times that event had occurred over the person's entire life history (prevalence).

Levels of Reporting for Child Maltreatment

In examining the incidence of child maltreatment, different levels of official recognition or public awareness must be delineated. The methodology used for the National Incidence Studies (NIS-1, -2, and -3) was based on a model that used five levels of official recognition or public awareness of abuse or neglect.[1] These levels are described below and are illustrated in Figure 5.1.

Level 1. Those children reported to Child Protective Services (CPS) where the allegation of abuse and neglect is either substantiated or unsubstantiated after an investigation.

Level 2. Those children who are not known to CPS but who are known to other "investigatory" agencies, such as police, courts, or public health departments. These agencies may have overlapping or even conflicting responsibilities concerning certain situations, such as felonious assault, homicide, delinquency, dependency, domestic disputes, "children in need of control," or nutrition and hygiene problems. Although Level 2 children are, in some sense, "officially known," they are not necessarily regarded by the community as abused or neglected in the same sense as Level 1 children are, and they do not necessarily receive assistance that specifically targets the abuse or neglect problems.

Level 3. Abused and neglected children who are not known to CPS or to any Level 2 agency, but who are known to professionals in other major community institutions, such as school, hospitals, day care centers, and social services and mental health agencies. Children may remain at this level for any number of reasons. One reason may be definitional ambiguities as to what types of cases should be reported to CPS (or to other investigatory agencies). Other reasons relate to the attitudes and assumptions of the professionals who are aware of these situations. For example, they may feel that they are in the best position to help, may not trust CPS to handle the problem appropriately, or may have apprehensions about becoming involved in an official investigation.

Level 4. Abused and neglected children who are recognized by someone outside the purview of the first three levels, such as a neighbor, another member of the family, or by one or both of the involved parties—the perpetrator and the child. However, none of the individuals recognizing the maltreatment at this level has made it known to persons at Levels 1 through 3.

Level 5. Children who have not been recognized as abused or neglected by any-

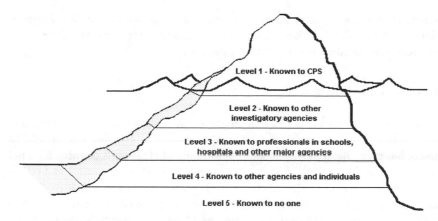

Figure 5.1. Levels of recognition of child abuse and neglect. *Source:* NCCAN (1998). *Study findings: Study of national incidence and prevalence of child abuse and neglect—1988* (p. 2.2). Washington, DC: U.S. Department of Health and Human Services.

one. These are the cases in which the individuals involved do not regard their behaviors or experiences as child maltreatment and where the situations have not yet come to the attention of outside observers who would recognize them as such (NCCAN, 1988, pp. x–xi).

Statistics collected by the National Center of Child Abuse and Neglect Data System (NCANDS) currently are the most accurate "official" reporting data. The NCANDS data, however, include only Level 1 type cases. The NIS-3 study uses data pertaining to Levels 1 through 3. It includes "countable" data that pertain to child abuse and neglect that is reported to CPS law enforcement or other "official" agencies, as well as those cases known to other professionals or agencies. Thus, both studies are important sources of data regarding incidence and reporting.

Neither study, however, reflects the total amount of child maltreatment. The pyramid depicted in Figure 5.1 can be used to illustrate the "iceberg effect," a phenomenon in which the number of cases that are reported (i.e., visible) may represent only the tip of the iceberg of cases that occur but are unreported. In other words, the official statistics of the NCANDS and NIS-3 national surveys almost certainly underestimate the actual numbers of cases in the United States and must be viewed with caution.

There are at least three major reasons for this lack of accurate and comprehensive data. First, there is a failure to detect injury caused by abuse due to parent avoidance of medical care, switching physicians, and other factors. Second, there is a failure to recognize abuse as the cause of the victim's injuries. Part of this relates to medical personnel reluctance to label middle and upper income parents as abusers (Pelton, 1978). And third, even after an injury has been reported and recognized as child maltreatment, the proper agency may not be notified (Zigler & Hall, 1989, pp. 48–49). These and other factors argue for viewing current child maltreatment statistics as conservative estimates.

Types of Child Maltreatment

This chapter will use the definitions employed in some recent national reporting and incidence studies, supplemented by current research findings. It should be noted, however, that a universal set of definitions of child maltreatment does not exist currently in the United States. Giovannoni and Becerra (1979) and others have demonstrated that different professional groups define child maltreatment in varying ways. Although nearly all states adhere to the basic definitions of child maltreatment provided in the Child Abuse and Neglect Prevention and Treatment Act (as amended), individual state definitions reflect their own state laws and service emphases. Furthermore, law enforcement, education, medical, mental health, and other allied professionals may hold different views and apply slightly different definitions, not only within but between states. Clearly, this makes it difficult to design uniform reporting practices and standards for agency intervention (Hutchinson, 1989; Panel on Child Abuse and Neglect, National Research Council, 1993).

The forms of child maltreatment, however, have been consistently grouped into approximately five major categories: physical abuse, sexual abuse, physical neglect, educational neglect, and psychological (including emotional) maltreatment. Furthermore, a more universal typology of child maltreatment with specific subtypes is gradually being established, as evidenced by the practice literature and recent studies that have used practical case record review typologies (e.g., Barnett, Manly, & Cicchetti, 1993). One such typology, presented in Table 5.1, focuses on the basic types of maltreatment rather than causal dynamics or the actors involved. For example, incest and sexual assault by a stranger are not distinguished, even though they present two different forms of sexual abuse. More specific definitions of each form of maltreatment are presented in Chapters 6 and 7, but it should be emphasized how difficult it is to define when certain parenting practices are considered child maltreatment.

WHO IS SERVED? CURRENT STATISTICAL DATA
ON CHILD ABUSE AND NEGLECT

Early Studies

A number of studies have been conducted to provide estimates of the incidence of child maltreatment in the United States. David Gil conducted one of the first

Table 5.1. Major Types of Child Maltreatment[a]

Physical Abuse
    Major physical injuries (e.g., broken bones, fractured skulls, serious burns)
    Minor physical injuries (e.g., small bruises, minor burns)
Sexual Abuse[a]
    Intrusion (penile penetration: oral, anal, or genital)
    Molestation with genital contact
    Molestation without genital contact
    Sexual exploitation (e.g., participation in prostitution or filming of pornographic movies)
Physical Neglect
    Refusal of health care
    Delay in seeking or obtaining health care
    Abandonment
    Expulsion from the home (e.g., child is locked out of the house)
    Inadequate supervision
    Inadequate provision of food, clothing, or personal hygiene care
Educational Neglect
    Permitted chronic truancy (some states limit this to children aged 12 and under)
    Failure to enroll children or other truancy (e.g., requiring child to care for siblings instead
        of attending school)
    Inattention to special educational needs
Psychological Maltreatment
    Isolating (e.g., tying, binding, or locking child in their room or a closet)
    Denying emotion responsiveness (e.g., failing to provide sensitive, responsive caregiving
        by avoiding child hugs or through mechanistic touch)
    Terrorizing (e.g., child is threatened repeatedly with severe injury, child is made to fear
        objects or people in inappropriate ways)
    Rejecting (e.g., actively refusing a child's request for help, ignoring a child)
    Degrading (e.g., calling a child "stupid," labeling)
    Corrupting (e.g., teaching and reinforcing racist, immoral, or criminal behaviors)
    Exploiting (e.g., using a child as a servant, sexual molestation).

Sources: American Association for Protecting Children (1988), Garbarino et al. (1986), Hart, Germain, and Brassard (1987), NCCAN (1988).
[a]Note that for many of the statistics reported in the following tables, incest [proscribed sexual conduct between culturally specified relatives (Korbin, 1987, p. 247)] is grouped with the larger category of sexual abuse: "contact or interactions between a child and an adult when the child is being used for the sexual stimulation of that adult or another person" (NCCAN, 1981).

national studies of child abuse in 1967–1968 by screening more than 13,000 cases of child maltreatment that met his definition (deliberate injury inflicted on children by a parent or other caretaker aimed at harming the child). Gil estimated that there was a nationwide reporting rate of 8.4 children per 100,000 in 1967 and 9.3 children per 100,000 in 1968 (Gil, 1970, pp. 98–99). More importantly, he projected that between 2.5 and 4 million families either failed to act or used inappropriate physical force with the intent of hurting, injuring, or destroying their children (Gil, 1971).

In 1985, Straus and Gelles (1986) estimated that a minimum of 1 million children ages 3–17 (residing in two-parent families) were subjected to serious physical abuse. If children maltreated in single-parent homes were added, this figure would be increased significantly, given the greater prevalence of child maltreatment in single-parent homes.

More Recent Data on Rates of Child Maltreatment

Reports of Maltreatment.   Over the past two decades, the number of children reported as victims of maltreatment has also increased substantially. From 1976 to 1987, the American Humane Association collected reporting data from the states under a federal grant. In 1976, an estimated 669,000 children were reported to child protective services agencies, and by 1987, that figure had increased to 2,178,000 children. By 1997, the number of American children who were the subject of a report of abuse or neglect rose to 2,923,374 according to NCANDS data (U.S. Department of Health and Human Services, 1999, p. E-4); with approximately 984,000 child victims (U.S. Department of Health and Human Services, 1999, p. xii). A few states and cities account for much of the numbers. For example, in New York City alone, there were 52,106 reports of child maltreatment in 1996 (New York City Administration for Children's Services, 1998, p. 8).

The NCANDS figure of 984,000 victims represents a 18% increase in the number of confirmed victims of abuse or neglect since 1990. On average, based on data from 1976 to 1993, there has been a 9% annual growth rate in the reporting of child maltreatment. The reasons for this vary, but the steady increase (until very recently) in reporting appears to be due to both an increase in public awareness of child maltreatment and an increase in the incidence of maltreatment. But over the past 5 years this annual rate has leveled off; and it actually decreased from 1995 to 1996—most likely due to the low unemployment and other generally positive economic conditions in the United States.

The NIS-3 (summarized in Appendix A), however, indicates that the actual incidence of child maltreatment is much greater than the number of cases cited in published studies or "official" reports. Even the nature of reporting skews estimates of the incidence of maltreatment because allied professionals, on average, report less than half of the cases of suspected maltreatment of which they are aware. For example, the range of cases known and reported by allied professionals in the second national incidence study (NIS-2) varies from a low of 16% for day care providers to 24% for school personnel, 56% for mental health staff, 61% for police officers/sheriffs, and 66% for hospital personnel [National Center on Child Abuse and Neglect (NCCAN), 1988, p. 6.12]. In contrast, a number of studies have documented that minority and poor families are more likely to be labeled abusive or neglectful (cf. Turbett & O'Toole, 1980, as cited in Gelles, 1987).

The need for a comprehensive and coordinated response to the problem of child maltreatment is all the more apparent given the number of children and families involved.

Types of Maltreatment. Among children substantiated as victims of maltreatment in 1997, 440,944 (55.9%) were victims of neglect, 197,557 (24.6%) were physically abused, 98,339 (12.5%) were victims of sexual abuse, 49,338 (6.1%) were emotionally maltreated, and 18,894 (2.3%) were victims of medical neglect. Medical neglect and "other" forms of maltreatment, such as abandonment, congenital drug addiction, or threats to harm a child, accounted for 12.2% of substantiated maltreatment reports (U.S. Department of Health and Human Services, 1999, p. 4-2) (see Figure 5.2 and Table 5.2). According to NCANDS data, an estimated 1,197 children died in 1997 as a result of abuse or neglect (this is an extrapolation from the 967 child maltreatment deaths reported by 41 states) (U.S. Department of Health and Human Services, 1999, p. xiii).

It is important to note that reporting rates for sexual maltreatment (until just in the past year or two) have been steadily increasing in the 1980s. For example, the proportion of sexual abuse cases reported nationally increased from 9% in 1983 to 15.7% in 1986 (AAPC, 1988, p. 22). But using NCANDS data, it decreased slightly from 1990 (14.9%) to 1997 (12.5%) (U.S. Department of Health and Human Services, 1999, p. 4-2). Whether these figures indicate an *actual* increase or a recent slight decrease in the number of cases, an increased willingness to report, or

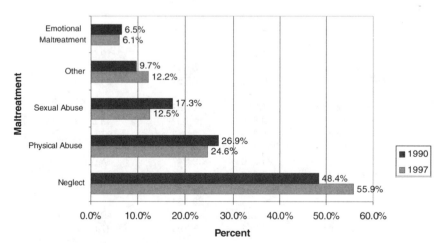

1990: N = 611,924 victims in 35 states.
1997: N = 689,513 victims in 35 states.

Figure 5.2. Comparison of victims by type of maltreatment, 1990 and 1997. *Source:* U.S. Department of Health and Human Services. (1999). Child maltreatment 1997: Reports from the states to the National Child Abuse and neglect Data System. Washington, DC: U.S. Government Printing Office, 4–2.

Table 5.2. Victims by State, 1990 and 1997

State	1990[a]	1997[b]	Percent Change
Alabama	16,508	22,204	34.5
Alaska	5,217	9,017	72.8
Arizona	24,244	24,005	−.9
Arkansas	7,922		
California	48,512	174,215	259
Colorado	7,906	8,935	13.0
Connecticut	12,481	36,638	193
Delaware	2,065	4,417	113
Washington, DC	3,210	5,332	66.1
Florida	79,086	99,639	25.9
Georgia	34,120	45,504	33.3
Guam			
Hawaii	1,974	2,559	29.6
Idaho	2,667	8,283	210
Illinois	37,539	45,133	20.2
Indiana	26,818	15,624	−41.7
Iowa	8,215		
Kansas		18,592	
Kentucky	22,239	22,662	1.9
Louisiana	15,383	14,825	−3.6
Maine	4,133	5,721	38.4
Maryland			
Massachusetts	28,621	33,759	17.9
Michigan	25,774	22,030	−14.5
Minnesota	9,256	11,840	27.9
Mississippi		17,559	
Missouri	21,732	17,463	−19.6
Montana		3,611	
Nebraska	5,595	4,757	−14.9
Nevada	7,703		
New Hampshire	1,056	1,382	30.8
New Jersey	19,546	10,982	−43.8
New Mexico	4,379	8,213	87.5
New York	57,931		
North Carolina	24,880	33,347	34.0
North Dakota	2,893		
Ohio	49,434		
Oklahoma		23,564	
Oregon	8,126	12,128	49.2
Pennsylvania	7,951	5,799	−27.0
Puerto Rico			
Rhode Island	5,393	4,378	−18.8
South Carolina	9,632	10,927	13.4
South Dakota	4,132	2,894	−29.9
Tennessee	11,473	10,803	−5.8
Texas	53,939	45,676	−15.3

(*continued*)

Table 5.2. (Continued)

State	1990[a]	1997[b]	Percent Change
Utah	8,524	9,437	10.7
Vermont	1,500	1,121	−25.2
Virginia	14,174	11,792	−16.8
Virgin Islands			
Washington		23,303	
West Virginia			
Wisconsin	14,165	17,592	24.1
Wyoming	2,478	986	−60.2
Totals	**760,526**	**908,648**	**19.5**

[a]1990: N = 760,526 victims in 44 states.
[b]1997: N = 908,648 victims in 44 states.
Sources: U.S. Department of Health and Human Services. (1996). *Child maltreatment 1994: Reports from the states to the National Conference on Child Abuse and Neglect.* Washington, DC: US Government Printing Office, pp. 2-6 and 2-7. U.S. Department of Health and Human Services. (1999). *Child maltreatment 1997: Reports from the states to the National Child Abuse and Neglect Data Systems.* Washington, DC: US Government Printing Office.

an increased capacity for school and child welfare authorities to detect such cases is the subject of some debate in the field. A number of authors have written about how sexual abuse has been a common social problem (even if not defined as one by a particular society at that time) across cultures and historical periods (e.g., deMause, 1988; Korbin, 1987).

Service Responses

In 1997, about 16% of children who were investigated following a maltreatment report were removed from their homes in the 36 states reporting this data (U.S. Department of Health and Human Services, 1999, p. E-11). Twenty-six states reported that court actions were initiated involving 19.2% of the child maltreatment victims in 1997. And 32 states reported that 656,280 (49.1%) of child victims received additional child welfare services (U.S. Department of Health and Human Services, 1999, p. E-8).

Recidivism

Recurring child abuse and neglect, the subsequent or repeated maltreatment of a child after identification to public authorities, is a major concern with rates varying among states and local areas:

Recurrence plays a key role in both research and practice. For example, recurrence is used to describe and to measure child safety outcomes by some statistical agencies. Recurrence is used in the development of predictive and actuarial risk assessment instrument as a criterion (Baird, 1988; Baird, Wagner, & Neuenfeldt, 1992; Wagner & Squadrito, 1994). It has been used as part of administrative decision making in evaluating the efficacy of alternative workload reduction policies (Fluke, 1995).

One of the most disturbing aspects of child maltreatment is its tendency to recur. Studies examining abusers in treatment have reported recurrence rates ranging from 16% to 66.8% (Cohn, 1979; Herrenkohl, Herrenkohl, Egolf, & Seech, 1979; Green, Power, Steinbook, & Gaines, 1981; Fryer & Miyoshi, 1994; Levy, Markovic, Chaudhry, Ahart, & Torres, 1995; Wood, 1997).

Levy and colleagues (1995) found that the most common form of recurrent maltreatment was neglect, followed by physical abuse, with sexual abuse recurring less frequently. They also found some evidence that children insured by Medicaid (standing in for socioeconomic status) were 2.6 times more likely to recur compared to children not insured by Medicaid.

Event history analysis techniques were used in a study of as safety assessment protocol in Illinois (Fluke, Edwards, Johnson, & Wells, 1997) designed to examine short-term recurrence pre- and postimplementation. The results of the study provided evidence that a 23% reduction in rates of short-term recurrence (substantiated recurrence within 60 days of the initial report) could be attributed to the protocol.

A recent study of 10 states (Illinois, Louisiana, Massachusetts, Missouri, Maine, North Carolina, New Jersey, Pennsylvania, Texas, Vermont, and Washington) using 1994 and 1995 NCANDS data found that the average recurrence at 6 month was 14.7% and at 12 months it was 19.6% (with the average weighted by the number of child victims in a particular state). States varied significantly in their rates of recurrence (3–22%) and in the increase in rates of recurrence from 6 to 12 months (1–7%) (Fluke, Yuan, & Edwards, 1999, pp. 634, 640).

CHILD MALTREATMENT SEVERITY AND REPORTING

Serious and Fatal Maltreatment

The estimated number of seriously injured children essentially quadrupled from 141,700 to 565,000 in the intervening 7 years between the NIS-2 and the NIS-3 (a 299% increase) (see Sedlak & Broadhurst, 1999). Yet it should be noted that chronic neglect in the form of nonsupervision, nonorganic failure to thrive, inadequate nutrition, or poor medical care has been termed the "silent killer" because of the significant number of child fatalities that result from untreated neglectful situations (see Chapter 7).

As mentioned earlier, the most tragic outcome of our society's inability to ensure child safety is the death of a child from abuse or neglect, as contrasted with other forms of traumatic child deaths (Rivara & Grossman, 1996). Forty-one states reported that 967 fatalities resulted from child maltreatment in 1997, with a 50 state plus District of Columbia estimate of 1,197 fatalities. Please note that states have different methods of tracking fatalities. It is also important to note that fatalities attributed to abuse or neglect typically reflect only the death of children known to child protective agencies; not all child deaths are reported to child protective services. Seventy-seven percent of children who died from abuse or neglect were less than 4 years of age; 10% of the child victims were age 8 years and older (U.S. Department of Health and Human Services, 1999, p. 6-2).

What disturbs many child welfare professionals and child advocates is that a substantial number of these families had been reported to or served by CPS at least once before the child's death. What complicates targeting services is the lack of a definitive set of risk factors for predicting child fatalities. For example, one study compared all child maltreatment fatalities in New York City in 1984 (73 children) with a random sample of 114 nonfatal cases. Researchers identified 11 child, parent, and family characteristics that distinguished fatal from nonfatal child abuse cases in 71.2% of the cases. The authors caution the field that even this list of factors was not complete enough for screening purposes, as 17% of the fatality cases were incorrectly classified as nonfatal (Fontana & Alfaro, 1987, pp. 8, 69–73). Another concern was raised in a Michigan study that found that a disproportionate number of infants died from preventable deaths in foster care compared to the general population (Siefert, Schwartz & Ortega, 1994.)

Although many child fatalities cannot be predicted, better worker training regarding the risk factors currently known and the use of more realistic workload standards would probably allow CPS staff to better ensure the safety of children for those families under the supervision of the child welfare agency. More importantly, universal prevention programs for all first-time parents, crisis services, and better case management would help minimize child deaths (Mitchel, 1989, p. 4).

CHILD PROTECTIVE SERVICES AS A MAJOR PROGRAM AREA IN CHILD WELFARE

Mission and Scope of CPS

Child maltreatment represents a significant social problem in the United States. And to child welfare personnel it is commonly seen as "driving" the service delivery system, as these families are reported to Child Protective Services through both generic and specialized intake units. Technically, states and countries vary somewhat on how they define CPS, with many jurisdictions including all investigatory functions and the short-term services associated with those, but excluding more extensive family support and placement services. CPS today remains one of the most controversial yet important areas of child welfare practice. No other program area is as frequently assailed by the press, criticized by citizen advocacy groups, and viewed with mixed feelings by child welfare staff. Yet all of these groups acknowledge the importance of this service for protecting children and providing services to families.

What are the purpose and mission of CPS? This program area operates on the philosophical basis that all children have a right to live in a safe environment and receive protection from abuse and neglect. CPS was defined by DeFrancis (1955, p. 2) as "a specialized casework service to neglected, abused, exploited or rejected children. The focus of the service is preventive and nonpunitive and is geared toward a rehabilitation through identification and treatment of the motivating factors which underlie the problem."

At the most general level there is a firm consensus regarding the mission of CPS: the program is designed to protect children from child maltreatment committed by their parents or other caretakers. But in translating this broad mandate into practice, the consensus breaks down in a variety of areas such as defining what is child abuse or neglect, establishing standards for agency intervention, and specifying what constitutes a minimum standard of parenting (popularized by the question, What is a good enough parent?).

In an attempt to bring clarity to the mission of CPS, a group of child welfare administrators began work in 1986 to identify and clarify some of the major issues facing CPS programs and their parent child welfare agencies. In 1988, this group, the National Association of Public Child Welfare Administrators (NAPCWA), published a set of guidelines for a model CPS delivery system. This document (revised in 1999) contained the following definition of the CPS mission statement:

> *CPS Agency Mission.* The mission of the child protective service agency is to assess the safety of children, intervene to protect children from harm, strengthen the ability of families to protect their children, or provide an alternative safe family for the child. Child protective services are provided to children and families by CPS agencies in collaboration with communities in order to protect children from abuse or neglect within their families. (National Association of Public Child Welfare Agency Administrators, 1999, p. 12)

We view the child protective services as a vital part of the larger child welfare agency, and is charged by state legislation with the responsibility for responding to reports of alleged child maltreatment and children "at risk of maltreatment," determining the safety of the child who is the subject of the report, and determining what initial response is needed. Any intervention into family life on behalf of children must be guided by the legal bases for action responsibilities of the intervening agency. But this mission statement reflects a growing consensus in the child welfare field regarding the parameters of CPS intervention and yet reveals the dynamic tension between family support and child safety. Because of legal, funding, and staffing limitations, most child welfare agencies are clarifying and narrowing the scope of their involvement with respect to child maltreatment. For example, many CPS units are not offering services beyond possibly an initial assessment for third-party abuse or neglect, abuse perpetrated by teachers, coaches, or day care providers (Harris & Warner, 1988). What can be considered educational neglect has been narrowed by some states to reduce the number of truancy-related cases. In most states, the police are being requested to handle the investigation and prosecution (if necessary) of cases of child maltreatment in publicly licensed child care facilities.

Emphasis currently is being placed on intervening in case situations in which the child is at risk of serious harm and/or where the level of child care falls below a minimum standard of parenting (NAPCWA, 1999; Stein & Rzepnicki, 1983). This approach to service contrasts with the more traditional child welfare approach in which the agency offers assistance to whomever requests it for whatever reason. Agencies instead are placing primary responsibility for care and protection of children with their parents. When parents are unwilling or unable to protect their children, the CPS agency is authorized to intervene. But this authorization also carries with it a responsibility to provide "earnest and persistent efforts" to prevent the child's placement (see Chapter 1), as well as a responsibility to provide a child with some form of a permanent placement if he or she cannot return home safely.

INTAKE IN CHILD WELFARE AND CHILD PROTECTIVE SERVICES

Child Welfare Intake

The intake function is part of a larger service delivery process (see Figure 5.3) concerned essentially with screening requests for service from individuals or referrals from allied agencies, such as schools, law enforcement, mental health, and hospitals and private medical offices. Intake staff provide information, make referrals for service, accept service applications, screen reports of child maltreatment, and may accept financial or heat assistance applications, as well as determine the client's next contact with the agency (Jenkins & Schroeder, 1980, p. 13).

CPS Intake Process

Most state laws require that child abuse and neglect be reported to a law enforcement agency or to the CPS office of the public child welfare agency. The responsibility to investigate referrals lies primarily with CPS workers, although in many jurisdictions, serious cases of neglect or abuse (including sexual abuse) may be jointly investigated by a law enforcement officer and the CPS worker. The CPS worker will typically assess such things as the child's home environment, child and

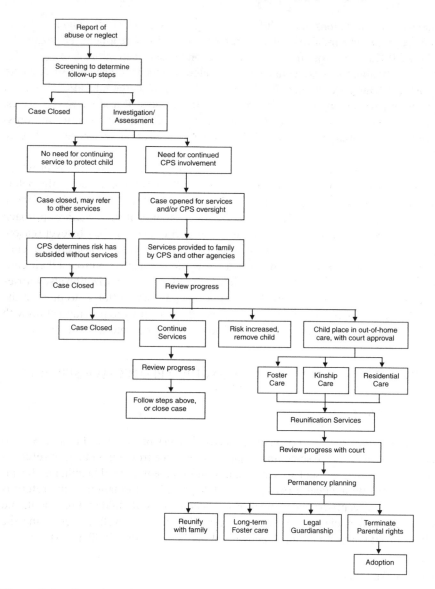

Figure 5.3.   Overview of steps followed by cases through the child protective services and child welfare systems. *Source:* Schene (1998, p. 31). Reprinted with permission.

parent emotional functioning, the nature and extent of the injuries, the physical safety of the child, and the future risk of maltreatment. In addition, the worker will ascertain whether abuse and/or neglect has taken place, protect the child when needed, and make arrangements for ongoing services or closure of the case.

The actual casework process in terms of service delivery steps, court actions, and persons potentially involved in the case are much more complex. [See, for example, the American Humane Association (1999) and Stein & Rzepnicki (1983) for more detailed flowcharts of some of the decision-making steps in CPS.]

Intake is the first of the casework steps and is one of the most important decision-making points in the child welfare delivery system. Information gathered by intake personnel is used to make initial decisions about risk and the type of CPS response required. Intake workers also perform a critical public relations function by professionally responding to the concerns of the community, and by clarifying the role of the agency in regard to various types of CPS referrals. As with general referrals, CPS referrals are accepted from any source (written, telephone, walk-in) and each referral is treated as a potential report of children at risk. The intake worker attempts to obtain as much information as possible about the family being referred and the nature of the alleged maltreatment. Once the initial intake data are collected, a computer check is typically made for a central registry report, if the case is currently active within the agency or if there has been past agency contact with the family. All of this information is important for making a number of critical CPS-related decisions that must be made at the point of intake (see Table 5.3):

1. Is this referral appropriate for the agency? In other words, is there an allegation of abuse, neglect, exploitation, and/or abandonment of a child under the age of 18? (Note that the criteria for screening out reports vary with state law and agency policies. See the section on case screening below.)
2. Is the child in immediate risk of maltreatment or danger of some kind? Most CPS programs use an investigation priority system that weighs the seriousness of the case to determine how quickly the CPS worker must respond (e.g., 1 hour, 1 day, 3 days).
3. Should law enforcement be notified immediately? In serious cases of maltreatment or sexual abuse, CPS and local law enforcement personnel may need to be immediately notified and may team up during the initial stages of the investigation.

The service needs of a considerable number of families in America demand that child welfare and other professionals implement well-designed programs that will be sufficiently powerful to address this serious social problem. To be most effective, these interventions should be based on a well-conceptualized theoretical model of what factors contribute to the maltreatment. Consequently, to help lay the foundation for a discussion of causal factors specific to each major form of child maltreatment, a discussion of the major theoretical perspectives in this area will be presented.

Table 5.3. Stages of CPS Decision Making and Casework

Although terminology and organizational structures vary across jurisdictions, caseworkers typically follow these steps when responding to an allegation of child abuse or neglect. At each step, the caseworker documents actions and decisions in the case record.

Intake

- Receive the report
- Explore appropriateness of the referral
- Check for previous reports
- Decide whether to investigate
- Determine the urgency of response
- Assign the report to an investigator or assessor

Initial Assessment/Investigation

- Make contact with the child and family
- Assess the harm to the child and other children in the home
- Assess the risk for future harm
- Determine the evidence of abuse/ neglect
- Provide emergency services
- Identify resources that could be tapped to protect the child while at home
- Decide on removal of the child
- Find an appropriate placement
- Involve law enforcement and courts, as indicated
- Decide whether to keep case open for continuing protective services or refer to other services
- Provide feedback to parents and other relevant individuals
- Provide results of the assessment/ investigation to the state child welfare information system

Service Planning

- Specify changes needed to ensure the child's safety

- If a child is in placement, decide on permanency goal and develop resources
- Explore the family's strengths and needs
- Identify the outcomes anticipated through services
- Determine what will be provided by whom, for how long, with what frequency
- Establish dates for review
- Continue to review safety of child

Service Provision

- Contract for or coordinate services provided by other agencies
- Clearly communicate service goals
- Deliver selected services directly
- Prepare for court hearing, as needed
- Continue to review safety of child

Evaluating Progress

- Review progress with all service providers and court, if involved
- Obtain client perceptions of progress
- Determine which services in the plan are still needed, new referrals needed
- Continue to review safety of child

Case Closure

- With the family, evaluate progress
- Assess continuing risks to the child
- Identify steps to be taken if protective issues reemerge
- Decide whether to close the case
- Communicate decisions to all relevant agencies and persons
- Document the rationale for case closure

Source: Filip, J., McDaniel, N., and Schene, P. (Eds.) *Helping in child protective services: A competency-based casework handbook.* Englewood, CO: American Humane Association, 1992.

THEORETICAL PERSPECTIVES REGARDING THE CONTRIBUTING FACTORS TO CHILD MALTREATMENT

Overview

Although it is likely that there are a number of causal factors that are specific to a particular form of child maltreatment, it is informative to examine the major theoretical perspectives that attempt to explain why parents and other caretakers may physically abuse, neglect, or sexually maltreat the children in their care. These perspectives include (1) the *psychiatric or psychological* model, (2) the *sociological* model, (3) the *social situational* model (also known as the ecological *or "effect-of-the-child-on-the-caretaker"* model), and (4) the *ecological* or *integrative* model (Belsky, 1978, Goldstein, Keller, & Erné, 1985; Parke & Collmer, 1975). As might be suspected, no one theory has been sufficiently developed or empirically tested to qualify as a conclusive unifying framework. But each perspective does contribute to a better understanding of the phenomena of child maltreatment, and the ecological model does attempt to integrate to some degree the perspectives of the other three models.

Psychiatric or Psychological Model

Much of the early work in the field approached abuse and neglect from the perspective of the medical model, subscribing to a psychiatric view of the causes of maltreatment (Kinard, 1987). The psychiatric of psychological model views the parent's traits or upbringing as the major causes of child maltreatment. It assumes that abusive parents have certain personality characteristics that separate them from nonabusive parents (Belsky & Vondra, 1989; Goldstein, Keller, & Erné, 1985). The model suggests that the abuser is mentally ill and attributes maltreatment to the psychopathology of the abuser, ranging from severe mental illness to deviant personality traits. It relates to special characteristics of parents that contribute to their inability to provide adequate child care.

Although psychiatric disorders corresponding to major categories in the revised *Diagnostic and Statistical Manual (DSM-IV)* are found in only approximately 10% of the child abuse cases, "borderline and marginal personality disorders" are more common among certain classes of abuse and neglect cases (Garbarino, 1980, p. 66). For example, the "apathy-futility" syndrome may play an important role in explaining some of the chronic neglect cases with which child welfare caseworkers struggle (see Chapter 7, Polansky et al., 1982). Physical abusers may be subject to some type of "aggressive-impulsive syndrome" (Spinetta & Rigler, 1972), although more recent conceptualizations of aggressive behavior emphasize that cognitive, physiological, and social-situational factors may together account for some of this behavior (Goldstein & Keller, 1987).

The major limitation of this perspective is the inadequate evidence showing personality characteristics of abusive parents to be the *primary* causal agents of child abuse. Goldstein, Keller, and Erné (1985, p. 24) state that "personality attributes of abusive parents even if found consistently with further research, do not seem to be sufficient to cause child maltreatment in the absence of other predisposing factors within the family and larger social systems." This is a reason for the development of another major theoretical model—one that attempts to explain the importance of societal norms, role models, and environmental stresses on parents.

Sociological Model

The sociological model, instead of focusing on the attributes of abusing parents, emphasizes the social context in which maltreatment occurs (Garbarino, 1977; Gil, 1970). To do otherwise merely "blames the victim" (Belsky, 1978). In particular, socioenvironmental factors such as societal norms and attitudes toward violence, socioeconomic status, unemployment, financial difficulties, housing and living conditions, family size, family structure, adolescent parenting, and social isolation are seen as major precipitating agents of the stress that leads to maltreatment (Gil, 1970; Kinard, 1978; Light, 1973).

This model also focuses on cumulative environmental stresses and their relationship to family isolation from social supports and community resources from inside or outside the family, and how all these factors are associated with child abuse. It has also been suggested that social isolation reduces the social controls that inhibit the use of violence in families (Giovannoni & Becerra, 1979). Some of the most compelling evidence in support of this model derives from studies linking unemployment, labor market shrinkage, and social isolation with child abuse and/or neglect.[2] According to this viewpoint, parents must be considered the victims of these social forces. The basic premise of the sociological model of child abuse is that in a society in which violence is rampant and frequently encouraged as a strategy for settling human relations disputes, in which children are regarded as property of their parents, and in which beliefs such as "spare the rod and spoil the child" are promulgated, the fact that parent–child conflict eventuates in child abuse should not be surprising. In essence the cultural soil is regarded as fertile when it comes to fostering the mistreatment of children (Belsky & Vondra, 1989, p. 155).

This conceptual framework, more than any other, discourages "blaming the victim." Although families and ultimately children, are the victims, the larger society is viewed as a major contributor to child abuse and neglect. Two essays have provided a scathing review of the societal trends regarding child maltreatment. Lloyd deMause (1988) has discussed the paradox of the 1970s and 1980s: that at the time of greatest public outcry against child abuse there was also widespread official planning to cut basic services to families ("the sacrifice of children" in public policy). Scheper-Hughes and Stein (1987) have added to this perspective by discussing how American society is more concerned with the morally clear-cut actions associated with punishing the "abusers" than focusing on the larger problem of child neglect and the lack of employment, housing, and other basic supports for families.

Garbarino and Hershberger (1981) have viewed this phenomenon from the perspective of "collective evil" in terms of institutional insensitivity and greed.

> We tolerate and even profit from the alienating and personally crushing aspects of American life. We permit people to be part of a socially defined *Lumpen proletariat,* the hard-core clients, so long as they don't make a public show of shocking or assaulting us. David Gil [1970, 1973] and Edward Zigler [1979] are two voices linking the mistreatment of children to evil in our social order. Their message is our message here: to protect children we must do more than cure individuals. (p. 212)

Social-Situational Model

Another theoretical perspective, the social-situational model, focuses not only on the characteristics of the abuser and the child but also on their interactional patterns. That is why this perspective has also been termed the "effect-of-the-child-on-the-caregiver" model, in particular because this model emphasizes the role the child's own behavior plays in determining the course of parent–child relations (Belsky & Vondra, 1989, p. 155).

Particular characteristics of the child, such as low birth weight, prematurity, physical or mental handicaps or illness, "temperamental incompatibility," and inappropriate child behaviors may place stress on parents and interfere with the development of a positive parent–child relationship (Friedrich & Einbender, 1983; Parke & Collmer, 1975):

> Evidence to suggest that children might be responsible for the mistreatment they experience comes from reports that a single child within a family is typically the recipient of abuse (Kadushin & Martin, 1981); that mistreated children exhibit deviations in social interaction and general functioning prior to their reported abuse (Starr, Dietrich, Fischhoff, Ceresnie, & Zweier, 1984); and that prematurity and low birthweight characterize the perinatal histories of a disproportionate number of abused children (Fontana, 1971; Klein & Stern, 1971; Martin, Conway, Breezley, & Kempe, 1974). (Belsky & Vondra, 1989, p. 155)

More often, it is the combination of a parent with certain traits with a particular child that may be at the root of the problem. In other words, "temperamental incompatibility" may be a problem. A colicky baby under the care of a hypersensitive parent may be at higher risk of maltreatment than one born to a more calm, less vigilant parent (Garbarino, 1980, p. 66). Children who need a more flexible parenting style that tolerates loud play may be at higher risk with a strong authoritarian parent. In addition, dysfunctional family dynamics may also be at work in some cases:

> Families involved in mistreatment appear to become enmeshed in patterns of interaction that reinforce whatever destructive elements are present in the family. Burgess & Conger (1978) found that families involved in mistreatment had half the level of overall interaction, twice the propensity to respond to negative behavior, and half the likelihood of responding to positive behavior than were similar families not involved in mistreatment. (Garbarino, 1980, p. 66)

Integrative or Ecological Models

Views of the child as a contributor to the occurrence of abuse have broadened recently to consider abuse as a sequence of interactions between parent and child that escalates into abuse (Burgess & Conger, 1978; Kadushin & Martin, 1981). Kinard (1987) suggests that regardless of whether the child manifests such special characteristics, if the parent perceives the child as different or difficult, that perception may increase the risk of maltreatment. This broader approach views child maltreatment as a multidimensional phenomenon resulting from the interaction of several elements: characteristics of the parent and the child, family interactional processes, family socioenvironmental stresses, and the larger community and societal contexts (Belksy & Vondra, 1989; Nasuti, 1990).

Another variation of this broader, more integrated approach was developed by Belsky (1980) based on an adaptation of Bronfenbrenner's (1979) ecological framework:

> While abusing parents enter the microsystem of the family with developmental histories that may predispose them to treat children in an abusive or neglectful manner (ontogenic development), stress-promoting forces both within the immediate family (the microsystem) and beyond it (the exosystem) increase the likelihood that parent–child conflict will occur. The fact that a parent's response to such conflict and stress takes the form of child maltreatment is seen to be a consequence both of the parent's own experience as a child (ontogenic development) and of the values and child-rearing practices that characterize the society or subculture in which the individual, family, and community are embedded [the macrosystem]. (Belsky, 1980, p. 33)

This model can best be illustrated by Figure 5.4 and it presumes that parenting

> is directly influenced by forces emanating from within the individual parent (personality), within the individual child (child characteristics of individuality), and from the broader social context in which the parent–child relationship is embedded— specifically the marital relations, social networks, and occupational experiences of parents. Further, the model assumes that parents' developmental histories, marital relations, social networks, and jobs influence their individual personalities and general

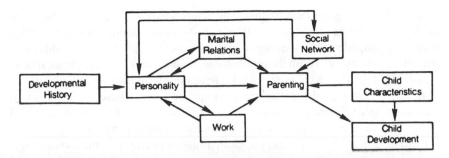

Figure 5.4.   The determinants of parenting: A process model.

psychological well-being and, thereby, parental functioning and, in turn, child development. (Belsky & Vondra, 1989, pp. 156–157)

Thus, although some of the major risk factors associated with special forms of maltreatment will be summarized in this chapter and Chapters 6 and 7, we believe that any one risk factor must be viewed within a broader ecological context. This perspective is also supported by some of the more sophisticated perspectives on risk assessment that recognize interactions among parent, child, and situation variables (e.g., Howing et al., 1989; Sedlak, 1991b). The preceding sections have presented the definition and incidence of the major forms of child maltreatment, and have described some of the processes of intake and CPS investigation in child welfare. The following sections of the chapter will present an overview of reporting rates and risk factors for physical abuse of children, highlight some of the major practice, policy, treatment, and evaluation issues related to physical abuse. Readers, however, are cautioned that the definition and causal factors—let alone treatment or prevention—of physical abuse is extremely complex, and space limitations preclude in-depth discussion of any one topic.

PHYSICAL ABUSE

Definition and Reporting Rates of Physical Abuse: General

In terms of incidence and reporting rates, this chapter will draw from the federal NCANDS database of state reports and from statistics from the NIS-3 study that is described in Appendix A. Although nearly all states adhere to the basic definitions of child maltreatment provided in the Child Abuse and Neglect Prevention and Treatment Act (as amended), individual state definitions reflect the their own state laws and service emphases. Furthermore, law enforcement, education, medical, and mental health allied professionals may hold different views and apply slightly different definitions, not only within, but between states.

As might be imagined there are many difficulties in defining physical abuse. Do we define it in terms of injuries sustained? Or do we also include violent acts that could have but did not cause injury (e.g., a hurled chair that missed a child)? Victims suffer either way—from the psychological impact and from the physical blow (Straus, 1991, p. 19). In contrast, what is "legitimate" violence? Corporal punishment may be sanctioned, but slapping your spouse is not. These are just a few of the serious issues that need to be addressed by researchers, CPS workers, and staff members of law enforcement and family violence-related agencies.

One strength of the NIS studies of child abuse, however, was the use of operational definitions of various types of child maltreatment, so that reporting would be more consistent across the national data collection sites. These definitions will be used in each of the sections to describe a particular form of child maltreatment (e.g., physical abuse, neglect). In addition, the projected number of reported cases nationally are provided.

Definitions and Reporting Rates: Physical Abuse

Physical abuse has been defined generally as nonaccidental injury inflicted by a caretaker. The severity of the injury in relation to what is categorized as abusive may vary according to different community or societal contexts. In other words, in the United States, there remains a "gray area" in which decision-making practice may vary: some cultures believe in severe corporal punishment that may leave welts and bruises for a few days. If carried out within the context of a loving parent–child relationship, when does this behavior constitute physical child abuse? In contrast, sometimes certain ethnic medical practices are not child maltreatment, but to the uninformed may appear to result from abuse. For example, pinching a child's forehead or rubbing a child's chest with heated coins that produce bruise-like marks are both viewed by some Asian cultures as a form of healing. Thus the definition of physical abuse is not precise and the incidence statistics for this and other types of maltreatment should be viewed with caution.

A total of 197,557 children were physically abused in 1997. For the NIS-3 study the estimate was 381,700 under the harm standard and 614,100 under the endangerment standard for a total projection of 614,180 cases in 1986 (see Note 1 for information about the different standards) (Sedlak, & Broadhurst, 1999, p. 8).

A special form of physical child abuse has been identified that deserves special attention, even though it may be clustered within the NIS-3 and other definitions—"Munchausen by proxy syndrome." This form of maltreatment is characterized by subjecting children to medications, surgery, and other medical procedures for which there is no justification (Meadow, 1985; Shnaps, Frand, Rotem, & Trosh, 1981). This is a relatively rare but dangerous form of maltreatment in that some children have died from poisons or injections administered to them by one or both parents.

Spousal Abuse as a Correlate with Child Abuse

It is not uncommon for there to be spousal abuse occurring at the same time a child is being maltreated, particularly if physical child abuse is being committed:

> The scene is the emergency room of a major children's hospital. This evening, like so many before, and so many that would follow, the staff is hovering over a suspected case of child abuse. A three-year-old boy is being examined. He has a number of cuts and abrasions, but what catches everyone's attention is the outline of a hand on the side of his face. A young intern suddenly turns to the boy's mother and yells at her. "How could you do this?" he begins, until he finally concludes, "I will see that your child is taken away from you and this will never happen again!"
>
> The senior social worker on duty moves in and takes the young physician aside. Beginning with the obvious statement, "You seem to be upset," the social worker then asks the intern if he can describe the mother. "Tell me what she looks like," the social worker asks. The physician, a little calmer, could offer only the briefest description. "Come back with me," the social worker offers, and they return again to the mother and the child. "How did you lose your front teeth?" the social worker asks the mother. "Oh, my husband knocked them out last week," the mother replies in a flat, emotionless tone. Turning to the intern, the social worker notes, "You have two victims here." (Gelles & Cornell, 1985, p. 64)

Family violence is a major social problem that, until relatively recently, was basically ignored by the child welfare, medical, and law enforcement fields (Mullender, 1996). It is a program area in which sensitivity to cultural issues are only recently being attended to (Agnetu, 1998). Contrary to the notion that the family is a "haven in a heartless world," the home is a violent place. Within families, killings account for about 25% of all homicides. In Canada, the figure is about 50%. The U.S. rate is comparatively low because of the huge number of homicides we experience as a country every year (Straus, 1986, as cited in Straus, 1991, p. 20; also see Herzberger, 1996).

A national survey in 1985 of 6,002 currently married or cohabiting couples revealed that 16 of every 100 couples reported a violent incident during the year of the survey. The definition of violence was "an act carried out with the intention or perceived intention of causing physical pain or injury to another person" (Gelles & Straus, 1979, p. 554). This is a conservative estimate, yet it is projected that 3.4 million of these incidents were "severe" assaults such as kicking, punching, choking, or use of weapons (Straus, 1991, pp. 21–22).

The *prevalence* rates are even higher as they estimate "the proportions of couples who, *over the course of the marriage,* experienced a violent altercation" (Straus, 1991, p. 21). The most conservative estimate is 30%, with an estimate of 60% plausible because violent events may be forgotten, particularly if they occurred only once and at some time in the past. Unfortunately, when wife abuse occurs, violent events are committed on an average of about five times per year. With shelter populations, the rate dramatically increases to about 60 assaults per year (Giles-Sims, 1983; Okun, 1986, as cited in Straus, 1991, p. 23). In addition, these statistics often do not include physical violence committed against women by their husbands to force them to have sex with them (Finkelhor & Yllo, 1982; Russell, 1980, as cited in Gelles & Cornell, 1985, p. 70).

Research on the Link between Spousal Abuse
and Child Abuse[3]

When spousal abuse occurs in the home, children may witness the violence, may be injured in the course of a spousal assault, or may become targets for victimization themselves. Prior research into this topic points to increased likelihood of child abuse in cases in which spousal abuse is present (e.g., Edelson, 1999; Ross, 1996; Straus & Smith, 1990). As Belsky observed, "Since the parent–child system (the crucible of child maltreatment) is nested within the spousal relationship, what happens between husbands and wives—from an ecological point of view—has implications for what happens between parents and their children" (1980, p. 326).

Much of the early literature on the link between spousal abuse and child abuse focuses on the impact of witnessing spousal assault on emotional, behavioral, and school problems in children (e.g., Hershorn & Rosenbaum, 1985; Hughes, Parkinson, & Vargo, 1989; Holden & Ritchie, 1991; Sudemann & Jaffe, 1997). Findings indicate that children of maritally violent homes have more internalizing and externalizing behavior problems than those in nonviolent homes, with the greatest distress reported by abused children who also witnessed domestic violence (termed the "double whammy") (Hughes, 1988). Factors such as age, coping style, and severity of the violence witnessed mediate the effects on a given child. However, as Sudemann and Jaffe (1997) report, many children present full-blown symptoms of posttraumatic stress disorder after witnessing violence.

Many studies on the relationship between woman abuse and child abuse rely on nonrepresentative samples such as residents of battered women's shelters (e.g., O'Keefe, 1994; Giles-Sims, 1985; Holden & Ritchie, 1991). Clinical studies indicate that between 40 and 70% of men who batter their partners also abuse their children (40%, O'Keefe, 1994; 63%, Giles-Sims, 1985; 70%, Bowker et al., 1998), while rates of abuse committed by battered women reportedly range from 44% (O'Keefe, 1994) and 45% (Stacey & Shupe, 1983) to 55.6% (Giles-Sims, 1985). (Tajima, 1999).

Contributing Factors to Physical Child Abuse

As discussed earlier in this chapter, it is difficult to say definitively what set of factors "causes" a parent to physically maltreat their child in some way. The conceptual framework employed to a great degree can influence what causal factors are most emphasized and what prevention or treatment strategies are selected. For example, if you place emphasis on the psychiatric or psychological model, then you might look at the presence of certain personality traits in the parents.

A cognitive–behavioral approach might lead one to examine whether a lack of certain skills may be contributing to the situation. More specifically, for some parents it is a lack of knowledge regarding approaches to parenting that results in their inability to manage the child's behavior. Their frustration may build in the absence of other social supports and this situation may result in an angry outburst that injures the child. What may be a factor is that the parent might have been disciplined in a severe manner as a child, with no exposure to healthy role models for parenting (see Note 2). A lack of anger management skills may be one of the main contributors for another parent who lashes out at his or her child. For others, it is an attitude that children have no inherent rights; therefore, they can be treated as mere property.

A sociological approach would encourage a social worker to also look for environmental stressors and cultural determinants that may be interacting to produce abusive behaviors. What is the immediate home environment like? Is spousal abuse present? Is violence pervasive in the neighborhood and viewed as an acceptable means of settling differences? Is the family a member of a culture in which the use of severe corporal punishment is viewed as part of being a "responsible"parent?

The more integrative or ecological approaches would build on these two important perspectives by looking at the interactions of these and other factors as they may contribute to a situation in which physical abuse is more likely to occur. As part of this approach, the worker might examine how finances, child characteristics, parenting knowledge and skills, household routines, social supports, neighborhood characteristics, and other factors may increase or lower the risk of physical abuse. This approach might draw from some of the research literature summarized in Table 5.4 to assess the family.

In reality, a considerable number of the factors that predict risk of physical abuse act in an interactive or nonlinear manner (see Table 5.4). For example, an analysis of the National Incidence Study (NIS-2) data found that the age of the child was systematically related to the risk of being physically abused, but that the nature of the relationship depended on the child's race/ethnicity and family structure. Compared with white children, black/Hispanic children were more likely to be maltreated as they increased in age beyond 8 years old if both parents were present, family income was less than $15,000, and there was only one child in the household. Furthermore, in general, the relationship between family structure and risk of physical abuse was not linear in that children from one-child families *and* children from families with four or more children were at higher risk than children from families with two or three children (Sedlak, 1991b, Chapter 3) (see Note 2).

These findings also question the appropriateness of viewing single-parent families as automatically high risk, as evidenced by their inclusion in risk matrices in the high-risk categories, and in terms of the attitudes that seem so prevalent in the

Table 5.4. Selected Risk Factors for Physical Abuse Categorized by Force Field

Child

- Developmental or physical disability (Diamond & Jaudes, 1983; Gabinet, 1983; Zigler, 1979)
- Premature birth and/or difficult prenatal or perinatal period (Hunter, Kilstrom, Kraybill, & Loda, 1978; Klein & Stern, 1971)
- Child level of behavior difficulty or misconduct (Kadushin & Martin, 1981; Reid, Taplin, & Lorber, 1981; Stratton, 1985)
- Child was placed previously

Parent

- Inadequate knowledge of child care, unrealistic expectations of the child (Johnson & L'Esperance, 1984)
- One or more caretakers view the child as "evil," "bad," or otherwise unwanted (Bakan, 1971)
- Substance abuse (Bradford & McCleon, 1984; Fein, 1979; Pierce & Pierce, 1984).
- Parents maltreated as children (Deighton & McPeek, 1985; Hunter et al. 1978) (see Note 2 however.)
- Young mother (Anderson, Ambrosino, Valentine, & Lauderdale, 1983; Miller, 1985).

Family

- Low family income (Garbarino, 1976; Giovannoni & Billingsley, 1970; Sedlak, 1991a)
- Marital conflict (Goode, 1961)
- Domestic violence
- Isolation from relatives, friends, or other social support systems (Salzinger, Kaplan, & Artemyeff, 1983; Wahler, 1980)

Maltreatment (this refers more to the likelihood of further maltreatment)

- Multiple bruises, lacerations, or broken bones are present (degree of severity)
- Cruel or premeditated maltreatment (surrounding circumstances)
- Frequent and multiple forms of maltreatment, or abuse has been occurring for a long time (extent of maltreatment)
- Precipitous rather than patterned maltreatment (ability to predict when maltreatment occurs) (Barth & Blythe, 1983; Kadushin & Martin, 1981)

Intervention

- Low parental cooperation or motivation to change their behavior
- Unavailability and/or low accessibility of necessary services in the community (e.g., homemaker, mental health, crisis nursery)
- Nonoffending parent is unwilling to protect the child from abuse
- Lack of necessary informal support systems (Wahler, 1980)

professional and nonprofessional communities currently. Recent graphs of the NIS-2 data indicate that risk of physical abuse increases as the age of the child increases for two-parent households, compared to very slight or nonexistent increases for one-parent households.

For physical abuse, it appears that the single-parent stereotype as a high-risk category may need to be reexamined given these results. In addition, in examining the types of children underserved by CPS agencies, greater numbers of children from two-parent families were not being served. For physical neglect, it was interesting that older aged children from father-only and two-parent homes were at higher risk (Sedlak, 1991b, Chapters 3 and 4). The bottom line is that being a single parent should be a risk factor, but possibly more because of its relation to other variables such as degree of social support, family income, positive parenting role models, and other variables (see Table 5.4). In fact, family income is increasingly being recognized as one of the most important factors contributing to all kinds of child maltreatment (Pelton, 1989). Yet various risk assessment models and intervention frameworks often fail to take the power of this factor into account (Sedlak, 1991b).

Protective Factors and Children at Risk

One promising approach that takes a different perspective compared to examining risk factors is to study what "protective" factors help a child avoid or successfully cope with various kinds of child maltreatment; Rutter (1985) defines "protective factors" as those "influences that modify, ameliorate, or alter a person's response to some environmental hazard that predisposes him/her to maladaptive outcome." Examples of general protective factors include "rapid responsivity to danger," "the conviction of being loved," and an attitude of "optimism and hope."

For children of color, in particular, some of the research is beginning to show that factors such as having an "active extended family of fictive or blood relatives," "religious affiliation," and "biculturalism" (has values and beliefs in at least two cultures, knows when to use which behaviors) are important (Hodges, 1991). This is a fascinating and worthwhile approach to prevention and treatment of child maltreatment because the focus is on building child, family, and community strengths.

TREATMENT OF PHYSICAL ABUSE

General Observations

One of the fundamental treatment principles related to physical child abuse is to recognize that it often occurs within a context of *family* violence, where one spouse (often the father or boyfriend) is physically abusing the mother. As mentioned earlier in this chapter, to prevent or treat child abuse, the conditions that promote this type of interpersonal violence must be addressed as well. Similarly, no one treatment approach will be universally effective for all types of child maltreatment, let alone physical abuse specifically. For some parents, their expectations may be totally unrealistic with respect to a child's crying behavior, eating difficulties, or toilet training. Educational and supportive approaches may then be most effective, possibly supplemented with counseling and training to increase parental empathy (e.g., Cameron & Vanderwoerd, 1997; Wiehe, 1997). In contrast, living conditions in some families may be so impoverished that food, clothing, and utilities may need to be provided at the same time as counseling to reduce the anxiety or stress levels of the parents. Effective treatment for some parents may require a blend of intensive in-home services (see Chapters 10 and 11) as well as some office-based groupwork to build social support networks.[4]

So although the broad-based changes in community development and societal support are important on one level, direct intervention with parents as early as possible as summarized by Daro (1988, p. 129) is also essential:

> Programs offering instruction in specific parenting skills such as discipline methods, basic child care, and infant stimulation; child development education; familiarity with local support services; and linkages to other new parents in the community address a number of interpersonal and situational difficulties which are precursors to abusive and neglectful behavior. While the content and structure of these programs vary, ranging from in-home visitor programs to center-based services, the most effective of these efforts include the following service goals:
>
> - increasing the parent's knowledge of child development and the demands of parenting;
> - enhancing the parent's skill in coping with the stresses of infant and child care;
> - enhancing parent–child bonding, emotional ties, and communication;
> - increasing the parent's kills in coping with the stress of caring for children with special needs;
> - increasing the parent's knowledge about home and child management;
> - reducing the burden of child care; and
> - increasing access to social and health services for all family members. (Cohn, 1983)

Building Anger Management and Self-Control Skills

The social-situational and ecological models both suggest that many environmental stressors such as unemployment, crowded living space, children that are difficult to care for, and other factors all may act to increase the likelihood of anger and aggression. There are a variety of strategies for addressing these problems, including reinforcement of incompatible nonangry responses, modeling and role-playing of nonangry reactions, relaxation, systematic desensitization in the presence of the anger-evoking situations, and cognitive–behavioral strategies, including stress inoculation, thought-stopping, and self-control (Borrego, Urguiza, Rasmusser, & Zebell, 1999; Goldstein, Keller, & Erné, 1985, p. 32).

Some of these treatment methods have been recently incorporated into an intervention sequence that uses a broad social-situational approach consisting of the following:

- Anger control training
- Relaxation training
- Communication training
- Negotiation training

- Contracting
- Contingency management training
- Prosocial skill training
- Prosocial values training (Goldstein & Keller, 1987).

Although this treatment approach demands both assessment and intervention skills, it has been succinctly described by Goldstein and Keller (1987, pp. 4–5). An aggressive act begins, in their view, with a stimulus event and its interpretation as aversive by an individual. This "trigger" is accompanied or followed by kinesthetic and other physiological cues that idiosyncratically signal "anger" to the person, and result in heightened levels of certain feelings. These two initial stages of the aggressive behavior sequence may be effectively controlled by the parent by two main strategies: (1) anger control training aimed at reducing anger-arousing self-statements, and (2) relaxation training to counteract the physiological cues of anger arousal. Both procedures, therefore, seek to short-circuit the aggressive behavior sequence via interventions early in its development.

However, Goldstein and Keller (1987) point out that aggression is most typically a dyadic event, with the aggressor and aggressee reversing roles and spiraling upward in an escalating conflict. This is particularly true for some forms of adolescent maltreatment. To be effective, aggression reduction efforts must include not only methods for aiding the parent in efforts to reduce his or her own anger level, but also in how to do likewise for the child. A series of calming techniques can be useful for this purpose. Armed with such techniques, individuals are better prepared to lower the anger arousal level of their children, and move on to more constructive means for conflict reduction: communication, negotiation, and contract training. In effect, having begun to control undesirable behaviors, the individual can proceed to master desirable alternative responses that are focused on communication processes.

Other reliable means exist for accelerating desirable behaviors and decelerating undesirable ones:

> Means for both providing and withdrawing contingent reinforcement, as well as for providing aversive contingencies, will be examined. These several contingency management approaches to aggressive behavior each assume that desirable, prosocial alternative behaviors exist in the individual's behavioral repertoire, but are rarely expressed overtly. A rather different perspective on prosocial behavior, following from a behavior deficit model, holds quite the contrary that prosocial behaviors may be rarely expressed by an individual because he/she literally does not know how to do so. Such behaviors, in this view, are weak or lacking in the person's repertoire and must be taught quite directly. Prosocial skill training . . . will be examined for this purpose. (Goldstein & Keller, 1987, p. 5)

However, a person may be competent in controlling his or her anger, reducing others' anger, communicating effectively with others, and so forth, but may still *choose* to behave in an aggressive manner. Consequently, underlying values may

also have to be altered, particularly those concerned with the needs and perspective of others. Moral education can be designed explicitly for this purpose (see
Goldstein & Keller, 1987, Chapters 8 and 9). What distinguishes this approach, besides the well-designed interventions, is the attention paid to transferring the learning to a variety of abuse-evolving situations and the strategies being developed for
maintenance of the cognitive, emotional, and behavioral gains made during the
initial treatment.

Other Treatment Approaches

As mentioned earlier, different clusters of risk factors often require different combinations of interventions. Substance abuse treatment may be a first step for some
parents, while in many cases child management training, increasing prosocial child
behaviors, and teaching alternatives to physical punishment may also be necessary.

PROGRAM CHALLENGES

Preventing or treating physical abuse demands skill and perseverance because of
the complexities of many abusive situations, the inability of any one treatment
modality to be used for every family, and the lack of guidelines from interventive
research. Just a few of the other major challenges are highlighted below.

Protecting Children from Abuse by the System

The child protection field has not done well in protecting victims of child maltreatment from further *emotional* abuse in that frequently multiple investigative interviews are conducted without sufficient coordination, interviewers are not
trained sufficiently, and prosecutory requirements often subject children to insensitive medical or psychological examinations and emotionally upsetting cross-
examination. Child welfare, law enforcement, family court, and criminal court personnel have much work to do to help ensure that children are treated with sensitivity, and yet the individual rights of those accused are adequately protected (see,
for example, Dziech & Schrelson, 1991).

False Allegations

There is increasing concern on the part of citizens and certain professionals that
persons accused of sexual or physical abuse are not being treated fairly (Schultz,
1988), or may be the victim of false allegations by children or adolescents. Although there are ample reasons to cautiously investigate all reports of child mal-

treatment because of this possibility, the bulk of the evidence indicates that in the vast majority of cases children are reporting the essential facts (see, for example, Robin, 1991).

Conflicting Roles in CPS

CPS workers have been concerned for some time about how their authority to place children (with judicial or law enforcement authorization) conflicts with their other major role of counseling the parents and children (Whitman, 1919, as cited in Anderson, 1989, p. 228, Costin, Karger, & Stoez, 1996). Complaints from CPS experts that the field has placed too much emphasis on the investigative and law enforcement activities echo criticism of one of the earliest studies of CPS services, where the author of the report was assailed for placing too little emphasis on the treatment aspects of the work. "Scientific casework . . . is just as applicable to all types of cases coming before a protective agency as it is to child-placing or institutional work" (Williamson, 1931, p. 387, as cited in Anderson, 1989, p. 232).

Unfortunately, community pressure to prosecute sexual abuse and serious cases of physical abuse has resulted in new pressures to collect certain types of evidence during the investigation that will assist law enforcement personnel and local prosecutors. Many leaders in the CPS field are concerned that the basic helping functions of CPS are being undermined by the demands of allied agencies. Program advocates and social work leaders are calling for a reemphasis on promoting child development through a variety of prevention and family support programs in child welfare, rather than being overly concerned about risk assessment and gathering evidence for courtwork. Indeed, some advocates are calling for a clear demarcation of tasks, with law enforcement assigned the task of investigation, and caseworkers in child welfare focused more on helping the family through concrete and clinical services (Corey & Holder, 1986; Pelton, 1991; Waldfogel, 1998).

Lack of Intervention Research

The field has a long way to go in terms of evaluating (Oates & Bross, 1995) and then refining the range of interventions so that parenting skills and other gains made in treatment are maintained and recidivism rates of between 30 and 50% are reduced (see, for example, Cohn, 1979, p. 518). Long-term follow-up studies of sexual abusers are particularly needed to answer a variety of questions about why adults molest children and the efficacy of various treatment modalities (Finkelhor, 1986, pp. 136–142).

In light of the critical decisions that are made in child welfare intake and CPS, it is surprising that so few intervention-oriented research studies have been funded by the federal government and other organizations. Studies using methodologically sophisticated designs, rigorous statistical analyses, or careful qualitative research approaches are still few in number, despite the following critical questions facing the field: What are the most critical determinants of various types of child maltreatment? What treatment approaches have the lowest recidivism rates? How can informal support networks be used most effectively in treatment? Under what conditions can substance- abusing parents be helped while leaving children in the home? Yet as future chapters will describe, there is a body of intervention technology to implement, including some growing clarity about the key CPS decisions to be made (Wilson & Morton, 1997, p. 13).

Clearly, politics have played an important role in limiting the availability of funds for addressing these and other pressing issues. But the availability of trained researchers in this field is not great, and will remain small without educational stipends and research grants to encourage doctoral students in social work and psychology to focus on these areas in their training. In addition, public and private child welfare agencies need to be involved in agency-based research projects to test out different assessment and intervention models that will yield the most gain for the funds invested (Morton & Holder, 1999). However, a growing body of research-based practice wisdom is emerging (e.g., Briere, Berliner, Bulkley, Jenny, & Reid, 1996; Panel on Child Abuse and Neglect, 1993; Waldfogel, 1998).

Workload Standards

Service delivery standards in child protection were first adopted in 1931 by the American Humane Association (AHA; National Humane Review, 1931, as cited in Anderson, 1989) and in 1936 by the Child Welfare League of America (CWLA, 1937). More recent standards emphasize increasing the availability of ancillary services and setting more reasonable caseloads: 12–14 cases per worker (CWLA, 1989a, p. 52) or 20–25 families (National Association of Social Workers, 1981a). Strengthening hiring standards, with respect to educational preparation, and improving worker training are also being advocated.

Due to worker turnover, poor working conditions, high caseloads, and a number of other factors, there remains a shortage of treatment personnel able to use specialized skills in working with maltreatment parents. The landmark research conducted by Berkeley Planning Associates in the late 1970s found that protection of children while they were in treatment was most strongly associated with the utilization of highly trained professionals during the intake and treatment planning phases. In terms of treatment it was a blend of professional, paraprofessional, and Parents Anonymous services that was most effective in reducing parent propensity to reabuse (Cohn, 1983, pp. 518–519).

Because of a variety of reasons, CPS reports have been steadily increasing while agency funding has not increased at nearly the same rate. Caseloads in most agencies are too high, and in some states, CPS caseloads for investigation or supervision are over 45 cases per worker, preventing any form of professional casework to be carried out. Many child welfare administrators are reluctant to set firm standards, in part because they are mandated by law to respond to all credible referrals. Legislators resist supporting agency operating procedures where staffing levels are tied to caseload size, with increases mandated as caseloads increase. Thus it might be viewed as fortunate that some of the consent decrees emanating from class action suits in over nine states are establishing court-imposed service standards on many child welfare agencies, which have implications for caseload size, worker training, and other program components (American Public Welfare Association, 1991; Stein, 1987). If staff turnover and service quality are to increase in child welfare, and CPS in particular, caseload limits must be implemented (see Chapter 14).

Agency and Worker Liability

CPS staff members have been justifiably concerned about the increasing number of lawsuits brought against them and their agencies. Implementation of risk assessment systems in and of themselves will not address this situation, and in fact may make matters worse. Without high-quality training, reasonable caseloads, and consistent professional supervision, the new risk assessment procedures will not be implemented adequately because the best risk assessment systems require a rather specific set of investigation actions, supervisory review, and careful documentation of decisions. As the specificity of the casework protocols increases, so does the agency vulnerability to lawsuits, particularly if worker training, supervision, and other program requisites are not in place. Yet experts have stated that sound casework practice is the agency's best approach to minimizing liability, along with promoting good working relationships with clients (see Chapter 14 and Holder & Hayes, 1984).

RECOMMENDATIONS FOR CPS PROGRAM IMPROVEMENT

Overview

Waldfogel (1998) analyzed the current child protection system and argues for revamping it. The centerpiece of her proposal is a *differential response paradigm* for child protection consisting of the following central features:

- a *customized response to families,* built on the availability of skilled social workers who are capable of functioning autonomously;
- a *community-based system of child protection,* in which frontline workers have access to services that cross agency lines and the boundaries between the public and private sectors; and
- a *larger role for informal and natural helpers,* based on assessment of the family's needs and available resources.

The above paradigm explicitly recognizes the diversity and complexity of families coming to the attention of child protection agencies. Furthermore, in contrast to current approaches, "It sees child protection as the responsibility of the local community, as well as the state" (Waldfogel, 1998, p. 138). Public agencies would be responsible for child protection "in collaboration with a broad range of community partners, including formal resources such as police, other public agencies, private agencies, and informal sources of help such as neighborhood and associations, congregations, and families themselves" (Waldfogel, 1998, p. 138). Additional recommendations for improving CPS are listed below. But a major reform effort that merits consideration are the efforts underway to build community partnerships to improve the protection of children through strengthened families:

> rather than one agency—the public child protective services agency—bearing sole responsibility for protecting children, a broader array of parents, public and private agencies, organization, and individuals should join together to carry out this fundamental public responsibility. The hearts of this improved system is a community partnership for child protection. (Farrow with The Executive Session on Child Protection, 1997, p. vii).

Developing and implementing these partnerships may differ in terms of starting points and the degree and pace of change; but there are a number of key factors involved in the reform process:

1. *Agreeing on the direction for change.* Reaching out to the public makes it more likely that the partnership will be accepted and sustained. An essential first step for CPS administrators, legislators, and other policy makers is to recognize that the CPS agency alone cannot successfully protect children.

2. *Starting the partnerships.* Partners should include all the people and organizations in a community that are required to keep children safe. Chief among these are parents. And although all partners are important, protecting children requires that schools, substance abuse prevention and treatment providers, the police, domestic violence service providers, and welfare services be part of this new agency from the start. Broader public consensus is needed regarding goals and public responsibilities for child protection. If CPS is to be effective, state legislature must establish clear, manageable, and stable parameters for it and provide resources befitting the responsibilities assigned.

3. *Creating differential responses to the varied needs of families for child protection.* Government's responsibility to protect children from abuse and neglect requires long-term steps to reduce family poverty. In the short term, child protection and welfare reform caseworkers should collaborate to ensure that children and adults benefit from welfare reform and are not jeopardized by deep poverty. CPS agencies must be able to respond to children's safety needs in a way that makes sense for each situation. When abuse and neglect are severe, and coercive services and an investigation are essential, cases are assigned to an "investigative" track.

However, when children are not at immediate risk and families will benefit from voluntary services, needs can be met through a second track that emphasizes a comprehensive assessment of family strengths and needs. For example, flexible funds are essential to address urgent child needs and remedy family problems. At state and national levels, noncategorical funding streams allow communities to establish the array of services vulnerable families need. At the local level, reserves of unrestricted funds enable CPS caseworkers to respond promptly to pressing needs. Because informal community ties and kin can help prevent and respond to child abuse and neglect, government agencies should include informal resources in case planning, and link informal helpers to professional service systems and financial resources.

4. *Developing comprehensive neighborhood-based supports and services.* Effective neighborhood-based services require the use of family networks, friends, and other informal supports, the commitment of a wider array of formal services, and a willingness to change the way public services are now organized. Drawing on family networks and other informal resources is as important as expanding formal services. These networks, often including friends, relatives, and neighbors, are closer to and more trusted by struggling families than are most traditional formal services. Equally important is the need to reorganize service delivery. Moving services into neighborhoods and creating teams of public agencies and community resources make services more accessible. Having a community partnership for child protection that focuses on each specific community builds bonds of accountability, trust, and knowledge between service providers and community residents.

5. *Transforming public child protection agency services.* CPS agencies must change their internal policies and practices while playing a leadership role in creating and sustaining the community partnership. The mainstays of practice become (a) using more comprehensive assessments, (b) engaging families and natural networks of support, (c) understanding the dynamics of substance abuse, domestic violence, and other risks to children, and (d) teaming with colleagues in other systems and the community.

In addition, to improve case-by-case decision making in CPS, agencies should raise training and professional qualifications for caseworkers. Legislatures should provide the funds required to allow CPS agencies to make their pay scales professional and competitive. The AHA standards in 1951 required a master's degree (AHA, 1951, pp. 6–7, as cited in Anderson, 1989, p. 231). More recent standards for CPS recommend that child welfare administrators and supervisors should have a master's degree in social work and previous child welfare experience. A number of states require that CPS workers have a minimum of a bachelor's degree in social work or one of the closely related social sciences, in addition to specialized agency training. Attracting these professionally trained persons to public child welfare agencies, however, remains a challenge, due to low salaries and poor working conditions in some states. Unfortunately, this problem is not being systematically addressed, as studies have found that most child welfare and CPS workers do not have professional social work training or master's degrees in other job-related areas such as clinical psychology (Shyne & Schroeder, 1978; Russell, 1987).

Specialized training for CPS workers, however, has received renewed attention in the past 10 years. Many states are implementing CPS training academies (modeled after police academies) or "certification" programs to better prepare newly hired and veteran CPS staff. There are a variety of factors promoting these developments, including the fact that CPS is becoming more of a specialized endeavor, with a growing technological base and a higher proportion of serious cases being reported. A continuing high rate of worker turnover and the hiring of people without specialized educational backgrounds represent additional factors. Finally, class action lawsuits are also resulting in greater state support of training and caseload reductions (Stein, 1987).

Existing knowledge regarding child maltreatment and intervention effectiveness must be translated into operational guidelines for staff. New research should be funded to fill knowledge gaps, resolve inconsistencies, link interventions to child and family outcomes, and show how caseworkers use knowledge. To guide case planning, evaluations of interventions for abusive and neglectful families should identify the effects of specific services on families with differing risk profiles.

6. *Shifting intake and follow-on services for lower risk cases to a community-based system.* A well-established community partnership for child protection creates the possibility that some of the families now served by the CPS agency may be served by other members of the community partnership, without formal CPS involvement. This reduces the workload that is now overwhelming CPS agencies.

7. I*nstituting community governance and accountability for protecting children.* Even as communities begin to build partnerships, they must ensure clear responsibility for the safety of children, for the effectiveness of the system as a whole, and for generating and acting on data produced for the purposes of accountability. As partnerships mature, they may organize formal boards that assume responsibility for keeping children safe (abstracted from Farrow with The Executive Session and Child Protection, 1997, pp. viii–x; Larner, Stevenson, & Behrman, 1998, pp. 4–21).

Definitions and Statistics

Because of a lack of federal leadership, funding, and variations in state reporting, there is a paucity of accurate data regarding the incidence and prevalence of child maltreatment in the United States. Although a number of organizations and researchers have been making progress in this area, much more work must be undertaken to develop better definitions of various forms of maltreatment and, at the same time, be sensitive to various cultural differences in the country.

Implement More Culturally Sensitive
Child Protection Services

The reanalyses of the NIS-2 data revealed that the older black children became, the less likely they were to be reported to CPS or investigated by CPS for service compared to white, Hispanic, and other groups, even when their circumstances merited such action (Sedlak, 1991a, Chapter 2). The pattern remained, even when other characteristics such as gender, household composition, and severity of injury were entered as part of the multivariate equations.

This underreporting or selective screening of black teenagers merits further study. Is this another indication of continuing institutional racism that is played out through a discounting of the safety needs of black children? For example, severe corporal punishment by black parents that is, in fact, abusive may be viewed by largely white, culturally uninformed reporters and investigators as merely a culturally appropriate form of corporal punishment.

Conversely, part of the effect may be due to differences in the criteria used by the reporter versus those staff members responsible for conducting the investigations (see Appendix A). Forms of corporal punishment that are thought to be abusive by largely white, culturally uninformed citizens and professionals may, on reporting, be recognized as within the realm of allowable corporal punishment by CPS staff members. In addition, there were also a large number of white adolescents who were estimated to be underserved in the NIS-2 report (Sedlak, 1991a, Chapter 5).

Although the erroneous referral process described above may be occurring with a small number of cases, differential referral and service delivery patterns may actually account for the majority of this phenomenon. Older black teenagers may be viewed as less important to society and less worthy of services as they grow older. This finding may help explain some of the manifestations of racism in the United States and partially explain the huge rates of black teenage unemployment across this country. For CPS administrators, it certainly merits careful study of referral patterns and a determination of the extent to which certain groups of children are not receiving services to which they are entitled.

Devote More Attention to Adolescent Victims

It was not until the 1970s that maltreatment of adolescents was recognized by the helping professions as a distinct category, and they remain an underserved group. Risk factors and family dynamics may differ from younger children. Prevention and treatment strategies therefore need to be tailored according to the adolescent's developmental level, type of maltreatment, and other factors (for reviews, see Derezotes & Barth, 1990; Doueck, Ishisaka, Sweany, & Gilchrist, 1987).

CONCLUSION

Despite the problems in definition and data collection, some facts and trends can be noted. Conservative estimates of child maltreatment indicate that over two million cases become known to community agencies and child welfare personnel each year. The number of actual cases is probably higher due to the existence of cases known to other agencies and knowledgeable individuals. We also know that child maltreatment is not found just among low income families (although their lack of income increases their risk). Yet part of the increased risk for ethnic-minority families is the heightened societal monitoring of their parenting, along with an increased level of erroneous reporting (Gelles, 1987, p. 22).

In 1999, the U.S. Children's Bureau noted an overall decline in the rate of increase in reporting for many states compared to the tremendous increases found in the 1970s and early 1980s (U.S. Department of Health and Human Services, 1999). Nevertheless, over the past decades the steady increases in the number of reported and substantiated cases, without a concomitant increase in staff and other resources, has placed a huge burden on child welfare agencies, particularly for those cases involving serious physical abuse or chronic physical neglect.

In addition, cases are more complex, particularly with respect to the service coordination required. For example, the number of substantiated cases of sexual abuse has been increasing. These cases require huge amounts of worker time to handle sensitively. Workers must collaborate with law enforcement officials, medical personnel, and other professional staff. It is ironic (and tragic) that child welfare agencies have been overwhelmed by increases in child maltreatment reports and budget cuts at a time when our knowledge of both prevention and treatment programs has substantially increased.

In Chapters 6 and 7, issues regarding the specific prevalence, and etiology, treatment of sexual abuse, neglect, and psychological maltreatment will be discussed.

NOTES

1.   The 1993 NCCAN National Incidence Study (NIS-2) was similar in many respects to those conducted in 1986 and 1980, but a major difference between the two earlier studies was that data for the 1986 study included two major types of cases that were tabulated separately: (1) where demonstrable harm to a child occurred and (2) where the child's health and safety were endangered through abusive or neglectful treatment. For a summary of these and other differences in the two NCCAN studies, see NCCAN (1988, pp. 4-1–4-4). The definitional standards used in the NIS-3 were identical to those used in the NIS-2. These standards imposed a number of requirements, including the restriction that the abuse or neglect be within the jurisdiction of CPS (i.e., perpetrated or permitted by a parent or caretaker), and they applied uniform classification systems to index the type of maltreatment and the severity and type of injury or harm. Two sets of definitional standards were applied: the Harm Standard and the Endangerment Standard. The Harm Standard was developed for the

NIS-1, and it has been used in all three national incidence studies. It is relatively stringent in that it generally requires that an act or omission result in demonstrable harm in order to be classified as abuse or neglect. Exceptions are made in only a few categories where the nature of the maltreatment itself is so egregious that the standard permits harm to be inferred when direct evidence of it is not available.

The chief advantage of the Harm Standard is that it is strongly objective in character. Its principal disadvantage is that it is so stringent that it provides a view of abuse and neglect that is too narrow for many purposes, excluding many children whose maltreatment is substantiated or indicated as abuse or neglect by CPS. To meet the need to include the full set of substantiated/indicated children in the incidence statistics, the Endangerment Standard was developed as a definitional standard during the NIS-2 to supplement the perspective provided by the Harm Standard. The Endangerment Standard includes all children who meet the Harm Standard but adds others as well.

The central feature of the Endangerment Standard is that it allows children who were not yet harmed by maltreatment to be counted in the abused and neglected estimates if a non-CPS sentinel considered them to be endangered by maltreatment or if their maltreatment was substantiated or indicated in a CPS investigation. In addition, the Endangerment Standard is slightly more lenient than the Harm Standard concerning the identity of allowable perpetrators in that it includes maltreatment by adult caretakers other than parents in certain categories as well as sexual abuse perpetrated by teenage caretakers. The Endangerment Standard was used in both the NIS-2 and the NIS-3 (Sedlak & Broadhurst, 1996, p. 6).

2. Unfortunately, much of the research that identifies characteristics of physically abusing parents is correlated in nature in that it identifies which characteristics are associated with maltreatment, rather than taking a more prospective approach, in which parents with various characteristics are followed over time to determine if maltreatment takes place. Prospective studies, however, are more difficult to conduct (for more information, see Kolko, 1996; Leventhal, 1982; Plotkin, Azar, Twentyman, & Perry, 1981; Miller, Williams, English, & Olmstead, 1987).

Furthermore, caution should be exercised in assuming that just because a parent was maltreated, he or she will then later abuse a child. Studies have found that about 70–89% of parents maltreated as children do not abuse their own children (Egeland & Jacobvitz, 1984; Hunter & Kilstrom, 1979; for an excellent discussion of this issue, see Zigler & Hall, 1989, pp. 52–53, 63–64).

3. Abstracted from Tajima (1988).

4. Addressing these social support and other needs requires training and an earnest desire to empower families (see, for example, Gutiérrez, 1990; Miller & Whitaker, 1988; Polansky, Chalmers, Buttenwieser, & Williams, 1982; Kinney et al., 1990; Tracy & Whittaker, 1987; Wahler, 1980; also see Barth, 1991; Daro, 1988, pp. 125–146; Miller et al., 1984; Olds, 1988b; Whitey, Anderson, & Lauderdale, 1980). For more information about blending group work and home-based interventions, see Daro (1988, pp. 129–137) and Olds and Henderson (1989). For research regarding home-based interventions, see Gray, Cutler, Dean, and Kempe (1979) and Chapters 8 and 9 in this book.

FOR FURTHER INFORMATION

Ascione, F.R., & Arkow, P. (Eds.) (1999). *Child abuse, domestic violence, and animal abuse: Linking the circles of compassion for prevention and intervention.* Purdue Research Foundation. West Lafayette, IN: Purdue University Press. Presents a nontechnical collection of readings that links issues of animal abuse, child mistreatment, and domestic violence, with an emphasis on animal abuse.

Briere, J., Berliner, L., Bulkley, J.A., Jenny, C., & Reid, T. (Eds.) (1996). *The APSAC handbook on child maltreatment.* American Professional Society on the Abuse of Children. Thousand Oaks, CA: Sage Publications. Provides concise summaries of the major types of child abuse and neglect, including psychosocial treatment, medical issues, legal aspects, prevention, and organization of services.

Cicchetti, D., & Carlson, V. (Eds.). (1989) . *Child maltreatment: Theory and research on the causes and consequences of child abuse and neglect.* New York: Cambridge University Press. Presents a cogent overview of the history and definition of various types of child maltreatment, causal factors, and the developmental consequences for children.

Daro, D., & McCurdy, K. (1994). Preventing child abuse and neglect: Programmatic interventions. *Child welfare: A research agenda for child welfare. LXXIII*(5) 405–430. Presents a concise but useful overview of prevention approaches.

Dubowitz, H., & DePanfilis, D. (Eds.) (2000). *Handbook for child protection practice.* Newbury Park, CA: Sage Press. Provides extremely concise 3–5 page summaries of 124 aspects of child protection practice.

Fernandez, E. (1996). *Significant harm—Unraveling child protection decisions and substitute careers of children.* Aldershot, England: Avebury—Ashgate Publishing Co. An intensive study of the perspectives of child welfare workers and biological parents on decision making in child welfare. It includes implications for practice and research, particularly in relation to paying greater attention to societal processes and environmental factors that perpetuate poverty for children and families at risk.

Morton, T.D., & Holder, W.C. (1999). Supplemental paper: Practice considerations in child protective services. In *Guidelines for a model system of protective services for abused and neglected children and their families* (pp. 43–48). Washington, DC: National Association of Public Child Welfare Administration. Presents an excellent summary of the issues involved in improving decisions in CPS, the key decisions, and how to approach this work.

National Association of Public Child Welfare Administrators. (1999). *Guidelines for a model system of protective services for abused and neglected children and their families.* Washington, DC: American Public Welfare Association. An excellent summary of the purposes and direction that CPS in the United States should be taking.

Sedlak, A.J., & Broadhurst, D.D. (1996). *Executive summary of the third national incidence study of child abuse and neglect.* Washington, DC: National Clearinghouse on Child Abuse and Neglect. Part of a series of reports (a "Final Report" and four technical reports on the NIS-3: Revised Study Design, Sample Selection Report, Data Collection Report, and Analysis Report), as well as reports on the NIS-3 policy substudies (Court Referral Study, CPS Screening Policy and Record-keeping Study, Sentinel Questionnaire Follow-Up Study), or the NIS-3 public use data tape, contact the National Clearinghouse on Child Abuse and Neglect Information, P.O. Box 1182, Washington, D.C. 20013-1182, (800) FYI-3366 [also http://www.calib.com/nccanch/data/nis3. txt]. Reports the methodology and findings of the most recent national study of the incidence of various forms of child maltreatment, based on data collected in 1993 and 1994. It is best used in conjunction with the NCANDS data report summarized below.

U.S. Department of Health and Human Services, Administration on Children, Youth and Families. (1999). *Child maltreatment 1997: Reports from the states to the National Child Abuse and Neglect Data System.* Washington, DC: U.S. Government Printing office. [Web: *http://www.calib. com/nccanch*]. Otherwise known as the NCANDS system, this annual publication and website, sponsored by the National Center on Child Abuse and Neglect, reports the most recent national incidence levels regarding various forms of child maltreatment.

6

Sexual Abuse: Prevention and Treatment

INTRODUCTION

Defining Sexual Abuse: Major Components

In the previous chapter, various theoretical perspectives regarding physical abuse were presented. Building on that information, this chapter will focus on the definitions, incidence, prevalence, contributing factors, and promising approaches to addressing sexual abuse.

Sexual abuse is an area of child maltreatment marked by some debate over incidence levels and treatment approaches, and with considerable controversy over methods of investigation, case substantiation, treatment of the offender, and other areas. In light of the general public's tolerance of soft pornographic and sexist themes in television, movies, and even music videos, it is no surprise that American citizens as a whole are reluctant to address sexual victimization of children. The area of sexual abuse is extremely complex, and only a few of the major issues can be addressed in this brief chapter. Readers are therefore encouraged to read the more specialized publications on etiology and treatment that are available.

As with the other forms of child maltreatment that have been discussed, the behaviors and situations that make up sexual abuse range from those that might be considered abusive in some situations to those that would always be considered sexual maltreatment. Conte (1986) has described some of the activities that constitute child sexual abuse:

> *Exhibitionism,* in which an adult exposes his genitals to a child.[1] This may be in the context of some other activity (e.g., bathing or undressing), or may be carried out without reference to such activities (e.g., an adult opens his pants to expose himself to a child he sees walking on the street). In cases where the adult and the child are not related, exhibitionism is usually regarded as abusive behavior. In family cases it is sometimes difficult to determine whether a situation is abusive because family norms vary considerably about how much nudity is appropriate, or how much privacy is expected during bathing or dressing. With only a description of what took place, it is often difficult to determine the intent of behavior.
>
> *Voyeurism,* in which an adult watches a child undress, bathe, or use the bathroom. As in the case of exhibitionism, this is often a situation that is difficult to label as abusive. Parents and other adults in some situations (e.g., day care centers) may appro-

171

priately observe children dressing or going to the bathroom. When the intent of the observation is the sexual gratification of the adult, however, then the situation is sexually abusive. Even though adults may have a difficult time determining when these situations are abusive, children oftentimes can tell that "something is funny" if you ask them.

Kissing, in which the adult gives the child lingering or intimate kisses, particularly on the mouth and perhaps with the adult's tongue stuck in the child's mouth. This is another example of behavior that is difficult to define as abusive without knowing more about the context within which it takes place. Families differ. Some proscribe kissing other family members on the mouth. Others don't. You need some information about how long the kiss lasts and what feeling the child has about it before making a judgment about its potential abusiveness.

Fondling, in which an offender touches, caresses, or rubs a child's genitals or breasts, or has the child similarly touch his body. Fondling may occur in the context of some other activity such as bathing or reading a story to the child. In such a case, the adult uses the context to be close to the child, and uses the closeness to rub against the child's body. Rubbing a child's back, head, or other "nonsexual" part of the body may be abusive if its intent is to engage the child in a situation that will ultimately lead to actual sexual behavior. If the purpose is to relax the child, communicate support, or otherwise share positive emotions with the child, it is not abusive.

Fellatio or cunnilingus, in which an adult forces a child to have oral–genital contact with him.

Vaginal or anal intercourse, in which the adult penetrates the child's vaginal or anal opening with a finger, penis, or object.

Pornography can be a special instance of child sexual abuse, when it involves the use of pictures, videotape, or film depicting graphically specific sexual acts between adults, adults and children, or children. These materials may be shown to children as part of a situation in which their own abuse takes place, or pornographic pictures or film may be taken of them. With the increasing availability of "adult only" channels on cable television networks, some people have suggested that parents who allow access to this programming are abusing their children. Unless the intent of the parents is clearly for their own gratification, however, such situations are not child sexual abuse, although they may reflect poor judgment and even be considered child neglect in some cases. (Conte, 1986a, pp. 2–4. Reprinted with permission of the National Committee for the Prevention of Child Abuse)

A variety of specific definitions of sexual abuse have been developed, and they vary somewhat depending on whether they were developed for research, professional, or legal purposes. For example, molestation in many state laws is defined to include touching the anus or any part of the genitals of a child or otherwise taking indecent liberties with a child, or causing a child to take indecent liberties with the perpetrator or another with the intent to arouse or gratify the sexual desire of any person.

Sexual exploitation of minors means knowingly employing, using, persuading, inducing, enticing, or coercing any minor to pose in the nude for the purpose of sexual arousal of any person or for profit; or to engage in any sexual or simulated sexual conduct for the purpose of photographing, filming, recording, or displaying in any way the sexual or simulated sexual conduct. It also includes displaying, distributing, possessing for the purpose of distribution, or selling material depicting minors in the nude or engaging in sexual or simulated sexual conduct.

Federal Versus Professional Definitions of Sexual Abuse

Child sexual abuse was redefined in 1984 by the federal government to include

> (i) the employment, use, persuasion, inducement, enticement, or coercion of any child to engage in any sexually explicit conduct (or any simulation of such conduct) for the purpose of producing any visual depiction of such conduct or (ii) the rape, molestation, prostitution, or other form of sexual exploitation of children, or incest with children, under circumstances which indicate the child's health or welfare is harmed or threatened thereby. (Child Abuse Prevention and Treatment Act 42 as Amended by Public Law 98-457, 98th Congress, 9 October 1984; as cited in Tower, 1989, p. 105)

The use of more specific terms, although possibly helping the professional community to be aware of the range of behaviors that constitute sexual maltreatment, can be confusing:

> Numerous other words are used synonymously with sexual abuse. Sexual exploitation, for example, can be not only the actual genital manipulation of a child and the request to touch an adult, but also compelling the child to observe sexual acts or have pictures taken for pornographic purposes. Some authors use the terms assault (Burgess et al. 1978), molestation (Sanford 1980), victimization (Finkelhor 1979), and child rape (Rush 1980). Rape, in the commonly understood sense, denotes sexual intercourse usually undertaken with violence to the victim. The laws of many states, however, define child rape as the intrusion of any part of the perpetrator's body (e.g., penis, fingers, tongue) into an orifice of the child's body. (Tower, 1989, p. 106)

Sexual abuse may be committed by a nonrelated stranger to the child or by a family member. Generally, intrafamilial sexual abuse can also be termed incest.[2] In some states, other persons (e.g., paramours) who live with the family may also be charged with sexual abuse under the child welfare codes (as well as under the criminal codes). Incest, or sexual abuse committed by a family member, can be defined to include blood relationships of the whole or half blood without regard to legitimacy, relationship of parent and child by adoption, and relationship of stepparent and stepchild while the marriage creating the relationship of a stepparent and stepchild exists. Although sexual abuse of a child by a family member is often given more publicity, proportionally more children are victimized by nonfamily members. Thus, both types of abuse need to be addressed in prevention and treatment. What distinguishes sexual abuse and contributes to the child's harm are some of the qualities or circumstances that accompany it (Korbin, 1987, pp. 249–250).

Many forms of incest—sexual abuse among "culturally specified relatives" (Korbin, 1987, p. 247)—involve a violation of family roles and structure: It is the "wrong way to act in a relationship: as father-son, as father-daughter, as mother-son" (Schneider, 1976, p. 166). For both intrafamilial and the other forms of sexual abuse, coercion is often present, although in some situations the victimization takes on a gentle, comforting tone. In most situations, there is a considerable amount of coercion used in terms of threats to tell the child's parents, to hurt the child physically, or other intimidating statements. In few cases is the child's consent obtained. The age difference between the victim and the adult both make coercion and lack of consent more possible, and this is another feature of sexual abuse.

In addition, sexual abuse is an act that most often takes place secretly in extremely private situations (as contrasted with an adult's loss of temper and spanking a child in a grocery store). The degree of secrecy is an important factor in multicultural situations as well. For example, a Vietnamese mother's stroking of her 2-year-old child's genitals in a living room with company present can be viewed as a culturally acceptable means of showing affection to a child (Q. Nguyen, personal communication, September 19, 1991).

In summary, three major dimensions are often used to define sexual abuse with children: (1) age differences between the child and the offender (5 years or more), (2) specific sexual behaviors, and (3) sexual intent, where the intent is sexual gratification of the adult (Conte, 1991; Finkelhor, 1979).

Cross-Cultural Definitions

The variety of definitions noted in the preceding sections may be confusing to readers, but they reflect the current status of the field. As indicated by the case example described above, viewing sexual abuse from a cross-cultural perspective can add both clarity and complexity to the situation. For example, in the cross-cultural literature, incest refers to proscribed sexual conduct between culturally specified relatives (Korbin, 1987, p. 247). The term sexual abuse can be defined as "proscribed sexual conduct between an adult and a sexually immature child for the purposes of the adult's sexual pleasure or for economic gain through child prostitution or pornography" (Korbin, 1987, p. 248).

Each of the emphasized terms, however, is culture bound and needs to be defined for specific cultures. For example, in some cultures, sharing food in certain situations may constitute incest, while other behaviors considered sexual in the United States may be forms of greeting in other cultures. Because of the varied definitions of the term incest, from anthropological and other perspectives (Finkelhor, 1984, p. 224), the term intrafamilial sexual abuse will be used instead through-out this chapter when referring specifically to incest as a subtype of sexual mal-treatment. Clearly, defining sexual abuse is complex and studies in this area should be examined carefully in relation to the particular definition employed by the re-searchers.

Incidence of Sexual Abuse

The difficulty in defining sexual abuse also hinders our ability to collect reliable data on its incidence and prevalence. Yet a number of both kinds of studies shed some light on the extent of this form of child maltreatment. For example, in 1997, the most recent year for which the federal government was able to collect state re-porting data, a total of 98,339 cases of sexual abuse were identified (USDHEW, 1999, p. 4-2).

The NIS-3 study found a high incidence level of sexual abuse, 217,700 cases under the harm standard and 300,200 victims under the less stringent endanger-ment standard (see Note 1 in Chapter 5) (Sedlak & Broadhurst, 1996, p. 8). The NIS-2 study also found that the reporting rates for sexual abuse increased 125% from 133,600 in 1986, compared with projected total estimates of 300,200 in 1993. For the NIS-2 and NIS-3 studies, children who experienced any one of three spe-cific forms of sexual abuse were counted in estimates of the overall incidence of sexual abuse. The three forms of sexual abuse reflected different kinds of acts:

1. Intrusion: Evidence of actual penile penetration—whether oral, anal, or genital, homosexual or heterosexual—was required for this form of mal-treatment. [Evidence means credible information (e.g., the perpetrator ac-knowledged his actions). As in the 1980 study, the term does not have a technical meaning here, either legal or medical.]
2. Molestation with genital contact: This form of maltreatment involves acts in which some form of actual genital contact had occurred, but where there was not specific indication of intrusion. When intrusion had been coded for a given child, molestation was not also coded unless it reflected a distinct-ly different type of event in the child's experience (e.g., if it involved differ-ent perpetrators).
3. Other or unknown sexual abuse: This category was used for unspecified acts not known to have involved actual genital contact (e.g., fondling of breasts or buttocks, exposure) and for allegations concerning inadequate or in-appropriate supervision of a child's voluntary sexual activities.

Prevalence of Sexual Abuse

Another way to approach estimating the extent of a social problem is to identify how many people from a sample of persons have experienced the event over time.

Prevalence rates are higher than incidence rates because they report a cumulative occurrence of the event for a certain time period, rather than for a year. Choosing representative samples, designing precise interview questions, enhancing memory accuracy, obtaining adequate response rates, and using skilled interviewers are just some of the major issues that have not been carefully addressed in many studies. So as readers review various estimates of prevalence, they need to keep in mind that definitions, sample characteristics, and other important factors make simple comparisons of studies unwise.

Probably one of the earliest studies was conducted by Kinsey et al. (1953) as part of his national survey of sexual behaviors in the United States. Kinsey found that 24% (1,075) of the 4,441 female respondents had as preadolescent girls (ages 4–13) experienced sexual contact between themselves and adult men (men at least 15 years old and at least 5 years older than the girls) (Kinsey et al., 1953, p. 118, as cited in Leventhal, 1988, p. 768). If a "more narrow" definition is used, where noncontact cases (verbal abuse or genital exhibition) are excluded, the prevalence is reduced to 12% (Kinsey et al., 1953, p. 119, as cited in Leventhal, 1988, p. 768). But even these figures underestimate the problem because adolescent abuse is excluded.

In contrast, a survey in 1980 by mail of 1,054 license-holding Texas drivers reported rates of 3% for males and 12% for females (Kercher, 1980, as cited in Finkelhor, 1984, p. 1).[3] A 1981 survey of 521 Boston parents of 6- to 14-year-old children found that 6% of the males and 15% of females had responded yes to one of two questions, the first dealing with sexual things being done to or with them before age 16 by a person at least 5 years older, and the second with similar wording with the exception that the question focused on "attempts" to do something to or with them (Finkelhor, 1984, pp. 71, 72).

Russell conducted interviews of 930 San Francisco women and found that before age 14, 28% of them had experienced intrafamilial or extrafamilial sexual abuse (unwanted sexual experiences). Experiences that involved sexual contact with a relative that were wanted and with a peer (less than 5 years older) were regarded as nonexploitative (Russell, 1983, pp. 135–138). A lower percentage (12%) had been victimized by a relative before age 14. A substantial proportion of women (16%) reported experiencing intrafamilial sexual abuse before age 18. These studies reflect that sexual abuse of children is a serious problem in this country, one that probably increased from World War I to 1960 (Russell, 1984, pp. 198–214).

In-person interviews with a national survey of 1,099 noninstitutionalized women who were age 21 and older in 1991, which was recently republished, found a prevalence rate of child sexual abuse (CSA) that varied according to the specific criteria used (also see Table 6.1):

> CSA was identified by two sets of criteria, from Wyatt (1985) and Russell (1983). The Wyatt criteria included: (a) any intrafamilial sexual activity before age 18 and that was unwanted or that involved a family member 5 or more years older than the respondent; and (b) any extrafamilial sexual activity that occurred before age 18 and

Table 6.1. Estimated Prevalence of Childhood Sexual Abuse (CSA) in Women

CSA Definition	Women Reporting CSA (%) Method 1[a] (95% CI)	Women Reporting CSA (%) Method 2[b] (95% CI)	Women Reporting CSA (%) Method 3[c] (95% CI)
Wyatt Criteria	21.4	24.0	32.1
	(18.4–24.4)	(20.6–27.4)	(28.4–35.8)
Russell Criteria	15.4	17.3	26.1
	(13.0–17.8)	(14.5–20.0)	(22.7–29.5)

Source: Vogeltanz et al. (1999), p. 583.
[a]Method 1: Cases with insufficient information treated as no-CSA.
[b]Method 2: Cases with insufficient information are excluded.
[c]Method 3: Cases with insufficient information treated as CSA.

was unwanted, or that occurred before age 13 and involved another person 5 or more years older than the respondent. The Russell criteria included: (a) any intrafamilial sexual activity before age 18 that was unwanted or involved a family member 5 or more years older than the respondent; and (b) any unwanted extrafamilial activity that occurred before age 14, or any unwanted sexual intercourse occurring at age 14–17. (Vogeltanz et al., 1999, p. 582)

Prevalence rates for the more inclusive CSA definition ranged from 21% to 32%, depending on how respondents who provided incomplete information about their sexual experience were classified. The less inclusive CSA definition resulted in prevalence rates ranging from 15% to 26%. Additional information about the types of abuse experienced, perpetrator characteristics, age at first abuse, and physical and affective consequences of the abuse experience are reported. The risk of CSA was related to higher scores on a measure of father's rejection, and the interaction between parental drinking status and whether the respondent had lived with both parents during childhood. Further analysis of this interaction suggests that when respondents reported living with both biological parents, they were most at risk for CSA when their father was a nondrinker and their mother was a drinker. (Vogeltanz et al., 1999, p. 579)

Sexual abuse has likely been increasing since 1960 as well because of family structure changes that may make children more vulnerable, changes in sexual behavior, and more permissive attitudes in society (Finkelhor, 1984, pp. 2–3). But what do these studies tell us about the victims? First, it is important to point out that the vast majority of victims are girls. The number of boys to girls ranges from 11 out of 100 to 48 out of 100, depending on the study (Finkelhor, 1984, p. 168). The most common ages are between 8 and 12, although both younger and older children are victimized as well (Finkelhor, 1984, p. 23). All socioeconomic classes are represented, and ethnic-group rates vary in some complicated ways. So it is not accurate to state that sexual abuse occurs only among low-income or ethnic-minority families.

Contributing Factors to Sexual Abuse

In trying to understand why sexual abuse occurs, a number of researchers have been identifying factors that may contribute to a child's risk of being sexually maltreated. As with the other areas, the risk factor research with respect to sexual abuse must be viewed with extreme caution. Many risk factors have been identified through retrospective or correlation-based studies, which are not able to document causal linkages (Leventhal, 1982). For example, whereas child situational factors (e.g., family structure, age) can be researched, it is difficult to identify emotional and psychological vulnerabilities because "without measures of pre- and post-abusive functioning (e.g., depression, emotional well-being), it would be virtually impossible to determine what is a risk factor for abuse and what is an emotional consequence of being abused" (Conte, Wolf, & Smith, 1989, p. 299).[4]

Most multivariate studies have not been replicated with other samples to test the accuracy of their predictive models. Furthermore, it is likely that some of the risk factors do not act in a simple linear fashion, but may interact in certain ways for children of different ages, gender type, ethnicity, geographic area, and other characteristics. Finally, another limitation of many lists of risk factors is that they do not communicate which factors under which conditions are most important. So although a number of risk factor summaries will be presented, they should not be used as simple checklists but should be viewed as preliminary models to be replicated with other samples and research designs.

A number of major risk factor assessment research projects have been conducted in the area of sexual abuse and have begun to identify some of the factors, including one by Finkelhor in 1979 based on reports from 796 college students and one by Landis in 1956 using 1,800 college students. Landis used comparison groups to determine what factors place a child at risk. It was interesting to note that both studies cite roughly similar risk factors.

Finkelhor's (1984, pp. 28–29) eight strongest predictors were the following:[5]

- stepfather in the home,
- victim has at one point lived without a mother,
- victim not close to mother,
- mother never finished high school,
- mother sexually punitive,
- no physical affection from the father,
- income under $10,000,
- two friends or less in childhood.

Children with none of the factors had no sexual abuse. Among those children who had five factors, two-thirds had been victimized. The presence of each additional risk factor increased the chance for sexual abuse by 10 to 20% (Finkelhor, 1984, p. 28). Similarly, Landis's strongest indicators (statistically significant compared to the nonvictim group) were the following:

- victims came from unhappy homes,
- victims had mothers who worked full or part time,
- victims had poor relationships with the mother,
- mothers had less education,
- victims did not receive sex education from mothers,
- fathers had lower job status (Landis, 1956).

The two studies of risk factors listed above identified risk factors of children who are victims of both intrafamilial and extrafamilial sexual abuse. When looking specifically at risk factors for intrafamilial sexual abuse, the following factors are commonly identified by many recent studies:

- violence in the family, including the spouse as well as the children,
- role reversal with the child,
- alcohol/substance abuse of the father/stepfather,
- poor marital history, separation, or divorce,
- presence of stepfather
- mother absent, ill, or depressed,
- parents were abused as a child,
- mother's rejection of the daughter or poor relationship with daughter,
- family isolation,
- low socioeconomic status or father unemployed,
- mother did not finish high school,
- patriarchal family or father seen as "domineering."

Much more research needs to be conducted to refine the risk factors for specific forms of abuse with specific subgroups related to gender, race, and age. But, in general, when thinking about risk factors for sexual abuse, child welfare staff should consider status conditions (e.g., being in a particular family situation, age), emotional characteristics (e.g., emotional vulnerability, shyness), and situational factors (e.g., child was alone and unprotected) (Conte et al., 1989).

Explanatory Models

So given the risk factors discussed above, what dynamics account for why an adult would sexually maltreat a child? Neither research nor theory is developed enough to address this, and more research is needed that is both qualitative in design as well as quantitative. Some preliminary models have been proposed that build on the general models described in Chapter 5 to specify causal dynamics for specific forms of maltreatment. Although they are not without their limitations, these more specific models do help to explain some of the causal factors and dynamics in this area.

One model that has been proposed uses a particular form of a family systems perspective where family interaction patterns and experiences over multiple generations are emphasized, the sexual abuse is viewed as a symptom of a dysfunctional family rather than a dysfunctional individual, and there is a strong belief that the behavior is actually more of a symptom of another problem (e.g., sexual abuse is used as a tension reduction mechanism). Although some of these dynamics may reflect certain aspects of some families, this model is largely based on small-sample studies of intrafamilial incest, it allows the abuser to avoid personal responsibility by blaming the family system, and it may oversimplify case situations in a number of ways (e.g., by not considering cognitive distortions, learned behaviors, or community or societal contributors) (Conte, 1986a, pp. 115–121).

Another model that has received a great amount of attention was developed by Finkelhor (1984, p. 54), and it groups risk factors for sexual abuse into one of four preconditions that need to be met before sexual abuse can occur:

1. A potential offender needed to have some motivation to abuse a child sexually.
2. The potential offender had to overcome internal inhibitions against acting on that motivation.
3. The potential offender had to overcome external impediments to committing sexual abuse.
4. The potential offender or some other factor had to undermine or overcome a child's possible resistance to the sexual abuse.

Finkelhor's model is summarized in Table 6.2 and Figure 6.1. A brief summary of the major components is presented below, but readers should consult Finkelhor (1984, pp. 53–68) and related articles for a more comprehensive explanation.

Precondition 1: Motivation to Sexually Abuse. A model of sexual abuse needs to account for how a person (an adult or adolescent) becomes motivated for or interested in having sexual contact with a child. There appear to be three components to the source of this motivation: (1) emotional congruence—relating sexually to the child satisfies some important emotional need; (2) sexual arousal—the child comes to be the potential source of sexual gratification for that person; and (3) blockage—alternative sources of sexual gratification are not available or are less satisfying.

Precondition 2: Overcoming Internal Inhibitors. For sexual abuse to occur, a potential offender not only needs to be motivated to commit abuse, but the offender must overcome internal inhibitions against acting on those motives. Most members of society have such inhibitions, but many cultural factors can act to reduce those (see Finkelhor, 1984, pp. 44–46). So although emotional congruence, sexual arousal, and blockage are sources of the motivation to sexually abuse, without the lessening of internal inhibitors, the motivation will not be unleashed.

Precondition 3: Overcoming External Inhibitors. The first two preconditions try to account for the behavior of perpetrators. But it is quite clear that such accounts do not fully explain to whom or why abuse occurs. A man fully motivated to abuse sexually who is also disinhibited may not do so, and he certainly may not do so with a particular child. There are factors outside himself that control whether he abuses and whom he abuses. Preconditions 3 and 4 are about these.

Table 6.2. Preconditions for Sexual Abuse[a]

Precondition	Level of Explanation		
	Individual		Social/Cultural
Precondition 1: Factors related to motivation to sexually abuse			
Emotional congruence	Arrested emotional development		Masculine requirement to be dominant and powerful in sexual relationships
	Need to feel powerful and controlling		
	Reenactment of childhood trauma to undo the hurt		
	Narcissistic identification with self as a young child		
Sexual arousal	Childhood sexual experience that was traumatic or strongly conditioning		Child pornography
			Erotic portrayal of children in advertising
	Modeling of sexual interest in children by someone else		Male tendency to sexualize all emotional needs
	Misattribution of arousal cues		
	Biologic abnormality		
Blockage	Oedipal conflict		Repressive norms about masturbation and extramarital sex
	Castration anxiety		
	Fear of adult females		
Precondition 2: Factors predisposing to overcoming internal inhibitors			
	Alcohol		Social toleration of sexual interest in children
	Psychosis		Weak criminal sanctions against offenders
	Impulse disorder		Ideology of patriarchal prerogatives for fathers
	Senility		Social toleration for deviance committed while intoxicated
	Failure of incest inhibition mechanism in family dynamics		Child pornography
			Male inability to identify with needs of children
Precondition 3: Factors predisposing to overcoming external inhibitors			
	Mother who is absent or ill		Lack of social supports for mother
	Mother who is not close to or protective of child		Barriers to women's equality
	Mother who is dominated or abused by father		Erosion of social networks
	Social isolation of family		Ideology of family sanctity
	Unusual opportunities to be alone with child		
	Lack of supervision of child		
	Unusual sleeping or rooming conditions		
Precondition 4: Factors predisposing to overcoming child's resistance			
	Child who is emotionally insecure or deprived		Unavailability of sex education for children
	Child who lacks knowledge about sexual abuse		Social powerlessness of children
	Situation of unusual trust between child and offender		
	Coercion		

Source: Finkelhor, D. (1984). *Child sexual abuse: New theory and research* (pp. 56–57). New York: Free Press. Reprinted with permission.

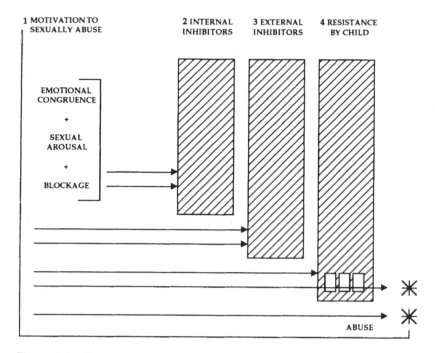

Figure 6.1. Four preconditions of sexual abuse. *Source:* Finkelhor, D. (1984).
Child sexual abuse: New theory and research (p. 55). New York: Free Press.
Reprinted with permission.

Precondition 3 concerns external inhibitors in the environment outside the offender and outside the child. The most important of these external forces is the supervision a child receives from other persons. Family members, neighbors, and children's own peers all exert a restraining influence on the actions of a potential abuser.

Precondition 4: Overcoming the Resistance of the Child. Children themselves play an important role in whether or not they are abused, and any full explanation of why abuse occurs needs to take into account factors related to the child. Children have some capacity to avoid or resist abuse. Unfortunately, since professionals are mostly in contact with children who were abused, the importance of this capacity is not often realized. If professionals dealt with more children who had had close calls but had escaped, this capacity might be more apparent. Some of the factors noted in the literature as compromising children's capacity to resist are listed as part of Finkelhor's model in Table 6.2, including emotional insecurity and a lack of knowledge about sexual abuse.

Another way of viewing the dynamics of Finkelhor's model is presented in Figure 6.1. Although some may view this as oversimplifying what is generally a complex interaction of factors, this diagram suggests that the preconditions are encountered in a somewhat logical sequence:

Only some individuals have strong motivation to become sexually involved with children. Of those that do, only some overcome their internal inhibitions to act on these motives. Of those who overcome their internal inhibitions, only some overcome external inhibitions—the surveillance of other family members or the lack of opportunity—and act on the motives.

At this point, three things can happen. (1) Any particular child may resist either directly or indirectly, for example by running away or by having a confident, assertive, or invulnerable demeanor, and in such a way avoid abuse. This is shown by the arrow that stops before Precondition IV. (2) Any particular child may fail to resist and be abused. This is shown by the lowest line in the figure. (3) Any particular child may resist but may have his or her resistance overcome through coercion. This is shown by the line drawn through Precondition IV.

All four preconditions have to be fulfilled for the abuse to occur. The presence of only one condition, such as lack of protection by a mother or social isolation or emtional deprivation, is not enough in itself to explain abuse. To explain abuse requires the presence of all four prior conditions. (Finkelhor, 1984, pp. 61–62)

Finkelhor presents a useful approach to considering some of the dynamics of sexual maltreatment and what process might be involved in many situations. This model needs explicit testing to establish its validity more firmly. But many of the components have been supported by other researchers such as Faller (1988), who believes that sexual abuse is the result of an interaction between certain prerequisites (sexual attraction to children, will to act out sexual feelings) with contributing factors such as cultural, environmental, individual, and family conditions (also see Russell, 1984, pp. 233–268).

We may find that models containing special risk factors need to be modified, given specific data regarding families of color, and use of more gender-sensitive variables. For example, the risk for sexual abuse in one study (Sedlak, 1991c) increased with age for white/black/Hispanic families, and for families with a father-only household, but not for other ethnic groups (e.g., Asian, Native American, Alaskan Native). What characteristics of these groups lower the risk of child sexual abuse? What cultural factors may be at work that fit some of the aspects of Finkelhor's model? Are there any data peculiarities or limitations that might account for this finding? For example, is this pattern consistent with basic incidence rates among the various ethnic subgroups found in other studies? Clearly, the explanatory models in this field need additional refinement and testing.

TREATMENT OF SEXUAL ABUSE

Victim Treatment

Treatment methods vary according to the theoretical (psychoanalytic, cognitive–behavioral, attachment-focused) and practice perspective of the therapists (Murray, 1999; Sgroi, 1988, 1989). Because of the short- and long-term problems shown

by victims of sexual abuse (see Chapter 5), a variety of interventions may be needed at different points in the child's development to help him or her overcome the
effects of the abusive experience. The therapeutic process is complicated by the
guilt that many children feel about their inability to stop the victimization and the
family stress (and possibly separation of family members) that their disclosure has
increased.

To cope with the abusive situation, many children separate themselves emotionally from the events. Although this process is functional for minimizing emotional trauma, it may interfere with their ability to trust and form healthy emotional
relationships. For some children, their behavior becomes "sexualized" and they
need to learn new ways of behaving toward other children or adults. One 5-year-
old girl frequently wanted to play with the breasts of her therapist, and when placed
in a preschool was found kissing and hugging a little boy in the bathroom with both
of their pants pulled down. Unfortunately, victimized children may act out in ways
that go beyond what is normal exploratory sexual behavior. However, the degree
of dysfunctional behaviors and emotional distress vary with the degree of "traumatic sexualization":

> Traumatic sexualization is the process by which a child's sexuality become distorted
> over the course of the abuse. This process can occur to a child when the offender:
> (a) repeatedly rewards a child for inappropriate sexual behavior, (b) exchanges gifts,
> affection, privileges, or attention for sexual activity with the child, (c) overly attends
> to or distorts the meaning and importance of certain parts of the child's body, (d) con-
> veys misconceptions and confusion about sexual behavior and accepted morality to
> the child, and (e) abuses the child to a degree that the child associates fearful mem-
> ories and events with sexual behavior.
>
> Children tend to evidence greater degrees of sexual traumatization when the of-
> fender attempts to arouse the child's sexual responses rather than merely interacting
> with the child as a passive object. Additionally, children appear to experience more
> severe levels of traumatization when they are enticed to participate, when high lev-
> els of fear become associated with sexual experiences, and when they have a better
> understanding of the implications of the sexual behavior. (Walker et al., 1988, p. 145)

According to Finkelhor and Browne (1986, pp. 181–185), traumatic sexualization is one of the dynamics that therapists must deal with for sexually abused victims in particular, along with three other relatively unique issues: stigmatization,
betrayal, and powerlessness.

Careful assessment of the child and his or her situation is essential, and efforts
must be taken to protect the child from further abuse. Most child welfare experts
recommend that in cases of intrafamilial sexual abuse the offender leave the household to minimize the emotional trauma on the child. Although sometimes child
placement may be the only way to protect the child reasonably, it should be the least
preferred alternative (see Haugaard & Reppucci, 1988, pp. 210–215; Sgroi, 1982).

Treatment methods and areas of emphasis will vary according to the child's developmental stage, cognitive ability, duration and nature of the abuse, degree of

family support, and other factors.[6] Some children may need to resolve the guilt they feel, learn to express anger toward the offender, and resolve specific areas of anxiety (e.g., sleeping in their own bed). Play therapy using fairy tales, drawing, and other art forms may be extremely useful. It is also important for these children to acquire assertiveness and other skills for self-protection. The family's ethnic culture and gender differences must be considered carefully or they may affect what treatment approaches will be successful (Fontes, 1993).

For older children, group therapy may be a particularly effective therapeutic modality to help them resolve conflicted feelings with family members or to work through their anger with peers in an adolescent victim group (Goodwin & Flanagan, 1983). By meeting with other children who have had similar experiences, the children learn that their situation is not unique and that secrets do not have to be maintained. The group experience becomes a place for the child to relate in a meaningful way with peers, thereby reducing the child's feelings of isolation.[7] A case vignette from Haugaard and Reppucci (1988) illustrates one child's experience:

> A nine-year-old girl was repeatedly molested by her uncle. Although she has made some progress during individual therapy in expressing and understanding her reactions to the abuse, she remains withdrawn from her peers at school and has not made much progress in understanding that her experiences are not unique. A place in an ongoing group treatment program of sexually abused girls becomes available, and she reluctantly joins. She interacts little during the first few sessions but listens intently to the experiences of the girls who have been in the group for a while. She gradually begins to interact in the group and makes friends with some of the other members. She begins to involve herself with her peers at school and attributes this interaction to her realization that other sexually abused children appear normal to her and that they are able to keep their friends in school. (p. 262)

Methods for treating male victims of sexual abuse are less developed, although more studies of the surrounding circumstances, effects, and promising treatment approaches are being published along with practical treatment manuals (e.g., Karp & Butler, 1996a,b). What is important to note, even in this brief review, is that boys may suffer from other effects in addition to the shame, depression, guilt, and inappropriate sexual behavior discussed earlier and in Chapter 5. Walker et al. (1988) summarize the clinical findings of one of the few available studies:

> Rogers and Terry (1984) have described other issues encountered in the treatment of boy victims, which include: (a) confusion over sexual identity and fears of homosexuality; (b) the tendency of boy victims to reenact their victimization by sexually abusing other children; (c) increased aggressive behavior; and (d) strong denial or minimization of the impact by the boys' parents. . . . They recommend providing a clear cognitive framework to increase the victim's and family's understanding of the abuse. This approach may help reduce the parents' blaming the child and the child's self-blame. Another recommended technique is to help the boy channel his need for assertiveness into socially acceptable outlets. This might include joining a sports

team or taking a course in self-defense techniques. These authors suggest that intervention with boy victims may be a productive long-term approach to preventing
sexual crimes. (p. 153)

Despite some of the promising results of the Daughters and Sons United, Parents United, and other group approaches, insufficient intervention research has
been conducted. Part of the problem lies in the need to refine the conceptual frameworks for describing and explaining the effects of abuse on boys and girls, despite
the recent advances, made by a number of researchers (e.g., Finkelhor & Browne,
1986; VanderMey & Neff, 1986). In addition, the research on the sexual abuse of
children and its treatment, while growing, is still underdeveloped (e.g., Maddock
& Larson, 1995; Walker et al., 1988). Much work remains to be done in developing services to victims, siblings of victims, the family as a whole, and adults molested as children. Consequently, at this time it is not possible to make definitive
statements about what treatment approaches are the most effective, although the
individual and groupwork strategies cited earlier are promising.

Treatment for Offenders

Treatment of sexually abusing adults is complicated by the multiplicity of problems that they may be experiencing. Roundy and Horton (1990) present an excellent summary of some of the most common symptoms and treatment issues
drawing on the professional literature (see Table 6.3).

In addressing these symptoms, child welfare staff members must be aware of
any professional and personal biases that will affect their ability to work with offenders and their families. For example, what gender biases do they have that may
need to be examined? How willing is the caseworker to explore issues with clients
that may be extremely powerful for the caseworker, but necessary for effective
treatment? (See Roundy & Horton, 1990, pp. 168–182.)

A variety of treatment modalities are being used to help offenders address the
treatment issues listed in Table 6.3 and to avoid reabusing. Insight therapy to help
the offender understand and take responsibility for the abusive situation has been
employed, along with a variety of behavioral approaches to reduce the offender's
sexual arousal to children. These behavioral approaches include aversive conditioning and masturbatory reconditioning to appropriate sexual fantasies (Abel,
Becker, & Skinner, 1987; Marshal, Earls, Segal, & Darke, 1983). A variety "community containment approaches" (English, Pullen, & Jones, 1997) of sentencing
procedures, such as the use of suspended sentences pending completion of sex
abuse treatment, are being used to encourage higher treatment usage and lower recidivism. But the evaluation research remains sparse (e.g., National Institute of
Justice, 1997).

Group approaches for treating offenders are gaining recognition for their effectiveness in help offenders overcome their denial and for the utility of involving

Table 6.3. Treatment Issues of Incest Offenders

The interpersonal dynamics that precede and are a result of incestuous behaviors are indicative of a variety of treatment issues. Therapists who work with incest perpetrators will do well to be prepared to recognize and address one or more of the following possible presenting symptoms.

1. *Confusion of sex and love.* Members of incestuous families very commonly believe the following equation: Sex = Love = Closeness (Intimacy). If perpetrators accept this statement as true, they may attempt to meet their love (closeness) needs through sexual contact with family members (Mayer, 1983).
2. *Sexual identity conflicts.* Conflicted sexual identity is common with offenders who may not perceive themselves as adequate in "masculinity" (Mayer, 1983; Williams & Finkelhor, 1988).
3. *Fear of adult females.* Perpetrators of incest may have been exposed to mothers or other significant adult females who were hostile toward, rejecting of, and superior to the males in their lives (i.e., their fathers, husbands, and so on), and, consequently, a generalized fear of all adult females may result (Finkelhor, 1984).
4. *Sexual addiction.* Incest offenders may exhibit symptoms of sexual addiction and have scores on sexual addiction scales that link them with such an addictive pattern (Benson, 1985; Carnes, 1983, Chapter 9 of this book).
5. *Previous history of abuse.* As in-depth histories are gathered with incest perpetrators, it is not uncommon to discover that offenders are also victims of prior physical or sexual abuse (Williams & Finkelhor, 1988). Groth (1979) found that 32% of offenders convicted of sexually abusing children had experienced sexual trauma in their youth (Steele & Alexander, 1981). De Young (1982) found that 43% of incestuous fathers had been physically abused, and 37% reported sexual abuse in their childhood years (Mayer, 1983).
6. *Other forms of abuse.* Men who sexually abuse their own children may also exhibit other types of abusive behavior, that is, emotional abuse, physical child abuse, or spouse abuse (de Young, 1982; Dietz & Craft, 1980; Herman, 1981).
7. *Substance abuse.* Alcohol and drugs are often associated with incest offenders. These substances may serve to reduce normal inhibitions, allowing the tendency for abuse to emerge. Perpetrators may also attempt to excuse their sexual behavior by blaming it on the abused substance: "I didn't know what I was doing! I was drunk" (Deighton & McPeek, 1985; Herman, 1981; Mayer, 1983; Williams & Finkelhor, 1988).
8. *Sexual irresponsibility.* Many fathers who become sexual with children have failed to assume personal responsibility for their own sexual behavior. They seem to evidence an egocentric attitude, which might be expressed as: "I must have sex. If my wife won't give me what I have to have, then I'll have to go someplace else and get it" (Mayer, 1983).
9. *Poor stress management skills.* Men who sexually abuse their children often lack the ability to manage their lives and do not possess skills for coping with and reducing the amount of stress or anxiety they encounter. They often seem to be in a chronic state of near overload (Justice & Justice, 1979; Mayer, 1983; Williams & Finkelhor, 1988).
10. *"Compartmentalization" (dissociation) of abusive episodes.* Abusers may employ "compartmentalization" as a defense against the unacceptable feelings that would be experienced if the incestuous episodes were allowed to enter their conscious awareness. They simply place the abuse in an unconscious compartment, and they are thereby not required to face the full weight of personal responsibility. They may also use this defense as a way of being honest in their denial of involvement in the abuse (Justice & Justice, 1979).
11. *Denial of involvement in or responsibility for abusive behavior, often with high degree of*

(continued)

Table 6.3. (Continued)

defensiveness. Whether or not offenders have conscious awareness of their involvement in incestuous activities, they may vigorously deny any complicity. Their efforts may include attempts to depict accusing victims as habitual liars, as seductresses, as sexually promiscuous with their age-mates, or as children simply having "bad dreams" or fantasies (Mayer, 1983; Sanford, 1982). Defensiveness is not uncommon with incest offenders. Perhaps they have some realization of the magnitude of their offense and, fearing the consequences, they take a defensive posture, especially when confronted.

12. *"Mamma's boy."* Because of unresolved issues related to their relationships with their mothers, incestuous fathers often present as "wimpy" or as "momma's boys," dependently tied to their mothers and lacking the normally developed masculine independence and strength usually associated with males (Mayer, 1983; Williams & Finkelhor, 1988).

13. *Isolation: Poor social skills with few significant relationships.* Some men who sexually abuse their own children exhibit varying degrees of social isolation. They may be uncomfortable in social settings, especially those where significant social interaction is normal. They may imitate a form of surface social skills; that is, they may be known as the friendliest member of their social or religious group due to their ability to shake hands with everyone, a social interaction requiring little or no real communication. This factor may influence where they live, as well as their choice of employment. Offenders may choose to live in small rural communities where social contacts would be minimal, or they may work as auto mechanics, carpenters, and so on, where their work requires little interaction with people (Justice & Justice, 1979; Williams & Finkelhor, 1988; see also Chapter 5 of this book).

14. *Egocentricity/narcissism.* This factor is best illustrated in the seeming lack of awareness of the significant pain and suffering incestuous fathers cause their child victims directly and the entire family indirectly. Fathers often react with apparent genuine shock and dismay as they are brought to an awareness that their actions have been devastating to others. They seem to have been tuned in only to their own needs and concerns (Crewdson, 1988; de Young, 1982).

15. *Jealousy of daughter's association with boys.* Fathers in incestuous families frequently play the role of "jealous lover" to their daughters when they become involved with other age-mate males. They may discourage or restrict dating and may project their own sexual issues onto their daughters' boyfriends, accusing them of sexual intentions (Justice & Justice, 1979).

16. *Authoritarian parenting, often with submissive servitude outside of the home.* Incestuous fathers may present contrasting interactional patterns in and out of the home. In the home they may rule supreme, demanding absolute obedience and dealing out swift and harsh punishment for those who do not respond properly. Out of the home they may present as submissive and overly solicitous, eager to please, and anxious to avoid confrontations and conflict, especially in dealings with those who are perceived to be in power positions, that is, police, employers, religious leaders, therapists, and so on (Cormier, Kennedy, & Sangowicz, 1962; de Young, 1982; Herman, 1981).

17. *Low impulse control at home, with appropriately managed behavior elsewhere.* Offenders frequently claim to be unable to control themselves in their abusive behavior: As one perpetrator explained, "I feel like I'm in the St. Lawrence River, in an inner tube, headed toward Niagara Falls, and all I have to stop me from going over is my hands. No matter how fast I paddle I can't stop myself" (de Young, 1982; Mayer, 1983). By contrast, they often seem able to appropriately manage their behavior outside of the home, suggesting a voluntary (though perhaps unconscious) determination of what type of behavior is acceptable where.

(continued)

Table 6.3. (*Continued*)

18. *Highly manipulative manner.* Perhaps no single descriptive trait is used more often in describing incestuous offenders than "manipulative" or "slick." Perhaps in an effort to give appearances of being in control of their chaotic lives, they become master manipulators of their victims, wives, family members, and associates. In order to maintain the sexually abusive activity in the face of such powerful social taboos, they must be persuasive with respect to their innocence when suspicions arise, or when the secret is out. They may be very effective in their efforts to portray postures of circumspect character and may convince others and themselves (Mayer, 1983).

19. *Minimization of abusive behavior.* Perpetrators often attempt to minimize either the severity of their abusive acts or the number of such contacts. "It was just a little simple messing around" might be the offenders' way of characterizing several incidents of oral, digital, and penile sexual contact with their daughters (Mayer, 1983; Sanford, 1982).

20. *Rationalization.* This common defense mechanism is frequently used by sexual offenders to justify their activities: "I couldn't help myself. She was dressed in a skimpy nightgown" (de Young, 1982; Mayer, 1983; Sanford, 1982).

21. *Self-deception.* Some perpetrators are so effective in their use of defense mechanisms that they successfully deceive even themselves into believing their distortions. For example, some offenders deceive themselves into assuming their daughters want the sexual contact and benefit by it in order to justify their continued involvement or reduce their own guilt (de Young, 1982; Sanford, 1982).

22. *Poor relationship with parents.* Incestuous fathers frequently describe histories of early childhood parental deprivations, which might have been economic, or more commonly, emotional or interpersonal in nature. These parental relationships were often negative or ambivalent in character (de Young, 1982). Common themes from childhood include abandonment, powerlessness, maternal seduction, and paternal rejection (Williams & Finkelhor, 1988).

23. *Possessiveness.* Incestuous fathers may believe that children are their "possessions" and therefore they have a right to do whatever they wish with them (de Young, 1982).

24. *Blurring of generational boundaries.* Incestuous fathers may, in interactions with their daughters, act impulsively or immaturely. They may act as if they were young suitors to their daughters (Justice & Justice, 1979).

25. *Low self-esteem.* Sexual offenders seldom have a high regard for themselves and often consider their behavior as indicative of the lowest form of life possible (Mayer, 1983; Williams & Finkelhor, 1988).

26. *Depression.* Upon disclosure of the sexual abuse, with the threat of potential disruption to the family system, court-ordered treatment, possible incarceration, and a beginning realization of the potential devastation resulting from the abusive behavior, it is not uncommon for incest offenders to experience periods of significant depression (Williams & Finkelhor, 1988).

27. *Paranoia.* Perhaps due to the virtually universal societal revulsion of incest, offenders commonly appear paranoid in their interactions with intervening individuals. Motives of helping professionals are often suspected by perpetrators to be negative. Claims of being persecuted are frequent (Williams & Finkelhor, 1988).

28. *Irrational reasoning or behavior.* Sexually abusive men may evidence "quick fix" mentalities. They may expect complete forgiveness from their spouses and victims in response to simplistic apologies, such as, "I'm sorry. Please forgive me" (Williams & Finkelhor, 1988).

(*continued*)

Table 6.3. (Continued)

Issues Clinically Observed But Not Documented in the Literature

29. *Sexual validation.* Offenders often see their value as persons corresponding to their sexual involvement with females. From that perception they may have difficulty validating themselves, depending on external sexual reinforcement for their sense of well-being.
30. *Control issues.* Many perpetrators of incest have significant issues regarding control of themselves as well as significant others. This may have originated in their own victimization as children.
31. *Dysfunctional guilt.* Sexual offenders may direct significant amounts of emotional blaming at themselves often in the form of a psychologically dysfunctional guilt response. This effort may represent attempts to do penance for sins committed; however, the actual effect is often to waste energy, leaving offenders stuck in their behaviors.
32. *Rigid moral or religious values.* Perpetrators may have very rigid moral and religious values and demand strict compliance with little or no flexibility. Their own sexual irresponsibility is highly inconsistent with this position.
33. *Sexualization of emotions.* Stress, anger, fear, insecurity, and other emotional states may be tied to offenders' sexual states. As these emotions rise so do their needs for sexual release. After heated arguments with their wives, they may suggest going to bed and making up by having sex. If these sexualized emotions are not resolved sexually with spouses, husbands may turn elsewhere, perhaps to children.

Source: Roundy, L. M., & Horton, A. L. (1990). Professional and treatment issues for clinicians who intervene with incest perpetrators. In A. L. Horton, B. L. Johnson, L. M. Roundy, & D. Williams (Eds.), *The incest perpetrator: A family member no one wants to treat* (pp. 182–187). Newbury Park, CA: Sage. Reprinted with permission.

other adult offenders in supporting each other through the process of scrutinizing why the abuse occurred and how relapses can be prevented, and exploring ways to reestablish health relationships with family members.

For example, Groth (1983) has developed treatment intervention for some of the most difficult offenders in correctional settings. He believes that sexual assault is the result of developmental defects and a lack of life management skills in certain areas. Although the person's assaultive inclinations will never be eliminated, they can be controlled to prevent reoffense. Groth and his colleagues focus on three areas of treatment with different treatment components incorporated into each area:

1. reeducation (sex education, understanding sexual assault, personalizing the victim),
2. resocialization (improving interpersonal relations, management of aggression, parenting skills),
3. restitution (e.g., offenders speak to law enforcement CPS workers, and other professionals about their situations to help in designing preventive and protective programs for children; see Groth, 1983, for information about the clinical interventions).

Despite the existence of many excellent treatment programs for offenders, many communities lack well-conceptualized and concerted approaches. Besides the lack of rigorously designed treatment effectiveness studies, sexual abuse offenders are not appealing clients to work with—they generally deny their offense and are difficult to bring to justice or treatment (Finkelhor, 1984). But progress is being made and a summary of some of the practice wisdom emerging from programs around the country is indicative of a growing body of knowledge:

1. Success for both prosecutors and therapists seems to be enhanced by mutual cooperation. This notion has received increasing endorsement in jurisdictions throughout the country, and new models are being developed and implemented, although entrenched institutional patterns have slowed their adoption.
2. It is not true that effective treatment can occur only with offenders who are "motivated" to get help, even though this attitude is widespread. Programs have been successful in treating offenders who were pressured into treatment through threats of prison or parole revocation.
3. Many incestuous abusers require more than family therapy to insure against reoccurrence of abuse. Some of the important issues that lead to incestuous abuse, such as a history of childhood trauma, may not be adequately dealt with in family therapy and require individual treatment of offenders as well.
4. There now exists a wide variety of treatment technologies for dealing with child sex offenders, many of which have proven successful (Kelley, 1982). These include techniques such as masturbatory reconditioning (Laws & O'Neil, 1979), desensitization (Abel, 1978), heterosocial skills training (Marshall & McKnight, 1975; Whitman & Quinsey, 1981), insight therapy (Kelley, 1982), and antiandrogen drug therapy (Berlin & Meinecke, 1981). Although there are controversies about the effectiveness of various approaches, the issue for many experts is not whether any effective approach exists, but rather how to mix and match approaches to types of offenders.
5. The treatment of child sex offenders is a highly specialized field, and most clinicians, including many who treat other types of offenders, are not skilled enough to treat them. In spite of this, many child sex offenders are routinely remanded by courts and attorneys to therapists with only limited experience in this kind of treatment. This misplacement needs to be monitored and changed (Finkelhor, 1984, p. 235).

Thus, although many gains in research and the need for refining intervention must be addressed, progress is being made. In the meantime, practitioners must choose carefully both the assessment and treatment paradigms to be employed, as well as what aspects of prevention most merit our attention.

CURRENT PROGRAM CHALLENGES

False Allegations

There is increasing concern on the part of citizens and certain professionals that persons accused of sexual or physical abuse are not being treated fairly (Schultz, 1988) or may be the victim of false allegations by children or adolescents. Although there are ample reasons to investigate all reports of child maltreatment cautiously because of this possibility, the bulk of the evidence indicates that in the vast majority of cases children are reporting the essential facts (see, for example, Robin, 1991). But practitioners should receive special training to ensure that child interviews are conducted in such a way that the emotional trauma is minimized and no leading questions are used. Conducting assessment or corroborative interviews with law enforcement personnel is a controversial area with few empirically defined guidelines.

> Children are often the only available sources of information about possible abusive experiences. Research has shown that children can, in fact, be remarkably competent informants, although the quality and quantity of the information they provide is greatly influenced by the ways in which they are interviewed.
>
> Interviewers can take advantage of children's strength, tendencies, and limitations when conducting investigative interviews. There is a gradual increase with age in the likelihood that young children can be found competent to testify, however. Few developmentalists would wonder, for example, whether a 1 year old could be competent or assume that (absent other disabilities) a 12 year old is likely to be incompetent. Disagreement might well emerge, however, concerning the age at which most children could be presumed competent. Most children of or under the age of 3 lack the communicative and memorial capacity to be competent witnesses, although competence rapidly increases over the remaining preschool years and Jones and Krugmen (1986) have persuasively documented the ability of one 3 year old victim to provide compelling information about her experiences and to identify her abuser. The rate of change in competence appears to decrease substantially once children attain 6 years of age, with the majority of children in this age group being capable of providing useful information when questioned competently (see Lamb et al., 1994 for a review). Indeed children are often more competent informants than adults realize. Interviews conducted in ways that clearly communicate the unique purposes of investigative interviews, minimize the burden placed on children's capacities, and take maximal advantage of children's abilities and our growing knowledge of memory and communication demonstrate that children can be invaluable sources of information. Because alternative sources of information about alleged or suspected events are seldom available, only improvement in the average quality of investigative interviews are likely to bring about improvement in our ability to protect children. (Lamb, Sternberg, & Esplin, 1998, p. 813, 821)

Treatment Effectiveness

The field has a long way to go in terms of refining intervention strategies so that parenting skills and other gains made in treatment are maintained, and recidivism rates of between 30 and 50% are reduced (see, for example, Cohn, 1979, p. 518). Long-term follow-up studies of sexual abusers are particularly needed to answer a variety of questions about why adults molest children and the efficacy of various treatment modalities (Finkelhor, 1986a, pp. 136–142).

Staffing

Due to worker turnover, poor working conditions, high caseloads, and other factors, there remains a shortage of treatment personnel able to use specialized skills in working with parents. The landmark research conducted by Berkeley Planning Associates in the late 1970s found that protection of children while they were in treatment was most strongly associated with the utilization of highly trained professionals during the intake and treatment planning phases. In terms of treatment efficacy, it was a blend of professional, paraprofessional, and Parents Anonymous services that was most effective in reducing parent propensity to reabuse (Cohn, 1983, pp. 518–519).

CONCLUSION

This chapter has discussed the etiology, prevention, and treatment of child sexual abuse. These are program areas in which family members are experiencing much stress and pain. Professional skill and sensitivity are essential for helping the victims and their families overcome the trauma of the maltreatment. In contrast, the next chapter addresses two less dramatic but nevertheless damaging forms of maltreatment: (1) physical and medical neglect and (2) emotional abuse and neglect.

NOTES

1. As Conte (1986) notes, "For general convenience, offenders will be referred to throughout this work in the masculine and victims in the feminine unless specifically intended otherwise. Males can also be victims and females, on rare occasions, may be offenders."

2. Definitions of sexual abuse and how to distinguish the more general term from intrafamilial abuse ("incest") are current challenges in the field. Much confusion exists and terms such sexual abuse and incest are often used interchangeably without proper distinctions being made. For a discussion of these issues, see Conte (1991), Haugaard and Reppucci (1988, pp. 13–31), and Korbin (1987).

3. The question in the Texas study was "Were you ever sexually abused as a child?" sexual abuse being defined as "contacts or interactions between a child and an adult when the child is being used for the sexual stimulation of the perpetrator or another person. Sexual abuse may be committed by a person under the age of 18 when that person is significantly older than the victim or when the perpetrator is in the position of power or control over another child." There was no specified age range for "child" and no specified age difference for "significantly older" (Finkelhor, 1984, p. 237).

4. Also see Daro (1988, pp. 139–142), Gilbert et al. (1989, pp. 115–137), and Reppucci and Haugaard (1989) for discussions about mixed effectiveness and/or funding decisions for sexual abuse prevention programs.

5. The multiple R for Finkelhor's predictive model for sexual abuse was 0.32 (see Finkelhor, 1984, p. 28).

6. For more information about treating victims of sexual abuse, see Berliner and Ernst (1984), Burgess et al. (1978), Finkelhor and Browne (1986), Faller (1988, pp. 265–391), Haugaard and Reppucci (1988), Justice and Justice (1979), Oates and Bross (1995), Sgroi (1988, 1989), and Walker et al. (1988, pp. 142–164).

7. Group work approaches require highly trained and skillful coordinators but appear to be one of the most important treatment components along with individual and family therapy. See Blick and Porter (1982), Haugaard and Reppucci (1988, pp. 261–292), Giarretto (1981), MacFarlane et al. (1986), and Sgroi (1989).

FOR FURTHER INFORMATION

English, K., Pullen, S., & Jones, L. (1997). Managing adult sex offenders in the community—A containment approach. (National Institute of Justice Research in Brief.) Washington, DC: U.S. Department of Justice.

Faller, K.C. (1988). *Child sexual abuse: An interdisciplinary manual for diagnosis, case management, and treatment.* New York: Columbia University Press. This volume represents one of the most practical volumes available currently on sexual abuse diagnosis, evaluation, and intervention. The book includes numerous case vignettes as well as chapters on medical evaluation and legal interventions.

Friedrich, W.N. (Ed.). (1991). *Casebook of sexual abuse treatment.* New York: W. W. Norton. Fifteen case descriptions of sexually abused children in treatment are discussed by nationally recognized treatment experts. Each case includes a description of the therapist's theoretical perspective, assessment, intervention approach, case outcome, and personal reactions.

Haugaard, J.J., & Reppucci, N.D. (1988). *The sexual abuse of children.* San Francisco: Jossey-Bass. Presents practical guidelines regarding the diagnosis and treatment of sexually abusing families and victims. This book is distinguished by a number of informative case examples and information for treatment strategies.

Karp, C.L., & Butler, T.L., (1996). *Treatment strategies for abused children: From victim to survivor.* Newbury Park, CA: Sage Publications. A practical book with accompanying activity guide for treating sexually abused children.

Maddock, J.W., & Larson, N.R. (1995*). Incestuous families: An ecological approach to understanding and treatment.* New York and London: W.W. Norton & Company. Focuses on clinical issues in treating sexual abuse.

Margolin, Judith A. (1999). *Breaking the silence—Group therapy for childhood sexual abuse—A practitioner's manual.* This manual provides a detailed curriculum for conducting short-term psychoeducational groups for survivors of childhood sexual abuse.

National Institute of Justice. (1997). *Child sexual molestation: Research issues.* Washington, DC: U.S. Department of Justice. Discusses evaluation issues associated with assessing and treating sexual abuse.

Videos

Faller, K.C. (1998). *Interviewing for child sexual abuse—A forensic guide.* A color video (35-minute VHS). Available from Guilford Publications, 72 Spring Street, New York, NY 10012.

Faller, K.C., & Scarnecchia, S. (1998) *Testifying about child sexual abuse—A courtroom guide.* A color video (35-minute VHS). Available from Guilford Publications, 72 Spring Street, New York, NY 10012.

7

Child Neglect and Psychological Maltreatment

This chapter will examine various forms of neglect and psychological maltreatment in relation to the following areas:

- definitions and subtypes
- rates of reporting and estimated incidence in America
- causal typologies and major risk factors
- strategies for prevention
- promising treatment approaches
- current policy, practice, and research issues[1]

In terms of incidence and reporting rates, the chapter will draw from statistics from the NIS-3 study that were summarized in Chapter 5, supplemented by statistics from the American Association for Protecting Children. As discussed in Chapter 5, the definitions of child maltreatment used in this chapter, although representing the best available, oversimplify the cultural and gender factors that affect how we define which parental behaviors (or lack thereof) constitute child maltreatment. In addition, Giovannoni and Becerra (1979) and others have demonstrated differences among professional groups in their operational definitions of child maltreatment.

Although nearly all states adhere to the basic definitions of child maltreatment provided in the Child Abuse and Neglect Prevention and Treatment Act (as amended), individual state definitions reflect individual state laws and service emphases. Furthermore, law enforcement, education, medical, and mental health allied professionals may hold different views and apply slightly different definitions, not only within, but between states. Mandatory reporting is not standardized regarding required reporters or the training they are required to have. This variability contributes to the inconsistency in the definitions of child neglect.

One strength of the NIS-2 and NIS-3 studies, however, was the use of reasonably specific operational definitions of various types of child maltreatment, so that reporting would be consistent across the national data collection sites. These definitions will be used in each of the sections describing a particular form of child maltreatment (e.g., physical neglect), and supplemented by other studies that contain either comparable data or more comprehensive definitions.

PHYSICAL NEGLECT

Definitions and Reporting Rates

Precise definitions of neglect are difficult to develop as people disagree about where to draw the dividing line between responsible or minimal but adequate parental care and that considered "neglectful" (see Zuravin, 1989, and Chapter 5). Nevertheless, a number of definitions will be presented. In 1974 neglect was defined by the federal government as "an act of omission by a parent or caregiver that involved refusal or delay in providing health care; failure to provide basic needs such as food, clothing, shelter; affection and attention; inadequate supervision; or abandonment. This failure to act holds true for both physical and emotional neglect" (Public Law 93-247). Another definition that is helpful to consider follows:

> Child neglect may be defined as a condition in which a caretaker responsible for the child either deliberately or by extraordinary inattentiveness permits the child to experience avoidable present suffering and/or fails to provide one or more of the ingredients generally deemed essential for developing a person's physical, intellectual, and emotional capacities. (Polansky, Hall, & Polansky, 1975)

Child neglect is generally thought of as an act of omission and it has been divided into several categories, including the types mentioned in the definition above that relate not only to food, shelter, and medical care but to emotional deprivation as well. Zuravin and Taylor (1987) have proposed the set of definitions listed in Table 7.1. Note that Zuravin and Taylor have added age qualifiers to the definitions to further improve their specificity (see Zuravin, 1989, Appendix I).

These major categories of neglect can subdivided into 14 more discrete subtypes to help clarify research and practice in this area (see Table 7.2). This is particularly useful when examining the causes and effects of each form of neglect.

In attempting to define various types of maltreatment it is easy to see how they overlap and interact with one another, particularly regarding psychological maltreatment. For example, Zuravin (1989) and others (e.g., McGhee et al., 1989) feel that abandonment/desertion is more than just psychological maltreatment and that this form of maltreatment should be given a discrete category for neglect as well.

Physical neglect is the most frequently reported type of maltreatment and is generally seen as occurring when parents or the child's primary caretaker do not provide children with basic life needs, i.e., food, clothing, and shelter. Educational neglect is generally seen as occurring when parents fail to comply with laws that require regular school attendance. Medical neglect is present when there is a failure to provide a child with necessary medical care. Emotional neglect occurs when parents are responsible for an impairment of a child's intellectual, psychological, or emotional functioning or an impairment of a child's ability to view him or herself as a separate individual with dignity and self-worth. Viewed in the longer term,

Table 7.1. Zuravin and Taylor Definition of Neglect

Neglect: includes eight types of omissions in care by parents (*perpetrators*) that *may* or do result in physical, emotional, social, and/or cognitive harm to the child *or* harm to others or their property (as a result of the child's actions).

Physical health care: failure to obtain or delay in obtaining medical attention for acute illnesses, injuries, physical disabilities, and chronic problems; *or* failure to comply with professional recommendations (medical, school, or social work) regarding treatment.

Mental health care: failure to obtain or delay in obtaining professional attention for *obvious* mental health problems and developmental problems; or failure to comply with professional recommendations regarding treatment.

Supervision: inadequate supervision of child activities both inside and outside of the home, parent is in the home with the child but is not monitoring the child's activities closely enough to keep the child from behaving in ways that could have negative consequences for herself or himself, others, and/or property, *and* parent is not aware enough of the child's activities when he or she is out of the home to ensure that the child is not at risk for negative personal consequences or engaging in behaviors that could harm others or other's property. Includes truancy, being consistently late for school, and failure to enroll in school. Age Graded.

Substitute child care: abandons child, leaves child alone to fend for himself or herself, leaves child in the care of an inappropriate caretaker, leaves child with any caretaker for more than 48 hours without either telling the caretaker in advance that the child(ren) would remain for 2 days or calling during the first 2 days. Age Graded.

Housing hazards: e.g., leaking gas from stove or heating unit, hot water/steam leaks from radiators, dangerous substances (household cleaning agents, insect and rodent poisons, medications, anything that, if swallowed, could cause death or serious illness), and dangerous objects (guns and knives) stored in unlocked lower shelves or cabinets, under sink, or in the open, etc.

Household sanitation: e.g., garbage is not kept in a receptacle—instead it is strewn around the house or kept in bags that are rarely taken away, perishable foods are not refrigerated and are frequently found spoiling, roaches, mice, and/or rats are frequently seen in the home, toilets are not functioning with human excrement spilling on floor, animal excrement is visible around the house, etc.

Personal hygiene: constant and consistent inattention to child's personal hygiene (e.g., child's hair is matted or tangled and dirty, child's skin is dirty, child's teeth are encrusted with green or brown matter, infant/toddler's soiled diapers are not changed for hours/days, child's clothes, which are soiled and stained beyond cleaning, are worn for days).

Nutrition: Failure to provide regular and ample meals that meet basic nutritional requirements (meals have not been provided at all for several days, children eat spoiled food or nonfood items such as starch, dogfood, or catfood, or are frequently seen begging for food), and failure to provide the necessary rehabilitative diet to a child with particular types of physical health problems (lead poisoning, severe diarrhea, etc.).

Source: Zuravin and Taylor (1987, as cited in Zuravin, 1989, pp. 17–18).

emotional neglect may be the most damaging type of neglect. Abandonment occurs when a parent or parent substitute leaves a child alone with no intention of returning.

Child neglect was reported for 1,817,665 children in 1997, based on 43 reporting states (US DHEW, 1999, p. 4-2). A total of 1,335,100 of children were pro-

Table 7.2. Neglect Subtypes

Refusal to provide physical health care
Abandonment/desertion
Delay in providing physical health care
Failure to provide a permanent home
Refusal to provide mental health
Personal hygiene neglect
Delay in providing mental health care
Housing hazards
Housing sanitation
Supervisory neglect
Custody refusal
Nutritional neglect
Custody-related neglect
Educational neglect

Source: Zuravin (1989, p. 23).

jected to have been neglected in the NIS-3 study using the endangerment standard and 879,000 under the harm standard (Sedlak & Broadhurst, 1996, p. 8). See Note 1 in Chapter 5 for a definition of each standard.

Related studies have confirmed the importance of parental supervision. Nelson et al. (1989) found that lack of supervision of preschool children was the most frequent category noted in their sample of 171 primary caretakers who were suspected, newly confirmed, or categorized as chronically neglectful in Allegheny County (Pittsburgh). A significantly higher proportion of the chronic group was referred for inadequate housing and medical neglect (pp. 2–3). Nelson and colleagues confirmed these results in a later study (1993) that found that chronically neglecting families were poor, frequently receiving public assistance, lived in inadequate housing, exhibit poor hygiene, poor financial management, poor nutrition, poor medical attention, and parent–child conflict. Neglecting caregivers are frequently unemployed, depressed, and exhibit emotional problems. Investigating allegations of neglect and assisting caregivers where lack of supervision (a manifestation of child neglect) is a problem may present a variety of challenges to child welfare staff, due to the complex needs of these families. However a significant number of children sustain injuries each year due to nonsupervision (Jones, 1987).

Education neglect was also fairly high in 1996, as it was projected to involve 292,100 cases. Defining and responding to this form of maltreatment vary among the states and are controversial in the field. Many child welfare administrators want school systems to assume more of the responsibility for working with families whose children are experiencing difficulty in school attendance. Currently, many school systems facing budget cuts in counseling and social work services refer families to public child welfare agencies that should be served within the school system. The result is that child welfare staff are pressured to serve these children despite large caseloads of other families, families whose needs are appropriately addressed by the agency. This problem offers opportunities for schools and child welfare agencies to partner in order to better serve these families. Some local school districts have partnered with child welfare agencies to colocate child welfare workers in schools that experience a significant number of problems. These programs have yet to be rigorously studied, but offer promising alternative approaches.

Causal Typologies and Major Risk Factors

Neglect tends to be chronic and long term—not an isolated "act of commission" (Gaudin, 1993; Polansky, Chalmers, Buttenweiser, & Williams, 1981, p. 16). So statistics usually reflect *prevalence*—the level of neglect that exists as an ongoing, chronic phenomenon.

Wolfe (1993) argues that parents' maltreatment of their child follows a predictable course and can be viewed in three stages: (1) Parents experience reduced tolerance for stress and aggression. The parents' degree of preparation for their role as parents influences this stage. (2) Parents experience poor management of acute crisis and provocation. Neglecting parents may begin to avoid their children in an effort to cope with crisis. (3) Parents experience habitual patterns of arousal/avoidance and aggression with family members. Neglecting parents feel trapped and, thus, justified by further avoidance.

Nelson and colleagues (1993) found significant differences in chronically and newly neglecting caregivers. Newly neglecting caregivers report confused thinking and more dread than other caregivers. Approximately one-third of neglecting caregivers are assessed as having a substance abuse problem at the time a referral is made to child protective services. Newly neglecting caregivers have the lowest perception of the quality of their family relations and nearly 42% of these families are assessed as needing intervention services. Chronically neglecting parents tend to be older; more likely to be unemployed; more likely to be receiving public assistance; more likely to be married, have more children, and have less knowledge of child development; and more likely to have had a child placed out of the home. Chronically neglecting caregivers exhibit poor hygiene of the children, money management problems, inadequate housing, unemployment, mental retardation, and parent–child conflict. Chronically neglecting caregivers reported more perceived health problems than other caregivers.

Causal factors include *economic* conditions (lack of material goods and income); *ecological* or community factors (family behavior seen as responsive to the larger social context in which it is embedded); and *individual/family* (e.g., personalistic, where poor child care is attributed to differences in parental personalities, particularly their character structures) (Polansky et al., 1981, p. 21) (Table 7.3).

Poverty may be a major causal factor in most neglect cases. However, the disorganization, apathy, and lack of interpersonal and job skills of many neglecting parents make merely increasing income a necessary but insufficient condition for

Table 7.3. Major Risk Factors for Child Neglect

In the NIS-3 (1996) it is reported that child neglect accounts for 56% of all the referrals to child protective services. It is by far the most common form of child maltreatment. These families are the most difficult to engage in services. Chronic neglecting families tend to have several referrals to Child Protective Services; some families may have as many as 50 referrals. The specificity of the definitions, the risk assessment method used, and agency response procedures can significantly impact a social worker's intervention with a neglecting family. Some risk factors from a range of research studies are summarized below:

Paget and colleagues (1993) found that parent–child attachment in neglecting families has been specified as anxious/avoidant. Neglecting mothers tend to use less speech, shorter incomplete sentences, direct imperatives, and less praise with their children. Children reciprocate with low rates of positive social behavior, less verbal interaction, and high rates of physical aggression. Brown and colleagues (1998) found that neglected children where at increased risk for being anxious and withdrawn in early childhood. Neglected children exhibit expressive and receptive language deficits, they have difficulty with cognitive and physical activities, and they engage in less prosocial behavior with peers. Neglected children are at increased risk of low verbal IQ scores. Benard (1989) found that a critical variable influencing a child's level of self-esteem and psychosocial development is the degree of parental conflict in the family. The parent–child relationship, life stress, and social support available to the mother also influence child self-esteem.

Individual Risk Factors

Margolin (1990) found that male children under 3 years of age living with a mother and two siblings were at greatest risk to die from child neglect. Margolin also found that preschool aged children are at greatest risk of child neglect. English (1998) found that children under 1 year are more likely to be reported to child protective services than are older children. Of the child fatalities between 1993 and 1995, 85% involved children under 5 years of age. Liaw and Brooks-Gunn (1994) found that children's IQ scores were negatively correlated with low birth weight. Nelson and colleagues (1993) found that children of chronically neglecting caregivers had more problems with mental illness, truancy, and school.

Family Risk Factors

Cowan et al. (1996) found that severe pathology in parents or dysfunctional interaction in families is associated with greater risk of poor outcomes for children. Liaw and Brooks-Gunn (1994) identified risk factors for children associated with the following characteristics of the mother: noncompletion of high school, low reading scores, depression, and low social support. Brown and colleagues (1998) identified demographic risk factors such as ethnicity, large family size, low income, low maternal education, maternal youth, single parenthood, and recipient of welfare. Familial risk factors identified in this study include early separation from mother, maternal alienation, maternal anger, maternal dissatisfaction, maternal external locus of control, maternal hostility, low self-esteem of the mother, maternal sociopathy, parental conflict, paternal psychopathology, paternal sociopathy, marital discord, and serious maternal illness. Parenting risk factors are low paternal involvement and low paternal warmth.

Wolfe (1993) argues that parents' maltreatment of their child follows a predictable course and can be viewed in three stages. (1) Parents experience reduced tolerance for stress and aggression. The parents' degree of preparation for their role as a parent influences this stage. (2) Parents experience poor management of acute crisis and provocation. Neglecting parents may begin to avoid their children in an effort to cope with crisis. (3) Parents experience habitual patterns of arousal/avoidance and aggression with family members. Neglecting parents feel trapped and, thus, justified by further avoidance.

(continued)

Table 7.3. (Continued)

Nelson and colleagues (1993) found that there are four general categories of factors that contribute to child neglect. (1) Family demographics: family size, parents' educational attainment, marital status, age of caregivers, and age of the children. (2) Financial and housing status. (3) Psychological profile of the caregivers: childhood experience of abuse, substance abuse, stressful life events, and psychological distress. Chronically neglecting caregivers are older, more likely to be unemployed, more likely to be receiving public assistance, more likely to be married, have more children, have less knowledge of child development, and are more likely to have had a child placed out of the home. Chronically neglecting caregivers exhibit poor hygiene of the children, money management problems, inadequate housing, unemployment, mental retardation, and parent–child conflict. Neglecting caregivers tend to provide inadequate nutrition and medical attention for their children. Neglecting caregivers are more likely to be depressed or have emotional problems at the time a referral to child protective services is made. Chronically neglecting caregivers reported more perceived health problems than other caregivers. Newly neglecting caregivers report confused thinking and more dread than other caregivers. Approximately one-third of neglecting caregivers are assessed as having a substance abuse problem at the time a referral is made to child protective services. Newly neglecting caregivers have the lowest perception of the quality of family relations and nearly 42% of these families are assessed as needing intervention services.

Gaudin (1993) identified risks associated with child neglect as a parent's mental retardation, depression, lack of money management skills, lack of menu-planning and cooking skills, and personality characteristics. Paget (1993) found that a mother's promiscuity, alcoholism, and temporary financial problems were found to be correlated with abandonment of biological children. Neglecting parents have been shown to exhibit poor problem-solving skills. Research consistently shows that neglecting mothers have problems with alcohol, violence, low self-esteem, and isolation. Neglecting caregivers have low quality or no support from spouses and fathers of the children. They tend to be less involved in informal helping networks, more lonely, do not interact with neighbors, and have a multiplicity of problems—money management, housing, medical care, unemployment, mental retardation, and conflict with child.

Zuravin (1987, 1988) found that as the number of unplanned conceptions increases the likelihood of child neglect also increases. English (1998) reports that substance abuse by a caregiver is likely to be present in 50–80% of the referrals to child protective services. The use of crack cocaine has also increased referrals to child protective service agencies. Maltreating parents are more likely to exhibit low self-esteem, poor impulse control, aggressiveness, anxiety, and depression.

Community Risk Factors

According to the data reported in the 1996 Study of the National Incidence and Prevalence of Child Abuse and Neglect, children living at or below the established poverty line are 40 times more likely to be harmed by physical neglect. Poverty, as a significant risk factor for child neglect, is confirmed by a number of studies (Gaudin, 1993; Paget et at., 1993; Nelson et al., 1993; English, 1998; Brown et al., 1998). Liaw and Brooks-Gunn (1994) identified risk factors for children associated with the child's socioeconomic status. These characteristics included race and ethnicity, and employment of the head of household. They found a significant correlation between poor child outcomes and socioeconomic risk factors.

Paget and colleagues (1993) found household crowding and community instability to be associated with child neglect. Nelson and colleagues (1993) found that 70% of the neglecting caregivers in their study had moved at least once in the previous 3-year period.

Source: Rector, F. (1998). *Balancing risk and resiliency in neglecting families: A review of the literature.* Seattle: University of Washington, School of Social Work (mimeograph).

reducing the level of neglect (Polansky et al., 1981, p. 25). This is particularly true given that most poor families do not neglect their children (Nelson et al., 1993; Zuravin, 1987; Gaudin, 1993). Ecological factors may interact with personality or behavioral factors as evidenced by the "social distancing" that seems to occur with some families, where the surrounding community shuns them because their lifestyles differ significantly from community norms (Gaudin & Polansky, 1986; Polansky & Gaudin, 1983). Yet it may not be the community per se that is rejecting the family, as family isolation may be due in major part to their feelings and behaviors. A study by Polansky, Gaudin, Ammons, and Davis (1985), which controlled for race, economic well-being, and other factors, found that one of the major differences between neglectful and nonneglectful parents was that the neglectful parents felt they lacked emotional support and were lonely. Unusually large numbers of neglectful parents were placed in substitute care as children. Many neglecting parents also had frequent moves after marriage. These families are also more socially isolated from informal and formal helping networks (Polansky et al., 1981, pp. 90–95).

Neglect is seen more as a permissive style of life than as an isolated or discrete symptom of distress. Children, and in particular infants, sometimes are used as a "bulwark against loneliness." As the child grows older and more independent, the possibility of neglect increases with these parents. Detachment and impulsivity (behavior or decisions without much forethought) also seem to be common maternal characteristics (Polansky et al., 1981, pp. 35–36). Some of the following character traits are common to many neglectful mothers and represent major components of the "apathy–futility" syndrome:

1. A pervasive conviction that nothing is worth doing. The feeling of futility predominates, as in the schizoid personality. As one patient used to say, "What's the use of eating supper; you'll only be hungry before breakfast."
2. Emotional numbness sometimes mistaken for depression. It is beyond depression; it represents massive affect-inhibition from early splitting in the ego.
3. Interpersonal relationships typified by desperate clinging; they are superficial, essentially lacking in pleasure, and accompanied by intense loneliness.
4. Lack of competence in many areas of living, partially caused by the unwillingness to risk failure in acquiring skills.
5. Expression of anger passive-aggressively and through hostile compliance.
6. Noncommitment to positive stands; even the stubborn negativism is a last-ditch assertion that one exists.
7. Verbal inaccessibility to others, and a related crippling in problem solving because of the absence of internal dialogue.
8. An uncanny skill in bringing to consciousness the same feelings of futility in others; this is used as a major interpersonal defense against efforts to bring about change (Polansky, 1979).

An intergenerational cycle may be at work here as well—a "passing on of infantilism, mother to daughter, through processes of deprivation leading to detachment (the 'deprivation–detachment hypotheses'), failure to provide stimulation, and the child's identification with an inadequate role model. Hence the cycle of neglect might be said to drive from a cycle of infantilism" (Polansky et al., 1981, p. 43). Although it must be emphasized that generalizing these families is not wise because of their diversity, some of the research data depict a group of neglectful caregivers who are generally (1) less able to love, (2) less capable of working productively, (3) less open about feelings, (4) more prone to living planlessly and impulsively, (5) more susceptible to psychological symptoms and to phases of passive inactivity and numb fatalism, (6) less organized and more chaotic, with more family conflict, (7) less verbally expressive, and (8) less positive and show more negative affect (Erikson & Egeland, 1996; Polansky et al., 1981, p. 109; Gaudin, Polansky, Kilpatrick, & Shilton, 1996; Polansky, Gaudin, & Kilpatrick, 1992). Although many families involved with substance abuse never come to the attention of child welfare agencies, when they do they very often are identified as having problems related to child neglect (DHHS, 1999a).

In a sense, the parenting/nurturing instinct has been weakened or distorted in its aim, or overwhelmed by the parent's struggle in personal survival. This stunting or crippling of parenting or nurturing is not often an emergent response to current stress but predictable from the social history of the parent and the lack of nurturance in their childhood (Polansky et al., 1981, pp. 147–157). Some of those risk factors (and family strengths and resources) are illustrated by the following case example:

Children Who Are Not Headliners

The family consists of Mona Stay, twenty-three, and her common-law husband Frank Brown, aged twenty-six. There are three children: Frank Stay, three and a half, Sylvia Stay, eighteen months, and Wilma, seven months. The Stay-Browns have been together over five years. Although they quarrel and separate periodically, they seem very mutually dependent and likely to remain a couple.

Their original referral was from a nurse who had become aware of the eldest child's, Frank's, condition. He was difficult to discipline, was eating dirt and paint chips, and seemed hyperactive. Although over two, he was not speaking. His father reacted to him with impatience. He was often slapped, and hardly ever spoken to with fondness. The case worker got Mona to cooperate in taking young Frank in for a test for lead poisoning, and for a full developmental evaluation. This child had had several bouts with impetigo, had been bitten through the eyelid by a stray dog, and had a series of ear infections resulting in a slight hearing loss. Although physically normal, developmentally he appeared already nearly a year retarded.

Often this child was found outside the house alone when the caseworker came to see the family. On one occasion he was seen hanging from a broken fire escape on the second floor. The worker was unable to rouse his mother, or to enter the house until she got help from the nearby landlord, after which she ran upstairs and rescued the child. Only then did the sleeping Mona awaken!

With much effort having been expended on his behalf, this child had been attending a therapeutic nursery. His speech is already improved after four or five months, and his hyperactivity has calmed. He comes through as a lovable little boy.

Sylvia is surprisingly pale . . . and indeed, suffers from severe anemia. This child has had recurrent eye infections, and had a bout with spinal meningitis at age three months which, fortunately, seems to have left no residua. Much effort has gone into working with Mona concerning Sylvia's need for proper diet and iron supplement. After a year of contact this is still a problem.

The baby was born after the family had become known to the agency. Despite the agency's urging, Mona refused to go for prenatal care until she was in her second trimester, but she did maintain a fairly good diet, helped by small "loans" from the agency when her money for food ran out. When Wilma was born, she had to remain for a time at the hospital for treatment of jaundice. After she went home, she was left to lie most of the time in her bassinet, receiving very little attention from either parent. At four months of age, Wilma weighed only five pounds and was tentatively diagnosed as exhibiting "failure to thrive" by the hospital. Thereafter the mother avoided going to the clinic, and the caseworker spend much effort concerning the feeding and sheer survival of Wilma. The baby is now slowly gaining weight but is still limp and inactive.

In addition to an active caseworker, a homemaker was assigned to this family for months. Much more was involved than trying to help Mona learn to organize her day: she had almost no motivation to get started. Rather than learning how to manage, she tried to manipulate the homemaker into doing her housework for her. However, with time and patience, Mona has been persuaded to go with the caseworker on shopping trips, is learning how to buy groceries to best advantage, and from time to time manages to get the laundry into and out of the laundromat. So far as her plans for herself, Mona has talked of seeking training as a beauty operator, but has never followed through on this or on other positive plans.

The family's sole support is public assistance. Frank Brown, the father, was on drugs earlier in their relationship, but managed to get off them. Now, however, he drinks heavily, and although he manages to work, he never contributes to the household.

Mona, apparently, was herself a neglected child, and was removed from her parents in infancy. Placed with an adoptive family, there was constant friction during her growing up, and she ran away from home several times. During her teens, she was placed in an institution for incorrigible girls. Later she spent a period in a mental hospital during which she was withdrawn from heroin addiction. It is a commentary on her life that she regards this period in the adolescent ward as one of her happiest ever. Her adoptive mother is now dead, and her father wants nothing more to do with her, so she was more or less living on the streets when she met with Frank and set up their present establishment.

Frank and Mona, despite his obvious exploitativeness, seem to love each other and their children, and to want to keep the family together. They are able to relate to those who try to help them, so at least one is not operating constantly against hostile resistance. Mona is an intelligent woman and now shows adequate ability to handle the children. She can be an excellent cook—when there is food. Yet this remains a disorganized household. Bills are never paid, clothes are thrown around, the children never sleep on clean sheets, trash is piled around the house so that flies and maggots abound. Mona still leaves the youngsters quite alone for brief periods. There is no heat in the house, and the family will soon have to move, with neither any idea where to go nor funds for rent deposits and the like. Mona, at least, is currently wearing an IUD.

The Stay-Brown menage was not invented, although of course we have altered names and some facts to protect all concerned. These are real people, and they are clearly involved in child neglect. The failures center on poor feeding, uncleanliness, extremely bad housing, filthy circumstances which make the children prone to infections, lack of medical care, inadequate supervision and protections from danger, lack of intellectual stimulation, inattentiveness to the children bordering on rejection—one could go on. What chance does a Wilma, malnourished to the point of near death in infancy, have of resolving her first life crisis on the side of Erikson's (1959) Basic Trust? By what models is young Frank to acquire control over his impulses, and joy in productive work?

These are obvious questions, but it is hard to ask them without seeming to sneer. There are those in the legal profession who believe we have no right to intervene in families like this one because our ability to predict the future harm to the youngsters is so poor. And what would they predict? Three Nobel Prize winners? Three factory workers? Three happy adults of whatever sort? Yet, these are people about to miss on their only chances for happy lives, unless something is done to save them. Indeed, it is hard simply to condemn their parents, given what we have learned about Mona's history. Frank, who is not an admirable man, does not talk. But something about his background might be gleaned from the fact that his own parents have recently asked to move in with him!

What we see, in other words, is that these are very real people, that there must be many, many Mona–Frank households, and "something should be done." We also see, immediately, that the problem is not easy, and that our knowledge concerning what to do is inadequate. The fine staff trying to help Mona improve her child care finally gave up and closed her case after about fifteen months of effort. The care was improving slowly, if at all, and there were recurrent instances of regression. Frank proved superficially amendable to suggestions when he could be seen, but in fact evaded any real responsibility for the household. The time, money, and—more importantly—motivation for hard work with such families are chronically in short supply. So the decision was made to try to help someone else who might be more treatable.

Meanwhile these children are with their parents. Since they have not literally been abandoned, it is uncertain whether a local judge would decide the home is so bad that the children must be removed. If a catastrophe were to occur, if one were to read that that these three children had burned to death in a fire, one would be saddened but not greatly surprised. If one of the three were to die of an infectious disease or an undiagnosed appendicitis, one would not be surprised either. For the present, however, they are among the group child-protection workers know well, but that the public does not, because they do not make headlines—or at least not yet. (Polansky, Chalmers, Buttenweiser, & Williams, 1981, pp. 5–7)

Promising Treatment Approaches

Most neglectful parents are not reacting to a situation-specific crisis such as the illness or death of a family member. Most often the problems are long-standing ones connected with how parents think and feel about themselves. With many of these families, unless some form of intensive in-home treatment or support group is initiated, specific treatment goals cannot be quickly formulated, and casework is certainly going to require a period of time longer than 6 months. Thus treatment generally is not short term and neglectful parents often do not change in response to a threat as they expect others to change the situation for them (Polansky et al., 1981, p. 161). Multiple types of intervention may be needed (DePanfilis, 1997).

Treatment "leverage."   These methods for building client rapport and investment in the change process assume a special prominence in casework with neglecting families. Some critical principles include the following:

1.   The social worker can often use him or herself as the entering wedge in beginning the treatment by posing some form of threat to the client (persistent visitation, child placement) or by disrupting the client's level of system balance.

2.   Practical or "concrete" services such as housecleaning, transportation, or securement of household goods are often one of the best forms of treatment leverage provided that the parent wants them and that there is as direct a connection as possible between the service rendered and the social worker's action (i.e., indirect referrals are less potent forms of treatment leverage). Concrete help is an obvious but often underutilized form of leverage.

3.   When clients like their workers personally, another form of casework leverage is present. Client attachment to workers is difficult because of clients' poor prior experiences and their feelings of hostility or suspicion. Nevertheless, continued supportive contact (particularly when accompanied by the provision of concrete help) often generates some positive relationship.

From this positive relationship there emerges a client who wishes to stay in contact with the worker and to please him or her. Because child removal is a realistic and ethical option in so few neglect cases, "the workers only leverage becomes what he or she has to offer in the way of wanted services or the ability to give or withhold approval, like a living parent."

4.   Identification with the worker, homemaker, or members of a parent group may also be a form of leverage for change. Clients begin to assimilate and use "standards of child care and other values that the worker has, in a process that is typically unconscious and certainly unspoken." This form of identification should not be identified and discussed per se (Polansky et al., 1981, pp. 190–191).

The concept of client homeostasis is a key one for understanding case dynamics and how clients often deliberately create external turmoil to distract themselves from inner conflicts. Caseworkers need to help the client break up the old equilibrium ("unfreeze"), move to a new level of child care, and "refreeze" the equilibrium (Polansky et al., 1981, pp. 196–199).

A large percentage of neglectful parents suffer from the "apathy–futility syndrome." This character disorder is characterized by severe immaturity and infantilism. A high percentage of the parents may appear to be "impulse-ridden." Parents who scored high on character disorder scales had much poorer "indices of child care" as measured by the Childhood Level of Living scale. So what we have are parents who are apathetic, feeling futile, who dull their wants and feelings, and whose only way of asserting themselves is through negativism. What Polansky and his colleagues observed is that in treating these people, social workers should recognize that many will have a fear of closeness because of parent rejection and deprivation as a child. Also, expect to see a poorly developed sense of independent self.

In building a close working relationship, it is only natural that some caregivers may become dependent on the support of the caseworker. Although encouraging client dependency is frowned on in some treatment circles, this may be one of the more helpful benefits of effective rapport building. Encouraging caregiver dependency in terms of reliance on the caseworker for understanding the situation and providing some resources may be one of the best casework strategies because some parents who had extremely negative past experiences or relationship problems, if they relate at all, will relate first at that level (Polansky et al., 1981, p. 202).

Alleviating Client Loneliness.   Probably one of the most useful treatment principles relates to the notion that many neglecting parents are lonely people because of past maltreatment, a lack of social skills, or an inability to risk closeness (Polansky, Ammons, & Gaudin, 1985). These last two points are connected as the Bowen Center in Chicago found that one of the most important aspects of their treatment was the ongoing and stable relationship that the caseworker formed with the parents.

As the parents at the Bowen Center received concrete services such as homemaker, day care, public assistance, and emergency child care, and expanded their social networks, the social worker remained for them the primary helping individual, consistently relating to their needs and feelings. So although there is a need for recreational and educational services for these parents, the social worker still plays a key role in providing a stable relationship to the parents. In a sense the social worker renurtures the parents to build up or unleash their capacity to parent their children (Polansky et al., 1981, pp. 206–207).

But in conjunction with this, the staff member should be helping the parents to examine their social network and to learn skills that will allow them to build and maintain strong and supportive informal social networks when the service has ended. This can be achieved in a variety of ways, including personal networking, mutual aid groups, volunteer linking, neighborhood helpers, and social skills training (Gaudin, Wodarski, Arkinson, & Avery, 1989, pp. 6–7). So one aspect of the helping relationship with neglectful patents is the treatment of loneliness through building positive social networks.

Helping parents deal with the sources of anxiety and hostility within themselves is another important treatment focus as these parents often harbor deep-seated feelings of hostility to their parents and anxiety in a wide range of areas. Given a sufficiently stable and trusting relationship, parents may be willing to attempt major attitude changes and self-exploration of their feelings and motivation if a therapist is available to help and is aware of the client's willingness to engage in treatment in a new way. Finally, the *advocacy and companion* role in helping to advocate for the client cannot be overlooked as it is both a source of concrete support and means to combat loneliness. Once a tie of affection and trust has been established, the societal values and minimum standards of child care may then be transmitted, partly through identification with the worker.

Transitional Relationships.   The concept of a *transitional relationship* is an important one in which clients use their relationship with you to learn how to form relationships and to learn skills for relating to others that they can use in other relationships. Clients then can generalize the changes made in a casework relationship to relationships with others. Marital counseling (with some emphasis on improving communication) can be used to help parents to *nurture* each other. Both parents need to share the "mothering" they both need (Polansky et al., 1981, p. 216).

Use of Groups and Parental Prostheses.   Approach group modes of treatment with some caution as most neglectful parents have poor self-images, are wary or phobic of group situations, and are notoriously unorganized in relation to keeping appointments. But if started with special support such as transportation and day care, groups can be very effective and rewarding to the parents and children, as progress will generally be made more quickly compared with more traditional counseling approaches (Cole, 1985; Polansky et al., 1981, pp. 218–220).

Concrete services and counseling ("parental prostheses") may be necessary to supplement a child's care. This occurs normally across America to the degree that parents use music lessons, day care, and other services to enrich childrearing. If any one of a variety of parental prostheses are used, it is important that the primary worker be supported and involved in setting up, coordinating, and reviewing the treatment process to minimize the workers vulnerability to manipulation and to increase the workers' treatment leverage and power (Polansky et al., 1981, pp. 224–225).

In neglectful homes a variety of things may need to be addressed to ensure that children receive adequate care in the following areas:

- Basic Physical Care (including food, warmth, medical attention, rest, protection, basic hygiene).
- Basic Psychological Care (including love, attentiveness, talking, teaching, and limiting).
- Predictability (people and things will stay in place; meal and bedtime routines are established; promises will be kept and children's actions have consequences they can count on).

- Organization [day-to-day things get done because someone in the family knows how to help get them done; problems in daily living are addressed reasonably well (Polansky et al., 1981, pp. 226–227)].

There are a variety of services that can act as parental prostheses (DePanfilis, 1997; Gaudin, 1993). Homemaker services (on a daily or hourly basis) is an important service because a significant number of neglectful mothers lack knowledge about basic household skills and because homemakers are great role models. But one should expect some possible transference to occur with the homemaker viewed as the "good mother" and the caseworker seen as the "bad mother." Day care is useful for providing additional child physical and emotional nurturance, parental respite, and an enjoyable means of parent participation in the nurturing of children. But workers should realistically expect that some parents may, at least initially, need someone to help wake, dress, and transport the children to the Day Care Center.

Emergency services such as emergency in-home or foster care may be needed to provide some families with a temporary coping mechanism. Finally, institutional placement and foster care may be utilized for specialized treatment or out-of-home care. However, be aware that many neglectful parents will have an all-or-none relationship with their children. The child is treated as part of the parent, or the child loses meaning entirely. So unless ongoing parental visitation and involvement are encouraged, client change and reunification are not likely to occur (Polansky et al., 1981, pp. 221–237).

NONORGANIC FAILURE TO THRIVE AS A SPECIAL CASE OF NEGLECT

Definition and Diagnosis

Failure to thrive (FTT) is defined as a syndrome of infancy and early childhood that is characterized by malnutrition, poor physical growth, and retardation of motor and social development. There is no "universal" or standard definition of FTT, but the following are usually listed as diagnostic criteria:

1. Weight or height below the third percentile.
2. Weight is less than 80 to 85% of the ideal for that age.
3. Failure to maintain previous growth—usually indicated by the patterning of the child's growth—where his or her growth line drops below previous percentile lines (see Figure 7.1).
4. Duration of failure to maintain growth (2 months for infants less than 5 months of age, 3 months for infants 5 or more months of age).
5. Delayed psychomotor development (English, 1978; Metcalf, 1989).

**BOYS: BIRTH TO 36 MONTHS
PHYSICAL GROWTH
NCHS PERCENTILES***

Figure 7.1

NAME _____Nathan Jones_____ RECORD # ___522

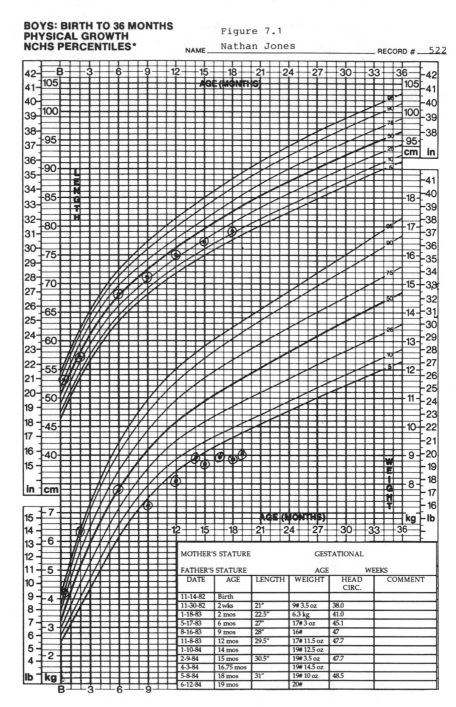

MOTHER'S STATURE			GESTATIONAL		
FATHER'S STATURE			AGE		WEEKS
DATE	AGE	LENGTH	WEIGHT	HEAD CIRC.	COMMENT
11-14-82	Birth				
11-30-82	2 wks	21"	9# 3.5 oz	38.0	
1-18-83	2 mos	22.5"	6.3 kg	41.0	
5-17-83	6 mos	27"	17# 3 oz	45.1	
8-16-83	9 mos	28"	16#	47	
11-8-83	12 mos	29.5"	17# 11.5 oz	47.7	
1-10-84	14 mos		19# 12.5 oz		
2-9-84	15 mos	30.5"	19# 3.5 oz	47.7	
4-3-84	16.75 mos		19# 14.5 oz		
5-8-84	18 mos	31"	19# 10 oz	48.5	
6-12-84	19 mos		20#		

In essence, FTT involves the starvation of a child. Weight generally precedes height in their falling off, with head circumference the last to decrease. Thus, growth charts are critical in determining failure to thrive. Children who are approximately in the third percentile in weight for their age are likely candidates (see Figure 7.1). In Figure 7.1, the height and weight patterns of a child recently diagnosed with failure to thrive are illustrated. The child's length (height) is plotted according to percentile curves on the upper lines. The pattern of height growth indicates that the child is beginning at the 75th percentile at birth but has dropped to the 10th percentile at 18 months (see the percentile scale at the far right of the graph).

The lower percentile lines are used to chart changes in the child's weight over a 36-month period. The pattern of weight gain or loss indicates that the child's weight percentile has dropped significantly (birth, 90–95th percentile; 6 months, 50th percentile; 9 months, 5th percentile). The extreme decrease at 9 months occurred when the infant was mistakenly put on 2% milk by his mother. Note that only a momentary weight gain to the fifth percentile was made at 14 months, before dropping to dangerous levels after that (medical intervention would have begun much earlier had the pattern been recognized, but the parents saw a variety of different health care providers). The pediatric specialists reconstructed this chart by contacting the various health care providers as part of their diagnostic assessment.

Some of the behavioral signs exhibited by infants and children include an unusual "frozen or radar-like" watchfulness. The child may smile rarely or not at all, and resist being cuddled. Their body posture may be immature, assuming a newborn-like position (e.g., frog-like posture on their back). These children are frequently tired, appear apathetic, and may have problems with vomiting and diarrhea.

Failure to thrive can be due to a variety of reasons. Socioenvironmental or nonorganic factors are present in approximately 50% of the cases. Organic factors include some types of physical illness or disability that do not allow the infant or child to process or retain sufficient nutrients; these factors may be present in about 25% of the cases. In contrast, genetically linked factors may be involved, such as small stature or slow maturation. Some cases, however, involve a mixture of organic and nonorganic factors. Some of the most common nonorganic and organic factors are listed below, roughly in their order of prevalence in FTT cases.

Figure 7.1.   Height and weight growth percentile chart for boys, birth to 36 months. Adapted from Hamill, P.V.V., Drizd, T.A., Johnson, C.L., Reed, R.B., Roche, A.F. & Moore, W.M.. (1979). Physical growth: National Center for Health Statistics percentiles. *American Journal of Clinical Nutrition, 32,* 607–629. Data from the Fels Research Institute, Wright State University School of Medicine, Yellow Springs, Ohio. © 1982, Ross Laboratories. Reprinted with permission of Ross Laboratories, Columbus, OH 43216. From *NCHS Growth Charts* (1982).

Nonorganic (Psychosocial-environmental)

1. Improper feeding
2. Child abuse or neglect
3. Multiple births
4. Emotional deprivation

Organic

1. Central nervous system (CNS) (e.g., degenerative disease, spastic quadriplegia, subdural hematoma)
2. Gastrointestinal (e.g., celiac disease, giardiasis, lactose intolerance, cystic fibrosis)
3. Renal (e.g., chronic pyelonephritis)
4. Congenital heart disease
5. Intrauterine growth retardation
6. Tumor (e.g., leukemia, Wilms, neuroblastoma)
7. Metabolic (e.g., glycogen storage, galactosemia)
8. Pulmonary (e.g., cystic fibrosis)
9. Endocrine (e.g., diabetes, hypothyroid, hypopituitarism)
10. Syndromes, numerous—e.g., hypochondroplasia, etc.
11. Familial small stature
12. Familial slow maturation (constitutional delayed growth)

In distinguishing organic from nonorganic failure to thrive, English (1978) specifies that it may be characterized by a deceleration in physical growth from a previously normal standard and , not attributable to disease or systemic problems. It is distinguished by symptoms of failure to grow and gain weight, developmental slowness, occasional vomiting and/or diarrhea, and frequent feeding difficulties.

To determine if organic factors are involved, the medical team must determine if the child is unable to eat, digest, or use a sufficient amount of food calories if they are provided to him or her. For example, the child may refuse to eat because of a neuromuscular disorder or mental retardation. The child may swallow the food, but later vomit because of some obstruction, intestinal disorder, or some other factor.

In contrast, the food may be retained but is losing calories as fecal material because of cystic fibrosis, inflammatory bowel disease, or other illness. "End organ" unresponsiveness may also be a problem in that the child's organs cannot absorb or process the nutrients in sufficient quantities to maintain or increase growth (e.g., hormonal disturbances such as hypothyroidism, renal disease, growth anomalies, and neurological disorders). Finally, the child may have an illness that requires more energy than can be generated by what he or she can normally consume, such as congenital heart disease, chronic infections, or hyperthyroidism.

All of these possible factors must be examined through a complete child and family history (e.g., parental, prenatal, perinatal), physical examination, child growth patterns, developmental assessments (e.g., Bailey Developmental Assessment, Denver Developmental Screening Test), and a series of laboratory tests (e.g., urinalysis, CBC, culture, sedimentation rate, and pediatric profile). Yet FTT can be difficult to diagnose. Constitutionally delayed growth sometimes accounts for a temporary (1–5 month) leveling off in height, weight, and head circumference.

But the overall pattern is such that the child fails to maintain any growth after that. Caseworkers and physicians need to be able to differentiate short stature, ethnic differences, congenital midgets (they are proportionally small), or prenatal illnesses (e.g., congenital rubella, cocaine addiction of mother). These children may be born with a reasonable length, but are skinny and are likely to grow slowly. Most FTT patients have reasonably normal height and head circumference, but are below normal weight and fail to gain weight over time.

Family Dynamics of Nonorganic Failure to Thrive

Nonorganic FTT accounts for a significant percentage of FTT cases. Assessing specific factors in these cases involves obtaining an understanding of who the parents are and answering questions such as the following: (1) What are their lives like? Is there a history of maltreatment? (2) How do the parents feel about the infant or child? (3) How do the parents hold, feed, and interact with the child? Many parents of FTT children hold the child facing away from them, rarely vocalizing or smiling at the child, and use improper feeding routines such as having the child hold the bottle. There are standardized assessment tools available to assist child welfare workers in better understanding the risks for FTT, e.g., NCAST feeding scales (Barnard, 1983; 1998) and the various parental stress checklists (e.g., Abidin, 1983).

Medical and social service professionals strive to identify the social and emotional components of FTT. For example, attachment between parents and child is often impaired in some way due to emotional deprivation in the family, death of a family member or friend, or family isolation. The parents may have experienced previous miscarriages, may be very poor, or may suffer from some form of mental illness. In addition, the child may have had a difficult delivery or postpartum period. The child's nonresponsiveness or irritability may reinforce the parent's low sense of self-esteem through their behavior.

This tension also inhibits the formation of healthy parent–infant attachments. Mother–infant interaction is one of the more important parent or family factors. Moore (1982) believes that:

> Failure to thrive is rarely the result of willful neglect, but instead . . . is most frequently a symptom of family dysfunction, wherein the infant at risk becomes the receptacle of (usually unconscious) resentments, fears, conflicts, and stress points.

Thus, the parents respond with anxiety and tension to this child, who often reacts with similar rigidity, becoming fussy, unresponsive, and irritable. (p. 390)

More specifically, the maladaptive behaviors of both mother and infant may contribute to a child's failure to thrive. A clash of temperaments may occur at feeding time that produces a vicious cycle that usually accelerates (English, 1978). Failure to thrive becomes a process in which mother and infant both contribute to the other's problem through a series of problematic interactions. For example, mothers may provide inadequate amounts or types of food, as well as not hold or burp the infant. So, the infant develops an upset stomach, cries, and may suffer from diarrhea. Mothers are often unaware of the proper stimulation required by an infant. In addition, some mothers have unrealistic perceptions of their infant's condition and no awareness of the infant's development, progress, or lack of it. Infants can also contribute to this situation with behaviors that include resisting food, not sucking effectively, and remaining fussy after eating. The infant is often apathetic toward its environment, infrequently vocalizes, and does not smile. There may also be resistance to being held and/or cuddled (Harrison, 1976).

The family of a failure to thrive child is often isolated and has little support, whether from family or community. There is often economic deprivation and inadequate paternal emotional and/or economic support. Fulfillment in parental roles is not experienced and there may be ambivalence toward children (Evans, Reinhart, & Succop, 1983).

Impact on Children

Moore (1982) found that children who fail to thrive as infants are at a higher risk for developmental delays, personality problems, abuse, and even death. There is also evidence that suggests a higher risk of language delays, vocal unresponsiveness, and future problems in relating to parental figures (Mira & Cairons, 1981). These children may also be at higher risk for insecure attachment to others.

Treatment of Nonorganic Failure to Thrive

The traditional treatment approach has been hospitalization of the child, but recent literature emphasizes using more educational approaches, with follow-up support and supervision provided to the family (Moore, 1982). Even so, hospital personnel can play an important role in supporting the parents instead of ostracizing them. If the failure to thrive is rooted mainly in a disturbance of the parent–child interaction,

limited intervention approaches such as food distribution programs without personal contact for mothers can be expected to have little impact. The goal of intervention should be not only to give attention to the nutritional needs of the children, but also to provide the family with emotional supports that might prevent perpetuation of another generation of deprived parents. (Kerr, Bogues, & Kerr, 1978, p. 784)

Thus medical examination and treatment should be supplemented by educational and supportive approaches designed to improve parent–child interaction. For example, besides social work supportive services, an occupational therapist might work with the parents to point out and teach functional skills to the infant or child (e.g., use of both hands, balancing skill, interaction with toys), as well as helping parents to assist the child to interact with toys and to work on improving various physical skills. Since parent–infant dynamics shape the nature and rate of the child's development, a therapist, child development specialist, or child welfare caseworker might observe the feeding and recreational interactions between the parents and child in order to encourage prosocial types of interactions.

Parental counseling may also be necessary, particularly if the parent is suffering from some form of depression or irrational negative attitudes toward the child (e.g., "He's the black sheep of the family." "She reminds me of my terrible aunt." "He's skinny and stupid—just like me."). Although treatment of children and parents often requires at least 6 months or more to experience real progress, the prognosis in many cases is very good.

PSYCHOLOGICAL MALTREATMENT

Challenges in Defining Psychological Maltreatment

Psychological (emotional) maltreatment of children is a serious and widespread social problem in America. The term psychological maltreatment rather than emotional maltreatment is thought to be more appropriate because "it better subsumes all affective and cognitive aspects of child maltreatment" (Hart & Brassard, 1987, p. 160). Psychological maltreatment is an attack on the ability of children to fulfill their emotional and psychological needs. It undermines the child's emotional development as well as his or her need for love and self-esteem. In some severe and long-lasting cases, this form of child maltreatment is analogous to a form of slow torture, where a person's entire self-concept is broken down over time.

Many researchers and practitioners believe that psychological maltreatment is becoming recognized as one of the "core issues" in child maltreatment because of the following: (1) it is inherent in all forms of child maltreatment; (2) the major negative effects of child maltreatment are generally psychological in nature, affecting the victim's view of self, others, human relationships, goals, and strategies for living; and (3) the concept clarifies and unifies the dynamics that underlie the destructive power of all forms of child abuse and neglect (Brassard, Germain, & Hart, 1987, as cited in Hart & Brassard, 1987, p. 161).

Although there have been a number of attempts at defining psychological maltreatment, it is significant that the International Conference on Psychological

Abuse of Children and Youth held in 1983 developed the following working definition:

> Psychological maltreatment of children and youth consists of acts of omission and commission which are judged by community standards and professional expertise to be psychologically damaging. Such acts are committed by individuals, singly or collectively, who by their characteristics (i.e., age, status, knowledge, organizational form) are in a position of differential power that renders a child vulnerable. Such acts damage immediately or ultimately the behavioral, cognitive, affective, or physical functioning of the child. Examples of psychological maltreatment include acts of rejecting, terrorizing, isolating, exploiting, and mis-socializing. (Proceedings of the International Conference on Psychological Abuse of Children and Youth, 1983, p. 2, as cited in Hart & Brassard, 1987, p. 160)

Taxonomies of psychological maltreatment that are more operationally defined are in the process of being developed and will be described in this section (cf. Baily & Baily, 1986; Brassard et al., 1987; Garbarino, Guttmann, & Seeley, 1986). Defining precisely what constitutes emotional maltreatment, however, is a complex process that is limited by our lack of research and practice knowledge in this area. For example, the field must begin to address the following questions posed by a number of researchers and practitioners (cf. Bailey & Bailey, 1986; Garbarino, Guttmann, & Seeley, 1986):

1.   *What types of caretaker behaviors result in emotional damage or other psychological deficits in the child?* One of the central criteria used to help determine if a particular caretaker behavior or parenting practice constitutes psychological maltreatment is whether the child will suffer some form of "significant" emotional harm. (See Hart, Brassard, & Carlson, 1996, p. 78 for a concise summary of effects, and p. 81 for a discussion of legal issues.) This is complicated by the fact that there is usually no physical evidence of damage, and behavioral symptoms may be minimal, delayed, or able to be attributed to other factors. Related to this issue is the question of whether an identifiable relationship between adult behavior and child response can be established.

2.   *Will each child suffer a comparable amount of distress from the emotionally neglectful or abusive behaviors of the caretaker?* Children can be extremely resilient creatures, able to overcome severely abusive or neglectful situations with sufficient environmental and social supports (Rutter, 1987). Conversely, some children may be extremely vulnerable to psychological maltreatment, and will experience lasting emotional trauma.

This raises a number of important questions. What diagnostic paradigm can be used to differentiate these two types of children? What expert can determine which particular child will fall into one of these points on a continuum ranging from invulnerable to vulnerable? Does it matter; should society intervene when parents behave in ways that experts agree may damage children in a majority of cases?

3.   *What social and cultural circumstances must be taken into account when determining if psychological maltreatment is present?* Human service profession-

als and citizens alike view certain parental behaviors through a "cultural lens." "Any conclusions about *who* abuses and *how much* they abuse depend on a culturally validated definition of *what* abuse is" (Garbarino & Ebata, 1983, p. 773). For example, in a number of Scandinavian countries, any form of corporal punishment is considered bad and is illegal. In contrast in America, although many states have prohibited school personnel from physically disciplining children, all states currently allow parents to use corporal punishment. At what point are parenting practices that are acceptable in a minority culture unacceptable for the dominant culture, and thus defined as a form of psychological maltreatment?

These issues are significant and we have raised these questions to illustrate the complexity of this social problem and the challenges faced by child welfare personnel as they identify families experiencing difficulty, and prepare court petitions to allow children and their families to receive the necessary services. Fortunately, there have been some excellent studies that have focused on defining or measuring psychological maltreatment (e.g., Sanders & Becker-Larsen, 1995).

Types of Psychological Maltreatment

In examining the issues surrounding assessing and treating psychological maltreatment, Garbarino and his colleagues viewed it as a "concerted attack by an adult on a child's development of self and social competence, a pattern, of psychically destructive behavior" (Garbarino et al., 1986, p. 8). They developed the following operational definition that included five specific forms (examples of parental behavior were included with each form):

- *Rejecting* (the adult refuses to acknowledge the child's worth and the legitimacy of the child's needs).
- *Isolating* (the adult cuts the child off from normal social experiences, prevents the child from forming friendships, and makes the child believe that he or she is alone in the world).
- *Terrorizing* (the adult verbally assaults the child, creates a climate of fear, bullies and frightens the child, and makes the child believe that the world is capricious and hostile).
- *Ignoring* (the adult deprives the child of essential stimulation and responsiveness, stifling emotional growth and intellectual development).
- *Corrupting* (the adult "mis-socializes" the child, stimulates the child to engage in destructive antisocial behavior, reinforces the deviance, and makes the child unfit for normal social experience). (Garbarino et al. 1986, p. 8)

Two additional forms of psychological maltreatment have been identified:

- *Degrading* (to deprive of dignity, to bring into disrepute or disfavor, to depreciate —e.g., calling a child stupid, labeling the child).
- *Denying emotional responsiveness* (failing to provide the sensitive, respon-

sive, caregiving necessary to facilitate healthy social/emotional develop-ment; to be detached and uninvolved—e.g., ignoring a child's attempts to in-teract, mechanistic child handling) (Hart & Brassard, 1987, p. 7, also see Hart et al., 1996, p. 74).

To further characterize psychological maltreatment, it is necessary to examine these forms of maltreatment across different developmental levels as Baily and Baily (1986) and Garbarino et al. (1986) did in their studies (Table 7.4).

Incidence of Subspecialty Areas
of Psychological Maltreatment

Because of the complexities in defining what constitutes psychological maltreat-ment and because the effects on children are often more subtle than other forms of maltreatment, incidence rates are extremely difficult to determine and those re-ported must be viewed with caution. In fact a strong case can be made that some form of psychological maltreatment is present in almost all forms of child abuse

Table 7.4. Forms of Psychological Maltreatment by Developmental Level

Rejecting	In general, rejecting involves behaviors that communicate or constitute abandonment. For example, the parent or caregiver may refuse to touch or show affection to the child or to acknowledge the child's accomplishments. Rejecting is considered "mild" when it is confined or isolated (though perhaps poignant incidents. It becomes "moderate" when it is frequent and more generalized. When rejecting is categorical, absolute and frequent, it becomes "severe."
Infancy	The parent refuses to accept the child's primary attachment. That is, the parent resists the infant's spontaneous overtures and natural responses to human contact so as to prevent the formation of a primary relation-ship. Specific behaviors; abandonment; refusal to return smiles and vocalizations.
Early childhood	The parent actively excludes the child from family activities. Specific behaviors: not taking the child on family outings; refusing the child's affiliative gestures (such as hugging); placing the child away from the family.
School age	The parent consistently communicates a negative definition of self to the child. Specific behaviors: frequent use of labels such as "dummy" or "monster"; frequent belittling of the child's accomplishments; scapegoating the child as part of a family system.
Adolescence	The parent refuses to acknowledge the changing social roles expected of the child—that is, toward more autonomy and self-determination. Specific behaviors: treating the adolescent like a young child ("infant-ilizing"); subjecting the adolescent to verbal humiliation and excessive criticism; expelling the youth from the family.

Source: Garbarino, J., Guttmann, E., & Seeley, J. W. (1986). *The psychologically battered child: Strategies for identification, assessment, and intervention.* San Francisco: Jossey-Bass, p. 25. Reprinted with permission.

and neglect (Hart & Brassard, 1987). Using this perspective, psychological mal-treatment in one form or another was present in the over 1.5 million cases of child maltreatment that were estimated to have occurred in 1993 by the NIS-3 (Sedlak & Broadhurst, 1999). The 1997 Federal NCANDS database (which has data from fewer than 50 states) included 49,338 officially reported cases under the general heading of emotional maltreatment (US DHHS, 1999, p. 4-2). Emotional neglect was projected to involve 212,800 cases under the "harm standard" (see Chapter 5 for a definition of harm) (Sedlak & Broadhurst, 1996, p. 8). However, some of the National Incidence studies did attempt to estimate the incidence of some specific forms of psychological maltreatment. The following categories of emotional abuse and emotional neglect developed by NIS-1 and NIS-2 studies are included to bet-ter illustrate the dimensions of this serious form of child maltreatment.

Emotional Abuse. The category of emotional abuse had a total reported in-cidence rate of 211,100. It encompassed three distinct forms of maltreatment:

1. *Close Confinement* (Tying or Binding and Other Forms): Tortuous restric-tion of movement, as by tying a child's arms or legs together or binding a child to a chair, bed, or other object, or confining a child to an enclosed area (such as a clos-et) as a means of punishment. This definition did *not* include generally accepted practices such as use of safety harness on toddlers, swaddling of infants, or disci-pline involving "grounding" a child or restricting a child to his or her room.

2. *Verbal or Emotional Assault:* Habitual patterns of belittling, denigrating, scapegoating, or other nonphysical forms of overtly hostile or rejecting treatment, as well as threats of other forms of maltreatment (such as threats of beating, sex-ual assault, abandonment, etc.). This category was not used if verbally assaultive or abusive treatment occurred simultaneously with other abusive behavior (e.g., during a physical beating) unless adverse effects occurred that were separate and distinct from those in the other category (144,300; 2.3 per 1,000 children) (NCCAN. 1988, pp. 4.8–4.10).

Emotional Neglect. Seven specific forms of emotional neglect were differ-entiated in the NIS-3:

1. *Inadequate Nurturance/Affection:* Marked inattention to the child's needs for affection, emotional support, attention, or competence. Cases of nonorganic failure to thrive were classified under this form of maltreatment in addition to other instances of passive emotional rejection of a child or apparent lack of con-cern for a child's emotional well-being or development. Not included here were overt expressions of hostility and rejection, which were classified under verbal/emotional abuse.

2. *Chronic/Extreme Spouse Abuse:* Chronic or extreme spouse abuse or other domestic violence in the child's presence.

3. *Permitted Drug/Alcohol Abuse:* Encouragement or permitting of drug or al-cohol use by the child; cases of the child's drug/alcohol use were included here if

it appeared that the parent/guardian had been informed of the problem and had not attempted to intervene. Administering drugs to a child for nonmedical or nontherapeutic purposes was classified here when the child was of school age (and hence likely to behaviorally predispose the child to self-administer the drugs), but was classified under "other or unknown abuse" for younger children.

4. *Permitted Other Maladaptive Behavior:* Encouragement or permitting of other maladaptive behavior (e.g., severe assaultiveness, chronic delinquency) under circumstances where the parent or guardian had reason to be aware of the existence and seriousness of the problem but did not attempt to intervene.

5. *Refusal of Psychological Care:* Refusal to allow needed and available treatment for a child's emotional or behavioral impairment or problem in accord with competent professional recommendation.

6. *Delay in Psychological Care:* Failure to seek or provide needed treatment for a child's emotional or behavioral impairment or problem that any reasonable layman would have recognized as needing professional psychological attention (e.g., severe depression, suicide attempt).

7. *Other Emotional Neglect:* Other inattention to the child's developmental/ emotional needs not classifiable under any of the above forms of emotional neglect (e.g., markedly overprotective restrictions that foster immaturity or emotional overdependence, chronically applying expectations clearly inappropriate in relation to the child's age or level of development, etc.

Family Dynamics of Psychological Maltreatment and Major Risk Factors

Limited research has been conducted to identify the characteristics of families in which psychological maltreatment is present and, more importantly, how those characteristics interact as part of a causal chain of events. Results of a selected number of studies will be discussed in this section to describe some of the dynamics and risk factors of psychological maltreatment.

Caretaker characteristics, as compared with child factors, contribute in major ways to the incidence of psychological maltreatment. Parents who abuse drugs or alcohol are often "out of control" and are unable to care for themselves, their family, and, consequently, their children. They tend to ignore and neglect their children and are not aware of their parental responsibility (Jenewicz, 1983).

Frequently, psychological maltreatment also assumes a more active form of behavior. For example, Jenewicz (1983) found that parents of emotionally abused children create what he calls an "interactional stress environment." He describes this kind of environment as one in which there is tension in the parent–child relationship and each member "feels that the relationship might explode at any moment." These types of parents also create an environment that is disorganized and inconsistent. There are always power struggles between parents and the children.

Parents were often members of an impoverished family themselves (Garbarino et al., 1986, p. 59).

Another characteristic of parents of psychologically maltreated children is that many, themselves, were emotionally maltreated as children. Most of these parents have not received the emotional support needed during their childhood (Belsky, 1980; Fontana, 1973; Garbarino et al., 1986, p. 57; Gordon, 1979/80; Jacoby, 1985; McCarthy, 1979; Sweet & Resick, 1979). The way these parents raise their children is similar to the way they were raised. Consequently, these parents grow up to be emotionally needy and become dependent on their own child to satisfy their needs. When the child is unable to satisfy the parents' need for nurturance or emotional satisfaction, they feel rejected, insecure, and betrayed by their own child, forming the grounds for maltreatment (Garbarino et al., 1986, p. 58).

Parental impulsivity, low self-esteem, and identity also have an effect on children's development. These parents, unfortunately, project their own issues on the children, although blaming the environment for their own problems. In contrast, mentally ill or mentally retarded parents may lack some of the resources and knowledge to raise a child and, consequently, the child's needs are not met or satisfied (Garbarino et al., 1986, pp. 58–59).

It is important not to view maltreating families from a simplistic perspective. According to Egeland and Erickson (1987), abusive families do not just suffer from one problem but from many. These families experience instability in the environment. "Disruption, chaos, and deprivation" are used as common descriptors. The relationship between family members is unstable, and the members of the families are socially and emotionally deprived.

Social isolation also may play an important role. These families do not experience social support because they isolate themselves or because the community rejects them (Polansky & Gaudin, 1983). The families may suffer from a lack of belongingness and alienation because of the community conditions. Thus using an ecological perspective is important as child maltreatment is mediated by the presence and absence of community support. Other community characteristics of maltreating parents include a high poverty level, high percentage of unemployment, high crime rates, inadequate housing, and poor access to services (Brown, 1984; Brown, Whitehead, & Braswell, 1981). These conditions create a sense of frustration and powerlessness among parents and, consequently, establish the grounds for maltreatment (Belsky, 1980; Brown, 1984). Although these families may have some type of relationship with other families in the community, they all suffer from the same situation and may not provide positive support for each other (Garbarino et al., 1986; Stack, 1974).

The lack of parenting skills and methods is an important risk factor that needs to be considered (Belsky, 1980; Herrenkohl & Herrenkohl, 1981). These parents often lack knowledge about the psychological development of the child and therefore have irrational expectations. Parental frustrations are raised when the child is not able to perform what it is expected (Gordon, 1980). These observations might partially explain why teenage mothers have a relatively higher rate of psychological maltreatment of their children (Garbarino et al., 1986, p. 118). Hart and Brassard (1987) and Morgan (1970) have cited physical abuse, low family resources such as medical services and education, and poverty as factors that appear to be linked with psychological maltreatment.

According to Sturkie and Flanzer (1987), the age of the child correlates with the incidents of abuse. Children who are older than 11 years are twice as likely to be maltreated than children who are younger than 6 years. Adolescents are characterized by being more "rebellious" and, consequently, community standards change with the age of the child. What is categorized as maltreatment during childhood is accepted by society during adolescence. Furthermore, Olsen and Holmes (1986) found that teenagers are more often maltreated because there are more teenagers than children who live with stepparents. Changes in the family causes changes in the norms of power in the family and also in the roles that family members fulfill. But although child age and characteristics may play a role, parental upbringing, parenting skills, social supports, and other factors appear to be more important in explaining how and why psychological maltreatment occurs.

Prevention of Psychological Maltreatment

To prevent psychological maltreatment, we must first understand its causes and origins.[2] Historically, children have been considered the possessions of their parents. Parents who severely punished their children, who even corporally punished them, were not being deviant; they were making sure that their children obeyed—that they had a "good" upbringing (DiNitto & Dye, 1987).

According to Alice Miller, many parents who abuse their children were abused themselves. Miller (1985) contends that parents mistreat their children for psychological reasons and to meet their own needs. She points out that the way we were treated as children is the way we treat ourselves the rest of our lives. A child conditioned to be well-behaved must not notice what he or she is feeling, but what he or she ought to be feeling. Children who were unable to learn to recognize their authentic feelings and to be comfortable with them will have a particularly difficult time in puberty. Miller further maintains that even when people cannot talk about the cruelty they endured as a child because it was experienced so early that it is beyond the reach of memory, they may demonstrate that cruelty in their own current life.

Methods that are used to suppress spontaneity in the child (lying, manipulation, scare tactics, withdrawal of love, distrust, humiliating and disgracing the child, and coercion) parallel common definitions of psychological maltreatment. Miller argues that it is a basic assumption in our society that this treatment is good for children. However, in reality, this type of upbringing "contradicts every psychological insight we have gained, yet it is passed on from generation to generation" (1985, p. 16).

Miller (1985) further contends (as do many other writers on this subject) that children live what they learn. If they are humiliated or ridiculed, they learn how to humiliate or ridicule. This does not mean that children should be raised without restraints. For children to develop in a healthy fashion, they need the respect of their caregivers, tolerance for their feelings, awareness of their needs, and grievances and authenticity from their own parents, which will, in turn, set natural limits for children.

Children need both emotional and physical support from their parents, which includes

1. Respect for the child.
2. Respect for his or her rights.
3. Tolerance for his or her feelings.
4. Willingness to learn from his or her behavior
   a. About the nature of the individual child
   b. About the child in the parent themselves
   c. About the nature of emotional life, which can be observed much more clearly in the child than in the adult because the child can experience his or her feelings much more intensely and with less disguise than an adult (Miller, 1985, p. 100).

According to Miller (1985), "we do not need books about psychology in order to learn to respect our children; what we need is a revision in the theories of child rearing" (p. 133). Thus social change in our broader society must occur to prevent psychological maltreatment.

Garbarino also contends that social change is the forerunner of the prevention of psychological abuse. Major social changes such as full employment and improved day care are just two ways to enhance family functioning (Hyman, 1987). The topic of schooling as a source of maltreatment has been given more attention recently by researchers in this area. Studies point out that control through fear and intimidation, degradation, limited human interaction, and encouragement to remain dependent are ways in which institutions and school personnel are potentially psychologically abusive (Hart & Brassard, 1987). In contrast, schools can also be central places to offer support and treatment through colocated family resource centers and opportunities to engage students in prosocial activities (Hart et al., 1996, p. 82). Other changes that many researchers feel need to take place are changes in the media. Violence, racial/ethnic, and sexual stereotypes have a negative impact on children and need to be reduced.

Also important in the study and prevention of psychological abuse is that some children are more vulnerable to its negative effects than other children. Researchers (Rutter, Cox, Tuping, Berger, & Yule, 1975) have identified some factors that have protected children from psychiatric risk: positive personality dispositions, gender (girls were less vulnerable than boys), parental warmth, and a supportive school environment that reinforced children's coping efforts. Some additional potential protective factors include a positive relationship with the nonoffending parent or other positive adult relationships, the child's intelligence, emotional resiliency, and sense of self-efficacy, warmth and cohesion with extended family members, and the child's participation and mastery in community activities. Perhaps new interventions could consist of helping vulnerable children acquire or strengthen their capacity with respect to these protective factors.

Hart and Brassard (1987) point out a number of impediments to the intervention and study of psychological abuse. One is that our culture has a preference for crisis-oriented correction over secondary and primary prevention. Family privacy is an important value, so there also exists a resistance to interfere in family life. Lastly, valid definitions to support intervention criteria need to be refined. Operational definitions of psychological maltreatment and its subcomponents are just now being developed.

In summary, a huge gap exists between the high value our society places on children and the low value expressed in the allocation of resources (Gil, 1987; Hyman, 1987). Much of prevention will need to be composed of education in order to facilitate social change.

Promising Treatment Approaches

Psychological maltreatment accompanies most other types of child abuse, thus it is important to understand how to treat this issue in the context of addressing other forms of child maltreatment (see Note 1). Physical and psychological reactions to abuse cannot be easily separated from one another. Navarre (1987) has said that physical, psychological, and social survival are three components of the same struggle and that risks to any of these three may bring about similar consequences to the individual. Studies have found that family environments characterized by emotional maltreatment are not innocuous, but produce damaged human beings. Pervasive emotional deprivation and the destruction of the ego and self-esteem appear to be among the most outstanding factors in the background of adults who mistreat children (Garbarino et al., 1988). In general, it appears that psychological maltreatment in the early developmental period of a child has longer lasting and more detrimental effects on the victim than maltreatment at later stages of life (Montagu, 1970). Since psychological maltreatment is becoming one of the core issues in child maltreatment, intervention must occur on several different levels.

The common goals of all practitioners are to eliminate the occurrence of psychological maltreatment and help both victims and perpetrators to rebuild and restructure their lives (Garbarino et al., 1988). However, to provide adequate services, it is important for practitioners and agencies to become aware of the individual, family, and environmental contexts in which psychological maltreatment occurs.

According to Garbarino et al. (1988), we must look at three important factors in designing an intervention:

1. Assessment, which provides the information necessary to determine when and how to intervene effectively. In assessing families, practitioners identify the antecedents and consequences of psychological maltreatment.
2. Gaining family cooperation. The effectiveness of service is contingent on the motivation and willingness of family members to participate—thus it is important for social workers to try to create a positive atmosphere whereby client change and growth can occur.
3. Maximizing agency and community resources. Since so many fiscal cuts have been made in the area of social services, implementation of expensive new services is virtually impossible without major changes in social policy. Services are limited, so both agencies and practitioners must be innovative in packaging a mix of agency resources and informal network supports.

Finally, practitioners are focusing on a number of areas in their treatment of families including reducing environmental stress, improving patterns of family interaction, and individual counseling. Each of these areas will be briefly described below.

Interventions for Reducing Environmental Stress. In some families, attempting to meet day-to-day needs is a huge task for parents, leaving little time and energy for providing a positive environment for their children. Some environmental factors that contribute to psychological maltreatment include lack of financial resources, unemployment, inadequate housing, lack of appropriate medical care, unavailability of services, and community isolation. When families are stressed by limited financial resources or unemployment, workers may need to gather information for financial assistance or help parents locate educational or vocational training programs. Supportive activities such as these may be extremely helpful in dealing with psychological maltreatment.

In dealing with stresses other than lack of money, practitioners can bridge gaps to help meet other needs. For example, a worker can assist in locating services that provide clothing, rooms, meals, and emergency assistance as well as medical and nutritional services. Workers may also need to act as advocates for families who have been isolated from the community by providing or arranging transportation or by helping a system to recognize cultural and ethnic differences in clients.

Family Interventions. Psychological maltreatment is often a product of dysfunctional patterns of family interaction. Some interventions need to help resolve problems in interpersonal relationships and improve overall family functioning. Several therapeutic interventions exist for use in this context.

1. *Marital counseling.* When spousal conflict impairs the parent–child relationship, psychological maltreatment may occur.
2. *Family therapy.* This can be useful in reducing psychologically destructive family patterns of interaction and inappropriate coping behaviors. The goal with family therapy is to provide emotional support and nurturance to all members and to help the family function in a healthy manner.

3. *Parent–child interventions.* The goal of this is to eliminate dysfunctional interactive patterns.
4. *Interventions with infants and parents.* This focuses specifically on the infant–mother interaction. Skills are taught to the mother to help her become more nurturant in meeting the needs of the infant.
5. *Parenting interventions.* Parents can learn skills necessary to fulfill the parental role. Many models of parent education exist. The goals of these programs are to provide information, increase awareness, and teach practical skills to parents.
6. *Interventions with socially isolated families.* These interventions are designed to decrease isolation and increase social connectedness (Garbarino et al., 1988, pp. 125–154).

Intervention with Individuals. A parent or a child may have a personality disturbance that needs to be corrected to improve relationship functioning in order to eliminate psychological abuse. Interventions may address such parental characteristics as low self-esteem, feelings of futility or apathy, impulsiveness, and insecurity. There characteristics may have impaired personal and parental functioning. Workers can provide the basis for positive growth by establishing an atmosphere of respect, acceptance, support, and nurturance although teaching mature adult behavior and appropriate parenting skills.

Intervention with children is necessary as well. Enhanced therapeutic child care centers can provide cognitive, interpersonal, and motor experiences to compensate for the home environment. Workers serve as alternative role models and give nurturance and structure to children who do not receive these in their own homes. Children can also attend play therapy groups, behavioral counseling, and social skills training groups. Adolescents may need treatment services that are different from younger children. Individual therapy, youth groups, or more extensive treatment such as residential or drug/alcohol treatment may benefit adolescents with more severe problems. Warmth, acceptance, and nurturance demonstrated by practitioners are, again, of utmost importance. Programs such Early Head Start, Head Start, and HIPPY are popular examples of this kind of approach to meeting the needs of children at high risk of poor outcomes.

CURRENT POLICY, PRACTICE, AND RESEARCH ISSUES IN NEGLECT AND PSYCHOLOGICAL MALTREATMENT

Child Neglect

One the major challenges facing the field of child welfare is reducing inappropriate case referrals and caseload sizes to a level at which caseworkers have the time to provide services to the families where neglect is a problem. Although neglect cases tend to be lower in priority in many agencies, neglect-related situations are a major cause of death in almost 50% of all maltreatment-related child fatalities (see Chapter 5).

Part of the reason for the case overload is that the field has experienced great difficulty in developing operational definitions that provide clear guidelines for when parents are not meeting minimal standards of parenting (Stein, 1984; Zuravin, 1989). This lack of guidelines has hampered research to develop effective treatment methods because of incompatibilities in the way critical definitions and outcome variables are defined.

There has also been a lack of funding and public agency commitment for implementing groupwork-focused approaches to assisting parents where neglect is an issue. Among the factors limiting the use of this treatment method are the lack of child welfare staff with groupwork skills, the necessity of running some groups in the evening, transportation for parents, and simultaneously conducting groups for the children (or providing child care).

Psychological Maltreatment

Definitional issues and a lack of societal recognition that this is a major social problem are two of the major challenges facing program advocates in this area. Research in this field is at an early stage, with more developmental work needed in measuring what detrimental effects follow which forms of psychological maltreatment, for which ages of children, and under what circumstances. Treatment methods that are cost effective also need to be developed, and juvenile court judges and attorneys need to be convinced that psychological maltreatment cases can be successfully pursued through the court system in order to ensure that children receive protective services.

CONCLUSION

Although physical abuse and sexual abuse garner much of the public and professional attention, neglect and psychological maltreatment often cause more long-term damage to children. These social problems are more difficult to define operationally and there is less societal consensus about when to intervene in these situations. Nevertheless, they represent some of the more difficult prevention and service challenges in child welfare. Skilled casework is required to assist these families in overcoming what may be a lifelong pattern of behavior. Many of the families having difficulty in these areas are reluctant or unable to participate in the more traditional social services. This is one reason why a variety of "home-based" interventions have been developed, in which caseworkers are able to work with families in their home settings on an intensive basis. This new program model is the subject of Chapter 9, while intensive but equally helpful "family support services" that are less in some situations are described in the next chapter.

NOTES

1. Special thanks to Dr. James Gaudin and Oscar Haupt for their consultation regarding treatment of child neglect and psychological maltreatment, respectively.
2. Portions of this section were adapted from a summary prepared by Jane Peterson, MSW, for the Utah Child Welfare Training Project, University of Utah.

FOR FURTHER INFORMATION

Brassard, M.R., Germain, R., & Hart, S.N. (Eds.) (1987). *Psychological maltreatment of children*. New York: Pergamon Press. Presents a comprehensive set of definitions of psychological maltreatment, along with individual chapters on the various domains.

Garbarino, J., Guttmann, E., & Seeley, J.W. (1986). *The psychologically battered child: Strategies for identification, assessment and intervention.* San Francisco, CA: Jossey-Bass. One of the first books to thoroughly explore the dimensions of psychological maltreatment by developmental level. It presents a range of assessment and treatment strategies.

Polansky, N.A., Chalmers, M.A., Buttenweiser, E., & Williams, D.P. (1982). *Damaged parents—An anatomy of child neglect.* Chicago: University of Chicago Press. Presents one the best analyses of child neglect available based on a major research project. In addition to research data, family dynamics and treatment strategies are discussed.

Rose, S.J. (1999) Reaching consensus on child neglect: African American mothers and child welfare workers. *Child and Youth Services Review, 2*(6), 464–479. Presents a set of working definitions derived from conversations with public child welfare workers and African American mothers.

Zuravin, S.J., (1989). *Suggestions for operationally defining child physical abuse and physical neglect.* Paper prepared for a meeting on Issues in the Longitudinal Study of Child Maltreatment, Toronto, Ontario. Baltimore, MD: The School of Social Work and Community Planning, University of Maryland at Baltimore. Cogent summary of the major issues facing the field regarding defining various forms of child maltreatment. It also presents a set of excellent operational definitions of physical abuse and neglect.

8

Family Support and Other Prevention Services Related to Child Welfare

INTRODUCTION

Reform of the policies and systems that provide services to families and children is underway throughout the nation. Public agencies, not-for-profit agencies, and grass-roots organizations are developing new service approaches, integrating services across traditionally separate domains, and collaborating with new partners to demonstrate the potential of reform and to better serve families. Across most child-serving disciplines reform efforts address the more ecological and family-focused services as well as new approaches to management and financing. In the world of financing, there is broad exploration of the application of medical models of "managed care" across service delivery points with overlapping (but in some cases distinctive) emphases in different disciplines—in education the watchwords are "restructuring and site-based management," in mental health "quality assurance, capitation and outcome-driven systems," and in social services (and in some counties or states child welfare services particularly) "flexible funding, capitation, and benchmarking." The underlying themes of these reform efforts are remarkably similar: meeting changing family needs, maximizing limited resources, increasing program accountability for funds spent, and improving program effectiveness.

Family-centered services such as family support services, wraparound services, Family-Based Services (FBS), and Intensive Family Preservation Services (IFPS) represent some of the fastest growing program areas in child welfare, mental health, and juvenile justice. These services are designed to strengthen family functioning to achieve a number of outcomes. For some families it is prevention of child maltreatment, for others a reduction in parent–adolescent conflict, and for some families the goal is to improve some aspect of a child's behavior. One of the "distal" or ultimate goals is to improve the family situation to a point at which child placement can be prevented or the child can be returned from substitute care (e.g., family foster care, residential treatment).

This chapter will propose a typology of these innovative service models, and present some examples of family support and other preventive programs in child welfare. Chapter 9 will focus on the origins, program models, evaluation findings and current challenges of FBS and IFPS. But because these programs emphasize various aspects of "prevention," we provide an overall framework for prevention.

A FRAMEWORK FOR PREVENTION

A Framework for Prevention

Some of the best and most recent conceptualizations about prevention have emerged from *behavioral health care* (otherwise known as mental health). In this conceptualization, the traditional terms of primary, secondary, and tertiary prevention have been replaced with broader concepts that we believe make more useful distinctions (Mrazek & Haggerty, 1994). Although developed to describe prevention efforts in mental health services, we use examples from child abuse prevention and child wellness programs to illustrate these prevention concepts. *Universal* preventive interventions are targeted to the general public or a whole population group where individual risk is not an issue. The intervention is desirable for everyone in that group. Examples include provision of public information campaigns about the risks of shaking babies or options that are available if parents find themselves screaming at or humiliating their children (see Figure 8.1).

Selective preventive interventions for health needs, mental disorders, or other social problems are targeted to individuals or a subgroup of the population whose risk of developing these problems is significantly higher than average. The risk may be imminent or it may be a lifetime risk. Risk groups may be identified on the basis of biological, psychological, or social risk factors that are known to be associated with the onset of a mental disorder. Examples of selective preventive interventions include home visitation and infant day care for low-birthweight or medically fragile children, family resource centers in neighborhoods with high

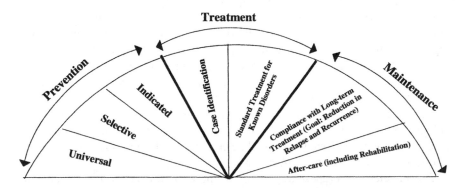

Figure 8.1. The mental health intervention spectrum for mental disorders. *Source:* Mrazek, P.J., & Haggerty, R.J. , eds. (1994). *Reducing risk for mental disorders: Frontiers for preventive intervention research.* Washington, DC: National Academy of Medicine Press, p. 33.

child abuse and neglect reporting rates, and "latchkey" school-based day care programs for working parents to prevent child abuse resulting from failure to supervise.

Indicated preventive interventions are targeted to high-risk individuals who are identified as having minimal but detectable signs or symptoms foreshadowing a social or physical health problem like child abuse and neglect, such as mothers who have not received prenatal care prior to entering the hospital or mothers who test positive for substance abuse at birth. Treatment services (e.g., family preservation) and maintenance services (e.g., long-term foster care) may be needed if prevention services are too little or too late.

A PROGRAM TYPOLOGY OF FAMILY SUPPORT AND FAMILY-BASED SERVICES[1]

Diverse Program Models Complicate Understanding

The use of a family support program such as "Healthy Start" (e.g., Breakey & Pratt, 1991) or a family treatment service such as family-based services reflects a philosophical stance that *a society should be willing to invest as many or more resources in prevention of problems in parenting as it would spend treating those problems or placing children in out-of-home care.* The distinguishing feature of many of these programs is the provision of a wide variety of selective or indicated preventive interventions to children and families in the home and community setting.

Within the broad framework of family support or FBS programs there is wide variation across the nation in the kind of interventions, duration of services, size of caseloads, and components of service that characterize these programs (see Figure 8.2). Perhaps this is inherent in all service innovations, but it is one of the reasons why research findings on family support and family-based service programs have been confusing. Despite a growing body of literature, it is not clear what these services are and who benefits from them. There is enormous variation in the service characteristics of these programs.

The programs themselves are often described using more specific terms such as *family support, family preservation, family-based, family-centered, home-based, and placement prevention services.* the term *family support* has been used as an umbrella under which clusters a broad range of family-based services programs. Over 44 states have launched these types of programs over the past 10 years (Government Accounting Office, 1997, p. 2). The number of family resource centers (the settlement houses of the 1990s) have been growing tremendously. According to the James Bell evaluation more than 65% of the federally provided Family Preservation and Support funds were used by states to fund family support programs rather than family preservation programs. From one perspective, these

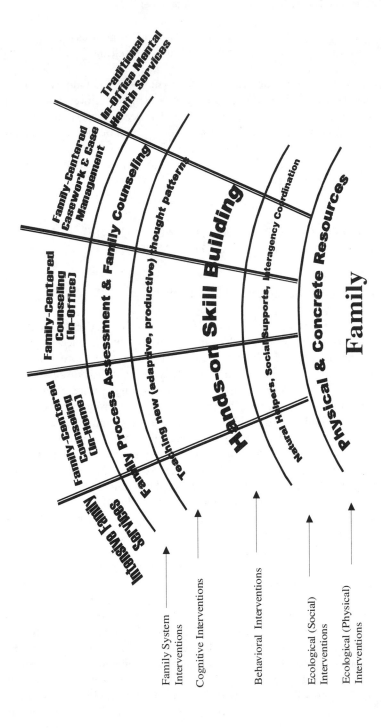

Figure 8.2. A sample array of family-centered services.
Source: Lloyd, J. (1993). Protecting children. *American Human Association* 10(3), 5.

program areas are in competition with each other for funds under the family preservation and support legislation.

In virtually all family-based services, the family is not seen as deficient but as having many strengths and resources (Kagen et al., 1987). Although family-based and intensive family preservation services have both been cited as family support programs, these programs are distinct from the primary prevention and child development-oriented family support programs such as prenatal care, home-visiting, early childhood education, parent education, home–school–community linkage, child care, and other family-focused services. A three-part typology of family-based programs is presented next:

1. *Family resource, support, and education services.* These community-based services assist and support adults in their role as parents. Services are available to all families with children and do not impose criteria for participation that might separate or stigmatize certain parents (Child Welfare League of America, 1989, p. 13; Family Resource Coalition, 2000). We will refer to these as "Family Support Services." Examples are the school- or community-based family resource centers being implemented in states such as Connecticut, Maryland, Kentucky, Minnesota, and Missouri (Farrow, 1991; Schorr, 1997, pp. 285–296).

2. *Family-based services.* These services encompass a range of activities such as case management, counseling/therapy, education, skill-building, advocacy, and/or provision of concrete services for families with problems that threaten their stability. (In some states, these kinds of programs are referred to as "family preservation" services). The majority are currently found in child welfare agencies, although a number have been initiated by mental health centers. FBS programs have recently been started in a number of new service arenas, including juvenile justice, developmental disability, adoption, and foster care reunification programs.

   Some programs straddle the definitions presented here and provide both family support and family based services. For example Hawaii's "Healthy Start" program initially provides services to all newborns and their families, irrespective of risk, and then provides a comprehensive array of health care, counseling, and concrete services to families judged to be at moderate to high risk of child maltreatment (Breakey & Pratt, 1991). For this reason, we generally categorize this program as a family support program. As mentioned earlier, the philosophy of these programs differs from the more traditional child welfare services in the role of parents, use of concrete and clinical services, and other areas (Child Welfare League of America, 1989, p. 29).

3. *Intensive family preservation services.* This grouping of services might be distinguished by the combination of case management with intensive therapeutic and other services. Some of these services are designed for fami-

lies "in crisis," at a time when removal of a child is perceived as imminent, or the return of a child from out-of-home care is being considered. Yet the reality is that this service model is also being applied to chronic family situations, involving child neglect or abuse, which do not involve crisis. These programs often share the same philosophical orientation and characteristics as family-based services, but are delivered with more intensity (including shorter time frame and smaller caseloads), so they are often referred to as intensive family preservation service or IFPS programs. Caseloads generally vary between two to six families per worker. Families are typically seen between 6 and 10 hours per week, and the time period of intervention is generally between 4 and 12 weeks.

So a three-part framework as outlined in these two sections distinguishes between family support (no case management), family-based services (includes case management), and intensive family preservation services (intensive services plus case management).[2]

Family Support Program Models and Their Prevalence

The term *family support* has been used as a generic category that often encompasses a broad range of family-centered or family-strengthening programs. In virtually all family-centered services the family is not seen as deficient but as having many strengths and resources (Kagen et al., 1987). Although family-based services and family preservation services have both been cited as family support programs, these programs are distinct from family support because family support services more appropriately fit the prevention categories of selective or indicated prevention. This seems particularly true for the child development-oriented family support programs such as prenatal care, home-visiting, early childhood education, parent education, home–school–community linkage, child care, and other family-focused services that tend to provide one type of service designed to prevent or mitigate a social problem or illness (e.g., education, housing, financial assistance, or counseling), or plan/monitor client services delivered by other agencies.[3]

Family resource, support, and education services, as community-based services, assist and support adults in their role as parents. Conceptually, at least, services are available to all families with children and there are no eligibility requirements that families or children must meet to participate. Yet, in practice, these services are just emerging and the new programs are typically situated in communities that have been identified as having a high need for the service. At some point, these services may be available to everyone (e.g., in Orange County California, there is a family resource center in a mall situated right next to Nordstrom for the ease of parents who are shopping with small children and have an interest in getting information about parenting). Examples of such programs that may be on their way to being delivered statewide are the school- or community-based family resource centers being implemented in Connecticut, Maryland, Kentucky, Minnesota, and Missouri (Farrow, 1991). Generally, however, these services are *not* available to all parents— they are almost always situated in communities of substantial need.

Estimating how widespread various types of family support programs are is difficult. For example, in 1999 the Family Resource Coalition estimated that there were roughly 20,000 Family Resource Centers (FRCs) that fall under formal state and regional family support networks. They indicated that it is difficult to define FRCs, which then impacts the total numbers, and there does not appear to be a list or number that is stratified by state. (Personal Communication, by Charlie Ferguson with Anthony Williams at the Family Resource Coalition.) This issue is borne out by state numbers. In California, the Office of Child Abuse Prevention has identified 479 FRCs in the state. Many of them are school-linked services (that is, the RC is at a school site) but it is unclear how many are in fact school based. If there are only 479 FRCs in California (which has about 10% of the nation's population) and FRCs are evenly distributed across the country, then there should be about 5,000 (not 20,000) FRCs nationwide. There may be many more in the east, however, where there are many more settlement houses. So although precise numbers are not currently available, family support services is a movement of some significant size—the size is just hard to determine.

A Closer Look at Defining Family Support and Other Prevention Services

This section will present a more detailed typology of family support services to help lay a foundation for highlighting some promising family support programs appropriate for the children and parent served by child welfare services.

> The 'Family Support Movement' is at this point more loosely defined than the more narrow 'Family Preservation' initiative. Indeed, there is some considerable debate in my state and others as to whether it ought at all to be associated with *specific* programmatic initiatives, or left as a set of guiding principles. On the programmatic side, family support typically includes: prenatal and infant development programmers; many child abuse and neglect prevention programmes; early childhood education; parent education and support; home and school community linkage programmes; family-oriented day care and many neighbourhood-based mutual help and informal support programmes. Key federal initiatives, such as the Family Preservation and Support legislation, and key private foundation initiatives, such as those from the Annie E. Casey Foundation and key voluntary associations such as the Family Resource Coalition—a national federation of family support programmes with headquarters in Chicago—have given impetus and sustenance to the family support movement. (Whittaker, 1997, p. 126)

A report to Congress from the General Accounting Office defines family support services thus:

Family support services are primarily community-based activities designed to promote the well-being of vulnerable children and their families. The goals of family support services are to increase the strength and stability of families, increase parents' confidence and confidence in their parenting abilities, afford children a stable and supportive family environment and otherwise enhance child development. Examples include: respite care for parents and care givers, early developmental screening of children; mentoring, tutoring and health education for youth; and a range of home visiting programmes and centre-based activities, such as drop-in centres and parent support groups. (General Accounting Office Report, 1995, p. 4)

Whittaker (1997, p. 127), therefore, argues that "family support" reflects a set of values more than a clearly defined program strategy. Chief among these values is a deep respect for the complex tasks involved in family care giving, particularly in parenting. The relationship between parent and professional is defined as essentially collegial: To paraphrase Heather Weiss at Harvard (Weiss, 1983), we no longer view parents as "empty vessels" waiting to be filled up with professionally derived child development knowledge, but as active partners in a search for the formal and informal supports necessary to carry out the difficult tasks of parenting. The following list of value statements from the Family Resource Coalition is illustrative:

- Parenting is not instinctive; it is a tough and demanding job.
- Parents desire and try to do the best for their children.
- Parents want and need support, information and reinforcement in the parenting role.
- Parents are also people with their own needs as adults.
- Programs should focus on and work with family strengths, not deficits.
- Programs should empower families, not create dependence on professionals. (Family Resource Coalition, 1983)

Such value shifts shape the ways in which we think and act as professionals. Yet much remains to be sorted out:

Suffice it to say that a broad spectrum of opinion exists on how to achieve more 'family support'—from arguments for provision of more entitlements and greater access to various and sundry support services, to arguments for a *de-emphasis* on formal programmes and professional involvement so that the 'mediation structures' of society (church, extended family, neighbours, informal associations and so on) can reclaim their 'natural function' as agents of (non-monetised) family support. The debate on how best to support families is, needless to say, scarcely settled. In addition to basic definitional issues, I believe a key question in family support revolves around the degree to which such services or helpful exchanges should be monetised versus provided voluntarily with minimal involvement of public dollars. (Whittaker, 1997, p. 127)

As described by Adams and Nelson (1995), Cameron and Vanderwoerd (1997), and Kagan and Weissbourd (1994), in recent years policy and program components have been more clearly delineated, as family support principles and strategies have been embraced by established agencies and institutions. Moreover, a growing body of knowledge is available to inform program decisions in settings such as schools, child health care, social services, and juvenile delinquency.

A Promising Typology for Categorizing Family Support Programs

Although a number of authors have attempted to categorize family support programs (e.g., Allen, Brown, & Finlay, 1992; Christopher, 1990; General Accounting Office, 1995; Kagan & Weissbourd, 1994), a typology developed by Manalo & Meezan (2000) illustrated in Table 8.1 is the most appealing one that we have found because of its clarity and practical use in helping program administrators to be aware of the program design choices they may be making:

Table 8.1. A Typology of Selected Family Support Programs Based on the Primary Recipient of Service

Service Recipient	Service Provided	Description of Selected Potential Services
Infant/toddler	Developmental preschool	School readiness; socialization; recreation remedial skills training
	Health services	Developmental screening; health screening
	Resources	Toy lending
Children	After school programs	Social, recreational, educational, therapeutic
	Human skills training	Problem-solving, assertiveness training, conflict resolution
	Mentoring	Use of adult volunteers for educational and social enhancements
	Services for special needs children	Developmental screening; educational screening; educational enhancement; advocacy for services; transportation
	Education	Remedial, enhancement; arts
	Counseling	Individual; group
Youth/Adolescents	After school programs	Recreation; arts; support groups around topical issues; leadership programs; vocational readiness.
	Human skills training	Problem-solving, assertiveness training, conflict resolution
	Educational	Remedial; enhancement; arts; GED preparation
	Counseling	Individual; group
	Employment services	Job training; job placement; work–study; vocational counseling
	Mentoring programs	Use of adult volunteers for educational and social enhancements
	Prevention programs	Substance abuse; teen pregnancy
	Health programs	Health promotion and prevention

(*continued*)

Table 8.1. (*Continued*)

Service Recipient	Service Provided	Description of Selected Potential Services
Adults	Counseling	Individual, group, couples
	Crisis intervention	Personal, interpersonal physical needs
	Emergency services	Psychological assessments; shelter, clothing, housing, food
	Drop-in-programs	Socialization and recreation, respite, networking, and information sharing; parent discussion groups; child development programs
	Employment services	Job training; job placement; vocational counseling
	Life skills training	Communication; self-esteem; stress reduction; home management; child-teaching skills; consumer education; health and nutrition; anger management
	Mentoring programs	Matches adult parents with new parents
	Newsletters	Childrearing tips; child abuse prevention
	Substance abuse prevention	Treatment services, relapse prevention, support groups, information and referral, counseling and therapy
	Program involvement	Peer facilitation, group leadership, paraprofessional training, program planning
	Transportation	Facilitation for service linkage
Families	Advocacy	Advocating in other service systems; work benefits and employment opportunities
	Counseling	Family counseling
	Emergency services	Food, clothing, medical care, energy assistance, housing
	Thrift shop	Provision at low prices of needed goods
	Health services	Health screening; primary health care; health education; well-baby care; immunizations; health and nutrition counseling; occupational, physical, and speech therapy
	Home-based services	Support education, counseling, child abuse prevention; case management
	Housing assistance	Weatherlzation, payment assistance, housing repair and rehabilitation, home financing
Parent–child	Service for young parents	Parenting classes; peer support groups; crisis intervention; information and referral; advocacy; case management; medical services; pre- and postpartum home visiting; hotlines
	Health services	Maternal–child health programs; prenatal care; Pre- and postpartum visiting; WIC program
	Parent–child activities	Recreational playgroups; infant stimulation; parent–child interaction training; role modeling
	Services for families with special needs children	Counseling and support; parenting skills; advocacy in other systems including education and health; transportation

(*continued*)

Table 8.1. (*Continued*)

Service Recipient	Service Provided	Description of Selected Potential Services
Agency	Training	Workshops, seminars; in-service training on child development; primary prevention; enhancement of social support; program planning and development; agency administration; evaluation; interprofessional training
Community	Advocacy	Public awareness; coalition building; community education
	Training	Leadership development for community members; institutes and workshops for the community

Source: Manalo, V., & Meezan, W. (2000). Toward building a typology for the evaluation of family support services. *Child Welfare, 79* (4), pp. 420–22. Reprinted with permission.

In column one, the service recipients are organized into the following categories: infant/toddler, children, youth/adolescents, adults, families, parent-child, agency, and community. The 'parent-child' category was conceptualized to capture those services which are truly focused on the relationship between the parent and the child, and to differentiate them from services specifically for parents (adults) or specifically for children (infant/toddler, children, youth/adolescents). In addition, the categories of 'agency' and 'community' incorporate into the typology the philosophical premises of family support which guides practitioners to empower families not only to improve their own families, but to improve the well-being of their community.

Column two of this new typology is the general type of service provided. Overlap in services between recipient categories such as counseling, health services, educational services, and employment services could not be avoided in this column, since such services can and should be provided to numerous populations. However, this issue is resolved in the third column, which describes in more detail the service provided for the recipient. For example, "health services" is found under three recipient categories: infant/toddler, families, parent-child, but the description of these services is specific to the target recipient. Health services for the infant/toddler includes developmental screening, although health services for families include primary health care and immunizations, and health services for the parent-child include maternal-child health programs and pre- and post-partum home visiting. In effect, this typology links specific, family support services with their intended recipients(s). (pp. 14–15)

FAMILY RESOURCE, SUPPORT, AND EDUCATION SERVICES

Overview

As mentioned earlier, prevention can involve efforts at the "universal," "selected," and "indicated" model of prevention levels (Mrazek & Haggerty, 1994). A variety of approaches have been developed to prevent further child maltreatment in families. A number of the early studies have less than ironclad methodologies, and the findings are not too positive (e.g., Olds & Kitzman, 1990). The National Academy of Sciences Panel on Research on Child Abuse and Neglect concluded that

> Evaluations of home visitation programs, school-based programs for the prevention of child sexual abuse and violence, and other community-based child maltreatment prevention programs are quite limited. Many evaluations are compromised by serious methodological problems, and many promising preventive interventions do not systematically include child maltreatment as a program outcome. Children and families who are most at risk for child maltreatment may not participate in the interventions, and those that do may not be sufficiently motivated to change or will have difficulty in implementing skills in their social context, particularly if they live in violent neighborhoods. (Panel on Research on Child Abuse and Neglect 1993, p. 14)

More recent evaluations are more encouraging. After considerable review, the leadership of the Packard Foundation's Center for the Future of Children asserted that "We believe that research findings are promising enough to recommend that the uses of home visiting should be further expanded and the evaluation of home visiting should be continued" (Gomby, Larson, Lewit, & Behrman, 1993, p. 7). Later they conclude that "Evidence for the effectiveness of home visiting programs is as good or better than the evidence of the effectiveness of many other programs which exist to serve children and families. We should move ahead to a time in which non-stigmatizing and supportive services for families, including home visiting, are available in every community" (p. 19). Still, they offer substantial caveats about the critical importance of having models with flexible intensity and duration, and with programs that are delivered by well-trained staff. A more recent review of these programs was generally positive but cautious:

> These findings are sobering. In most of the studies described, programs struggled to enroll, engage, and retain families. When program benefits were demonstrated, they usually accrued only to a subset of the families originally enrolled in the programs, they rarely occurred for all of a program's goals, and the benefits were often quite modest in magnitude [p. 6] . . . we believe that the results are a fairly accurate reflection of what can be expected from the home visiting programs that were assessed. This suggests two main implications: (1) existing home visiting programs should focus on efforts to enhance implementation and the quality of their services, and (2) even if those improvements are made, more modest expectations of programs are needed, and therefore home visiting should not be relied on as the sole service strategy for families with young children. (Gomby, Culross, & Behrman, 1999, p. 15)

Perinatal and Maternal Health Derived Programs: Some Ingredients for Success

Some of the best-conceptualized models for prevention or treatment arise from the perinatal research and programs in nursing and public health. At a most basic level, one might consider the value of the WIC Program (officially known as the "Special Supplemental Nutrition Program for Women, Infants, and Children"). WIC is a federal program, costing about 5 billion dollars per year, which provides food and counseling to millions of families to support good prenatal and perinatal care. Although the results may not be consistently positive (Besharov & Germanis, 1999), WIC services have had some important positive effects, particularly with their prenatal care programs.

Part of the theoretical underpinning for nursing and public health-based family support services is research demonstrating that successful mother–infant bonding may be important for preventing future parenting disturbances. Some of the program components of such an approach include providing a quiet place for the delivery of the baby, encouraging the father or other supportive person to be present, meeting the nurturance needs of the mother immediately after the delivery so that she is better able to bond with the baby, and providing a recovery room with enough privacy to allow the mother, father, and baby to spend quiet time together. These components can be followed with the offering of educational and skill development interventions during the postpartum period at the hospital and in the home. Parents are helped to deal with the inevitable stresses that a new infant brings to a family, and are helped to feel comfortable in caring for that child (Gray, undated).

A promising approach for universal, selected, or indicated prevention efforts has been the voluntary use of home visitors for families with newborns and young children at risk. Some of the better known and successful programs of this type have been operating since the 1980s in Elmira, New York, California, and the state of Hawaii (see the following summary). A cost/benefits analysis of the Elmira, New York program showed a savings of $1,708 per family for all families in the program, and $3,013 per family for low income families in terms of long term social costs (Fiscella et al., 1998; Olds et al., 1988, 1998a,b,c). A recent Rand Corporation analysis summarized the benefits but taking a longer term view:

For the Perry Preschool and the higher-risk families of the Elmira PEIP, our best estimates of the savings to government are much higher than the costs (about $25,000 versus $12,000 for each participating Perry family; $24,000 versus $6,000 for Elmira). Although there is considerable uncertainty with respect to the benefit estimates, from a statistical point of view we can be more than 95 percent certain that the benefits exceed the costs. There are however, other uncertainties that are not related to sample size and that cannot be measured with statistical methods. It is worth pointing out, however, that although benefits exceed costs, the costs accrue immediately, although the benefits are realized only as the years pass and children transition through adolescence to adulthood.

In the case of lower-risk participants of the Elmira PEIP, the savings to government are unlikely to exceed the costs. In fact, our best estimate of the net savings is that they are negative: The government savings, although positive, are not enough to offset program costs. This result illustrates the importance of targeting programs to those who will benefit most if the hope is to realize government savings that exceed costs.

We emphasize, however, that although we included the full costs of the programs, we could not account for all the benefits. The Elmira PEIP, which has followed participating children only to age 15 so far, provides no basis for calculating the amount these children may save the government in welfare costs, or the extra taxes they may pay as adults. We might expect such savings even for the lower-risk participants, although the longer-run savings may be less than those generated by children in the higher-risk families. The Perry savings may also be underestimated because benefits to mothers were not measured.

Furthermore, the programs generate additional benefits to society beyond the government. These include the tangible costs of the crimes that would eventually have been committed by participating children, had they not participated in the program. The benefits also include the extra income generated by participating families (not just the taxes on that income), which can be reckoned as a benefit to the overall economy. We estimated these two benefit sources combined as roughly $3,000 per family in the cast of the lower-risk Elmira participants, about $6,000 per family for the higher-risk Elmira participants, and over $24,000 per family in the Perry case. (Karoly et al., 1998, pp. xviii–xix)

Although some of the home-visiting findings are mixed, the program model is being clarified (e.g., Carrilio, 1998; Olds et al., 1998a), and improvements in some areas of parenting, increases in child safety, and reductions in emergency room visits have been found (e.g., Applebaum & Sweet, 1999; Olds, Henderson, & Katzman, 1994). Furthermore, Schuerman, Rzepnicki, and Littell (1994, p. 47) have summarized some other successful programs:

Taylor and Beauchamp (1988) conducted a randomized trial of a four-week program of postnatal visitation of first-time mothers by student nurse volunteers. Subjects were not screened for potential for abuse; 30 mothers participated in the study. Dependent measures were collected by research staff who were blind to group assignments. At 3 months postpartum, mothers in the experimental group demonstrated greater knowledge of child development, more democratic views of child rearing, and more liberal attitudes toward discipline. They provided their infants with more verbal stimulation and generated a greater number of solutions to child-rearing problems. Larson (1980) conducted a study in which 80 pregnant women were randomly assigned to three groups: (1) a prenatal home visit, postpartum hospital visit, home visits for the infants' first six weeks, and additional visits throughout the first year; (2) home visits during the child's sixth through fifteenth weeks; and (3) no visits. Children in the first group had significantly lower accident rates and were more likely to receive immunizations than those in the other two groups.

Evaluations of these types of programs have shown that, for first-time mothers, the educational efforts and home visits by trained volunteers can be effective in reducing a parent's unrealistic expectations of their children. The services appeared to help reduce role reversal as well, in other words, the expectation of mothers that their children would in some way take care of them (e.g., Kennell et al., 1974), and help some families avoid child placement (Marcenko, Spence, and Samost, 1996). These types of interventions have also been supplemented with opportunities for mothers to meet and network among themselves, thereby enlarging or building informal support networks.

Leventhal (1996), pp. 648–650 believes that although there is no consensus yet in the literature, the prevention of abuse and neglect requires nine essential ingredients, as described below.

1. *Services should begin early, preferably during the prenatal period or shortly after birth, and should extend through the first few years of a child's life.* Of course, no one knows what a "few years" means. The results from Olds' Elmira study in which home visiting continued to a child's second birthday showed that maltreatment occurred less frequently in a subset of the intervention group (Olds, Henderson, Chamberlin, & Tatelbaum, 1986) (presumably those at greatest risk), but that this effect disappeared when the children were reevaluated at 25 to 50 months of age (Olds, Henderson, & Kitzman, 1994). Thus, like many human service interventions for high-risk families, home visiting should not be viewed as an inoculation program that provide life-time protection, but rather as a service that may need to be continued (with varying degrees of intensity) for many years of the child's life.

2. *Home-based services need to occur frequently enough so that the home visitor gets to know the family, and the family gets to trust the person entering the home.* Frequent contact also enables the home visitor to recognize problems early and to provide the necessary services. In Olds' study, on average during the first 2 years of the child's life, each family received 23 visits (Olds, Henderson, Chamberlin, & Tatelbaum, 1986). In the Hawaii Healthy Start program, which screens families at birth and provide home-based preventive services to almost 50% of the state's high-risk families (until the child is 3 to 5 years of age), the frequency of visits is weekly at first and then is adjusted according to the family's needs (Breakey, Pratt, & Elliot, 1994; Department of Health, Hawaii, 1992). Although there will be a tendency to try to achieve the same results with fewer visits (usually because one is not given quite enough money) at least for now the successful models suggest that frequent contacts are important.

3. *The primary goal of the home visitor should be to develop a therapeutic relationship with the parents.* In the context of a trusting, helping relationship, parents will be able to feel better about themselves and in turn feel better about their children. One of the best descriptions of how this relationship develops was written by Selma Fraiberg who called home-based mental health care "psychotherapy in the kitchen" (Fraiberg, Adelson, & Shapiro, 1975). To help achieve this therapeutic relationship, home visitors need to be trained to work with vulnerable families and will need ongoing mental health supervision to help the visitor understand the dynamics of the relationship.

4. *The home visitor, believing that maltreatment can occur in families and knowing the early signs of abuse and neglect, can provide a watchful eye in the home.* This is different from the kind of oversight provided by a relative, such as a grandparent, who may be helpful to the family but who is untrained in this field

and often needs to deny the early signs of maltreatment because of the difficulty in believing that a loved one could abuse a child. Unusual bruises on an infant will be discussed by the home visitor with the family. Signs of spousal abuse will not be ignored. Frustration and anger related to raising a child will be addressed before such feelings escalate and lead to abuse.

5. *The home visitor should be able to model effective parenting.* Modeling is a process of observing behaviors and then suggesting alternative ways of managing the situation (e.g., a crying child or a toilet training accident) even of demonstrating how to hold a fussy infant. It does not mean taking over the care of the child or being overly critical, and it is best done after the home visitor has developed a relationship with the parent.

6. *The home visitor should not lose sight of the child's needs.* Of course, the balance between the parents' needs and the child's can be a difficult one in certain families. In many high-risk families, parents have substantial problems, such as domestic violence, depression, substance abuse, or unemployment. If the home visitor's focus is only on the parents' problems, then the child's needs, such as those related to appropriate safety, immunizations and health care, nutrition, and stimulation will be ignored. On the other hand, if the home visitor only helps with the child's needs and ignores the parents' problems, it is less likely that the parents will make the necessary life changes so that they can provide good enough parenting without the intensive help from the home visitor.

7. *The home visitor needs to be able to provide concrete service to the family.* High-risk families often need help with the organization of their lives, transportation, housing and so on. Helping the family receive these services can make a substantial difference although the relationship and the modeling develop.

8. *If home visiting is going to have any impact on the occurrence of serious physical abuse, strategies will need to be developed to include fathers (or boyfriends) as well as mothers.* Clinical experience suggests that the majority of the perpetrators of serious abuse are not the women, but rather the men in the household (Bergman, Larsen, & Mueller, 1986; Starling, Holden, & Jenny, 1995; U.S. Advisory Board on Child Abuse and Neglect, 1995).

9. *Home visiting should not be provided in a "one size fits all" approach, but rather should be tailored to the family's needs.* This means that assessments of the family's status and the level and types of services need to be made on a regular basis and appropriate adjustments made periodically in the goals for the family and in the services offered. It also means that home visiting may not be appropriate for some families in which the dysfunction is too great and thus, the children would be better served by placement outside the home.

Other Examples of Innovative Programs

Funding Schemes.   Many prevention programs are being supported by surcharges on marriage licenses, birth certificates, and other taxing mechanisms. As of 1988, Trust Funds were operational in 41 states (see Daro, 1988, pp. 126–127).

The programs funded by some of the trust funds vary widely in terms of the coherence of their conceptual model for prevention and the rigor with which they are being evaluated. In contrast, other programs have been supported by state-wide legislation and are trying to take a more comprehensive approach. For example, the Supportive Child Abuse Network (SCAN) uses a community-based approach that uses lay therapists and self-help groups as part of an effort to mobilize public awareness and support (Grazio, 1981).

Healthy Start in Hawaii.   Furthermore, some of the recent preventive efforts that have been developed are able to address not just physical abuse, but other forms of child maltreatment as well. The state of Hawaii has used the Trust Fund to develop a multidimensional approach to supporting and educating families to improve family coping skills and functioning, to promote positive parenting skills and parent–child interaction, and to promote optimal child development: "Healthy Start." With this program, home visitation services are offered to families of all newborns deemed at-risk via screenings performed in all hospitals in the state at the child's birth. Follow-up visits by paraprofessionals occur until children reach age 5 (school age), including linkage with a pediatric provider. This approach is illustrated in Figure 8.3.

Nine complementary components make up the Healthy Start approach (Breakey & Pratt, 1991, pp. 16–19):

1. *Systematic hospital-based screening* is used to identify 90 percent of high-risk families of newborns from a specific geographic area. The risk indicators used in the early identification include the following:
   1. Marital status—single, separated, divorced
   2. Partner unemployed
   3. Inadequate income (per patient) or no information regarding source of income
   4. Unstable housing
   5. No phone
   6. Education under 12 years
   7. Inadequate emergency contacts (e.g., no immediate family contacts)
   8. History of substance abuse
   9. Late (after 12 weeks) or no prenatal care
   10. History of abortions
   11. History of psychiatric care
   12. Abortion unsuccessfully sought or attempted
   13. Relinquishment for adoption sought or attempted
   14. Marital or family problems
   15. History of or current depression
2. *Community-based home visiting family support services are provided as part of the maternal and child health system.* These are home visits to help build trust, providing help with immediate needs such as obtaining food supplies and public housing, or resolving crises in family relationships. In fact, this program component is an excellent example of a specialized application of Family Support

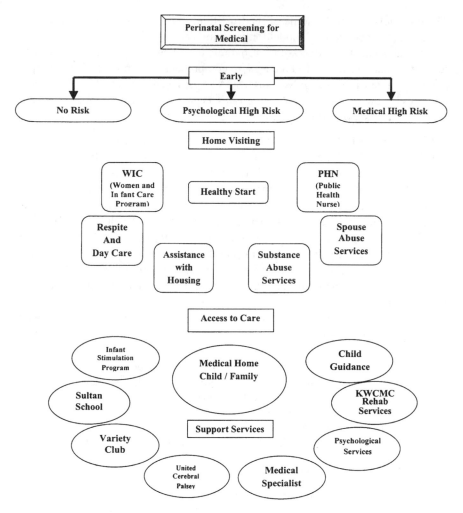

Figure 8.3.   The Healthy Start program model. Source: Breakey, G, & Pratt, B. (1991). Healthy growth for Hawaii's "Healthy Start": Toward a systematic statewide approach to prevention of child abuse and neglect. *Zero to Three* (April), p. 18. Reprinted with permission.

Services. Staff members model parent-child interaction and uses structured assessments (Barnard, 1983) to monitor parent progress.
3.   *The intensity of service is individualized and based on the family's need and lev-el of risk.* A system of "client levels" and "weighted caseloads" was implement-ed to help ensure quality service for families and prevent burnout among staff. All families enter the program at "Level I" and receive weekly home visits. The decision to change a family's level is based on criteria such as frequency of fam-

ily crises, quality of parent-child interaction, and the family's ability to use other community resources. As families become more stable, responsive to children's needs, and autonomous, the frequency of home visits diminishes. A family's promotion to Level IV means quarterly visit status, and quarterly visits continue until the target child is five years old. Thus, service intensity is constantly adjusted to the needs of the family, assuring that families who are doing well move along, and those needing more support are not promoted arbitrarily.

The system of client levels assists in caseload management. In the first year of a program, all families would be Level I; the caseload for each worker would be no more than 15 families. In the second year, some families would have progressed to Levels II and III; the average caseload would be 20 families. By the third year of a program, the average caseload would be about 25 families.

4. *Families are linked to a "medical home."* The concept of a "medical home" is important for work with vulnerable families (Sia & Breakey, 1985). As its name suggests, the Healthy Start program emphasizes preventive health care as an important aspect of promoting positive child development. Each family is assisted in selecting a primary care provider, which might be a pediatrician, family physician, or public health nursing clinic. Project staff use a special computer system to track both due dates for well care visits, using the child's age and the schedule of visits recommended by the American Academy of Pediatrics, and for NCAST visits. Each worker receives a monthly printout of the children in her families who are due for visits, and follows up to make sure that the visit is scheduled and the family has transportation.

5. *Coordination of a range of health and social services for at risk families is provided.* Coordination of services is a major feature of the Healthy Start program. Because high risk families generally lack trust in people and services and thus do not reach out for help, those families who need service most are the least likely to seek them. As it reaches out to and builds trust with high-risk families, Healthy Start is in a position to coordinate a wide range of services to families. The Healthy Start Model illustrates its approach to connecting families to the services most commonly available in communities.

6. *Continuous follow-up with the family is maintained until the child reaches age five.* An earlier service program stopped following families once they were no longer considered "high risk." In a number of these families, cases of child abuse and neglect were reported later. Family situations can deteriorate, and the birth of subsequent children can add to family stress. Learning from their early experience, the Healthy Start program was designed to maintain follow-up until the target child reaches age five and enters school. At that point, the educational system provides at least some link between the family and the larger community.

7. *A structured training program is provided in the dynamics of abuse and neglect; early identification of families at risk; and home visiting.* Staff members receive an extensive amount of training in three phases to promote uniform standards of service delivery and to share experiences with new teams.

9. *Staff selection and retention is carefully considered.* Teams consist of 5–8 paraprofessional and supervisory staff, based on an agreed on ratio. This ratio is 1:5 for supervisors and 1:3 for managers also carrying administrative responsibilities. For managers, the program selects masters level professionals who have

both clinical experience with dysfunctional families and supervisory experience, preferably with paraprofessional staff. Selecting the right staff for each role is critical to both program effectiveness and staff retention.

Preliminary evaluation results for the Healthy Start program are positive. For example, extremely few cases of abuse or neglect were reported among the families served and there was a significant reduction of the modifiable risk factors. Of the 2,254 families served by the program between July 1987 and June 1991, 90% of 2 year olds were fully immunized, and 85% of children were developing appropriately. Furthermore, among the 90 families in the program who were already known to child protective services at the time of intake due to a prior report of abuse or neglect of a sibling or imminent danger status, no additional reports occurred during the families' participation in the program (Earle, 1995).

A more recent report summarized the evaluation results:

> After two years of service provision to families, HSP was successful in linking families with pediatric medical care, improving maternal parenting efficacy, decreasing maternal parenting stress, promoting the use of nonviolent discipline, and decreasing injury due to partner violence in the home. No overall positive program impact emerged after two years of service on the adequacy of well-child health care; maternal life skills, mental health, social support or substance use; child development; the child's home learning environment, or parent-child interaction; pediatric health care use for illness or injury; or child maltreatment (according to maternal reports and child protective service reports). However, there were agency-specific positive program effects on several outcomes, including parent-child interaction, child development, maternal confidence in adult relationships, and partner violence.
>
> Significant differences were found in program implementation across the three administering agencies included in the evaluation. These differences had implications for family participation and involvement levels and, possibly, for outcomes achieved.
>
> The authors conclude that home visiting programs and evaluations should monitor program implementation for faithfulness to the program model, and should employ comparison groups to determine program impact. (Duggan et al., 1999, p. 66)

Center for Family Life's Preventive Services Program" Model.   Recently a 3-year study was funded to examine some of the results of the well-known Sunset Park neighborhood services center in New York City: The Center for Family Life. The Center's "Preventive Services Program" model was studied using a prospective sample of 189 families who received comprehensive yet individualized services provided directly and through referrals by a social worker in the preventive program. Hess, McGowan, and Botsko (in press) report that the program "uniquely integrates concrete and therapeutic services typical of family preservation programs with continuously available, intraagency comprehensive neighborhood-based family support services."

Since the inception of the Center for Family Life in 1978, its mission has been to help the families of Sunset Park, Brooklyn, remain intact. All families living in Sunset Park with a child under the age of 18 are eligible for the Center's free services, which are accessible 7 days a week, 24 hours a day. The range of services is extensive, including services to meet basic needs; employment programs; assistance with public benefits, immigration, and tax returns; a wide range of programs for children and youth, including recreation, arts, after school child care, and youth development; parent education and support groups; individual, family, and group counseling; neighborhood-based foster care; and initiatives designed to empower individuals, families, and the community of Sunset Park. Funded through government agencies, foundation grants, and gifts from corporations and individuals, the Center aims

> to sustain children and youth in their own homes by enhancing the capacity of parents, providing developmental opportunities for family members, addressing crisis in parent–child or spousal relationships, or intervening in a variety of ways to bring stability (social and economic) to the family household. The continuum of . . . activities embraces a large amount of preventive work and early intervention, as well as crisis management and remediation in instances of serious family disorganization and dysfunction. (Center for Family Life, 1997, p. 1)

The evaluation research found evidence of program effectiveness:

> At the conclusion of the study's data collection phase (30 months), almost all (98.6%) of the 423 study sample children remained with their families. All five families in which a child had been placed continued to receive Center services either in the preventive program, the neighborhood foster care program, or other Center programs. In addition 87.9% of the sample families' service needs had been addressed. (Hess, McGowan, & Botsko, in press)

In the 92 closed cases, statistically significant positive effects were found on five of eight child-centered problem/behavior factors as measured through the Family Assessment Form (McCroskey & Meezan, 1997; McCroskey, Nishimoto, & Subramanian, 1991): Relating Difficulties ($p = 0.001$) and Behavioral Difficulties ($p = 0.055$) (Hess, McGowan, & Botsko, 1997, pp. 183–184).

Hess et al. (in press) found three key program elements that differentiate the Center's preventive program approach from other family preservation programs and note that "these particular program characteristics are more typically found in family support programs rather than in family preservation programs (Allen et al., 1993; Schorr & Schorr, 1988; Weissbourd, 1987; Weissbourd & Kagan, 1989; Zigler & Black, 1989)." These include "broad inclusive accessibility to non-categorical services through multiple routes, including self-referral; the comprehensive nature of the within-Center community-based services provided through the preventive program; and flexibility in service duration, including continuing access to preventive program services over time." Hess et al. (in press) conclude that the Center for Family Life's "Preventive Services Program" model "provides a prototype for delivering comprehensive, integrated, and individualized services required by families with complex and varying sets of needs and problems."

Other Promising Programs. Although space does not permit a comprehensive review, well-designed school childcare programs (Nash & Fraser, 1998) and quality child care (e.g., Roditti, 1995) have been found to have value in teaching parents positive parenting approaches such as the use of mirroring, commentary on the child's behavior, praise (Eahler & Meginnis, 1997), and more positive family interactions (e.g., Kosterman, Hawkings, Spoth, Haggerty, & Zhu, 1997). In reviewing the Yale Child Welfare Research Program, Parents as Teachers, Avance Parent-Child Educators, Rural America Initiative Project, Infant Health and Development Program, and the Maternal Infant Outreach Worker Project, Comer and Fraser (1998) concluded the following:

> family support programs that attempt to control, ameliorate, and eradicate risk factors associated with socioeconomic, educational, and other disadvantages can be effective in strengthening families and increasing the well-being of children. In comparison to the control group families, program families demonstrated enhanced child, parent, and family functioning. Importantly, the data suggest that the effects of program services are cumulative and some "sleeper" effects appear to emerge two to three years after application of the intervention. For example, compared to control participants, families in the Maternal Infant Health Outreach Worker Project showed significant reductions in prenatal and pregnancy complications, improvements in the health of children, and growth in the development of more consistently caring and nurturing parent-child relationships. Gains made by participants in areas of child development, maternal behavior, and parent-child relations were maintained during the second year of program services. In addition, 24-month program outcomes showed advances in parenting skills (i.e., age appropriate expectations, less punishing of child). Thirty six month program services and follow-up data evidenced further gains in parenting knowledge.
>
> Although sample sizes are small and data are reported only for those families that fully completed service protocols (i.e., we know little about those families that dropped out of services), the findings suggest that well-conceptualized and implemented family support services have the capacity to improve family functioning. They appear to improve parent education and may have longer term effects on housing and income. Although the processes through which this occurs are not clear, the data indicate that family support programs may alter the knowledge and skills that parents bring to bear in solving child management and other family problems. (Comer & Fraser, 1998, p. 143)

In addition, Reynolds (1998) recently reviewed many studies of early childhood programs for children at risk and found positive influences when effective program components were present. The eight essential principles of effective early childhood programs identified by Reynolds are highlighted in this Figure 8.4. The implementation of these principles are directly associated with both short- and long-term social competence and school success for economically disadvantaged

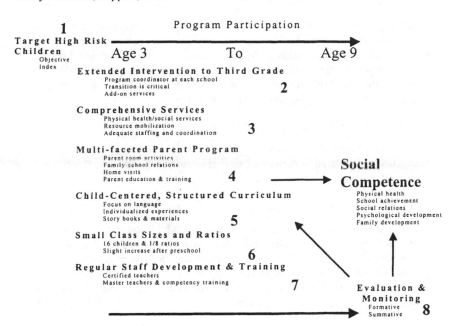

Figure 8.4. Eight principles of effective early childhood programs.
Source: Reynolds (1998).

children and families. They are based primarily on programmatic research conducted over the past two decades.

The relationship between the eight principles of effective programs and social competence derives from an extensive empirical research literature and from reviews of research and meta-analyses.[4] Early childhood was defined from ages 3 to 8. The targets of early childhood intervention are children who are at risk of developmental problems primarily due to economic disadvantage. Among the programs illustrated are large-scale programs such as Head Start, Follow Through, the less well-known Chicago Child Parent Center Program, and model programs such as the High/Scope Perry Preschool and the Abecedarian Project (Reynolds, 1998, pp. 504–505). The principles as articulated by Reynolds (1998), are listed below:

Principle 1: Target Children and Families who are at Highest Risk of School Difficulties

The better programs use objective instruments to screen children for risk factors associated with school underachievement and failure.

Principle 2: Begin Participation Early and Continue to Second or Third Grade

Both timing and duration of participation are associated with program effectiveness and performance gains. Because the preschool years are a time of rapid physical and cognitive growth, a stable learning environment offering stimulation language and social activities promotes a healthy foundation for the school entry and beyond. Early entry and greater program intensity are positively associated wit social competence (Ramey & Ramey, 1992; Wachs & Gruen, 1982; Zigler & Styfco, 1993). Most programs demonstrating long-term effects on child development provide more than one year of intervention services of a half-day or more.

Principle 3: Provide Comprehensive Child-Development Services

In order to promote and sustain good school performance, effective programs should assist children and families in meeting their physical health, nutritional, social psychological, emotional, and scholastic needs.

Principle 4: Active and Multifaceted Parent Involvement

Parent involvement is the cornerstone of many early childhood programs including the Child Parent Centers and Head Start. Evidence is accumulating that parent involvement helps increase the likelihood of long-term effects of early childhood programs (Reynolds, Maurogenes, Bezruczko, & Hagemann, 1996; Seitz, 1990). Moreover, parent involvement at home and in school also appears to be a good predictor of school achievement and grade promotion (Clarke-Stewart, 1988; Reynolds, 1991; Reynolds & Bezruczko, 1993).

Principle 5: A Child-Centered, Structured Curriculum Approach

No specific curriculum model is associated with successful early childhood intervention over the long term. The key is to implement an approach that is relatively structured, child-centered, and encourages developmentally appropriate practices and behaviors. Developmentally appropriate practices are those that emphasize (i) individualized work and choices, (ii) story-writing, story-telling, and drawing, (iii) hearing stories and books, (iv) cooperative activities, (v) reading and writing games, (vi) dramatic play, and (vii) teacher-child interactions to develop critical thinking skills.

Principle 6: Small Class Sizes and Teacher/Child Ratios

Almost all programs demonstrating long-term success into high school had teacher/child ratios of 1 to 8 or lower (Campbell & Ramey, 1995; Frede, 1994; Schweinhart et al., 1993). The benefits of low ratios for children most-at-risk may be particularly large. Small class sizes and teacher/child ratios encourage individualized learning experiences, increase contact between teachers and children as well as among children, facilitate better classroom organization, and improve satisfaction among teachers and staff. These characteristics are known to improve motivation, school commitment, curiosity, and later school achievement. In short, small class sizes increase the likelihood that Principle 5 is satisfied.

Principle 7: Regular Staff Development and Inservice Training for Certified Teachers

Another important feature of programs that promote longer-term effects is attention to staff development and training. Regular training (e.g., monthly) not only helps professionals stay abreast of the field and try new approaches but it builds cooperation and communication. The qualifications of staff are directly related to the quality of early childhood programs (Chafel, 1992; Frede, 1994). Teachers with bachelor's degrees or certification in early childhood education are more likely to provide developmentally appropriate practices in the classroom than teachers with other training experiences. In the well-known Perry Preschool Program, for example, all teachers had master's degrees.

Principle 8: Systematic Evaluation and Monitoring

If there is a truism about social programs, it is that good programs require commitment to evaluation. Effective social programs are those in which systematic evaluation is a high priority. Programs rarely are at their best in the first two years of implementation. Over the years, designers and evaluators have learned the hard lesson that programs are rarely ever implemented as well as they could be and only through systematic evaluation can programs be improved most efficiently. For example, the early evaluations of Head Start (cf. Zigler & Styfco, 1993) and other programs (e.g., Comer, 1993) are good illustrations of the importance of the timing of evaluation for program improvement.

Program evaluation helps determine: (i) whether the program and its services are being implemented as planned, (ii) if the program is achieving its short- and long-term objectives, and (ii) the best ways to improve the program. (Adopted from Reynolds, 1998, pp. 504–511)

Needs for Integrated Primary Health Care, Child Welfare, Mental Health, Substance Abuse Treatment and Other Services

As mentioned in Chapter 1, with the increase in substance abuse involved families, the need for prevention and treatment programs becomes critical and partnerships between child welfare, early childhood, education, mental health, primary health care, and substance abuse treatment facilities are crucial (see, for example, Office of Early Childhood, Substance Abuse and Mental Health Administration, 1998). The consequences (positive and negative) of the TANF and AFSA timelines for parents battling their addiction to drugs or alcohol must be monitored closely so public policy and intervention approaches are redesigned as needed (see an essay by Ira Chasnoff in Table 8.2).

Community-Based Approaches

Schuerman et al. (1994, p. xiii) have commented that "Family Preservation Services are often expected to solve major social problems one case at a time." Halpern (1999), Kamerman (1999), and O'Brien (1996), underscore the need to recognize that child and family well-being is affected immensely not only by public policies/service programs, but by funding strategies, local community conditions, and neighborhood supports. This recognition is stimulating a range of

Table 8.2. Prevention as a Moral Obligation: An Essay by Ira Chasnoff

---

The author Jonathon Kozol speaks of silent violence as a violence of inaction. This tendency to inaction, especially in situations in which substance abuse is present in a family, has become a characteristic of the health care system. The Lustbader article serves notice, however, that significant numbers of children are being exposed to toxic substances during early childhood. The physiological impact of that exposure is not fully understood, but the relational impact is clear: children in a family in which illicit drugs are being used or in which alcohol is being abused are at high risk for abuse, neglect, and behavioral problems that may interfere with long-term academic, emotional and social development. Is this a compelling reason for the state to enter family life at the infant's birth if the mother used drugs during pregnancy, or in the child's early years if he is found to be exposed to a toxic environment, and then to prescribe how the child shall be raised? What is a moral decision when there is a moral right on both sides of the issue, one side being the need for early intervention on behalf of the child, the other being the sanctity of the family and the right to raise children according to one's own beliefs? This is the quandary:

Given the complexity but immediacy of this issue, I propose that if a young child presents with a positive urine toxicology or a young child's family is found to be using illicit drugs or abusing alcohol, the family should be referred to treatment. If the family refuses treatment or fails to comply with treatment, CPS should be notified. For a first report to CPS, the family should be evaluated and referred to a structured educational and/or treatment program. If the family doesn't participate fully in treatment or continues to use drugs or alcohol, although family members have been offered treatment, parental rights should be reviewed and, when appropriate, terminated. For this approach to work, several issues must be directly addressed:

(1) Primary care physicians must talk with every family and screen every family in their care for alcohol and drug use, regardless of race, income, or social class. Screening should not depend on urine toxicology but on the use of a standardized self-administered screening instrument or one administered by a health care professional.

(2) The health care, child welfare, and substance abuse treatment systems must join forces to integrate services for families across the continuum of need. This joint effort must be supported by open dialogue and resolution of the differing perceptions and attitudes that drive each of these systems. The first step in bringing systems together is coming to agreement on an ultimate goal, in this case protection of the child, a goal that is high enough to avoid being mired in separate professional languages, but encompasses an ideal that all can acknowledge.

(3) Adequate treatment programs, both in numbers and quality, must be available to all families who need treatment. If a family fails to comply with mandated treatment because of the lack of adequate treatment facilities, this mitigating factor should be considered in any court proceedings that affect parental rights.

(4) Decisions to reunite parents with their children should be based on the family's adherence to and progress toward clearly stated treatment goals. These goals should be established collaboratively by the family, the treatment program, the CPS team, and the health care provider.

This proposal is compatible with The Adoption and Safe Families Act of 1997. This Act shifted emphasis from family reunification to safety of the child. Although child welfare agencies still must use reasonable efforts, specifically drug treatment for the parents, to keep families together or to reunify families, they also must concurrently identify an out-of-home permanent placement for the child. The court must decide within 1 year of the child's placement in the

---

(continued)

Table 8.2. (Continued)

child welfare system what the final placement goal will be. A Termination of Parental Rights petition is to be filed as soon as the court decides against family reunification, in any case no later than 15 months after the child's initial entry into the system. Parents are thus under obligation to make significant progress toward treatment goals within 1 year if they wish to keep their children. No one knows how this approach will work, but it cannot work unless there is a swift and thorough initial needs assessment of families reported to the child welfare system and credible treatment opportunities for the families.

The decisions that health care social service professionals must make on a daily basis are becoming progressively more complex and more intricate. We find ourselves knowing in our hearts what we believe, knowing through our advocacy what we support, but lacking many of the basic facts that must inform our actions. By improving access to treatment but tightening the consequences for parents who fail to take advantage of opportunities for treatment, we build on what knowledge we have, even though there is, and always will be, more to be discovered. Above all, we do know that there is an indisputable connection between child abuse and substance abuse. Silence may be violence.

Source: Chasnoff, I. J. (1998). Silent violence: Is prevention a moral obligation? *Pediatrics, 102,* 145–148. Used with permission of the American Academy of Pediatrics.

neighborhood and community-based initiatives, as exemplified by the child protective service initiatives reviewed in Chapter 6 and the programs discussed next.

For example, in a number of Chicago area neighborhoods, community councils are being forced to focus on neighborhoods in a way that is different from other community-directed change efforts that used reform frameworks proposed by outside policy researchers and funders:

The Children, Youth and Families Initiative sponsored by the Chicago Community Trust, is a ten-year, $30 million effort to enhance the development of children, families, and communities through the creation of community-directed infrastructures of services and supports.

This Initiative shares many characteristics with other comprehensive community-based initiatives, but it has some distinctive features. Chief among these is its *focus on the power of neighborhood resources*—afterschool programs, youth groups, sports teams, parent support and education programs, and the resources of parks, libraries, museums, community centers, and settlement houses. In developing the framework for the Initiative, Chapin Hall researchers chose to call these resources *primary sources* to indicate their potential to serve children and families and a need to redefine social services to include them in a pivotal role.

The Initiative proposes to enhance primary services and to join them as full partners with the traditional specialized services—including child welfare, mental health, and juvenile justice—to form a community-governed infrastructure of services. The idea is to reframe and reform social services so that they better serve children and families and so that they are better partners with other settings and sectors critical to enhancing outcomes for children, families, and communities—including schools, health care, housing and business. (Wynn, Merry, & Berg, 1995, p. 1)

Table 8.3. Outcomes, Assumptions, and Values of the Annie E. Casey Foundation Initiative for Family Development and Neighborhood Transition

Outcomes

We hope to promote the following five outcomes in each of the sites during the three-year Developmental Phase:

(1) Key stakeholders, residents and the community-at-large broadly embrace increasing neighborhood supports for families as a valued strategy for improving child outcomes.

(2) Leaders of both formal and informal organizations and institutions in the neighborhoods support this work in visible and meaningful ways.

(3) Key constituencies from outside the neighborhoods—including government, the private sector, foundations, and service providers—are actively engaged in the neighborhood's family strengthening enterprise.

(4) Programs and activities that contribute to neighborhood-scale family strengthening are increasing in quantity and quality.

(5) Neighborhoods are committed to and have the capacity to collect and use data to set priorities about the use of community resources, monitor neighborhood and family conditions, and advocate for change.

Assumptions

If we have learned anything from our past work in tough communities, it is that there is no cookie-cutter recipe for success. The kinds of activities it will take to reach the outcomes cited above will vary from site to site. But they should reflect a core set of assumptions and values that undergird our work and inspire us to believe we can make a meaningful difference in the lives of poor families and distressed neighborhoods.

We start off with the premise, first, that neighborhood conditions influence the way families raise their children, and that these conditions can be improved so that families have more opportunities and supports in their parenting roles.

Second, neighborhood conditions can promote or impede a family's access to these opportunities and supports. And it is our judgment that an explicit and central mission of any effort to change neighborhood conditions for the better should be to help make families stronger.

Third, some of the basics that families and communities need include access to jobs and economic security (which means not just surviving, but saving and building up assets), physical safety, time for families to bond with one another and with the larger community, connections to many different kinds of social networks, and access to informal and formal sources of support.

Fourth, one of the primary aims of this initiative is to restore and reinforce connections between families and supportive networks of kin, friends, neighbors, social groups, and communities of faith. At the same time, we recognize that "outside stakeholders"—including government, the private sector, and nonprofit agencies—have legitimate roles and responsibilities in providing critical support to families and communities. We also recognize that a family-strengthening agenda cannot be successful unless state and local governments are committed to reforms and policies that support and are responsive to community efforts to improve conditions for families.

Fifth, it is less important that we hold these beliefs about how critical strong families and neighborhoods are for children than that they resonate with communities committed to translating theory into action. We know from our own work and the work of others that any effort to impose a philosophy or set of strategies on communities is doomed to failure. The resources

(*continued*)

Table 8.3. (*Continued*)

we bring to the table are meaningless if they do not complement, supplement, partner, and link with what communities and their many sources of support and influence have to offer and are willing to negotiate.

Finally, an important part of our goal is to promote the kinds of changes in attitudes and organizations that lead to a common understanding of what it will take to create supportive communities and help generate the public and political will to support neighborhood-level efforts to strengthen families.

Values

Our Critical values include: The needs, desires, and wishes of families should be at the center of any community change agenda. Community ownership and participation in every step of the process is critical. The focus of this work should be the hardest to reach, most disenfranchised families: working in partnership with them to address needs they identify and helping them build the capacity to pursue their own vision for change.

Issues of race, class and gender inequities, and other forms of social injustice need to be surfaced and addressed as part of this work, rather than being allowed to simmer and become barriers to success. Racial and ethnic populations need to be represented in all aspects of our work. This work must respect and reflect the culture, history, language, and aspirations of communities.

Source: Annie E. Casey Foundation (1994). *Neighborhood Transformation/Family Development Project. Implementation Planning Group Operational Plan.* Baltimore, MD: Author, pp. 2–4.

As another concrete example of a community-based family support model, a new multiyear initiative by the Annie E. Casey Foundation that began in 1999 is described in Table 8.3. This initiative is investing over $60 million per year to help support families through strengthening the neighborhoods in which they live and work. Three primary strategies are being employed:

- *Opportunity* = connecting people to means for acquiring income and assets.
- *Networks* = connecting people to each other in the common task of problem solving.
- *Support* = connecting people to formal and informal sources of help (Nittoli, 1999, p. 3).

Desired outcomes include (1) the neighborhood has "embraced" the concept of family strengthening; (2) the community is mobilized in better ways; (3) stakeholders outside of neighborhoods understand that families matter and community conditions matter; (4) family activities in a neighborhood are increased; and (5) there is an increased capacity of community residents to have and use neighborhood data (Stark, 1999). These strategies fit with a likely community agenda related to key areas such as community safety, jobs, housing, and schools, with corresponding effects on neighborhoods and impacts on families.

To accomplish this work a *neighborhood context* is essential in which the following kinds of family supports are pursued:

- *Security* = stable, sufficient material conditions for family life.
- *Safe space* = living in a place families consider safe.
- *Time* = spending time together relaxing and participating in recreational, educational, and domestic activities as a family.
- *Civic society* = family and friendship ties, the range of formal and informal structures that gives communities a sense of order and organized formats to gather for common purposes.

How do such initiatives, goals, and strategies fit with a likely community agenda? Four areas are emphasized—safety, jobs, housing, and schools (Nittoli, 1999, p. 4). One cautionary note needs to be emphasized. This initiative is not summarized here to provide the ideal or even the most comprehensive model, but is included to provide a glimpse of some promising family support strategies based on over 10 years of experience (Walsh, 1997). Other promising community-focused programs have been described by Cameron and Vanderwoerd (1997), Kagan and Weissbourd, (1994), Kamerman and Kahn (1995, pp. 151–179), and Schorr (1997). On a more child-focused level, Greenberg, Domitrovich, and Bumbarger (1999) and Kumpfer, Molgaard, and Spoth (1996) have found effective programs for preventing mental disorders in school-age children. These are the youth who may end up in child welfare or juvenile justice placements without early intervention services.

CONCLUSION

The benefits to the families served by some family support programs parallel some of the other child welfare programs that use in-home teaching and other types of supportive interventions. But too few evaluation studies using rigorous experimental designs have been conducted, particularly those including both self-report and archival data on key outcome measures for randomly selected intervention and control groups (Helfer, 1982; Gomby, Culross & Berman, 1999; Olds, 1988a). In addition, evaluation results have been less positive for some of these programs that have served lower risk children (Karoly, Greenwood, Everingham, Hoube, Kilburn, Rydell, Saunders, and Chiesa, 1998) and those that have targeted child abuse prevention as a key outcome, particularly for those programs of short duration, with a less tightly specified parenting curriculum, and those focusing on families who have already been referred to child protective services (Barth, 1991).

Home visitation has been cited as the "single most critical element in a comprehensive approach to preventing child maltreatment" (U.S. Advisory Board, 1991; U.S. Government Accounting Office, 1992; Daro, 1993, p. 1). Substantial debate, however, continues as to various prevention services regarding length of services, intervention methods, provider training, and what combination of services is best for certain ethnic groups by problem area. Furthermore, there is the question of whether to continue to provide periodic bursts of services to vulnerable families with older children, given findings that older children are also at risk of child maltreatment, and are underserved by the CPS delivery system (Sedlak, 1991a; Jonson-Reid & Barth, 1999). Finally, Berliner (1993) and Daro (1988, p. 128) provide an important caution that prevention efforts must be multifaceted in design:

> Just as one treatment strategy is insufficient for all maltreating families, no one pre-vention effort can adequately address the various causal factors of maltreatment or provide effective inroads to all families at risk of different forms of maltreatment. Some families will respond to educational efforts, although other families initially will be more responsive to offers of material support. Although some families will welcome a service provider into their homes, others will prefer to attend classes of support group meetings in a local community center or church.
>
> Certain at-risk families or individuals, recognizing that they need assistance, will voluntarily enter a prevention program; other families will need more encourage-ment. Effectively preventing child abuse is a tall order and one that requires a differ-ential and flexible local response system. The most useful systems will be ones that address the multiple causal factors associated with various types of maltreatment, target services to both the potential perpetrator and the potential victim, and build on the experiences of others in designing specific prevention services.

Well-designed family support or other types of child abuse prevention efforts have the potential to be cost effective in terms of the health care, special educa-tion, legal, and other costs incurred by society in dealing with the social problem, not to mention the most important (and difficult to measure) costs of emotional harm to children. However, as discussed earlier, the evidence base, although grow-ing, is inconclusive. And recently, some program experts have been concerned not only about program fidelity, but also about the difficulty in certain areas of con-necting family support programs with child welfare programs. That is, they do not really serve the same clientele in many cases. Other serious questions are raised by the Rand analysis:

> On the basis of research conducted to date, we know that some targeted early in-tervention programs have substantial favorable effects on child health and develop-ment, educational achievement, and economic well-being. We also know that some of these programs, if targeted to families who will benefit most, have generated sav-ings to the government that exceed the costs of the programs. There is still much that we do not know about these programs, however, and this limits the degree to which these conclusions can be generalized to other early intervention programs. One of the big unknowns is why successful programs work—and others don't. In particular we do not know the following:
>
> - *Whether there are optimal program designs.* There have not been enough con-trolled comparisons that can support choices between focusing on parents versus children (or both), intervening in infancy versus the preschool years, integrating interventions versus running them independently, or tailoring to individual needs versus treating children the same but treating a greater number.

- *How early interventions can best be targeted to those who would benefit most.* It is not yet known which eligibility criteria would generate the most positive benefit/cost ratios. In addition, whatever criteria are used will have dramatic implications for program cost and implementation.

    There are other unknowns:

- *Whether the model programs evaluated to date will generate the same benefits and savings when implemented on a large scale.* The demonstrations have been undertaken in a more resource-intensive, focused environment with more highly trained staff than is likely to be achievable in full-scale programs.

- *What the full range of benefits is.* Typically, evaluations have focused on those aspects of development that the intervention was intended to influence. But we know from some studies that programs can have a broad array of effects beyond their principal objectives.

- *What the implications of the changing social safety net are.* Previous demonstrations were carried out under the now-superseded welfare system. To some extent, those interventions depended on that system for collateral support of families, and the savings generated were partly in terms of welfare costs that the government may not now be paying out anyway.

These unknowns will have to be resolved if wise decisions are to be made among early intervention alternatives and if the programs chosen are to be designed to fully realize their potential for promoting child development—and saving money. In particular, research is needed into *why* programs work. Otherwise, inferences cannot be drawn about new program designs, and every such design would be unproven until tested and evaluated. (Karoly et al., 1998, pp. xx–xxi)

Finally, we must identify the most important areas to be focused on rather than on secondary risk factors. For example, is it a lack of a parent's social network, employment skills, practical knowledge of child development, sense of self-esteem, and/or social skills that should be addressed? We need to avoid "single-variable" interventions in a complex area such as child maltreatment (Olds & Henderson, 1989). This is being shown to be particularly true as more community-based family support efforts are initiated and evaluated (see, for example, Schorr, 1997, pp. 301–379; Kamerman & Kahn, 1995; Wynn, Costello, Halpern & Richman, 1994). Theory-based interventions will help the field (Green & McAllister, 1997). The next chapter describes various forms of family-based services and the evidence base for those interventions.

NOTES

1.   This section is adapted from the following sources: Fraser, M. W., Pecora, P.J., & Haapala, D.A. (1991). *Families in crisis: Findings from the Family-based Intensive Treat-*

ment Project. Hawthorne, NY: Aldine de Gruyter, pp. 17–47. Pecora, P.J., Fraser, M.W., Nelson, K., McCroskey, J., & Meezan, W. (1995). *Evaluating family-based services.* New York: Aldine de Gruyter, pp. xiii–xxxvii.

2. For more information regarding the treatment philosophy and practice principles of FBS and IFPS, see Cole and Duva (1990), Dunst et al. (1988), Haapala and Kinney (1979), Kinney et al. (1981, 1990), Lloyd and Bryce (1983), and Pecora, Delewski, Booth, Haapala, and Kinney (1985).

3. For other examples of family support programs, see Jones (1985, pp. 27–34), Kagan and Weissbourd (1994), Weissbourd and Kagan (1989), Yale Bush Center in Child Development and Social Policy, and Family Resource Coalition (1983), and Zigler and Black (1989).

4. The major studies and analyses that Reynolds drew from are Chafel (1992), Frede (1994), Ramey and Ramey (1992), Schweinhart et al. (1993), Wachs and Gruen (1982), Zigler and Muenchow (1992), Zigler and Styfco (1993), Reynolds (1994), Haskins (1989), and White (1985).

FOR FURTHER INFORMATION

The David and Lucille Packard Foundation (1999). *The future of children home visiting: Recent program evaluations (9)*1. Los Altos, CA: The David and Lucille Packard Foundation. A concise and balanced look at the effectiveness and potential of home visiting programs.

Little, M., & Mount, K. (1999). *Prevention and early intervention with children in need.* Cambridge, England: Ashgate Publishing. Provides a concise synthesis of preventive services from a British perspective.

Schorr, L.B. (1997). *Common purpose: Strengthening families and neighborhoods to rebuild America,* 1st ed. New York: Anchor Books. Provides an inspiring summary of innovative approaches to family and neighborhood strengthening.

9

Family-Based and Intensive
Family Preservation Services

INTRODUCTION

As mentioned in Chapter 8, the term *family support* has been used as an umbrella under which clusters a broad range of family-based services programs. Over 44 states have launched these types of programs over the past 10 years (Government Accounts Office, 1997, p. 2). In virtually all family-based services the family is not seen as deficient but as having many strengths and resources (Kagen et al., 1987). Although family-based and intensive family preservation services have both been cited as family support programs, these programs are distinct from the primary prevention and child development-oriented family support programs discussed in Chapter 8 such as prenatal care, home-visiting, early childhood education, parent education, home–school–community linkage, child care, and other family-focused services. A three-part typology of family-based programs is repeated in part from Chapter 8 to initiate a more in-depth look at family-based and intensive family preservation services:

1. *Family resource, support, and education services.* These community-based services assist and support adults in their role as parents. Services are available to all families with children and do not impose criteria for participation that might separate or stigmatize certain parents (Child Welfare League of America, 1989, p. 13).

2. *Family-based services.* These services encompass a range of activities such as case management, counseling/therapy, education, skill-building, advocacy, and/or provision of concrete services for families with problems that threaten their stability. As mentioned earlier, the philosophy of these programs differs from the more traditional child welfare services in the role of parents, use of concrete and clinical services, and other areas (Child Welfare League of America, 1989, p. 29).

3. *Intensive family preservation services.* This grouping of services might be distinguished by the combination of case management with intensive therapeutic and other services. Some of these services are designed for families "in crisis," at a time when removal of a child is perceived as imminent, or the return of a child from out-of-home care is being considered. Yet the reality is that this service model is also being applied to chronic family sit-

uations, involving child neglect or abuse, which do not involve crisis. These programs often share the same philosophical orientation and characteristics as family-based services, but are delivered with more intensity (including shorter time frame and smaller caseloads), so they are often referred to as intensive family preservation service or IFPS programs. Caseloads generally vary between two to six families per worker. Families are typically seen between 6 and 10 hours per week, and the time period of intervention is generally between 4 and 12 weeks.

Comparing FBS and IFPS Programs

Family-based services and intensive family-preservation crisis services are described in this chapter. The emphasis of IFPS services is on providing intensive counseling, education, skills training, and supportive services to families, with the goal of protecting the child, strengthening and preserving the family, and preventing the unnecessary placement of children (Whittaker, Kinney, Tracy, & Booth, 1990). In some cases, however, the primary case goal is to reunite children with their families (Child Welfare League of America, 1989, pp. 46–47). We will refer to these programs as intensive family preservation services (IFPS), and they include programs such as HOMEBUILDERS™ in Washington, "Intensive Family Services" in Maryland, and certain types of "Families First" programs in various states. Although these programs may share core features, much diversity in treatment models exists among them; and a variety of program names have been used, which has added to confusion in the field: "family-based services," "home-based services," "services to children in their own homes," and "family preservation services."

Yet although program design and specific interventions differ, most of the programs fitting the broader name of Family-Based Services (FBS) share some or all of the following characteristics:

- A primary worker, advocate, or case manager establishes and maintains a supportive, empowering relationship with the family.
- A wide variety of helping options are used (e.g., "concrete" forms of supportive services such as food and transportation may be provided along with clinical services).
- Caseloads of two to twelve families are maintained.
- One or more associates serve as team members or provide back-up for the primary worker.
- Workers (or their back-up person) are available 24 hours a day for crisis calls or emergencies.
- The home is the primary service setting, and maximum utilization is made of natural helping resources, including the family, the extended family, the neighborhood, and the community.

- The parents remain in charge of and responsible for their family as the primary caregivers, nurturers, and educators.
- Services are time limited, usually 1–4 months (Bryce & Lloyd, 1981).[1]

So this framework distinguishes between family support (no case management), family-based services (includes case management), and intensive family preservation services (intensive services plus case management).

FAMILY-BASED SERVICES

Target Populations for Family-Based Services

The target populations for FBS and IFPS programs may overlap significantly. For example, although the target population for both programs is generally families in serious trouble, both program types may serve families no longer able to cope with problems that threaten family stability, families in which a decision has been made by an authorized public social service agency (or by the family) that there is substantial reason to place a child outside the home, and families whose children are in temporary out-of-home care. Although a "crisis orientation" may be emphasized by some programs, it must be recognized that many families who are served by these agencies are not in crisis and have been trying to cope with an abusive or neglectful family member, child mental illness, juvenile delinquency, or other problems for some time. Thus, these services may be appropriate for families seen by the child welfare, juvenile justice, or mental health systems, as well as for adoptive or foster families facing potential disruption.[2]

The distinction between the various program categories is not definitive, but the taxonomy does help to clarify some distinguishing features of the three types of programs and to suggest some of the program design questions facing practitioners and administrators in the field. Throughout the remainder of this chapter, when reviewing the general literature on family support, family-based or family preservation services we will use the term *Family-Based Services* (FBS). When referring specifically to programs that deliver both concrete and clinical services primarily in the home on an intensive basis, we will use the term *Intensive Family Preservation Services* (IFPS). Unfortunately, the distinction between the latter two categories is not definitive, but the taxonomy does help clarify the program design issues faced by practitioners and administrators in the field. A general typology that has been found helpful classifies family-based programs into three types, as shown in Figure 9.1. The first is family support services, the broadest category. The second is family-based services, which encompasses a wide variety of family-based programs, some of which focus on placement prevention although others focus on family strengthening. These programs may be office or home based, short or long term, intensive or diffuse.

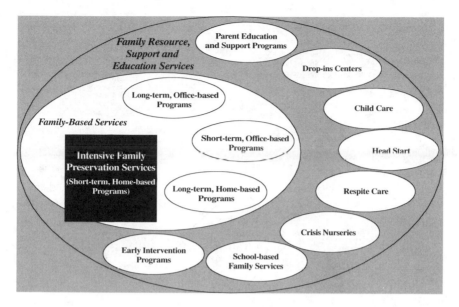

Figure 9.1. A typology of family-centered service programs

The third type is IFPS, which is short term and intensive, delivering both clinical and concrete services in the home setting and providing a more intensive service than other programs (e.g., provision of a minimum of 5 hours of client contact per week with a service duration of about 60 days or less; Edna McConnell Clark Foundation, 1985; Whittaker, Kinney, Tracy, & Booth, 1990) (see Figure 9.1). Note that some researchers have made a further distinction by highlighting which programs are home based. These models have many or all of the characteristics of the more general FBS programs, except that the majority of services are provided in the family's home setting. The IFPS programs listed in this chapter meet the criteria commonly listed for Intensive Family Preservation crisis services. Throughout the remainder of this chapter, when reviewing the general literature on programs that are home or office based and family based, the term Family-Based Services (FBS) will be used. When the service is also short term in terms of 1–4 months, and intensive, we will use the term Intensive Family Preservation services (IFPS).

HISTORY OF FAMILY-BASED SERVICES

Early Child Welfare Preventive Service Programs

The first foster care prevention or home-based service programs in America consisted of the "friendly visitors" of the Charity Organization Societies who worked

Figure 9.2.   An array of child and family supports
   Source: Pecora, P.J., Fraser, M.W., Nelson, K., McCroskey, J., & Meezan, W.
   (1995). *Evaluating family-based services,* p. xxii. New York: Aldine de Gruyter.

with immigrant and low income families in their own homes to promote self-
sufficiency and assimilation into American society in the late 1800s and early
1900s (Bremner, 1970–71). In the 1900s, settlement houses also were used to deliver a wide range of services to poor and immigrant families.[3]

   In the 1950s and 1960s, programs were developed to treat "multiproblem families" in order to improve family functioning and reduce welfare dependency (see
for example, Geismar & Ayers, 1958; Geismar & Krisberg, 1966; Overton, 1953).
But for many early programs, worker caseloads remained high and client contact

was limited to once a week or once a month for a 1- to 2-year period (Hutchinson & Nelson, 1985) (see Figure 9.2).

1960–1980 as Decades of Varying Developments in FBS and IFPS

The family-based services arose out of concern that traditional child welfare services were not meeting the needs of children and their families in America. More specifically, the field of child welfare was criticized during the 1960s and 1970s in the following areas:

- Children were placed in substitute care who could have remained at home
- Ethnic minority children were placed into substitute care at a rate far higher than their representation in the general public.
- Children in substitute care lacked clearly specified case plans.
- "Foster care drift" occurred with long-term placements, multiple placements, and no sense of permanence for many children (Gruber, 1973; Maas & Engler, 1959)
- Parental involvement and visitation were discouraged (e.g., Fanshel & Shinn, 1978).
- Termination procedures and adoption practices constrained the use of adoption as a bona fide case goal.
- Federal funding policies encouraged foster care maintenance services (i.e., placement) and did not adequately fund preventive or restorative services.
- Most state agencies did not have adequate management information systems in place; consequently program administrators did not know how many children were currently placed in substitute care, average length of placement, and other essential planning information (Knitzer, Allen, & McGowan, 1978; National Commission on Children 1991). (In some cases, program administrators did not even know what continent foster children were on—as evidenced by the massacre of foster children from San Francisco who had been taken to Jonestown in Africa.)

Exposés of the quality of child welfare services, and foster care in particular, were written and widely publicized by both child welfare experts and investigative reporters (e.g., Fanshel & Shinn, 1978; Knitzer, Allen, & McGowan, 1978; Maas & Engler, 1959; Mnookin, 1973). In addition, the growing incidence and costs of foster care, concern about the harmful effects of substitute care, the belief that some placements could be prevented, and the trend toward deinstitutionalization all prompted the development of a variety of foster care preventive programs (Emlen, Lahti, Downs, McKay, & Downs, 1978; Jones, 1985).

Family-based services arose in various service systems for somewhat different reasons. The fields of child mental health, juvenile justice, and child welfare were criticized during the 1960s and 1970s from a number of perspectives. In family services, FBS emerged out of concern that traditional child welfare agencies were not meeting the needs of children and their families in the United States. In mental health there was concern that services to some children were not adequate to meet their needs and that the use of largely restrictive treatment systems might not be necessary. In juvenile justice there has been a continuous emphasis on community-based treatment as an alternative to more traditional use of a more punitive "just deserts" model.

In the 1980s some of the same themes were continued. A foundation report charged that "children are separated from their families by default. Too few alternatives are available to help [families] stay together safely" (Edna McConnell Clark Foundation, 1985, p. 2). Many children were placed outside their homes not once but multiple times, using different family, group home, and/or institutional settings (Fanshel & Shinn, 1978; Rzepnicki, 1987).

One of the principal assumptions underlying foster care prevention and permanency planning efforts is that, in most cases, a child's development and emotional well-being are best ensured through efforts to maintain the child in the home of her or his biological parents or extended family (providing that at least minimal standards of parenting are maintained). Yet, child placement in some situations, where a minimal level of safety and well-being cannot be adequately ensured, is the more beneficial and necessary short-term option.[4]

As discussed in Chapters 2 and 3, a number of policy and program innovations have been instituted by federal, state, and local authorities to address critiques of the child welfare system. Most notable among these were Permanency Planning, and the related program and fiscal reforms promoted by the Adoption Assistance and Child Welfare Act of 1980 (AACWA: P.L. 96-272) and the Adoption and Safe Families Act of 1997 (ASFA or PL 105-189), and the Multi-Ethnic Placement Act of 1995 (MEPA: P.L. 103-382). For example, PL 96-292 mandated that a series of reforms be implemented in state child welfare agencies in order to qualify for special supplemental Title IV-B federal appropriations that helped to pay for in-home child welfare services. P.L. 96-272 also required, for the first time, that states implement a variety of placement prevention services as part of their strategy to ensure that "reasonable efforts" have been made to preserve the family before a child is placed in substitute care (Pine, 1986). Some constraints were placed on this reasonable efforts requirement and time limits to achieve permanency were shortened by the subsequent ASFA legislation.

As discussed in Chapter 3, permanency planning refers, first, to efforts to prevent unnecessary child placement, and second, to return children from foster care to their biological families or to some other form of permanent placement such as an adoptive home or long-term foster care family with guardianship. This emphasis took hold in child welfare agencies in the late 1970s and 1980s with the leadership of the Oregon Permanency Planning Project and other training efforts. Permanency planning has been helpful in reducing the numbers of children lingering in family foster care [as of 1985, 26% of the children who left substitute care had been there for 4 months or less; 46% of the children were in placement less than 6 months (Maximus, 1985, p. III-37)]. There is, however, growing concern about a lack of program alternatives for family reunification, foster care reentry, and, more importantly, placement prevention through improving child and family functioning (Goerge, 1990; Goerge, Wulczyn, & Harden, 1994; also see Chapters 12 and 13 in this volume).

Criticism of the child welfare service delivery system has been brought to public attention by the numerous class action suits filed by the American Civil Liberties Union and other advocacy groups. In fact, many would argue that the focus on permanency planning, creating service alternatives, and child stability has not been supported through staff training, supervision, and provision of the necessary resources (Fanshel, 1992). In 1995, the foster care population had an average daily census of 483,000 and the system was estimated to have served an annual total of 710,000 children and adolescents (Tatara, 1997). More recent statistics tabulated for March 31, 1998, estimate that 520,000 children were in foster care in the United States, with over one-third (34%) of these children in care for 3 years or more care (U.S. Department of Health and Human Services, Administration for Children and Families, Administration on Children, Youth and Families, Children's Bureau, 1999, p. 1). Some of this increase in placements is no doubt due to increased substance abuse among parents. A number of studies have found that various forms of child maltreatment are associated with abuse of alcohol or other drugs (Murphy et al., 1991). There have been large increases in the number of drug-exposed infants coming into foster care. In addition (prior to the economic boom in the 1990s for some soioeconomic groups in the United States), a declining economy, increasing rates of teen parenthood, a rise in never-married parents, AIDS, urban poverty, a growing shortage of affordable housing, and significant rates of unemployment all contributed to the continued need for foster care placements (e.g., Testa, 1992). Part of the "increase" in placements is actually due to the numbers of children who are remaining in care longer, particularly those placed with family members ("kinship care" placements) (see the Multi-state Data Archive Reports: Wulczyn, Harden, & Goerge, 1997).

Some experts believe that state agencies are already better at reducing the number of unnecessary placements. There are, of course, many ways to achieve such reductions. One way is to be sure that child welfare workers carefully assess the family environment for strengths that will allow them to provide a protective environment and supplement those strengths with useful services. Another way to achieve reductions in placement is to just allow a child to remain at home *without* providing any services to be sure that the home is safe. Although in many states the percentage of children placed in relation to the number of child protective service cases being reported appears to have decreased (Wald, 1988, p. 34), this may be due to a variety of reasons, including the lack of emergency placement resources. Child advocates, therefore, remain concerned that essential preventive services are not being provided. These advocates maintain that it is possible to identify families with a sufficiently high risk of maltreatment or harm to justify an intensive intervention to prevent further family deterioration or child placement. But these services are not being provided, in part due to ineffectual enforcement of P.L. 96-272, a general lack of funding for preventive services (Forsythe, 1992; Kamerman & Kahn, 1995), and continuing problems of targeting and screening of families most in need of the service. Consequently, many children have been placed outside their homes not once but multiple times in different family, group home, residential treatment, juvenile justice, and psychiatric hospital settings (Fanshel & Shinn, 1978; Rzepnicki, 1987).

During the late l960s and mid-1970s, new program models for strengthening family functioning began to emerge, many of which used the cognitive-behavioral and/or family therapy treatment techniques that were being developed during that time. For example, in 1969 the Home and Community Treatment Team was established at the Mendota Mental Health Institute in Madison, Wisconsin. The program worked with families with 3- to 10-year-old children who have emotional and behavioral problems. Both in-home (4 hours per week) and in-office (2 hours per week) services are provided for an average of 15 months (Cautley, 1979; Kaplan, 1986).

During the early 1970s, a number of child welfare agencies were also successful in preventing child placement through intensive counseling (Hirsch, Gailey, & Schmerl, 1976) or through the use of a variety of "emergency services" such as crisis counselors, homemakers, emergency shelters or foster homes, and emergency caretakers (Burt & Balyeat, 1974; National Center for Comprehensive Emergency Services to Children, 1978). These programs recognized the importance of crisis intervention and time-limited supportive services for families as means for preventing long-term foster care placement.

At the same time a multidisciplinary family-based approach to preventing child maltreatment and placement was developed in Philadelphia (the "SCAN" program or Supportive Child Adult Network). This program worked primarily with black single-parent families and renders services for a minimum of 2–4 hours each week over 9- to 15-month periods (Tatara, Morgan, & Portner, 1986).

A more time-limited and intensive home-based service, the HOMEBUILDERS™ program, was developed in mid-1970s at Catholic Community Services in Tacoma, Washington. Then and now, HOMEBUILDERS™ therapists receive referrals from the state child welfare agency for those cases in which previous counseling or other services have been provided, but the children are in "imminent danger of placement." In practice, this has been interpreted to mean that the children will be placed within 1 week or less if a more intensive service is not offered. The program is characterized by low worker caseloads, high intensity (provision of an average of 38 client contact hours in 30 days), and use of a variety of clinical and concrete services (e.g., Fraser et al., 1992; Kinney, Madsen, Fleming, & Haapala, 1977; Kinney, Haapala, & Booth, 1991).

Other less intensive family support programs have been effective in treating families in which child neglect is the major problem. One of the better known programs is the Bowen Center (Sullivan, Spasser, & Penner, 1977), which used a variety of services such as emergency shelter care, homemaker assistance, preschool day care, and laundry facilities at the center to reach out to parents and strengthen families. Initially, five-person teams were used with a dual focus on helping clients meet both concrete and psychosocial service needs. Later, the program model shifted to one that is more home based, with caseworkers seeing families individually for an average of 8.1 months, providing clinical, educational, and concrete services designed to promote healthy child development (Giblin & Callard, 1980; Kaplan, 1986, pp. 80-82).

The PACT program in Wayne County (Detroit) was successful in working with low income and ethnic minority families, and represents a successful partnership between a university-based program and a state department of social services (Cabral & Callard, 1982; Van Meter, 1986). Promising results were also found by using an ecobehavioral approach "Project 12-ways" (Lutzkert & Rives, 1984). Another less intensive approach used individual caseworkers as the primary service providers (the New York State Preventive Services Demonstration Project). This is one of the most well-researched home-based service programs, involving special units set up in two county departments of child welfare in New York City. These units delivered a variety of services that produced continuing beneficial effects for children and families, some 5 years after services were provided (Jones, 1985; Jones, Neuman, & Shyne, 1976).

Recent Developments

Currently in many states, only a small percentage of the children reported to CPS are ever placed in some form of substitute care. In six major states, about 4 in 1,000 children ages 0-4 will enter foster care and about 2 in 1,000 children ages 5-17 will enter foster care (Wulczyn, Harden, & Goerge, 1997). Some researchers argue that there are few "unnecessary" placements, and yet a proportion of those families experiencing the removal of their children could have been provided with FBS at an earlier time. Criticism of the child welfare service delivery system has continued with the continuing high rates of foster care placements or long lengths of stay for some children, particularly African-American children. (But some jurisdictions have seen a decrease in placement rates and an increase in adoptions or other permanent placements.)

To address these problems, as mentioned earlier, a number of policy and program innovations were instituted by federal, state, and local authorities. PL 96-272's requirement that every state implement a variety of placement prevention services as part of its strategy to provide "reasonable efforts" to preserve the family has led to some renewed use of traditional programs to support families, including homemaker, emergency day care, parent aide, and crisis nursery services. These services have also been supplemented by FBS, which are designed to help families to remain together safely.

As discussed in Chapter 3, the state of Oregon followed its implementation of permanency planning with FBS programs. The first four projects, which were viewed as IFPS programs, were implemented in 1980, based on a proposal approved by the 1979 legislature to divert money from the foster care budget to more preventative services. Although the original proposal was to train Children's Services Division (CSD) staff to provide family treatment, the legislature required the program to contract with private family therapy providers. Each of the four pilot projects was located in a different sociocultural area and was selected for its relatively high number of children in placement. Based on the pilot projects' success, the program was expanded in late 1981 and 1982 to 16 projects. During this expansion, qualified private providers were not available in five of the locations; at these sites, new CSD employees were hired to provide IFPS. Project standards and regulations are the same for the "in-house" (state-operated) projects as they are for the contracted programs.

The more intensive units were characterized by small caseloads (about eight families per worker) and a time-limited service period of 90 days, although it may be extended. The program operates from a treatment model based on principles of family systems theory. The behavior of one family member is seen as necessarily affecting the behavior of other family members; the presentation of a "problem child" is viewed as an indication of a problem family, with the child having been consciously or unconsciously selected by the rest of the family as the symptom bearer. Family treatment is directed toward healing relationships between parents, as well as between children and their parents, and is broken down into three phases: assessment, treatment, and termination. About a third of the work done with families was accomplished through co-therapy, and much of the counseling is provided using office-based sessions (Nelson et al., 1988, pp. 31–32).

In 1991, North Carolina began a process to implement family preservation programs in 100 counties, and as of 1996 was serving 32 counties at an average cost of $5,355 per family and $3,361 per at risk child. The state estimates that for every dollar spent on these services that $3.34 is saved (Division of Social Services, North Carolina Department of Human Resources, 1996, p. 42). In New York City, an FBS demonstration project that used a special form of FBS involving capitated prospective payments, greater flexibility in services, and lower worker caseloads resulted in accelerated parent–child reunifications (Wulczyn, Zeidman, & Svirsky, 1997). Although a complete description of the various states and agencies that have begun or funded FBS programs is beyond the scope of this chapter, the diversity of these programs is extensive. For example, in 1989 a form of FBS was designed and began operation by Boys Town. Their model of family preservation services is strengths based, builds on some of the well-recognized intervention techniques of their group care programs, but extends that work further in how their "Family Consultants" are trained and supervised (Peterson, Kohrt, Shadoin, & Authier, 1995). In Portland, Oregon, an IFPS program for families in which neglect is an issue that was designed for and by African-Americans is showing early signs of success (Ciliberti, 1998). Specially designed FBS programs are being implemented for other ethnic groups as well, such as Asian Americans (Fong, 1997) and

Native Americans (Miannes, 1990). Finally, one of the most well-researched models of IFPS is Multisystemic Family Preservation Services (MST), which uses a ecological-based intervention approach with specific treatment protocols to enable the worker and family to address individual, family, school, and community factors (Henggler, Schoenwald, Borduin, Rowland, & Cunningham, 1998).[5]

Current Status of FBS Programs

A large variety of FBS programs have been developed by both private and public child welfare agencies (some of which use more of an office-based approach to service delivery). The National Resource Center on Family-Based Services in 1988 published an annotated bibliography of 333 programs in over 25 states, a huge increase from the 20 programs listed in 1982 (National Resource Center on Family-Based Services, 1988). These programs are serving clients from child welfare, mental health, developmental disabilities, juvenile corrections, and other major service areas. A variety of staffing and treatment models were being employed, including those related to supporting families whose children are returning from foster care or residential treatment (e.g., Fraser et al. 1996; Pierce and Geremia, 1999), or are in danger of experiencing adoption disruption, as well as services tailored to special racial groups (e.g., Fong, 1997; Knox, 1996).[6] Although there has not been a recent cataloguing of such programs, we expect that they have continued to grow since the passage of the federal Family Preservation and Support Program in 1993. However, a recent analysis of where the funds were being spent under this legislation revealed that most of the spending was targeted at family support services rather than to FBS or IFPS.

Nevertheless, the field has therefore experienced a shift from a few small-scale and isolated demonstration projects to the use of FBS programs on a statewide basis in a number of states, for example, Florida, Illinois, Maryland, Michigan, Minnesota, and Tennessee (e.g., Grohoski, 1990; Holliday & Cronin, 1990). The implementation of these programs represents a commitment on the part of state and local governments to operationalize the principle stated earlier that society should be willing to invest as many resources in preserving families as might be spent for substitute family care (Lloyd, Bryce, & Schultze, 1980, p. 3). Thus, these services were developed to provide alternatives to out-of-home placement by improving family functioning as well as by linking families to sustaining services and sources of support (Bryce, 1979).

In response to the rising number of child placements, some juvenile court judges are ordering local departments of social services to provide housing assistance or FBS under the "reasonable efforts" mandate of P.L. 96-272 (Personal Communication, Judge Richard Fitzgerald, 1991). Furthermore, some states have continued to fund previously developed placement prevention efforts such as homemaker, emergency day care, parent aide, and crisis nursery services. These services have been supplemented recently by a new array of FBS programs that are designed to help families remain together safely. The program reforms

Table 9.1. Significant Events and Projects Related to FBS

Year	Event or Project
1800s	The use of "Friendly Visitors" becomes a popular approach for addressing the needs of the urban poor in the United States (Bremner, 1970, 1971)
1877	Charity Organization Societies are developed in the United States and Canada to begin to address the societal conditions creating poverty (Bremner, 1970, 1971)
1889	Hull House established in Chicago in order to help immigrants by addressing neighborhood living conditions, work opportunities, education, social activities, and other services
1954	Family-Centered Project in St. Paul, MN, is initiated to work with "multi-problem families" (Horejsi, 1981)
1959	Maas and Engler publish a research report criticizing foster care in the United States (Maas & Engler, 1959)
1969	Home-based treatment for emotionally and behaviorally disturbed children initiated by the Mendota Mental Health Institute, Madison, WI ("Home and Community Treatment Program," Cautley, 1979)
1972	The Lower East Side Family Union case management approach to HBS with multiethnic families in New York City is developed (Beck, 1979; Dun, 1979)
1973	Nashville-Davidson Emergency Services Project and other programs are created to provide a variety of services to prevent long-term foster care placement (Burt & Balyeat, 1974)
1974	The HOMEBUILDERS™ approach to intensive HBS first implemented in Tacoma, WA (Kinney et al., 1977)
1977	PACT (Parents and Children Together) HBS program is developed to address the needs of single-parent minority families in Detroit (Callard & Morin, 1979)
1980	The Adoption Assistance and Child Welfare Act of 1980 is passed (PL 96-272), which requires that "reasonable and persistent efforts" to preserve families be made by child welfare agencies before a child is placed in "substitute care" (Pine, 1986)
1980	Intensive Family Services is funded by the Children's Services Division, Oregon, involving the location of contract providers of HBS in the offices of local public child welfare agencies (Nelson et al., 1988)
1981	San Diego Center for Children begins FBS program for preventing residential treatment placement and for shortening the length of stay of current inpatient clients
1981	National Resource Center on Family-Based Services begins operation at the University of Iowa School of Social Work, with funding from the U.S. Children's Bureau
1987	HOMEBUILDERS™ begins a special IFPS program to serve adoptive families at risk of child placement and disruption (Haapala et al., 1988)
1987	First National Conference on Family-Based Services held in Minneapolis, MN
1987	Minnesota and other states form their own Family-Based Services Associations

promoted by P.L. 96-272, increasing placement rates, and a search for "revenue neutral" service innovations have all combined to produce an environment supportive of the development of FBS programs.

Although some program results may in certain areas be positive, it is important to note that FBS programs will not replace the need for other types of child welfare services. Some families will always be in need of one or more of the other services in the child welfare continuum of service, such as family foster care, day treatment, or residential treatment (see Table 9.1). But FBS, like some of the new family support programs, represents a significant departure from the more traditional categorical services that embrace a child-rescue philosophy, that place treatment within a narrowly "person-centered" perspective, and that give little attention to addressing the family's needs in a holistic manner (Farrow, 1991, Nelson, 1991, Whittaker, 1991). According to Whittaker (1991, pp. 295–296), these new ideas represent alternative conceptions of human services toward the following:

1. Establishing a service continuum—from preclusive prevention to secure treatment—with expanded capacity for individualized case planning through flexible funding and service eligibility.

2. Promoting competence and meeting basic developmental needs of children and families in "normalized" settings by teaching practical life skills and by providing environmental supports as opposed to uncovering and treating underlying pathology. Evidence for this trend is apparent in the explosion of educational or life-skills approaches (Danish, D'Angell, & Hauer, 1980), the move away from presumptive labeling and toward more developmentally focused, competence-oriented assessment, and the move in many fields toward "normalization" of both the location and focus of treatment (Wolfensberger, 1972).

3. Considering services as family supportive and family strengthening, not as "child saving." The rapid expansion of crisis-oriented family-support services (Whittaker et al., 1989), the family-support movement (Zigler & Black, 1989), and the renewed emphasis on family involvement in child-placement services (Jenson & Whittaker, 1987) all offer partial evidence of the strength of this idea.

4 .Reestablishing a person-in-environment perspective in theory, empirical research, and clinical practice as a foundation for intervention design. Bronfenbrenner's (1979) ecology of human development, the empirical work of Garbarino, Schellenbach, Sebes, and Associates (1986) on the environmental correlates of child maltreatment, and the rapid growth of preventive-remedial intervention designed to enhance social support (Gottlieb, 1988; Biegel, Farkas, Abell, Goodin, & Friedman, 1988) indicate a return to traditional social work paradigms (Whittaker & Tracy, 1989; Brieland, 1987).

INTERVENTION COMPONENTS

Interventive Methods

Clinical Services.   FBS practitioners have been creatively blending clinical techniques from a variety of theoretical paradigms to serve families involved with

Table 9.2. Clinical Interventions Checklist

Instructions: Indicate the major interventions you used with the family during this month, checking the appropriate column(s) to show which family members were involved. Please check only primary interventions, (e.g., those that were planned in advance or that had a major impact on the family). Do not include incidental interventions with minor impact on the family.

Interventions	Primary Caretaker	Other Adult	Child(ren) At Risk	Other Child(ren)
Therapeutic				
1. Drawing ecomaps/assessing social support				
2. Confrontation				
3. Behavior rehearsal/role play (practice for future use)				
4. Circular questioning				
5. Structured family interview				
6. Identifying behavioral sequences				
7. Speaking in metaphor				
8. Reframing (relabeling, positive connotation)				
9. Prescribing the symptom				
10. Predicting a relapse				
11. Drawing genograms (multigenerational history)				
12. Encouraging clients to get the family facts				
13. Positive/negative reinforcement				
14. Tracking or charting behaviors				
15. Multiple impact therapy				
16. Hypothesizing the function of the symptom (i.e. purpose, effect, or gain)				
17. Coaching verbal or nonverbal expression (e.g., "I" statements, direct requests)				
18. Blocking (e.g., refusing eye contact, moving seats, interrupting)				
19. Unbalancing (allying with subsystem, e.g., telling parents they managed a difficult situation well)				
20. Restraining change (e.g., suggesting clients go slow, speculating on the consequences of change)				
21. Developing a time line (chronology of problems, important events, developmental issues)				

Educational[a]

22. Child behavior management skills (consequences, behavior charts, token economies, PET, STEP)
23. Other parenting skills (e.g., age-appropriate care and expectations, nurturance, child development)
24. Communication skills (e.g., "I" messages, active listening, feedback, negotiation)
25. Cognitive interventions/self-management skills (self-monitoring, changing "self-talk," values clarification)
26. Assertiveness/self-advocacy skills (e.g., identification of emotions/areas of conflict, fair fighting)
27. Anger/conflict management skills (e.g. identification of emotions/areas of conflict, fair fighting)
28. Problem-solving skills (e.g., prioritizing problems, no-lose problem solving, problem ownership)
29. Home/financial management skills (e.g., cleaning, shopping, cooking, budgeting, daily routine)
30. Leisure time activities (e.g., teaching how to develop or use)
31. Sex education (e.g., birth control, avoiding victimization, dealing with sexual training)
32. Negotiating local service systems (what services are available, how to access)

Casework

33. Coordinating services
34. Accompanying family/member to appointment
35. Advocating for the family
36. Building informal support networks
37. Developing community resources
38. Testifying/attending court hearings
39. Providing or arranging for concrete services
40. Information and referral (not arranging for services)

Source: © Copyright 1992. The National Resource Center of Family Based Services, The University of Iowa School of Social Work, Iowa City, Iowa. Reprinted with permission.

[a]Educational interventions include the teaching of skills and behaviors so that they become part of the family member's) repertoire. Do not include interventions carried out by the therapist, but not taught to the family. Can include direct/didactic instruction, role modeling, coaching, cueing, role play, behavioral rehearsal, structured exercises, and homework.

child welfare services. Major treatment theories utilized by these practitioners include systems theory, crisis theory, communications theory, and cognitive–behavioral theory (e.g., Bryce & Lloyd, 1981; Kaplan, 1986; Kinney et al., 1991). Therapists in many programs are using concepts from social learning and cognitive–behavioral theory to teach client skills in areas such as anger management, parenting, stress reduction, conflict resolution, and household management. In addition, a variety of clinical techniques are being used, including rational emotive therapy; functional, structural, and strategic family therapy; guided imagery; Gestalt therapy; family sculpting; ecomapping; and genogram analysis.

In one study of services in a newly formed unit of an FBS program in a public child welfare agency, workers were asked to rate the frequency with which they used 35 different treatment techniques. A 5-point scale was used with 5 as the highest level of use. At the time of the study, this program used paraprofessionals to deliver concrete services, although the FBS therapists focused on providing individual and family therapy. The 12 techniques rated at 4.0 or greater are listed below with their frequency of use rating in parentheses:

1. Developing an assessment of the family's problem based on observation and interaction with the family system (5.0).
2. Work with family members to develop a mutually trusting relationship between you and them (5.0).
3. Identify and point out individual and family strengths (4.6).
4. Guide family and individual growth based on existing family strengths (4.6).
5. Encourage the establishment of the parents as authority figures in the family system (4.5).
6. Express interest and provide feedback to family members that indicates that the family members' messages are understood (4.5).
7. Feel and express empathy for members of the family system (4.3).
8. Elicit information from the family members to clarify the situation of the family and its members (4.3).
9. Attempt to delineate boundaries within the family (4.3).
10. Take a nonjudgmental stance to client's feelings, behaviors, or expressions [of] opinion (4.0).
11. Attempt to change the structure within the family system (4.0).
12. Let the client know that he or she is valued as a person (4.0) (AuClaire & Schwartz, 1986, pp. 17–18).

In examining the list of commonly used clinical techniques, note how client relationship and assessment techniques are rated high in frequency of use. The use of structural and strategic family therapy techniques is also represented because of the treatment orientation of this program. Other FBS programs may use more of a cognitive–behavioral approach, blending principles from Rogerian, ecological, and other theories. For example, see Table 9.2 for a list of clinical services provided by therapists in a number of states.

Concrete Services.   Concrete services or the provision of nonclinical assistance to clients is a very important component of FBS. Providing concrete services may be accomplished by the use of a paraprofessional FBS team member or, more likely, the FBS therapist. According to a number of studies, the most common concrete services provided by FBS therapists working with more intensive home-based programs include the following:

- providing transportation to clients
- providing or arranging for recreational opportunities
- helping clients obtain employment
- arranging for financial assistance
- doing housework with clients
- providing child care
- providing or coordinating food assistance
- securing medical care
- providing toys
- assisting with utility problems
- helping to obtain or providing clothing.

The type of concrete service that is provided will vary with each case, but in one recent study one or more types of these services were provided to families in over 74% of the cases and this service was correlated with the attainment of a number of treatment goals (Lewis, 1990, 1991). FBS workers feel that concrete services, although not provided in every case, can be a form of critical assistance for some families (e.g., providing a refrigerator, transportation, or assistance in cleaning up a kitchen). The importance of concrete services, in the context of the service philosophy of FBS will be discussed in the next section.

How the Service Philosophy Shapes Client Interventions

Overview.   One of the most important components of any treatment approach, whether it is permanency planning or FBS, is a supportive ideology that shapes certain worker attitudes toward clients and service delivery (Horejsi, 1982). The treatment goals and clinical techniques discussed in the previous section resemble much of what is currently provided in many of the most effective mental health or traditional child welfare agencies. Part of what distinguishes FBS programs from other child welfare programs is the set of treatment principles that many of these programs espouse (Henggler, et al., 1998; Kinney et al., 1990; Lloyd & Bryce, 1983). In other words, these clinical techniques are applied within an overall service philosophy that is relatively distinct from many traditional social service programs. Some of the treatment principles are listed below, and will be discussed in the following sections (see Note 6).

- deemphasizing previous diagnoses, use of labels, and professional jargon;
- emphasizing an understanding of the client's present situation;

- building on family strengths;
- providing "concrete" services such as moving, cleaning, and transportation;
- being available to clients 24 hours a day;
- seeing clients in their homes whenever possible;
- routinely working nights and weekends;
- never insisting that all family members participate in treatment sessions;
- encouraging clients, at least initially, to set service priorities with casework directed at the client's top priority.

Deemphasizing Previous Diagnoses, Use of Labels, and Professional Jargon. Many children and families are often given inappropriate and behaviorally nonspecific labels (GLOP) that interfere with objective clinical assessment and formation of treatment plans based on family strengths and resources (Stuart, 1970). Application of these labels has the following disadvantages:

1. GLOP terms are usually vague enough so that people disagree about what they mean and have difficulty specifying what needs to change.
2. Most GLOP is negative, value laden, and blameful. Such terminology can encourage clients to withdraw.
3. Therapists can become discouraged and frightened by a long list of negatives—there may be a tendency to expect the client to live up to the label.
4. Clients are often offended at what they consider to be an oversimplification of their situation.
5. It is poor modeling for clients who frequently already use name calling with each other and need help in using neutral, specific language.
6. The descriptions are so vague that often it is difficult to present evidence that discounts the label; once they are labeled, it is hard to reverse (Haapala, Kinney, & Gast, 1981, pp. 51–52).

In place of GLOP, therapists in many FBS programs are encouraged to approach the assessment of the family in a nonblaming manner and to listen to the clients' description of the situation carefully. Workers are cautioned not to let themselves be trapped into making quick judgments, but to spend large amounts of time "active listening" with the clients. In this way a more adequate amount of information is gathered from all family members before any diagnostic assessments or case plans are developed.

Emphasizing an Understanding of the Client's Present Situation.   Related to the above practice principle is the focus on the current family situation rather than spending large amounts of time investigating family or child history. The emphasis of the clinical assessment is on the dynamics that are currently operating in the family to produce certain patterns of behavior. In certain types of case situations, however, child or parent historical information is important, particularly if a long-standing pattern of behavior has been identified or if the case may involve intergenerational forms of maltreatment, particularly sexual abuse.

Building on Family Strengths.   Clinical interventions in this program area build on family strengths, as well as address problems. Programs at Boystown, Families First, the PACT program, SCAN, HOMEBUILDERS™, and others have adopted a family strengths perspective that is gaining increasing recognition in children's mental health as well.

Providing "Concrete" Services Such as Moving, Cleaning, and Transportation.   Transportation, employment, recreation, housecleaning, and other services are widely recognized in the child welfare field as important for working effectively with the types of family situations typically addressed by FBS (e.g., Kaplan, 1986; Levine, 1964; Polansky et al., 1982; Van Meter, 1986). IFPS therapists in particular have found that providing concrete services to address immediate family needs helps to ensure that better client relationships are developed, client trust is increased, and stress levels in the family are reduced.[7]

For example, in one IFPS case involving a young single parent, the infant born prematurely was at risk because the mother's level of anxiety had increased to a point where it was interfering with her ability to care for her and a 3-year-old boy who had been diagnosed as hyperactive. One of the contributing factors was the mother's recent move to a ground floor apartment. Someone in the neighborhood was staring into the apartment at night because she had no curtains. After spending some time listening to the mother, the IFPS therapist went with her to a local thrift store to buy some sheets to hang over the windows (using a special set of agency funds for concrete services). This assistance helped lower the mother's anxiety level to a point where she could begin to address the other issues in her family situation that were putting her infant at risk (Kinney et al., 1991, pp. 133–135). As this case illustrates, the provision of individual or family therapy with child welfare clients often cannot begin until more basic needs are addressed first. In addition, some of the most productive interviews with children and adolescents occur although driving to or visiting the local grocery store, public assistance office, or fast food restaurant.

Being Available to Clients 24 Hours a Day.   This characteristic may not be present in all FBS programs, but is common to all IFPS programs. If IFPS is viewed as partially a crisis intervention service, then it is important for clients to be able to contact their worker when a family crisis develops, or when they are feeling depressed and may act in a harmful manner toward themselves or another person. Crisis intervention theory and child welfare studies by Shapiro (1976) and others emphasize the importance of timely response to families in crisis. Individuals and families appear to be most amenable to change although they are in a state of crisis and when "normal" coping mechanisms for dysfunctional situations are not working (e.g., Smith, 1986). Thus, an immediate response by an IFPS therapist should result in better case outcomes.[8]

Yet in the most effective IFPS programs, workers are not spending large amounts of time during the evenings or weekends responding to crisis calls from families.

Because the therapist may spend 6 to 8 hours a week with the family, unanticipated crises needing immediate therapist attention are unlikely to occur for a number of reasons: (1) because clients practice treatment skills such as how to cope with various problem situations until the worker's next visit, the need to call between appointments becomes less crucial; and (2) as the bonds between the IFPS worker and clients become stronger, clients are reluctant to call the worker during the evening or weekends. For most clients, the fact that the worker is potentially available is reassuring.

IFPS programs address worker availability in various ways, with many programs using a 24-hour pager service and some form of worker and/or supervisor back-up. Some programs take this principle one step further, in that IFPS therapists provide clients with their phone numbers for the office, home, and pager. Other IFPS workers and supervisors act as backup for the on-call service to provide workers with breaks from on-call duty.

Seeing Clients in Their Homes Whenever Possible.   One of the key concepts of IFPS and some other FBS programs is that much of the service takes place in the client's home. There are a variety of advantages to an in-home services approach; one of the most important is that assessment of the family situation is significantly more accurate and more comprehensive when workers have the opportunity to observe family members interact within their own home. Issues or home conditions that clients may not think are important to mention probably will be noted by the worker (e.g., household sanitation, arrangements of furniture or living quarters that may decrease badly needed child or parental privacy).

Seeing families in their own home also increases family comfort (even though the comfort level for many therapists is decreased!). Parents and children are more likely to feel that they have some control and will be more able to talk about difficult issues with the worker. The home environment also provides opportunities to practice new parenting or anger management skills in a more realistic setting (i.e., it is much easier to "generalize" a new skill from the living room to the kitchen than from a sterile office environment to the home).[9]

The home environment also allows a worker to capitalize on what some have termed "teachable moments"—family situations that pose opportunities for clients to learn or practice a new skill (Kinney et al., 1991). For example, a therapist may have been discussing the discipline technique of using 2-minute "time-outs" to address angry outbursts in a 7-year-old boy. Although the mother and the worker are discussing the appropriate conditions and limitations of time-out in the kitchen, her son has an argument with his sister and begins a violent tantrum. The worker could demonstrate the use of time-out or, better yet, coach the mother as she applies the technique to help calm her son. Finally, CPS staff members in many states are justifiably concerned about referring certain high-risk cases to FBS programs. Increased family contact and in-home supervision are essential for helping to ensure that the child is protected in many of these high-risk cases.

Routinely Working Nights and Weekends. Because of the amount of time that is spent with clients in their own homes (2–10 hours a week), by necessity many FBS therapists must work nights and weekends when family members are most likely to be off work, out of school, and at home. Service feasibility and the principle of client empowerment are incompatible with requirements that one or both caretakers take time off from work to meet with the therapist during the day. Working some weeknights also allows the therapist to work with parents when they may need them most, such as assisting a mother referred for physical abuse to manage her child's bedtime tantrums.

Not Insisting That All Family Members Participate in Treatment Sessions. In contrast to some family therapy approaches, some FBS programs emphasize client empowerment and choice by working with whomever is available and willing to meet with the therapist. This treatment approach involves allowing family members to vary their participation in the treatment process in accordance with the issues being addressed in that meeting and the commitment of the family member. Ironically, this FBS treatment approach is actually more likely to involve all family members, because the service is delivered in the home setting and at times more convenient for family members.

Encouraging Clients, at Least Initially, to Set Service Priorities with Casework Directed at the Client's Top Priority. Most FBS clients have been involved with some form of service prior to being referred to the home-based service program. Many of the clients are disillusioned with the prior services, feel discouraged, and believe that nothing can be done to address their "real" family needs. Other than the fact that they are probably still in a form of crisis, these families are not very motivated to engage in treatment.

Part of increasing client motivation involves addressing needs important to the client and building hope. Consequently, workers may ask family members to identify one or two issues that are most important for them in order to focus the initial intervention efforts. Then a time-limited and feasible minicase plan may be established in order to address those needs, and to give the family a sense of accomplishment and hope. For example, the caseworker might assist the parents in obtaining a payment plan for utilities in order to restore telephone service. Alternatively the family's top priority may center around a child's refusal to do household chores. Thus a worker may help the child and the parents choose just one chore and develop a reinforcement plan to pursue for the upcoming week.

Sometimes this initial intervention may involve asking family members to specify one thing they could do to improve the family situation, along with what they think would be one little change or action that another family member could take that would make a difference. The emphasis is on specifying very small but important behavioral changes that, if acted on, indicate to family members that things can change for the better in the home (see Kinney et al., 1991). Then later interventions or follow-up service can focus on other areas.

(Although barriers to follow-up services must not be overlooked. See, for example, Straudt, 1999.)

Program Limitations and Policy Pitfalls
Need to Be Recognized

Although family-based and intensive family preservation services represent a significant step in the evolution of social services, and initial program results showed promise (although not uniformly so), it is important to note that FBS and IFPS programs cannot replace other types of child and family services or substitute for broader societal and service system reforms (Halpern, 1999). As mentioned earlier, although a number of case situations can be addressed by FBS programs alone, some families will always be in need of one or more other child welfare services such as day treatment, family foster care, residential treatment, or adoption; and most will need other preventive or supportive services such as income support, child care, parent education, substance abuse treatment, or job training (see Table 9.1).

Studies of FBS and other programs have repeatedly shown that many families need assistance with housing, food, medical care, employment, and basic financial support. Most of the families served by public systems live in communities with few resources to help parents or support healthy child development. In addition, many families experience other problems, such as ineffective communication among family members, poor self-esteem, serious mental illness, lack of social support, and pronounced deficits in parenting or basic social skills. Many of these derive from larger societal problems and/or significant psychological or social impairment (Polansky et al., 1983; Polansky, Gaudin, & Kilpatrick, 1992). As with other social service interventions such as home-visiting (Weiss, 1993), there is a danger that FBS will be oversold as a cure-all for families because of its emphasis on family strengthening and early reports of cost effectiveness.

Therein lies one of the major dangers of this movement—that public assistance, housing, health care, and other more preventive family support services that are essential to child and family well-being might be cut to fund the more intensive or residual forms of FBS. Although significant foster care and residential treatment program savings may be realized for some children, FBS programs are just one of an array of services that must be available to support families throughout the life cycle. Without a broader network of family supports available in the larger society and local community, families may not be able to maintain the gains made during FBS, and children may be vulnerable to continued abuse or neglect. Furthermore, some families need services on a long-term basis and are not well served by a short period of intensive work (Maluccio, 1991). Other families need high-quality foster care to help them through a difficult period or until an older child reaches adulthood (Fanshel, Finch, & Grundy, 1990).

It is incumbent on evaluators and program staff to locate FBS and IFPS programs within the larger network of services, and to emphasize to policymakers that both the short- and long-term success of these programs depends on the family's ability to access a range of community services and other societal supports. More immediately, an evaluator must consider how the availability of these services will affect the success of the program. Although some families may need just FBS, for many families maintenance of gains made in FBS is affected significantly by the availability of continuing FBS or other services in the community.

Policy and Program Questions

As the number of these programs has grown and claims of effectiveness have increased, agency administrators and policymakers have begun to ask a variety of questions:

- What specific services are we funding?
- How much of an "implementation gap" is there between design and what is actually provided (Barnard, 1998)?
- How effective are these services in relation to improving child, parent, or family functioning? Does the same reduce restrictiveness of care or prevent some out-of-home placement?
- Can the use of FBS and IFPS save child welfare service or other funds?

Responding to these questions has been difficult, in part because of the challenges associated with implementing rigorous evaluation designs, accurate targeting of the population of clients most likely to be placed without substantial service investment, and the problem of dissimilar programs using the same categorical title or description. For example, there is tremendous variation in the service characteristics of these programs, and they are sometimes described using terms such as "family support," "home-based," "family-based," "family preservation," or "placement prevention" services.

Empirical Data Regarding Effectiveness Remains Mixed

Some programs appear to provide a viable alternative to out-of-home placement for some children, and help to improve family functioning in specific areas. The program evaluation results, although promising, do not show dramatic differences between control and treatment groups, and are far from conclusive (see, for example, Fraser, Nelson, & Rivard, 1997; McCroskey & Meezan, 1997; Schuerman et al., 1994). As family-based services and the more intensive family preservations services have become more widely implemented, controversy over their effectiveness and suitability for protecting children in some family situations has grown.[10]

Table 9.3. Effect Sizes of Comparison- or Control-Group Studies in Intensive Family Preservation

Type of Outcome by Study	Data Collection Period	Experimental Group			Comparison Group[a]			Effect Size
		No. of Successes	Total	%	No. of Successes	Total	%	
Child welfare								
Prevention of placement								
Szykula and Fleischman (1985)[b]	Not reported[c]	16	24	66.6	14	24	58.3	+0.19
Less difficult cases		12	13	92.3	8	13	61.5	+0.76
More difficult cases		4	11	36.4	6	11	54.5	−0.38
Dennis-Small and Washburn, (1986)[c]	Not reported	72	87	82.8	64	85	75.3	+0.20
Mitchell, Tovar, & Knitzer, (1989)[c]	At 12 months	16	22	72.7	9	12	75.0	−0.05
Yuan et al. (1990)	8 months	276	338	81.7	291	352	82.7	−0.03
Schwartz, AuClaire, and Harris (1991)	At 12 months	24	55	43.6	5	58	8.6[d]	+0.88
Feldman (1991)	At 12 months	67	117	57.3	42	97	43.3	+0.28
Pecora et al. (1991)	12 to 16 months	15	27	55.6	4	27	14.8	+0.90
Schuerman et al. (1993, 1994)[c]	At 12 months	701	974	72.0	451	564	80.0	−0.19
University Associates (1995)	At 12 months	172	225	76.4	146	225	64.9[e]	+0.24
Family reunification								
Fraser et al. (1996)	Reunited at 6 months	55	57	96.5	17	53	32.1	+1.54
Fraser et al. (1996)	In home at 15 months	40	57	70.2	25	53	47.2	+0.47
Prevention of abuse and neglect								
Yuan et al. (1990)[c]	Eight months	110	143	76.9	113	150	75.3	+0.05
Schuerman et al. (1993)[c]	12 months	731	974	75.0	440	564	78.0	−0.07

Juvenile justice

Prevention of rearrest

Borduin and Hengeler (1990)	12 months	48	58	82.8	24	40	60.0	+0.52
Henggeler et al. (1992)[g]	59 weeks	25	43	58.1	16	41	39.0	+0.40
Henggeler et al. (1993)[g,h,i]	120 weeks	17	43	39.5	8	41	19.5	+0.42
Borduin et al. (1995)[g]	48 months	68	92	73.9	24	84	28.6	+0.93
Collier and Hill (1993)	12 months	32	40	80.0	23	40	57.5	+0.48

Prevention of incarceration

Henggeler et al. (1992)[g]	59 weeks	34	43	79.0	13	41	31.7	+1.01
Collier and Hill (1993)	12 months	33	40	82.5	24	40	60.0	+0.49

Source: Fraser, Nelson, and Rivard (1996), p. 143. Reported with permission.

[a]Except where indicated, treatment in the comparison group consisted of usual or routine services.

[b]Although all families were referred for child maltreatment, 13 of 24 families in the experimental group were rated as "less difficult" because parenting problems were viewed as related to serious conduct problems in children. In "more difficult" cases, parent problems were viewed as related to serious parental and environmental deficiencies that were not directly associated with child behavior. The differences between the experimental and control conditions were significant in the less difficult group ($p < 0.01$) and not significant in the more difficult groups.

[c]Most success rates are reported using total number of children as the denominator. However, if child-specific rates were not available, total number of families was used. Reports here are based on the family as the unit of analysis.

[d]Placement list.

[e]Child leaving substitute care.

[f]Alternative treatment.

[g]Withdrawals are included in analysis; otherwise, withdrawals are excluded from analysis.

[h]Same sample as Henggeler et al. (1992), but reports on different follow-up period.

[i]Individual therapy.

Table 9.4. Additional FBS Outcome Criteria and Findings from Selected Studies[a]

Days in Placement and Case Closure

- Children in the IFPS treatment group spent significantly fewer days in placement than comparison group children (e.g., AuClaire & Schwartz, 1986, pp. 39–40[b]; Nelson, 1984[b]; Yuan et al., 1990, p. v[b]).
- The likelihood of case closing for the FBS cases was 46% greater than for the control group cases (Littell & Fong, 1992; as cited in Rzepnicki, Schuerman, Littell, Chak, & Lopez, 1994, p. 61[b]).
- There is some evidence that FBS may shorten the placement time of those children served by the program. In one study in Connecticut, more than half of the children placed were home within 12 months compared to the state-wide average placement duration of 31 months (Wheeler, Reuter, Struckman-Johnson, & Yuan, 1992, p. 5.10).

Changes in Placement Rate

- In Michigan counties where IFPS programs were established using a "staging approach" in which some counties that did not yet have the service were used as comparison sites, out-of-home placement rates grew more slowly in the counties with IFPS than those in nonserved counties. In those counties in which IFPS programs were implemented later, placement rates also appeared to slow as a consequence of the service. Considerable costs were saved by the governmental agencies in those counties as a result of the placement trend decrease (Visser, 1991 as cited in Bath and Haapala, 1994).

Restrictiveness of Placement

- Treatment group used a larger proportion of shelter care days compared with other forms of placement (e.g., Yuan et al., 1990[b])
- Children in the FBS treatment group used "less restrictive" placement options (e.g., Kinney & Haapala, 1984[b]; Willems & DeRubeis, 1981, pp. 16–25[b]).

Further Reports of Child Maltreatment

- Treatment group children (*n* = 52) from chronically neglecting families had fewer subsequent reports of child maltreatment compared to control group children (*n* = 19) (Littell et al., 1992, pp. 8 and 16[b]).

Improving Child, Parent, and Family Functioning

- Improvements in child and family functioning were found, with the treatment group being rated as better in several areas compared with the control group (Feldman, 1991, pp. 30–33[b]). In some studies the differences in improvement found at about 7 months after FBS services began, however, did lesson over time, with few differences reported by parents at a 16 month follow-up (Rzepnicki, Schuerman, Littell, Chak, & Lopez, 1994, pp. 67–68[b]).
- In a quasiexperimental study, ratings by workers and clients indicated improvement in caretaker parenting skills, verbal discipline, knowledge of child care, child's school adjustment, child oppositional or delinquent behavior, and child's oppositional behavior in the home (Spaid, Fraser, & Lewis, 1991, pp. 139–156).
- In the Los Angeles study of two IFPS programs, there were improvements in the following areas of family functioning: parent–child interactions, living conditions of the families, financial conditions of the families, supports available to families, and developmental stimulation of children (Personal Communication, J. McCroskey and W. Meezan, January 4, 1994[b]).

(*continued*)

Table 9.4. (Continued)

- Parental use of new skills at 6-month follow-up was higher in a recent family reunification study using an experimental design (E = 62, C = 58) (Walton, 1991, pp. 113–114; Walton et al., 1993[b]).

Family Reunification
- Stein, Gambrill, and Wiltse (1978[b]) emphasized behaviorally specific case planning to achieve more permanent plans for children in family foster care. They found that more experimental group cases were closed (50%) than comparison group cases (29%), and a greater number of experimental group children were returned to their birth families.
- Lahti (1982, p. 558[b]) found that 66% of the treatment group children either returned home or were adopted, as compared to 45% of the comparison group children, when special efforts were made to provide services to birth families.
- A recent experimental study of IFPS focused on serving children who were in foster care for more than 30 days and who were randomly assigned to receive a 3-month IFPS intervention. These children were reunited more quickly, in higher numbers, and remained in the home for a greater number of days during a 12-month follow-up period than the control group youth (Walton et al., 1993).

Consumer Satisfaction
- Primary caretakers have reported relatively high satisfaction levels with most aspects of the FBS service (e.g., Hayes & Joseph, 1985; Magura & Moses, 1984, p. 103), including studies that involved comparison of the FBS-served parent ratings with those of parents receiving traditional child welfare services (McCroskey & Meezan, 1997, p. 6; Rzepnicki, Schuerman, Littell, Chak, & Lopez, 1994, p. 77[b]).
- Primary caretakers mentioned as positive the ability of the worker to establish a good rapport with them, as well as the teaching of communication, problem-solving, and chore chart/reward systems (Pecora et al., 1991).
- In a recent family reunification study using an experimental design (E = 62, C = 258) consumer satisfaction ratings in a number of areas were significantly higher for the experimental group families (Walton, 1991, pp. 106–109[b]); (also see Walton et al. (1993).

Juvenile Delinquency Reduction
- In a quasiexperimental study of a home-based service program, based on Alexander's behavioral systems family therapy (Alexander and Parsons, 1982), the FBS treatment group participants were assigned based on the need to prevent placement or reunify, and high likelihood of recommitting a delinquent offense within 1 year. Recidivism in juvenile delinquency differed between the FBS and comparison groups (11.1% treatment, 66.7% comparison group**). When the recidivism rates were adjusted for different follow-up periods, the differences were maintained (5%, 25%) (see Gordon et al., 1988, p. 250[b]).
- A home-based FBS program using the Multisystemic Treatment (MST) model was used as the treatment for 43 youth (an additional 41 youth were in the control group) to reduce rates of institutionalizing young juvenile offenders. At 59 weeks postreferral, youth who received MST had statistically significant lower arrest rates, had an average of 73 fewer days of incarceration, and had less self-reported delinquency (Henggeler, Melton, & Smith, 1992[b]).

[a]Adapted from Pecora, P.J. (1995). Assessing the impact of family-based services. In B. Galaway & J. Hudson (Eds.) *Canadian child welfare: Research and policy implications* (pp. 100–112). Toronto, CN: Thompson Educational Publishing.
[b]An experimental or case overflow research design was used in these studies.
**$p < 0.01$.

Regarding FPS effectiveness, a number of recent control group studies have not found much evidence that these services improve family functioning or prevent child placement (Meezan & McCroskey, 1996; Schuerman, Rzepnicki, & Littell, 1994; Yuan, McDonald, Wheeler, Struckman-Johnson, & Rivest, 1990). But it would be premature to dismiss this intervention model for these reasons as other studies have found that programs focusing on older youth with more opposition-al behavior problems, youth where delinquency is a major problem, and families with a child with schizophrenia or another severe mental illness are successful (for a review see Table 9.3 and Fraser, Nelson, & Rivard, 1996). When the list of criteria for success is expanded, more positive findings are found (see Table 9.4).

In fact, Borduin, Henggeler, and their colleagues have conducted an impressive series of experimental studies of Multisystemic Family Preservation Services that have found significant differences in child behavior improvement, including con-duct disorders and rates of child rearrest; peer relations; parent and sibling symp-tomatology; and family functioning in terms of cohesion, family interaction/ communication, and other areas (see Note 5).

As part of their comprehensive review of FBS research, Fraser et al. (1996) sug-gest that this kind of intensive and fairly short-term service may be most appro-priate for more child-related problems, and that longer and/or other types of interventions may be needed for younger children or situations involving serious child maltreatment. But policymakers and program administrators should not abandon new initiatives in this area. A number of authors (e.g., Meezan & Mc-Croskey, 1996; Pecora et al., 1995) have cautioned that more research is needed where the FBS or FPS intervention is well specified and implemented consistent-ly. In examining more closely subgroups of consumers, or special outcomes such as reducing the number of moves that a child has (Wells & Whittington, 1993), we may find that different forms of FBS or FPS programs are needed (e.g., Bath & Haapala, 1994).

Studies have been confounded by a number of administrative and evaluation problems, however. Problems in administration include referral, staff training, and community resources. Evaluation problems include the use of nonexperimental designs, small samples, poor case targeting, underuse of qualitative designs, and inappropriate assessment measures (see Note 10). Recent meta-analyses of labo-ratory and clinic-based studies of psychotherapy have also found a lack of dramatic differences between control and experimental groups (Weisz, Weiss, & Donen-berg, 1992). Across many different fields, evaluation studies appear to suggest that we cannot expect single services to produce dramatic changes in complex social problems. Most literature reviews report only a fraction of the research data gen-erated by this selected group of major studies. The full reports must be read to un-derstand the particular objectives, findings, and limitations of each study since intake criteria, treatment model, program maturity, services, and other critical pro-gram components differ.

SELECTED PROGRAM IMPLEMENTATION CHALLENGES
IN FAMILY-BASED AND INTENSIVE FAMILY
PRESERVATION SERVICES

Implementing Theory-Based Interventions

Despite the work of a number of program developers and researchers (e.g., Barth, 1990; Bryce & Lloyd, 1981; Henggeler et al., 1998; Jones, 1985; Kinney et al., 1991; Lindblad-Goldberg, Dore, & Stern, 1998), documentation of theories to guide FBS remains to be fully accomplished. Perhaps, this is where various qualitative approaches can make significant contributions (Wells, 1994). And yet, ideally, high quality evaluations use theory as a way of guiding the choice of dependent and independent variables, as well as the research design and measures.

> Emerging development theory suggests that lacking an intervention to strengthen the information-processing skills that aggressive children bring to bear on social problems, family-based services are not likely to alter a child's peer relationships. And peer relationships—particularly low peer social status and rejection by skilled peer groups—occupy central causal roles in the etiology of ungovernability, school failure, gang violence, and delinquency (Coie et al., 1992; Farrington et al., 1993; Farrington, Loeber, & Van Kammern, 1990; Roff, 1992). (Fraser, 1996, p. 23)

Case Targeting

Targeting services to cases at imminent risk of placement, if placement prevention is the purpose of the program, remains a serious challenge. Many of the largest FBS and IFPS studies with placement prevention objectives were unable to target services to children truly at risk of imminent placement, as evidenced by the fact that few children were placed within 30 days of referral to these studies.

Serious efforts are needed in programs with this target population to refine placement criteria, implement interdepartmental screening committees, involve juvenile court personnel, better manage the politics of implementation, and address staff concerns about child safety in order to improve case targeting and screening (Bruner & Scott, 1995; Pecora, 1991; Scott, Bruner, Hastings, & Perlowski, 1995). Otherwise we will continue to find only small differences in placement rates between treatment and comparison groups.

Being Clear about What Are Being Used as Criteria
for Success

In balancing a focus on outcomes and process, process objectives often are emphasized rather than results. Sorting out these issues is also complicated by differing policy emphases:

We wish to note here that workers often report that a case was a "success" because they did what they were supposed to do—they met the family within the first 24 hours, provided in-home and concrete services, and engaged the family in intervention efforts—even if there was no improvement or some deterioration in the family's situation.

Another important aspect of private agency staff views of program objectives is that they see the aim of their work as "helping families"—measures of success can vary from one family to another. In some worker's views, the Family First program is successful because it provides a flexible array of immediate and intensive services that can be tailored to a particular family's needs. In this view, virtually any policy goals (such as placement prevention) and aggregate measures of success are less relevant than families' progress toward the achievement of individualized goals. This reflects a general tension between policy goals, which prescribe generalized changes in a target group, and treatment goals, which tend do be highly individualized. (Littell et al., 1993, pp. 104–105)

Program Implementation

Another serious issue that has been inadequately addressed by many FBS initiatives is the need to achieve program consistency and rigor with respect to model specification, staff selection, staff training, program funding, quality control, staff turnover, and maintaining *planned* program refinement in contrast to model "drift" (Pecora, Haapala, & Fraser, 1991). For example, during the third year of implementation, when control groups were being formed, a major California FBS evaluation encountered staff turnover and decreased state administrative support. Other recent state-wide evaluation studies have also faced considerable methodological and implementation challenges (see Note 10).

The most comprehensive study so far, conducted in Illinois, found no significant differences in child placement rates between the experimental and comparison sites. But this was a likely finding given that only 7% of the comparison group cases was placed within 30 days and 16% at 6 months (Schuerman et al., 1993, p. 104). Despite some innovative approaches to random assignment and careful measurement strategies, a number of complications arose with the following: (1) considerable variation occurred among site characteristics in outcomes, possibly due to characteristics of cases and the services provided to them; (2) substantial differences were found between experimental sites in the risks of subsequent maltreatment, placement, and case closing; (3) patterns of case openings and closings differed substantially across sites; and (4) substantial variation was found across sites in the amounts, types, and duration of services provided to Family First and regular services cases (Schuerman, Rzepnicki, Littell, & Chak, 1993, p. 118).

As illustrated by the Illinois, California, Iowa, New Jersey, Utah, Washington, and other evaluations of FBS, the program implementation process, worker training, variation in services, and other implementation factors are critical in interpreting study findings and in developing effective research designs. Program consistency and quality must be at adequate levels prior to formal evaluations studies and replication of the model in other jurisdictions. This was recently documented in a replication study of MST (Henggeler, Pickrel, & Broudino, 1999). One of the immediate challenges for FBS is to better address the fundamentals of program implementation that will lead to more accurate evaluation studies:

- *Be careful and rigorous about how we specify the treatment model.* For example, program leaders need to be able to specify the theory base underlying the program, the major intervention methods, caseload size, intensity, and approach to the provision of concrete services (if applicable). We often do not take the time to consider what it will really take to make a meaningful difference for consumers. And yet in medicine, we often do not give someone half the prescription needed. So, program administrators need to be able to specify what it will take to make a difference in the lives of these families. Therefore, the field needs to have the data to say to legislators, for example, for high-risk families where neglect of young children is the issue, we need an average of 12 months of fairly intensive efforts, that are likely to be followed by some less intensive community services with occasional booster sessions to help get these children raised safely in a healthy manner. (Or if the parents are not showing substantial improvement and interest in the welfare of the children, termination of parental rights may need to be pursued.) Similarly, with wraparound neighborhood services some youth will be able to be maintained in their families. And that will save some funds that will need to be reinvested in the neighborhood in the way of housing, employment and health care supports so we can break the cycle. But if communities can not reinvest adequate dollars in infrastructure development, then do not expect child welfare agencies to be cost effective in their work.
- *Staffing can clearly make a difference.* Selection criteria, training, performance standards, and use of paraprofessional staff are all important to address. Staff turnover is very expensive, and programs need to use staffing-related cost data to support better pay, benefits, equipment, and working conditions.
- *Provide supervision and clinical consultation to staff to minimize treatment model drift.* (How many social service programs have begun as an apple, migrated to an orange, and ended up as a lemon?)
- *Establish an organizational and community climate supportive of continuing program innovation and ongoing quality assurance.* We have to constantly innovate to best meet consumer needs and to customize our intervention models for the community. In child welfare, we do not involve our consumers enough for program planning and refinement and yet they have much to offer us if we are willing to listen.
- *Collect benefit–cost data.* In times of continuing funding scarcity, we need

to be able to tie key outcomes to service costs. And if a service will be insufficient in power or intensity to have a major effect, than maybe we should invest in an intervention model that is more cost effective or its effects in terms of fiscal benefits outweigh program costs (Pecora, 1998).

These represent some of the major administrative and research challenges that the FBS and IFPS administrators and evaluators need to overcome. To date the field lacks conclusive evidence that FBS prevent child placement, and about which types of FBS programs are most effective with different client subpopulations including those involved in physical abuse, neglect, parent–child conflict, or other areas. We also need a better understanding of effectiveness with different age groups of children and of program components that contribute to success with different families (e.g., in-home services, active listening, client goal setting, concrete services). Studies are beginning to look at subpopulations and to estimate the value of different intervention components (see Note 6). These are all important evaluation goals, along with the fundamental need for FBS programs to assess effectiveness, to refine interventions, and to be accountable to funding agencies. Because the programs that have been evaluated varied significantly in target group, model consistency, program maturity, and services provided, it is premature to draw any conclusions about the effectiveness of any particular type of service for any particular clientele. But as mentioned earlier, there are a number of promising intervention models with supportive research data that can be used as a foundation for program refinement in this field of practice in child welfare.

CONCLUSION

Family-based services represent an enduring and valuable approach to working with families at a time when "orphanages" and quick termination of parental rights are being touted as easy solutions to complex problems. There remains considerable enthusiasm in the field, but with the caution that FBS should not be expected to address major social problems "one family at a time" as so aptly put by the FBS researchers at University of Chicago's Chapin Hall. There is growing attention to program and model refinements on the basis of careful experimentation and evaluation. These efforts are being complemented by the articulation of a variety of practice strategies available to families with diverse needs and characteristics. Regularly collected evaluation data, a strength-based approach to practice,[11] and the careful gathering of feedback from children and parents can help guide these kinds of service refinement efforts. As our ultimate "stakeholders" they have valuable information to share.

NOTES

1.   For more information regarding the treatment philosophy and practice principles of FBS and IFPS, see Berry (1997), Cole and Duva (1990), Dunst et al. (1988), Haapala and Kinney (1979), Kinney et al. (1981, 1990), Lloyd and Bryce (1983), and Pecora, Delewski, Booth, Haapala, and Kinney (1985).

2.   For more applications of FBS in various fields, see Evans, et al. (1997), Haapala, Mc-Dade, and Johnston (1988b), Hodges, Guterman, Blythe, and Bronson (1989), Keller, Huz, Marek, and Rejino (1997), Maluccio (1991c), and St. Lawrence Youth Association (1994).

3.   The current FPS casework philosophy differs from the belief of many Charity Organization Society workers. These workers tended to believe that social problems were the result of character flaws, and that such flaws differentiate the worthy from the unworthy poor. In contrast, most modern FPS programs share much of their philosophy with another early program that was more focused on community organization and was not necessarily home based—the Settlement House movement. Settlement House organizers established houses in poor or immigrant-filled neighborhoods by "socially concerned middle-class and upper-class university students and others, who . . . shared their lives with the poor—a kind of Peace Corps of the time" (Wood & Geismar, 1989, p. 47). Settlement Houses were begun about the same time as the Charity Organization Societies, but their philosophical approaches were significantly different (Leiby, 1978).

4.   One of the principal assumptions underlying foster care prevention and permanency planning efforts is that in most cases a child's development and emotional well-being are best ensured through efforts to maintain the child in the home of her or his biological parents and siblings (providing that at least minimal standards of parenting are maintained). Most child welfare practitioners and researchers would agree with this assumption. In addition, permanency planning has been praised for providing children with more permanent family relationships. However, the research literature in these areas is inconclusive for a number of reasons, such as the oversimplification of independent and dependent variables, need for clearly defined measures, lack of longitudinal research, and presence of confounding variables. For more information regarding these issues, see Barth and Berry (1987), Fanshel and Shinn (1978), Festinger (1983), Maluccio et al. (1986), Maluccio and Fein (1987), Seltzer and Bloksberg (1987), and Chapter 3.

5.   For other articles on MST, see Borduin and Henggeler (1990), Borduin et al. (1995), Brunk et al. (1987), and Henggeler et al. (1986, 1992, 1993).

6.   See Bath, Richley, and Haapala (1992), Feldman (1991), Fraser et al. (1991), Lewis (1991), Haapala (1983), Nelson, Emlen, Landsman, and Hutchinson (1988), and Scannapieco (1994). For more information regarding the treatment philosophy and practice principles of FBS and IFPS, see Berry (1997), Cole and Duva (1990), Dunst et al. (1988), Kinney et al. (1990), Lloyd and Bryce (1983), Pecora, Delewski, Booth, Haapala, and Kinney (1985), and Williams (1995).

7.   Few program evaluations, however, have examined the effect of concrete services within the context of FBS. Haapala's (1983) study and a recent doctoral dissertation by Lewis (1990) both found that the provision of concrete services was significantly associated with treatment success. Bryce (1982), as cited in Frankel (1988, p. 150), found that clients rated the provision of practical help as more useful than specific therapeutic techniques.

8.   The relative importance of responding quickly to referrals to the IFPS program and the implications that being in crisis have for treatment have not been firmly established by research in the crisis intervention, family service, and FBS research literature (Barth, 1990b). In fact the division of a crisis state may vary greatly, depending on the family situ-

ation. Some FBS supervisors have emphasized the value of using FBS with chronic child welfare cases, where children may have been performing poorly in school and/or at home over a year-long period of time. The sense of crisis is not present in such an acute manner, but the FBS intervention may assist the family to learn new skills to help the child improve his or her behavior.

9.   Indeed, Barth (1990b) highlights the power of social learning-based approaches to intervention for families with antisocial children, and how one social learning project concerned with improving the parenting behavior of parents referred for child abuse found success in transferring parenting skills only after moving the therapists into the home. It was necessary to present skill-relevant stimulus situations (usually involving the parent's own child) in the parent's home because changes in parenting witnessed in the clinic did not transfer to the home (for more information see Goldstein et al., 1985, pp. 153–155).

10.   For critical reviews of selected evaluation studies of family-based services or the research as a whole, see Bath and Haapala (1994), Frankel (1988), Henggler, Schoenwold, Bordvin, Rowland, and Cunningham (1998), Fraser, Nelson, and Rivard (1997), Jones (1985), Magura (1981), Rossi (1992), Stein (1985), and Wells and Biegel (1991). For an incisive discussion of similar challenges with home-visiting program research see Olds and Kitzman (1993). See Bath, Richley, and Haapala (1992), Fraser et al. (1991, 1997), Gershenson (1993), Littell, Schuerman, Rzepnicki, Howard, and Budd (1993), and Schuerman, Rzepnicki, and Littell (1991).

11.   See Depanfilis and Wilson (1996), Peterson, Kohrt, Shadoin, and Authier (1995), Ronnau and Page (1991), Ronnau and Poertner (1991), and Simpson, Korolof, Friesen, and Case (1999).

FOR FURTHER INFORMATION

Fraser, M., Nelson, K., & Rivard, J. (1997). Effectiveness of family preservation services. *Social Work Research, 21*(2), 138–1253. A sufficient summary of major studies of FBS and IFPS.

Henggler, S.W., Schoenwald, S.K., Borduin, C.M., Rowland, M., & Cunningham, P.B. (1998). *Multisystemic treatment of antisocial behavior in children and adolescents.* New York: Guilford. Describes a well-researched model of IFPS.

Lindblad-Golberg, M. Dore, M.M., & Stern, L. (1998). *Creating competence from chaos: A comprehensive guide to home-based services* (1st ed.). New York: Norton. Describes one pragmatic approach to working with families in crisis.

10

Family Foster Care

Family foster care, a phenomenon with ancient origins in human history, continues to affect the lives of millions of children, youths, and their families. Following a review of its evolution, this chapter examines contemporary foster care in the United States within the context of the family-centered orientation to child welfare practice presented in Chapter 3.

The central purpose is to provide a concise synthesis of current knowledge, practice, research, and issues pertaining to family foster care.[1] Other forms of foster care, such as the use of group homes or residential treatment, will be discussed in Chapter 13. The major areas to be covered in this chapter are (1) evolution, definition, and direction of family foster care; (2) children and youths in family foster care; (3) professionalization of foster parents; and (4) effectiveness of services. The chapter will conclude with consideration of the current status of family foster care. Content pertaining to family reunification and kinship care will be covered in the next chapter.

EVOLUTION OF FAMILY FOSTER CARE

Early History

Family foster care in one form or another has a long history (cf. Chambers, 1963; Hacsi, 1995; Kadushin & Martin, 1988) . Kinship care is probably the most common precursor to family foster care. Indeed, it has been noted that "under ancient Jewish laws and customs, children lacking parental care became members of the household of other relatives, if such there were, who reared them for adult life" (Slingerland, 1919, p. 27). Children from every culture continue to be raised by their kin when parents are unwilling or unable to fulfill the parental role.

In modern times in the United States, family foster care has been marked by a number of developmental milestones and federal laws, as outlined in Table 10.1. Family foster care began as an effort to "rescue" children who were "dependent"— or whose parents were "inadequate" and relying on charity; the movement was substantially stimulated by the Rev. Charles Loring Brace and the Placing Out System of the New York Children's Aid Society (Kadushin & Martin, 1988, p. 347). Brace and his associates planned and promoted the transfer by train of tens of thousands of children from the streets of New York to the West or South, where they were

Table 10.1. Milestones in the Evolution of Family Foster Care

Year	Event	Outcome	Reference
1853	New York Children's Aid Society organized with the Rev. Charles Loring Brace as its first secretary	Beginning of formal family foster care movement in the United States	Bremner (1971)
1854	Brace leads the placement of first group of children from New York City to the Midwest	100,000 children placed in foster homes in West and South between 1854 and 1929	Bremner (1970, 1971)
1872	Publication of Brace's *The dangerous classes of New York*	Popularized family foster care as a response to the plight of "dependent" children	Brace (1872)
1886	Charles Birtwell and the Boston Children's Aid Society pioneered the use of foster home placement as a means of restoring child to own family	Stimulated attention to the role and importance of natural parents, who had largely been neglected	Kadushin and Martin (1988)
1909	First White House Conference on Children	Proclaimed the goal of a "secure and loving home" for each child	Bremner (1971)
1959	Publication of *Children in need of parents*	Called attention to the inadequacy of the foster care system, particularly the danger of children drifting indefinitely, with no permanent family	Maas and Engler (1959)
1973	Establishment of the Oregon Project: "Freeing Children for Permanent Placement"	Demonstrated that children adrift in foster care could be reunited to own homes or placed in adoption; promoted permanency planning as a national movement	Pike (1976); Pike et al. (1977)
1974	Child Abuse Prevention and Treatment Act (PL 93-247)	Provided financial assistance for prevention and treatment programs and established National Center on Child Abuse and Neglect	Kadushin and Martin (1988); Stein (1984)

Year	Event	Reference
1978	Indian Child Welfare Act (PL 95-608)	Recognized tribal courts as having jurisdiction in child welfare issues involving Native Americans	Plantz et al. (1989)
	Publication of *Children in foster care*	Large-scale, longitudinal study that systematically examined the impact of foster care on a large sample of children	Fanshel and Shinn (1978)
1980	Adoption Assistance and Child Welfare Act (PL 92-272)	Established permanency planning for children and youths as the law of the land	Maluccio et al. (1986), and Pine (1986)
1986	Independent Living Initiative (PL 99-272)	Provided funding for services to prepare adolescents in foster care for independent living	Mech (1988)
1994	Adoption and Foster Care Analysis and Reporting System (AFCARS)	Established the first federally mandated data collection program regarding children placed in out-of-home care or adoption by the states.	http://www.acf. dhhs.gov/programs/ cb/stats/afcars/index.htm
1994	The Multiethnic Placement Act (PL 103-382) and the Interethnic Adoption Provisions Act (PL 104-88)	Forbid agencies that receive federal funds from making foster care and adoption placement decisions routinely on the basis of race, culture, and ethnicity	U.S. GAO (1998) and http://www.acf.dhhs.gov/ programs/cb/policy/ p1104188.htm.
1997	The Adoption and Safe Families Act of 1997 (PL 105-89)	Policies to improve the safety of children, promote adoption and other permanent homes, and support families.	http://www.acf.dhhs.gov/ programs/cb/policy/ pi9814.htm.

placed with farming families in which they would work and grow up (Brace, 1872). Although many children were orphans, others had one or both parents living. Most came from recently arrived immigrant families from southern Europe.

The transfer of those children created much controversy, including opposition of the Catholic church to placement of Catholic children with Protestant families, as well as resistance from child welfare professionals who were concerned about uprooting so many young people. As a result of these and other developments in child welfare services, such an approach eventually declined and Children's Aid Societies were established to provide and administer foster care programs within each state.

By the 1950s, a range of foster care options had emerged, including

- receiving or shelter homes—in which children were cared for on an emergency, time-limited basis;
- wage (or free) homes—particularly for older children who contributed some work in return for receiving care;
- boarding homes—for which the agency or parents paid a board rate to the foster parents; and
- group homes—for small groups of unrelated children.

In each of the above options, the emphasis was on providing a family setting for every child. Indeed, as early as 1909, the first White House Conference on Children proclaimed:

Home life . . . is the highest and finest product of civilization. It is the great molding force of mind and character. Children should not be deprived of it except for urgent and compelling reasons. (Bremner, 1971, p. 352)

In the efforts to achieve the goal of a "secure and loving home," following the 1909 Conference a complex child welfare system evolved encompassing both governmental and voluntary agencies. Gradually, family foster care, which had emerged in the latter part of the nineteenth century as a means of rescuing children from their "inadequate" parents, came to be considered a temporary service whose purpose was to reunite children with their families or place them, if necessary, in another family in which they could grow up.

The evolution of foster care as a temporary service, however, occurred more at the policy and philosophical levels than in practice. Particularly since the 1950s, it became apparent that the goal of a "secure and loving home" was not being realized for many children, despite the proliferation of new agencies and additional resources.

Foster Care and Permanency Planning

Practice experiences, research findings from landmark studies such as those of Fanshel and Shinn (1978), Maas and Engler (1959), and Shyne and Schroeder

(1978), and critiques of foster care in the 1950s and 1960s underscored a number of points:

- Despite its temporary purpose, foster care placement had become a permanent status for many children entering the system.
- Many children were drifting in foster care—going from one placement to another, with little sense of stability or continuity in their living arrangements.
- Children were inappropriately moved out of their homes—with little effort to help the parents to care for them. If anything, the system encouraged parents to abandon their children.
- Children from minority families—particularly black, Hispanic, and Native American—were disproportionately represented in foster care.
- Most of the children came from poor families—often families that were barely managing to survive on limited income from public welfare.
- Although some children were effectively helped through placement in foster care, for others the experience of separation from their families had adverse aspects, including losing track of siblings, feelings of inadequacy, unplanned school changes, and disrupted relationships.

As a result of these and other findings as well as the rapid increase in the numbers of children going into foster care, questions were raised about the effectiveness of the child welfare system. At the same time, there were other pertinent developments, such as the growth of the civil rights movement, which led to the child advocacy movement and to growing concern about the rights of children and parents. As discussed in Chapter 5, there was also the discovery (or rediscovery) of physical abuse of children by their parents or other family members—which led to a tremendous expansion of child protection services and, inevitably, an increase in the numbers of children going into out-of-home care.

Additionally, there was the rediscovery of the family—or rather the family became respectable again as a social unit to be supported rather than blamed (Lasch, 1977). For example, irrespective of the actual success of various family policy initiatives, the family was a major theme of the Carter administration in the 1970s. There also emerged conviction at the federal and state levels that needy people—including children—should be cared for in the least restrictive environment. And finally, as discussed in detail in Chapter 3, as a result of these and other related developments, by the 1970s there was much pressure to reform the child welfare system, in large measure as a result of the landmark Oregon Project, which contributed greatly to the promotion of permanency planning as a large-scale national movement (cf. Pike, 1976; Pine, 1986).

Legal and Policy Framework

Foster care practice and programs are governed by an intricate—and not necessarily coherent—set of policies and laws at the federal, state, and local levels.

These are described in Chapters 2 and 3, considered throughout this book, and outlined here as well as in Table 12.2. Also, Stein (1998, pp. 55–78) provides a useful, succinct summary.

At the federal level, policies that directly affect foster family care are embedded primarily in five major laws enacted by the U.S. Congress during the past three decades. First, the Indian Child Welfare Act of 1978 (PL 95-608) recognizes that tribal courts have jurisdiction in child welfare issues involving Native Americans. Second, the Adoption Assistance and Child Welfare Act of 1980 (PL 96-272) promotes permanency planning for all children and youths coming to the attention of public child welfare agencies. Third, the Independent Living Initiative of 1986 (PL 99-272), enacted as amendment Title IV-E of the Social Security Act, provides funding and opportunities for young people in foster care to prepare for independent living. Fourth, the Multi-Ethnic Placement Act (PL 103-382) and the Interethnic Adoption Provision Act (PL 104-88) forbid agencies that receive federal funds from making foster care and adoption placement decisions routinely on the basis of race, culture, and ethnicity. Fifth, the Adoption and Safe Families Act of 1997 (PL 105-89) clarifies and updates PL 96-272 and sets policies to protect the safety of children, promotion adoptive and other permanent homes, and support families. In conjunction with the Title XX Social Service Block grants, the above federal acts account for over two-thirds of all federal funding for child welfare services.

As Stein (1998) notes, the federal government is responsible for setting policy, issuing regulations, providing financial assistance to the states, and monitoring program operations. In turn, the states have major responsibility for development, administration, and operation of child welfare programs. In regard to foster family care, all of this occurs within the context of numerous and diverse laws, policies, processes, and procedures that often vary from state to state as well as from county to county in large states (cf. Stein, 1998, pp. 79–108). Systematic discussion of the above matters is beyond the scope of this chapter. Yet it is important to note that federal and state laws help determine agency practice in a number of areas of child welfare, including the following:

- state intervention into the family;
- prevention of out-of-home placement;
- foster care reviews;
- termination of parental rights;
- adoption of children in foster care;
- roles of courts and attorneys;
- interagency collaboration; and
- rights of children, birth parents, and foster parents.

Perhaps the most controversial, as well as sensitive, issue is that of balancing the rights of parents with those of children, particularly children placed in foster care because of parental abuse or neglect (cf. Banach, 1998; Goldstein et al., 1996;

Wald, 1980). Despite the proliferation of statutes, policies, and legal procedures, decision making in this area is heavily influenced by a number of idiosyncratic factors. These include, among others, availability of prevention and placement resources; values and biases of service providers; presence of strong advocates for the parents or children; attitudes of juvenile court judges toward placement; rigor of the screening process; ambiguities in definition of abuse, neglect, and child protection; and the imprecise nature of information about human behavior and impossibility of predicting the future. The consequences of such an idiosyncratic approach to decision making can be negative, as seen, for example, in some cases in which termination of parental rights is accomplished legally, but the child is then left to drift in foster care without any family connection or other permanent plan. Yet, discretion and flexibility can also be used for the greater good. For this reason, as suggested in Chapter 3, sound decision making in foster care, as in child welfare in general, requires not only a partnership between the family and service providers but also active collaboration among community agencies, child welfare workers, judges, attorneys, and others working with children and their parents.

DEFINITION AND PURPOSE OF FAMILY FOSTER CARE

Foster care is generally used as a term encompassing not only family foster care, but also placement of children and youths in group homes and residential settings—a topic covered in Chapter 14. Family foster care, the focus of this chapter, has been defined as

> the provision of planned, time-limited, substitute family care for children who cannot be adequately maintained at home, and the simultaneous provision of social services to these children and their families to help resolve the problems that led to the need for placement. (Blumenthal, 1983, p. 296)

The above definition reflects various principles that are increasingly accepted in the field of child welfare, as exemplified by the "CWLA Standards of Excellence for Family Foster Care" (Child Welfare League of America, 1995). First, family foster care is conceptualized as a comprehensive family support service, and the family is regarded as the central focus of attention, as discussed in Chapter 3. Second, family foster care is carefully planned, in order to maximize its potential as a vehicle for helping families and children. In other words, the central purpose is not simply to provide substitute care—as in the past; it is to provide services and opportunities that can help families to become rehabilitated and children to grow up and develop. Third, it is meant to be time limited for all but a small number of children, in order to avoid the drifting of children in care and to promote permanency planning for each child. The major functions of family foster care include emergency protection, crisis intervention, assessment and case planning, reunification, preparation for adoption, and preparation for independent living. To implement such functions, these diverse forms of foster care are required, including emergency foster care, kinship foster care, placement with unrelated foster families, treatment foster care, foster care for medically fragile children, shared family foster care, and small family group home care. Also, long-term family foster care is an option for a small number of youths for whom family reunification, kinship care, or adoption is not a viable permanency planning option.

In addition, there are indications that family foster care is at another turning point in its history and that its direction is beginning to change "from a largely custodial system to one that is essentially treatment oriented" (Woolf, 1990, p. 75). In response, we are seeing the development of specialized family foster care programs—particularly treatment foster care—for children and youths with special needs in areas such as emotional disturbance, behavioral problems, and scholastic underachievement. A current issue in the field, then, concerns whether family foster care should be considered and developed as a specialized or therapeutic service for all children in placement or as a multifaceted service, including supports to relatives raising children in a form of kinship care.

In regard to the above issue, it should be noted that there is a tendency to lump children needing family foster care into one category; there is, therefore, an urgent need to clarify the different types of family foster care appropriate for different children on the basis of factors such as nature of problem, reason for referral, situation of parents, and intensity of service required. In the past, calls for foster parenting focused on the importance of providing loving care for needy children and appealed to the altruistic feelings of adults. Today's youngsters with special needs and problems require different types of foster care, such as diagnostic placement to assess a child's needs, interim or respite care, preadoption placement, specialized care, therapeutic care, long-term care, and kinship care.

Kinship care, that is, placement of children with their relatives, needs to be distinguished from care in an unrelated family. As pointed out by the National Commission on Family Foster Care (1991) and the Child Welfare League of America (1994), kinship care, which is being used increasingly, raises a number of issues that need to be resolved in areas such as licensing and other regulatory procedures, administration, payments to the relatives as foster parents, and relationship between the caregivers and the child's parents. Some of these issues, along with related aspects of kinship care, will be considered in Chapter 11.

In addition to the question of different types, we observe that different outcomes are possible in family foster care, including reunification, foster parent adoption, adoption by other families, and preparation for independent living. Given the diversity in needs of children and families as well as desirable goals and outcomes, it is vital to define each type of foster care precisely and to delineate the differential purposes and components of each. This is an ongoing task for the profession and field of child welfare. A small but significant group of children, for example, may need high-quality long-term family foster care (Fanshel et al., 1990; Fein et al., 1990), although other children can benefit from a 2- to 6-month stay in a therapeutic foster home (Hudson & Galaway, 1995). With all children in foster care or being considered for foster care, a key question should be: What qualities of foster families, and what mix of services, do they need in order to promote their development in a variety of areas, including their social skills and preparation for adulthood?

CHILDREN AND YOUTHS IN FAMILY FOSTER CARE AND THEIR FAMILIES

In response to the above question, we should first understand the situations of children and families coming to the attention of the child welfare system, particularly in regard to their numbers, reasons for placement, age distribution, and race and ethnicity.

Numbers in Care

In the 1990s there has been a steady increase in children in foster care, including children in family foster care or group care. In 1989 it was estimated there were 360,000 children in out-of-home placement at any one time; this represented an increase of 29% in just a few years (Tatara, 1991b, p. 3). According to flow data collected by the Voluntary Cooperative Information Systems (1997) from all of the states, at the beginning of FY 1996 there were 488,000 children in care; during 1996, 218,260 children left care although 236,998 entered. At the end of FY 1996, the total number of children in care was 506,707.[2] The increase may have been due to cuts in preventive services, dramatic increases in crack/cocaine abuse, reduction in public housing and increase in homelessness, continuing unemployment in many geographic areas and among ethnic-minority groups, and other factors. Moreover, studies indicate that foster care reentry has contributed to the rise in foster care caseloads (Wulczyn, 1991).

A clear picture regarding children in out-of-home care nationally is not available, because of the newness of federal efforts in supporting the collection of data, leaving major gaps in reporting. In addition, available statistics tend to focus on children placed in out-of-home care through the child welfare system and neglect those placed through the mental health and juvenile justice systems as well as those in informal foster care. For example, some parents may allow the transfer of custody of their child to the state agency because they cannot afford the level of care necessary to treat a child who is severely emotionally disturbed. Although the federal government is now collecting data from most states through the Adoption and

Foster Care Analysis and Reporting System (AFCARS), not all states are reporting on all items. For these reasons, there are no accurate statistics but mostly estimates of the numbers of children in family foster care or in out-of-home placement
in general. (See Chapter 1 for further details.)

Reasons for Placement

Although precise data are not available, reports from the field document the
changes in the kinds of children entering placement. Most children still enter foster care because of the consequences of parent-related problems, largely child
abuse or neglect (Berrick et al., 1998; Kadushin & Martin, 1988). Some examples
follow:

- Gloria, 3-month-old daughter of a 16-year-old developmentally disabled girl
  without any family supports, has been placed in an emergency foster home
  since birth.
- Tyrone, age 2, was placed in a preadoptive foster home following the mother's death due to HIV/AIDS.
- Bobby and Gerry, ages 8 and 2, were removed from their family due to physical abuse of Bobby by his father, who visits him occasionally in the foster
  home. Gerry had not been abused but was removed as a precaution.
- Lucy, age 10, and her family have been referred to the child protection unit
  of a county welfare department following a teacher's complaint that the girl
  was neglected at home and an investigation showing that she was sexually
  abused by her mother's boyfriend.
- Steve, age 12, has been in a children's institution ever since his widowed father was hospitalized over a year ago for a psychiatric disturbance; the father
  had severely beaten him on at least two occasions for "misbehaving."

In addition, there is indication of increasing proportions of children entering
care—and remaining there—from these groups: children with special physical
or developmental needs, children with HIV infection, crack-addicted or drug-
exposed infants, children from multiproblem families and severely dysfunctional
families, children from substance-abusing families, and adolescents with serious
behavioral and/or emotional problems.[3] Furthermore, now as in the past, most
children in foster care come from poor families—families with multiple problems
in areas such as housing, employment, health, and education (cf. Fernandez, 1996).
Research has also shown that large proportions of children in foster care have major learning problems in school (Aldgate, 1990; Blome, 1997) and multiple health
problems (Belaver et al., 1999; Clausen et al., 1998; General Accounting Office,
1995; Halfon et al., 1994; Simms and Halfon, 1994).[4] Also, children entering foster care have a history of difficult birth circumstances: exceptionally high rates of
low birth weight, birth abnormality, no prenatal care, and families with three or
more children (Needell & Barth, 1998).

Age Distribution

We should also note the changing age distribution of children in out-of-home care and the consequent impact on service delivery. The proportion of adolescents in care, in particular, increased rapidly in the 1980s, as the permanency planning movement initially resulted in keeping younger children out of care, reuniting them with their biological families following placement, or placing them in adoption or other permanent plans (Maluccio et al., 1990, p. 6). Adolescents still constitute a major group in the foster care population, although their proportion is lower due to the marked rise in the numbers of younger children in foster care. Adolescents represent three different groups: those who were placed at an early age and have remained in the same foster home; those who were placed at an early age and have been moving from one placement to another; and those who were placed for the first time as teenagers, usually because of their behavioral or relationship problems.

The growing proportion of adolescents in family foster care in the 1980s, coupled with the greater sensitivity to their needs, has led to expansion of programs addressed to adolescents. Stimulated in part by federal enactment of the Independent Living Initiative of 1986 (PL 99-272) and the subsequent infusion of federal funds, agencies have been developing services focusing on the preparation of young people in care for "emancipation" or "independent living" (Cook, 1997; Mech & Rycroft, 1995). The concept of independent living, however, has been criticized as having various negative connotations or consequences, such as creating unrealistic and unfair expectations of adolescents, foster parents, and practitioners; regarding the need of adolescents for connectedness with other human beings as a sign of weakness; and placing the burden for preparation for adulthood largely on adolescents themselves (Maluccio et al., 1990, pp. 9–10).

As a consequence, it has been proposed that we shift to a mindset of *interdependent living* in work with young people in foster care. This concept is based on the assumption that human beings are interdependent in their functioning and relationships with others and with community systems and resources. Such a concept is useful for practice with adolescents in foster care for various reasons:

> It is much more realistic than independent living; it is fair; and it is more consonant with real life and with the ideal concept of a community in which all people are mutually and constructively dependent. It also helps to dispel the myth of total autonomy of individuals, families, and nations. It is consistent with the growth of the self-help movement, which stresses the value of learning to rely on one another, to serve as resources or each other. (Maluccio et al., 1990, p. 11)

Helping adolescents in family foster care prepare for interdependent living and competent adulthood requires a range of services, strategies, and skills. As various authors suggest (see, for example, Barth, 1990; Cook, 1997; Maluccio et al., 1990; Mech & Rycroft, 1995), the central thrust of practice should be to help adolescents develop qualities such as the following, through the combined efforts of foster parents, biological parents, social workers, and other service providers:

- competence and mastery of a range of tangible and intangible skills;
- satisfying and mutually gratifying relationships with friends and kin;
- ability to nurture their own children;
- responsibility for their sexuality;
- contribution to, and participation in, the community;
- making essential connections with others; and
- positive sense of self.

Yet, personal qualities alone are not sufficient—supportive services are also needed. New initiatives at the state and local levels are generating tutoring, scholarships, transitional supervised living, housing preference in county and local governments, and advocacy organizations for former foster youths, to name a few.

In recent years, the greatest growth in foster care has resulted from an influx of young children. But, as Berrick, Needell, Barth, and Jonson-Reid (1998) also explain in their extensive analysis of data from a range of studies, child welfare services, policies, and laws have historically paid limited attention to the unique developmental needs and characteristics of preschool children, particularly infants; the emphasis has been on school age children and on undifferentiated services and programs. This pattern has been reflected in federal and state laws, notably the Adoption Assistance and Child Welfare Act of 1980 (Public Law 96-272). For example, this pioneering federal legislation set a maximum of 18 months for making a permanent plan for a child coming to the attention of the child welfare system, thus overlooking the potentially destructive impact of temporary foster care placement on infants and other young children. (Conversely, the tighter time limits in ASFA may not adequately address the needs of older children and youths who enter foster care.)

When the above legislation was enacted nearly two decades ago, there were reasons for the lack of age differentiation in policies and services. In particular, there was great—and valid—concern about the plight of older children who had traditionally been placed in unstable, unplanned, long-term foster care that failed to promote their development. Understandably, the emphasis then was on the need of many of these youths for stability and permanence. In recent years, as mentioned above, there has also been a dramatic increase in the number of very young children coming to the attention of the child welfare system, including infants placed in foster care as a result of societal problems such as poverty, homelessness, family violence, child abuse and neglect, and substance abuse. The fastest growing population in child welfare consists of infants, who comprise between 20 and 29% of all children admitted to foster care (Goerge, Wulczyn, & Hardin, 1996; Schwartz et al., 1994; Wulczyn, Hardin, & Goerge, 1997).

Such an increase has served to underscore the inadequacy of existing laws, policies, and services. As a result, researchers, practitioners, administrators, and policy-makers have been challenged to serve young children in a more discriminating and responsive fashion and in accordance with their developmental needs. In particular, there has been further attention to the following question, which Michael Wald raised over two decades ago: "How can we build in *developmental knowledge* to make the laws more sophisticated and more likely to serve the best interests of children" (Wald, 1975, p. 628), In this connection, Silver et al. (1999) offer a comprehensive guide for professionals working with and on behalf of young children in foster care. In addition, Berrick et al. (1998) formulate ways of improving child welfare services by explicitly building a developmental perspective into child welfare research, policy, and practice; effectively using knowledge about child development to propose laws and policies pertaining to child protection; and leading the way toward redesigning child welfare services for very young children by taking into account their unique needs and qualities and developmental processes.[5]

Gay and Lesbian Children and Youths

Nearly a decade ago, a special committee of the Child Welfare League of America called attention to the needs of gay and lesbian children and youths in the foster care system:

> Because of negative societal portrayals, many gay and lesbian youths live a life of isolation, alienation, depression and fear. As a result, they are beset by recurring crises disproportionate to their numbers in the child welfare system. (Child Welfare League of America, 1991, p. 2)

Although their situations and needs are beginning to attract attention, gay and lesbian children and youths continue to be poorly understood and underserved. Ongoing challenges for practitioners include appreciating the uniqueness of gay and lesbian adolescent development; helping the adolescents to negotiate life within a hostile environment; helping them to confront the consequences of breakdown of the family system and the lack of family support (Mallon, 1997); and understanding the rights of lesbian and gay parents in regard to child custody and visitation (Stein, 1996).

Others have noted that many of these young people have a remarkable capacity for resilience (Savin-Williams, 1995). Yet, in an in-depth study of 54 gay and lesbian young people placed in out-of-home care in Los Angeles, New York, and Toronto, Mallon (1998) found that most were marginalized and struggling to function in society. On the basis of this study as well as other investigations, Mallon (1997, 1998) offers a number of recommendations for meeting the needs of those young people, including family foster care with gay and lesbian adults as foster parents and group homes designed for gay and lesbian adolescents for whom existing group home programs are not adequate. As Mallon (1998, p. 189) indicates:

> These programs offer nurturing and safe environments for young people who have had difficulty finding a good fit with their own families or within existing child welfare systems.

Similar program recommendations have been made by Ricketts (1991) and Ricketts and Achtenberg (1990). Ricketts (1991) discusses the psychological and legal issues associated with licensing lesbians or gay men as foster parents—a controversial topic in child welfare in many states. Mallon (1997) also recommends ongoing education and training for foster parents, child welfare workers, and often professionals. He notes that these and other groups need to have a good understanding of the impact of societal stigmatization of gay and lesbian individuals and their families and to develop basic competence for "preserving and supporting families and for the establishment of appropriate gay/lesbian-affirming child welfare services" (Mallon, 1997, p. 177).[6]

Children and Families of Color

As indicated in previous chapters, those coming to the attention of child welfare services include a disproportionate and expanding number of children, youths, and families of color.[7] There is, moreover, substantial evidence that minority children who enter the child welfare system are at greater risk for poor outcomes than their white counterparts.[8] In nearly every state, African-American children are represented in foster care in higher percentages than they are in the state's general population. In a study of six large states (California, Illinois, Michigan, Missouri, New York, and Texas), about 40% of all children entering foster care between 1988 and 1994 were African-American, about 18% were Hispanic, and about 34% were white, with the remainder being from a variety of groups (Wulczyn, Harden, & Goerge, 1997). In some states (e.g., California), the proportion of African-American new entrants is declining, whereas in other states (e.g., Illinois, Michigan, and Missouri) it is growing; on the other hand, in some states the Hispanic share is growing (e.g., California) and in others it is declining (e.g., Texas).

The length of stay in that first placement in foster care varies sharply by race and by state. In California, for example, African-American children have median lengths of stay of 28 months whereas whites and Hispanics have stays about 14 months. In New York, alternately, median stays for white children in foster care (12.6 months) are about one-third shorter than those for Hispanics (about 22 months), with African-American stays remaining the longest (about 32 months). Some of these differences in stay may be accounted for by the higher rate at which children of color are placed into family homes with relatives. Yet, when differential uses of kinship care were accounted for in an overall model, the results were not very different than they had been without accounting for kinship care. Either way, Hispanic children have stays that are very similar to white children and African-American children have substantially longer stays in care than other children (Wulczyn, Harden, & Goerge, 1997).

Along with being disproportionately represented in foster care and the child welfare system in general, children of color receive inadequate as well as differential treatment, and have different outcomes. Thus, a review of outcome studies carried out during the past 15 years suggested that "children of color and their families experience poorer outcomes and receive fewer services than their Caucasian counterparts" (Courtney et al., 1996, p. 99). In studies of exit rates among minority children in foster care, Avery (1998) and McMurtry and Lie (1992) found that black children returned to their families at only half the rate of white children.

When children—particularly young children—cannot go home from foster care, the policy expectation is that they will be adopted. The chances for adoption for children of color in foster care are considerably worse than they are for being reunified. Following young children for 6 years to understand whether they had been reunited with their biological parents, adopted, or remained in foster care (a few had other outcomes) provides a more informative analysis (Barth, 1997). So, among children who have not gone home by 6 years and remain in nonkinship foster care, the proportion of white children who are adopted is 2.18 times that of those who remain in foster care. For Hispanic children it is 1.00; for African-American children it is only 0.48. The latter figures means that African-American foster children have less than one-fourth the chance of being adopted than white foster children have and half the chance that Hispanic/Latino children have.

Comparable findings have been reported for decades. For example, on the basis of an analysis of data from the Shyne and Schroeder (1978) national study conducted over two decades ago, Olsen (1982, p. 583) concluded that minority children "are urgently in need of permanency planning, for they truly have been lost in the system." In particular, "Black children and their families showed several indications of neglect by the child welfare system," such as having fewer service plans and fewer contacts with their biological families (Olsen, 1982, p. 583).

Another study of children in long-term family foster care, from the 1980s, supported the above conclusions (Fein et al., 1990). This study found that black children and youths had fewer contacts with their biological families than white youngsters; Hispanic and black children were more likely to be placed in transracial foster parent adoptions than white children; and minority children in general were more likely to enter care as younger children. More recently, researchers have called attention to the special needs of children from such ethnic groups as Asian Americans (Fong, 1994), Native Americans (MacEachron et al., 1996), and children of mixed parentage (Folaron & Hess, 1993).

The difficulties in reducing the high use of foster care by children of color are substantial. Children of color more often than white children are likely to be placed into kinship foster care, which generally has longer lengths of stay prior to reunification and fewer exits to adoption. Further, African-American children, in particular, receive substantial benefit from placement in foster care. Recent studies that have endeavored to understand what happens to children outside of foster care demonstrate the protective capacity that foster care can provide. For example, African-American children in foster care have lower mortality than those who remain in their homes, despite the many health-related risk factors that children in foster care have (Barth & Blackwell, 1998). African-American children who have been in foster care and then reunified have higher rates of death from preventable conditions (abuse, homicide, accidents) than children who remain in foster care.

Another study shows that children of color (particularly African-American children) who were investigated for abuse and neglect and then went on to receive child welfare services (often meaning foster family care) had half the juvenile incarceration rate that children of color had who were investigated for abuse and neglect *but received no ongoing services* (Jonson-Reid & Barth, in press-a). Further, among children in child welfare supervised foster care, those who were reunified were far more likely to subsequently have experiences in probation foster care or youth corrections (Jonson-Reid & Barth, in press-b). Finally, among children who do go home from foster care, African-American children have the highest rate of reentry into care (Wulczyn, Harden, & Goerge, 1997). So, although we need new and better ways of providing services to families of color, these should be undertaken carefully before using them as a strategy that might reduce the powerful protective factors involved in foster care placements.

The increased recognition of the needs and risks faced by children and adolescents of color in family foster care has begun to influence policy, programs, practice, and training of staff, particularly in regard to identifying and building on the strengths of minority families and communities. For example, Carten (1990) delineates key principles and strategies for strengthening the contributions of African-American foster parents through culturally responsive training and agency practice. Further extending the work of Billingsley and Giovannoni (1972) as well as Hill (1972), she stresses the value of building on the strengths of black families. These strengths include strong achievement orientation, strong work orientation, flexible family roles, close kinship bonds, and strong religious orientation (Hill, 1972).[9] Fein et al. (1990) further note that, in particular, an affirmative action program on behalf of minority youngsters and their biological and foster families should be created to bring them added preventive services, decisive permanency planning, and increased financial and other supports.

Pinderhughes (1997) outlines principles for developing "diversity competence" in "interaction with culturally and socially different others, particularly where such others might be coworkers, colleagues, students or clients" (p. 19). In her formulation, diversity competence includes a range of components, such as knowledge and appreciation of—and respect for—the values, beliefs, and cultural practices of clients; readiness to be comfortable with racial, ethnic, and other differences in others; the ability to think and behave flexibly in working with clients from diverse groups; and skill in the application of knowledge about power, diversity, and human systems. Similarly, others have applied concepts of human diversity and cultural competence to child welfare training and practice with inner-city Latino families (Burnette, 1997), Native Americans (Bending, 1997), gay and lesbian adolescents and their families (Mallon, 1997), and unaccompanied refugee minors (Ryan, 1997).

In line with the greater emphasis on cultural sensitivity and diversity competence, there has emerged an awareness of the likely benefits of placing children and youths as much as possible with same-race families to help preserve their cultural identity. This resulted in part from the efforts of organizations such as the National Association of Black Social Workers, which as early as 1972 decried the placement of black children with white foster or adoptive families, calling such placement "a growing threat to the preservation of the black family" (Kadushin & Martin, 1988, p. 637). The National Association of Black Social Workers and, later, organizations such as the Child Welfare League of America strongly advocated the policy of same-race adoption and foster care placement for black children. In the 1990s, however, this policy was considerably weakened, following enactment of the federal Multi-Ethnic Placement Act in 1994 (MEPA) (PL 103-382) and its 1996 amendments. As considered further in Chapter 12, this "Act forbids discrimination in foster care and adoption decisions and provides a remedy under the Civil Rights Act of 1964 for potential foster or adoptive parents who believe they have been discriminated against" (Curtis & Alexander, 1996, p. 402).

At the same time, it should be noted that there have been only limited federal efforts to promote child welfare services that are more responsive to the needs of ethnic-minority children. One prominent example is the Indian Child Welfare Act (PL 95-608), which was passed in 1978 to reduce the number of Native-American children entering foster care, the majority of whom had traditionally been placed in non-Indian homes. As George (1997, p. 173) indicates, the "philosophy of the Indian Child Welfare Act calls for tribal heritage protection and family preservation by mandating an end to the out-of-culture placements of Native-American children." Although intended to benefit American-Indian children, the basis for the Act is the unique dual-nation status of children living in American-Indian tribes. Only these children are exempted from the provisions of MEPA based on issues of tribal sovereignty rather than race or culture matching.

As discussed in Chapter 2, the above Act makes the criteria for out-of-home placement more stringent and requires state agencies to relinquish case decision making to tribal courts, or at least to involve tribal child welfare staff in deciding child welfare matters involving Indian children. It specifies that preference be given to members of the child's extended family or tribe or other Native-American families in cases requiring substitute home or adoptive placement (Bending, 1997).

The Indian Child Welfare Act, however, has been inadequately funded and unevenly implemented. As noted by Bending (1997, p. 151), "noncompliance, juris-dictional indifference, and culturally insensitive services have hindered full im-plementation" of the Act. In the most recent—but over a decade old—national survey, Plantz et al. (1989, p. 25) concluded that "although the number of children of all races in substitute care decreased in the 1980s, the number of Indian chil-dren in care has risen by roughly 25% (from about 7,200 in the early 1980s to 9,005 in 1986)." Yet, American-Indian children are now far more likely to reside in fos-ter care with American-Indian families. (See Chapter 12 for further details.)

In addition, various authors propose specific child welfare training programs (Bending, 1997) as well as approaches for balancing child protection and family preservation in child welfare services for Native-American children and families (cf. Mannes, 1993).[10] Much more needs to be accomplished, however, in the field of child welfare in response to the needs and qualities of Native Americans and other ethnic-minority children and families. For instance, greater attention must be paid to use of flexible program funds to address housing and other environmental needs that prevent family reunification or provide a reason for child removal. Agen-cies also need to take a closer look at their cultural or ethnic competency, both as organizational cultures and in terms of staff recruitment and training (Anderson et al., 1997; Pinderhughes, 1991, 1997; Stovall & Krieger, 1990). In this regard, the Child Welfare League of America has developed a guide to assist agencies in their move toward cultural competence (Nash, 1999). There can also be more extensive use of intensive family preservation and other family-based services that are show-ing promise for meeting the special needs of ethnic-minority families through the provision of clinical and concrete services in the home setting (Fong, 1994; Fraser et al., 1991).

PROFESSIONALIZATION OF FOSTER PARENTS

A prominent development in recent years has been the trend toward professional-ization of foster parents. This has resulted from a number of interrelated changes in the field, including the complexity of the situations of children and families be-coming involved with foster care; the special needs and demands of children in care; the paucity of foster parents, partly because of the need for both parents to work and partly because their altruism has not been as valued in the 1980s "decade of greed" as in earlier years; the movement toward more treatment-oriented foster care; and the expanded and specialized roles of foster parents, including greater reliance on foster parents as role models and helpers for biological parents.

Accompanying these changes have been developments such as the growth of the Foster Family-based Treatment Association as well as the National Foster Parent Association, along with local and state foster parent organizations. Greater atten-tion to education and training of foster parents is being called for, along with con-sideration of a career ladder, including recognition of highly qualified foster parents as "master" foster parents. There is a beginning acknowledgment of foster parents, at least in some settings, as agency employees, with introduction of salaries for their services and efforts to delineate the range of foster parenting roles and competencies required to meet the diverse needs of children (Kufeldt, 1994). There is also inclusion of foster parents as members of the professional service team, giving them greater participation in the planning for the children (Child Welfare League of America, 1995; McKenzie, 1998) and having them serve parent aides in family preservation programs.

Although the concept of professional foster parenting has been widely talked about for some time as a means of upgrading foster family care, particularly for children with behavioral or other problems, it has not been precisely defined. However, there is general agreement that it refers to the provision of family foster care that encompasses characteristics such as the following:[11]

- systematic evaluation and selection of prospective foster parents;
- view of foster care as a goal-oriented service;
- adequate compensation, benefits, and rewards for foster parents based on training, experience, merit, and job expectations;
- training for foster parents on a continuing basis, including incentives for completion of training programs;
- careful matching of foster parents with the kinds of children whom they can most effectively help;
- participation of foster parents as members of the agency's service team;
- provision of supports to foster parents, such as quick access to social workers; and
- involvement of foster parents in helping biological parents.

The above characteristics, along with others, are described in details in the "Program Standards for Treatment Foster Care" promulgated by the Foster Family-based Treatment Association (1995). These standards provide a guide to quality programming and include a "Standard Review Instrument" that agencies can use to conduct a self-assessment.

Despite its growing acceptance at the philosophical level, professional foster parenting is far from being implemented in practice and not all "treatment" foster parents are professionalized. However, there are some exemplary programs, such as PATH in the midwest, PRYDE in Pennsylvania, Boystown in Nebraska, People's Places in Virginia (Meadowcroft & Trout, 1990), and the Casey Family Programs, based in Seattle (Massinga & Perry, 1994).

The greatest obstacle to the professionalization of family foster care undoubtedly is inadequate fiscal resources, particularly in public agencies, for things such as adequate compensation of foster parents, reasonable worker caseloads, respite care, and other support services. There has been discussion of—but little movement toward—payment of appropriate salary with full benefits for professional foster parents. Additional barriers include insufficient clarity in respect to the differential roles of foster parents and social workers, the limited training of most foster parents, and the natural inertia produced by any call for large-scale institutional change.

There is also a question as to whether the concept of professional foster parenting is accepted among parents themselves. In a study conducted in Canada, Miedema and Nason-Clark (1997) reported that mothers seemed reluctant to view themselves as "professional care givers," since they perceived the care that they offered to foster children as "mother care" or an extension of their mothering experience.

In addition to the ambivalence of some foster mothers regarding professionalization, there is a serious shortage of foster parents who are willing and qualified to work with the expanding population of children and youths requiring specialized care and treatment. In the face of expanding need, recruitment as well as retention of foster parents are becoming increasingly difficult. [These topics, which are beyond the scope of this chapter, are extensively considered elsewhere. See, for example, Rykus and Hughes (1998), Pasztor and Wynne (1995), and Rindfleisch, Bean, and Denby (1998)]. Also, as discussed in Chapter 12, the U.S. Children's Bureau has issued a set of guidelines to spur the recruitment of adoptive parents who are willing to adopt available foster children, as required under the Multi-Ethnic Placement Act of 1994 and its amendments.

The rapidly dwindling supply of foster families results from many factors, including the aging of current foster parents and the growing dropout rate of foster families, many of which are typically dissatisfied with the child welfare system. The "volunteer" labor pool, of which foster parenting is part, has been decreasing because of the increase in single-parent families and the movement of women out of the home and into the paid work force. In addition, the demands on foster families have increased substantially, because they are called on to deal with youngsters with special problems and needs; moreover, foster parents increasingly experience a lack of supports and rewards in the face of the difficult job that they carry out.

Noteworthy in this connection is the periodic publicity about abuse of foster children by foster parents—a phenomenon that creates considerable controversy—but about which little is known. Allegations of maltreatment involving foster families are of continuing concern, due to the need to protect already vulnerable children from mistreatment; agency and worker concern regarding legal liability; perceived problems of recruitment and retention of foster homes; and perceived harm to foster children, foster parents, and other foster family members owing in large part to how maltreatment allegations are handled. However, this subject has received little attention, even though it has been identified as an emerging problem since at least the mid-1980s by foster parent organizations and others (Carbino, 1991).

A study of an urban foster care population echoes earlier findings: reports of maltreatment in foster homes comprise a minuscule portion—1.1%—of all maltreatment reports; foster homes are at much higher risk of report than the general population; stricter definitions of maltreatment in foster care may influence report and substantiation rates; and foster homes have a lower substantiation rate—20% versus 35%—than the general public (Benedict, Zuravin, Brandt, & Abbey, 1994). In light of the limited information and controversial nature of maltreatment of children in foster care, it is clear that further research is needed on its nature, extent, and impact. There is, in particular, a need to support the well-being of foster children and their foster families when abuse is alleged.[12]

Agencies that have been able to implement professional foster parenting, generally voluntary agencies providing therapeutic foster care, report good results in terms of success in helping children and youths with serious emotional or behavioral problems (Meadowcroft & Trout, 1990). In light of the growing shortage of qualified foster parents noted earlier, it is imperative that further attention be given to issues involved in professionalization of foster parents, particularly issues of compensation, training and professional development, supports and rewards, and role clarification. In addition, there is empirical evidence that "foster parent involvement in service planning contributes to their satisfaction as foster parents" (Sanchirico, Lau, Jablonka, & Russell, 1998) and consequently their retention.

Another issue of concern is that professionalizing foster care may also lead to pressures to maintain children in foster care. In research done in California, children who were placed in specialized foster care—which have the most professionalized foster parents—had characteristics very similar to those children placed into conventional foster care but were reunified and adopted at rates that were dramatically lower. Indeed, even after controlling for some background factors such as reason for placement, birth weight, congenital abnormalities, ethnicity, and age, young children in specialized foster family care agencies had lengths of stay that were twice as long as children in conventional foster care (Webster, Barth, Needell, & Berrick, 1998). This study is not definitive, but raises concerns about the need to manage professional foster care so that families are willing to leave the ranks of professional foster care providers to become adoptive parents and so that they can work closely enough with the public agency responsible for a child's care toward accomplishment of permanence.

Although not everyone agrees that all foster parents should be regarded as professionals, there is growing consensus that the professionalization of at least some foster parents is an idea whose time has come. But there is an urgent need for national leadership—to explore this idea and its implications, to examine exemplary programs and strategies and their components, and to formulate pertinent policies and procedures. Additional demonstration projects are needed to disseminate knowledge about foster parenting in the context of the contemporary crisis in child welfare. Much more remains to be done to recognize explicitly the central roles of foster parents in achieving the goals of foster care. Foster parents must be involved more fully as an integral part of the services team, as partners with agencies and social workers. And society must be more willing to provide them with the supports and services they need to do the job. It is a national tragedy that we spend more per day to house our pets in kennels than we allocate to caring for our next generation of citizens.

TRAINING OF SOCIAL WORKERS AND FOSTER PARENTS

Another issue concerns the education and training of social workers and foster parents. By now it is widely recognized in the child welfare field that foster parents and social workers, as well as other service providers, need specialized training for practice in case situations involving family foster care. In most agencies, however, training tends to be fragmented and irregular. Extensive discussion of the purposes, content, and methods of necessary training is beyond the scope of this book and may be found elsewhere.[13] We would, however, like to stress several themes.

First, social workers, as well as foster parents, can best be helped to enhance their skills through a competency-based or performance-based approach to education and training (Hughes & Rykus, 1989). Such an approach stresses the development of practice-based competencies in the design, delivery, and evaluation of training in a specialized area of practice. There is considerable attention to selection of appropriate instructional methods, which typically include self-instructional materials, coaching, use of learning contracts, experiential exercises, and small-group interactions. Curriculum development is organized around what practitioners need to know, and is based on a thorough analysis of the knowledge, skills, and attributes required of staff members (Warsh et al., 1994, p. 6). Moreover, training is developed concerning areas identified as having highest priority for effective practice.

Second, training opportunities need to be offered within a supportive agency environment—an environment that encourages professional development; treats "trainees" as adult learners and involves them in assessment of their training needs and selection of appropriate learning opportunities; and offers incentives and rewards such as career ladders, certification, and salary increments corresponding with increased knowledge and skills.

Third, foster care practice requires that social workers and foster parents have knowledge and competencies in a range of areas, including

- child development;
- philosophy and practice of permanency planning;
- impact of separation and placement on children and their families;
- behavior management;
- appreciation of human diversity and sensitivity to issues of ethnicity, race, gender, sexual orientation, and sociocultural aspects; and
- involvement of children and their biological parents in decision making and goal planning.

Fourth, as practice in family foster care has evolved during the past decade, training programs have had to address a range of newer practice strategies and principles, in areas such as ecologically oriented assessment; goal planning that emphasizes contracting with clients and service providers; use of behaviorally specific, time-limited case plans; and case management.[14] In addition, training is increasingly required in relation to practice with children and parents having special needs in areas such as HIV/AIDS, substance abuse, and family violence.[15]

EFFECTIVENESS OF SERVICES

Although there has been considerable criticism of permanency planning as an ineffective and inappropriate perspective (cf. Pelton, 1991), there continues to be general conviction about its importance. As Barth and Berry (1994) remind us, the primary purpose of child welfare policy in general, and permanency planning policy in particular, is to create safe living situations that can potentially endure a lifetime. This purpose is reflected in the growing emphasis on using short-term treatment foster care as an intervention to help rehabilitate families (Hudson & Galaway, 1995; Meadowcroft & Trout, 1990; Meadowcroft, Thomlison, & Chamberlain, 1994). Above all, as discussed in Chapters 3 and 9, it is exemplified by the family-based movement, with its emphasis on preservation of families for children whenever safety concerns allow.

There has been little research, however, regarding the effectiveness of family foster care in relation to the current population of children and youths in care. Most—if not all—of the available evaluative research was carried out prior to the recent emphasis on permanency planning or it examined the situations of children who were placed prior to that emphasis. For the most part, such research dealt with children whose personal or family situations were not as dire as those of children currently in the foster care system. Although this research is not totally relevant in terms of the contemporary context, it may be instructive to review the central findings.[16]

Impact of Foster Care

There has long been concern in the field of child welfare over the impact of foster care placement on the development and functioning of children. As emphasized nearly 50 years ago in a classic paper by Ner Littner (1950), the assumption has been that the trauma of placement leads to lifelong negative effects. Research findings, however, have been inconclusive. Several early studies examined whether there are any differences in adjustment between children in permanent foster homes and those remaining in temporary foster care. No significant differences were found between these types of placements in one comprehensive study (Jones et al., 1976). Similarly, the follow-up study of the Oregon Project found no difference in adjustment between children in temporary foster care and those in permanent placements (Lahti, 1982).

Two later studies have explored the functioning of nearly 200 children placed in "short-term" foster family care (less than 2 years) (Fein et al., 1983), and nearly 800 children in long-term foster family care (that is, 2 years or over) (Fein et al., 1990). In both of these studies the children's functioning, based primarily on reports from the foster parents, was assessed in relation to each of the following areas: school functioning, behavioral functioning, emotional and developmental functioning, and family adjustment. In the study of short-term foster care, most children were reported by their foster parents to be functioning moderately well in all areas except for school functioning. There were, however, significant variations in functioning, depending on characteristics such as placement history, age at initial placement, family income, and marital status of foster parents (Fein et al., 1983, pp. 542–545).

In the study of long-term foster family care (Fein et al., 1990), an overall assessment of the children's functioning was obtained by summing up their individual scores in each of the areas noted above. As with those in short-term care, most children were reported by their foster parents to be functioning well. Higher overall functioning scores were obtained by female, black, and nondisabled children and youths. These youngsters were also likely to have spent more time in the current placement and to have had fewer placements. Higher functioning was also associated with youngsters who had more positive feelings about their biological parents and who lived with foster parents who were older, did not want the youngster to move to another home, and had seen an improvement since the child's placement with the foster family (Fein et al., 1990).

In another study, Fanshel, Finch, and Grundy (1990) examined the modes of exit from care and the adjustment at departure of 585 children who entered and left foster home placement through the Casey Family Programs in various western states between 1966 and 1984. This agency serves older foster children who are unlikely to go home because of significant family or behavioral problems. On the basis of content analysis of agency case records, the researchers concluded that over half of the children had remained in care until emancipation and that they left care in relatively good condition. In addition, as also noted in previous investigations (cf. Fanshel & Shinn, 1978), the researchers found that the child's adjustment at exit was significantly correlated with various characteristics of the child and the family prior to placement, including greater conflict with the biological parent, a greater number of prior living arrangements, and a boy's having been physically abused.

Other researchers have underscored the substantial damage that results from the tenuous status in which many foster children find themselves. Such status presumably makes it difficult for a child to develop his or her identity, achieve a sense of belonging, establish meaningful relationships with people, and deal successfully with developmental tasks. For example, in a small, nonrandom sample of foster graduates of various ages from the Casey Family Programs, a number of young adults reported experiencing problems with substance abuse and employment. But, without a comparison group, it is difficult to reach definitive conclusions about how they would have done at home had they remained (Fanshel et al., 1990). In fact, most follow-up studies of adults who grew up in foster care do not support the conclusion that out-of-home placement is damaging; but they do indicate that foster care alumni have difficulties in the area of self-sufficiency. On the whole, these studies "suggest that the initially negative effects of separation and placement in foster care can be counteracted or reduced through the influence of stable foster home placements and strong services to the children and their foster and biological parents" (Fein & Maluccio, 1992, p. 64).

Festinger examined the views, experiences, and functioning of 277 young adults who had graduated from foster care in New York City and concluded that, in general, they "were not so different from others their age in what they were doing, in the feelings they expressed, and in their hopes about the future" (1983, pp. 293–294). Generally positive outcomes for most graduates of foster care were also found in a follow-up study of children served by the Casey Family Programs, although, as mentioned earlier, a nonrandom sample was used and the follow-up period varied substantially among the young adults (Fanshel et al., 1990).

In a more recent study, Festinger (1996) described the situations of 210 children and families returning home from foster homes and group care facilities in 20 agencies in New York City. The researcher examined, in particular, whether a child's reentering foster care was associated with certain child, caregiver, and situational factors. She found that nearly 20% of the children reentered foster care within 2 years:

> Multivariate analysis showed that lower ratings of caregivers' parenting skills and less social support were the strongest predictors of reentry within 12 months of leaving care. (Festinger, 1996, p. 383)

Other researchers have suggested that many youths are served effectively in family foster care, view it as necessary for their well-being, and make significant improvements in behavioral functioning, emotional development, and academic achievement (see, for example, Courtney, Piliavin, Grogan-Kaylor, & Nesmith, 1998; Fanshel, Finch, & Grundy, 1990; Minty, 1999; Wedeven, et al., 1997). In other studies, however, children have reported that their placement in foster care was poorly handled. For example, Folman (1998) found that foster children encountered various risk factors, including a lack of information, terror of the unknown, and little acknowledgment of their feelings of pain and loss.

Although research on the functioning of children during or after placement in recent years has increased, it has not as yet led to consistent or definitive findings that can clearly guide policy and practice. For instance, in a synthesis of research on the long-term effects of foster care, McDonald, Allen, Westerfelt, and Piliavin

(1996) reported that the results are inconclusive. Moreover, most foster care studies conducted to date contain methodological limitations, such as small samples, lack of comparison groups, biased sampling, limited outcome measures, and retrospective data collection. Also, it is becoming increasingly apparent that "the outcome of foster care placement, whether measured in terms of children's functioning or stability and permanency, depends on a complex set of factors that are interactive" and difficult to measure (Fein et al., 1990, p. 76). At the same time, "we must recognize the complexity of human beings and that the instruments that measure functioning and the policies that guide interventions only approximate the complexities . . . when applied to individuals" (Fein & Maluccio, 1992, p. 345).

For all of these reasons, it is no wonder that in one of the most sophisticated longitudinal evaluations of the effects of foster care, Fanshel and Shinn (1978, p. 479) suggested the complexities involved in this type of evaluative research and the inconclusive nature of the findings:

> We are not completely sure that continued tenure in foster care over extended periods of time is not in itself harmful to children. On the level at which we are able to measure the adjustment of the children we could find no such negative effect. However, we feel that our measures of adjustment are not without problems, and we are not sure that our procedures have captured the potential feelings of pain and impaired self-image that can be created by impermanent status in foster care.

In short, it is clear that further research is required on the effectiveness of foster care as well as other permanency planning services, particularly in regard to its impact on the child's growth and development.

Adolescents Leaving Foster Care

Most adolescents in family foster care are discharged to another plan, typically some form of independent living, on reaching majority age at 18. Although it is unrealistic in our society to expect people to be independent at age 18, readiness to function independently is another criterion that has been used in studies of the effectiveness of foster family care. The results have largely been negative, in contrast to the more positive findings of studies cited in the preceding section that compared the functioning of foster care graduates with that of their peers in the general population.

First, foster parents and social workers have consistently reported that most adolescents approaching emancipation are unprepared for independent living (cf. Biehal & Wade, 1996; Fein et al., 1990, Hill & Aldgate, 1996; McMillen & Tucker, 1999). Second, follow-up studies of young persons who grew up in out-of-home placement have also pointed to their lack of preparation for life after foster care. For example, former foster youths have consistently highlighted their needs in the following areas: interpersonal and social skills, money management, planning a budget, job training, finding a job, finding housing, maintaining a household, learning to shop, and maintaining family ties (Barth 1990; Cook, 1997; Mech & Rycroft, 1995; Nollan, 1996). Also, in a longitudinal study that recently completed the first phase, Courtney, Piliavin, Grogan-Kaylor, and Nesmith (1998) found that children leaving care at age 18 face a difficult future, as they suffer from emotional problems, are without financial help from relatives, and become vulnerable to homelessness and other problems.

Third, it has been found that a high number of homeless persons have a history of foster care placement. For instance, 38% of the homeless in Minneapolis (Piliavin, Sosin, & Westerfelt, 1987) and 23% of those in New York (Susser, Struening, & Conover, 1987) reported a history of foster care placement during their childhood and/or adolescence. Perhaps of most concern, in a study of the homeless in Alameda county, those who had formerly been foster children were the least likely to have an expectation of ever achieving permanent housing (Piliavin, Wright, Mare, & Westerfelt, 1996).

In a study of the relationship between homelessness and foster care, Roman and Wolfe (1997) found that persons with a history of foster care placement are overrepresented in the homeless population. These authors also clarify the long-term implications of not providing permanent placements for children or adequate independent living programs for adolescents. Among those residents in homeless shelters who had children, the residents who had previously been in foster care were far more likely to have their current children in foster care than other residents. So, a heightened vulnerability to homelessness is a concern for former foster children and for their future children.

The challenges in regard to preparation for independent living include preparing youths earlier in their placement, obtaining flexible funding for work study programs, offering better vocational assessment and training, providing adequate health care, and maintaining supports to these young people as they move into adulthood (Barth, 1990; Cook, 1997; Maluccio et al., 1990; Mech & Rycroft, 1995). Such a panoply of services is required because adolescents in foster care generally have limited supports in their families and social networks and are often emotionally, intellectually, and physically delayed from a developmental perspective.

Foster Home Disruption

Finally, other investigators have focused on the phenomenon of disruption of foster home placement, that is, the need to replace a child, which in the child welfare literature is commonly (but we think erroneously) described as *breakdown*. Research in this area is limited and inconclusive. As Usher, Randolph, and Gogan (1999, p. 34) note:

Further research concerning placement disruption should give greater consideration to the representativeness of study samples and move beyond simply counting the number of placements children experience.

In a review of related research from Australia, the United States, and the United Kingdom, Berridge and Cleaver (1987) indicated that breakdown rates have been reported as high as 50% of placements. In their own study, Berridge and Cleaver found breakdown rates in different agencies ranging from 6 to 20% within 1 year and from 20 to 48% within 5 years. In a study in the United States, Fein et al. (1983) found that 50% of the cases of children placed in permanent foster care were disrupted within 1½ years. However, this was a small sample of 14 children, most of whom were teenagers. In the comprehensive study of the Casey Family Programs mentioned earlier, which involved nearly 600 children, 24.6% of the placements had apparently failed, as the children ran away or were returned to the courts (Fanshel et al., 1990).

In a California study, it was found that nearly half of all children who entered nonkinship foster care prior to age 6 and stayed for at least 4 years had three or more foster care placements during their stay (Needell, Webster, Barth, Armijo, & Fox, 1998). That means nearly one placement per year! This rate is lower (30%) for young children in kinship care but is 75% for children in specialized foster care and 85% for young children in group homes. (It should be recognized that some children in higher levels of foster care started off in lower levels of care and accumulated some of their placement count in those settings.) Clearly, *stable* or *permanent* are not words we would use to describe long-term foster care.

Although we cannot believe that all of these placements are necessary, it is difficult to know what these findings mean, because some placements are useful for reasons such as reuniting children with their siblings, finding potential adoptive homes, and attaining a better fit between children and families. Indeed, how should we view the breakdown of a placement? Also, even unplanned changes may not always be an experience with drastic and negative consequences, as generally assumed. Aldgate and Hawley (1986) contend that foster home breakdown should be redefined as a disruption in the placement and constructively exploited in the process of arriving at a long-term plan for the child. For example, according to these authors, workers can help child, birth parents, and foster parents learn more about themselves as well as learn new skills through the experience of disruption.

CURRENT STATUS OF FAMILY FOSTER CARE

Despite the enactment of public policies such as the federal permanency planning law of 1980 (PL 96-272) and the Adoption and Safe Families Act of 1997 (PL 105-89) as well as the infusion of federal, state, and private funds, the number of children in foster care and the extent and complexity of the problems faced by them and their families continue to grow. It is therefore no exaggeration to note that foster care needs new ideas, resources, and personnel. Some authors even speak of a crisis in foster care—a crisis that is reported in the mass media and argued in professional circles (see McKenzie, 1998).

Yet, the growth in foster care must be understood as having several parts—some of which show positive indicators of a more family-focused approach to services. In several of the major states (e.g., California) the number of children in conventional foster care has actually decreased in recent years, with increasing proportions of children in kinship foster care and treatment foster care. In the large states, the likelihood that any given child will enter foster care has gone up only modestly during the 1990s, although the likelihood of a child leaving foster care has decreased, too, resulting in the increase in the foster care population (Wulczyn, Harden, & Goerge, 1997). However, most of that decrease in exit rates is attributable to kinship care, suggesting that the proportion of children living with family members is growing. Fortunately, the massive growth in the foster care caseload witnessed in the late 1980s [that led the Select Committee on Children, Youth and Families (1989) to predict that the foster care census would now be 850,000 by the year 2000] has abated. In New York state, for example, the incidence of all children entering foster care was 6 in 1,000 in 1989, but in the late 1990s was less than 3 in 1,000 (Wulczyn, Harden, & Goerge, 1997).

This does not mean that there are not massive challenges ahead for providers of out-of-home care for children. Recruiting and retaining foster parents are necessities for an effective child welfare system; having well-trained child welfare workers who understand the importance of permanency for children and options for achieving it is essential; flexibility in funding and approach is central to responding to so many diverse child and family needs; and so is having adequate resources to help families and to accommodate a rapidly changing work environment for child welfare workers.

The challenges are evidenced in areas such as the typical pattern of dealing mostly with emergencies although the situations of other children and families deteriorate; the attrition rates of child welfare personnel, including foster parents; the substantial number of children who are further abused by the very foster care system in which they were placed because of abuse and neglect in their own homes; and the call for returning to a previously discredited orphanage system of care (McKenzie, 1998). At a time that work with birth families and relatives is being reemphasized, foster care workers and foster parents are too overwhelmed to respond. One tragic indicator of this crisis is the high proportion of children in placement, particularly those from minority groups, whose unmet cognitive, affective, and physical needs are interfering with their ability to learn and develop in a positive manner, as indicated earlier in this chapter.

Foster care services have improved in many ways in recent years, yielding more family-focused care, shorter lengths of stay, and higher adoption rates. Yet, the problems embedded in the child welfare system are evident throughout the country, as documented by Kamerman and Kahn (1990) in their national study of social services to children, youths, and families. Although noting that there are some exemplary programs and practices, these authors found that the efforts of social services are largely inadequate throughout the country:

> Available delivery systems, interventive methods, and line staffs are not equal to the legitimate and appropriate tasks which lie ahead for the social services. There is a need—on the basis of adequate resource commitments—for innovation and testing, for sharing and exchange, and for ongoing efforts to respecify mission and infrastructure. (p. 147)

CONCLUSION

In reflecting about the evolution and status of family foster care, readers may find themselves wishing for a set of more straightforward responses and solutions. Realities, such as resource limitations and the complexities of human behavior, make such solutions less viable. But an adequate system of family foster care is still a dream worth pursuing. A body of knowledge and clinical insights exists and can be applied so that the system may serve vulnerable children and families more effectively than at present, particularly as we listen to—and learn from—parents and children themselves.

To do so, however, family foster care must become an integral part of a comprehensive network of services. Extensive family supports, particularly concrete services such as housing, employment opportunities, health care, schooling, income assistance, and recreational services, along with substance abuse counseling, mental health services, and education for parenting must also be part of the network. As addressed in Chapter 14, such services would complement a more variegated, flexible network of out-of-home programs that can support families for varying periods of time by providing respite and a safe haven for children. If we are committed to the principle that no child's future is expendable, we have no choice but to be part of the efforts to improve family foster care services.

In addition, foster care must attract, support, and encourage adequately trained, supervised, and rewarded personnel, particularly foster parents—our front line of help for many children and families. The major goal of child development within a family setting must be articulated and reinforced through program, policy, and supervision. And organizational supports must be maintained, particularly by providing family-centered services, placing emphasis on services to clients although reducing paperwork and other bureaucratic constraints, and advocating for flexible and sufficient funding at the federal and state levels.

Some state and voluntary agencies are striving to address these concerns with innovative strategies such as family-based services and special reunification programs that are supported by a mix of public and private funding. But a more concerted effort at the legislative, policy, and programmatic levels must be made to maximize the quality of family foster care. Can we, as a society, rise to the challenge? As we reform our services, it is important that we listen to the perspectives of birth families and their kin, as discussed in the next chapter on family reunification and kinship care and as articulated by a birth mother in a classic article.[17]

NOTES

1.   As recommended by the National Commission on Family Foster Care (1991), in this book we refer to *family foster care* rather than *foster family care,* in part to emphasize the focus on the family. Portions of Chapters 3, 10, and 11 were adapted from the earlier writings of Anthony Maluccio and his colleagues; we therefore thank the coauthors and publishers as follows:

*   Maluccio, A.N., Fein, E., & Olmstead, K. A. (1986). *Permanency planning for children—Concepts and methods.* London and New York: Routledge, Chapman and Hall.
*   Fein, E., Maluccio, A.N., & Kluger, M. (1990). *No more partings: An examination of long-term foster care.* Washington, DC: Child Welfare League of America.
*   Maluccio, Anthony N., Krieger, R., & Pine, B.A. (Eds.). (1990). *Preparing adolescents for life after foster care: The central role of foster parents.* Washington, DC: Child Welfare League of America.
*   Warsh, R., Maluccio, A.N., & Pine, B.A. (1994). *Teaching family reunification—A sourcebook.* Washington, DC: Child Welfare League of America.

2.   For further details on numbers of children in care, see Voluntary Cooperative Information System (1997) and ww.acf.dhhs.gov/programs/cb/stats/afcars, 9/23/98.

3.   Information is available on children with special needs and/or from multiproblem families (Anderson et al., 1998; Berrick et al., 1998; Dore, 1999; Fine, 1995; Kupsin & Dubsky, 1999; Select Committee on Children, Youth and Families, 1989; Pilowsky, 1995; Schneiderman, Connors, Fribourg, & Gonzalez, 1998; Simms & Halfon, 1994).

4.   See Chernoff et al. (1994) and General Accounting Office (1995) for reports on the health needs of young children in foster care; Battistelli (1998) for the views and recommendations of state child welfare commissioners regarding the health of children in out-of-home care; DeWoody (1994) for a report by the Child Welfare League of America documenting the need for health care reform in relation to children and youths in the child welfare system; and Simms et al. (1999) for recommendations on delivery of managed health care for children in foster care.

5.   For additional suggestions regarding services and policies that promote the development of young children, see Berrick et al. (1998) and Fraser (1997).

6.   See also Ryan and Futterman (1998) for a hands-on guide to counseling lesbian and gay youths.

7.   See Jackson and Brissett-Chapman (1997) for a series of articles on research studies and policy and practice issues pertaining to African-American children and their families.

8.   The term at "greater risk" has a variety of facets, from the increase in the disproportionate numbers of children being placed to the threat of remaining longer in foster care to the greater likelihood of death, reabuse, or incarceration after leaving care. See Anderson, Ryan, and Leashore (1997), Barth and Blackwell (1998), Jonson-Reid and Barth (in press-a), McMurtry and Lie (1992), Olsen (1982), and Stehno (1990).

9. Hill (1997) recently revised his 1972 study, focusing on the implications of societal focus and policies and social and economic changes and their impact on African-American families.

10. Bending (1997) reports on a training program, "Teaming for Indian Families," which is aimed at child welfare workers working with Native Americans and was developed in collaboration with federally recognized tribes in the state of Washington. The training covers these six areas: collaboration between tribal and state workers; the history of federal Indian policy; federal and state laws governing implementation of the Indian Child Welfare Act of 1978; the Washington State Tribal-State agreement; cultural factors in risk assessment of Indian child welfare cases; and culturally relevant models of intervention and prevention of child abuse, sexual abuse, and neglect.

11. These and other characteristics of foster parenting are described, for example, by Maluccio et al. (1990), Meadowcroft and Trout (1990), and Rykus and Hughes (1998).

12. The authors thank Rosemarie Carbino for sharing a summary on abuse allegations in foster care, from which the above section was adapted.

13. See, for example, Zlotnik, Rome, and DePanfilis (1998) for a discussion of education for child welfare practice in general; Anderson et al. (1997) for training child welfare workers for practice with children and families of color; Rykus and Hughes (1998) for consideration of training programs for foster parents and social workers; and Warsh, Maluccio, and Pine (1994) for suggestions on training social workers for family reunification practice.

14. Practice principles and guidelines regarding assessment, case planning, goal planning, contracting, and case management are considered by, Maluccio et al. (1986), Pecora et al. (1996), and Warsh et al. (1996).

15. See Merkel-Holguin (1996) for agency guidelines for adoptive and kinship placement of children whose parents die of HIV/AIDS.

16. See Pecora and Maluccio (2000) for a more extensive summary of outcome research in family foster care.

17. McAdams (1972) vividly depicts the feelings and views of birth parents and offers thoughtful suggestions for reshaping policies, improving services, and enriching staff development in family foster care.

FOR FURTHER INFORMATION

Barth, R.P., & Berry, M. (1994). Implications of research on the welfare of children under permanency planning. In R. Barth, J.D. Berrick, & N. Gilbert (Eds.), *Child welfare research review—Vol. 1.* New York: Columbia University Press, pp. 323–368. Extensive review of research evidence concerning the outcomes of placement prevention, reunification, adoption, guardianship, and long-term foster care.

Fanshel, D., Finch, S.J., & Grundy, J.F. (1990). *Foster children in life course perspective.* New York: Columbia University Press. Retrospective study of the experiences of a large sample of children placed in long-term foster family care and the impact on their growth and development.

Jackson, S., & Brissett-Chapman, S. (Eds.) (1997). Perspectives on serving African American children, youths and families. Special Issue of *Child Welfare, 76* (1) (January–February 1997). A series of articles on research, policies, and programs affecting African-American families and children coming to the attention of the child welfare system.

Kadushin, A., & Martin, J.K. (1988). *Child welfare services,* 4th ed. New York: Macmillan Includes a chapter that thoroughly reviews the literature on foster family care and delineates trends and issues in policy, practice, and research prior to the mid-1980s.

Maluccio, A.N., Fein, E., & Olmstead, K.A. (1986). *Permanency planning for children: Concepts and methods*. London and New York: Routledge, Chapman and Hall. Integrative discussion of the emergence, philosophy, theory, and practice of permanency planning for children and youths within a family-centered orientation.

McDonald, T.P., Allen, R. I., Westerfelt, A., & Piliavin, I. (1996). *Assessing the long-term effects of foster care—A research synthesis*. Washington, DC: CWLA Press. Extensive review of the findings of 29 studies of out-of-home care published between 1960 and 1992. The authors identify what is known and unknown concerning the impact of out-of-home care, provide a framework for assessing trends and policies, and offer recommendations for research as well as program and policy development.

McKenzie, B. (Ed.). (1994). *Current perspectives on foster family care for children and youth*. Toronto: Wall & Emerson. Comprehensive review of issues in the development of policy and practice in the field of family foster care, with contributions from Canada, the United States, and European countries.

Meadowcraft, P., & Trout, A. (Eds.). (1990). *Troubled youth in treatment homes: A handbook of therapeutic foster care*. Washington, DC: Child Welfare League of America. A handbook of therapeutic foster care, covering topics such as recruitment, selection, and training of foster parents; organization of programs; and services or children and their birth families.

Palmer, S.E. (1995). *Maintaining family ties—Inclusive practice in foster care*. Washington, DC: Child Welfare League of America. Building on an intensive study of social workers in two Canadian child protection agencies, the author delineates practice principles for helping children in foster care and their parents maintain their "connections" and cope with the impact of separation.

11

Family Reunification

Family reunification, as noted in the preceding chapter, has been attracting considerable attention in recent years in the field of child and family welfare. Although it has been regarded as an integral component of the philosophy and practice of permanency planning for children and youths coming to the attention of the service delivery system, reunification has become increasingly controversial, particularly as there has been a growing backlash against family preservation following highly publicized failures to protect children from harm and deaths of children in their own homes.

Despite such controversy, family reunification is often viewed as the desired outcome of out-of-home placement of children and youths. Successful family reunification, however, requires a full range of efforts that is supported by well-grounded theory and that targets and responds carefully to the needs of children and their families.[1] This chapter presents a redefinition of reunification, outlines pertinent principles and guidelines, reviews evaluative research, and examines the increasing use of formal and informal kinship care. The chapter builds on the view of preservation and child protection as, in many cases, *complementary* and, in essence, two sides of the same coin. When this is not so, child protection has a higher priority. The ideal of complementarity is illustrated in this chapter by the example of reunification of children in out-of-home care with their birth families. This ideal is tempered with a strong emphasis on children's safety.

AN EXPANDED DEFINITION OF FAMILY REUNIFICATION

The theory, policy, and practice of family reunification have traditionally been based on the premise that children and youths in out-of-home care need to be either returned to their families of origin or placed in another permanent setting. This either-or orientation appears to be supported by the legal framework of federal laws that have been reviewed in previous chapters, particularly PL 96-272 and—even more so—PL 105-89. In particular, termination of parental rights and responsibilities is expected to be sought when families have been unable to care for children in their own homes, even though there may have been a meaningful relationship between parents and children and even when no other permanent family has been, or was likely to be, found.

There are, however, many parents who love their children and want to nurture them, but are unable to be full-time caregivers. The child welfare system's response to these parents has often been to test them beyond their limits by returning their children home, or to terminate their parental rights and forever sever their family bonds. Such an either-or orientation is too simplistic and not in the best interests of the child or the families involved in foster care. In its place, a family reunification orientation is needed that embodies a flexible approach to working with children in out-of-home care and their families—an approach that recognizes and meets children's and families' individual needs.

This rethinking of family reunification has led to the development of the following expanded definition:

> Family reunification is the planned process of reconnecting children in out-of-home care with their families by means of a variety of services and supports to the children, their families, and their foster parents or other service providers. It aims to help each child and family to achieve and maintain, at any given time, their optimal level of reconnection—from full reentry of the child into the family system to other forms of contact, such as visiting, that affirm the child's membership in the family, and to contact with the family even following termination of parental rights and responsibilities. (Modified from Maluccio, Warsh, & Pine, 1993, p. 6)

This expanded definition views family reunification as a dynamic process and suggests that practitioners should use a flexible approach that seeks to meet the unique needs of children and their families in an individualized and carefully thought through way. It underscores the value of maintaining and enhancing connectedness or reconnectedness between children in foster care and their families or members of their extended kinship system. At the same time, it recognizes that not every parent can be a daily caregiver and that some families, though not able to live together, can still maintain kinship bonds. Such a view of family reunification suggests a flexible approach to preserving family bonds by responding to each child's and family's individual qualities and needs. In particular, it calls for fully respecting human diversity, particularly culture, race, and ethnicity, and involving the family and its kin through approaches such as family group decision making and provision of "wraparound" services, as considered further in Chapter 3.

It should, of course, be acknowledged that there are situations in which children must be protected through temporary, or even permanent, separation from their parents. Guidelines have been developed for identifying such situations, including those in which a child has previously died due to abuse or neglect; cases involving sexual abuse when the abuser continues to reside in the child's home; and situations in which parents refuse to recognize the need for services, such as substance abuse treatment, despite repeated efforts on the part of agencies. Even in these extreme cases, however, attention paid to preserving as much of the child's family as possible may help support the child's well-being. In short, reunification can occur in a variety of ways—and differing degrees—beyond physical reconnection.

The redefinition of reunification should be accompanied by an expanded definition of *family,* as discussed in Chapter 3. The terms *parents* and *families* are used in a generic sense to refer to those parents or caregivers who are *meaningful* to the child and with whom family reunification is being considered. Although for the most part this refers to biological parents or families, reconnections can also include adoptive parents and families, grandparents, primary caregivers, or other significant attachment figures the child may have, including foster parents.

UNDERLYING PRINCIPLES AND GUIDELINES

Redefining family reunification leads to a number of principles and guidelines for family reunification policies, programs, practices, and training. As illustrated through the case example in Table 11.1, the principles and guidelines include the following (Warsh, Maluccio, & Pine, 1994, pp. 3–4):

- Family reunification is an integral part of the philosophy of preserving families and of permanency planning, with their emphasis on ensuring continuity of care for children. Family reunification should be systematically considered and planned for by the child welfare and legal systems as early as possible in a child's placement in out-of-home care.
- Family reunification is a dynamic process that must be based on the child's and family's changing qualities, needs, and potentialities. It should be viewed by all who provide services to the family as a continuum, with levels or outcomes ranging from full reentry into the family system to partial reentry to less extensive contact. At any point during the child's placement in out-of-home care, the most appropriate or optimal level of reconnection should be identified and actively pursued. At the same time, it should be recognized that reconnection is not possible or desirable in some situations that may appropriately require termination of parental rights and responsibilities. Even in such instances, however, children should at the least be helped to move into new permanent families with some tangible tie to their past in the form of pictures, a lifebook, or other family memorabilia.
- As a form of preserving families, reunification embodies (1) conviction about the role of the biological family as the preferred child-rearing unit, if at all possible; (2) recognition of the potential of most families to care for their children, if properly assisted; (3) awareness of the impact of separation and loss on children and parents; and (4) involvement, as appropriate, of any and all members of the child's family, including members of the extended family or others who, although not legally related, are considered by the child and themselves to be "family." As noted in Chapter 3, *family group conferences* can be used to promote involvement of the extended family in the care and protection of "at risk" children.
- Reunification practice is guided by an ecologically oriented, competence-

Table 11.1. Case Example in Family Reunification

To illustrate some of the principles and issues in family reunification, a case example is presented.[a] In this case, reunification of the child with the biological parents was accomplished, after a brief foster family placement as well as temporary placement with a maternal grandmother.

The case illustrates the family-centered approach presented in Chapter 3, along with a number of the issues and trends considered in the present chapter and the previous one, particularly the emphasis on involvement of biological families; the range of potential permanency planning options; the complementary roles of various service providers; and the urgency of timely, carefully planned, and well-coordinated case management. In addition, the case exemplifies a recurring theme from Chapter 3, namely, the importance of explicitly adopting a permanency planning perspective. This helps practitioners to focus more clearly on timely decision making and enhance parental functioning, even when alternative permanent plans become necessary.

The Sawyer Family

Robert and Olivia Sawyer, an African-American couple in their early 20s, were referred by a hospital's social service department to the public agency charged with protecting children, because their 3-year-old son John had been severely burned. John, who had been in his mother's custody following the parents' separation, was then temporarily placed with his maternal grandmother, after a brief time in a foster home. Both parents, who were still separated, had visited John for 1½ hours per week while he had been placed. The parents were in conflict and presented discrepant information regarding how, and with whom, the burn occurred. In working with the mother, the agency worker focused on assessing the mother's ability to resume care of the child. A court date was scheduled for 3 months later regarding this issue.

The worker followed a permanency planning perspective and consulted regularly with her supervisor and the agency's child psychologist. An initial interview was scheduled with Mr. and Mrs. Sawyer to discuss the reason for the referral and what was expected of them. Individual roles and responsibilities were clarified, emphasizing the availability of parent aide services for the mother. During this session, Mrs. Sawyer expressed a wish to resume care of her child, whereas Mr. Sawyer also made it clear that he wanted to remain involved with John through visiting as much as possible.

While John remained with his maternal grandmother, weekly parent aide visits and counseling sessions with Mrs. Sawyer followed, to develop parenting and child management skills, alternative ways of handling stress, the ability to ask for help and utilize appropriate community resources, confidence in being able to understand the needs of the child, and better communication among family members. In addition, the worker held monthly family sessions with both parents, maternal and paternal grandmothers, the child, and the parent aide; the purpose was to discuss issues and facilitate communication among family members. The maternal grandmother was found to be particularly concerned and supportive. Parent–child visiting progressed from 1½ hours per week to two overnight visits with the mother and monthly weekend visits with the father. A service agreement was used, which listed what the mother had to do to resume care of her child and what the worker's responsibility was in keeping records of scheduled appointments and notes indicating progress. There was also weekly contact with the maternal grandmother regarding the child and the visitation schedule, and the mother was helped to otain needed furniture for her apartment.

Throughout this process, the worker assessed Mr. and Mrs, Sawyer's emotional and behavioral functioning and helped the mother in particular to deal with her sense of inadequacy and streghten her parenting skills. In addition to her therapeutic functions, the worker's role

(*continued*)

Table 11.1. (Continued)

involved advocating on behalf of child and mother, collaborating with a court monitor and a parent aide assigned to the case, and using community resources to assist the other in developing the skills and confidence she needed to care for her child. Within 8 months, Mrs. Sawyer resumed care of her child. The outcome was dependent on several factors: an awareness of permanency planning, effective consultation, appropriate use of collateral resources, timely intervention, and sensitivity to the needs of the mother as well as those of the child.

aThis case example is adapted from Maluccio et al. (1986, pp. 39–42) and reprinted with permission of Tavistock Publication, London, England.

centered perspective that emphasizes promoting family empowerment, engaging in advocacy and social action so as to achieve societal conditions and structures that enhance family functioning, reaching for—and building on—the strengths and potentialities of parents and other family members, involving parents as partners in the helping process, and providing needed services and supports.

- Children in care, biological families, foster families and other caregivers, social workers, court-appointed special advocates, attorneys, parent aides, and other service providers constitute an ongoing partnership, promoted by effective teamwork. The differential roles of all parties should be clearly spelled out and understood.
- Human diversity—for example, culture, race, ethnicity, sexual orientation, and ability—should be respected. Life-styles and child-rearing methods that might be considered different or unusual should be accepted so long as they promote a child's health and safety. This principle is particularly crucial because a disproportionate number of children in care come from low-income families or families of color, whereas most practitioners are white and from the middle class.
- A commitment to early and consistent contact between the child and family is an essential ingredient in preparing for and maintaining a successful reunification. Child–family contact can serve as a laboratory in which both parties work on the problems that may have contributed to the need for placement and learn new ways to be together again.
- Family reunification services should be offered for as long as they are needed to maintain the reconnection of a child with the family. For many families, intensive family reunification services may need to be followed by less intensive services. For a few families, some level of service may be necessary until the child is ready for independent living.

As the above principles suggest, it is essential that we think broadly and flexibly about family reunification in response to the unique qualities, needs, and situations of each child and family. Thinking in these terms is useful for various reasons. For instance, reflecting about an optimal degree of reconnection can encourage practitioners to consider a range of family members, including not only parents and siblings but also relatives and significant others who constitute a family for a particular child. As another example, ambivalent parents can be helped to identify the optimal degree of reconnection that they and the child can tolerate and prepare for it through means such as trial visits.

Furthermore, the reunification of children and their families is more likely to be successful when an agency articulates its mission through a comprehensive framework of policies, in line with the principles and guidelines delineated above. In addition, effective reunification programs involve the commitment of agency administrators to hiring social workers with a range of family reunification competencies, empowering them through appropriate decision-making authority and opportunities to further develop their skills, facilitating all aspects of service delivery, and continually seeking new directions and pursuing program improvements.

An agency context that supports family reunification practice needs to address numerous aspects in relation to agency policy, direct practice with children and families, collaboration with other systems, and staff development. As considered in detail elsewhere (Warsh, Pine, & Maluccio, 1996, pp. 71–180), such a supportive context includes agency policies that, among other aspects, provide adequate resources for supporting practitioners in their outreach to children and families; promote collaboration with other community systems, including other child and family agencies, judicial and legal personnel, state and local legislators, and schools of social work; and offer ongoing staff development programs focusing on family reunification and directed not only to its workers but also to other service providers and community representatives. We need to consider, in particular, how to provide effective services for vulnerable families such as those coming to the attention of child welfare agencies. As Halpern (1999, p. 253) has indicated:

> We have now had more than a century of experience with supportive social services for poor families. . . . Reform efforts have yielded many helpful new approaches and programs. Nonetheless, such efforts have not brought us closer to a service system that is coherent in purpose and design, and responsive to families, particularly poor families.

FAMILY REUNIFICATION COMPETENCIES

Following the definition, principles, and guidelines delineated in the preceding sections, family reunification practice requires a range of specialized competencies for social workers. As discussed elsewhere,[2] practice competencies, which involve a set of knowledge, attitudes, and skills necessary for successfully reunifying families, are organized into four major parts. Building on the values delineated in the preceding section, practitioners and administrators

- evaluate the family's readiness to reunify;
- use the results of the assessment to formulate goals and service agreements;
- work directly with children and parents and collaborate with other service providers; and;
- prepare the family to remain connected, end the service, and evaluate the work.

It should be noted that family reunification practice—like other forms of child welfare practice—is a dynamic process. Assessment, goal planning, implementation, and evaluation are interrelated activities that occur throughout work on a family reunification case. For example, social workers need to use their assessment skills when they plan case goals, their intervention skills when they help children cope with their feelings during the assessment phase, and their evaluation skills throughout the reunification process.

In addition, as already noted, it should be stressed that although these competencies are *specific* to family reunification practice, they build on generic or core child welfare competencies in areas such as assessment, case planning, and the impact of separation and placement. Family reunification practice also requires practitioners to possess specialized competencies in related practice areas, such as family therapy, child abuse, and legal issues in child welfare. In short, the competent family reunification practitioner, whether serving families as a line worker in a public agency or as a social worker in a family preservation program, is a specialist equipped with the full range of generic child welfare competencies as well as the competencies that are specific to family reunification. The generic competencies are extensively described and illustrated in a series of four volumes by Rykus and Hughes (1998a).[3] The specialized reunification competencies, described in detail by Warsh, Maluccio, and Pine (1994), are outlined below. Their use is most effective in conjunction with approaches such as *concurrent planning,* which, as discussed in Chapter 3, can facilitate and expedite the implementation of a timely permanent plan for the child.

First, there should be careful *assessment of the readiness of family and child to be reunited,* particularly assessment in regard to aspects such as

- the family's willingness to be reunited with the child;
- the child's willingness and readiness to return;
- the strengths and resources of the parents and child that can make reunion possible;
- the parent–child and family–child interaction and relationship;
- resources available to the family through its extended kin networks as well as the social service and community network;
- the qualities of the family's home, the community, and the broader environment that may affect reunification;
- the obstacles and supports that may impinge on a child's reentry into the family; and
- the obstacles between parents and foster parents that impede reunification.

Second, on the basis of the assessment, there should be *goal planning* that is guided by principles such as the following:

- goal planning as both a product and a process that involve the child and family in mutual decision making; occur throughout work with a family up to case closure; and require continual monitoring, reassessment, and revision;
- helping children, parents, and other family members cope with their feelings about—and reactions to—the experience of loss and separation;
- working with the family to identify the optimal level of reconnection that is possible—from actual reunification of the child with the family to visiting or other forms of contact;
- explaining to family members, children, and others as appropriate why the child is being reunited with the family, including reasons for original placement, what has changed or needs to change to make reunification possible, what is involved in the process of family reunification, and why the particular level of reconnection is being sought;
- working with family members to help them develop and prioritize the goals that must be reached in order to effect a reunification;
- incorporating the requirements of the legal system into goal planning with the family and helping to ensure that the court's decision-making process is in concert with professional recommendations;
- working with the parents, the child, and the foster parents and other service providers to develop a service agreement for implementing the plan; and
- regularly convening formal and informal reviews of progress toward the goals delineated in the service agreement, and revising or amending the goals as needed.

Third, *implementing the family reunification plan* is guided by the following principles:

- working directly with the children, parents, and other family members to prepare them for the desired form of family reunification;
- working specifically with the parents in order to help them, among other aspects, to identify those behaviors they might expect to see in their children following reconnection and to learn the parenting skills necessary for achieving the particular level of reconnection;
- arranging for their child's access to adequate food, clothing, housing, health care, and education;
- helping parents to learn how to discipline in a constructive way;
- encouraging parents to use and interact with community resources in behalf of their child;
- working specifically with the child by helping her or him to deal with a sense of divided loyalty toward biological and foster families; providing opportunities to learn coping skills and positive behaviors for family reunification; and helping the child cope with feelings that may be reactivated as departure from the foster family approaches;

- using visiting to prepare for reunification through means such as structuring visiting in such a way that parents' caregiving skills are enhanced; arranging visiting along a continuum of increasingly stressful times; recognizing and overcoming those obstacles that make visiting difficult for children, parents, and other family members; progressively increasing the length of visits and parental responsibilities; and evaluating and altering the visiting plan in accordance with the family's and child's progress and needs;
- promoting the foster family's collaboration and participation in family re-unification by clarifying and negotiating the complementary roles of biological parents and foster parents; helping foster parents to serve as resources to the biological family; convening to the foster parents the importance of their giving the child "permission" to reconnect with the biological family; and
- collaborating with other service providers, so as to facilitate teamwork and provision of services to the family.

Fourth, *maintaining the reunification and ending the service* are guided by principles such as the following:

- preparing and assisting family members to remain connected with one another, in ways such as helping them to form or strengthen linkages with formal and informal social supports;
- engaging foster parents in the postreunification phase by helping them cope with their feelings regarding the child's reunification;
- dealing effectively with any disruption of a reunification plan by using the disruption to learn more about a child and parents in order to make another permanent plan; recognizing that disruption in some cases may be a temporary setback and not necessarily a failure; and helping parents and children cope with the reality of disruption of reconnected families;
- holding a closing session with the family and others to summarize accomplishments, elaborate on family strengths, prioritize the work that remains, and review the supports that can help the family carry out the tasks ahead; and
- building on the agency's experiences with each case by assessing and analyzing what was learned, evaluating program implementation as well as impact, and disseminating what is learned, ultimately influencing agency policy and practice.

EFFECTIVENESS OF FAMILY REUNIFICATION SERVICES

In recent years there has been increasing research on the processes and effectiveness of family reunification services; however, the findings of studies on the results of family reunification are inconsistent.[4] A selective review, for example, revealed "a wide range of reunification rates (from 13% to 70%) and of rates of reentry into out-of-home care (from 10% to 33%)" (Maluccio, Fein, & Davis, 1994, p. 494). The main reason for such an inconsistent picture seems to be

> the inappropriateness of comparing and aggregating findings of diverse studies in regard to operational definitions of crucial study variables, study samples, timing of the studies, geographic locations, length of placement and follow up periods, and service factors as well as child and family characteristics. (Maluccio et al., 1994, p. 494)

Because human interactions are so complex, it is not surprising that research in the human services reflects that complexity, often producing insufficient and sometimes contradictory information. Nevertheless, without expecting panaceas or simplistic answers, some order can be created out of the apparent chaos. The findings that emerge from studies on family reunification can be applied with insight—albeit with caution—to policy and practice planning. Although they may have methodological flaws, the studies reviewed below make noteworthy contributions that can help guide the decisions and actions of practitioners as well as policymakers.

Exit from Foster Care

Children exit from foster care in a number of ways that are qualitatively distinct. In an analysis of longitudinal data from a cohort study of 8,625 children in foster care, Courtney and Wong (1996) examined the factors that affect discharge to their original family or guardian, placement in an adoptive family, or running away. This methodologically rigorous study shows the complexities and subtleties of the exit process in foster care. The authors reported that a large number of children returned to their homes or to the homes of guardians in the first few months after placement. Later, however, fewer children returned home and an increasing number were adopted, although others ran away. A related study from Australia found that the probability of reunification decreases as the child remains in care longer (Fernandez, 1999).

It is not clear from the above studies or related research by Davis, Landsverk, Newton, and Ganger (1996) whether some children return home earlier because they and their families are functioning at a higher level and thus make better use of services than is the case with other families. Also, some studies indicate that children who return home sooner are more likely to reenter foster care (Berrick et al., 1998; Wulczyn, Harden, & Goerge, 1997), suggesting that these families are in substantial need. Nevertheless, these studies call attention to the importance of providing comprehensive and easily accessible supportive services to children and their families in both the preplacement phase and early in the placement period in order to promote family reunification (Pierce & Geremia, 1999).

Child welfare workers have long recognized the need to address the traumatic impact of separation and placement on children and their parents and other family members as a means of helping them move toward reunification (Kadushin & Martin, 1988). As the above studies suggest, equally vital is involving both children and parents actively in the helping process, by providing not only therapeutic services but also concrete assistance with their everyday needs (Staff & Fein, 1994). Traditionally, the emphasis in child welfare practice has been on services to the children, in response to their immediate need for care and protection. Although this is appropriate, parents also need special attention; help to them should be provided on an intensive basis, so as to enhance their rehabilitation and increase the likelihood that they will be able to take their children back home, keep them there, and function as competent parents.

In this regard, successful outcomes depend on treating parents as individuals with problems and needs of their own, rather than solely as caregivers with responsibility for their children. In addition, parents and other family members need to be involved as partners in the change process and as active agents in preparing for reunification, "including having an understanding of the reasons for placement, participating in developing goals, sharing in determining visiting plans and purposes, and evaluating their own progress" (Warsh, Pine, & Maluccio, 1996, p. 125).

Aftercare Services

The value of providing supportive services to parents and children following reunification is demonstrated in a number of studies. For example, Fraser, Walton, Lewis, Pecora, and Walton (1996) report on an experimental evaluation of a state program established to reunify children in foster care with their biological families. These researchers randomly assigned the cases of foster children to (1) a control group of 53 children whose families received routine agency services as a component of an overall foster care plan and (2) an experimental group of 57 children whose families received intensive reunification services, with the goal of family preservation.

Fraser et al. (1996) found that children in the experimental group receiving intensive services were more likely to be reunited successfully with their families than those in the control group receiving routine services. These differences proved to be statistically significant at the conclusion of treatment as well as during the follow-up period. In particular, relatively brief but intensive, in-home, family-based services positively affected reunification rates and outcomes. Such services involved building strong worker alliances with family members, providing skills training to parents, and meeting the concrete needs of the children and other family members. The findings suggested that reunification is promoted through *in vivo* family-strengthening services. Similarly, Jones (1998) found that the provision of adequate housing reduced the risk of failure of reunification efforts.

A series of descriptive follow-up studies of children and adolescents discharged from foster care was also conducted in Great Britain, with emphasis on reunification issues (Biehal & Wade, 1996; Farmer, 1996). Despite certain methodological limitations, these investigations are quite informative in regard to the after care period. In the Farmer (1996) study, the sample consisted of 321 children reunited with their families after a period of court-ordered out-of-home placement. The researcher employed qualitative methodology, specifically intensive review of the children's case records and in-depth interviews with a small number of birth parents and social workers. She found that there were two distinctly different groups of children: the "disaffected" adolescents who had been removed due to juvenile offenses or truancy and the "protected" younger children who had been removed for abuse, neglect, or family breakdown. The research revealed that the most successful reunifications in both groups were first attempts; later reunifications had higher failure rates.

Biehal and Wade (1996), on the other hand, conducted a longitudinal study of adolescents leaving care in several public child welfare agencies. Their project involved both an initial survey of 183 youths during their first 3–9 months of independent living and semistructured interviews with 74 of the adolescents, conducted soon after leaving care and on two later occasions during a 2-year period. In addition, the young people's social workers were interviewed on each occasion. In each phase, the researchers focused on the varied patterns of family contact and the quality of the children's and youths' relationships with their families.

Since the study by Farmer as well as the study by Biehal and Wade employed qualitative methodology, their findings and conclusions should be viewed with caution. For example, as with other such investigations, there are questions about the reliability and validity of the data and the extent to which one can generalize to other populations. Nevertheless, these studies are useful for policy and practice, as they shed light on the supports required by children and adolescents as well as their families. In particular, it should be noted that supportive services such as special education contributed to the success of reunification efforts. Also prominent in the young people's postdischarge functioning were ongoing connections with one or more family members and a sense of belonging to and identification with a family unit, that is, their original family or a foster family with which they maintained contact.

Emphasis on the provision of follow-up services after reunification is also the most common theme in the findings of other studies on aftercare. The results point to a number of policy and practice strategies. Most notable are providing brief, time-limited but intensive services (Fraser et al., 1996; Pierce & Geremia, 1999); offering a range of social supports to the families, including concrete services in areas such as health, housing, and income, as well as counseling services in areas such as parent–child conflicts and the challenges presented by the children's behavioral difficulties (Fraser et al., 1996; Festinger, 1996); and facilitating ongoing supports to children and youths in regard to special education, treatment of emotional/behavioral and developmental/learning problems, and other special needs (Biehal & Wade, 1996; Landsverk, Davis, Ganger, Newton, & Johnson, 1996).

As various studies indicate, the services provided to children and their families in the postreunification phase can be critical in helping to keep them together. Furthermore, it has been found that in most child welfare agencies postreunification services are at first intensive, but then taper off to a less frequent contact. "A few families, however, may need some level of services indefinitely to maintain their children at home" (Warsh, Pine & Maluccio, 1996, p. 137). These may now be more obtainable than ever because of funding available under Title IV-B, Part II (The Adoption and Safe Families Act—P.L. 105-89). In addition, research has shown that strategies such as the following can be useful in maintaining the reunification (Warsh et al., 1996, pp. 136–137):

- helping the child to cope with feelings of fear, guilt, grief, and anger that may be reactivated as separation from the foster home or residential placement approaches;
- developing a postreunification safety plan for protection of a child who was originally placed because of harm in the biological home;
- assisting the child and other members of the biological and foster families to clarify—and plan for—their continuing relationship following reunification;
- helping the child and parents and other family members to anticipate and deal with conflicts that are likely to develop once the child returns home; and, above all,
- ensuring the family's access to services following reunification and eventual termination of their case.

Parent Education and Training

As suggested by several studies cited in the preceding section, parent education and training should occupy a central position in work with parents and family members of children in out-of-home care, along with more traditional services. Parent education and training can be effective, particularly when implemented with sensitivity into the qualities, needs, and expectations of parents from diverse racial, ethnic, and cultural groups (Banks, Hicks, Marlowe, Reid, Patterson, & Weinrott, 1991). Superior results have also been obtained by programs that utilize behavioral approaches rather than simply relying on didactic instructional techniques (Berry, 1988). A study of the effectiveness of parent education and training programs that compared problem-solving versus behavioral training approaches reports that the behavioral training groups produced the best results (Magen & Rose, 1994).

The above findings suggest that participation in a formally constructed parent education and training program may well have to be a fundamental element of a reunification plan. The essential motive is to empower parents and family members so that they can safely reassume caring for their children. In describing the *Family Empowerment Training Program,* the authors note that this program is based on the conviction that parents of children in out-of-home care must

- sustain involvement with and responsibility for their children if at all possible;
- feel empowered in their role of caretakers in order to preserve and possibly reunify their family;
- become advocates for their children's needs; and
- believe that they can be good parents for their child although they are in . . . care (Struhsaker, Schatz, and Bane, 1991, pp. 671–672).

The added value of a formally constructed program such as the above is that it allows parents and family members to meet other parents in a similar position. Importantly, "when this takes place parents see that they are not alone and that other families have difficulties. Through discussions that arise naturally in these situations, parents experience a sense of community and support (Ainsworth, Maluccio, & Small, 1996).

An interesting example of this approach from a residential treatment center in California provides a key as to how such a program may need to be constructed (Carlo, 1993). This agency provides an education/support group, jointly led by a social worker and a child care worker, for parents of children placed in the group care program. The group

> is used to didactically provide information about child management and to introduce parents to a range of behavior shaping and relationship building techniques. The parents are then provided with experiential opportunities through participating in daily life events, meal preparation, birthday parties, games and sports in the living unit in which the child resides. Here, they observe how child care workers manage children and have the opportunity to practice what they have heard talked about in the parent education/support group. (Ainsworth, 1996, p. 25)

In two studies conducted to measure the effectiveness of the above approach, the data collected revealed that separately applied, neither the didactic (cognitive) nor an experiential only approach is "as powerful as both conditions conjoined. . . . The two components have complementary value, and the effects of each is enhanced when they are together" (Carlo, 1993, p. 110). This supports the notion that for these parents learning takes hold best when it is embedded in experience. These studies suggest the need for practitioners to use formally constructed parent education, training, and support programs as part of the reunification process of children in foster care.

Parental Visiting

During the placement period it is also crucial to sustain and enhance connections between children and their families, particularly parents or other caregivers. Parent–child visiting in foster care has been described as a crucial determinant of the outcome of foster care services (Hess & Proch, 1988) and as the "heart of family reunification" (Warsh et al., 1994, p. 49). Also, in an in-depth study of the impact of separation on children in foster care, Palmer (1995) documented the importance of maintaining family ties between children and their birth families.

In an extensive follow-up investigation of permanency planning for children in foster care, Davis et al. (1996) examined the relationship between parental visiting and reunification. The majority of children who had visited with their parents at the level recommended by the courts were reunified with their families. However, there was no significant relationship between parent–child visiting and whether the child remained in the biological home at a follow-up point a year after the reunification.

The findings of the above study suggest that explicit policies and practices should be instituted to facilitate parent–child visiting throughout the placement process and to use visiting deliberately as a therapeutic vehicle in preparation for reunification. Visiting helps maintain family ties and provides opportunities for family members to learn and practice new behaviors and patterns of communicating with each other, with the assistance of social workers and foster parents. Yet, visiting continues to be a problematic aspect of practice in foster care, with at best ambivalent attitudes by foster parents toward birth parents (cf. Erera, 1997). Moreover, in many cases parent–child visiting is infrequent and irregular or nonexistent (Fernandez, 1997).

Authors such as Hess and Proch (1988) and Warsh et al. (1994 and 1996) offer guidelines for employing parent–child visiting as a strategy for reuniting children in out-of-home care with their families of origin. These authors emphasize that visiting should be carefully planned and implemented, with attention to its different purposes during each phase of the foster care placement. These purposes include providing reassurance to the child and the family that the agency is concerned with reuniting them, if at all possible; assessing the children's and parents' capacity for reunification; offering opportunities for staff members to help parents and children to reconnect with each other and learn or relearn skills for being together; and documenting the progress of children and parents in becoming reunited. As Warsh et al. (1996, p. 133) note, "Whether or not children are able to return home, visiting maintains family ties which may contribute to a child's healthy development." The natural bonds between children in foster care and their parents continue to be prominent for parents as well as children long after they are physically separated.

Researchers have identified a number of pertinent policies and strategies for facilitating visitation and promoting connectedness between children in placement and their families (Hess & Proch, 1988; Warsh et al., 1996):

- placing children near their parents and other significant kin;
- placing siblings together, unless otherwise indicated;
- encouraging foster parents to allow family visits in the foster home, unless contraindicated;
- requiring written visiting plans that specify aspects such as the purposes, frequency, length, and location of each visit;

- selecting visiting activities that provide children and parents with opportunities to learn more effective patterns of interaction; and
- preparing children, families, and foster parents for visits and giving them opportunities to work through their reactions before and after each visit.

Reentry of Children into Foster Care

Reentry of children back into foster care following reunification is a central dynamic of child welfare services. Although a critic of the child welfare system (Pelton, 1989) has noted that there is a revolving door with children repeatedly going home and returning to care, determining the ideal reentry rate is not a simple matter. Although every discharge from care should be expected to be successful, an overly cautious reunification program might not give any families the benefit of the doubt and only send children home when there is evidence beyond a reasonable doubt that the reunification will succeed. Such a standard would prevent many children who could be successfully reunified from going home. Low reentries into foster care following reunification might also show that there are insufficient follow-up services to detect the need for reentry and could mean that children who went home were remaining there unsafely. The ideal reunification program has the resources to provide ongoing support to families that have a reasonable chance at reentry and, coincidentally, provides the vigilance necessary to see that postreunification harms are rapidly observed and addressed.

In a descriptive study conducted in New York City, Festinger (1996) investigated recidivism in a sample of 210 children from 20 agencies returning to their families from foster homes and group care settings. The study explored whether there were any differences between children who reentered care within 2 years of discharge and those who did not reenter, taking into account the characteristics of the children, their caregivers, and their social situations. There were several limitations in the above research. "All data came from one large city at a particular point in time. Also, the 20 agencies were not selected on a random basis but were included to provide a range of agency types of varying size, sectarian and non-sectarian auspices, levels of care, and child populations served" (Festinger, 1996, p. 397). In addition, since it was not possible to gather data directly through the children and their families, the researcher relied primarily on the social workers' perceptions and observations and on data obtained from computerized files of the state agency. Although these subjective and typically unreliable data sources weakened the study, some noteworthy findings did emerge. In particular, the strongest predictors of reentry into foster care within 1 year of discharge were lower ratings of parenting skills by social workers and few social supports available to the families. The strongest predictors of reentry within 2 years were the number and the severity of problems experienced by the biological parents or substitute caregivers.

Recent work on foster care caseload flows indicates that about 20% of children who leave foster care will return to care within a 3-year time frame (Berrick et al.,

1998; Wulczyn, Harden, & Goerge, 1997). Reentry appears to be most likely when foster care stays were short. About 25–30% of children who leave foster care before they have stayed 6 months will return to foster care. Children are also more likely to reenter during the first 2 years after they go home. Children who exit care as infants have particularly high reentry rates—in one large urban county in California, this rate approximated 40% (Berrick et al., 1998). In addition, there also appears to be a higher rate of reentry among minority adolescents (Fein, Maluccio, & Kluger, 1990; Wulczyn, Harden, & Goerge, 1997).

Preventing entry back into the child welfare system is not the sole goal of the foster care program. Foster care and reunification are tools to be used to protect the safety and well-being of children. There is growing evidence that longer stays in foster care may have beneficial effects and that reunification can result in risks far greater than reentry to foster care. In two studies in California using different samples and methods, investigators found that children of color who were reunified from foster care had higher mortality rates (Barth & Blackwell, 1998) and higher likelihood of transitioning to juvenile justice programs (Jonson-Reid & Barth, 2000) than children who remained in foster care. Although these studies are not a reason to change dramatically the course of what we do, they are a cautionary note that we should not be basing child welfare decisions primarily on the goal of reducing the numbers of children in foster care. To sharply accelerate reunifications, we would first need to be sure that funding mechanisms were there to support postreunification services, that service models were in place to adequately assist families, and that monitoring was sufficient to look after the safety needs of children following foster care.

Child Psychosocial Functioning

A recurring question in the field of child welfare concerns the potential impact of the child's psychosocial functioning on the outcome of her or his placement in out-of-home care. Landsverk et al. (1996) explored this theme in a descriptive, longitudinal study of 669 children who had been removed from their families and placed in either foster care or kinship care at a large county agency in California. The study was enriched by the use of standardized measures to assess the children's psychosocial functioning. The researchers examined emotional/behavioral difficulties, developmental/learning problems, and physical handicaps or acute medical problems.

The findings indicated that children with behavioral or emotional difficulties were half as likely to be reunified with their families as children without problems, regardless of their type of maltreatment, family circumstances, and other background characteristics. Developmental and medical problems did not have an effect on reunification. The authors stress the importance of assisting parents in coping with the challenges of behavioral problems presented by children following reunification, underlining the role of after care services discussed earlier in this chapter.

The findings of the above study are consistent with the results of an earlier demonstration project conducted at the Florida Mental Health Institute, which examined the efficacy of intensive, individualized services in improving the functioning of foster children with emotional and behavioral problems (Clark, Prange, Lee, Boyd, McDonald, & Stewart, 1994). The latter study involved a controlled experiment, with children assigned randomly to an experimental group receiving specialized services and a control group of children receiving standard agency services. It was found that the outcomes, in terms of the children's adjustment and the stability of permanency plans, were significantly more positive for subjects in the experimental group than those in the control group. In light of the findings, these researchers emphasized the importance of providing intensive services and supports as well as individualized permanency plans for children with, or at risk of, emotional and behavioral disorders.

The studies reviewed in this section pertain to the developmental needs, multiple problems, and disruptive behaviors of the children. The results point to various implications for practice and policy, particularly in regard to the timely provision of mental health and other services to the children. By the same token, it should be emphasized that the problems faced by the families of these children, particularly the birth parents, must be acknowledged and confronted through adequate services and supports in each case as well as through societal reforms. As concluded in an earlier article recommending a range of family reunification services, a focus on the child is not enough:

> Service delivery must take into account the competing interests of adults and children. In particular, the treatment of substance abusing adults needs to be reconciled with their role as parents. On a larger scale, the social and economic conditions that produce our addicted adults and our children in need of permanency planning must be addressed for families to survive. (Fein & Staff, 1991, p. 342)

KINSHIP CARE

Kinship care is an ancient phenomenon. In many cultures the practice whereby grandparents, older siblings, aunts and uncles, or other adults or elders assume responsibility for children unable to live with their parents is a time honored tradition (Child Welfare League of America, 1994; Hegar & Scannapieco, 1999) (see Table 11.2). Kinship care for children who must be separated from their biological parents is attractive for many reasons, as it

- enables children to live with persons whom they may know and trust;
- reduces the trauma children may experience when they are placed with persons who are initially unknown to them;

Table 11.2. A Child's Yearning for Placement with Her Grandmother

Decision making and planning in child welfare cases require listening to the voices of children. The poem that follows reflects children's yearnings for security in their lives, and especially for connections with their kin and with their familiar environments.

Grandma's House

By Chiemi T. Davis[a]

I'm scared . . . yesterday they came and got me.
I'm scared . . . my mom's using again and nobody's home.
I'm scared . . . where they going to put me?
I'm scared . . . . who's going to take care of me?

I want to go to Grandma's house
Where I know the smells.
She'll cook my food and do up my hair.
She'll sing my songs, I can sleep in her bed,
She'll hold and rock me all night long

I want to go to Grandma's house
Where I can go to my store.
Ms. Robinson, she'll be there
She'll yell and tell me to "git"
but first she'll give me a free soda and some "sugar" to go.

I want to go to Grandma's house
Cause my mom will know where I am.
She'll say "sorry baby" and kiss my hand.
Grandma will tell her "enough is enough"
She'll know she can't smoke here
Shell get straight and do what's right.

I'm scared . . . and I want to go to Grandma's house.

[a]Chiemi T. Davis is Director, Portland Division, The Casey Family Programs, Portland, Oregon.

- reinforces children's sense of identity and self-esteem, which flows from their family history and culture;
- facilitates children's connections to their siblings; and
- strengthens the ability of families to give children the support they need. (Wilson & Chipungu, 1996, p. 387).

Although it is not a new phenomenon, kinship care may be viewed as a new child placement paradigm due to "its recent embrace by the child welfare field, social work, and public policy" as a "model governing thought and practice" (Hegar, 1999, p. 225). In recent years it has become the first choice—rather than the last resort—in the continuum of services for children requiring out-of-home care (Ingram, 1996).

Definition

The Child Welfare League of America's Kinship Care Policy and Practice Committee has defined kinship care as

> the full-time nurturing and protection of children who must be separated from their parents by relatives, members of their tribes or clans, godparents, stepparents, or other adults who have a kinship bond with a child. (Child Welfare League of America, 1994, p. 2)

Scannapieco and Hegar (1999, pp. 2–3) further explain that there are different perspectives on what constitutes kinship care, a phrase that was originally inspired by Carol Stack (1974) in her work on extended kinship networks in the African-American community. In particular, they note that kinship care includes both care entered into by private family arrangement and care provided through auspices of a public child welfare agency with legal custody of a child. Some authors prefer the terms "kinship" and "kinship caregivers" for private care and "kinship foster care" and "kinship foster parents" for care that falls within the formal child welfare system (Scannapieco & Hegar, 1999, p. 3).

According to Nisivoccia (1996, p. 1), kinship foster care can be regarded as "a form of extended family preservation that offers continuity of family ties and maintains culture and ethnic identity although cushioning the trauma of foster care placement for children." Whether provided through informal or formal arrangements, it can be a culturally sensitive response that respects the child's and family's origins. Toward this end, Crumbley and Little (1997, pp. 65–71) delineate a series of questions that must be addressed to implement kinship care that respects culture, race, and ethnicity. For example, they urge workers to consider aspects such as the roles and authority of relatives in child rearing, the family's hierarchy of responsible relatives, and the impact of gender and cultural traditions on the family's decision-making patterns.

Kinship Care under ASFA

Kinship care was a relatively unobserved part of the child welfare system when the first major child welfare reform law was passed in 1980 (PL 96-272). By 1997, however, when the Adoption and Safe Families Act (ASFA) was passed, almost as many children were in kinship care as any other kind of care. Whereas Congress decided not to become involved in a major analysis of kinship care at the time ASFA was debated, ASFA does include language about kinship care that is crucial to understand.

ASFA requires that states file or join a petition to terminate parental rights and responsibilities when a child has been abandoned (in foster care for 15 of the most recent 22 months), or the parent has been convicted of a very serious crime against his or her own child. Yet, there are three exceptions and the first one mentioned is that the "child is placed with a relative (at the option of the State)" (Administration for Children and Families, 1998). This is an acknowledgment that being in the care of kin may provide a permanent plan with many desirable features.

At the same time, state and county agencies are reexamining their use of long-term kinship foster care because children who enter kinship care have such long stays and are dominating their caseloads. In a few places (e.g., New York City and Los Angeles County) renewed efforts are being made to explain the options of legal guardianship and adoption to kin in order to encourage them to follow those paths to permanency if appropriate. Several states (e.g., Illinois and California) are also using the flexibility provided by IV-E waivers to allow children to "exit" from the formal reunification or permanency planning program by giving the foster family a payment that is higher than the Temporary Assistance for Needy Families (TANF) payment but lower than a full foster care payment and by helping kinship caregivers to care for the child but not requiring that they continue to have a child welfare worker or go to court on behalf of their child. We can expect to see considerably more innovation regarding reunification and kinship care in the years ahead.

Increase in Kinship Care

Although kinship care has long been used on an informal basis, there is an increasing number of children placed with relatives who become their permanent or long-term primary caregivers. As Crumbley and Little (1997, p. xiii) indicate, "This increase . . . has been attributed to parallel increases in divorce, marital separation, alcohol and other drug abuse, parental incarceration, child abuse, and AIDS-related parental incapacity or mortality." In particular, there has been a major increase in the numbers of children cared for by their grandparents (Anderson, Ryan, & Leashore, 1997; Burnette, 1997; Goldberg-Glen, Sands, Cole, & Cristofalo, 1998). Burnette (1997), for example, reviews studies of grandparent caregivers and offers recommendations for direct practice and public policy on behalf of grandparents raising grandchildren in the inner city. Others delineate the application of strength-based case management to practice with grandparents raising grandchildren (cf. Whitley, White, Kelley, & Yorke, 1999).

In Illinois, for example, formal kinship care increased sevenfold between 1986 and 1995 (Testa, 1997), resulting in a policy change that limits the amount of foster care payments to relatives. A larger analysis conducted in 1993 of the policies of 32 states in regard to kinship care also indicated that this is the fastest growing type of placement (Gleeson & Craig, 1994). In Philadelphia, relative homes constituted over two-thirds of all foster care homes by 1992 (Takas, 1993). In Los Angeles, nearly 60% of all children in care are with relatives (Needell, Webster, Barth,

Armijo, & Fox, 1998). In addition, it has been estimated that between 1 and 4 million American children live with relatives (Everett, 1995). Many of these children live apart from their parents in their grandparents' homes.

The positive aspect of the trend toward greater use of kinship care is that it may indicate that child welfare agencies are becoming more sensitive to family, racial, ethnic, and cultural factors and the importance of family continuity in child development. Given that out-of-home care, whether family foster care, kinship care, or group care, needs to be both "child centered and family affirming" rather than solely child focused, this may represent an improvement in the quality and efficacy of these services (Ainsworth & Small, 1994). Less positively, the trend may be a response to the increasing difficulty in recruiting and retaining foster families. This long-standing difficulty and the rise in the number of children entering care, particularly adolescents, indicate that without a growth in kinship care the child welfare system, in recent years, would have experienced a major placement finding crisis (U.S. Department of Health and Human Services, 1996).

Kinship care, as previously noted, has traditionally provided for children separated from parents due to family impoverishment, neglect, abuse, or abandonment. A reemphasis on kinship care is of course in line with the emergence of the political rhetoric associated with conservative family values. This rhetoric is also associated with efforts to reduce the influence and cost of governmental services. Kinship care appears to fit this political paradigm, as it may be cheaper than nonrelative foster care, particularly if support services, including financial payments to kinship families, are less than those provided to nonrelative foster parents. This may be so even though the pattern of service to kinship carers by comparison to nonrelative foster carers indicates that kinship caregivers often receive low levels of service (Berrick, Barth, & Needell, 1994). Yet children in care with relatives— particularly if the latter are paid the same as foster parents—stay much longer than other children, which means that kinship care is becoming quite expensive in many places (Berrick et al., 1998).

The combination of a decline in the availability of nonrelative foster care placements and a reemergence of conservative family values is not a good omen for children who need out-of-home care. On demographic characteristics kinship carers, at least in the United States, appear to be older and less well off financially and to have more health and mental health problems than nonrelative foster parents. In a California study of 29 kinship parents and 33 nonrelative foster care parents designed to assess the quality of care, nonrelative placements were rated on a number of measures as more physically safe than kinship placements (Berrick, 1997). This study also reported that drugs and alcohol use and violence were more likely to occur in kinship care than in nonrelative foster care situations.

As kinship carers also are frequently single women from minority groups who, unlike unrelated foster parents, receive little training or support for this role, a question about the extent to which kinship care is an exploitation by the state of these women is worthy of consideration (Berrick, Barth, & Needell, 1994). What we may have once again is a good practice idea being overwhelmed by political ideology and fiscal considerations before it has been adequately examined.

In particular, the increase in formal or agency-based kinship care has created considerable confusion and controversy:

> of concern are the complex dynamics that lead to placement (in kinship care); internal family relationships; family-agency relationships; legal and child welfare factors concerning both protection and nurturing, permanency planning, monitoring and supervision; and equity and financial costs. (National Commission on Family Foster Care, 1991, p. 92)

The role that "the state should play in support and supervision of relatives as caregivers is also controversial" (Hornby, Zeller, & Karraker, 1996, p. 410). For instance, should support be primarily financial or also service-related? Should relatives be required to receive counseling or other services if they simply request financial assistance? Should relatives be formally assessed, as with unrelated foster parent applicants?

Practice Standards

Although the use of kinship care has greatly increased, there are no established protocols to guide decisions about placing children with kinship carers. The Kinship Care Policy and Practice Committee of the Child Welfare League of America (1994) did, however, develop a series of recommendations, as outlined below.

- *Assessment of the kinship family:* assessing "the willingness and ability of kin to provide a safe, stable, nurturing home and meet the child's developmental needs" (p. 44).
- *Approval/licensing of kinship homes:* approval and licensing are necessary to ensure "a basic level of care for children in the custody of the state" (p. 47).
- *Services for children:* "kinship services must meet the range of needs of children cared for by kin" (p. 51).
- *Services for parents:* "Child welfare agencies should provide the services that parents need for support, rehabilitation, and enhancement of their functioning as parents" (p. 53).
- *Services to kinship families:* "Child welfare agencies should provide kin with the supports and services they need to meet the child's needs, assist the child's parents, and meet their own needs as caregivers" (p. 54).
- *Financial supports:* Financial supports for children in kinship care should be provided "at a level appropriate to meet the children's physical, mental health, and developmental needs" (p. 56).
- *Support for kinship parents:* there should be "orientation programs and dis-

cussion groups to ensure that kinship parents are prepared to meet the needs of children for whom they are caring, to manage their relationships with the child's parents, and to work effectively with the agency" (pp. 63–71).

- *Monitoring and supervision:* there should be "regular and frequent contacts between the agency social worker and the child and kinship parent to continually address the health, safety, and well-being of the child and the service needs of the kinship family" (p. 62).
- *Permanency planning:* The "child welfare agency should arrange the most appropriate permanent plan for the child—that is, reunification with parent, adoption by relatives, subsidized guardianship by kin, long-term kinship care, or nonrelative adoption" (pp. 63–71).
- *Competency-based training and other supports for staff:* "To provide effective kinship care services, staff must participate in competency-based pre-service and in-service training and strong supervisory leadership must be available" (p. 73).
- *Program coordination:* "Child welfare agencies should coordinate services at both an intra-agency and inter-agency level to ensure effective, timely service provision, and a smooth transition when case transfer between programs is required" (p. 77).

Various authors have formulated useful principles for practice. Nisivoccia (1996) delineates a range of principles, approaches, and strategies to enhance agency staff relationships with kinship parents, build on the strengths of kinship members, and facilitate empowerment of families. Crumbley and Little (1997) discuss in depth clinical issues, assessment and intervention strategies, and case management approaches in kinship care. Hegar and Scannapieco (1999) offer a comprehensive analysis of kinship care, including practice models that build on available research. Jackson, Mathews, and Zaskin (1998) delineate a service delivery model for kinship care that is culturally sensitive, strength based, and family centered. Gleeson and Hainston (1999) describe the findings of research projects that can help improve kinship care practice.

In addition, the Child Welfare League of America (1994) specifies the major components of a policy and practice framework, from recruitment and licensing to monitoring and supervision. Wilson and Chipungu (1996) examine kinship care policy, practice, research, and advocacy. Finally, building on a demonstration project, Bonecutter and Gleeson (1997) have developed an extensive training manual and a series of training tapes designed to prepare child welfare caseworkers in "achieving permanency for children in kinship foster care." These materials reflect a broadened view of the family, an ongoing striving for cultural competence, a collaborative approach between members of the child's kinship system and the formal child care and protection agency, and building the case management capacities of the kinship networks, so as to provide family continuity and long-term permanency planning for the child.

Research Considerations

Since formal kinship care has begun to be widely used recently, there has been limited research regarding its effectiveness. For example, only recently has the outcome of kinship care versus nonrelative foster care been examined in terms of the
impact on adult functioning of these children. In a Maryland study involving 214
children who were in care and whose foster families had previously been part of
a study of abuse and neglect by foster parents, Benedict, Zuravin, and Stalling
(1996) examined levels of education, employment status, income, stability of
housing, homelessness, physical and mental health, life stresses and social support, and drug use and violence. The results were inconsistent and the researchers
concluded that "young people placed with kin and nonrelative care were functioning similarly in their current lives" (Benedict, Zuravin, & Stallings, 1996,
p. 545). Without some assessment of how they were doing at intake, however, this
is hard to interpret—particularly since the children in kinship care in this study
and several others apparently had fewer problems at the time of placement (cf.
Brooks & Barth, 1998). For this reason, it is not possible to conclude that children
in kinship care with the same level of difficulties as children in nonrelative foster
care would do as well. In the Brooks and Barth (1998) study, for example, children
who were born prenatally exposed to drugs and were in kinship care were not faring as well as children who were born drug exposed and were residing in nonrelative care.

    Other studies have shown that the rates of family reunification for children in
formal kinship care are actually lower than those from foster care with nonrelatives (Goerge, 1990). A further study of all 525 children placed in kinship care in
one county in New York state confirms these findings (Link, 1996). Similarly, other investigators have found that children placed with relatives remain in state custody longer and are less likely to be returned home or adopted than children in the
care of nonrelatives. What this means is unclear, as Gleeson, O'Donnell, and Bonecutter (1997) reported in a study of kinship care at two private agencies in Illinois.
In the latter study, in-depth interviews with caseworkers "revealed the complex nature of practice in this area and identified potential obstacles to permanency planning for these children" (p. 801). The latter included parental problems, such as
substance abuse in over 80% of the biological mothers; the lack of cultural competence among caseworkers; and complexities and delays inherent in the child welfare and juvenile justice systems. Moreover, as Needell and Gilbert (1997, p. 93)
have underscored, the "lack of appropriate service provisions to birth parents and
structural problems in the child welfare system . . . no doubt contribute to the low
reunification rates."[5]

    Although the practice guidelines and research findings noted above are useful,
various research questions require attention. For example, when kinship care is being considered, should practitioners require the same type of assessment of kinship carers as is required of potential nonrelative foster carers, or can it be less

intensive? In addressing this issue, Scannapieco and Hegar (1999) identify a range of personal, family, and parenting characteristics that should be examined prior to placement of a child, much as is done with unrelated foster parents. These include the nature of the attachment between the child and the kinship carer and the extent to which a permanent kinship placement will allow for ongoing contact with birth parents, siblings, and others in the child's extended family network.

As kinship care practice is further developed along the lines noted above, it can be further informed through research addressing issues such as the following:

- What are the factors that indicate that kinship care is a desirable option?
- How do the characteristics of the children being placed and their caregivers influence the outcome of kinship care?
- What safeguards should be put in place to ensure that children in kinship care who have been abused by a family member will be protected from further abuse?
- How should legal matters relating to custody and access issues be managed by kinship carers?
- How does placement in kinship care affect the long-term functioning of the child? Does it produce better outcomes for children than nonrelative foster care?
- What should be the roles of the child welfare agency and other service providers in kinship care cases?
- Should kinship care be viewed as a prelude to adoption by the family providing it?
- What is the impact of formal kinship care on birth parents and siblings?

The above questions go to the heart of kinship care and warrant answers that can help guide the actions of practitioners. In addition, kinship care raises a number of issues that need to be resolved, in areas such as licensing and other regulatory procedures, administration, payments to the relatives as foster parents, and relationships among child, birth parents, and kinship families. Although there is much that we need to learn about its application and effectiveness, kinship care is a promising approach to placement of children in need. If provided in a high quality manner with adequate parent supports, it can offer stable placements that maintain family continuity and promote child well-being.

THE REUNIFICATION OF VERY YOUNG CHILDREN FROM FOSTER CARE

Reunification of young children from foster care requires special consideration. The incidence rate for admissions to foster care among young children (ages 0–4) is now twice what it is for children 5–17 years of age. Young children comprise nearly 25% of all entrances into foster care (Goerge, Wulczyn, & Harden, 1994).

Much of the child welfare literature addresses families with older children and explains ways to assist them in the transition back to living with their biological families (e.g., Folaron, 1993). The vulnerability of young children to harm means that safety considerations, and the possible need for placement of a child in foster care, must be given a higher weighting than is generally given for older children.

Although shorter stays of younger children in foster care are apparently consistent with permanency planning goals, they are more likely to be followed by reentry into foster care (Wulczyn, Harden, & Goerge, 1997). Other studies also indicate that children who were infants at exit from foster care (i.e., they entered and left care prior to 1 year of age) were 25% more likely to reenter care than older children (Barth, Needell, Berrick, Albert, & Jonson-Reid, 1995).

About half of all those who reentered within 4 years did so within the 6 months after they had returned home. This suggests that since few postreunification services last longer than 6 months, these reentries were not primarily a result of the ongoing supervision and heightened vigilance of the child welfare workers who oversaw the reunifications. The fact that the majority of children who reenter foster care typically do so after 6 months of being returned home suggests, instead, that they may become gradually reexposed to living conditions below the minimum standard of care for lengthy periods of time. That nearly one in four young children reenter care after reunification is, alone, cause for considerable concern; the actual number of children who are exposed to marginal living conditions is likely to be even higher, given the probability of underidentification and underreporting. Unfortunately, research now tells us little about the circumstances of reentry—that is, how much harm has befallen children who were in foster care prior to their reentry. It is plausible that the threshold of reentry is higher than the threshold of initial entry for children never before in foster care, and that children are coming back into care on the basis of relapsed parental behavior rather than actual harm to the children.

Family Preservation vs. Short-Term Foster Care

The finding of high reentry for very young foster children, particularly those who stay a short time, is vexing. One critique of the child welfare system has been that family reunification programs too often serve families that could have been served with in-home services. That is, if a family's problems can be resolved after only 1 to 3 months of foster care, why were temporary in-home services not provided to bridge the crises instead? On the other hand, the findings cited above suggest that short foster care episodes are often not resolving the crises either.

Another criticism is that foster care episodes, even short ones, may further destabilize families, who might have remained together for a longer period of time had family preservation services been provided instead of foster care. This hypothesis may be tested, in part, with the advancement of family preservation programs.

These programs should help to divert families that do not need foster care and, by so doing, could reduce the number of short foster care episodes. If the foster care entry rate among those who receive family preservation services is lower than the reentry rate for those who have short foster care stays, we would have evidence to suggest that short episodes of foster care are less helpful than family preservation services. Further research would then be needed to confirm this possibility. At this point, we do not know whether in-home service or reunification-focused foster care is ultimately more likely to result in family preservation.

Foster care placements occur because of a child welfare worker's judgment that this is the best possible way to protect a child from harm. Very young children are placed into foster care following fewer child abuse reports than other children (Barth, Needell, Berrick, Albert, & Jonson-Reid, 1995). This suggests that they are brought into foster care with some understanding of their age-based cognitive and physical vulnerability. Yet, their high reentry rate into foster care after returning home suggests that their development vulnerabilities may not be considered as carefully at discharge as at intake.

The quandary is profound. Pressure to return infants and young children home comes from at least two child-centered concerns: (1) concern about multiple placement that may result when the foster care system acts to transition children out of the first, and more expensive, emergency foster care placements, and (2) concern about disrupting the child's relationship to the biological parent(s). Consequently, some children may be reunified too soon, which appears to place them at increased risk and result in excessive reentries. Given the high reentry rates for very young children, the physical dangers of premature reunification seem to outweigh the psychological dangers of multiple placements and prolonged uncertainty. The evidence suggests that final decisions about reunification should be made between 6 and 12 months whenever possible, with full reunification services continued for at least 12 months. Brief foster care spells for children younger than 3 should be discouraged. Also, although in care, an effort should be made to limit a child's placement to one home—ideally one that is committed to becoming an adoptive home if reunification fails after no longer than 6 months.

Perhaps more intensive family reunification services can yield more lasting reunifications. Two recent evaluations have considered the use of intensive services to reunify children from foster care in Illinois (Rzepnicki, Schuerman, & Johnson, 1997) and Utah (Fraser, Walton, Lewis, Pecora, & Walton, 1996). The models and findings are similar. Services were akin to those in family preservation programs, although they were provided for a longer period of time than some family preservation services. Still, they were intended for only 90 days in Utah and about 180 days in Illinois. In Utah, significantly more children returned home if they received intensive services. In both settings, approximately 20% of cases reentered foster care within about 1 year. These results do not suggest that more durable reunifications will result from more intensive reunification services.

Colorado has adopted legislation (HB 94-1178) that enhances reunification services but shortens the review period for young children so that a facilitated, early permanency planning decision can be made. The agency cites as its rationale the "numerous studies establishing that children undergo a critical bonding and attachment process prior to reaching the age of six" (Colorado Revised Statute, 1994, p. 1). In the Colorado demonstration in Jefferson County, the agency will conduct permanency planning hearings at 3 months after the dispositional decree, at which time the court may ask the county to show cause why it should not file a motion to terminate the parent–child legal relationship. A child is to be returned home or placed in a permanent home no later than 12 months after placement (unless the court determines that a permanent placement is not in the best interests of the child at that time).

Postreunification Services

As noted earlier in this chapter, the reunification process needs to be conceptualized as one that extends well beyond the time that a child returns home. Conventional "trial visits" were initially developed in order to integrate the older child back into the home. This involved helping the child gradually sort out the role confusion of transitioning back to the biological family and supporting and supervising the biological family's transition back to the parenting role. For younger children, and families involved with substance abuse and neglect as the primary reasons for removal of their children, these are necessary but not sufficient postplacement services. Additionally, families need continued contact and treatment to identify the reemergence of self-destructive and child endangering behavior patterns.

Reunification of very young children also requires that the social worker or provider of postreunification services be knowledgeable about the developmental status and needs of small children. The practitioner must be comfortable holding the baby, checking the baby for bruises and infections, interviewing the families, and understanding signs of relapse. If young children are involved with early intervention services, the link needs to be made between the intervenor (who would previously have worked with the child and foster parents) and the biological parent. If there have been no early intervention services, assessment for and enrollment in them should be pursued prior to ending reunification services. Additionally, given the high recidivism rate, no child should be returned home without establishing a relationship among the child, family, and outside agencies in order to ensure ongoing support and surveillance.

Another option is to bring biological parents into foster care. In such arrangements, families have the opportunity to reestablish living arrangements with the support and mentoring of foster families, as discussed in Chapter 10. Another innovation that appears to be getting increasing attention is one that involves using the foster family as a respite family during the transition to reunification (see Barth, 1991). All means of connections between the reunified family and supportive services provide children and their families with protection from the calamity of further disruption.

A Longer Vision

Our understanding of the perils of short foster care episodes combined with short postreunification services calls for a longer vision of services. Besharov (1994) argues that brief services are not sufficient for many child welfare families and that we must think long term. He concludes that the greatest barrier to that is not budgetary, but conceptual. New York, among other municipalities, encourages reunification and allows agencies to provide necessary aftercare services without incurring new costs by paying a fixed rate per case (Wulczyn & Zeidman, 1997). Even if the use of a capitated rate is not feasible, local funds, along with new funds available under the Family Preservation and Support Program, could be used to provide postreunification services. We should aim to establish a minimum length of combined out-of-home and in-home aftercare. However, since, each year in the United States as many as 25,000 children are reunified from foster care after stays of less than 6 months, IV-B funds would not be sufficient to extend postplacement services for these families unless funds were available to supplant nearly all other uses of IV-B (i.e., placement preservation). Clearly IV-E funds must also be brought to bear if we are to routinely provide in-home postreunification services. Support for these very needed services could be enabled by allowing Title IV-E funds to pay for case management for up to 1 year after reunification of children younger than 5 years at the time of exit from care. Failing that, states may want to experiment with extended postplacement services under the new IV-E waiver provisions.

Programs that guarantee extended periods of case management have been developed in lean fiscal times and have been shown to be cost effective. In general, a dose–response relationship does exist for services, and longer services are better (Barth, 1993). The current clientele in child welfare is younger and more vulnerable than ever before. Their child protection needs are extensive and so must be the services they receive.

RECURRING ISSUES AND DILEMMAS

In reexamining the area of family reunification, it is necessary to take into account recurring issues and dilemmas in child welfare. In family reunification practice, social workers, attorneys, judges, and others face a major challenge—deciding whether children, who have already been deemed to have been at a risk significant enough to necessitate their placement, *can* return home, and *when*.

This challenge raises a number of issues that must be taken into account in the development of policy, program, and practice in family reunification, although the Adoption and Safe Families Act of 1997 provides some guidelines. For example, the issues include the following:

- What evidence can help us assess the risk of returning children to their families versus the risk of prolonging their stay in out-of-home care?
- What is the minimum level of care and parenting that is adequate for family reunification? What constitutes "good enough" parenting?
- How can we assess the risks of returning children to their families versus the risk of prolonging their stay in out-of-home care?
- Where do we draw the line between providing continuing supports to reunited families and perpetuating their dependence?
- How can we maintain or restore optimism and a belief in the potential of even the most challenging families to do what is best for their children, although also accepting that some parents cannot care for their children?

To answer these and other related questions, *practitioners* as well as researchers need to be involved in outcome evaluation, thus contributing to the dynamic interaction of research and practice for the purpose of enhancing services to children and families. In this regard, Warsh, Pine, and Maluccio (1996) have developed a self-study guide to strengthening family reunification services that incorporates a substantial evaluation component. The guide is designed to help administrators, practitioners, and community representatives in efforts to examine their agency's family reunification policies, programs, and services; assess their strengths and limitations; and plan for required changes. It is an example of an evaluative tool that can be used directly by agencies in the regular course of providing services, so as to contribute to knowledge building as well as program enhancement in the area of family reunification.

CONCLUSION

Family reunification of children from kinship and nonkinship care must occur in a way that protects children's safety and well-being. Increasing the number of children in foster care who are reunited with their families of origin or with relatives will often safely promote their growth and development. The studies reviewed in this chapter highlight a number of implications for policy and practice that can contribute to these purposes, particularly through serving children and parents during the out-of-home placement episode, maintaining connections between children and their parents, and providing supports following reunification or placement in kinship care.

As reflected in this chapter as well as throughout the book, attention to family reunification and kinship care is but one expression of the emphasis in child welfare and related fields on preserving families although also protecting children and maintaining their safety. The unique challenges of preserving families that have been separated through placement, however, require new thinking, informed policy changes, supportive programs, revised practice strategies, systematic attention to developing the competence of family reunification practitioners, collaboration among service providers, and emphasis on hope and compassion.

NOTES

1. Sections of this chapter have been adapted from Warsh, Maluccio, and Pine (1994).
2. See Warsh, Maluccio, and Pine (1994) for detailed discussion of family reunification competencies as well as curriculum modules for teaching them through courses and workshops for child welfare practitioners, foster parents, and other providers.
3. The *Field Guide to Child Welfare* (Rykus & Hughes, 1998) consists of four volumes on "Foundations of Child Protective Services," "Case Planning and Family-Centered Casework," "Child Development and Child Welfare," and "Placement and Permanence." It is designed for competency-based in-service training for child welfare practitioners.
4. For British studies on the outcome of reunification services, see Bullock, Gooch, and Little (1998), Hill and Aldgate (1996), and Pinkerton (1994).
5. For further studies on the use and outcome of kinship care, see Barth, Courtney, Needell, and Jonson-Reid (1994), Testa (1997), and Wulczyn and Goerge (1992).

FOR FURTHER INFORMATION

Bonecutter, F.J., & Gleeson, J.P. (1997). *Achieving permanency for children in kinship foster care: A training manual.* Chicago: University of Illinois at Chicago, Jane Addams College of Social Work. A series of training modules and videotapes designed for child welfare caseworkers. The manual is comprised of six units covering formal and informal kinship care; its sociocultural contexts; the impact of substance abuse on family systems; convening the kinship network; decision making and empowering families; and supporting permanent plans. The tapes portray casework interviews with a family.

Child Welfare League of America (1994). *Kinship care: A natural bridge.* Washington, DC: Author. Based on recommendations of the Child Welfare League of America's North American Kinship Care Policy and Practice Committee, this report provides a framework for kinship care policy and practice, including steps to further advance kinship care as a child welfare service through legislation and research.

Crumbley, J., & Little, R.L. (Eds.) (1997). *Relatives raising children—An overview of kinship care.* Washington, DC: CWLA Press. The authors describe social work practice in kinship care, with emphasis on clinical issues, assessment, intervention, and case management. They also consider dimensions of race and culture, examine issues of legal relationships, and offer recommendations for policy and practice.

Hegar, R.L., & Scannapieco, M. (Eds.) (1999). *Kinship foster care—Policy, practice, and research.* New York: Oxford University Press. A comprehensive analysis of kinship care, by researchers, policy advocates, and practitioners from child welfare and related fields. Particularly informative is a section with reports of research on kinship care. In addition, the editors thoughtfully define kinship care and place it in context "as the most recent of the paradigm shifts in child placement practice that have been necessitated by societal and demographic trends, as well as directed by changing professional beliefs and norms" (p. 11).

Jackson, S., Mathews, J., & Zuskin, R. (1998). *Supporting the kinship triad—A training curriculum.* Washington, DC: CWLA Press. A five-day curriculum for training child welfare workers for working with the kinship triad: child, parent, and caregiver.

Palmer, S.E. (1995). *Maintaining family ties—Inclusive practice in foster care.* Washington, DC: Child Welfare League of America. Building on an intensive study of social workers in two Canadian child protection agencies, the author delineates practice principles for helping children in foster care and their parents maintain their connections and cope with the impact of separation.

Warsh, R., Maluccio, A.N., & Pine, B.A. (1994). *Family reunification—A sourcebook.* Washington, DC: Child Welfare League of America. Contains curriculum modules, handouts, and a bibliography aimed at training social workers, foster parents, and other providers working with families and children toward reunification from foster care. Major topics include a conceptual framework for reunification practice, family reunification competencies for social workers, differing perspectives on family reunification, developing policies and programs, and parent–child visiting.

Warsh, R., Pine, B.A., & Maluccio, A. N. (1996). *Reconnecting families—A guide to strengthening family reunification services.* Washington, DC: CWLA Press. A step-by-step guide showing administrators how to set up work teams of staff members from all levels of their agency so as to carry out a comprehensive self-assessment of their family reunification policies, programs, and resources. The teams engage in activities designed to identify system strengths, recommend improvements, and implement action plans for change.

Wilson, D.B., & Chipungu, S.S. (Eds.) (1996). Kinship care. Special Issue of *Child Welfare, 75*(5) (September–October 1996). A collection of essays on kinship care policy, research, practice, and advocacy. The authors help clarify the role of kinship care as a child welfare service and consider strategies for maximizing the use of kinship care as a positive resource in permanency planning for children.

12

Adoption

INTRODUCTION

Children deserve willing and able families to love and protect them. Adoption is a legally sanctioned procedure for ensuring that an adequate family life is provided when the family into which a child is born is unable or unwilling to parent. Adoption is not only a program for children. In its intent, adoption benefits are equally shared by adopting parents. Adoption creates or expands new families by bestowing the rights and responsibilities of parenting from children's birth parents to new parents. Birth parents who place their child with a new family also benefit from the relief from parenting responsibilities, which they or others judge themselves unprepared to assume, and from the hope for a better life for their child. At its best then, adoption serves the three members of the "adoption triangle," the child, the adoptive parents, and the birth parents.

But adoption is more than an interpersonal or familiar triangle. Adoption is a social institution that reflects the status, interests, and moral views of nearly every social entity. Social communities are a fourth point in the adoption configuration. The future of our larger society, and the communities that comprise it, depends on our children. Our children's future requires an adequate family life. Our society and many communities within it—particularly Native-American tribes, ethnic communities, other self-defined communities (e.g., foster parents, grandparents, and gay and lesbian persons), and the domain of child welfare service providers— also have an interest in adoptions. For Native-American children, the delivery of adoption services has been powerfully influenced by tribes and also has an important influence on them. In the case of other service providers and communities of color the presumption of a special interest in adoption continues to evolve.

Types of Adoption

Adoption is possible today through a variety of means and involves different types of agencies and auspices, each with unique procedures and requirements. Although this chapter emphasizes older child adoptions, an overview of other variants of adoptions places older child and special needs adoptions in the larger sphere of child and family services. Generally, adoptions are grouped into four categories: *independent, intercountry, stepparent, and relinquishment or agency.* Independent adoptions occur when parents place children directly with adoptive families of their choice without an agency serving as an intermediary. Independent adoptions held steady at about 20% of all adoptions in the 1960s and 1970s (Meezan, Katz, & Russo, 1978) but appear to have increased recently as more states have come to allow adoptions without agencies. (A few states still require agency involvement and outlaw independent adoptions.) Stepparent adoptions refer to the adoption of the children of one's spouse. Stepparent adoptions differ from most other adoptions, and are most like foster child adoptions, by involving the adoption of a child already in the home. In most states, stepparent adoptions are the most numerous form, comprising about 40% of all adoptions (Flango & Flango, 1995).

Nationally, about 53,000 children are adopted by relatives or stepparents and another 25,000 children are adopted independent of agencies each year. Another 50,000 U.S.-born children are adopted through agencies. Intercountry adoptions involve the adoption of foreign-born children by adoptive families. Nationally, almost 19,000 foreign-born children were adopted in the United States in 1997 (Immigration and Naturalization Services, 1998). This is the firmest number in an area in which few national data are available.

Relinquishment or agency adoptions are those that follow the voluntary or involuntary legal severance of parental rights to the child and are overseen by a public or private agency. The Adoption Assistance and Child Welfare Act of 1980 endeavored to increase the number of relinquishment adoptions, and has succeeded in doing so. Rosemary Avery's (1998) study of the foster care and adoption dynamics in New York state shows that the median length of stay in foster care prior to adoption has been halved since 1980, indicating that past child welfare and adoption reforms have had a major impact on the likelihood of adoption. Overall, relinquishment adoptions of children in foster care were estimated to have grown from 25,693 in 1995 to 31,030 in 1997 (see Table 12.1). An informal survey of states indicates that more than 36,000 children were adopted in 1998 (Kroll, 1999). Relinquishment adoptions do seem to be increasing, but adoption statistics, particularly at the national level, still require many caveats and inspire little confidence (www.acf.dhhs.gov/programs/cb/stats/afcars). The new Adoption and Foster Care Analysis and Reporting System is the first federally mandated data system and will improve our counts each year. That being so, this chapter will often rely on state statistics.

Adoptions can also be classified across types as either infant or older child adoptions. Infant adoptions (whether private, independent, or intercountry) are popular but somewhat controversial programs because they are sometimes perceived as principally for parents rather than for children and often provide well-to-do parents with the babies of disadvantaged mothers. Infant adoptions are perceived as requiring little social commitment on the part of parents; yet adoptive parents do provide a vital service to newborns and their parents by freeing them from a situation viewed as untenable.

Table 12.1. Number of Adoptions by State (1995–1997)

State	1995 Adoptions			1996 Adoptions			1997 Adoptions		
	IV-E	Not	Total	IV-E	Not	Total	IV-E	Not	Total
Alabama	35	93	128	50	103	153	38	98	136
Alaska	68	35	103	94	18	112	93	16	109
Arizona	161	54	215	311	72	383	160	114	474
Arkansas	61	23	84	165	20	185	140	6	146
California	2,157	937	3,094	2,617	536	3,153	2,468	1,146	3,614
Colorado	286	52	338	378	76	454	266	192	458
Connecticut	164	34	198	121	25	146	230	48	278
Delaware	23	15	38	28	18	46	19	14	33
District of Columbia	18	68	86	32	81	113	60	72	132
Florida	363	541	904	424	640	1,064	406	586	992
Georgia	172	211	383	263	274	537	306	252	558
Hawaii	31	11	42	47	17	64	110	40	150
Idaho	38	8	46	30	10	40	41	6	47
Illinois	1,647	112	1,759	1,148	998	2,146	1,615	1,080	2,695
Indiana	333	187	520	248	125	373	385	207	592
Iowa	179	48	227	301	82	383	414	26	440
Kansas	122	211	333	222	70	292	302	119	421
Kentucky	139	58	197	152	62	214	152	70	222
Louisiana	281	11	292	309	12	321	298	12	310
Maine	76	9	85	128	16	144	85	11	96
Maryland	112	212	324	236	177	413	148	142	290
Massachusetts	535	538	1,073	612	501	1,113	657	504	1,161
Michigan	1,463	254	1,717	1,695	255	1,950	1,744	303	2,047
Minnesota	535	117	232	184	55	239	228	74	302
Mississippi	19	90	109	32	69	101	83	48	131
Missouri	417	121	538	421	179	600	408	125	533
Montana	72	32	104	83	15	98	112	31	143
Nebraska	96	112	208	90	78	168	112	68	180
Nevada	98	57	155	86	59	145	97	51	148
New Hampshire	41	10	51	48	11	59	20	4	24
New Jersey	326	290	616	405	273	678	367	203	570
New Mexico	106	35	141	111	37	148	114	38	152
New York	4,295	284	4,579	4,217	373	4,590	4,697	282	4,979
North Carolina	173	116	289	258	159	417	458	236	694
North Dakota	32	10	42	29	12	41	40	17	57
Ohio	1,110	92	1,202	1,151	107	1,258	1,168	232	1,400
Oklahoma	163	63	226	298	73	371	264	154	418
Oregon	325	102	427	356	112	468	325	116	441
Pennsylvania	836	182	1,018	983	144	1,127	1,332	194	1,526
Rhode Island	174	42	216	205	136	341	119	107	226
South Carolina	115	116	231	132	88	220	190	128	318
South Dakota	27	15	42	49	23	72	33	22	55
Tennessee	336	122	458	228	102	330	134	61	195
Texas	443	361	804	412	334	746	676	415	1,091
Utah	130	153	283	87	37	124	174	94	268

(continued)

Table 12.1. (Continued)

State	1995 Adoptions			1996 Adoptions			1997 Adoptions		
	IV-E	Not	Total	IV-E	Not	Total	IV-E	Not	Total
Vermont	53	9	62	79	4	83	68	12	80
Virginia	183	137	320	191	107	298	196	80	276
Washington	397	248	645	361	160	521	518	138	656
West Virgina	50	89	139	71	117	188	119	101	220
Wisconsin	285	75	360	421	90	511	432	98	530
Wyoming	6	4	10	5	15	20	3	13	16
Total	18,887	6,808	25,893	20,604	7,157	27,781	22,829	8,206	31,030

In contrast, older children adoptions—of abused, neglected, or abandoned children who cannot go home—are considered children's programs because the decision to place a child with a family addresses the child's welfare most and because parents' needs are secondary. The Child Welfare League of America's *Standards for Adoption Services* (CWLA, 1998) asserts that adoption is a means of finding families for children, not finding children for families. Yet, this dualistic appraisal of adoptions is somewhat unfortunate and makes it too easy to ignore the needs of the child or infant in independent adoptions, the needs of the parents in older child or agency adoptions, and the needs of consenting parents or abandoned children residing in a range of countries and communities. The future of improved adoption services rests on renewed attention to each program's ability to meet the needs of all parties to the adoption.

Regardless of the type, adoptions follow some general guidelines based on the premises that every child has a right to a family and that the child's needs are paramount. Arising from this fundamental right are other agency principles: that finality of adoption be made as soon as possible (after a sufficient trial of the placement's viability), that every party have options and assistance in weighing these options, that confidentiality be ensured as far as possible, and that agency services be available before and after placement.

A Brief History of Adoption

Moses is the best known adopted child. His placement was not trouble free, but was permanent. The earliest known adoption laws are in the Code of Hammurabi: "If a man takes a child in his name, adopts and raises him as a son, the grownup man may not be demanded back" (cited in Sorosky, Baran, & Pannor, 1978). Informal adoptions are also part of U. S. custom, although children were at one time probably more likely to be indentured than to be adopted. The end of slavery and indentured servitude was followed by the growth of orphanages and the emergence of legal adoption. Children were sometimes purchased and newspaper ads for children were common. At least a few of these adoptions resulted in scandalous abuse of children. Regulations followed that protected the right of birth parents to give or withhold permission for the child's adoption, the right of adopting parents not to have their child reclaimed, and the right of children not to be placed with unsuitable adopting parents. Judges made decisions after meeting the interested parties, but no other investigations occurred (see Table 12.2 for a summary of historical highlights in adoption).

Although some adoptions did not succeed, most did. Zainaldin's (1976) history of the earliest periods of adoption concludes that 70% of the children beginning adoptive placements from 1851 to 1893 were still in their adoptive family as they entered adulthood. The 30% noncompletion rate includes the high infant mortality rates of that era. Placements of infants with strangers had lower completion rates than the more robust placement of children with relatives or friends. A more recent study comparing independent and agency adoptions found few differences in outcomes between them (Meezan et al., 1978).

Individual states first began to legislate and regulate adoption practices in the 1850s (Whitmore, 1876), and by 1929 every state had adoptive statutes. Statutes varied on several accounts, but all reflected concern that adoption promotes the welfare of the child. The statutes allowed children who had been adopted through private arrangements to assume new family homes (and rights of inheritance) without an express act of the state legislature. Concern that the adopted child's welfare could not be adequately protected without the oversight of public agencies arose later, but is most clearly reflected in the report of the Wisconsin Children's Code Commission (cited in Breckenridge, 1934): "Adoption proceedings are, for the adoptable child, next to birth itself, the most important single transaction in his life. It is imperative, therefore, that the child at this time has the benefit of the most thorough and careful work in the procedure that is to determine his whole future. Essential to this is the need that the court shall have for its guidance full and complete facts about the child and the adopting parents. This can be secured only through skillful investigation by completely trained persons."

Regulations requiring social investigations of prospective adoptive parents and trial placement periods in prospective adoptive homes were written between 1923 and 1933 (Heisterman, 1935). A few states also required visits by agents of the state child welfare department. The mandates of the visits were rarely clarified (and the use of visits is still poorly conceptualized today), although most contained some language similar to Wisconsin's: "so the court is satisfied that the home of the petitioner and the child are suited to each other" [Wisconsin General Laws 1932 (Ter. Ed.), C. 210, Sec. 5A].

In the United States, the process of older child adoption dates back at least to Charles Loring Brace (1859). Foster care and adoptions were intertwined in the late nineteenth century. The middle-class leaders of child care agencies expected to save both souls and money by placing poor children in good homes (Clement, 1979, p. 409). Placing agencies were concerned less with the individual, personal

Table 12.2. Chronological History of Adoptions in the United States

Year	Event
1851	Massachusetts becomes first state to pass adoption legislation
1891	Michigan law requires judge's investigation before finalization of adoptions
1909	First White House Conference on Dependent Children resolved that "Children not be deprived of home life, except for urgent and compelling reasons"
1910–1920	Establishment of first private adoption agencies
1917	Minnesota law requires detailed investigation by Department of Public Welfare regarding advisability of permitting the adoption
1929	All 50 states have adoption legislation
1938	Child Welfare League of America publishes first edition of adoption standards
1949	Children's Home Society of North Carolina begins older child adoptions
1950s	First transracial and international adoptions through agencies
1958	Ohio is first state with statewide adoption resource exchange
1964	H. D. Kirk writes *Shared fate: A theory of adoption and mental health,* which highlights key aspects of the adjustment to infant adoptions
1967	Child Welfare League of America establishes Adoption Resource Exchange of North America, first national exchange
1968	The *Detroit Sunday News* begins "A Child Is Waiting" series
1968	New York is first state to enact adoption subsidy legislation
1970	175,000 adoptions in the United States-highest number of adoptions ever (half are nonrelative)
1970	Kadushin's study of older child adoption finds that most adjust well
1972	National Association of Black Social Workers releases a statement that opposes transracial adoptions as "a threat to the preservation of the black family"
1973	Child Welfare League of America Adoption Standards not acceptability of foster parent adoptions
1973	Lutheran Child & Family Services in Illinois begins first fost-adopt program
1975	North America Center on Adoption coordinates the Family Builders Agencies, national network of agencies for special-needs adoptions
1978	PL 95-608, Indian Child Welfare Act of 1978, establishes federal standards for removal of Indian children to protect Indian culture
1978	New York City Department of Social Services Policy Statement on Adoption states that no proof of infertility can be required of adoptive applicants
1979	North Dakota law establishes mechanism by which an adult adopted can contact birth parents through a Registry
1980	Passage of PL 96-272, the Federal Adoption Assistance and Child Welfare Act of 1980
1981	H. D. Kirk writes *Adoptive kinship: A modern institution in need of reform*
1981	43 states gives preferences to foster parents in adoption, 9 by legislation
1984	North America Post-Legal Adoption Committee prepares "Model Statement on Post-Legal Adoption" stressing lifelong services for adoptive families
1987	Michigan legislature outlaws surrogate parent contracts
1991	U. S. Office of Civil Rights finds that adoption decisions made solely on the basis of race violate the civil rights of minority (black) children
1991	National Conference of Commissioners on Uniform State Laws updates 1965 Uniform Adoption Act
1994	OBRA institutes tax deductions for adoptions
1994	Adoption and Foster care Analysis and Reporting System begins implementation
1995	Multi-Ethnic Placement Act
1996	Passage of Inter-Ethnic Adoption Provisions that further limits routine use of race in foster care and adoption decision making
1997	Passage of Adoption and Safe Families Act (PL 105-89)

problems of the children than with the problems they might eventually pose in the larger community. Many children were placed out by agencies for indenture—their birth families gave the child to the agency and relinquished all rights to visit or correspond with the youngster. The most common reason for placement was poverty—not protection from child abuse. Older child adoptions took a back seat to infant adoptions for many years. In 1949, the Children's Home Society began a "new type of child care program in North Carolina to provide ways and means of placing older children in institutions, in family homes for adoption" (Weeks, 1953, p. i). This effort was partly in response to waiting lists to place children in orphanages. Today orphanages are all but closed, and foster and group care are the typical sources of older children awaiting adoption.

MAJOR ADOPTION LEGISLATION

Most adoption law is local to states. This can be grounds for much confusion as was shown in the very high profile "Baby Jessica" case in which a child was placed from Iowa into Michigan in violation of the Iowa state law, but would not be returned by the parents in Michigan until forced to do so by the Supreme Court's ruling. Although there is much interest in improving the efficiency of matching children with homes, this must be done against a backdrop of state laws that vary dramatically. Adoption laws remain inconsistent from one state to another, despite an enormous amount of effort in past decades to achieve greater uniformity in procedures and in substantive laws. This is harmful for people when they are involved in consensual adoptions—that is, people who are not in litigation and who have agreed on what they want to do—because it adds to costs, delays procedures, introduces unanticipated risks, and leaves the status of children in limbo for too long. Some progress has been made—a Uniform Adoption Act (UAA) has been designed by the National Conference of Commissioners on Uniform State Laws to save as a model for state legislature. The UAA has now been implemented—at least in part.

As of late 1998, Vermont has enacted it; much of the UAA has been enacted in Michigan, Oklahoma, Montana, and some sections in North Carolina. A substantial number of states are enacting what may be the most important provision, which limits the amount of time for challenging a final adoption (from between 6 and 12 months, after which *no* challenges are allowed). Some states have enacted provisions that clarify that postadoption contact agreements are allowable (even if not enforceable in court), and that their existence does not provide a basis for challenging the validity of an adoption. Some states have agreed in law that provisions requiring preplacement evaluations (home studies) of prospective parents are required in all cases. Also well adopted are provisions that strengthen the requirements for disclosing medical and social background information and provisions that require the court to pay more attention to needs and welfare of child during the proceedings. Nonetheless, according to Joan Hollinger, who led the effort to draft the Uniform Adoption Act, "the laws from one state to another for both private and public adoptions remain a ridiculous patchwork of inconsistent and often contradictory provisions" (Personal Communication, October 14, 1998).

The Indian Child Welfare Act

The first major piece of national legislation influencing adoption of children in foster care was PL 95-608, the Indian Child Welfare Act (ICWA) of 1978. As discussed in Chapters 1 and 3, the legislation provides legal guidelines to promote the stability and security of Indian tribes and families and to prevent the unwarranted removal by adoption of Indian children from their homes. The passage of the ICWA was fueled by the recognition that as many as 30% of Native-American children were not living in their homes, but were residing in boarding schools, foster homes, or adoptive homes. In South Dakota, for example, 40% of all adoptions between 1967 and 1977 were Indian children whereas they comprised only 7% of the population (Barsh, 1980); in Minnesota in 1972, nearly one in four Indian children were adopted (Fischler, 1980); and in Montana in 1976, the ratio of Indian children to non-Indian children in placement was 13:1. The viability of Native-American tribes that had survived despite disease, war, and poverty was dissipating in the face of the removal of its children. Although tribal Indians represent only about half of all Native Americans, the emphasis of the Act is to protect tribal communities and institutions.

Historically, the rationale for removing Indian children from their homes has, at times, combined ingredients of (1) disdain for or ignorance of Indian childrearing practices, (2) concern about the effects on children of the debilitating poverty and substance abuse in many Indian families, and (3) demonstrable physical and sexual abuse and neglect. Extreme poverty, alcohol abuse, homicide, and suicide rates affect many youth (Bachman, 1991; Sandefur & Leiblur, 1997; Beals et al., 1997; Costello et al., 1997). Child abuse and neglect may be at least as common on Indian reservations as in the general population (Fischler, 1985) and probably more so given the higher rates of substance abuse. If American-Indian children are going to receive adequate protection they need highly effective child welfare services.

Within this broad Act are protections specific to adoption. Most notably, termination of parental rights and responsibilities requires the highest standard of proof: child welfare authorities must show beyond a reasonable doubt that the continued custody of the child by the parent or Indian custodian is likely to result in serious emotional or physical damage to the child. Thus, the court must find with 99.5% certainty that the child will be seriously harmed in the future before the child can be freed for adoption. This very high standard leaves little latitude for overseeing the child's right to be safe.

Section 1915 of the Act also legislates the adoptive placements of Indian children subsequent to the termination of parental rights. Preference is given to a placement with (1) a member of the child's extended family, (2) other members of the Indian child's tribe, or (3) other Indian families. Some Native-American mothers choose to place their children for adoption with non-Indian families off the reservation. If the mothers are tribal members, then they do not control the right to do so; placement of tribal children is governed by the tribe.

More fundamentally, that tribal rights supercede mother's rights has been ICWA's most controversial feature. Bakeis (1996) and others argue that tribal interests should not supercede the interests of each child. Fischler (1980) critiques the Act as follows: "It is unfortunate that the means of greater sovereignty for American Indian adults places American Indian children in jeopardy. By regarding children as the property of parents, families, and tribes, the Indian Child Welfare Act will not protect them adequately. On the wisdom of American Indian adults depends a generation of American Indian children, and no society can afford to waste its children" (p. 348).

In response to Fischler's concerns that the ICWA fails to protect children's rights, Blanchard and Barsh (1980) argue that a child's right to a lifelong cultural affiliation deserves at least as much protection as the right to household permanency. They propose that the choice to protect culture is what tribal child welfare professionals have made explicit in their report of the ICWA. The future of the ICWA should be tied to better funding of Native-American child welfare services and evaluation of the impact of the Act on children.

Congress has considered reforms of the ICWA on several occasions—much of that focus has been on the rights of parents to express their preference for their child if the child is also a tribal member. The ICWA expresses a strong preference that Indian children, including those who have one non-Indian parent, belong in Indian tribes and homes. Placement with a non-Indian family is not barred, but it is discouraged. There are, however, "good cause" and "parental preference" exceptions that allow an agency to place a child for adoption if no suitable Indian adopters are available and that allow the placement choice of parents to prevail over tribal and statutory preferences, respectively.

The courts are divided about whether the preferences apply to Indian children who have never been exposed to Indian society or culture. Congress has considered whether the length of time since a child has resided in an Indian community or the remoteness of the proposed Indian home can be considered, for example, when determining whether good cause exists (Hollinger, 1990).

Research on the extent to which permanency in an adoption has been achieved for Indian children has not been well developed. Plantz et al. (1989) provided the first empirical analysis of the Indian Child Welfare Act, with a survey that focused on implementation of the ICWA and on the foster care dynamics for American-Indian children. They found that under the ICWA—between 1975 and 1986—American-Indian children were placed into foster care at a rate that was 3.6 times higher than that of other children. This may well have been a reduction from the pre-ICWA years when American-Indian children were being placed into foster care at rates in some states that were estimated to be 5 to 18 times as high as the general population of children (Byler, 1977).

Plantz et al. also found that the number of children in substitute care rose by 25% even though the number of non-Indian children had not grown during that time, although there was no clear explanation for this effect. It may be related to a lack of exits from foster care for Indian children. If entry rates are going down for Indian children, but relatively more Indian children are remaining in care, this may be due to longer lengths of stay, which could be, partially, related to fewer exits by adoption for American-Indian children than other children.

Plantz et al. (1989) also determined that more American-Indian children were being cared for by American-Indian caregivers. They conclude that "Indian children's rights to their tribal and cultural heritage are being protected better than in the past and the role of Indian parents and tribes in protecting those rights has been strengthened" (p. 28).

MacEachron and her colleagues (1996) drew on four different data sources before concluding that the adoption rate of American-Indian children had dropped by an estimated 93% between 1978 and 1986: "all state adoption rates had declined to near zero, with the exception of Alaska, whose rate had actually increased" (p. 457). They judged this to be a sign of the effective implementation of the ICWA. The discrepancy between adoptions rates for American-Indian and non-Indian children had also decreased because as of 1986 they concluded that 2.64% of non-Indian children in foster care would be adopted as compared to 2.9% of Indian children in foster care. They infer that ICWA implementation has been successful because both the "foster care and adoption rates for Indian children decrease substantially since the implementation of the ICWA" (p. 458).

This conclusion that fewer adoptions is a *good* result highlights a new challenge facing the Indian Child Welfare Act—the need to better understand how to integrate its mission and practices with that of the Adoption and Safe Families Act. Longitudinal research on the adoption of American-Indian children in foster care indicates that young children have relatively low rates of adoption (Barth, Webster, & Lee, 1998). Because the majority of them are served in state—rather than tribal—child welfare systems they are clearly covered by the expectation that they will have parental rights terminated if they have been in foster care more than 15 of the last 22 months. Yet, the parental right termination standard is higher for American-Indian children, which poses a challenge. Also, although ICWA clearly states that preference is to be given to placing children with kin, within the tribe, and with other American-Indian families, there are no clear guidelines or timelines about when American-Indian children should be identified as available for adoption by non-American-Indian families. Much of this uncertainty is likely to be addressed in future legislation.

The Adoption Assistance and Child Welfare Act of 1980

More encompassing national adoption legislation was passed in 1980 as the Adoption Assistance and Child Welfare Act (PL 96-272). Although this legislation has since been replaced by the Adoption and Safe Families Act (as discussed in Chapter 3), some attention to its adoption-related principles is well worthwhile. This Act mandates that child welfare agencies implement preplacement preventive services, programs to reunify placed children with their biological families, subsidized adoption, and periodic case reviews of children in care. The legislation, focused on permanency planning, was in part a reaction to indications that children were spending unnecessarily long periods in foster care, with no real plan for reunification with their families. The legislation was also a legal assertion of the child's right to a permanent home—a condition that child welfare professionals have long agreed is important to a child's development (Slingerland, 1916). In describing the rationale for the new legislation, Senator Alan Cranston explained that "Our efforts from now on will be to reduce the foster care load by supporting programs that promise to restore children to their families, that prevent unnecessary foster care, or that promise the opportunity for adoption" (*Congressional Record*—Senate, June 13, 1980).

The impact of permanency planning legislation since 1980 has been an increase in the number of children legally freed from their parents for adoption (U.S. Department of Health and Human Services, 1984). In 1982 there were over 50,000 children legally free from their parents and waiting to be placed (Maza, 1983). Approximately 17,000 of these children had the specific permanent plan of adoption (Maximus, 1984). That year, approximately 14,400 older children were placed for adoption in the United States (Maximus, 1984). (Although impressive by conventional standards, 71% of children available for adoption at the time of the survey had not been placed.) The placement of older children for adoption has greatly changed the historic purpose and scope of adoptions.

When adoptions were focused on finding infants for infertile couples, healthy babies were prime candidates for adoptions, and older children or children with special needs were not considered adoptable. The increase in older children moving out of foster care over the past decade has changed this practice, and more and more older children are considered adoptable. Although varying by state, about 10% of children who enter foster care will be adopted within 7 years of entry into care (Wulczyn, Harden, & Goerge, 1997). This varies sharply by state as a result of the proportion of children in kinship care (kin adopt less) and by age—children placed into nonkinship foster care as infants in California have about a one-in-three chance of being adopted by the time they are 6 years old (Barth, 1997a).

Adoption Subsidy Policy and Issues

PL 96-272 encouraged states to develop adoption subsidy programs for special-needs adoption and reimburses the state for 50% of the subsidy costs. Subsidies were originally initiated in the states to help foster families meet the financial necessities of adoption and not to be disadvantaged by the decision to adopt a child in their care. Federal reforms to make subsidies available to families that adopt special-needs children were passed over the objections that sentiment should be the only consideration in adoption. Adoptions of older children with special needs are a large proportion of all publicly supervised adoptions and are the focus of federal law. State regulations generally identify special-needs adoptions as involving the adoption of children aged 3 or over, minority children, or sibling groups of three or more. The North American Center on Adoption offers a more limited definition of special-needs children: black children over 10, white children over 13, emotionally disturbed or mentally retarded children of all ages, physically handicapped children, or sibling groups of three or more (Shyne & Schroeder, 1978). These are also called "hard-to-place" children or "children who wait," due to their typical placement history. The notion is that subsidies can facilitate the adoption of special-needs foster children and promote new adoptions. Title IV-E adoption assistance is now provided in all states when the child and family are eligible.

Subsidies are meant to encourage families to adopt. Families that adopt special-needs children are entitled to subsidies without a means test (although their financial condition can be taken into account). The law insists, however, that "a reasonable but unsuccessful search has been made to place the child with appropriate adoptive parents without providing adoption assistance" [42 USC 673 (c) (2) (B)]. Agencies, concerned about making speedy and culturally consistent placements, and at least generally aware of the value of adoption, do not always pay this requirement of reasonable search great heed. Yet this requirement can work against continuity for children when foster parents of small children will adopt only with a subsidy and other families will adopt without one. Ironically, PL 96-272, which stipulates that adoption is preferable to long-term foster care, requires that foster parents who decide to adopt can receive absolutely no more money that the foster care rate and subsidies are almost always less than the foster care rate. Federal policy also refuses to pay any portion of a temporary group care placement that a parent might need to help preserve their adoption. The best that can usually be done is to get an increase in the subsidy to help pay for some of the placement costs. Some states have committed to pay for time-limited group care placements in nonprofit residential treatment or group care programs. Given the history of state leadership in developing adoption policy, this is a consideration that the federal government might eventually examine.

Unfortunately, the attitude that a placement without a subsidy is better than a placement with a subsidy is still held by some adoption workers, as well as by some local and state policy setters. Some social workers state that they try to wean families off subsidies within a few years. This notion that the award depends on families' means rather than on the child's needs in the context of families' resources remains even though the federal law states otherwise. Some states have begun to use fixed schedules of payment levels based principally on family income. This fails to consider the expenses that are associated with adequate care of children with different needs. Further, this ignores the point that the subsidies are designed to minimize disincentives to adoption and to help children tap the vast pools of emotional and material resources that adoptive families provide across life's very long haul.

When they were conceived more than a decade ago, adoption subsidies were a risky and refreshing departure. The results have since refuted concerns that adoption would become a racket and that subsidies would open the door for the entrance of deceitful and disturbed families. Hage (1987) adopted a three-sibling group of children (aged 4, 6, and 8 years old) with the aid of subsidies, after previously adopting four children. She writes:

> One thing is certain, without the prospects of a subsidy, we could not have considered adopting the last time. We would have had to change the standard of living of the children we already had in order to meet the expenses of three more children with problems. And we simply would not have done it. We would have lived comfortably with six children instead of extending our resources to cover nine. In all likelihood, Jamie, Jesse, and Amber would have been split up. (pp. 18–19)

As Waterman (1987) documents in the *Renewal Factor,* when leaders anticipate and articulate responsible behavior on the part of employees, the employees typically live up to that respect. Our years of distrust of adoptive families should become part of our past. Although the subsidy arrangement is imperfect, income requirements no longer narrow the adoptive parent pool to upper and middle-class parents. The availability of subsidies illustrates the recognition that low income should not be a barrier to adoption. More than half the families adopting older children receive subsidies. Subsidies continue to be paid to families even when families move across state or national boundaries. The concern among legislators and administrators about "paying people to be parents" has not been vanquished, however, and federal and state lawmakers continue to pursue ways to curtail subsidies.

Nationwide, adoption assistance funding rose from $442,000 in 1981 to $300 million in 1995 (aspe.hhs.gov./96gb/intro.htm). Because of federal guidelines, state eligibility requirements for subsidies show little variation in the amount paid to families. A majority of states have, however, expanded their adoption subsidy programs to include certain children not eligible for federal reimbursement.

The set of standards used to decide the eligibility, duration, and size of subsidies is a question open to many interpretations. One mother had to pursue a fair hearing aggressively to get a subsidy for her special-needs adoption, at which time she was granted a subsidy. The following year her subsidy was reviewed and terminated by an agency administrator. Agencies should be sure that administrators, supervisors, and line workers all support the rights of families to receive subsidies. Further, policies should be examined to ensure that the state and local shares of adoption subsidies are shouldered primarily at the state level so local entities are not penalized by moving children from long-term foster care to adoption.

Federal law requires a formal written agreement that constitutes a binding contract between the state and the adoptive parents that ensures the continuity of the subsidy. The agreement must specify the amount of the assistance payment, the types of services or other assistance to be provided to the child and the family, and the duration of the agreement. The agreement must also stipulate that the subsidy will remain in effect if the family leaves the state or country. Other significant provisions of the agreement should include procedures for recertification of eligibility, the bases and mechanism for future benefit adjustments, and the parents' right to a fair hearing in the event of disagreement with the agency about the subsidy. All adoptive parents should have a copy of such an agreement in their possession (Segal, 1985).

With the trend in adoptions shifting from infants to older, special-needs children has come a shift in the philosophy and purpose of adoption. The recent legislation toward permanency planning recognizes the importance of permanent homes for children. Practitioners are recognizing that no child who needs a permanent home should be considered unadoptable because of his or her problems (Cole, 1984). Efforts to place older children for adoption are very gradually becoming more mainstream with evolving adjustments in all aspects of the adoption process. Still, the chances of an older child getting adopted are quite slim.

The Multi-Ethnic Placement Act and the Inter-Ethnic
Adoption Provisions

To address perceived discrimination in adoptive and foster placement, the Multi-Ethnic Placement Act (MEPA) prohibited federally funded agencies and entities from, on the one hand, denying anyone the opportunity to become a foster or adoptive *parent* due to the race of either the parent or the child, and, on the other hand, denying a *child* the opportunity to be placed due to the race of either the parent or child. In addition, the legislation required states to develop plans for the diligent recruitment of potential foster and adoptive families that reflect the diversity of children in need of placement. MEPA did not prohibit *all* consideration of race, however; it merely prohibited "*categorically*" denying placement "*solely*" on this basis. The race of the child, and the capacity of prospective adoptive or foster parents to meet the needs of a child of this background, could be considered along with other factors in determining the child's best interest.

Primarily to address the concerns of civil rights advocates that race was not an appropriate tool for policymaking unless there was clear evidence of discrimination against minority groups, MEPA was revised 2 years later by the Inter-Ethnic Adoption Provisions (IAP), which limited further the extent to which race could be considered in adoptive and foster placements. The new law did this by deleting just a few words from the language in MEPA. Now, the prohibition is on federally funded agencies and entities denying placement "on the basis of race" rather than "*solely* on the basis of race." In addition, agencies may not "deny to any person the opportunity to become an adoptive or foster parent," whereas under MEPA they could not "*categorically*" deny such an opportunity. MEPA's requirements regarding the recruitment of foster and adoptive families remained unchanged.

Precisely how MEPA and the Inter-Ethnic Adoption Provisions will affect placement practices is unclear, but the general rule favoring inracial placement is no longer legal. Now, a decision to place a child inracially must be specifically justified with regard to the needs of the particular child and the parents' capacity to meet the child's needs. Thus, in each individual case, the child welfare worker must begin with no presumptions. The most immediate impact of the new laws, then, is likely to be on the *process* of making and implementing a decision. Whether the number of transracial adoptions will increase is difficult to predict.

The recruitment provisions could have a substantial impact on the number of inracial foster and adoptive placements, however, Congress did not appropriate additional funds for recruitment efforts, instead requiring states to be proactive and use existing resources. Second, the law's antidiscrimination provisions may interfere with targeted recruitment efforts in communities of color.

Adoption 2002

In response to an announcement by President Clinton in late 1996, the U.S. DHHS created a document describing a blueprint for the Adoption 2002 initiative that is intended to double the number of adoptions and guardianships by 2002. The principles of the initiative underscore the federal government's commitment that every child deserves a safe, permanent family; that the child's health and safety should be paramount considerations in all placement and permanency planning decisions; and that foster care is a temporary situation—it is not an appropriate place for children to grow up. Major provisions of the legislative package that followed included clarification in Adoption and Safe Families Act, ensuring that children are entitled to reasonable efforts to adoption (just as they are to reunification) when a child cannot safely go home; providing states with fiscal incentives for increasing their adoptions (by providing $20,000,000 a year in incentives for increasing adoptions over 1996 baselines); and aggressively implementing MEPA, as amended by the Inter-Ethnic Adoption Provisions of the Small Business Job Protection Act (discussed above).

Adoption and Safe Families Act (PL 105-89)

As described in Chapter 2, the Adoption and Safe Families Act (ASFA) of 1997 represents a substantial retooling of the Adoption and Child Welfare Act of 1980. The desire to achieve some of the goals highlighted in Adoption 2002 was central to the development of ASFA. The adoption provisions of ASFA include (1) permission to use concurrent planning—that is engaging in reunification and adoption planning at the same time for children who are unlikely to go home—as a legitimate tool and not as an infringement of reasonable efforts provisions of PL 96-272; (2) acknowledging that children are entitled to "reasonable efforts" to an adoptive home if they cannot go home; and (3) provisions that agencies must be willing to allow their children to participate in the interstate compact—that is, that if a child can be adopted into another county or state more expeditiously than in their home county or state then cooperation is required.

Safe and Stable Families Act (PL 105-89)

One of the great germane opportunities of the Safe and Stable Families Act (SSFA) is that it will help to develop the infrastructure needed to support postadoptive services. With these funds supplemented by some of the incentives available to states from Adoption 2002, postadoptive services may finally have a dependable funding base, at least until 2002 when SSFA and Adoption 2002 expire. Up-to-date information about the emergence of regulations related to ACF adoption policies can be found at www.acf.dhhs.gov/programs/cb/policy.

CURRENT ADOPTION PRACTICE

Adoption is changing as rapidly as any element of child welfare services. Although practices vary broadly, practitioners struggle to decide how to keep pace with emerging trends in a way that fits their agency and is best for children, families, and the community.

The Paths to Adoption

Three paths lead to adoption of older children (see Table 12.3). Birth parents decide that they are unwilling or unable to parent—or the court determines that they are unable to care for their children. This decision can be made before the child's entry into the child welfare system (e.g., when the child is relinquished or abandoned), soon after the child enters it (e.g., when the parent has brutally battered or raped a small child), or following a maximum of 15 months of failed efforts to reunify the child with the parents. In many states the decision that the child should

Exhibit 12.3. The Path to Older Child Adoption

Steps	Adoptive Parent(s)	Child	Birth Parent(s)
1	Parent contacts agency requesting information or home study	Child enters child welfare system via abuse, abandonment, or relinquishment	Parent is determined to be neglecting or abusing child
2	Group or individual home study begins	Child is determined unsafe at home and enters foster care	Parent should receive all reasonable efforts to prevent placement
3	Parents and agency identify type of child most suited to family		Parent is determined to be likely to continue to endanger child or child is removed to enable correction of health or behavior
4	Agency completes home study and approves family		Parents should be offered as opportunity to participate in reunification services, e.g., drug treatment, public housing provision, parent training
5	Parents review		
6	Available children presented by social worker		
7	Visits with child begin	Child is determined unlikely to return home and enters foster/ adoption home	
8		Child is determined to be unable to return home	Parent's progress in rehabilitating home and self is reviewed and found inadequate with no allowance for additional time
9		Child is transferred to the adoption program	Birth parent's rights are terminated by law
10		Adoption placement begins with supervision	
11		Adoption is legalized	

be placed into a preadoptive home occurs in juvenile court and well before the parents' rights are finally terminated in superior court. This step is not taken lightly. Many judges often find the responsibilities of terminating parental rights and responsibilities to be onerous, some even comparing these cases to capital punishment cases. Some social service departments are reluctant to meet the legal and time-eating requirements of documenting the search for absent parents and of appeals by disgruntled birth parents. For these reasons, only the most egregious instances of parental failure to care for their child were ever used to terminate parental rights in the years before PL 96-272. Since then, the rate of parental right terminations has increased and is likely to increase again under ASFA because reunification is no longer expected in all cases.

The older child who is adopted is increasingly likely to be adopted by his or her foster parent. Most often the child is placed with a family interested in adopting as soon as a decision is reached in juvenile court that the child is likely to be freed for adoption—that is, he or she will not go home or to relatives who will become the child's guardian. Such fost-adopt placements now comprise roughly two-thirds of older child adoptions. Children in such a program are buffered from the personal tumult that arises during reunification efforts and parental rights terminations, since their living situation does not change. Perhaps, most important, they are already in adoptive placements when their parents' rights are finally terminated and do not have to look for a new home at an older age. Given that the likelihood of getting and staying adopted is strongly related to a younger age, this is a critical advantage of fost-adopt or concurrent planning placements. These placements have also been known as "risk" placements (Lee & Hull, 1983), however, because some children are reunified with birth parents and the adoptions never occur. In a celebrated case in Chicago, a child in fost-adopt status with an alderman and an appellate court judge was returned home despite their efforts because the mother had completed drug treatment and maintained her involvement in therapy and work. ("Judge sides with woman in heated Chicago foster family fight," November 4, 1998; Associated Press.)

Children who are adopted by parents who are not their foster parents or relatives are likely to be older and the adoptions are somewhat more likely to break down (Barth & Berry, 1988). Many of them are adopted out of group or residential care, from previous adoptions that disrupted, or from foster homes that decide not to adopt the child. Many of these children have remained in foster care for a considerable amount of time because they entered care before the time limits of permanency planning. Since those limits were instituted, the numbers of children who live with foster parents for a long time and are then placed for adoption have dropped markedly.

Adoptive parents also come to adoptions from many different experiences. According to Nelson (1985), one-fourth of adoptive parents fit the archetype of couples who did not want to wait for a healthy infant and decided to adopt a special-needs child, and more than one-third mentioned their infertility as a reason for adopting. This validates Barth and Berry's (1988) findings, which also determined that older children were sought because they fit in better with the family in more than half of the adoptions, and almost two-thirds of adoptive families had other children in the home. Increasingly, parents will enter the world of adoption through the foster parent role. Recruitment and preparation for foster parenting and adoption are often combined. Persons who expressly want to become foster parents are told that they may change their minds and become adoptive parents and should know about that possibility. Persons who expressly want to adopt (and they usually outnumber those who want to provide only foster care) are oriented to the social service system and the legal and moral responsibility to facilitate the child's reunification with the birth family when this is the case goal.

Screening of families for older child adoption results from agency and family initiatives. Historically, most agencies have refused to allow some parents to be studied as potential adoptive parents because they judge that some element of their lives makes them unsuitable. For many years, race, religion, and parental age were used in such a way. Today, such arbitrary preconditions are less often applied but they do remain—sexual orientation is still used as a screen by some agencies. For example, after or during orientation, some parents will decide—after self-examination and a better understanding of the types of children available—that older child adoption is not for them. Some parents will be counseled away from adopting by the agency. The grounds for agency actions to exclude a potential adoptive family may be shaky and controversial. What makes a good adoptive parent is a question that every social worker answers differently, and there is no single, certain answer. (This question cannot be answered any more easily for birth parents.) It is the fit between the parent, the child, and the services that is most critical to the success of an adoption. Single parents have better than average success with children adopted when they are older than 9 (Barth & Berry, 1988); parents with very high expectations may be less likely to succeed with older children who have learning problems (Barth & Berry, 1988; Boyne, Denby, Kettenring, & Wheeler, 1984); middle-class families with developmentally disabled children already in the home are considered more desirable as adoptive families for other such children (Coyne & Brown, 1986). There are few outright reasons to disqualify an adoptive parent applicant. On the other hand, few parents are ready for the challenges of adopting without considerable preparation and postplacement services. If services are not provided, a child has many difficult characteristics, and the parents' resources are overloaded, a problem is likely to occur (Zwimpfer, 1983).

Illegal Adoption

Illegal or black market adoptions involve purchasing a child from a third-party seller (that is, not the child's parent). Such adoptions are illegal across the globe; nor can babies be legally bought from their mothers (although surrogate parenting is still legal in most states). Pregnant women cannot be paid to relinquish their children (although the health care and lodging of pregnant women can be provided by adoptive parents-to-be). The community and professional consensus is that such efforts to obtain children by making outright payments compromise the mother's integrity and endanger the child's well-being. No direct evidence about the outcomes of such practices for children or parents is convincingly in support of or opposition to this consensus. Legal decisions that some forms of reimbursement are illegal and other forms of reimbursement are legal are value driven, and are based on the concerns of the community as translated by the political process.

Information Sharing with Adoptive Parents
and Wrongful Adoption

Social workers must provide adopting parents with all available information about the child. Because of the inevitable coordination problems, much valuable information that is gathered on each of the parties is not told to the others. This inefficiency is not necessary and could be redressed by rethinking the type of information that is collected and how it is summarized and transmitted to the families. Worse, some social workers have withheld information to increase the likelihood of adoption. A better approach is to increase information and preparation.

The strong confirmation by researchers of the inadequacy and importance of information sharing calls for prompt action (Nelson, 1985; Barth, 1988). One family adopted a boy with a history of sexual assaults who molested their other boy with Down's syndrome (also adopted). Parents have argued that social workers who knowingly deny available information to an adoptive applicant should be suspended from their job and reviewed for dismissal. We share their sentiment although not their policy recommendation. (We would allow agency review and employee discipline policies to govern the consequences.) Families are suing to show their outrage.

Agencies can prepare an information-sharing checklist (see Table 12.4) for use by social workers and adoptive parents. The checklist could be included in every case record and would allow each party to provide and initial that they have received information about a given child. Information that is not available can be duly noted. This should reduce the confusion about whether information was known but not shared or was not available. Use of a simple device such as this may lead to better placements and lower family stress in a way that is now followed by disruptions.

A few families have been so unhappy with the result of their adoptions that they have sued the agency that placed the child for adoption. These suits are (1) extremely unlikely events; (2) they can be prevented in almost all cases with additional attention to a few best practices (see Table 12.5); (3) they can be quite demoralizing to agencies and workers; and (4) they do not need to prevent any child

Table 12.4. Information Checklist

Child's First Name_____   Case ID
Adoptive Applicant_____   Social Worker

Social worker initials column A or B to indicate the availability of information and parent(s) initial column C to indicate that you did discuss or receive a written report on the following:

	(A) Not Available	(B) Available	(C) Provided
Child History			
Characteristics of birth family	_____	_____	_____
History of physical abuse	_____	_____	_____
History of sexual abuse	_____	_____	_____
History of neglect	_____	_____	_____
Child Problems			
Physical or medical disability	_____	_____	_____
Developmental disability	_____	_____	_____
Learning disability	_____	_____	_____
Emotional or behavioral problems	_____	_____	_____
Subsidy			
Eligibility			_____
Amount			_____
Duration			_____
Other			
Availability of postplacement services			_____
Legalization			_____
Postlegalization services			_____
Risk of disruption			_____
Laws regarding set aside			_____
Discuss disruption			_____

Worker: Please describe plans to obtain additional information on items initiated as not available:

_____

_____

_____

_____

Source: Barth and Berry (1988). Reprinted with permission.

from being adopted. In the past 20 years, nearly 400,000 adoptions of former foster children have occurred. In Blair's (1992) review, only 17 cases were known to be pending in five major states and 6 appellate cases were pending.

Assuming that the addition of cases from other states would double the number of cases, there were still about 1 wrongful adoption case for every 10,000 adop-

Table 12.5. Steps to Avoid Liability

Convey the information that is known, fully, accurately, and with specific attention to the family that is hearing the information
Get good information from the biological parents including medical questionnaires, and interviews (which should be checked against each other)
Be forthright about information that is not known and the limitations of the process of collecting information (particularly as the birth mother may be the sole source of background information)
Children should receive medical examination prior to placement (or at least be given the opportunity to do so)

Source: Adapted from Freundlich, M., & Peterson, L. (1998). *Wrongful adoption: Law, policy, and practice.* Washington, DC: Child Welfare League of America.

tions. Since an adoption worker is involved in about 10 adoptions per year, it will take 1,000 years of adoption practice before a typical adoption worker had a wrongful adoption case.

Most of the wrongful adoption cases were for children who were adopted when the standard was not to present full information to adoptive parents. Indeed, the thinking then was that adoption is so successful that the important thing was to get a child into an adoptive home and then the mood of adoption would take over and any sins committed in getting that child into the home would be absolved by the bliss of the adoptive relationship. We now know better. Adoption may be very successful, but adopted children and the parents often struggle to overcome children's biogenetic and environmental disadvantages. A classic wrongful adoption suit can help clarify what can go wrong. In 1964 the Burrs applied to an Ohio county welfare department to adopt a male child younger than 6 months old; a few days later the caseworker called the Burrs and told them that a 17-month-old nice, healthy, baby boy who had been born at a city hospital to an 18-year-old unwed mother living with her parents (who were mean to the boy) was being made available for adoption. It turned out that the child was born in a psychiatric hospital to a dually diagnosed schizophrenic and developmentally disabled mother!

Avoiding Wrongful Adoptions

It is important to provide all the information that is available (see Table 12.4). Provide it systematically. Develop a form that indicates what you do and do not have on the child. Offer the family the opportunity to tape record the information to be gathered from the child. The key issue is that families should not be deprived of information that they might need to make an informed decision about the adoption.

Although we do not have research on who files wrongful adoption suits, research has been gathered on this issue in the medical malpractice world. In many hospitals, insurers now require that every physician attend training every year on avoiding malpractice. The centerpiece of that discussion is developing and sustaining a good relationship with parents followed by good record keeping. So maintaining a supportive relationship with excellent documentation is vitally important to avoiding wrongful adoptions.

Open Adoption

The practice of open adoption, or the continuance of contact of the adopted child with birth parents, is particularly applicable among older children who still have ties to their parents, siblings, and extended family. On "ideological" grounds, since outcome data on open adoptions are very scarce, Pannor and Baran (1984) call for "an end to all closed adoptions" (p. 245). They view the secrecy of conventional adoptions as an affront to the rights of adopted children. More pragmatically, Borgman (1982) argues that open adoption may be a more realistic alternative for older children since many of these children have demonstrated their need and ability to continue prior relationships. This argument seems to be winning the day; in about half of non–foster parent adoptions in California in 1988–1989 there was contact with the birth family in the 4 years following placement (Berry, Dylla, Barth, & Needell, 1998). Even among children adopted from foster care, about 35% continued to have contact with their biological family 8 years later (Frasch, Brooks, & Barth, 1999); the levels of contact are very modest, however. Kraft, Palombo, Woods, Mitchell, and Schmidt (1985), among others, counter that open adoptions necessarily interfere with the process of bonding between the adoptive parent and child. The dialogue will continue as experience with open adoption mounts, although there is increasing support for them. Whereas most open adoptions continue to be voluntary on the adoptive parents' part, recent case law has added stipulations to adoption decrees that provide birth parents with visitation rights, but at present, none of these had been upheld in court. This is in stark contradiction to the historic notion of adoption as a parent–child relationship equivalent to the birth parent–child relationship and without condition.

The potential benefits of open adoptions are that they provide a resource for coping with the typical transitions as the adopted infant marches across time to adulthood. The danger is that continued contact with birth parents may prevent the cement that bonds the child to the new family from drying. The presumption for open adoption parallels the presumption in divorce custody proceedings—a far more common event than adoptions—toward joint custody. The situations are comparable, but more different than similar insofar as the child in divorce custody cases is not attempting to develop a bond to the family, but rather is trying to maintain bonds to her or his parent(s). The adoptive child and parent are endeavoring to become a family and need a structure to do so. The older a child becomes, the less detrimental and more natural it would seem to be to retain ties to former caretakers. The danger in this logic is that older children also have a more difficult time developing ties to their new family—since they are also pushing toward independence—and this may be preempted by contact with birth families. Open adoption can be viewed as an enrichment to a stable placement, not a palliative of a troubled one.

Matching of Parent(s) and Child(ren)

Adoption workers have a long history of endeavoring to match children with adopting families, so as to maximize the comfort of family, child, and community. Most of these matching principles have lost influence in recent years. As recently as 1974, 35 states had "religious protection" statutes (Gollub, 1974) that required agencies to place a child in a family with the same religion as their birth parent(s). Although most professionals agree that the child be allowed spiritual and ethical development, religious matching is increasingly disfavored (CWLA, 1978). Only a few agencies still require that the child and parent be of the same religion, although many adoption agencies will attempt to adhere to birth parents' religious preferences in selecting an adoptive home.

Families with and without children adopt older children. We have moved beyond the days when a note from a physician indicating infertility was required by the agency. Among a large sample of California older child adoptions, 73% of adoptive families had other children (biological, foster, stepchildren, or other kinds) in the home at the time of placement (Barth & Berry, 1988). Many adoption workers are still concerned, however, that some families are making a career of adoption, and refuse to place a fourth, fifth, or sixth child with a willing family. To some extent these concerns are to best serve waiting parents; a very few agencies still require that the adoptive couple be infertile, and that no other biological children be present in the home, yet this has also lost ground.

Transracial adoptions involve the adoption of a child by parents of a race different than the child, and are mostly found among older child adoptions. From the 1970s until the mid-1990s, racial matching had the highest weighting in adoption decision making. Until 1998, many states even had laws requiring that same-race placements be extensively pursued before transracial adoptions occurred (O. Golden, Personal Communication, September 1998). Transracial adoptive placements are currently used only in exceptional circumstances as a result of concerns that children will be denied exposure to their own cultural heritage and preparation to cope with racism—a position espoused in 1972 and maintained for a long time by the National Association of Black Social Workers.

The Multiethnic Placement Act arose in part because of the concern of the civil rights community that African-American children were being denied equal access to adoption. The evidence base grew increasingly clear that adoption was a good thing (and was no less good when it was transracial) and that African-American children were being adopted at rates far lower than their ages in care would indicate. Figure 12.1 shows that young children in nonkinship foster care—

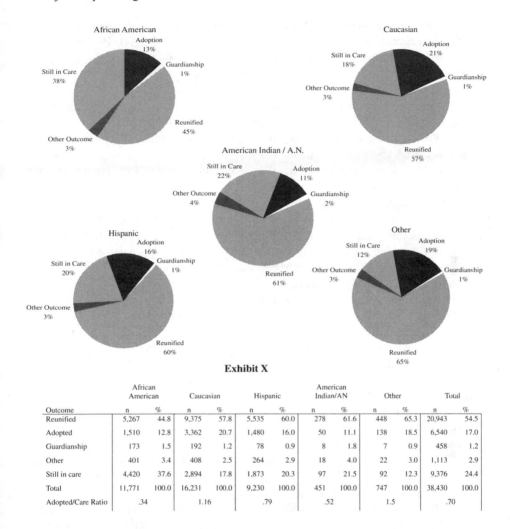

Exhibit X

	African American		Caucasian		Hispanic		American Indian/AN		Other		Total	
Outcome	n	%	n	%	n	%	n	%	n	%	n	%
Reunified	5,267	44.8	9,375	57.8	5,535	60.0	278	61.6	448	65.3	20,943	54.5
Adopted	1,510	12.8	3,362	20.7	1,480	16.0	50	11.1	138	18.5	6,540	17.0
Guardianship	173	1.5	192	1.2	78	0.9	8	1.8	7	0.9	458	1.2
Other	401	3.4	408	2.5	264	2.9	18	4.0	22	3.0	1,113	2.9
Still in care	4,420	37.6	2,894	17.8	1,873	20.3	97	21.5	92	12.3	9,376	24.4
Total	11,771	100.0	16,231	100.0	9,230	100.0	451	100.0	747	100.0	38,430	100.0
Adopted/Care Ratio	.34		1.16		.79		.52		1.5		.70	

Figure 12.1. Outcomes at 4 years from nonkin care of children less than 6 years at entry for California.

chosen because their need for adoption, should they not be able to return home, is least equivocal—continue to have grossly unequal access to adoption depending on their race or ethnicity (Barth, Webster, & Lee, 1998). Each of the pie charts allows us to directly examine the likelihood that children who do not go home will be adopted. This can be done by isolating the children who went home or had other outcomes from the analysis and by comparing the two remaining groups (those who remain in foster care and those who are adopted) with a simple ratio. So, among children who have not gone home by 4 years and remain in nonkinship foster care, the proportion of white children who are adopted is 1.16 times that of those who remain in foster care. For Hispanic children the ratio is 0.79, for American-Indian children, 0.52, and for African-American children only 0.34. The latter figure means that African-American foster children have only a little better than one-fourth the chance of being adopted than white foster children.

Because adoption provides a far more satisfactory setting for growing up than does long-term foster care (Barth, 1997b), it seems unfair that children's access to this valuable resource depends so much on their race. Clearly, adoption reform such as MEPA and its amendments was very likely to have been needed in order to give children of all ethnicities equal access to this resource. Previous efforts to improve the opportunity of adoption for all children were not sufficient. Whereas additional recruitment of minority adoptive parents is an important contributor to more placements for African-American children—as there is clearly a preference by many adoptive parents to adopt a child like them—it is unlikely to be sufficient to redress these long-standing imbalances in adoption. Indeed, adoption rates were falling prior to the introduction of MEPA and IAP. A successful approach must be broader and include ways of engaging a far larger proportion of the American public in welcoming foster and adoptive children of all types into their homes.

The expectation that families match on race was controversial, as is the Multiethnic Placement Act, which forbids routine use of racial matching—and all state laws that encourage it. Practitioners generally agree that children benefit from the cultural education provided by members of their own race, but some practitioners stress the overriding importance of finding adoptive parents regardless of race (Brooks & Barth, 1999).

In all likelihood, there is no single factor that determines the outcome of an adoption—not even race. Numerous investigators (e.g., Grow & Shapiro, 1972; Shireman & Johnson, 1986; Feigelman & Silverman, 1983; Simon & Alstein, 1987) have suggested that children adopted transracially are as well adjusted as other adopted children. There is no significant research to the contrary. The burden of proof has shifted to the opponents of greater flexibility in racial matching.

MEPA and the Inter-Ethnic Adoption Provisions that strengthened MEPA are now the law of the land and foster care and adoption workers are struggling to change practice models that routinely used race in placement decision making (Brooks, Barth, Bussiere, & Patterson, 1999). The law alone will not generate new perspectives or approaches. This is a challenge for everyone in the field.

Efforts to make the home study process more intensive, to screen adoptive families more rigorously, or to require extensive agency review of placements rest on little evidence. Whereas fingerprint checks for felonious criminal behavior and assessments of the safety of the household are undoubtedly warranted, adoption services must be circumspect about past and future efforts to add barriers to the recruitment, approval, and retention of adoptive families. Adoption agencies should use a light touch in guiding children to specific families based on their assumptions of the best matches. Families should be helped to see their strengths and limits and to make good choices. Additional screening is unlikely to reduce the very low rates of child maltreatment by adoptive parents and are likely, instead, to frustrate potential parents into giving up on adoption of foster children.

Nontraditional Adoptions

The traditional requirement that adoptive parents be a married couple who own a home with a full-time mother at home severely narrowed the field of possible adoptive parents. Although these requirements might have been helpful in reducing the field of applicants during the infant adoption boom, they were also erroneously promulgated to protect children from unsuitable parents. Instead, they limited the placement of special-needs children. A bigger pool of parents is needed for these waiting children, and is certainly not attainable without flexible requirements. Requirements for adoptive parents have typically been more flexible in public agencies than in private ones. It appears that public agencies supervise adoptions with parents with lower incomes, lower education levels, higher ages, and more children in the home than do private agencies (State of California Department of Social Services, 1987).

Agencies now recognize the potential of unconventional adoptive parents, such as single parents, foster parents, and gay or lesbian parents. An early study of single-parent adoptions (Branham, 1970) found that applicants have high levels of emotional maturity, tolerance of frustration, and independence, although still linked to a supportive network of relatives. Barth and Berry (1988) found that single parents adopted older and more difficult children with no more adoption disruption than couples.

Older parents may want older children. With the greater length of time couples are waiting to begin having children, and the long waiting lists for infant adoption, a couple could be approaching 40 before they are aware of their infertility, or of the long delays in adoptions. Social workers indicate that older parents are particularly more suitable for adopting developmentally disabled children (Coyne & Brown, 1986). Agencies are less likely than in the past to exclude parents who may have already raised some children, and want to complete their families.

Interest in adoption by gay and lesbian individuals and couples has become more common in all likelihood (although no good data are available), but remain limited by policy and practice constraints. A few states have developed statutory proscriptions against adoption by homosexuals and others have endeavored to go further and discourage adoptions by single people, partly on the grounds that they may be in gay partnerships. These policies run counter to the growing evidence that gay and lesbian parenting of children is quite common and successful, and that the outcomes are largely indistinguishable from parenting by heterosexuals (Bailey, Bobrow, Wolfe, & Mikach, 1995; Chan, Raboy, & Patterson, 1998; Golombek, Tasker, & Murray, 1997). The demand for more adoptive families that is being generated through federal and state permanency planning initiatives, and the growing emphasis on assessing the appropriateness of adoptions based on individual needs of a child rather than categorical factors such as race or age, is likely to generate a counteraction to statutory limits on who can adopt. Such policies might prevent the denial of an adoption on the basis of any single categorical factor, as long as there was an adoption agency's agreement that the placement was in the child's overall best interest.

Foster Parent Adoptions and Fost-Adoption

Recruitment efforts are eased by the use of foster parents as adoptive parents. Foster parent adoptions increased in the 1970s as special-needs children freed for adoption increased, without an associated increase in adoptive applicants. Prior to that, foster parents were considered inappropriate for adoption. Sometimes the foster parents knew at the initial placement that the placement could become an adoptive placement; at other times they decided to adopt after the child had lived with them as a foster child for some time. Some foster parents have felt pressured by the agency to adopt the child (Meezan & Shireman, 1982), although others intended to adopt from the very beginning. At least 80% of adoptions are now by foster parents (Barth, Brooks, & Iyer, 1996).

Fost-adopt or legal-risk adoptions involve placing a child into a foster home with the plan for adoption, assuming that the child will not go home to birth parents. Although fost-adopt placements are becoming more commonplace and agencies are developing guidelines for these kinds of placements, many controversies surround them. The major objection is that foster parents hoping to adopt will not work toward the child's reunification with the biological family, one of the major goals of foster care (Lee & Hull, 1983). The dual goals of reunification with the biological family and the integration of the child into the fost-adopt family may impose a strain on foster parents' and children's loyalties. In fact, some professionals believe that beginning an adoption as a foster parent reduces a sense of entitlement to be a parent, resulting in less commitment to parenthood and a weaker parent–child bond (Ward, 1981). Foster families are also not screened as carefully for compatibility with the child (Meezan & Shireman, 1985). The time constraints involved in some foster placements allow little matching or placement preparation, both thought to be important to adoption success. Also, confidentiality is less protected in a foster home adoption, where the foster parents and biological parents have met. Fost-adoptions may also be disquieting to other foster children present in the foster home.

The advantages of fost-adoptions are the continuity of home life afforded the child, the retention of a familiar community, the ability for ongoing assessment of the placement, and the involvement of the child in the decision to adopt. Fost-adoptions can begin when the children are younger and are more able to adjust to a new family—even if custody battles stretch out in the courts over years. Adoptive parents who were previously foster parents are also reported to be more accepting of ongoing contact with the agency—particularly when problems arise.

Given these advantages and disadvantages, several situations lend themselves to fost-adoptions, generally where there is little likelihood of children's reunification with their biological parents (Katz & Robinson, 1991). Those cases in which the child has been relinquished by the mother (and the father is unknown, absent, or likely to relinquish in the future) are appropriate for fost-adoptions, as are cases in which the child has been abandoned or parental rights have been terminated but are being contested. If the child's birth parents have gone through parental rights terminations for siblings or are unlikely to be able to parent the child, fost-adoption is also now often considered an appropriate option and is more clearly allowable under ASFA.

Fost-adoptions are gaining wider acceptance among professionals, particularly concerning older child adoptions, and these placements compare favorably to conventional adoptive placements in terms of stability (Barth, 1988a). The cost of potential removal of the family from the foster family network seems to be overshadowed by the continuity and stability proffered the adopted child.

MODEL PRACTICES AND PROGRAMS

The adoption field is "wide open" in terms of opportunities for developing creative solutions. The past two decades have witnessed the emergence of adopting handicapped children, fost-adopt, open adoption, and postlegal adoption services. The field continues to pursue new initiatives. This section will discuss some of these areas of innovation, including recruitment, home study approaches, adoption planning for the child, postplacement, postlegalization, and intensive adoption preservation services.

Recruitment of Adoptive Parents

This challenge to find additional foster and adoptive parents is growing greater every day as the United States is becoming a country in which every adult is working outside the home, family size is dropping, understanding and misunderstanding about the contribution of genetics and prenatal environments are making adoptive parent more wary, reproductive technologies are promising more alternatives to adoption, and the cost of raising a child is soaring. Given the lengthening preparation period to adulthood that children are now experiencing, the value of a permanent family that can support them until they are on their own is growing. Adoption is clearly the ultimate public–private partnership on behalf of children and offers them impressive opportunities and resources (Barth, 1997b). We will need far better information in the future to guide us in maximizing the use of this very valuable, yet scarce resource.

The ultimate implementation of MEPA, with its requirement to accelerate recruitment of families that will adopt the children in foster care, will eventually bring in more adoptive families that would have been discouraged or, perhaps, have become involved in international adoptions. Yet, the gains in adoptive placements for America's foster children will be small unless we work to better understand the responsiveness of the general public to interethnic adoption. There appears to be considerably more acceptance of interethnic and cross-racial placements among the general public than among the professional adoption community (Brooks & Barth, 1998b; Howard, Rowse, & Skerl, 1977). Indeed, in California, African-American children who are placed for adoption by their own biological parents are about three times more likely to be placed into homes with at least one white parent than are children placed by adoption agencies (Barth, Brooks, & Iyer, 1996).

With the increase in the pool of adoptive children, adoption exchanges and networks have begun to fill the need for adoptive parents. Exchanges serve as matching resources, which list children waiting for adoption and their special needs, and parents seeking to adopt. They often include descriptions and pictures of children on the World Wide Web that emphasize children's interests and strengths (e.g., The National Adoption Center's site: www.adopt.org).

In addition to exchanges, parent recruitment is also effected through community education. There are two types of community recruitment. First, the broad education of the community can reach general groups of potential parents that may never have considered adoption. The *One Church, One Child* program, which involves black churches, exemplifies this method. The second method is child-specific recruitment that involves identifying children who have become free for adoption (or are likely to become free) and finding homes for those children.

Although children of all colors need permanent homes, black children are drastically overrepresented in foster care and continue to wait the longest for homes. Finding them adoptive homes requires the most innovative recruitment efforts. Beginning in 1979, Father George Clements, a priest in Chicago, challenged every black church in Chicago to accept the responsibility and opportunity to have one member of each congregation adopt a child. With support from the state, the One Church, One Child program was presented at 50 black churches, in the early years of the program, resulting in 37 adoptive homes (Veronico, 1983). The program included aspects of child-specific recruitment via slide presentations of available children and also focused on linking private and public agencies and church and community representatives to generate ideas for streamlining the home study and adoption process. The federal government subsequently provided several years of support to One Church, One Child to encourage its dissemination and has funded many replications. More than 20 states now have a version. Other agencies sponsor periodic recruitment drives aimed to encourage African Americans to adopt. These drives may consist of evening meetings advertised in local newspapers or presentations to organizations with substantial participation by African Americans.

The second mode of recruitment is more individualized: to find the right parents for a particular child. This is attempted by using the media, television or newspapers, to present a particular child and a description of his or her strengths and needs (e.g., through special features often titled something like "Wednesday's Child"). These media campaigns are quite successful and inexpensive. Recent efforts focus on improving the speed and quality of the agency's response to parents once they call and inquire about adoption. Also, the requirements in ASFA that parental rights be terminated after 15 months in foster care spring from the needs of child specific recruitment because it is far more effective when children are free and can be readily identified as available on the media and on websites.

Corporate and other groups' newsletters have begun to address older child adoptions, with the hope of interesting group or company members in adoption of these children (Walton, 1985). These newsletters have not had much success, but are a very recent development, and agencies are fine-tuning their efforts to better reach their audience. "Adoption fairs" bring interested parents and eligible children together in a picnic-type situation.

In November 1998, the president directed the Department of Health and Human Services (HHS) to develop a plan to expand use of the Internet to share information about children who are legally free for adoption in order to shorten the time needed to find them adoptive families. His remarks follow.

Between 1996 and 1997, the number of adoptions increased by 10 percent, from 28,000 to 31,000. We know, however, that that cannot be the sole measure of our progress. We also must ask ourselves whether our child welfare system always puts the health and safety of our children above all else; whether children have the chance to live out their dreams and fulfill their potential; whether families who open their arms can actually reach to embrace a child in need. As we celebrate National Adoption Month, Americans can take pride in the progress we're making—but we know there is much more work to be done. We know geographic and other barriers to adoptions still exist. We know we have to do a better job in informing America's families about the many children who wait in the foster care system for adoption. To give those children the permanent homes they need, to give our families the opportunity to give them those homes, we must make technology a partner and propel the public welfare system into the 21st century. Today, therefore, I am directing the Secretary of Health and Human Services to work with the states, the courts, the private agencies, to report to me within 60 days on a plan for a national Internet-based registry of children waiting to be adopted everywhere in the United States. (President Clinton announces expansion of the internet to increase adoptions, November 24, 1998; http://www.acf. dhhs.gov/news/whfsn24.htm)

Despite innovative strategies, recruitment is often hampered by current fiscal arrangements and policies. Particularly troublesome is the failure of most states to reimburse private adoption agencies adequately for making and maintaining the placements of high-risk children. When state governments are serious about capitalizing on the exceptionally generous in-kind contributions made by adopting families, they would double their reimbursements to agencies and even pay churches, civic organizations, or private agencies that develop placements of high-risk older children. Michigan has developed a related rate structure, paying agencies higher rates for placing children who have been in foster care longer. This would provide an additional incentive to other organizations to find homes. (To be sure that the placements were not contrived only for the welfare of the agency or organization would, of course, require oversight by public child welfare services.) The benefits to the state would far exceed the costs. Whether or not this cash payment seems abhorrent or appealing, readers should consider whether the current rate structure for home finding is inadequate given the value of adoptive homes to children and society (Barth & Berry, 1988).

Also, other barriers to adoption must be addressed. Some adoptive families will eventually require a residential treatment program for their adopted children, but the federal government does not provide for this cost. Should the option to us be to have tax credit spread across all the years of the adoption in order to help meet these costs? Basic research would help us know if such an option would increase the adoption pool and by how much.

Home Studies and Preplacement Preparation
for the Parents

Conventional home studies and selections of adoptive families double as preplacement preparation. In the name of efficiency, this is a sensible approach. The requirements of the two activities, however, are not singular. Many adoptive parents are still interviewed under a format that has survived the change in agency practice from a concentration on infant adoptions. As such, agency staff commonly may interview couples together, then each member of the couple alone, and then the couple together again. The intent is to understand if they have views that they cannot express in front of their partner and that reflect on uncertainty about adopting. This procedure, like many others that emerged when home studies also included much counseling for infertility, assumes that one spouse would tell a nearly complete stranger of concerns that he or she would not tell the other spouse. Much streamlining of adoption practice beckons and some agencies now require only one interview if the family has participated previously in a home study or was previously approved as a foster care home.

Couples or individuals that meet with others in a like situation can more effectively challenge their false expectations. The earliest group model is Barbara Tremitiere's (1979). The nine-session format includes the following:

1.   Informing the five to seven couples or single applicants of the purpose of
      the group and what will follow;

2. Exposure to panels of adoptive parents who present the challenges (and threats) of adoptive parenting;
3. Clarification of family and individual values about adoption;
4. Visits with a family that has adopted a child with characteristics similar to the child of interest to the adoptive parent(s); and
5. Completing the writing of the home study, which is a joint effort by the applicant and social worker.

Another version of group preparation is the Model Approach to Partnership in Parenting (MAPP), which prepares participants to become adoptive or foster parents. The group approach to preplacement provides opportunities for ongoing support. Adoptive families who begin the process in such multifamily groups have often maintained contact with one or more families—many times well beyond their time of contact with their social worker. However, many agencies still do not use such a model despite the evidence that it strengthens high-risk placements (Barth & Berry, 1988).

Adoption Planning for the Child

Permanency planning legislation has freed many children for adoption, yet agencies have been slow to implement the specifics of the legislation. Whereas more has probably changed than remained the same, many barriers to placement and permanence remain. Determining a child's eligibility for adoption continues to be a confused mixture of answers to three questions. Is the child (1) easily interested in adoption, (2) likely to be adopted, and (3) likely to remain adopted? Some children are never considered for adoption because they seem content in a less permanent situation. Social workers with narrow ideas about "adoptability" may reject some children as too severely handicapped or too old to be adopted. Adjusting practice to the needs of these older children includes recognizing that some disruption is inevitable. As Betsy Cole has commented, "The only failed adoption is the one you didn't try" (Cole, 1986, p. 4). Workers who recognize and accept the possibility of disruption in adoption will find creative ways to facilitate adoptions for all waiting children, and will support the placement in accordance with the risk involved.

Proof that a child will be better off adopted than in long-term foster care or guardianship is unattainable. The best any social worker, foster parent, and child can do is try to land on the right side of the likelihood that a placement will work out for the best. In general, the value of adoption and the relatively modest disruption rates (about 10%) shown in several studies (e.g., Barth, 1988a; Partridge et al., 1986) make adoption the clearly and convincingly superior plan over foster care. Yet children are casually resigned to foster care, given little encouragement to consider adoption, and their promising tomorrows are readily swapped for a "manageable placement" today.

Speedy efforts to place children although they are young and more able to fit into an adoptive family's home represent the starting point for successful adoption. ASFA supports efforts to terminate parental rights and responsibilities more quickly when reunification is improbable, to move children into fost-adopt situations, and to pursue speedier termination of parental rights when reunification is not likely. These efforts deserve full support and dissemination. Court reform is already in the works, but some states still require an evidentiary hearing in family or juvenile court to determine that the child should be freed for adoption, and then a separate civil court hearing to terminate parental rights. This is virtually triple jeopardy for children. The first jeopardy is that the family court will return them to a situation that is least likely to promote their well-being and allow them to grow unharmed. This is the jeopardy that we condone in public policies that are overly protective of parental rights. If they avoid that jeopardy, the second jeopardy is that the civil court—in its inexperience in these matters—will, after much delay, overturn the family court decision. The third jeopardy is that the child will grow without a plan, without the right to join a family, and without the freedom of permanence. Separating the hearings, but conducting them all consecutively in juvenile court is a sensible way to proceed that protects parental and child rights.

Practitioners need the tools and the support to work with foster children and parents toward adoption. Younger children are likely to get referrals to adoption units and older foster children are increasingly referred for emancipation services. Agencies neglect latency-age children in care. These are children whose likelihood of adoption is judged to be low and whom agencies are hesitant to free from their birth parents because they will become "legal orphans" unless an adoptive home awaits. These children are thus not transferred to adoption units, entered into adoption books, or referred to adoption fairs. They very often miss the opportunity of a lifetime family. ASFA's requirement that these children are entitled to reasonable efforts to find adoptive homes could change that.

Postplacement Services

Important to successful adoption placements, agency support after placement is also essential. Any placement will have challenges. The goal is to be close enough to the family to remain aware of these problems and guide the family to resources to aid in their resolution. However, many families are reluctant to seek services until it is too late because they are afraid they will lose their child.

Both the child and the parents have needs in postplacement services. The agency should maintain close contact with the family during the first 6 months to reassure the child of continuity with his or her past and to enable the family to explore uncertainties without feeling lost (Fitzgerald, Murcer, & Murcer, 1982). The goal is to catch problems early in the placement before they escalate into unsalvageable disasters. The evidence is increasingly clear that 3 months is far too brief a time (Barth & Berry, 1988). Indeed Howard and Smith (1995) found families struggling with the possibility of disruption an average of 9 years after adoption. Mechanisms must be established in agencies to provide services for high-risk placements throughout the adolescent years. This is not simply a call for more postlegalization counseling services. These may be useful, but are not specifically aimed at preserving placements on the verge of disruption. They tend to serve adoptees placed as infants—not older child adoptees—and help them with reconciling their adoptions and making decisions about searching for birth parents, and other concerns of adopted children when they become adolescents and young adults.

Many agencies have introduced support groups of adoptive families for parents and children. It is often helpful for new adoptive parents and children to talk to fellow adopters and adoptees, to know what is normal in adoption, and to share realistic expectations and feelings about the process. These groups also facilitate supportive relationships that parents and children can fall back on in individual need. Support groups probably operate best when started during the homestudy, but successful versions have also been developed after placement to support high-risk placements.

Parent self-help groups are also becoming more numerous in this country. There were 250 such groups for adoptive parents in 1980 (Meezan, 1980). One example is Adoptive Families of America (AFA). Adoptive Families of America (previously known as OURS, Inc.) is a nonprofit organization of over 9,000 families and professionals recognizing a need to share information, support one another, and keep the children in contact with one another. AFA provides adoption information, a "helpline," resource materials, a bimonthly magazine, and donations and support to children in need of permanency. Parents and children find it helpful to meet and talk with people in similar circumstances. Often, members of groups that go through a group home study prior to placement voluntarily maintain regular contact after placement (Tremitiere, 1979). Other groups are more structured and closed-ended, although long-lasting supportive relationships are often formed.

Many postplacement services involve fostering a support system for adoptive families. In addition to parent groups, agencies offer individual and family counseling, retreats, "helplines," reading lists and materials, and video information (Spencer, 1985). The North American Post-Legal Adoption Committee considers postlegal services as a logical extension of preplacement services, which should be offered "at whatever point in their lives these [needs] may arise" (Spencer, 1985, p. 5). They argue that postplacement services should be available, for a (sliding) fee, for the rest of an adoptive family's life. The call for more available and continuous postplacement services is coming from many quarters, although existing evidence is fuzzy about the type, timing, and effectiveness of such services for older child adoptions.

A program that pairs experienced adoptive parents with those new to adoption was developed by the North American Council on Adoptable Children (NACAC). The "buddy system" is a cooperative effort between adoption agencies and adoptive parents (Boersdorfer, Kaser, & Tremitiere, 1986). Bringing these families together provides opportunities for preadoptive families to learn what to expect in their own adoption, enables them to develop lasting supportive relationships, and helps the more experienced (but still in progress) adoptive families to benefit from a review of their adoptive accomplishments. Buddies are often drawn from an adoptive parent organization, but this is not necessary. Families known to the adoption unit can be solicited for participation as buddies. Foster parents can also make good buddies and can be recruited through their associations (which are more numerous than adoptive parent organizations). Buddies are assigned according to the type of adoption anticipated. For instance, a family planning to adopt a sibling group of three children might be assigned to another family that had adopted a large sibling group. Ideally, the buddy participates in some of the parent and home study process since this is a time when families are deciding what kinds of children they want to and can parent. Supportive postplacement activities include occasional phone calls and cards, invitations to cookouts, sharing books and articles, referrals to other resources, and explaining the many mysteries of the agency. Another strategy for providing support to adoptive families is via an adoption "warm-line" staffed by other adoptive families or, as the Tressler-Lutheran Agency calls it, a "listening ear." The model is designed to help families reach out to needed resources without calling the social worker whom they may perceive as a threat to their placement.

Development of community resources knowledgeable about adoption can help make the promise of treatment for an adopted child more than just a prayer. Mental health practitioners often do not understand the special family dynamics and natural developmental stress points experienced over time by families built through adoption. Community-based mental health and educational service providers can be invited to participate in the group home study process and during agency adoption training. Part of that training should involve participation in in-house reviews of each disruption. Adoption workers and the therapists to whom social workers refer adoptive families need greater understanding and commitment to working with educational systems—particularly special education. Numerous families in Barth and Berry's 1988 study identified obtaining an appropriate public or private special or regular education program as a turning point away from a disruption. Typical postplacement services that are limited to office or kitchen counseling and fail fully to explore the child's broader world suggest that many social workers do not recognize or know how to respond to the importance of schools in the lives of parents and children. Collaborative training with educators, school social workers, and school psychologists would benefit adopted children.

Adoptive and foster parent associations are beginning to develop respite care arrangements as another important postplacement service. Families agree that they would be willing to provide care for a child in their home for a time—some families designate 3 weeks and some designate 3 hours. Arrangements are made for reimbursement of meals and other expenses. For children in fost-adopt programs, agency guidelines about the use of respite must be clarified so it is in keeping with foster parent obligations to the agency.

Adoption affects the child and his or her family all their lives. Adolescence, for example, is a time of heightened awareness and concern about identity, and the need for counseling may be acute during this time. Postlegalization services are those focused on helping families after the first year of placement when the placement is legally finalized. A recent committee on postlegal services (North American Council on Adoptable Children, Post-Legal Adoption Committee, 1984) offered this list of methods for the provision of postlegal services:

1.   individual and family counseling;
2.   intermediary in legal matters;
3.   workshops on topics such as transracial and intercountry adoption;
4.   support groups;
5.   classes;
6.   retreats;
7.   social events;
8.   intermediary in "adoption triad" matters, such as specifics of visitation;
9.   professional consultation;
10. information;
11. films and other materials for distribution; and
12. research on evaluation of services as well as other postlegal concerns.

Searching for birth families is another key component in those agencies that do provide postlegal services. Although laudatory and helpful to facilitate adjustment to adoption, this is only a small part of the spectrum of services needed by families in crisis.

There is a clamor for the development of postplacement and postlegalization services that meet the demands of supporting older child adoptions. The clarion call is for something far more than mandatory visits soon after the adoption. Although this principle is sound, a few concerns arise. First, postadoption services should not be staffed at the expense of recruitment and home study efforts. Dollars spent on conventional postplacement services are probably not as valuable to agencies and families as dollars spent on recruitment. Second, whereas referral to services is often useful, social workers involved with the family should be primarily available to assess the situation and coordinate postplacement services from other providers. Families are less likely to request timely assistance from the agency when they lose contact with the worker who did their home study (Barth & Berry, 1988). The home study is a poignant process that builds strong bonds between the worker and family. The organization of services should facilitate a continuous relationship between the family and social worker. In addition, to study and orient families appropriately, adoption workers need to know about the legal delays and challenges that await families.

Adoption Preservation Services

The adjustment to older child adoptions is often difficult. At times, the future of the adoption is in doubt. With so much riding on the outcome of such an adoption crisis, reliance on conventional social casework counseling or office-based psychotherapy is unwise. At times, intensive in-home adoption preservation services may be needed. Over the past decade, family preservation services have emerged in most of our states but have been primarily reserved for preventing entrance into the child welfare or mental health systems. As previously described, programs such as HOMEBUILDERS™ have had some success in preventing the placement of children who are at "imminent risk." The contributors to the success are not fully understood, but IFPS (as described in Chapter 9) involve a crisis time-limited orientation, use of social and cognitive methods of intervention, intensive work that occurs in the home (sometimes exceeding 15 hours per week per family), and linkage to other resources. Adoption agencies have generally not called on these services to help preserve adoptive placements. Medina Children's Services (the Seattle-based agency specializing in adoption of older and special-needs children) and the Behavioral Sciences Institute (the organizational sponsor of HOME-BUILDERS™) collaborated to develop and evaluate intensive adoption preservation services and provide training in their use. As in all HOMEBUILDERS™ interventions, each full-time therapist in the project had a caseload of two families, the intervention consisted of 4 weeks of in-home therapy, and the therapist saw the family as often as needed—typically three to five sessions of 2 hours or more. After 6 months, 89% of adoptive families who were experiencing an adoption crisis and were at risk of a disruption had been helped to maintain the placements. (By the end of 1 year, depending on the definition of placement preservation, the success rate was only about 50%.) These data and the experience of the adoption presentation program in Illinois (Howard & Smith, 1995) suggest that longer term interventions are more optimal for adoption presentation services (Barth & Miller, in press).

Few adoptive families now have the benefit of intensive or long-term home-based, family preservation services to prevent adoption disruption. Iowa, Massachusetts, Illinois, and Oregon have developed promising programs to support families in times of crisis (Barth, 1991a). For families in crisis, in-home interventions reduce the likelihood of alienation that can occur during out-of-home care. The specific presenting problems that precipitate adoption disruptions are those that signal the breakdown of other families, particularly assault, running away, and noncompliance of latency and teenage children (Barth & Berry, 1988). Although such postadoption services are costly, if they finally prove successful, those costs can be favorably weighed against the lifelong benefits that follow adoption. Barth and Brooks (1997) have found that parental satisfaction with adoption reaches its low point during the years from 12 to 18 with fewer than 60% of parents reporting feeling somewhat or very close to their child. After age 25, this figure approaches 90%. The challenge is to see families through these low times.

Illinois was among the first states to devote family preservation resources to preserving adoptions—starting with their statewide family preservation initiative in 1991 that began modestly and eventually was operating in 11 sites across the state. The short-term family preservation model used for biological families was adapted during the project and eventually yielded to a model that had the flexibility to provide years of services (Howard & Smith, 1995). Most of the families served had histories of receiving counseling services and had many accommodations to try to preserve their adoptions, but 45% raised the possibility of dissolution of their adoptions during the course of services. Eventually, about 17 of the 57 families (30%) that could be contacted had placed their child outside the home since service ended. (This does not mean that they dissolved their adoptions, however, as placement of adopted children in residential care is not an uncommon strategy for maintaining family unit—only seven families had given up legal guardianship.) The data from Illinois are much more like those from Oregon in suggesting the capacity of longer term adoption preservations services to prevent disruptions.

Some adoptions cannot be saved and children are returned to the agency. The costs of disruption to the child, family, and agency are substantial. The most recent study of adoption disruptions moves the field forward by using administrative records to determine how many children who left foster care with an exit reason of adoption subsequently reentered foster care. Since these children may have changed their names (usually only their last names) through the adoption, a probabilistic record linkage technology was used to give weight to other factors in their case histories (Goerge, Howard, & Wu, 1996). The administrative records covered the years from 1976 to 1994—the longest follow-up study yet. The findings that about 16% of adoptions end in disruption are largely consistent with the shorter studies of adoptions (Barth & Berry, 1988; Partridge et al., 1986; Urban Systems Reseach & Engineering, 1985). Taken together with other research on the high rates of placement changes for children in foster care, the findings on the relative rarity of adoption disruptions is quite promising. The best prediction for any adoption is that it will last a lifetime.

The risk of disruption is linked with the child's age, prior disruptions, behavioral problems (particularly cruelty, fighting, disobedience, and vandalism), and nonfoster parent adoptions. Also linked to disruption are higher education of parents, higher expectations on the part of adoptive parents, and preplacement information about the child that was scanty or too favorable. Perhaps the best adoption outcome is to make and sustain a very high-risk placement. Better information, adequate subsidies, and more experienced social workers are associated with lower than expected disruptions. These findings should encourage clinicians to continue to place older, special-needs children for adoption.

Perhaps the worst outcome of an adoption is to have a low-risk placement that disrupts. The lack of adequate information about the child, multiple workers, and the lack of a subsidy are associated with low-risk placements that disrupted. (Contrarily, provision of subsidies was associated with adoptions that were predicted to disrupt but did not.) The equitable and efficient delivery of adequate subsidies should be supported.

CURRENT PROGRAM CHALLENGES

Cost Effectiveness

Adoption appears to be quite cost effective, although there are considerable "start-up" costs. Research suggests that the investment required to complete an adoption is considerable. California data suggest that adoptions cost (Allphin, Simmons, & Barth, 1998), on average, about $16,000 each in additional agency efforts—not including court costs. Given that adoptions provide a major environmental intervention, the value of each dollar spent to make or maintain a placement may comprise one of government's greatest returns. Yet, because agencies incur considerable expense when they make adoptive placements and the long-term benefits are great, agencies should see that at every point in their child-serving system they nurture family preservation services for use by families at risk of breaking up. Nearly every child welfare system has standing arrangements to provide in-home services to families just entering the child welfare system but has no mechanism for using them to prevent the disruption of existing adoptions. This should be remedied in every agency.

Recognizing Other Adoption Benefits

Some adoptions do disrupt despite the best services. The effects of failed adoptions on children and parents are currently impossible to assess. Further, the success of adoptions cannot be evaluated only on the basis of placement stability. Although this provides a basis for estimating the quality of the adoption, other indicators of success in child welfare include protection from reabuse, achievement of developmental outcomes, and child satisfaction. The outcomes of adoptions, whether disrupted or not, must be compared to long-term foster care, guardianship, or residential care on these criteria. Fortunately, the evidence suggests that adoptions do have advantages over other permanency planning options and appear worth the calculated risk that they might disrupt (Barth, 1997b).

Once placements are made, adoptive families typically receive fewer services than do birth families with less chance of providing adequate developmental resources to a special-needs child. Adoptive families are given equivalent statutory rights to birth families, but not equivalent services. Wider use of intensive adoption preservation services would correct this imbalance.

As this chapter has shown, the child welfare "system" is a fragile weave of programs. The outcomes of efforts to prevent out-of-home placements, to reunify families, and to provide long-term care all depend on the quality of programs from which they receive children and to which they send them. Each program must work if the other programs are to do what they intend. If older children in the child welfare system are not adopted or able to stay adopted, then the rationale for moving quickly to terminate parental rights (after a determination that children cannot go home) is weakened. Indeed, the pressure to leave or return children to unsafe birth families is intensified when permanent adoptive homes are unavailable. Many agencies will not free children until a stable home is all but guaranteed. Without confidence in the benefit of terminating parental rights and freeing a child for adoption, judges lose their tenuous conviction to do so, time limits on foster care are rendered insignificant, and mandates for speedy permanency planning become moot. To argue that successful services to promote older child adoption are the hub of effective child welfare services may be excessive. Still, they are critical.

Need for Community Support

Adoption services can provide effective care to children only by addressing the mandates and needs of the community. The recent trend to focus only on the service needs of the adoption triad is too narrow. Instead, services must enhance the capacity of the community to support the family's capacity to protect and nurture their children so they do not require placement or adoption. Second, for children who do need care, the care and concern of the community must be harnessed to insist that barriers to adoption be jackhammered into dust, that children be provided with adoptive homes, and that prejudice against nontraditional homes not prevent a single adoption. Third, the community of adoptive parents must be enlisted to strengthen the agencies' capacity to study, prepare, and support new adoptive parents. Finally, services to adoptive placements that are in trouble must go beyond counseling about adoption and include the broad array of educational, social, recreational, and financial services warranted in a community-centered intervention to rescue the dream of a forever family.

CONCLUSION

The bulk of evidence on adoption outcomes informs us that older child adoptions outperform the most heralded and successful of our early intervention programs such as Headstart when measured according to criteria such as the child's developmental progress. Adoption is a total intervention. Adoptive families can have a great and lasting influence on children. The success of intensive preschool educational programs such as the Perry Preschool Program and Headstart is in much part attributable to enhanced family involvement (Berrueta-Clement, Schweinhart, Barnett, Epstein, & Weikart, 1984). Older child adoption can be expected to outperform those programs on that account because the child gains a new family for life. Still, the challenges that children adopted from foster care bring to adoption may call for an ongoing investment in postadoption services.

Arguing that adoption is of great value may seem obvious. It is not. Many social workers and judges are not convinced of adoption's advantages over long-term foster care or guardianship, and fail even to try to make a case about its value to foster families and children. Consistent with this ambivalence about adoption, some states give children veto power over an adoption at the age of 10. Whereas good sense always calls for engaging children in choices of placements, the implication of this change is to indicate that adoption is just one of basically equal alternatives and, given this equivalence, even a 10 year old cannot fail to make the right decision. This has serious implications, as comprehending the lifelong value of adoptions is not easy. At minimum, it requires careful contemplation of the information about the long-term benefits of adoption.

FOR FURTHER INFORMATION

Barth, R.P., & Berry, M. (1988). *Adoption and disruption: Risks, rates, and responses.* Hawthorne, NY: Aldine de Gruyter. Describes the results of the largest study of adoption disruption rates and risk factors and offers program and policy recommendations that are still useful.

Banks, R. (1998). The color of desire: Fulfilling adoptive parents racial preferences through discriminatory state action. *Yale Law Journal, 107,* 875–1025. This provocative analysis argues that adoptive parents should be expected, like other recipients of public resources, to accept children into their families without racial bias and should be excluded from the adoption pool if they are not willing to commit to nondiscrimination. Elizabeth Bartholet's critique of Bank's argument—in the same volume of the *Yale Law Journal* (pp. 2351–2356)—is also informative. This is likely to develop into a substantial debate in the post-MEPA era.

Center for the Future of Children. (1993) Overview and major recommendations. *The Future of Children, 3,* 4–16. This article is one of 14 in this special issue that is very scholarly and balanced. It is available at no cost (while they last) from the Circulation Department, Center for the Future of Children, 300 2nd Street, Suite 102, Los Altos, CA 94022 or at www.futureofchildren.org.

Hollinger, J. (Ed.) (1988). *Adoption law and practice:* This is the only work to cover all the legal aspects of adoption, including: who may adopt and be adopted; consent; placement; independent adoptions; agency adoptions; contested adoptions; adopting children with special needs; adopting children from other countries; adopting native American children; the effect of the new reproductive technologies; and economic, legal, and psychological consequences of adoption. First published in 1988, this two-volume set is updated annually with supplements and revisions.

Jewett, C. (1978). *Adopting the older child.* Cambridge, MA: Harvard Common Press. Discusses issues and program strategies for facilitating older child adoptions.

Meezan, W., Katz, S., & Russo, E.M. (1978). *Adoptions without agencies: A study of independent adop-*

tions. New York: Child Welfare League of America. Remains the best study of independent adoptions.

U.S. General Accounting Office. (September 14, 1998*). Foster care: Implementation of the Multiethnic Placement Act poses difficult challenges.* Washington, DC: GAO/HEHS-U.S. General Accounting Office. Cogent analysis of the challenges of this act and of the issues regarding this legislation.

13

Residential Group Care Services

> Group care of normal children was, for all intents and purposes, off the profession-
> al's agenda either as a solution to some types of problems or even as a theoretical
> concern. Like Lamarckian genetics or the demon theory of mental illness, it had been
> laid to rest. (Wolins, 1974, p. 2)

THE AMBIVALENCE TOWARD GROUP CHILD CARE
AS A HELPING SERVICE

Twenty-five years later and at the dawn of the twenty-first century, the late Martin
Wolins, perhaps group child care's most brilliant, passionate, and articulate theo-
retician, researcher, and advocate for the latter half of the twentieth century, would
in all likelihood drop the qualifier "normal" and simply admit that group care for
any children was "off the professional's agenda."

This probably would only have deepened Wolins' resolve to pursue legitimacy
for a form of service he deeply believed deserved a full and rightful place in the
overall continuum of care. As colleague and collaborator, the Israeli scholar
Yochanan Wozner said it best:

> A large part of Martin's scholastic energy was devoted to a sometimes lonely, often
> unpopular, but always vigorous and data based advocacy for responsible and ac-
> countable social work in general, and child and youth care in particular. His main
> thrust was directed toward the understanding of residential settings and their intelli-
> gent, controlled and planned use. (cited in Gannon, 1987)

In the spirit of Martin Wolins, it is the thesis of this chapter that a full and rigorous examination of the theoretical and empirical underpinnings of residential
group care with respect to their implications for current service policy, practice,
and future research is long overdue and ought to receive high priority on the child
welfare agenda for the new century.

What Is Meant by "Residential Group Care"
and What Are Its Current Parameters?

> The traditional definition of group care services for children describes: a child wel-
> fare service that provides 24 hour care for a child in a residential facility designed as

a therapeutic environment. Within this setting are integrated treatment services, educational services and group living on the basis of an individual plan for each child who cannot be effectively helped in his or her own home , (or) with a substitute family. (CWLA, 1982, p. 15)

Two of the most dominant forms of group care include campus-based residential treatment centers and community-based group homes (Braziel, 1996). Programs and services are provided in a wide range of settings including community-based apartments, group homes, campus-based facilities, and other self-contained facilities including secure units. Within these settings, children and families obtain a mix of services including counseling, education, recreation, health, nutrition, daily living experiences, independent living skills, reunification services, aftercare services, and the like (CWLA, 1991, cited in Braziel, 1996).

Recent efforts by the Child Welfare League of America and other groups have placed great emphasis on the quality of links between the child, the residential setting, and the family (Braziel, 1996; CWLA, 1990). Group care services are provided under public, voluntary nonprofit, and proprietary auspices. Group care services are provided by child welfare, child mental health, and juvenile justice systems often to similar populations of youth. As Melton, Lyons, and Spaulding (1998, p. 10) point out, the traditional divisions between children's service systems reflect somewhat arbitrary regulatory and payment structures more than they do differences in purpose, type of services, clientele, or even source of referral. As these authors point out, children in residential treatment tend to be, or have been, clients of all or most of the major children's service systems. As Lerman (1980), Schwartz (1989), and others have pointed out, attempts to limit residential placements in one sector of care through systematic efforts at deinstitutionalization have often resulted in an increase of residential placements in another sector of care— underscoring the need for a cross-system perspective.

Accurate population figures for children and youth in residential group care placements are difficult to obtain. Within child welfare services, a recent national study commissioned by the U.S. Children's Bureau indicates a total population of approximately 500,000 children in out-of-home care in the mid-1990s, the majority of whom were served in family foster care arrangements, with something less than 25% in residential group care facilities broadly defined. These proportions for children in out-of-home care have remained constant since the late 1970s, as Figure 13.1 indicates. Such figures most certainly undercount mental health and juvenile justice placements and mask what some have described as the "hidden sector" of residential care, particularly children in private residential care or psychiatric hospitalization (Melton, Lyons, & Spaulding, 1998, p. 25.). As we have argued elsewhere in this text, creation of an accurate, comprehensive, national, up-to-date database for all children and youth in residential group care remains a critical requisite for any serious service reform efforts.

Percentage

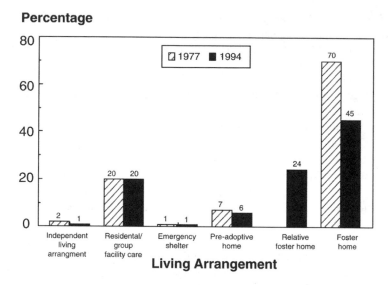

Figure 13.1. Living arrangements of children in foster care on April 1, 1977 and March 1, 1994. Reprinted from U.S. Department of Health and Human Services Children's Bureau. (1997). *National Study of Protective, Preventive and Reunification Services delivered to Children and Their Families.* Washington, DC: U.S. Government Printing Office.

Group Care, Marginalization, and the Climate
of Distrust

"Pariah care" was the term the late Morris Fritz Mayer, executive director of Bellefaire, a large campus-based residential treatment center in Cleveland, Ohio, and a leading advocate for high-quality residential services, used to describe group care programs for troubled youth (Mayer, 1975). Mayer's intent was to describe both the marginalization and stigmatization of acting out youth and the group services designed to meet their needs. Uttered near the end of his career, his comment reflected frustration at the field's inability to raise the level of discourse about group care and accord it the theoretical and empirical attention it deserved. Wolins' contemporary observation probably reveals the reason this was so:

> Over the years, full and part time group care programs . . . have fallen into disuse—an occurrence that most professionals, who saw little good and much evil in their impact on children, greeted with considerable satisfaction. As professionals withdrew their approbation the programs deteriorated; innovation ceased, and cycles of prediction of bad results, and their fulfillment, spiraled the programs downward. (Wolins, 1974, p. 1)

The roots of such a negative view extend deep in American culture and history and suggest a distrust of institutions of all kinds as fit places for the care and nurture of children. Indeed, the appalling health conditions that existed in large, congregate child caring institutions in the mid-nineteenth century suggest some basis in fact and help to explain in large measure the zeal of reformers such as Charles Loring Brace to develop an alternate system of placing out where children might be "rescued" from their institutional confines or from the dangers of the city streets and given a wholesome and healthy new life on the expanding American frontier with upright farm families eager for additional hands to help with the many tasks that confronted them.

For a fuller explication of the placing out movement and its relationship to the development of group child care, see Bremner (1970, 1971), particularly volumes 1–3, and Hacsi (1997). For a series of milestones in the development of group care services, see Table 13.1. Ironically, one consequence of the "placing out" move-

Table 13.1. Historical highlights of residential child care services

For group care and treatment services, some of the more important historical milestones are as follows:

- The establishment of an orphanage by the Ursuline nuns of New Orleans (1729) to care for children orphaned by an Indian massacre at Natchez—the first children's institution in the present boundaries of the United States [Bremner 1970: 60–61; Whittaker 1971a]
- The house of Refuge, first instituion for juvenile delinquents founded in New York. Similar institutions founded in Boston (1826) and Philadelphia (1928) [Bremner 1970].
- The Lyman school, first state reform school for boys, founded in Westborough, Massachusetts (1847) on the model of the German agricultural reformatory. It is not without irony that Lyman School was also the first state training school to close in the now famous "Massachusetts experiment" in deinstitutionalization in the early 1970s [Bremner 1970: 697–711, and Bremner 1974: 1084–1086; see also Coates et al. 1978].
- New York Children's Aid Society sends its first band of children to the west in 1855. What Charles Loring Brace and others saw as saving children from the evil influences of the city and congregate institutions, others—notably, the Irish Catholic community in New York City where children were most affected—saw it as a nativist plot to separate their children from their culture, family, and religion. One direct outgrowth of this placing-out movement was the growth of Catholic and other denominational institutions to care for destitute, dependent, and neglected children [Bremner 1970: 669–670; 747–750].
- The move in the late 19th century from congregate ot cottage-style institutions with an attempt to achieve a more family-like atmosphere [Rothman 1980: 265–283].
- The inception and growth of the mental hygiene movement, beginning with the work of Healy in Chicago, with its emphasis on classification of childhood disorders, differential diagnosis and treatment [Bremner 1970: 536–538; Whittaker 1971b].
- The slow transition of many children's institutions in the 1930s, 1940s, and 1950s from care of, essentially, dependent children to residential treatmemt of emotionally disturbed children.
- Recent exposure of abuse/neglect in residential institutions for disturbed and delinquent children, coupled with and, in part, repsonsible for efforts to deinstitutionalize service programs in mental health, juvenile correction, child welfare, and mental retardation.

ment may have been to serve as a catalyst to the creation of new, sectarian child care institutions many of them reflecting recently arrived immigrant and Catholic families who saw Brace and his movement as a nativist plot to deprive children of their cultural and religious birthright.

As noted in Chapter 10 on family foster care, by the 1920s, and following the pronouncement of the first White House Conference on Children (1909), a consensus developed on children in need of out-of-home placement that suggested the desirability of family foster care over group care placements wherever possible and particularly so when child dependence was the primary reason for placement. By the middle of the twentieth century, less than 10% of children in group care settings fit the description of "true orphans" and by far the greater proportion of purely dependent children were being served in foster care—a reversal from the beginning of the century. Group care settings were left to develop more specialized treatment programs for children with emotional disturbance and/or conduct problems and for whom family foster care was deemed insufficient or inappropriate. For at least the latter half of the twentieth century, group care in one of its many treatment forms constituted the bulk of such services and the object of whatever attention was given to the residential field. The reasons why residential settings continued to be viewed within the professional domain with skepticism are summarized as follows:

1. A lack of clear-cut diagnostic indicators for residential placement, as opposed to a family based alternative.
2. The perception that some service systems, left to their own devices, continue to use residential placement too freely without first providing services to the child and family in their home and community.
3. The perception that residential placement is an intrusive and disempowering intervention, particularly with respect to families.
4. The potential for physical and psychological abuse and institutional neglect, sadly and frequently the subject of exposés in the popular press.
5. The absence of hard evidence for comparative treatment efficacy, particularly long term.
6. The difficulty in identifying core components of residential treatment services and their codification in commonly agreed on treatment protocols.
7. The high cost of residential treatment services relative to the numbers of children served, which some argue retards the growth of more effective preventive, "front end" services (Whittaker, 2000).

For perhaps some or all of these reasons as well as for the belief advanced by social historians such as David Rothman (1980) that institutions of all kinds are, essentially, unreformable, group care has, for at least the past 25 years, been off limits to serious inquiry. The following anecdotal indicators offer illustration.

*   In the late 1980s, a major division of the American Psychological Association commissioned and then declined to publish a thoughtful, balanced, and

substantive report on the state of the art in residential treatment, presumably because it might in some way be seen as promoting residential placements.

- The last attempt at a comprehensive census of children and youth in residential care first ably executed by Donnell Pappenfort and colleagues at the University of Chicago in the mid-1960s (Pappenfort et al., 1973, 1983) was greatly limited in its scope and dissemination in its second implementation in the early 1980s in large measure because of the reluctance of any single national agency to take leadership and responsibility in seeing the study through to adequate completion. The results were never published by the original sponsoring agency.
- The U.S. Children's Bureau, long a beacon for standard setting for the children's field, focused only minimal attention on group care services during the late 1970s and 1980s when, by contrast, an impressive network of regional and national centers was created around adoption services, child abuse and neglect, and in-home services.
- During the period of the late 1980s and early 1990s, private foundations such as Edna McConnell Clark and the Annie E. Casey Foundation devoted millions to system reform efforts, intensive family preservation, and family support. Very few foundation resources, other than those of the regionally oriented Duke Endowment, went to support model development in group care.
- The National Institute of Mental Health (NIMH) did provide support in the early 1970s for development of a model group home program (Achievement Place), but has since focused its attention elsewhere in developing community-based systems of care, a contrast to the 1950s when Fritz Redl developed a laboratory model for residential treatment in Bethesda and the early 1960s when Nicholas Hobbs developed Project RE-ED, in part with support from NIMH.

THE RESEARCH BASE FOR GROUP CHILD CARE

As a result of inattention to group care, model development, treatment innovations, development of treatment and training protocols, and controlled empirical studies of residential group care have all languished. This is no doubt the reason that the General Accounting Office in a recent study concluded as follows:

Not enough is known about residential care programs to provide a clear picture of which kinds of treatment approaches work best or about the effectiveness of the treatment over the long term. Further, no consensus exists on which youths are best served in residential care . . . or how residential care should be combined with community based care to serve at-risk youths over time. (GAO, 1994, p. 4)

Yet concerns about residential provision continue to mount: from those who argue it is being overused, or inappropriately used, to those who argue that its absence for certain types of youth with multiple diagnoses amounts to service deprivation and system neglect.

Fathoming and synthesizing the patchwork of studies that constitute the empirical research base of residential care is an exercise that is itself often colored by the predilections of the analysts involved. Although a summary review of outcome research appears later in this chapter, it is important to note here that several detailed reviews of group child care (Whittaker & Pfeiffer, 1994; Curry, 1991, 1993) underscore the powerful impact of the postdischarge environment, particularly with respect to community and familial supports, in determining youth outcomes identified in many earlier hallmark studies (Allerhand, Weber, & Haug, 1966; Taylor & Alpert, 1973; Wells, Wyatt, & Hobfoll, 1991). Other factors, such as program specificity (Curry, 1993), underscore the problems highlighted in the above quoted GAO study (1994) on the absence of any firm consensus in the residential field on what might be thought of as *necessary,* as distinct from *sufficient* program components. Such program specification, in our view, ought to precede further controlled outcome studies.

Less sympathetic reviews tend to focus on negatives. For example, Melton, Lyons, and Spaulding (1998, p. 47) conclude that "there is little evidence of the effectiveness of residential treatment, particularly relative to well conceptualized nonresidential alternatives, but the primary problem of residential treatment may be *avoiding negative effects.*" These and similar reviewers seem to proceed from the assumption that any residential program will, by definition, be more restrictive and less community connected than its nonresidential community counterpart. Such assumptions need to be tested empirically particularly given some recent work that failed to find evidence of some prevalent negative beliefs about residential placement for troubled adolescents (Friman et al., 1996).

So what does the outcome research on residential child care tell us about the effectiveness of that service in remediating the problems of troubled children and youth? The answer is, of course, "it depends": on how you read the evidence, when you read the evidence, and how confident you are in the methodological rigor of the various studies. For example:

- Do you include in your analysis objective indicators of postplacement adjustment such as school performance and contact with police (residential care fares rather poorly on these measures), or do you include more subjective indicators such as therapist judgment of "progress," or parental satisfaction (residential care looks rather more effective)?
- Do you sample behavior during residential care, or at the point of discharge from the therapeutic milieu (residential care looks reasonably effective at the point of discharge)? Or do you sample behavior at regular intervals in more distal environments such as school, neighborhood, and family (the "decay"

of treatment effects appear both rapid and progressive when measured in this way)?

On the question of methodological rigor, there are numerous threats to the reliability and validity of outcome studies in this area. These are so substantial that only a few consistent conclusions can really be trusted. Some of the more prominent methodological problems are as follows:

Absence of Controls

For ethical and practical reasons, many studies omit the use of control groups required in the classic experimental design. Although this omission leaves the interpretations of results open to question—particularly with respect to "success"—it is often difficult to argue for a control group, if this design is seen to deprive troubled children of needed care and treatment. Some outcome studies have tended toward a comparison group design—testing differential approaches to residential and nonresidential treatment on a similar population of referrals. Caution must be taken in evaluating the results of such comparisons, as youth in residential settings may be drawn from a more troubled population to begin with.

Poorly Defined Service Units

In such an all-encompassing service strategy as milieu treatment, it is often difficult to specify exactly what a service unit consists of and also to identify which interventions are most potent in changing behavior. Although such questions are not of paramount interest to the clinician concerned primarily with positive movement in an individual case, they are of concern to executives and planners charged with the responsibility for program expansion. An often-heard refrain in the field is "We know we are doing some things right—but we are not sure which ones."

Improper Selection of Outcome Criteria

All too often, residential programs have allowed themselves to be evaluated on a narrow range of criteria—grades in school, recidivism, absence of police contact—that either are not directly related to services offered or that occur in community environments in which the residential program has little involvement, much less control. Such outcome studies typically show discouraging results and lead to the nihilistic conclusion that "nothing works" with these kids. The opposite problem is reflected in some outcome studies in which extremely diffuse and poorly defined measures of community and personal adjustment have been used. These ratings often are based on the clinical judgment of the therapists who provided the services and are open to questions of reliability and validity.

Sample Selection

Troubled children and youth are seldom randomly assigned to different residential programs; instead, placement depends on factors such as severity of problem, prognosis for positive change, and available bed space. These factors may definitely bias sample selection in a number of ways. For example, some programs may engage in what is known as "creaming-off"—accepting only the best-risk children—in order to positively dispose toward program successes. This problem of nonrandom assignment, particularly when coupled with the absence of a control or comparison group, can confound the interpretation of results from a program—particularly a demonstration project seeking funds for expansion on the basis of a high degree of success in the pilot phase.

Lack of Utility

Because many of the studies of residential child care are outcome studies—often conducted by outside researchers—many practitioners doubt the value of the research enterprise and feel that its findings are of little use in shaping day-to-day practice. Almost by definition, outcome research cannot be directly useful, since it does not focus on the treatment process as it is occurring but on a "payoff" that occurs, if at all, long after children have left care.

To control for some of these methodological problems, Durkin and Durkin (1975) proposed a multilevel approach to evaluation in residential child care including the use of descriptive case studies, outcome and follow-up studies, process evaluation, and system analyses (1975). Some group care models, such as the Family Teaching Model at Boys Town in Nebraska and the residential program at Boysville of Michigan, have incorporated formative (process) evaluation directly into their training procedures and operational policies so that program staff and supervisors receive continuous feedback on treatment effectiveness (Fixsen, Collins, Phillips, & Thomas, 1982; Savas, 1999).

Many residential programs are now actively soliciting consumer feedback from the children, their families, referring agencies, and collateral helpers on treatment effectiveness. The "Who Cares" project of the British National Children's Bureau pioneered the approach of regularly bringing together children and youth in substitute care settings to elicit their views on a wide range of concerns, including which staff are most helpful to them and their degree of "connectedness" to the broader community (Paige & Clark, 1977).

Despite these advances, many of the extant studies suffer from one or more of these methodological problems. The existing corpus of research on residential care is fairly sizable, but fragmented. Studies vary widely in scope and quality and most suffer from one or more deficits that plague much research in human services: absence of control or contrast conditions, poorly defined service units, limited samples, improper selection of outcome criteria, lack of perceived relevance, and utility by practitioners. An earlier review of the residential literature (Pecora, Whittaker, & Maluccio, 1992) yielded the following conclusions:

1.   The quality of supports available in the postdischarge environment appears to be associated with a youth's subsequent community adjustment irrespective of status at discharge.
2.   Contact and involvement with family appear to be positively correlated with postplacement success.
3.   In general, neither the severity of the youth's presenting problem nor the specific treatment modality employed appears to be strongly associated with postdischarge adjustment.
4.   Youth with supportive community networks are more likely to maintain their treatment gains than those who lack such supports.

A thoughtful review by Curry (1993) expands our understanding of the implications of existing outcome research for future residential evaluations. For example, in reviewing an earlier attempt by Pfeiffer and Strzelecki (1990) to tease out implications from over two dozen published outcome studies, Curry notes:

> Results showed that several variables were consistently and powerfully related to outcome. These included having a specific treatment program, having a supportive postdischarge environment and the three subject variables of non organic, non psychotic and reactive symptomatology. Healthier family functioning was also strongly related to outcome. By contrast, age, gender, intelligence and length of stay were only weakly related to outcome. (Curry, 1993, p. 10)

These findings hark back to pioneering residential studies such as those by Allerhand, Weber, and Haug (1966) and Taylor and Alpert (1973), particularly in their emphasis on the postdischarge environment. Kathleen Wells and her colleagues at Bellefaire, site of the original research by Allerhand et al. on "adaptation and adaptability," conducted a carefully designed outcome study that advances our understanding of the critical components in the postplacement environment (Wells, Wyatt, & Hobfoll, 1991). This study looked at the postdischarge adaptation of 50 former residents 1 to 3 years after leaving the institution. Family support was found to be the most strongly related to the multiple measures of adaptation utilized. Wells and her colleagues (1991) describe the practice implications of their study as follows:

> [A] failure to respond in some way to the conditions in the environments in which youths were discharged may well undo the hard won gains youths make in treatment. . . . [W]e need . . . the reconceptualization of residential treatment as a family support system and to identify the potential stressors and stability of the environments to which the youth are returned. (p. 214)

Studies such as those by Wells and her colleagues buttress recent initiatives by The Child Welfare League of America and others to increase family involvement in group care placements before, during and after treatment. Particularly in the face of growing pressures for shorter lengths of stay, however, a reinvigorated focus on the postplacement, particularly the familial environment, cannot substitute for the careful specification of salient treatment variables *within* the milieu that Curry and others have called for.

In sum, the evidence on the effectiveness of group child care is inconclusive at this time, though the bulk of studies point up the importance of specifying and operationalizing treatment methods and putting more resources into real world community environments where the majority of children and youth will return following placement. This follows a general trend in social services to place a much greater emphasis on "environmental helping" (Kemp, Whittaker, & Tracy, 1997) and, in particular, identification of "social supports" and "life skills," along with risk and protective factors, as critical elements in intervention (Whittaker, Schinke, & Gilchrist, 1986).

Future Directions for Group Child Care Research

In attempting to tease out implications for future research from the existing research base on group child care, Whittaker and Pfeiffer (1994, pp. 588–597) attempted to generate some suggestions relevant at the level of individual, agency, and policy practice. These include the following.

Dissemination and Adoption of New Knowledge/Research Findings Relevant to Group Care. Too often, findings from the laboratory are not followed by translation into clinical practice. Practitioners do not readily adopt innovations, regardless of how worthwhile the research findings may be (Backer, Liberman, & Koehnel, 1986). There are a number of reasons why research findings are not readily translated into clinical practice. The following three points are but a subset of reasons why research findings do not influence practice:

- Most practitioners continue to rely on techniques learned in graduate school and during their field placement training. Clinicians are not frequent consumers of research literature (Cohen et al., 1986), and therefore are not utilizing a rich source of new knowledge. However, even after exposure to continuing education, practitioners are reluctant to adopt new techniques (Barlow, 1981).
- Research often lacks obvious programmatic and clinical significance, and therefore is not viewed as relevant to practitioners. Furthermore, research articles are often oriented more toward other researchers, and typically do not provide readily translatable action plans.
- Quite often, research findings that could improve clinical practice are not

available to practitioners because the studies are never published, or the research takes years to appear in print because of the delays inherent in the editorial process (Backer et al., 1986).

A recent national survey of clinicians in residential treatment centers found that practitioners possessed very favorable attitudes toward research (Pfeiffer, Burd, & Wright, 1992). For example, 88% agreed that the integration of research and practice is important, and more than half of the sample stated that they would like to be doing research in their setting. At the same time, however, the great majority of respondents perceived significant barriers to conducting research in their residential settings. The three top-rated barriers were (1) insufficient time, (2) research not formally part of the job, and (3) lack of financial support. Taken together, a picture emerges of a gap between scientific knowledge and clinical practice (Whittaker & Pfeiffer, 1994).

As a result, very little research is being conducted within residential settings, and residential settings, in turn, too infrequently utilize research findings from studies conducted at other types of settings. Other topics identified by the authors include the following:

Research on Subgroups Who Might Be Better Served in Residential Settings.   Residential treatment programs usually have specific criteria to exclude children and adolescents considered inappropriate for placement. However, criteria for admissions are often vague and vary considerably across residential centers (Apsler & Bassuk, 1983; Wells, 1991).

Three broad factors typically affect the admissions decision-making process. These are (1) characteristics of the child or adolescent, (2) available resources within the family, and (3) type, quality, and availability of alternative services.

Among the criteria that have been suggested in the literature as warranting residential placement are

- extremely severe behavioral and emotional problems requiring the expertise of highly trained professionals;
- clear and imminent danger to the child, others, or to society;
- an inadequate fit between the needs of the child and the resources available in the environment; and
- self-perpetuating cycles of dysfunctional behaviors resistant to less intensive treatment (Barker, 1988; Lyman, Prentice-Dunn, Wilson, & Taylor, 1989; Rinsley, 1980).

Research on Improving Coordination of Residential and Community Programs.   Children and youth who require residential treatment present with challenging and multiple needs that often require a comprehensive spectrum of mental health, education, child welfare, juvenile justice, and related services (Burns & Friedman, 1990; Pfeiffer, 1993). Unfortunately, even when services in the community are available, they typically are fragmented with little if any coordination between agencies (Epstein et al., 1993; Knitzer, 1982, 1984; Nelson & Pearson, 1991).

A critical challenge is the need for better interagency coordination, with the goal of ongoing linkages between residential facilities and community agencies (Duchnowski & Friedman, 1990; Jacobs, 1990). It is apparent that a coordinated, multiple agency approach that pools resources can best provide a comprehensive system of care that meets the challenging and multiple needs of the child who might require a residential placement.

Research on Successful Community Transitions and Maintaining Treatment Gains.   Research on outcomes of residential treatment is sorely lacking (Burns & Friedman, 1990; IOM, 1989; Pfeiffer, 1989; Pfeiffer & Strzelecki, 1990). Few residential programs conduct systematic follow-up studies and, as a result, there are few data concerning the maintenance of residential treatment gains after the child returns to his or her home and community, much less what factors best predict a successful transition.

Policy (Systems Level) Research on Residential Group Care.   Basic service systems research on group care is needed to answer the following questions:

- Who comes into care?
- For what reasons?
- How long do they stay?
- What characterizes the families of youth entering group care?
- How are families involved with the service: pre-, during, and postplacement?
- What factors are associated with youth discharge?
- Into what types of community living situations do youth return?
- What types of services do they receive and how do they fare in postplacement adjustment?

The pioneering work of Fanshel and colleagues in foster care (1978, 1982, 1990) and the recent efforts by the Dartington Research Group in Great Britain (Bullock, Little, & Milham, 1993) and Richard Barth and his colleagues (Barth, Berrick, Needell, & Webster, 1996; Webster, 1999) offer some potential models for research of this type. Ideally, such systems research—particularly that segment that amounts to a census of children and youth in care—is a governmental responsibility. Since the Pappenfort studies in the mid-1960s (repeated in the early 1980s), we have had no such systematic database for either children in group care or group care facilities.

Research on Family Involvement in Residential Group Child Care.   The empirical work of Baker, Pfeiffer, and colleagues (Pfeiffer & Baker, 1994), Wells et al. (1991), and others illustrates the need for further studies that focus *specifically* on the involvement of parents and extended family in the course of residential placement including (1) types of contact, (2) when initiated and by whom,

(3) level of consumer satisfaction, and (4) contribution to youth outcome. To us, this includes greater specification of the *content* of family work, as well as greater clarity about its *timing:* preplacement, during placement, and after discharge.

Research Focused on the Continuum of Child and Family Services and the Proper Place of Residential Child Care within It.   It would be extremely helpful to have some comparative research to shed light on the question of where residential services "fit" in an overall continuum of care and service. For example, what proportion of beds should exist relative to community placements? It would also be useful to know what levels of severity of youth/family problems appear to justify the temporary loss of community "connectedness" that invariably accompanies placement. We are particularly interested here in children and youth who are dually diagnosed: severely emotionally disturbed and delinquent and major involvement in sexual abuse and substance abuse. How do effects for such youth differ from those achieved, say, in intensive in-home services, or in treatment foster care? Are there subpopulations of children/youth for whom residential treatment *is* the treatment of first resort rather than last?

Studies on Prevention of Child Abuse and Neglect in Residential Settings. Children in residential placement are in care as well as treatment. Studies are needed of the relative efficacy of procedures and programs to prevent abuse and neglect from occurring in the residential setting and uncovering it swiftly when it does.

Longitudinal Research on Residential Outcomes.   As difficult as it is to fund and implement, there is a need for life course research including qualitative studies on the effects and meaning of group child care placement on individual development. Fanshel's work in long-term foster care (Fanshel, Finch, & Grundy, 1990) offers one template for conducting such research, as does the foster care alumni survey currently underway at the Casey Family Programs (Pecora et al., 1999).

VARIETIES OF RESIDENTIAL SERVICES

What do the following services have in common?

- a group home for adolescent status offenders;
- a residential treatment center for emotionally disturbed children;
- a state training school for adolescent delinquents;
- a shelter care facility for street children;
- a respite care group home for developmentally disabled adolescents;
- a group residence for "dependent/neglected" children; and
- a boarding school for troubled adolescents.

Despite their differences, all of these services fall under the general heading of group child care. This segment of the service continuum is comprised of a number of types of service, each sharing the common element of caring for groups, however small, of special-needs children on a 24 hour a day basis. The component of 24-hour care is the most obvious commonality. National standard-setting associations recognize several different types of group care settings for children who are dependent and/or have behavioral/emotional difficulties. These include residential treatment centers, group homes, crisis and shelter care facilities, children's psychiatric facilities, and respite care facilities (Child Welfare League of America, 1991). Depending on state and local jurisdictions, group care services for children might be provided under mental health, juvenile correction, child welfare, developmental disabilities auspices, or a combination of two or more of these. Accordingly, there is considerable overlap between group care services provided by these different authorities, as well as a lack of precision in various definitions of group care.

Concepts used to describe residential care, such as "therapeutic milieu," are not well specified, nor is the implied progression of serving the most "severely disturbed" child in more sophisticated and restricted residential treatment centers empirically borne out in existing programs in which severely disturbed children are increasingly being treated in less restrictive, more family-oriented settings (Invisible Children, 1989, p. 7). Moreover, Maluccio and Marlow's (1972) observation over a quarter century ago regarding the placement process in institutional care is still largely correct:

> The decision to place a child in residential treatment is presently a high individualized matter based on a complex set of idiosyncratic factors defying categorization. The literature does not indicate agreement on consistent criteria or universal guidelines and it is not certain whether institutions diverse in origin, philosophy, policy, and clientele can agree on a basic set of premises. (p. 239)

In sum, we must be wary of references to "group and institutional care" as though it were a single entity. It is not. Rather, this segment of the service continuum contains a range of different kinds of residential placements that overlap considerably in terms of definition, purpose, population served, and bureaucratic responsibility.

Much group care is therapeutically oriented—group homes and residential treatment centers—and services children and youth with a wide range of behavioral and emotional problems. Some work has been done to conceptualize such therapeutically oriented residential child care. For example, the term "therapeutic milieu" has been used to describe this process of environmental group treatment. Whittaker (1979/1997) defined it as

> a specifically designed environment in which the events of daily living are used as formats for teaching competence in basic life skills. The living environment becomes both a means and a context for growth and change, informed by a culture that stresses learning thorough living. (p. 36)

Teaching formats here include rule structures, daily routines, play and activities, as well as more individualized education, counseling, and treatment services for children and their parents. Models of residential treatment so defined typically avoid strictly psychological explanations of problem behavior and proceed, instead, from an essentially developmental—educational base. This typically involves identification of skill deficits and the teaching of social competence in areas such as managing emotionality, developing more effective interpersonal skills, and mastering proximate and distal community environments. Examples of such residential programs include Project RE-ED, developed by the late Nicholas Hobbs (1982) in the early 1960s, and the Walker School in Needham, Massachusetts, developed by the late Albert Trieschman (Small, Kennedy, & Bender, 1991; Trieschman et al., 1969; Whittaker, 1979/1997).

Exploring Group Care as a Powerful Environment

Groups have a powerful influence on individual behavior. Ironically, as self-help groups and support groups have gained great favor for providing the support and modeling needed for people to recover from a variety of problems, structured group care has lost influence. Part of the differences may be that support groups are considered to be operated in such a way that people draw on the *strengths* of others, whereas group care is considered to be a setting in which youth learn the maladaptive behaviors of others. Yet the truth is more complicated, and support groups can have negative impacts (e.g., Galinsky & Schopler, 1994) just as group care can have positive impacts.

One key to harnessing the powerful group environment is to have high standards for youth, to ask youth who have greater skills to teach those with fewer skills, and to endeavor to offer youth enough opportunities for growth that they can remain in a program even after they have developed the capacity to be a role model and leader. When all the successful youth leave, group programs have the most difficulty (Wolins, 1974).

Many American parents agree that their children should "go away to college" because they will benefit from the intensity of the college environment and the benefits of meeting new peers. In New England, Belgium, and Great Britain, parents see boarding schools as opportunities to focus the mind, learn discipline, master arts and sports, and stay safe. These environments are considered to typify the positive side of institutional life.

The Hyde Schools (in Connecticut and Maine) are boarding schools for adolescents that also focus on challenging their students—most of whom have recently been in residential treatment programs, wilderness programs, and hospitals (Gauld, 1993; www.hydeschools.org). The emphasis in these coeducational schools is on character development, including a "brother's keeper" emphasis that holds everyone accountable for seeing that their classmates achieve their best. Freshmen, sophomores, and juniors are supervised by seniors who must earn the privilege of being leaders. If they fail to provide the requisite level of leadership, they may be asked to repeat their senior year no matter how good their grades. Students may be sent to a wilderness program component of Hyde to challenge them, if they are getting high, not attending classes, or not providing as much leadership as they could. Families are also challenged to grow and change. Many students remain at Hyde even after they have dramatically changed their behavior. Some students' far-less troubled siblings also attend because of the school's opportunity to build character. The Hyde Schools are just one example of the type of program model that we may need to develop—one that bridges between worlds and provides a broad range of opportunities so that successful students do not need to rush away but are willing to share their successes with others. Other agencies experimenting with a variety of group care options include the Walker School for Children in Needham, Massachusetts, Boysville of Michigan, and Boys Town in Nebraska.

Obviously, not all residential treatment centers adopt such an integrated approach to the therapeutic milieu. For example, in definitions by the Child Welfare League of America, "treatment services" are listed as separate from "work in behalf of or directly with children . . . in a therapeutic milieu." This separation of treatment functions—often along disciplinary lines—has from the beginning been a source of staff conflict and has plagued the development of a unified and consistent total milieu approach to working with children (Piliavin, 1963; Whittaker, 1971b; Whittaker & Trieschman, 1972). Some residential programs, like Project Re-Ed, attempted to overcome this separation of service by combining educational and treatment functions in a single role: the "teacher counselor" (Hobbs, 1982). The Family Teaching model of group home treatment has, similarly, combined all significant helping functions in a single pivotal role, the "teaching parent," with auxiliary support services provided by a training consultant (Boys Town: http://www.boystown.org; Phillips et al., 1974).

Ultimately, debate on the efficacy of residential treatment programs will improve with the ability to specify the essential dimensions and components of both kinds of services. Wells (1991) called for a new partnership between researchers and practitioners and Curry (1991) delineated the types of studies that need to be implemented to answer the question of what comprise the critical components of any form of residential child care.

The national study of families and children receiving child welfare services, cited in previous chapters (U.S. Department of Health and Human Services: *National Study of Protective, Preventive and Reunification Services Delivered to Children and Their Families,* 1997), included a comparison of children served in various forms of out-of-home care for the focal years 1977 and 1994. The study indicates that although substantial changes have occurred in the relative proportions of children served in in-home versus out-of-home services, the number of children receiving out-of-home services was "roughly similar" and, within the population receiving out-of-home care, the relative proportion receiving foster family care versus group residential care remained relatively stable (Figure 13.2).

Number

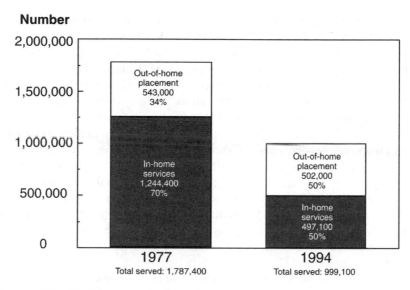

Figure 13.2. Children served on April 1, 1977, and on March 1, 1994. U.S. Department of Health and Human Services, Children's Bureau (1997). *National Study of Protective, Preventive and Reunification Services Delivered to Children and Their Families.* Washington, DC: U.S. Government Printing Office.

Those data indicate that approximately 20% of the total number of children requiring out-of-home care received that care in a group residential setting as opposed to a foster family home in both study years. Such apparent similarities must be taken cautiously, however. Overall, figures indicate a much higher proportion of the total population of children served received out-of-home services in 1994. In fact, some child welfare researchers urge restraint on the uses of group care for very young children entering the system. For example, Berrick, Barth, Needell, and Jonson-Reid (1997) note that in their recent California study, comparing a primary placement in foster homes with group care, for young children, results indicate less stability, lower rates of adoption, and a greater likelihood of remaining in care:

> Given that placement into group care costs much more, provides less stability of caregiving, and does not increase the likelihood of adoption, very young children should not be placed in group care. (p. 27)

The increasing use of computerized information systems has allowed researchers to examine patterns of placement in group care settings and the cost of group placements as compared with family foster care.

One of the historic changes from the era of orphanages to today is the lengths of stay in group care. Analyses of group care in the 1990s suggest that periods of stay tend to be far shorter than they are in other forms of out-of-home care. In a study of 10 states (Alabama, California, Illinois, Iowa, Michigan, Missouri, New Mexico, New York, Ohio, and Wisconsin) group care stays were about 17% shorter than stays in conventional foster care (Wulczyn, Brunner, & Goerge, 1999). However, there was wide variation between states. In Michigan, New York, and Alabama the stays in group care are 45% shorter than stays in foster care, whereas in Iowa group care stays are twice as long as stays in foster care.

The study by Wulczyn et al. (1999) found no difference in reunification rates between group care residents and children placed in foster care. Perhaps because there was a different age distribution in the two populations, 16% of the group care residents ran away although just 4% of the children place in foster care ran away; 19% of the children in foster care were adopted compared with less than 2% of the children placed in group care. When the outcomes for just young children (ages 1–6 years) in California were compared (Berrick, Barth, & Jonson-Reid, 1998), group care placement demonstrated substantially lower adoption rates (6%) than did foster care placement (16%).

Children returning home from group care have higher reentry rates that do children reunified with their families after foster care. Among children who entered out-of-home placement between 1988 and 1993 and were eventually discharged from care, 30% of those children in group care had returned to welfare-supervised care by the end of 1997, whereas 25% of children placed in nonkinship foster care returned to care (Wulczyn, Brunner, & Goerge, 1997). Children placed in group care are, in general, difficult to care for and by virtue of their age able to get into more serious trouble at home. We know that shorter stays in care are associated with a higher likelihood of reentry to care (Barth, Courtney, Berrick, & Albert, 1994), so the short stays in group care may be a contributor to higher reentry rates.

Placement Uses and Costs

The use of group home care does not seem to be changing sharply. In California, recent research shows that the proportion of children in group home care has been between 8% and 10% between 1988 and 1997 (Needell, Webster, Barth, & Armijo, 1996; Needell, Webster, Cuccaro-Alamin, & Armijo, 1998). The fastest growing setting for children in out-of-home care is treatment foster care, which has increased from less than 2% to 12%. Coupled with evidence that conventional foster care has declined from 45% to 30%, the growth in treatment foster care ought not to be seen as substituting for group care, but as an increase in residential services for troubled youth. In other sections of care such as juvenile justice and mental health, some policymakers note with alarm the growth of residential services and their utilization replace more preventative, community-based alternatives (Melton, Lyons, & Spaulding, 1998).

In certain streams of out-of-home care, nongovernmental services play an increasingly important role. For example, in 1983, 92% of the children in group care services for the emotionally disturbed were in voluntary, nonprofit, and proprietary agencies. Proprietary care is apparently on the rise and presently serves 4.5% of all children in group care and 8.5% of all children in nongovernmental group care (Pappenfort et al., 1983). Some analysts are concerned with what appears to be a shift of youngsters (particularly status offenders) from more traditional streams of care (e.g., juvenile justice) to private drug rehabilitation and psychiatric residential settings that are often proprietary (Melton et al., 1998; Schwartz et al., 1983). Similarly, several investigative accounts in recent years have documented abuses in voluntary agencies, particularly some religiously oriented group care services, which often avoid not only public funding but also public licensing (Taylor 1981; Wooden 1976). These latter two categories of group care–private psychiatric placements, often funded directly by third-party payments, and private, voluntary placements in religious institutions that avoid both public funding and licensing— constitute what some have called the "hidden sector" of group care (Melton et al., 1997, p. 25).

Looked at in the aggregate, group care seems not to be expanding out of control; yet, in fact, it represents the smaller proportion of children in all substitute care who, in total, comprise less than 1% of all U.S. children aged 0–18, the overwhelming majority of whom live with their families (Whittaker, 1988). Looked at another way, a very different image emerges. Charles Gershenson, a respected researcher and former chief of evaluation for the U.S. Children's Bureau, observed that

> about one child enters substitute care every 35 seconds: during the year 750,000 will be admitted to juvenile facilities, 200,000 to child welfare facilities and at least 50,000 to psychiatric hospitals or residential treatment centers. (Gershenson, 1990, p. 1)

By any measure, this is a significant and disturbing number of children removed from their families—albeit, temporarily and (for some) voluntarily, given that, as numerous reports have documented, these children are being placed without benefit of preventive, intensive in-home services that may have ameliorated the need for placement (Invisible Children, 1989). Children entering group care settings exhibit a range of problems, including serious emotional disturbance, substance abuse, all forms of child abuse and neglect, delinquent behaviors, and learning disabilities. These labels mask the intensity of what it is like to experience the child coming into residential care. A clinical view helps fill in needed detail of these "children of action and impulse" (Ekstein, 1983):

> Their records are replete with litanies of behavior so dangerous that one marvels that they have so far survived physically intact. These are children who throw chairs at their teachers when asked to sit down, dismantle principal's offices when sent there; and strike out with fists, rocks and teeth at other children, at parents, at grandparents. Their classic response to the WISC stimulus question inquiring what they would do

if threatened by a younger child is "get a big stick and beat him to a pulp." These are children who treat their own bodies with total disregard for safety, hurling themselves into busy streets on bicycles without brakes, climbing to dangerous heights in trees and buildings. Many of their families have other equally impulsive and aggressive members who lash out verbally and physically without regard for social conse-quences. . . . In one family with two boys in placement, the eight year old had been hit by a car while riding his big wheeled tricycle in a major thoroughfare; the six year old had attempted to throw himself out of a second floor window; and the father was in jail for throwing the two year old out the window in a fit of rage. (Small, Kennedy, & Bender, 1991, pp. 328–329)

Intake studies of children entering residential care settings typically show a high percentage coming from single-parent-headed families, often faced with a host of psychological, legal, and financial problems of which having a difficult child was but one component of an overall constellation of problems (Fitzharris, 1985; Wells & Whittington, 1993; Whittaker, Fine, & Grasso, 1989). This poses a special chal-lenge to policymakers and practitioners alike in forging a partnership with "par-ents as partners" that approximates the family-centered philosophy outlined earlier in this volume. Consideration of family involvement raises an even more funda-mental question about residential care: is it best seen as a substitute for a family that has failed, or as a support for a family in crisis?

FUTURE CHALLENGES FOR RESIDENTIAL CHILD
AND YOUTH CARE SERVICES

As practitioners, program planners, and policymakers assess the history, research base, and current status of residential care, several challenges emerge. Some of these will involve long-term research that will benefit children and families in the future. Others will have more immediate impact on the lives of children presently in residential care. Many apply equally to family preservation, family foster care, and the other services described in this book. Given the history of concerns about residential care, it is imperative that they begin to be addressed here:

1. *Prevention of abuse and neglect.* As physicians are warned: "First (physi-cian), do no harm." With an at best tentative record of treatment effective-ness, a *minimalist* goal for policy development in placement suggests that at least youth removed from their biological caregivers will not be subject to abuse/neglect in their out-of-home placements. The task will be to prevent not only physical and psychological abuse, but the special kind of institu-tional neglect that deprives youth of developmental opportunities that chal-lenge their growth. Many resources exist for addressing the special problem of abuse and neglect in out-of-home care settings—screening procedures, case review mechanisms, reporting requirements, training modules—a

good many of which were developed by the National Center on Child Abuse and Neglect. The best guarantor of safety, however, remains a high level of program quality throughout the milieu that adheres to the highest level of professional standards and is monitored through citizen review.

2. *Documentation of outcomes.* As noted earlier, a critical challenge for residential services involves specification and documentation of intervention outcomes. How do we document change during and after placement? In what settings? By what criteria is success measured? Among the many methodological problems that exist in the research base on residential care is the narrow and inconsistent range of outcome indicators that makes cross-study comparisons extremely difficult. It has been argued elsewhere that a good criterion for residential provision ought to include multiple time points and multiple measures (Whittaker, Overstreet, Grasso, Tripodi, & Boylan, 1988). A related task involves presentation and dissemination of this outcome data to a range of consumers: practitioners, board members, policymakers, families, and youth themselves.

3. *Specifying intervention components.* What combination of treatment and educational service components, delivered at what levels of intensity, for what duration will produce given outcomes for different types of youth and their families? Residential services are both difficult to specify and to measure. Yet the advent of computerized management information systems holds great promise for what might be thought of as the systematic analysis of routinely gathered data. For example, as noted earlier supportive family contact during treatment has been shown to correlate with successful postplacement adjustment. To what extent does timing, e.g., frontloading vs. focus on aftercare, make a difference? Given the significance of recent research (Wells et al., 1991) does the *intensity* of family work matter (e.g., does structural family therapy vs. liaison work or even telephone contact matter? Does it make a difference who initiates the contact? Are there race/ethnic differences in effective family work?)? These are difficult questions to disentangle, but they are all, ultimately, "answerable" given the capacity to analyze routinely gathered data. We could, for example, empirically determine a minimum threshold amount of contact for any youth entering care and set in place a tracking system to ensure that it was actually delivered. Similar questions could be raised for group interventions within the milieu, for special education services, life space interventions, and more individualized forms of therapy. Currently, agencies such as Boysville of Michigan are experimenting with the use of computerized information systems and "logic modeling" of program components to inform residential and other forms of practice (Savas, 1999).

4. *Maintenance and generalization of gains.* The real test of change is, of course, in the postplacement environment. How do we design learning experiences that are "portable"? How do we design effective aftercare pro-

grams that include work with extended family, friends, and other collateral helpers? To what extent do staff members facilitate the use of self-help? Are there patterns of residential care that yield more long-lasting outcomes: Michigan, for example, is experimenting with a form of residential placement that is short term and intensive followed by extensive community follow-up. Finally, how does our assessment of pluses and minuses in the youth's environment figure in our overall determination of risk and acuity?

5. *Quality assurance.* There is enormous variation in residential care in the United States. Licensing standards speak only minimally to quality of care issues and standards from national professional bodies are only a little bit better. Due to the huge costs of in-patient psychiatric hospitalization, many insurance companies are instituting "utilization reviews" to help ensure that the appropriate type and length of care are provided. Other remedies include peer review as pioneered in the California and North Carolina associations of voluntary agencies, more criterion-based training that is actually tied to staff career advancement, and more frequent use of program audits. Also needed are more systematic assessments of "model" service programs and a search for technologies from companion services such as family preservation that might have application to residential services.

Finally, it is clear that service agencies themselves cannot address these challenges effectively without help from university professional schools, public sector services, and private foundations. A partnership between voluntary service agencies, public sector, and university professional schools is one that holds great promise for the future development of quality residential care services for troubled youth and their families. Given the ambivalence toward group residential care noted earlier in this chapter and the resultant lack of model development and experimentation in residential provision, the task of renewal will require a fully comprehensive effort. The following questions might serve as a starting point:

1. Under what conditions should any of the varieties of group care be considered a treatment of first or last resort?

2. In its multiple forms, what is the effectiveness of group care in ameliorating specific behavioral problems and improving life outcomes among youths and preventing their reintroduction into deeper end services?

3. What is the relationship between the varieties of residential group care that exist and therapeutic fostering, multisystemic therapy, wraparound services, and similar community-based interventions?

4. Of the varieties of residential group care, what relative proportions of each should exist in an overall continuum of care and what factors should direct a youth/family to one or the other?

5. What are the critical ingredients in the varieties of successful residential care? How can these be empirically validated, captured in treatment protocols and standards, and monitored through quality assurance procedures?

6. How should "success" be measured across the varieties of residential pro-
    vision and what is a proper metric for assessing benefits/costs relative to
    nonresidential alternatives?
7. How do we balance and integrate care and treatment needs of children and
    what implications does each raise specific to group residential settings?
8. Are there possibly offsetting benefits to some of the presumed negatives
    associated with residential placement (e.g., a separation from family/com-
    munity/culture) such as *intensity* of the treatment provided, *physical safe-
    ty* of the child, and *protection* of the community?
9. Are there situations in which long-term residential care and treatment are
    warranted? If so, for what types of children? How should such treatment
    be articulated with family, community, and cultural supports?
10. Do models of residential care and treatment exist in other cultural contexts
    that show potential for adaptation here?

CONCLUSION

As discussed in this chapter, residential care and treatment remain essential but,
nonetheless, controversial components in an overall continuum of child welfare
services.

In a recent review of residential group care, Whittaker (2000) notes:

> Given the manifest needs of children, youths, and their families for high quality and
> effective services, the greatest tragedy would be to extend into the next century the
> polarizing debate that has engulfed group care throughout much of the last hundred
> years. With hindsight and with an eye toward the lessons of history, we can and should
> do better. Group care, in any of its forms, is no panacea. Yet, it deserves thoughtful
> critical review to determine its proper place and function in an overall continuum of
> care and services. (pp. 11, 12)

Several recent developments offer hope and promise in developing new foci for
group care in the twenty-first century.

*   A group of historians, child welfare experts, and family service providers
    meeting around the needs of children orphaned by AIDS in New York City
    envision a role for group care as one of several long-term care options avail-
    able. Far from recreating the Dickensian orphanage, the group suggests the
    following minimal standards for any group services extended to this popu-
    lation:
    1. Continuity of developmentally appropriate caregiving with stable adult
        caregivers.
    2. Stability of the sibling group wherever possible.
    3. A structured, safe, and predictable living environment;

4. Continuing connections with family and continuity with community and culture (Levine, Brandt, & Whittaker, 1998, pp. 39, 40).

Such suggestions bring forth the vision of group child care as a support to families struggling to fulfill their responsibilities as caregivers, rather than as a substitute for a family that has failed.

*   Writing from an Australian perspective, Ainsworth (1997) argues for renewed model building around models of "family centered group care" and highlights among other projects The Carolinas Project, a cooperative effort of a number of group care agencies in North and South Carolina, and the Trieschman Center of the Walker School in Needham, Massachusetts to expand the range of linkages between families and children temporarily placed in group care (Ainsworth & Small, 1994). Such action projects as described in the volume of family centered practices in group care published by the Child Welfare League (Braziel, 1996) offer great promise for breaking down the historical barriers that have existed between group care agencies and families.

*   Experimentation with group models of wilderness camping, boarding schools, transitional living arrangements, and specialized treatment facilities for youth with multiple problems, as well as the many efforts to rethink the continuum of care provide a new opportunity to recreate the functions of group care services.

Our basic policy goal should be nothing less than a clearly articulated set of conditions under which group care in any of its multiple forms should be used to meet the needs of children and families in the context of a fully integrated continuum of care and services that extends from preclusive prevention to secure residential placement for those few children who require such services.

NOTE

Portions of this chapter appeared previously in Whittaker (2000) and Whittaker and Pfeiffer (1994).

14

Organizational Requisites
for Child Welfare Services

INTRODUCTION

The preceding chapters have outlined the major concepts and principles for providing family-centered services in a variety of child welfare program areas. Child welfare does not operate in isolation and is affected by unemployment rates and community infrastructure such as housing, police and fire protection, public transportation, and other community risk, protective, and infrastructure factors. The availability and quality of ancillary services are critical as well, for example, mental health, health care, education, vocational development, and juvenile justice.

Community levels of racism, sexism, ageism and other forms of discrimination also affect the ability of child welfare services to succeed in protecting children and strengthening families. These issues should be mentioned as a cautionary note that agency capacity will be affected by these factors, and supplemental agency supports may be needed if the community infrastructure is not adequate for supporting families.

To deliver effective services, a number of *organizational components* must also be in place. Workers and supervisors need to be supported in specific ways that complement a family-centered approach to child welfare practice. Unfortunately, too many child welfare practitioners work in "toxic organizational environments" characterized by unclear organizational missions, overcrowded office space, poor supervision, low salaries, large caseloads, and troubled working relations between co-workers or other program units (Cole, 1987; Esposito & Fine, 1985; Government Accountants Office, 1995). These child welfare organizations do not adhere to many of the administrative standards published by the Child Welfare League of America or other organizations (CWLA, 1998; NASW, 1981b). In contrast, a number of public and private child welfare administrators have paid attention to how the following community capacity, organizational, or management components support the effective delivery of child welfare services.

Some of the organizational capacity issues that need to be addressed include the following:

1. Articulating a clear organizational mission and program philosophy.
2. Developing effective organizational designs and service technology, including paying attention to program capacity.

3. Careful personnel recruitment, selection, and training, including professionalizing child welfare staff members by promoting key staff competencies. (What staff knowledge, skills, and attitudes are essential? What personnel recruitment and selection capacity must be in place to attract the right staff members? What in-service and ongoing training, coaching, and consultation are necessary? What minimum qualifications should staff in various positions possess at entry? By the end of training?)
4. Reasonable caseloads.
5. Adequate clerical support.
6. Supervisory capacity and supports.
7. Clear and measurable performance criteria and worker appraisal methods (with regular staff—supervisory "check-in" sessions and staff professional development plans to support this work).
8. Collection and use of practical program performance data, including consumer feedback information as part of a continuous quality improvement (CQI) process.
9. Organizational standards of quality. (Whether this is the set of Council on Accreditation of Services for Families and Children standards or another framework, what standards of quality need to be in place?)
10. Organizational and worker liability protection. (Risk management and other preventive programs are in place and these issues are assessed and addressed.)
11. High-quality clinical consultation.
12. Technology. [What kinds of communication (e.g., office and mobile phone, fax, e-mail, portable computers, teleconference facilities, data-capturing white boards, voice-activated computers, dial-in web-based assessment measures) and other technological infrastructure does a child welfare agency need to function most cost effectively in today's work world?]
13. Political supports and protection. (This is related to the agency liability factor. What kinds of political support are essential to buffer child welfare administrators and staff from the day-to-day controversies of this work? Despite the best efforts, children will be hurt and agencies need to be supported to a point where staff are not hesitant to make the right decisions about placement or reunification.)

Some of these and other organizational requisites will be discussed in the following sections along with their importance for effective delivery of social services. The emphasis, however, will be on the utility of these requisites for child and family-centered social services, because this appears to be the major direction that many public and private child welfare agencies are taking in relation to all their program areas, including intake, child protective services (CPS), foster care, group care, and adoption.

ESTABLISHING A CLEAR AGENCY MISSION, PHILOSOPHY, AND PROGRAM OBJECTIVES

Agency Mission and Philosophy

One of the most common characteristics of effective human service organizations is their use and commitment to a clear, well-defined, value-driven organizational mission (Peters & Waterman, 1983; Selznick, 1984). Only a few child welfare agencies have been able to define and sustain their mission in ways that promote staff, client, and public understanding of what it is that they do. This image and clear sense of mission are bolstered by a supportive ideology: a particular set of values and beliefs about the organizational mission, service technology, and the clients served. Patti (1987) in commenting on some of the literature on organizational excellence emphasizes that an organization needs

> not only clear objectives, structured roles, competent personnel, and adequate resources to perform well, but more importantly, the organization needs values, symbols, and beliefs that attach a social significance to the organization's outcomes and processes, and that help to reconcile ever present ambiguity and uncertainty. (p. 378)

The strong commitment to client empowerment and family strengthening held by some family-centered agencies enhances such an approach to organizational design. Yet, as with virtually all human service programs, child welfare agencies function within a political and organizational context that heavily influences their organizational mission and philosophy. For example, a variety of family-centered child welfare services such as special-needs adoption and family preservation services have expanded during the past 10 years, in part because it was recognized that permanency planning was a necessary but insufficient way to minimize the number of children being placed in substitute care. The extent to which a family-centered approach is a cost-effective alternative to more traditional child welfare services has also increased its popularity, as fiscal austerity and program accountability have become some of the important themes during the 1980s and 1990s.

An agency mission that places priority on a family-centered approach is also being promoted because of the "ideological fit" of such an agency mission with some of the concerns that were raised during the past two decades. Many of these concerns were translated into law by a diverse group of advocates as part of PL 96-272 (the Adoption Assistance and Child Welfare Act of 1980). As discussed in Chapters 1, 2, and 3, some of the principles that were promoted by this law and the child welfare reform movement that accompanied it were that services should be provided in the least restrictive environment and with "reasonable and persistent efforts" to prevent child placement. Where possible, agencies should deemphasize categorical provisions of services that force families to work with numerous programs and case managers (Pine, 1986). The Adoption and Safe Families Act (AFSA) also had important effects on services. It shortened time frames for family reunification and increased attention to child safety, permanence, and well-being. It also reinforced the need for agencies to have a clearly articulated mission that drives the agency's philosophy and programs.

The choice and operationalization of an agency mission have important implications for how state laws mandating certain services should be formulated, as well as how intake criteria are specified. Many child welfare agencies operate like the Statue of Liberty: "Give us your tired, your hungry, your poor . . . and anyone else your school or agency thinks needs help and we'll work with them."[1] This approach promotes a nonspecific agency mission and results in an "open door" intake policy that guarantees an impossible workload for most programs, particularly for CPS (the program area most used for referrals that do not fit typical service criteria).

One of the dysfunctional phenomena that we are seeing in some child welfare organizations across the country is the lack of a well-articulated vision or clear agenda for action on the part of administrators. This approach is used as a power retention device by limiting organizational communication, fragmenting program units, and maintaining institutional confusion. What results besides massive organizational confusion is a tendency to try to serve everyone although providing effective services to relatively few. Many social scientists believe that institutional innovation and change occur on a regular cycle of 30, 60, or 100 years (depending on the changes under examination), as societal institutions develop, grow, and decay. Child welfare organizations in the late 1990s are indeed struggling to fight this decay and to articulate a coherent program structure that flows directly from a well-designed organizational mission statement.

In contrast, some child welfare agencies are reformulating the agency mission in order to clarify and narrow intake criteria. Although this process often requires changes in state law, administrators and line staff feel it is worth the effort in terms of more effective targeting of services and lowering unreasonably high worker caseloads. For example, some of these agencies are focusing their services in relation to a core mandate such as child protection (American Public Human Services Association, 1999). Intake criteria and operational policies have been revised to refer cases involving truancy or delinquency to other agencies. These administrators feel that child welfare staff should not act as school attendance enforcement agents or family therapists for local school systems for cases that do not involve child abuse or neglect. In addition, case referrals requiring services for emotionally disturbed or developmentally disabled children are being referred to mental health departments or the agency responsible for handicapped children's services, unless the family situation involves actual or potential child maltreatment. Other agencies are attempting to limit their child protection types of cases because of concern for abrogating parent rights and the need to allocate resources to primary and secondary prevention programs. A variety of innovative program designs have recently been proposed along those lines (Pelton, 1991; Waldfogel, 1998), along with a call for client-centered (Thomas, 1990; Weissbourd, 1996) and outcome-oriented (Patti et al., 1987; Rapp & Poertner, 1988) services.

Some child welfare agencies are building "logic models" that describe the interventions necessary to accomplish the desired service results. Assuming that the philosophical principles, outcomes, and performance measures for child welfare have been outlined, the next set of challenges appears to be determining what community and organizational capacity/funding is needed to achieve those results. These logic models are backed by concise practice protocols or guidelines where possible, within a management philosophy that "manages to outcomes rather than to process." As part of state funding eligibility reviews, the Federal Government (The U.S. Children's Bureau) developed a new set of performance outcomes. Each state will have a set of measures to assess how it is ensuring safety and permanency for children in care.

There is insufficient space here to explain adequately the important strategies of the child welfare experts cited above or of others who are developing new approaches in this area, but one thing is clear: Many child welfare agencies as currently organized are just beginning to become outcome focused and client centered in terms of involving children and caregivers meaningfully, and implement what the empirical literature has documented as effective. Although almost every agency can point to an innovative or highly effective unit in a particular area, few agencies have designed and maintained a high level of quality across all of their programs (for some exceptions, see Fisher et al., 1999; Kamerman & Kahn, 1989; Schorr, 1988, 1997).

Because of funding limitations and the need to focus program efforts, child welfare agencies cannot afford to be all things to all people. Yet what is or should be the central mission of child welfare services? Is it to place children, protect children, and/or to strengthen families? Should child welfare agencies continue to be involved in cases that do not involve maltreatment? Has public child welfare abandoned its responsibility to assist vulnerable non-CPS-related families, as charged by Kamerman and Kahn (1989)? The answers to these questions will shape the agency mission as it is (or should be) described in program brochures, and reflected in program policies, program literature, intervention technology, and choice of staff. In fact, the choice of a central program mission directly affects the choice of program and position titles, as discussed in the next section. Implementing a strategic business plan focusing on an agency's mission is increasingly important in nonprofit organizations. (Kluger, Baker, & Garval, 1998).

What's in a Name? The Importance of Program Names
and Position Titles

To many organizational design and public relations specialists, the answer to the question above is everything. Program names and position titles take on a life of their own and influence how staff members, consumers, and the general public view the agency's mission and method. Consider the difference in image between the following two programs: Substitute Care (staffed by "placement workers") versus a Family Support or Preservation Program (staffed by a permanency planning specialist or family consultant).[2] What would you prefer to be called? The first program name and position title communicate that the purpose of the program is to place children in foster care (or at least work with foster children). The second name and title emphasize family support as the major goal with staff members working to preserve families and ensure a sense of permanence for children.

Some child welfare agencies across the country are recognizing the importance of program names and job titles. Position titles have been changed from those tied to categorical programs such as protective supervision or foster care worker, to new titles such as family specialist, family support worker, or permanency planning worker. These changes more accurately communicate the message of the programs that have been redesigned to emphasize family strengthening, and the new terminology contributes to a more positive image of the agency within the community that it serves.

Selection of Effective Service Technology

As child welfare agencies move to implement fully a family-centered approach, there is a greater emphasis on family empowerment and teaching families new skills for living (see Chapters 3, 10, and 11). Service approaches that are based on neighborhood offices, service delivery teams, community development specialists, and use of informal helping networks are being reexplored (Briar-Lawson, 1998; Brown & Weil, 1992). In addition, administrators recognize that "maximizing productivity through people" is critical for the human services. This requires a concentration of effort, and the use of a well-formulated treatment technology. Despite limitations of our knowledge of human behavior there is a growing body of empirical research and practice wisdom that some agencies are aggressively tapping to provide their staff with the most powerful change technologies available (e.g., Curtis, 1994; Kluger, Alexander, & Curtis, 2000).

Child welfare administrators and workers, in designing their service approach, should be making careful decisions about the intervention technology to be used. The empirical evidence and practice wisdom supporting various approaches should be carefully examined before implementation. Indeed, many studies of policy and program implementation have emphasized how the need to choose the most effective service technology has been fatally overlooked (Bardach, 1977; Williams, 1980; Williams & Elmore, 1976). Unfortunately, determining which theoretical models should guide treatment interventions is complicated by the lack of evaluative research in the child welfare field. Nevertheless, there are a variety of interventive models and practice techniques that can be applied, if previous practice demonstrations, available research findings, and current practice wisdom are examined and synthesized (Rothman & Thomas, 1994).

Ancillary services essential for success must also be identified and provided. For example, what specific kinds of mental health, health care, education, vocational development, juvenile justice, and other services are needed? What kinds of integrated behavioral health services are essential?

Services Integration

Organizational climate and interorganizational coordination can have mixed results in service quality and outcomes (Glisson & Hemmelgarn, 1998). Integrating essential child welfare and ancillary services also includes integrating behavioral health services. Since it has been demonstrated that collaborative efforts are seldom successful based solely on participants' good will or intentions (Eisenhardt, 1989; Kagan, 1993; Lindblom, 1990), a team approach of providing services to children and families requires that participating agencies demonstrate that each has economic or other incentives to communicate, cooperate, and coordinate activities so that collaboration can occur. Some mechanisms for promoting collaboration include (1) funding and accountability criteria based on outcomes achieved, (2) setting program goals across disciplines, (3) encouraging the use of informal ties among managers to get things done across organizational lines, and (4) working together on outcomes with no one organization having control over all the processes involved. (Sylvia Pizzini, Personal Communication; Zlotnik et al., 1998).

RECRUITMENT, SELECTION, AND TRAINING OF CHILD WELFARE PERSONNEL

If service technology is so important and clients are the "raw material" for human service organizations, then child welfare workers comprise the major "production equipment." As such, frontline workers represent one of the organization's most precious resources. It is useless for a particular child welfare program to select the most effective service technology if it is unable to hire and train staff members capable of applying the treatment technology in their work with families.

One of the first tasks involved in hiring capable staff members is the specification of the major job tasks to be performed in the position. Accurate position descriptions are essential for communicating to workers what is expected of them. The descriptions should accurately reflect the difficult job tasks that must be performed and the worker competencies—the major knowledge, skills, abilities, and attitudes—necessary for effective job performance.

Unfortunately, although some progress is being made in specifying the worker characteristics of successful child welfare staff, additional research needs to be conducted to specify more fully the competencies necessary for workers (and supervisors) to possess both at the time they are initially hired, and later as full-fledged or "journeyman" staff members.[3] Lack of these data has contributed in some state agencies to the weakening of educational standards for child welfare positions.

In fact, given changes in state hiring standards for child welfare that weaken hiring requirements ("reclassification" or "declassification"), poor working conditions, and high staff turnover, the number of child welfare staff with undergraduate and graduate degrees in social work has declined between 1978 and 1988 to less than 28% (Lieberman et al., 1988, p. 487; NASW, 1980; Teare, 1983). Furthermore, the hiring registers in many states lack BSW or MSW applicants, particularly for rural areas. Thus, child welfare services are being provided by personnel with a wide variety of educational backgrounds: some that are job related such as social work, psychology, or marriage and family counseling, and many that are not. Although child welfare agencies are attempting to find qualified personnel and to assign tasks differentially to workers with varying levels of professional education, the federal government and many human service professional organizations have become concerned about the growing scarcity of professionally trained child welfare workers and supervisors to fill the large number of position vacancies.

This trend of underutilization of social work-trained staff is ironic in light of a small but growing number of studies that document the job relevance or superior job performance of workers with social work degrees (e.g., Booz-Allen & Hamilton, 1987; Teare, 1987; Albers, Reilly, & Rittner, 1993; Rittner & Wodarski, 1999). However, there still remains a need for more research that assesses the differential effectiveness of BSWs, MSWs, and other types of educated personnel in child welfare.[4] And the continuing lack of professionally trained child welfare staff is to be expected, given high caseloads, deemphasis in some states on worker provision of treatment-oriented services, fiscal pressures to keep salaries low, reduction in agency programs for tuition reimbursement and administrative leave, misinterpretation of Equal Employment Opportunity and Affirmative Action regulations, friction between unions and professional organizations, and other factors (Karger, 1983; Pecora & Austin, 1983; Teare, 1983). These issues are discussed in the next section.

Cultural Competence at an Organization Level

Child welfare agencies certainly differ in their staff composition and dedication to addressing issues of diversity, and yet this is clearly an essential factor in effectiveness (Gutierrez & Nagda, 1996). On a "Cultural Competence Continuum" how would the agency you work with rate?

- Destructiveness: An agency that behaves in culturally destructive ways demonstrates evidence of blatant racism and genocide.
- Incapacity: An agency that avoids working with ethnic minorities and is inaccessible to people of color is culturally incapable.
- Blindness: An agency that believes that everyone is the same is culturally blind.
- Precompetence: An agency that tries to educate employees, but has no real

knowledge about how to educate them, is culturally on the precompetence level of the continuum.

- Basic Competence: An agency that is aware of and accepts differences, promotes cultural knowledge, has the ability to adapt practice skills to fit the cultural context of children, and understands the dynamics of culturally destructive ways.

Supervisor–Staff Ratios

Supervisory workloads are also an issue. What should be the minimum supervisor to worker ratios in various program areas, and how are these affected by geographic and other community factors? What supervisory knowledge, skills, and attitudes are essential? What in-service and ongoing training, coaching, and consultation are necessary? What minimum qualifications should supervisors in various positions possess at entry? By the end of training?

CHALLENGES TO PROFESSIONALIZING CHILD WELFARE STAFF[5]

Despite the advantages of hiring professionally educated child welfare workers, many factors may account for the consistently low number of trained social work staff—not the least of which are poor working conditions in many child welfare agencies and problems in social work education (see Figure 14.1). These factors, and strategies to change the situation, are discussed in this section. (Examples of states in which these strategies are being implemented are given in parentheses.[6])

Low Minimal Qualification for Child Welfare Positions

A national survey of 26 states and 1 major city revealed that educational requirements for child welfare positions have been reduced since 1975. For example, 12 states or 44% do not require their entry-level child welfare workers to have any kind of degree to perform direct service functions in their states. For upper-level casework positions, 7 of the 12 states required an MSW degree (Russell, 1987, pp. 15–16). That study also showed that turnover rates are higher in states that do not require baccalaureate degrees or MSWs for upper-level positions and do not engage in professionally oriented recruitment and retention activities (Russell, 1987, pp. 35–38). Strategies for change include the following:

- forming realistic career ladders with positions for technicians, midlevel practitioners, and family intervention and CPS specialists, as well as developing pay grades that do not require people to move to supervisory positions to obtain equitable salary increases (New Mexico and Massachusetts);

Figure 14.1. Challenges to professionalizing child welfare. *Source:* Pecora, P.J., Briar, K.H., & Zlotnick, J. (1989). *Addressing the program and personnel crisis in child welfare: A social work response* (p. 3). Silver Spring, MD: National Association of Social Workers. Reprinted with permission.

- implementing and publicizing job validation or job effectiveness studies that document the knowledge and skills required for particular positions in child welfare (Florida, Kentucky, Louisiana, and Maryland) (Dhooper et al., 1990; Ellett, Kelly, & Noble, 1995);
- educating administrators regarding the increased costs involved in supervising undereducated or undertrained workers and the agency's increased vulnerability to and expenses incurred in defending charges of malpractice (California, Hawaii, Rhode Island, and Utah); and
- encouraging social workers to apply for child welfare positions by using special recruitment campaigns and job announcements that specify that social work degrees are preferred.

High Worker Caseloads and Worker Turnover

A major reason why child welfare staff resign is their workload. The unwillingness of the state and federal governments to invest in child welfare services results in a shortage of staff and high caseloads. Personnel standards may play a role as well.

A vicious cycle is created when poor working conditions cause staff members to leave. Rycraft (1994) found that key factors in retaining workers in child welfare include the caseworkers' commitment to helping others, the goodness of fit between job assignments and the workers' preferences, supervision, and investment between the worker and the agency. This turnover and other forms of organizational "churning" in terms of transfers and promotions (Rycraft, 1994) increase the caseloads for other staff, requiring a longer period to recruit qualified staff because of heavy caseloads (Russell, 1987). Worker turnover rates for all levels of workers, except administrators, were found to be higher in states with no degree requirements. Strategies to lower caseloads include

- examining turnover rates and their causal factors (e.g., Dickinson & Perry, 1998; Ellett, 1999; Ellett & Ellett, 1997);
- prompting statewide adoption of national caseload standards and obtaining agency accreditation (Illinois, Kentucky, and Texas);
- designing and implementing more sophisticated studies of workload standards;
- passing state legislation to limit caseload sizes;
- encouraging class action, civil rights, or other forms of lawsuits that argue for reduced caseloads (Massachusetts and New Mexico); and
- using more paraprofessional technicians to assist with casework tasks.

Poor Working Conditions

Recruitment and retention of professionally trained child welfare staff are difficult because social workers often are forced to work out of converted department stores or huge noisy rooms with desks but no walls. One child welfare worker in a midwestern city recently purchased a telephone answering machine of her own, because the "new" telephone system was so poor that clients were unable to leave messages when she was out on appointments. This example, although significant, may seem trivial when compared with situations in other offices in which social workers may have to share phones, clerical services, and computer support. In child welfare other agency supports that are taken for granted in the private sector are missing or so grossly underfunded that they are ineffective.

Child welfare staff should be provided with facilities and services that enhance their job performance. Strategies include the following:

- advocating for better clerical, computer, and phone answering services, such as desk phones with three-way conference capability and speed dialing features;
- devising creative use of sound insulation and office divider materials;
- allowing workers to divert phone calls during interviewing sessions;
- instituting flextime that includes some flexibility in the start of the workday;

- allowing extended lunch hours two or three times a week if employees use the time for exercise;
- increasing and making better use of clerical staff, technology, technicians, and volunteers to reduce paperwork demand;
- using electronic mail or fax machines to facilitate interoffice communication;
- "nesting" forms so that demographic and other information is typed or entered once into the management information system, even though this system may require waivers or exemptions from state or federal authorities for permission to alter existing forms (Florida);
- provision of lap-top computers; and
- distribution of cell phones.

If a family-centered approach to service delivery is to be implemented, part of that approach involves empowering clients. Workers need to be empowered, as well, if they are expected to aid in the empowerment of others. Basic office and clerical supports are two important components of this support.

Low Worker Salaries

Curtis and Feagans (1999), Lindsay (1988), and others have documented that although there are agencies with adequate salaries, public child welfare worker salaries in many agencies are low, compared with other similar professions and positions. In a national study (Russell, 1987, p. 45), salaries and promotion opportunities were two of the major factors identified by child welfare administrators that contribute to a positive or negative organizational climate. With the expansion of social work jobs in the private nonprofit and for-profit sectors, the competition for social workers puts the low-salaried child welfare positions at a distinct disadvantage. Licensing programs in many states have contributed to a situation in which child welfare agencies become a training ground that enables new graduates to accrue the necessary clinical hours, but not stay with the agency beyond the point of clinical licensing. Attracting qualified staff will require a multifaceted campaign involving public education, merit system refinements, administrator advocacy, and possible use of collective bargaining agreements (Karger, 1988, 1989). Some states (Louisiana) or counties (Hennepin) have established adequate salaries for entry-level positions. Other strategies include

- supporting unionization and other advocacy efforts by professional organizations to raise salaries and increase benefit packages (Michigan and Missouri);
- studying pay equity studies and bringing lawsuits (Washington and California); and
- requesting social services departments to reclassify position descriptions and other types of job analyses so that better descriptions of the social worker

competencies required for effective service for child welfare positions are included.

Opportunities for Professional Education and Training

When budgets are tight or reduced, many child welfare agencies are forced to cut programs that provided staff members with opportunities to return to school on a part-time or full-time basis to pursue MSW or other job-related degrees. Although the federal government funds some child welfare training programs, this initiative alone is unable to meet the need. For example, it is difficult for staff to return to school, particularly in rural areas where staff members must take a leave of absence to obtain their educational degree on-site as full-time students. The agency-sponsored educational stipend programs in the 1960s and 1970s were some of the most efficient methods for upgrading social worker skills and retaining effective staff. These programs were cut in the 1980s, and in hindsight, these cuts may have saved money in the short run, but in the long run they were costly, given the supervisor, training, and staff recruitment expenses associated with coping with undertrained workers and high worker turnover rates.

Recently, with growing concerns about the competency of staff and high rates of staff turnover, child welfare agencies and universities, particularly social work education programs, have established partnerships to address these issues. Often capitalizing on the availability of federal Title IV-E training funds, these partnership efforts have worked to expand opportunities to provide professional education for current child welfare staff and to attract new BSW and MSW students into child welfare fields. Many of these partnerships provide stipends for students, carry out on-going research, provide opportunities for agency staff to teach and serve as advisors, and keep university faculty connected to what is occurring in the child welfare agency. These partnerships often also provide the aegis under which the agency carries out its staff training program.

A related issue is the need for ongoing staff training. Training is an important component, at least for maintaining staff capability and morale. High-quality preservice and in-service training has assumed new importance as agencies attempt to provide new staff with essential practice skills, particularly since many new child welfare recruits lack educational training in social work or psychology. Provision of ongoing training opportunities is crucial if workers and supervisors are to keep abreast of the latest developments in service technology. Some child welfare agencies view staff development as one of the few remaining fringe benefits for workers during times of fiscal restraints when salaries cannot be increased adequately (Austin, Brannon, & Pecora, 1984). The current efforts that state departments of social services are investing in worker certification programs and continuing-education training for their staff members are examples of the agency investment that is necessary to operationalize the service technology that is chosen.

Training, however, should not be used to substitute for necessary social system or agency changes (Maluccio, 1985; Tracy & Pine, 2000). In addition, certification and other staff development programs cannot substitute adequately for the foundation of knowledge and skills gained through professional social work education. A full range of education and training initiatives are needed:

- creating part-time evening and weekend MSW programs—some on a "satellite" basis (nationwide);
- providing more opportunities for admission of applicants currently working in public social services (California, Illinois, Maryland, Minnesota, Missouri, New Jersey, Ohio, Oklahoma, Utah, and Washington);
- ensuring field placements and other practice opportunities in public child welfare settings through paid practicum stipends, scholarships, student research projects, or administration-related student projects (nationwide);
- expanding course options in schools of social work regarding family-centered child welfare practice, including family preservation services (Iowa, New Jersey, New Mexico, Ohio, Utah, and Washington);
- improving the supervision of students in agency-based field placements, by allowing for more instructor release time and instituting special field seminars;
- creating summer employment programs for MSW students to involve more students in child welfare practice, policy, administration, and research;
- using federal discretionary grants to provide tuition stipends for current employees or child welfare-oriented students (nationwide);
- creating agency-subsidized loan tuition programs and procedures for educational leave for those employees enrolled in professional degree programs (Illinois, Ohio, Tennessee, and Utah);
- using Title IV-E funds to support public assistance and social service workers to enroll as part-time or full-time MSW students (IV-E is being used in over 40 states); and
- creating child welfare training academies and certification programs (Florida, New York, Oregon, Tennessee, Texas, Utah, and Washington).

Poor or Controversial Public Image

Media coverage about child welfare agencies often is controversial and unfair. For example, child welfare staff are criticized for removing children from their homes and for leaving children at home who "should have been placed in shelter or foster care." Child welfare agencies also have earned a poor public image in some areas because of poor services, overloaded telephone systems and receptionists, "inaccessible" workers, terrible office facilities, and other service delivery problems. Professionally trained social workers, like other professional groups, prefer to work in agencies with strong public support and a solid reputation for delivering effective services. Strategies for addressing this problem include the following:

- improving child welfare agency use of the media through special public relations campaigns, publication of "success stories," newspaper columns authored by child welfare personnel, and talk show appearances (see Brawley, 1983; Jones, 1983);
- using agency ombudspeople or constituent affairs representatives to listen and respond to client complaints or recommendations (nationwide);
- making focused legislative efforts with state and local policymakers;
- developing, implementing, and publicizing public as well as private agency family preservation service and adoption programs to emphasize that public child welfare agencies preserve families and find permanent homes for children, rather than merely investigating reports of maltreatment and placing children in foster care; and
- promoting attitudes among social work practitioners and faculty that emphasize child welfare as a vital and exciting area of practice, one that is often more challenging than mental health and private practice.

Educational Reforms Are Needed

Schools and programs of social work can play major roles in addressing the personnel crisis, as well as reforming service delivery in the public child welfare system. Over the years, BSW and MSW graduates have been hesitant to take public child welfare jobs. Rome (1997) found that exposing social work students to child welfare (through volunteer, work, or personal experience) increased the likelihood that the student would consider a child welfare career. Despite such trends, the rise of schools and programs of social work is integrally related to the demand for trained child welfare practitioners. Federal government efforts to increase support for child welfare traineeships for BSW and MSW students have risen and fallen and risen again over the past 30 years. Social work education is the only academic program with a central mission to prepare students for child and family welfare. Increasingly, schools and programs of social work are being asked to address the personnel crisis through increasing child welfare course content and paid practicum placements. The promotion of public child welfare practice helps to familiarize students with and attract them to permanent jobs in public child welfare agencies. But child welfare agencies must designate only the best staff as field instructors and decrease their workload so that they can provide high-quality training and supervision to the students. And the students need to be exposed to a healthy work environment, with reasonable caseloads, working hours, salaries, and benefits. Through the use of Title IV-E funding, university-funded field instructors are staffing agency-based field units.

Not only are schools and programs of social work being encouraged to form new partnerships with public child welfare agencies, but in many cases in-service training programs as well as credential and degree acquisition initiatives are outgrowths of this sense of shared responsibility between the social work educational program and public child welfare agencies. Over the past decade, a majority of states have begun to draw on state and federal dollars from Title IV-E of the Social Security Act to help workers acquire MSWs, and to interest a new cadre of BSWs and MSWs in child welfare careers.

Increasingly, schools and programs of social work are promoting a family support focus in the curriculum so that graduates are prepared not only to do public child welfare work, but also to be private providers of contracted services. Problematic variations in clinical services occur when some social workers are trained to work with the entire family in various types of family preservation services, and other social workers prefer to adhere to a one-to-one service model that focuses only on the child. Strengthened education programming will lead to more effective services for child welfare clients. The Council on Social Work Education, the National Association of Social Workers, the Child Welfare League of America, the National Association of Public Child Welfare Administrators, the Association for Baccalaureate Program Directors (BPD), and the National Association of Deans and Directors of Schools of Social Work (NADD) have worked together to promote joint projects and educational initiatives to address the public child welfare crisis. Social work programs have increased their course offerings in child welfare and have increased the number of public child welfare placements available. The use of Title IV-E training funds has facilitated student preparation for child welfare careers. The California Social Work Education Center (CALSWEC) at the University of California at Berkeley coordinates a statewide effort between 14 MSW programs and the County Child Welfare Directors to prepare students for child welfare practice and to train current staff. Similar efforts are on-going in other states including a certification effort for BSW students in Kentucky that readies them to enter a child welfare position on graduation.

Educational programs and educators are also addressing this crisis, in ways such as faculty and deans of schools of social work are on loan as administrators. In other cases, faculty are pioneering research in effective child welfare practice. Many educational programs also provide much of the continuing education and in-service training for child welfare staff.

The crisis in child welfare outstrips individual responses by agencies or schools of social work. Newly developed protocols and agreements between education programs and public child welfare agencies regarding the various staffing, research, program development, educational, and administrative requirements are essential to meet the current crisis. The willingness of schools and programs to present their partnership plans to elected officials is of utmost importance. In turn, these officials may be increasingly reluctant or more motivated to invest in critical child welfare resources as educational institutions sign on to help.

The challenges associated with recruiting, selecting, and retaining qualified child welfare staff are formidable but must be addressed, as effective child welfare services require personnel capable of providing skilled interventions. Low worker turnover is essential for providing a consistent level of service. Furthermore, the importance of adequate salaries (which require not only political advocacy, but also thorough documentation of the worker competencies necessary for effective job performance) was highlighted by a national study as an important factor not only for minimizing worker turnover, but also for increasing job satisfaction as well (Jayaratne & Chess, 1985).

SPECIFYING MEASURABLE PERFORMANCE CRITERIA AND APPRAISAL METHODS

Job effectiveness and worker motivation are shaped, in part, by reasonable caseload sizes and worker competence, as well as the following two factors: (1) clarity of performance expectations, and (2) the type and quality of feedback that workers receive (Siegel & Lane, 1982; Taylor, 1988). Some of the organizational components necessary for maximizing the clarity of performance expectations and worker feedback include developing measurable performance criteria and practical performance appraisal methods.

Worker performance appraisal is essentially concerned with systematically assessing how well agency staff members are performing their jobs over a specified period of time. In child welfare (and in other areas of the human services), developing measurable performance criteria that are realistic and job related is a major challenge. For example, consider what performance criteria would be applicable to a family-based services therapist, as well as how these criteria would be measured or their attainment documented. Some of the more gross measures of performance would be the number of children at risk of placement who were appropriately maintained in their own homes, the number of families in which another report of child maltreatment was reported although the family was being treated, and the number/nature of client complaints. Yet, in relation to the first criterion, placement prevention rates must be examined carefully, taking into account that some placements represent positive case outcomes. This involves deciding how to weigh the viewpoints of various persons: children, parents, workers, supervisors, and allied professionals.

Furthermore, contrast the performance criteria listed above with the difficulties involved in specifying what constitutes adequate provision of crisis intervention services, effective teaching of assertion skills, or handling the client termination process in a "professional and sensitive manner." Developing measurable performance criteria for many child welfare job responsibilities is very difficult, which is why open-ended and personality trait types of appraisal methods are still being used in various forms and combinations in some child welfare agencies (Wiehe, 1980). Nevertheless, measurement of worker performance is possible, particularly when client outcome measures are carefully chosen and linked to worker performance criteria in ways that take into account agency and resource limitations (Rapp & Poertner, 1988). In fact, to better specify the standards and the behaviors associated with superior versus unacceptable performance, some social work agencies are developing systems that use behaviorally oriented, competency assessments, and behaviorally anchored rating scales (Pecora & Wagner 2000).

In addition to selecting performance criteria and methods, the meaningfulness of the various performance criteria must be considered. "If the client values one kind of outcome, the worker values another, and the funding agency yet another outcome, whose definition of success will be used to determine whether the service has been effective?" (Patti, 1987, p. 378). This is no easy task in child welfare given the controversial mandate of maintaining family privacy whenever possible although protecting children. Choice of both performance criteria and appraisal methods should be considered knowing also that the provision of feedback to workers that is timely, easy to understand, and caseload specific is associated with both worker motivation and service effectiveness (Hackman & Lawler, 1971; Patti, 1987; Schoech & Schkade, 1980).

EVALUATION OF SERVICES

Another organizational requisite for child welfare services that supports effective practice is the systematic collection and use of program evaluation data by program planners, supervisors, and line staff. At a minimum, the evaluation data should at least be used to (1) ensure that care and services provided are in accordance with the purpose of the agency service, (2) assess the adequacy and efficiency of agency resources to carry out the objectives of the services, (3) ensure that each service carries out the intent of the agency in making it available, and (4) determine whether services are effective by using a valid research design to measure case outcomes for clients (CWLA, 1984a, p. 20).

In setting or examining program performance levels, Thomas McDonald cautions that a balance needs to be maintained. A healthy success rate includes a certain percentage of cases that do not meet the program effectiveness criteria. For example, if rates of client recidivism are too low, then workers are not taking enough risks to fully refine their intervention skills (Thomas McDonald, personal communication, February 15, 1990).

Now more than ever, child welfare agencies are being urged to increase the amount of evaluation effort in all program areas to refine prevention, treatment, and administrative efforts in this field (Pecora, Seelig, & Zirps, & Davis, 1996; Mulenn & Magnabosco, 1997). Research efforts must, however, be realistic, be carefully fitted to the program objectives, and incorporate a variety of approaches, quantitative and/or qualitative (Chambers, Wedel, & Rodwell, 1992). Administrative experts are urging that a more consumer-oriented management and service delivery system be adopted, where client outcome becomes more of the program focus rather than how much service was provided (Rapp & Poertner, 1988). Finally, systematic gathering of client feedback, both positive and negative, through brief but focused consumer satisfaction interviews or surveys is also being recognized as important (Magura & Moses, 1984; Maluccio, 1990).

The extent to which program evaluation is incorporated into the agency management information system will help determine how frequently such data are available and the degree of supervisor or worker access. The value of timely information regarding client outcomes is being emphasized increasingly in the child welfare field because of its value for refining service interventions and maintaining worker motivation (see, for example, Carter, 1988; Grasso & Epstein, 1992; Chobar &Wallin, 1984). Organizational integrity is increased when programs are validated through using measures of client accountability. Cost-effectiveness data allow the organization more clearly to advocate for program funding. Short practice assessment instruments such as the Hudson, Achenbach, and Child Well-Being scales are increasingly in use; and management information systems and required paperwork in many child welfare agencies are being redesigned to reduce duplication and provide more useful information regarding both client outcomes and worker performance.

Some Cautions about Performance Assessment:
The Need to Focus on Quality and Understand
What the Outcomes and Quality Indicators Mean

Outcomes assessment should not pursued at the cost of ignoring the quality of the services that are provided. Use of better outcome measures can help determine and improve the quality of service. On the other hand, there is danger in overreliance on outcomes, given the present state of the field. For example, some state or local governments have turned over child welfare services to a private provider, with minimal process guidelines or standards of quality but instead using a few semi-defensible outcome measures to guide agency practice and to govern their level of payment to the private agency. This may be particularly likely to occur when there are capitated payments and few process requirements governing placement and service delivery.

It is a useful idea to strip away needless process requirements, if that is done thoughtfully. Many agencies have thick manuals that are intended to substitute for the individual judgment of qualified workers. On the other hand, there are essential legal or other process requirements that must be spelled out and for which private agencies must be held accountable.

Unlike child welfare, the medical profession has vast, extensive, and scientifically defensible requirements for practice that must be obeyed by any managed care medical provider even if they are not included in a contract with a managed care provider. In addition, there are strict requirements governing the education and training of caregivers. If practice does not meet accepted medical standards or if medical caregivers do not have the proper credentials, providers are at great risk of medical malpractice. Medical providers are not free to manage their practice solely based on achieving particular outcomes. In child welfare, as Feild (1996) points out, there are few equivalent protections. Using outcome measures as a wholesale substitute for requirements governing things such as staff qualifications, case planning and review procedures, and due process protections can literally be very dangerous to children.

Another danger in the wholesale substitution of outcome measures for quality standards or process requirements (such as licensure, qualifications, protocols for service selection, or required arrays of services) is that this prevents child welfare from becoming a mature field of practice. If there is no consistency in training or qualifications of staff, service selection, and available services, then we do not develop expertise in our field (Mark Hardin, Personal Communication, January 22, 1999).

We must also understand the limitations of this new emphasis on assessing child welfare services outcomes by examining the implications of measuring and achieving indicators such as *whether preventive services were provided, how long children stay in foster care, what proportion go home within 6 months, 1 year, and 2 years,* and *how many visits they received from child welfare workers.* Whereas we can celebrate that we are now developing the technologies to routinely record and analyze such indicators of services, we have a long way to go in understanding their relationship to the welfare of children. For some children, for example, shorter lengths of stay in foster care expose them to higher likelihood of incarceration and early death (Barth & Blackwell, 1998; Jonson-Reid & Barth, in press). One of the challenges ahead is to link the daily activities and observable outcomes of child welfare services to their impact on the lives of children when they are no longer under the supervision of child welfare services. A focus on outcomes must never be allowed to become a focus on *child welfare services* outcomes—vulnerable children need our vigilance and assurances that we care about their individual outcomes.

PROVIDING QUALITY SUPERVISION

Importance of Supervision

Many child welfare cases involve families who are in crisis and have many needs. A high degree of worker autonomy is required as practitioners spend the vast majority of their time out of the office. Because a substantial number of the cases served by both public and private agencies involve child maltreatment, workers are required to make critical decisions regarding the risk of future child maltreatment. Workers in diverse program areas such as protective-services intake, youth services, foster care, and adoption often need to develop strategies to maintain child safety at different points in the case process, including case closure (Holder & Corey, 1986). Consequently, supervision of child welfare workers is one of the most demanding jobs in the human services—so much so that a number of organizations have developed training curricula regarding supervision in child welfare generally, or for family-centered practice and CPS specifically (e.g., Abramczyk, 1983; Day & Cahn, 1988; Drews, Salus, & Dodge, 1981; Holder & Costello, 1987). Yet even these programs cannot compensate for supervisors who lack practice experience, sound analytic skills (Gambrill, 1990), or a commitment to supporting (and empowering) their line workers.

Because of budget cuts, many human service agencies have increased the supervisory span of control to where supervisors are unable to fulfill the administrative, clinical, and educational functions of their position (Kadushin, 1985). The ratio of workers to supervisors is one of many important indicators of an agency's capability to supervise their line staff adequately. Given the degree of case difficulty and the amount of clinical consultation required, and because child welfare supervisors must balance such diverse roles, what is an equitable number of supervisees? The answer to this question clearly depends on the nature of the services provided, including the type of clients, clinical interventions employed, worker caseloads, and intensity of the service. This issue is also difficult to address because workloads vary by program area, amount of paperwork, and the capabilities of line workers. Yet the extent of supervisory control is important along with the quality of supervision that is provided.

Components of Effective Supervision

The importance of quality supervision for supporting effective worker practice is often overlooked in terms of the budget allocation and staff development planning process. Yet supervision can have a substantial impact on worker performance if certain supervisory functions are carried out well. For example, as part of a workshop at the Second National Conference on Family-Based Services, a group of supervisors identified some of the important components of effective supervision of family-centered workers that appear to be useful for virtually all areas of child welfare practice:

- Promoting a consistent application of family-centered service philosophy (e.g., by setting the overall tone of the supervisory unit, reinforcing the philosophy through case analyses, tactfully confronting inconsistencies in practice behavior as they arise).
- Empowering workers (e.g., emphasizing that workers "own" the program by

promoting a team approach, assisting workers in brainstorming practice strategies, delegating responsibility and credit, providing necessary resources such as "protected time," maximizing training opportunities).

- Balancing the supervisor's degree of directiveness (so that workers are able to maximize their autonomy and make decisions).
- Encouraging both professional and personal growth of workers (e.g., by incorporating both types of objectives into performance appraisal plans).
- Being available to line staff as much as possible for consultation and support (this complements the emphasis in home-based services of being on-call in order to be responsive to clients).
- Acting as an ally and advocate for staff (shifting the major role of the supervisor as an "expert" or agent of social control to one of being an advocate for workers—a person who tries to remove organizational, resource, or other barriers to effective work, and one who "supervises up" to educate upper-level managers regarding program issues and resource needs).
- Acknowledging effective job performance (ensuring that workers are acknowledged for providing a quality service under stressful conditions).
- Preventing large amounts of overtime or compensatory time from being accumulated (i.e., prevent worker burnout, in part, by making sure workers are taking care of themselves).
- Helping staff set priorities regarding their work in a supportive manner (e.g., a supervisor acts as a resource person to a worker who, after working more than 40 hours that week must struggle with choosing which of four tasks to accomplish at 4:00 on a Friday afternoon when only one task can be done effectively in the time remaining) (Day & Cahn, 1988).

Another critical supervisory component is the degree to which a supervisor is able to balance the provision of staff "consideration" with "setting task structure." According to studies of supervisory effectiveness, both of these functions must be carried out. Providing consideration involves building relationships, as well as sympathizing with, supporting, and individualizing workers. Providing task structure is concerned with setting objectives, clarifying tasks, monitoring and evaluating performance, and providing task-specific feedback (Patti, 1987). In other words, it is not sufficient for supervisors to be supportive alone: A set of structuring actions is essential as well.

Agency and Supervisory Support Minimizes
Worker Burnout

Listed above are just a few of the supervision-related components necessary for providing effective child welfare services. A related concern of many program planners and administrators is minimizing worker burnout. Because of the intensive nature of many child welfare services, workers may work long hours, including evenings and weekends. Families in crisis place many demands on the line staff, which are accentuated by program requirements to close the investigation promptly or to limit the service to a short period of time. To counteract these pressures, many child welfare agencies provide large amounts of training, supervisory consultation, and supervisor backup of workers. Teaming certain types of cases is useful, along with increasing the availability of clinical consultation. Because child welfare practice can be extremely stressful (e.g., occasionally child injury or death occurs despite the best efforts of a staff member) some agencies have followed the example of law enforcement agencies in implementing "critical incident debriefings" to analyze why the events occurred, to develop program and policy revisions, and, most importantly, to support the staff member involved in the case realistically to assess his or her role and deal with the usual feelings of guilt and inadequacy (Katherine Briar-Lawson, personal communication, February 24, 1990).

Some child welfare programs such as the Behavioral Sciences Institute (which is the sponsor of the HOMEBUILDERS™ Program) also assist workers to recognize the gains that clients have made through goal attainment scaling and interviews conducted with clients at case termination. In addition, this agency has recognized individual therapists through awards and the typing of positive client comments on multicolored hearts and stars, which are posted on a special agency bulletin board. Given that large salaries, plush offices, and a 9-to-5 workday will not be possible for most child welfare workers, one of the important managerial challenges is devising creative strategies for enhancing worker effectiveness and motivation through quality supervision, increased vacation time, participatory decision making, and other organization supports.

Technology

What kinds of communication (e.g., office and mobile phone, fax, e-mail, portable computers, teleconference facilities, data-capturing white boards, voice-activated computers, dial-in web-based assessment measures) and other technological infrastructure does a child welfare agency need to function most cost effectively in today's work world? These challenges relate to the next section on liability.

Political Supports and Protection

This is related to the agency liability factor. What kinds of political support are essential to buffer child welfare administrators and staff form the day-to-day controversies of this work? Despite the best efforts, children will be hurt and agencies need to be supported to the point that staff are not hesitant to make the right decisions about placement or reunification.

ADDRESSING ORGANIZATIONAL AND WORKER LIABILITY

Child welfare administrators are becoming concerned about minimizing the areas of "exposure" regarding liability because of the increasing number and cost of lawsuits. These areas of exposure may relate to the use of facilities, services rendered (or not provided), staff decisions or actions, or use of vehicles in an improper manner. Although the chances of an individual child welfare staff person being sued are extremely low, the most common sources of liability in child welfare fall into four major categories:

1. Liability for inadequately protecting a child:
   - Failure to accept a report for investigation
   - Failure to investigate adequately
   - Failure to place a child in protective custody
2. Liability for violating parental rights:
   - Conducting professional duties such as CPS investigation in a slanderous manner
   - Wrongful removal of children
   - Malicious prosecution
3. Inadequate provision of foster care services:
   - Use of dangerous foster care placements that result in a child's injury or harm of some kind
   - Failure to meet a child's needs for special care
   - Placement of dangerous children without sufficient warning or supportive services
4. Children remaining in foster care unnecessarily:
   - Failure to treat parents
   - Failure to arrange the child's adoption in a timely manner (Besharov, 1984, 1985b).

Another source of liability relates to federal laws mandating certain services. The Adoption Assistance and Child Welfare Reform Act of 1980 (PL 96-272) mandates that a number of program reforms be implemented in child welfare, including "earnest and persistent efforts" to provide children with preventive services before they are placed. Providing the placement prevention services necessary under this act requires supervisors with graduate social work or closely related training, and a large proportion of professionally trained workers. Parents and child advocates across the United States have begun to sue state and local social services agencies for not providing adequate child welfare services (Besharov, 1985b; Stein, 1991). Although some lawsuits have forced program reforms to be implemented in a number of states (e.g., New Mexico), the costs of defending these lawsuits represent a tragic waste of public funds that could have been spent on upgrading working conditions and hiring more qualified staff. Unfortunately, many state agencies are unable to obtain adequate legislative support and fail to reform their services until the American Civil Liberties Union (ACLU) or some other organization sues them to obtain a "consent decree," which facilitates the judicial-led reform of services. Connecticut and Washington, D.C., are two recent examples in which such an outcome occurred.

There are a variety of strategies that can be used to prevent unnecessary risk of malpractice and liability, including paying attention to how state laws and policies are formulated in relation to resources provided and agency capacity to fulfill the legal mandates. Proper screening, training, and supervision of staff members is critical, as well as the use of shared (teamed) decision making. "Competent practice is your best defense": Many child welfare agencies are developing more specific practice protocols for service, which act as practical guides for worker action. One danger in this approach is that if the protocols are not followed carefully, the agency can be more successfully sued because the service requirements are more clearly specified. Similarly, casework decision-making and recording systems can either lower or increase liability by affecting how workers develop treatment goals, document casework actions, and identify the evidence justifying their decisions. Finally, one of the often overlooked but most important preventive strategies is maintaining good rapport and working relationships with clients (see Besharov, 1985b; Holder & Hayes, 1984).

Liability concerns increasingly overshadow child welfare practice. Poor working conditions and job stresses are compounded by a litigious environment. Social workers are sued for doing their job and carrying out agency policy. Few states offer complete immunity to social workers and case law is often unclear. Thus, liens may be placed on social workers' homes, or they may find they are prevented from selling their property. Many suits undergo lengthy court procedures, resulting in an intrusion into a social worker's personal life for several years. After such a long ordeal, cases often are decided in favor of the social worker and agency. Unfortunately, by the time the case is decided, there have been great psychological and financial costs to all involved. The emotional aspects of liability often are unrecognized by the public, administrators, and the courts.

When a social worker has acted in good faith to protect a child or to perform a service and then is the subject of a suit or even prosecution, emotional trauma may follow. Not only does the stress of court proceedings and appearances erode professional functioning, but the impact on an overburdened workload often goes unmitigated. The trauma not only affects the worker being sued, but the whole department. Few child welfare agencies have developed trauma response systems to address the effects of litigation on the social worker. Moreover, the effects of rising litigation on creative practice, which involves more risk-taking to keep children and families together, go undocumented. (Rising foster care placements in some states sometimes are attributed to more cautious practices because of the litigious environment.) These are all reasons why the NASW offers liability insurance and helps provide risk management consultation. In addition, the American Bar

Association is beginning to work with NASW, the American Public Welfare Association, and other organizations to address the issue of agency liability and worker immunity (Pecora et al., 1989).

CONCLUSION

This chapter has highlighted some of the organizational requisites for family-centered child welfare services. Many challenges associated with designing and managing child welfare services remain to be addressed, such as securing adequate program funding, using a more universal intake process, designing supportive work environments, developing powerful intervention technologies, ensuring reasonable caseload sizes, and implementing supervision strategies that promote "best practice." If child welfare agencies are going to be able effectively to implement the service strategies described in the previous chapters, these organizational components must be in place to support those efforts. Family-centered approaches to child welfare practice involve various strategies for supporting parents and children. But in order to empower families, practitioners must first be empowered by the organizations within which they work.

NOTES

1. Special thanks to Michael Corey of ACTION for Child Protection for this analogy.
2. The title family consultant is used by Boystown of Nebraska for its home-based services program (K. Authier, Personal Communication, January 3, 1990).
3. For information regarding what worker competencies may be important for effective job performance in various child welfare program areas, see Booz-Allen and Hamilton (1987), Rykus and Hughes (1998a,b), Maluccio (1985), Pecora and Wagner (2000), Rittner and Wodarski (1999).
4. For summaries of the gaps in the research regarding the effectiveness of social work-trained staff, see Costin, Karger, and Stoesz (1996, pp. 158–161), National Center for Social Policy and Practice (1989, pp. 16–18), and Rittner and Wodarski (1999).
5. We appreciate the consultation of Joan Zlotnik for her review and advice on this and many other sections in this chapter.
6. This section is adapted from Pecora et al. (1989, pp. 3–7). We thank NASW and the coauthors of that report: Pecora, P.J., Briar, K.H., and Zlotnik, J.L. (1989). *Addressing the program and personnel crisis in child welfare—A social work response.* Washington, DC: National Association of Social Workers.

FOR FURTHER INFORMATION

Austin, M.J. (1981). *Supervisory management for the human services.* Englewood Cliffs, NJ: Prentice-Hall. A thorough, but practical discussion of the major roles and principles associated with supervisory management in the human services. The book contains a variety of case examples and checklists pertinent to child welfare.

Glisson, C., & Hemmelgarn, A. (1998). The effects of organizational climate and interorganizational coordination on the quality and outcomes of children's service systems. *Child Abuse and Neglect, 22* (5), 401–421. This quasiexperimental, longitudinal study found that positive organizational climate, rather than increased interorganizational service coordination, is a significant factor in improving the psychosocial functioning of children involved in the system of care. Findings suggest that caseworkers have improved success when they can make decisions based on the child's unique needs, can respond to unexpected problems, and have the tenacity to navigate bureaucratic and judicial hurdles.

Munson, C.E. (1993). *An introduction to clinical social work supervision.* New York: Haworth Press. One of the most comprehensive and practical texts available for structuring and providing clinical supervision (as opposed to administrative or educational-focused supervision). It is helpful for both novice and experienced practitioners.

Patti, R.J. (Ed.) (2000). *Social welfare administration: Managing social programs in a developmental context.* Newbury Park, CA: Sage Press. This book describes the major phases of designing, implementing, and managing human service programs.

Patti, R.J., Poertner, J., & Rapp, C.A. (Eds.). (1988). *Managing for service effectiveness in social welfare organizations.* New York: Haworth Press. Highlights the empirical literature regarding factors associated with administrative effectiveness in the human services in selected areas. Topics include measurement of client outcomes, social program design, as well as managing people, information, and environmental relations.

Rittner, B., & Wodarski, J. (1999). Differential uses for BSW and MSW educated social workers in child welfare services. *Children and Youth Services Review, 21*(3), 217–238. This article examined curriculum standards for BSW and MSW education and the tasks required of child protection services workers to determine which functions should be carried out by a BSW and which should be carried out by an MSW.

Appendix

Special Issues in Child Abuse and Neglect

HISTORICAL OVERVIEW OF CPS IN THE UNITED STATES

The legal principle of parens patriae was used to form part of the statutory authorization for CPS intervention in the United States. According to this principle, the child welfare agency has been given the right to intervene in family matters in order to protect the child. This principle reportedly was first used in 1696 in England to justify the king's care of "charities, infants, idiots, and lunatics returned to the chancery" (Areen, 1975, p. 898). The powers associated with parens patriae were gradually expanded to justify court interference to protect wards from the misdeeds of testamentary guardians, and eventually to justify government intervention to protect a child from exploitation by third parties despite the fact that his or her father was alive and able to protect his or her interests.

The use of parens patriae, however, was restricted to cases involving property until 1847, when the English court in the case of in re Spence held that intervention to protect the child from his or her parent or guardian was proper in the absence of property [41 Eng. Rep. 937 (Ch. 1847), as cited in Areen, 1975, p. 898]. But it should be mentioned that during these times in England and later in the American colonies, the principle of parens patriae was widely used to justify state intervention with poor families although state authorities rarely separated parents from children in higher income families except under extreme circumstances (Areen, 1975; Broek, 1964). (See Table A.1 for a historical summary.)

As early as 1692, various towns and states recognized the responsibility of local government and private institutions to care for abused and neglected children. For example, the state of Massachusetts extended the provisions of the colonial poor laws to ensure that all persons under the age of 21 years live "under some orderly family government" (Axinn & Levin 1982, p. 32). The city of Boston in 1735 received legislative approval for the care of neglected children through a process of indenture where children could be given to responsible families for upbringing. But local agencies generally lacked specific legal authority for intervening in cases of child abuse until the early 1800s—beginning in 1825, states began to legislate the right of social welfare agencies to remove children (Folks, 1903, reprinted 1978). For example, New York was the first state to pass legislation to protect and safeguard the rights of children as part of the Protective Services Act and the Cruelty to Children Act, passed in 1874 (Katz, Ambrosino, McGrath, & Sawitsky, 1977; Schene, 1998).

Table A.1. Some Historical Highlights in Child Protective Services

Year	Event
1696	Principle of parens patriae used to protect children in England (Areen, 1975)
1825	States in the United States begin legislating the right of social welfare agencies to remove children (Folks, 1903)
1940s	Child abuse in the form of the "battered child syndrome" begins to be recognized by pediatric radiologists (Caffey, 1946; Silverman, 1957)
1953	Kinsey conducts national studies of sexual behavior and reports significant rates of sexual abuse (Kinsey et al , 1953)
1955	CPS defined as a specialized form of casework (DeFrancis, 1955)
1974	Child Abuse Prevention and Treatment Act (P.L. 93-247) is passed (Stein, 1984)
1975	Sexual abuse identified with the phenomenon of rape, with a "victim advocacy approach" promoted that is based in part on service models for rape crisis counseling and victim witness programs (Brownmiller, 1975; Finkelhor, 1984; Nelson, 1982)
1982	State of Illinois develops a risk assessment system
1993	The Family Preservation and Support Initiative (P.L. 103-66) is passed to fund state family preservation and support services.
1997	The Adoption and Safe Families Act (P.L. 105-89) is passed to amend and reauthorize P.L. 103-66 to move children into permanent homes more quickly and to increase child safety from child maltreatment.

Ironically, these laws were established with the help of the Society for the Prevention of Cruelty to Animals (i.e., the American Humane Association). It has been reported that the impetus for this movement arose with a widely publicized case of a girl indentured to a couple who were abusing her (the "Little Mary Ellen case"). The case was brought to the court under the premise that the child was covered by laws protecting all "animals." That premise was recently debunked as an historical myth (Watkins, 1990). That the Little Mary Ellen case was the first child protective service (CPS) court intervention on behalf of a child is also not correct. Although the girl's case was finally addressed by a court of law in 1875, reported criminal cases involving child abuse date back to 1655 (Bremner, 1970, pp. 123–124, as cited in Watkins, 1990, p. 500). In 1840, a parent in Tennessee was charged with excessive punishment of a child; and in 1824 New York passed legislation allowing child indenture to remove neglected children from their parents or the streets. Thus laws to protect children were on the books in many states, but were not enforced (Watkins, 1990, pp. 500–501; Thomas, 1972).

The Humane Society founded the National Federation for Child Rescue Agencies in 1835. The focus of these early child rescue societies was on investigating complaints of neglect, exploitation, or cruelty. Child commitment to institutions was frequently recommended, and the programs assumed the appearance of private law enforcement agencies. Foster family care and "friendly visiting" (an early form of social casework services) were not emphasized. This led to a split among the various agencies beginning in about 1906, with some agencies implementing more casework services and advocating for public child welfare programs with a CPS specialization (Anderson, 1989).

In the 1930s, service delivery standards, worker training, and the differential roles of public and private family service agencies were emphasized (Anderson, 1989). Public child welfare and CPS as a major program area became recognized as a specialized endeavor. Federal involvement in addressing child maltreatment dates from 1935, when the Social Security Act first funded public welfare services "for the protection and care of homeless, dependent, and neglected children and children in danger of becoming delinquents" (Kadushin, 1978, p. 5).

Child maltreatment was also recognized in the United States in the early 1800s by the child rescue society workers and family agency caseworkers. During the 1950s and 1960s, social work and other professional disciplines began to try to specify the type and nature of this syndrome (e.g., Young, 1964). However, "child abuse" or "the battered child" as a specific syndrome was first publicized by pediatric radiologists in 1946 (Caffey, 1946). The term in use by child rescue societies and social caseworkers previous to this was cruelty to children or abuse of children (Anderson, 1989, p. 241). The article that received widespread attention, however, was published in 1962 in the *Journal of the American Medical Association* (Kempe, Silverman, Steele, Droegemueller, & Silver, 1962) and highlighted a suspicious pattern of injuries that was being seen in certain children. This article and the editorial that accompanied it publicized the importance of this problem and helped focus both professional and media attention on this area. Kempe and other pediatricians were a major force in the passage of reporting laws and PL 93-247, the Child Abuse Prevention and Treatment Act (Giovannoni, 1989).

Although child abuse was being publicized more during the early 1960s, not until the mid-1960s did states enact mandatory reporting laws for child abuse and offer reporters protection from being sued by those being accused. By 1966, however, 49 states enacted such reporting laws (Sussman & Cohen, 1975). The lack of reporting laws is just one of a number of reasons why accurate statistics regarding historical trends with respect to child maltreatment are not available.

In 1974, the Child Abuse Prevention and Treatment Act (PL 93-247) was passed by the United States Congress. It represented federal recognition of this social problem and the beginning of a series of federal initiatives to address it. The legislative intent of the act was to provide for the following:

- A broad and uniform definition of child abuse and neglect.
- Nationwide coordination of efforts to identify, treat, and prevent child abuse and neglect.
- Research leading to new knowledge and demonstration of effective ways to identify, treat, and prevent child maltreatment.
- Compilation of existing knowledge and dissemination of information about successful methods and programs.
- Training of professionals, paraprofessionals, and volunteers.

- Encouragement of states, as well as private agencies and organizations, to improve their services for identifying, treating, and preventing child maltreatment.
- A complete and full study of the national incidence of child abuse and neglect (U.S. DHEW, 1975, as cited in Daro, 1988, pp. 15–16).

The Child Abuse Prevention and Treatment Act defined child abuse and neglect as "the physical or mental injury, sexual abuse, negligent treatment, or maltreatment of a child under the age of eighteen by a person who is responsible for the child's welfare under circumstances which indicate that the child's health or welfare is harmed or threatened thereby." Laws in each state mandate that CPS be provided by state or local departments of social services. Protective service workers comply with these laws by investigating each report of suspected child abuse, neglect, and/or exploitation. Services are available 24 hours per day, through the use of "on-call" type workers. How staff fulfill the mandates of this act is described in the next section, which focuses on the intake process in CPS.

CHILD ABUSE AND NEGLECT

Who Reports Child Abuse and Neglect?

Allied professionals from schools (16.3%), law enforcement (13.3%), anonymous or unknown (11.7%), social services (10.7%), medical personnel (9.1%), and other relatives (9.0%) comprise the majority of persons reporting child maltreatment to CPS agencies (U.S. Department of Health and Human Services, 1999, p. 3-1, 2). According to the AAPC, until 1984 the majority of reports originated with nonprofessional individuals. Although this pattern of reporting has shifted, the victim's own friends, neighbors, and relatives still constitute a sizable group of reporters (19%). Only a tiny percentage of reporters were the alleged perpetrators (0.2%) or the alleged victims (1.2%) (U.S. Department of Health and Human Services, 1999, Figure 3-1). Although public awareness campaigns and reporting laws have increased, the public's and allied professional community's recognition of the problem of child maltreatment reporting remains a problem in most states. A significant number of serious cases were not reported that should have been. For example, the *Third National Incidence Study of Child Abuse and Neglect* (NIS-3), conducted under the auspices of the National Center on Child Abuse and Neglect, surveyed 5,600 community-level professionals who come into contact with children; it estimated that almost three times as many children are maltreated as are reported to child protective services agencies (Sedlak & Broadhurst, 1998, p. 2).

Why is not a higher proportion of cases reported by community agency staff and others? Perceptions of what constitutes child maltreatment vary across the community. For example, some medical personnel may believe that the case is not serious enough to warrant reporting, even if the situation meets legal criteria. In some schools, the principal acts as a gatekeeper, limiting the types of reports that are made. Some teachers have not been trained and some teachers feared the legal ramifications of false allegations, the negative consequences of reporting, and parental reprisals, or had other concerns such as experience that nothing happened as a result of reporting (i.e., child was not removed from the home) (see Abrahams et al., 1989, pp. 7–10; Rodwell, 1988).

Some citizens may recognize that CPS agencies are overwhelmed and believe that CPS staff are not likely to be able to address the family situation in a comprehensive manner; others feel that involving public child welfare agencies unfairly stigmatizes parents. If involvement of CPS staff remains our society's last chance for protecting children in these situations, then underreporting is a major problem that seriously endangers the thousands of at-risk children who are known to allied professionals and citizens but not reported.

Reporting Rates for Child Maltreatment, Until Recently, Have Been Rising

Until recently, reports of child maltreatment have been steadily increasing by 4% to 17% each year from 1983 (AAPC, 1989; USDHHS, 1999). Public awareness campaigns have been a factor, along with the increased use of child abuse hotlines, crisis nurseries, and prevention programs in the schools and community, which act as case-finding mechanisms. Some of the state agency CPS liaison officers have stated that reports were increasing in their state because concerned professionals, family members, and neighbors lacked a clear sense of available service alternatives and so were "turning to child abuse reporting systems in an effort to secure help for children they considered to be at risk or to be victims of maltreatment" (Daro & Mitchel, 1989, p. 3). A state-by-state breakdown of reporting rates for both families and children from 1997 is presented in Figure A.1. An examination of the child report rates per thousand children reveals wide variation from state to state (e.g., in 1997 Pennsylvania had a rate of 7.9 per thousand children, whereas the District of Columbia had a rate of 107.4 per thousand children). Some research experts caution that these statistics do not necessarily indicate that one state has a much higher incidence of child maltreatment because how reports are counted, public awareness, reporting laws, community programs, media efforts, and other factors affect these statistics (AAPC, 1988). It is possible, however, to conclude that more children were identified through the reporting system in Washington, D.C. as compared to Pennsylvania.

The increases in case reporting, however, may be slowing. Some of this decline may be due to the implementation of case screening mechanisms or other changes in investigation procedures that attempt to address CPS workload by decreasing the number of cases investigated compared to previous years (Wells, Stein, Fluke, & Downing, 1989). However, because of state differences in how these data are

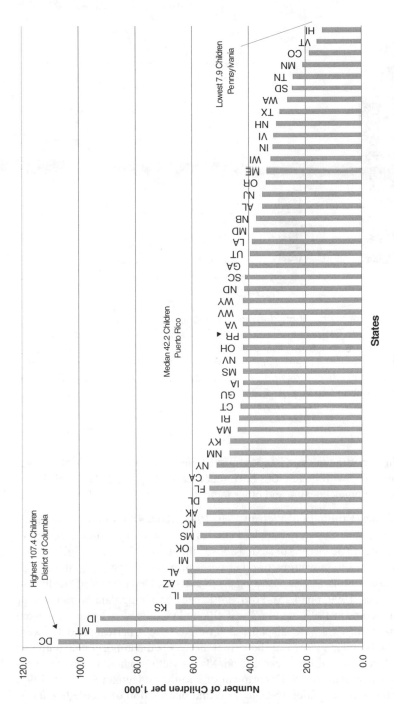

Figure A.1. Children reported as abused or neglected and referred for investigation, 1997 per 1,000 children in the population, (N = 54). Adapted from U.S. Department of Health and Human Services, Children's Bureau, National Center on Child Abuse and Neglect. (1999). *Child maltreatment 1997: Reports from the states to the National Child Abuse and Neglect Data System.* Washington, DC: Government Printing Office, p. E-4.

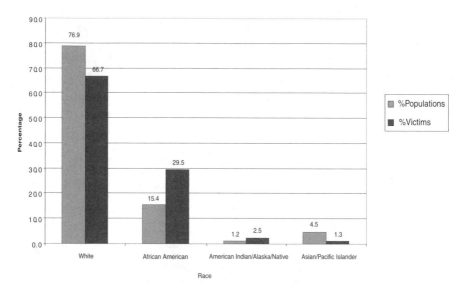

Figure A.2. Comparison of children in the population and child victims by race, 1997 (*N* = 585,512 victims in 40 states). Adapted from U.S. Department of Health and Human Services, Children's Bureau, National Center on Child Abuse and Neglect. (1999). *Child maltreatment 1997: Reports from the states to the National Child Abuse and Neglect Data System.* Washington, DC: Government Printing Office, p. 4–6.

collected, the reporting rates and trends must be viewed with caution. Furthermore, a number of states with large cities have recorded a jump in CPS reports due to increased use of crack cocaine and other factors.

Gender/Race/Ethnicity of Victims.   In 1997, about 48% of maltreated children were male and 52% were female. Females were more than three times more likely than males to be victims of sexual abuse, although males were slightly more likely than females to be victims of other types of maltreatment, with the exception of emotional maltreatment (49% versus 51%) (U.S. Department of Health and Human Services, 1999, pp. 4–5). For the 40 states providing data on the race or ethnicity of victims in 1997, about 67% of all child victims were white, 30% were African American, 13% were Hispanic, 3% were Native American, and 1% were Asian/Pacific Islander. Figure A.2 shows that there were disproportionate numbers of African American and American-Indian/Alaska victims, about twice their proportion in the population (U.S. Department of Health and Human Services, 1999, p. 4-6). Demographic data on the age, sex, and distribution of race/ethnicity of victims has been similar for all 6 years of NCANDS data collection.

The Third National Incidence Study of Child Abuse
and Neglect

Study Overview. The most recent national incidence study involving multiple levels of reporting was conducted by Westat, Inc., for NCCAN. This section is extracted from the executive summary of a report from the Children's Bureau authored by Sedlak and Broadhurst (1996). This study (cited hereafter as the NIS-3 study) was the third of three studies to attempt to assess the incidence of child abuse and neglect. The first NIS (NIS-1) was conducted in 1979 and 1980 and published in 1981. The second NIS (NIS-2) was conducted in 1986 and 1987 and published in 1988.

The NIS-3 data were collected in 1993 and 1994, analyses were conducted in 1995 and 1996, and these results were published in 1996. A key objective of the NIS-3 was to provide updated estimates of the incidence of child abuse and neglect in the United States and measure changes in incidence from the earlier studies.

Design and Methods. The NIS-3 offers an important perspective on the scope of child abuse and neglect. The NIS includes children who were investigated by CPS agencies, but it also obtains data on children seen by community professionals who were not reported to CPS or who were screened out by CPS without investigation. This means that the NIS estimates provide a more comprehensive measure of the scope of child abuse and neglect known to community professionals, including both abused and neglected children who are in the official statistics and those who are not (see Sedluk & Broadhurst, 1998).

General Findings. There have been substantial and significant increases in the incidence of child abuse and neglect since the last national incidence study was conducted in 1986. For example, an estimated 1,553,800 children in the United States were abused or neglected under the Harm Standard in 1993. The NIS-3 total reflects a 67% increase since the NIS-2 estimate, which indicated that the total was 931,000 children in 1986, and it corresponds to a 149% increase since the NIS-1 estimate for 1980 of 625,100 children (Sedlak and Broadhurst, 1996, Executive Summary).

Significant or close-to-significant increases were found in both abuse and neglect. For example, the number of abused children who were countable under the Harm Standard rose by 46% from an estimated 507,700 in the NIS-2 to 743,200 in the NIS-3. The number of neglected children who fit the Harm Standard increased significantly from 474,800 during the NIS-2 data collection in 1986 to 879,000 at the time of the NIS-3 data period in 1993. In the estimates given here and below, children are included in all categories that apply to them (i.e., those who were both abused and neglected are included in both estimates). Under the Harm Standard definitions, the total number of abused and neglected children was two-thirds higher in the NIS-3 than in the NIS-2. This means that a child's risk of experiencing harm-causing abuse or neglect in 1993 was one and one-half times the child's risk in 1986.

Child Characteristics.   Girls were sexually abused three times more often than boys. Boys had a greater risk of emotional neglect and of serious injury than girls. Children are consistently vulnerable to sexual abuse from age 3 on. There were no significant race differences in the incidence of maltreatment or maltreatment-related injuries uncovered in either the NIS-2 or the NIS-3.

Family Characteristics.   Children of single parents had a 77% greater risk of being harmed by physical abuse, an 87% greater risk of being harmed by physical neglect, and an 80% greater risk of suffering serious injury or harm from abuse or neglect than children living with both parents. Children in the largest families were physically neglected at nearly three times the rate of those who came from single-child families. Children from families with annual incomes below $15,000, as compared to children from families with annual incomes above $30,000 per year, were over 22 times more likely to experience some form of maltreatment that fit the Harm Standard and over 25 times more likely to suffer some form of maltreatment as defined by the Endangerment Standard. Furthermore, children from the lowest income families were 18 times more likely to be sexually abused, almost 56 times more likely to be educationally neglected, and over 22 times more likely to be seriously injured from maltreatment as defined under the Harm Standard than children from the higher income families.

Substantiation Criteria Affect Statistics
Regarding Child Maltreatment

One of the major issues related to the incidence of child maltreatment focuses attention on why so many of the reported and investigated cases are not serious enough to be substantiated. Substantiation rates reflect the proportion of the cases reported in which workers determine that child abuse or neglect was present or had occurred. Program critics have stated that child abuse and neglect laws are too vague and too inclusive. Because the substantiation rates are too low, family privacy is being violated and too many children in seriously abusive situations are not receiving adequate protection (Besharov, 1986, Fernandez, 1996). But vague reporting laws and society's preference to protect children contribute to this situation. In light of limited resources to serve clients, many states are narrowing their definitions to screen out more of the inappropriate CPS reports; some states, such as Washington, are referring low-risk cases to community agencies instead of investigating them (AAPC, 1989, p. 14).

Furthermore, the way in which substantiation is defined affects the statistics obtained. For example, NCANDS data estimated that 33.8% of the reports in 1997 were substantiated or indicated, compared to a much larger number reported (U.S. Department of Health and Human Services, 1999, pp. 3–4). State substantiation rates do vary greatly; for example, substantiation rates in 1993 varied from 13% in New Hampshire to 83% in Connecticut (U.S. Department of Health and Human Services, National Center on Child Abuse and Neglect, 1995), and the median substantiation rate was 35% for the subset of states supplying these data (U.S. DHHS and the National Center on Child Abuse and Neglect, 1995). This difference may largely be due to differences in the definition of substantiation versus unfounded and inconsistencies among workers.

Some workers find that child abuse or neglect has occurred, but that the parents are using resources to ensure that the maltreatment will not occur again. These workers are reluctant to substantiate the case because they believe that it would unfairly place the names of those parents on the central registry for the state.

Another issue is how substantiation rates are computed; many states use categories other than substantiated and unfounded (e.g., suspected). How they count the cases in the other category affects the rates. Another source of confusion relates to the definition of the term substantiated. Some CPS supervisors and workers substantiate a case only when they have sufficient evidence to file the case in criminal court, as compared to having obtained enough information for filing the case with juvenile court. These and other serious problems in regard to using a uniform approach to substantiating cases are present in many states. If the accuracy of state as well as national statistics is to be improved, more consensus and consistency in this area must be achieved.

SPECIAL GROUPS AND CHILD MALTREATMENT

Juvenile Perpetrators of Child Maltreatment

One of the more worrisome trends is the increasing number of cases of child maltreatment in which the perpetrator is 18 or under, particularly in relation to acts of sexual abuse committed by adolescents. Many of these adolescent perpetrators are victims themselves, which indicates a lack of effective interventive efforts to stop the cycle of maltreatment (McKenzie, English, & Henderson, 1987). It is tragic that in some states services may be vulnerable to funding reductions when the provision of treatment at this time in an adolescent's development could help make the difference in whether he or she makes a healthy adjustment to living independently as a functioning adult in the community.

Child Maltreatment among Specific
Ethnic-Minority Groups

Relatively few rigorous studies of prevalence and family characteristics have been conducted for specific ethnic-minority groups. But differences in how various cultures distinguish acceptable from unacceptable childrearing practices is crucial to ethnically sensitive assessment (Gray & Cosgrove, 1985; Hong & Hong, 1991; Korbin, 1981). Sample sizes and research methodology vary significantly, making summarization difficult.

Child Maltreatment in Out-of-Home Care

Society expects that children will be safe if they are removed from their birth parents. Child welfare agencies have a reasonably good record in most states in this area, but the serious cases of child maltreatment by foster or adoptive parents or by staff members in group care programs often bring intense media attention and public outcries. Reliable data about rates of child abuse or neglect in larger foster care population are sparse, so it is difficult to gauge agency performance in this area. Studies differ greatly, ranging from 0.27 to 7% maltreatment rates by caregivers in out-of-home settings (see Bolton, Laner, & Gai, 1981; Rindfleisch & Rabb, 1984; Nunno & Motz, 1988; Ryan, McFadden, & Wiencek, 1987).

Spencer and Knudsen (1992) reported that rates of child maltreatment varied by setting—with 16.93 children per 1,000 in foster homes, 120.35 per 1,000 children in residential care, 8.88 per 1,000 children in state institutions, and 15.66 per 1,000 in hospitals and other placements. Oregon reported a rate of 4–5 children per 1,000 in a recent year period (as cited in Poertner, Bussey, & Fluke, 1999, pp. 550–551). In one set of analyses for the state of Illinois over a 5-year period the rates varied between 1.7% and 2.3% (Poertner, Bussey, & Fluke, 1999, p. 549). More comparable data need to be gathered, including using anonymous or confidential surveys of children, before definitive judgments can be made about the true incidence levels of child maltreatment in out-of-home care.

Effects of Child Maltreatment

If child fatalities due to child maltreatment are relatively low compared to other social problems, why should society be concerned about this social problem? Although the evidence base is not complete and most children who are abused or neglected grow up to be healthy functioning adults, there can be a number of short- and/or long-term negative consequences (see Anderson et al., 1993; Lamphear, 1985; Silverman, Reinherz, & Giaconia, 1996 for reviews). For physically abused children, there is greater incidence of brain damage, learning impairments, and growth retardation (Kempe, Silverman, Steele, Droegemuller, & Silver, 1962; Martin, Conway, Brezzle, & Kempe, 1974). Increases in aggressive, delinquent, and antisocial behaviors have been noted for children in the general population (Kinard, 1980; Lewis, Shanok, Pincus, & Glaser, 1979; Mathews & Pearce, 1998), as well as for children growing up in long-term foster care (Fanshel, Finch, & Grundy, 1990). The economic consequences are immense in terms of medical costs, special-education services, counseling, delinquency, and employment problems (Daro, 1988, pp. 153–162).

For children who have been sexually abused, the issue is more controversial but no less serious. Finkelhor and Browne (1986) point out that children suffer from sexual abuse due to at least four "traumagenic dynamics" or factors:

- traumatic sexualization, in which they are introduced to sexual experiences that are developmentally inappropriate—they learn to use sexual behavior in manipulating others;
- betrayal or a loss of their sense of security and trust;
- powerlessness—feelings of fear, anxiety, and helplessness because they cannot terminate the abusive situation; and
- resulting stigmatization, where they distort their own sense of value and worth because they realize that the victimization is socially unacceptable and they feel ashamed, guilty, and worthless.

A variety of short- and long-term effects of sexual abuse have been identified (see Fergusson & Lynskey, 1997; Mathews & Pearce, 1998; Golding, 1999; Schaaf & McCanne, 1998). Sexually victimized boys (and to a lesser extent girls) may molest other young children as they grow older (McKenzie et al., 1987) as well as suffer from depression, aggressive behavior, fire-setting, substance abuse, and social withdrawal (for more information, see Finkelhor & Browne, 1986; Kunitz, Levy, McCloskey, & Gabriel, 1998; Pecora & Martin, 1989, pp. 79–81; Walker, Bonner, & Kaufman, 1988, pp. 111, 113–114).

For children who have been neglected, the effects may vary with the neglect but include malnutrition, health problems, serious physical illness due to medical neglect or food poisoning, learning disabilities, injury due to hazardous living conditions, and victimization of various kinds (Polansky, Chalmers, Buttenweiser, & Williams, 1982).

Emotional maltreatment is even more controversial in that the effects of this form of abuse or neglect may be even more subtle. Yet the very justification for agency intervention in this type of family situation is predicated on the ability to document significant emotional trauma, behavioral effects, or some other form of reaction. Needless to say, as discussed further in Chapter 7, poor self-esteem, various physical disorders, school problems, adolescent suicide, and a number of other problems are consequences of this form of maltreatment (Garbarino, Guttmann, & Seeley, 1986).

CPS INTAKE CHALLENGES

A number of problems are hampering intake units across the country, such as turnover in agency staff members with a knowledge of community resources, controversy over the minimum qualifications necessary for intake staff, insufficient agency or community services to meet the needs of families, lack of specialized and culturally relevant treatment programs, and insufficient amounts of low-cost housing (see Table A.2). The last challenge is particularly problematic in many of the large urban areas and Native-American reservations where placement ostensibly cannot be based on poverty alone, but families are forced to live in overcrowded and dangerous living conditions although waiting for affordable housing. These situations limit what intake staff can recommend to families inquiring about services, forcing CPS staff members to weigh the risks to the children of leaving them with their parents versus the psychological and other benefits of preserving families.

Factors That Affect the Provision of CPS

It should be noted that many child welfare advocates have been concerned about the conflicting roles of investigator and helper (e.g., Pelton, 1989; Lindsey, 1994; Waldfogel, 1998). Costin, Karger, and Stoesz (1996) propose major restructuring of child abuse policies and services. In particular, they advocate establishment in each locality of a "children's authority." The latter would have "a clear and unambiguous mandate to protect the rights and well-being of children ... in a geographically circumscribed catchment area" (Costin, Karger, & Stoesz, 1996, pp. 173–174). Such an authority would incorporate the following major functions:

- family support
- prevention/education services
- child placement
- investigation
- enforcement; and
- research and development.

CPS are affected by several factors, including the following: agency policy and statutory limitations, service delivery standards, services available, and client ability or willingness to use the service. No matter what an agency or individual worker would like to do to assist a family, both operate under agency policy and statutory limitations. For example, a worker may wish to assist a child who he or she feels is being emotionally maltreated by parents, but if the case situation does not meet the requirements for a petition, it may be impossible for a worker to intervene unless the family agrees to cooperate voluntarily.

Standards used in case decision making seriously affect provision of services. Historically, the standard used for CPS intervention was based on the "best interests of the child" (Goldstein, Freud, & Solnit, 1979). Such a broad and subjective standard skewed social worker's actions toward frequent removal of children. This approach to practice resulted in an emphasis (and a public expectation) that child welfare services should be used to improve all areas of family functioning. In addition, child placement was also justified because it was the "best" plan for the

Table A.2. Major Problems of CPS: by Jane Waldfogel

Overinclusion

For a variety of reasons, some families are unjustly or inappropriately reported to CPS, exposing them unnecessarily to coercive and intrusive investigations. That problem can be termed "overinclusion." For instance, according to parents' rights groups, the current abuse and neglect statutes and practices lead CPS to intervene in the disciplinary decisions of some families that do not warrant public intervention; in addition, both parents and CPS agencies worry that individuals may file baseless, vindictive reports as part of ongoing custody disputes, fights with neighbors, and so on.[a] Child protection professionals also express concerns about the disproportionate representation of children from poor and minority families in the CPS system. These families may be at higher risk for conditions of poverty-related neglect, such as inadequate housing or child care, and they also may be more likely to come to the attention of reporters.

Contributing to the problem of overinclusion is the perception on the part of some community advocates that families stand a better chance of getting services such as child care or therapy if they are identified as CPS cases.[b] This perception leads some to refer low-risk families to CPS, even though that referral is no guarantee of receiving any services at all. Together with false reports of abuse and neglect, reports concerning relatively low-risk families unnecessarily add to the volume of cases flooding the CPS system. These inappropriately referred cases are problematic not only because of the potential harm to the families involved, but also because they may impede the ability of the system to respond effectively to other, higher-risk cases.

Capacity

The second problem, then, has to do with capacity. Put simply, the number of families involved with the child protection system far exceeds the capacity of the system to serve them responsibly. Both federal mandates and state laws require that CPS agencies accept and respond to reports of child abuse, yet the resources devoted to this activity have not kept pace with the rapidly rising demand. As a result, even the systems with the best resources have been unable to keep up with the increased caseloads. There is consensus that the system is at or near the breaking point.[c]

Underinclusion

The third problem, paradoxically, is underinclusion. Some children and families who could benefit from child protective services are not reached, or are not reached adequately, by CPS agencies. Even the best reporting and screening systems will miss some abusive families who should be subject to child protective intervention. . . . Moreover, child welfare professionals and community advocates point out that another group is underincluded: low-risk families who voluntarily contact CPS to ask for help, only to have their request denied because they are not high-risk.

Given the limited availability of preventive services such as child care or family therapy, excluding these families from CPS all too often means that they will not receive help until they cross the line into abuse and neglect. At that point, their problems may be more intractable, and more damage will have been done to the child.

Service Orientation

The fourth and fifth problems have to do with services for families. The basic service orientation of the child protection system has long been twofold: to investigate and remedy abuse and neglect in an authoritative way, and to keep families together whenever possible. Re-

(*continued*)

Table A.2. (Continued)

flecting the tension between these competing goals, CPS agencies have tended to alternately emphasize child rescue (by promptly removing the child from home to a safer setting) or family preservation (by keeping the child at home and providing services to strengthen the family). Yet, neither orientation is correct for all families, and as CPS follows swings of the pendulum from one approach to the other, some families are ill-served.

Service Delivery

In many instances, needed services simply are not available. Service delivery tends to be uneven across communities, with particular shortages of services delivered in languages other than English. An overarching service delivery issue is that families often have multiple and overlapping problems, while services for them tend to be fragmented, delivered in separate locations by different professionals.[d] Although this issue is not unique to child protection, the lack of service integration is particularly problematic for CPS. Many families need services, such as substance-abuse treatment, housing, or child care, that the agency does not provide directly and must obtain through the cooperation of other service providers. CPS caseworkers typically cannot access funds to buy services on a case-by-case basis. . . . Because they are large public bureaucracies engaged in a high-stakes enterprise, CPS agencies tend to adopt a uniform approach to all cases, prescribing specific procedures that must be followed in each case rather than encouraging a customized approach that takes into account the fact that families coming to the attention of CPS are a varied group whose needs change over time. Although standardized procedures exist to ensure that the delivery of services is fair, responsible, and equitable, they often mean that families do not get a response that is sufficiently tailored to their needs.

Source: Abstracted from Waldfogel (1998, pp. 107–109).

[a]Myers, J.B. (Ed.) (1994). *The backlash: Child protection under fire.* Thousand Oaks, CA: Sage.

[b]Kamerman, S., & Kahn, A. (1990). Social services for children, youth, and families in the United States. *Children and Youth Services Review 12* (½), 1–184; Kamerman, S. & Kahn, A. (1990). If CPS is driving child welfare—Where do we go from here? *Public Welfare 48,* 1, 9–13.

[c]In fact, the U.S. Advisory Board on Child Abuse and Neglect declared that CPS was in a state of emergency. See note no. 10, U.S. Advisory Board on Child Abuse and Neglect (1990, p. 2).

[d]See, for instance, Kamerman, S., & Kahn, A. (1992). *Integrating services integration: An overview of initiatives, issues, and possibilities.* New York: National Center for Children in Poverty; and Waldfogel, J. (1997). The new wave of service integration. *Social Service Review, 71*(3), 463–484.

child. The public and certain community agencies expected that the grade for family functioning had to be improved from an F to an A before the case was closed.

That expectation is no longer feasible or ethical. CPS and child welfare staff are instead focusing on minimum standards of parenting, with a requirement that involuntary CPS intervention proceed only if there is evidence that children have been harmed or will be at risk of maltreatment in the near future (Stein & Rzepnicki, 1983).

To summarize, in child welfare and particularly in CPS, the main goals that guide worker assessment and action are (1) to protect children at risk and (2) to strengthen the family to prevent recurrence of maltreatment (Maluccio, Pine, & Warsh, 1994; NAPCWA, 1999). Therefore, even when children are removed from the home, every effort should be made to work toward reducing risk of maltreatment to a level that allows reunification of the family. Where there is no risk of maltreatment, involuntary intervention is not possible.

Court Involvement in CPS

Juvenile or family courts fulfill an important role in serving children and families in child welfare. These court systems review agency recommendations regarding important decisions such as child removal, transfer of child custody to state agencies, choice of placements, family reunification, termination of parental rights, and adoption of children. Each jurisdiction of the court has specific requirements, and different judges within the same jurisdiction may require different types of information in reports made to them. For the purpose of this book, judicial requirements will be described in general terms; child welfare practitioners need to become familiar with the specific needs of the juvenile court in their state locality. In CPS, the types of hearings or court appearances that a worker may be involved in may include the following: shelter hearing, preliminary hearing or arraignment, pretrial conference/hearing, dispositional hearing or trial, and review hearing. (For more information, see Costin, Bell, & Downs, 1991, pp. 59–99; Stein, 1991.)

At a shelter hearing in most states, the worker will be required to present an oral report regarding the immediate safety of the child and to present the court with the juvenile referral report and request for petition. These forms contain the information needed for the court worker to file a petition. In some cases, the state or county attorney will already have approved the filing of a petition. In other cases, the worker will need to meet with the attorney to obtain support for filing a petition. In either case the family situation and risk factors that necessitated the placement of the children are described and used to help determine whether to file the petition.

The juvenile court requires information about how the jurisdiction of the court can best be used to help this child and family. For example, in the case previously discussed, some background information drawn from the case assessment documents regarding the high risk factors and the worker's appraisal of the case will be helpful as he or she recommends a particular case plan to the court. If the parents deny the allegations at the preliminary hearing, the judge will often schedule a trial on the allegations. At the trial, the worker will likely be called as a witness. Careful analysis and documentation of case facts will help the worker focus on the most important elements of the case when testifying. For example, in the case previously discussed the question may be asked, What did you see when you arrived at the home? If the worker has prepared her testimony by reviewing accurate case notes and a thorough assessment of the family situation, she would answer in specific terms regarding what was seen that affected risk in a critical way, rather than answering in a rambling and unfocused fashion.

When the worker is questioned by the defense attorney, the worker can draw on the risk assessment factors and specific details regarding child or family functioning to justify her judgment and conclusions. For example, it is sometimes difficult to determine if a 9-year-old child is safe being left alone, but by examining family resources and the major risk factors that are present (e.g., availability of neighbors, dangerousness of the neighborhood, the child's level of maturity), a worker can make and justify a judgment about the safety of the 9-year-old child if left with her family without supplemental services.

Judicial Case Review

Judicial case review represents one of the more important program reforms of the Adoption Assistance and Child Welfare Act of 1980 (PL 96-272) and the Adoption and Safe Families Act (PL 105-89), and is required of all child welfare cases, including CPS-related cases. Every 6 months in most states, the case situation must be reviewed, progress (or lack of progress) noted, and the case plan updated. For the final review, the risk factors should have been well addressed, along with documenting progress on the various treatment methods as they affect those areas of child, parent, or family functioning. In other words, when recommending the termination of the court's jurisdiction, the caseworker should be able to justify this decision because the risk factors that brought this situation to court have been reduced to an acceptable level of risk.

Case Screening and Risk Assessment

Many state and local CPS agencies are beginning to establish formal risk assessment criteria for use in case screening reports. Preinvestigative screening is one major way that agencies are attempting to screen out inappropriate reports and reduce the number of unfounded cases.

In fact, according to a one national study (Wells, Stein, Fluke, & Downing, 1989, p. 47), states are developing policies to address three aspects or steps in the intake decision-making process. The first step, classification of reports, involves using a set of guidelines to help clarify which types of referrals meet the legal definitions of an official report of child abuse or neglect. For example, cases involving only truancy or with no specific allegations of abuse or neglect would not be accepted. A second phase was termed preliminary assessment, where information in the report is weighed against relevant policy and legal mandates to determine if the referral merits investigation. Case situations that might meet the legal criteria but are contradicted because of other information might include referrals that repeat previous unsubstantiated reports, complaints that are an attempt to harass, and insufficient information to proceed.

A third type or phase of screening, selection for investigation, is exemplified by the state of Washington's use of risk assessment guidelines to refer valid but low-risk referrals to community agencies specifically funded to handle these cases instead of investigating them directly. Thus the referral may meet state criteria for investigation but the agency screens the case out because of a low risk rating and insufficient staff resources to investigate the case at the time. Community agencies are then used to assist the family.

There are a number of challenges that must be overcome to develop valid approaches to screening CPS referrals at intake. Currently, many agencies are concentrating on developing standardized intake protocols that will gather the most pertinent data in the most concise manner possible in a way that helps the CPS investigation process (Children's Research Center, 1999; Holder & Corey, 1986; Doueck, English, DePanfilis, & Moote, 1993). One of the most serious challenges is the insufficient research regarding which risk factors are most associated with child maltreatment (see the risk assessment section that follows). These research data are essential for developing valid intake criteria and screening instruments. With the inability of the field to develop screening frameworks that are valid and reliable enough to structure worker assessments and that have low numbers of misclassified cases, worker discretion in this area will remain relatively high.[1]

More objective screening frameworks are necessary because of the generally negative research findings regarding the use of "professional judgment" in decision making:

> In the last 50 years or so, the question of whether a statistical or clinical approach is superior has been the subject of extensive empirical investigation; statistical vs. clinical methods of predicting important human outcomes have been compared with each other, in what might be described as a 'contest'. The results have been uniform. Even fairly simple statistical models outperform clinical judgment. The superiority of statistical prediction holds in diverse areas, ranging from diagnosing heart attacks and predicting who will survive them, to forecasting who will succeed in careers, stay out of jail on parole, or be dismissed from police forces.
>
> ... objections (to using statistical models) ignore the data from well over 100 studies, almost all of which show the superiority of prediction based on statistics rather than on experts' intuition. For example, undergraduate records and test scores alone predict performance in graduate school better than do the ratings of admission committees. *The objections to using statistics also ignore the ethical mandate that, for important social purposes such as protecting children, decisions should be made in the best way possible. If relevant statistical information exists, use it. If it doesn't exist, collect it.* (emphasis added) (Dawes, as cited in National Council on Crime and Delinquency, Children's Research Center, 1999, p. b-2).

This research documents relatively low levels of interrater reliability or agreement regarding case diagnosis and other areas (Gambrill, 1990; Stein & Rzepnicki, 1984). The degree to which the use of these criteria will aid in case screening remains an open question at this point, but growing data from the Alaska, California, Vermont, and other states appear promising.[2]

RISK ASSESSMENT CONCEPTS AND ISSUES

Defining Risk in Child Welfare

We use the term risk factor to describe child, parent, family, and other influences that increase the likelihood that a child will be maltreated in a certain way. Risk assessment is used to denote a particular form of assessment useful for child welfare practitioners. Risk assessment and case decision making have recently received increased attention as two of the main challenges facing workers and administrators in CPS and in child welfare generally. The term risk assessment actually is being used to define a number of different assessment and decision-making processes in various agencies. Risk assessment essentially is concerned with predicting whether a child will be maltreated at some future point in time. It involves examining the child and family situation to identify and weigh various risk factors, family strengths, family resources, and available agency services. This assessment information can then be used to determine if a child is safe, what agency resources are necessary to keep the child safe, and under what circumstances a child should be removed from the family. In some cases, risk assessment instruments can be used to help judge whether a child who has been in foster care can safely return home. Thus child welfare staff assess risk although working with children in their own homes or in substitute care as they examine the extent or likelihood of future child maltreatment (Holder & Corey, 1986).

The term risk assessment refers both to a structured form of decision making as well as to the specific instruments that are used in this process. A number of child welfare agencies and organizations have developed models and instruments for assessing risk. What is supporting the development of risk assessment systems is the increasing amount of research and rapidly accumulating "practice wisdom" regarding what factors are associated with various forms of child maltreatment.[3] Some of these risk factors are used to predict the likelihood of maltreatment, although other "indicators of maltreatment" are important for identifying children or adolescents who are currently being maltreated. Both types of information are useful to child welfare workers as they assess risk to children. Given these developments in research and the need for agencies to implement better procedures for screening and prioritizing reports, four basic types of risk assessment systems have emerged (Pecora, 1991a). Each of these will be briefly described in the sections below.

Matrix Approaches.   The first type to be widely publicized was developed in Illinois in 1982 (Martinez, 1989) and has been revised since then in Illinois and other states (e.g., English et al., 1998). This approach uses a risk matrix, comprised of 16–32 factors that are rated in terms of their severity or risk to the child using 3- to 5-point scales. An adaptation of this approach that includes some multicultural assessment guidelines was developed a few years ago (Pecora & English,

1991). The factors chosen for inclusion in the matrix represent some of the more commonly cited factors associated with one or more forms of child maltreatment. Workers use the matrix to assess the family in relation to these and other factors to make casework decisions and formulate initial casework plans. In certain states, the scores for each factor are added together, averaged, or displayed by area. Most states do not total or average the scores because that would imply a greater degree of precision than the matrix is capable of at this time.

A number of states (e.g., Montana, Oregon, and Florida) have adopted a matrix approach, patterning their systems largely after the pioneering state in this area— Illinois. Although many risk matrices are relatively compact and easy to use, some are hampered by anchors that are not written clearly or that contain multiple concepts within an individual anchor. One of the most serious limitations is that without additional guidelines and space on the forms, workers may not be encouraged to consider and record information about other risk factors that may be present but not contained on the risk matrix. (Many states using the risk matrix approach, including Washington, have recently added additional recording sections to address these limitations.) Finally, as with all predictive instruments in the social sciences, the predictive accuracy of the instruments varies widely and is largely untested. However, a variety of reliability and validation studies are being conducted on the matrix approaches to refine the factors and scales.[4]

Empirical-Predictors Method. A second and (probably the most parsimonious approach) is modeled after the risk studies conducted in juvenile corrections. These systems focus on identifying the risk factors most predictive of child maltreatment. Thus parent, child, or family characteristics associated with child maltreatment are considered but are not included in the final set of risk factors unless they actually predict the occurrence or recurrence of one or more types of maltreatment (or only cases of severe maltreatment). Thus these systems try to include only those factors actually predictive of child maltreatment, as opposed to including factors "associated" with child maltreatment through prospective or other types of studies (see Leventhal, 1982; Miller et al., 1987). With this approach, the risk factors that are identified are provided to CPS intake personnel, and, in some cases, CPS investigators, to assist them in assessing the risk of future maltreatment (e.g., caretaker abused as a child, mother figure's parenting skill, presence of more than one child in the home, reasonableness of the mother figure's expectations for the child). Part of the rationale for this approach is that the agencies want to use an empirically derived set of factors, and workers can realistically assess only a small number of factors over the phone or as part of a time-limited investigation.

Ideally, the risk factors incorporated into these instruments would be the same factors that predict first-time occurrences of maltreatment, as well as recurrence, because often the CPS worker is investigating cases in which child maltreatment has already occurred and the primary concern is whether the child may be maltreated again. Much more research, however, must be undertaken to confirm whether the same set of factors for various forms of child abuse and neglect can be used for both types of situations. CPS risk assessment studies conducted thus far in over 12 states by the National Council on Crime and Delinquency are promising in that a reasonable percentage of the cases for various forms of child abuse or neglect have been correctly classified by the sets of risk factors.[5] But any set of predictors will misclassify a number of cases; a number of methodological limitations in most validation studies need to be addressed (Pecora, 1989; Rodwell & Chambers, 1989). Nevertheless, the empirical-indicators approach is very promising for providing workers with additional information for making assessment decisions.

Family Assessment Scales.   The third approach uses behaviorally anchored scales to assess the levels of parent, child, family, and household functioning to identify areas of concern. The assessment scales typically use the Child Well-Being or Family Risk scales developed by the Child Welfare League of America (CWLA; Magura & Moses, 1986; Magura, Moses, & Jones, 1987) or assessment scales developed by the Children's Bureau in Los Angeles (McCroskey & Nelson, 1989). These various packages contain some of the most clearly anchored assessment scales available in the field. For example, the Child Well-Being scales address concepts related to one or more physical, psychological, or social needs that all children possess. The degree to which these needs are not being met is intended to help define a child's state of overall "well-being." Each scale has between three and six levels of child, parent, family, or other capability ranging from an adequate level to increasing degrees of inadequacy (Magura & Moses, 1986). Each level of a scale is explicitly defined using observable or behaviorally specific anchors. The descriptors for any given scale are intended to be mutually exclusive in that a family or child is best described by only one of them.

Generally, this approach to assessing risk is more of a structured assessment system than a risk assessment system per se; assessment of child and family functioning is the primary focus of the instrument, not identification of risk factors. The family is rated at multiple points during the casework process and workers are requested to identify a range of risk factors present in the case, as well as family strengths and resources.

Although these scales are promising for family assessment, they are less appropriate for use as a technical risk assessment instrument because of their lack of predictive validation research, length, and relevance. For example, with respect to the CWLA scales, although interrater reliability studies have been conducted (Downs & Hirayama, 1988; Nasuti, 1990), no criterion-related studies that evaluate how well the scale scores predict further reports of child maltreatment have been conducted. Consequently, in contrast to the Alaska, Washington, and Alameda County approaches, the anchored scales address factors that may not in fact predict child maltreatment, and the scale packets are very long because of the lengthy scale descriptors.

Child at Risk Field.   The fourth major approach to risk assessment is the Child at Risk Field (CARF), which was developed by Wayne Holder and Michael Corey of ACTION for Child Protection. This risk assessment system uses an ecological approach and is organized around five "force fields": child, parent, family, maltreatment, and intervention. A series of 14 open-ended questions and anchored rating scales are used to help workers identify "risk influences" that may be present in the case (Holder & Corey, 1986):

1. How is the child viewed by the parent?
2. How does the child present self, specifically as related to behavior/emotion?
3. What is the child's current status and vulnerability?
4. What are the pervasive behaviors, feelings, or levels of adaptation apparent in the parents?
5. What is the history of the adults (parents) in the family (recent and past)?
6. What are the parenting practices in this family?
7. How do parents relate to others outside the home (nonrelatives)?
8. What are the demographics of the family?
9. How does the family function, interact, and communicate?
10. How does the environment, which includes extended family, support the family?
11. What surrounding circumstances accompany the maltreatment?
12. What form of maltreatment is apparent?
13. How does the family perceive or respond to intervention?
14. What influences, external to the family, will reduce intervention effectiveness?

The CARF is probably one of the most comprehensive approaches to risk assessment available in that it promotes the consideration of a variety of risk influences, reinforces an analytical approach to assessment that considers interactions among factors, considers family strengths/resources, helps workers make decisions about initial safety, and promotes the use of risk assessment throughout the entire casework process. Limitations of the system include the amount of paperwork required and use of a large number of risk factors, some of which—depending on the situation—may not be predictive of future maltreatment. Although interrater reliability and implementation studies have been conducted (Allen, 1988; DePanfilis, 1988), evaluation studies with sufficient sample sizes to assess its predictive criterion validity need to be carried out (English, 1997).

Risk Assessment Methodological Challenges

Although certain risk assessment approaches seem more promising than others, a lack of rigorous validation and implementation data precludes definitive answers at this time regarding how much faith to place in the ability of these systems to predict the likelihood of future child maltreatment. Many of the available systems need to be customized for use with particular ethnic groups (Horejsi, 1987; Horejsi & Pablo, 1991; Zuravin & Starr, 1991), tested for gender bias, assessed for urban/rural and other geographic differences, and adjusted for specific types of child maltreatment. In addition, some of the matrix items and their scaling are not supported by current research. For example, in many types of maltreatment an older child is more likely to be abused than a young child, given certain other factors such as race and family structure. Yet most risk matrices treat older children as at low risk. For physical abuse, two-parent families may pose a higher risk for children above 5 years of age. Most risk matrices reflect just the opposite (Sedlak, 1991c). Adjusting for how factors interact, "threshold effects" and nonlinear relationships remain additional challenges to be addressed (Howing, Wodarski, Gauding, & Kurtz, 1989), some of which might be solved via use of automated expert consulting systems (e.g., Schuerman, 1987).

Most of the scales do not include ethnicity as a variable, and virtually none has any culturally specific guidelines regarding their usage. What makes it difficult to address ethnic factors in the current systems is the lack of empirical research in this area. This research is complicated by the degree of interactive effects observed thus far, such as family income and education (Hegar, Zuravin, & Orme, 1991). The need for a significant amount of worker training to provide staff with the necessary interviewing and assessment skills has also not been addressed by most agencies. The focus on risk factors and structured decision making is, however, having a number of positive benefits on worker practice, including focusing worker attention on critical areas for assessment, structuring documentation, improving decision-making procedures, minimizing worker bias in decision making, and reminding workers to examine family strengths as well as limitations. Some of the practice principles emanating from the risk assessment approaches are described below.

CULTURAL ISSUES IN CHILD PROTECTIVE SERVICES

Need for Specialized Training

Among the many problems with the CPS delivery system is the lack of staff training in working with different ethnic or racial groups. For example, any risk assessment matrix is only as useful and valid as the skill of the person responsible for gathering the information used in the assessment rating and analysis. The availability of risk assessment instruments does not constitute a substitute for providing staff persons with the essential training, supervision, and consultation. There are at least three areas of competence that a person should have (Quynh Nguyen, Personal Communication, September 19, 1991):

Knowledge of the Culture and How It Affects the Family within It. In this competency area, staff members need to know some of the major traits of the cultural group with which they are working, along with knowing something about the following aspects of the family:

- how the family system is organized
- family member roles and expectations of each other
- family dynamics (e.g., how families relate to each other in certain situations)
- life-styles that are expected (e.g., how families eat, sleep, socialize, and discipline their children).

These are essential areas of knowledge for effective and humane service to children and families. For example, when should what appears to be a home health care remedy be viewed as potentially dangerous behavior requiring CPS intervention? Being culturally competent also requires knowing the issues associated with acculturation and assimilation, as well as being aware of how individuals may differ along these dimensions.

Intervention Skills. Caseworkers need to be able to approach and interact with family members in culturally appropriate ways. These are actually both knowledge and skill areas that are expressed through specific behaviors. For example, where and how does one sit (e.g., requesting permission, distance from client, direction of lean in the interviewer's body posture)? What family member should be spoken to first? What is appropriate eye contact, tone of voice, and use of questions?

Consultation and Community Resources. Staff members need to have someone readily available with whom they can consult for advice about family situations and dynamics. Each caseworker should be aware of resources for ethnic-sensitive counseling, as well as other culturally appropriate community resources.

Culturally Sensitive Approaches to Risk Assessment

Risk assessment approaches, and the matrix-based instruments in particular need to be redesigned so that they

- recognize cultural values, principles of child development,[6] child caring norms, and parenting strategies;
- include specific multicultural guidelines that should be considered
- in assessing each risk factor, with attention to some specific ethnic minority groups;
- incorporate space for rating the presence of family strengths; and
- help workers differentiate limitations in child, parent, or family functioning that may be caused by poverty or the environment, versus those due to family conditions or behaviors, such as abnormal functioning.

This last feature of the design would be used to highlight areas in which additional resources need to be made available to meet the most pressing needs of the family and for the agency to meet the "reasonable efforts" standards of PL 96-272 and AFSA (see Pecora & English, 1991, for an example of one such approach). It should be emphasized that the multicultural guidelines represent a sample of the pertinent issues and need to be supplemented with more extensive knowledge and skill-based training. The matrix items or risk factors that are listed will need to be revised based on empirical studies of what predicts various types of maltreatment. These risk factors certainly vary in terms of their significance for specific ethnic groups and types of maltreatment. Much more predictive criterion research is necessary to establish more firmly which risk factors are the most important for predicting future serious child maltreatment.

A narrative analysis is also essential to make sense of the information and ratings, so that the issues of interacting factors, ethnic differences, counteracting family strengths, and the availability of resources can be documented. For example, why was a case in which a 10-year-old Native-American girl supervises her 4-year-old brother for part of the evening every Saturday able to be closed? The answer might be the existence of a number of supportive relatives in the neighborhood that the child is able to turn to for assistance, and the child's level of maturity regarding hazardous situations and emergency procedures. For CPS staff members, in many case situations, it is difficult to balance the provision of culturally sensitive services and child protection despite some of the materials available to guide such efforts (e.g., Abney, 1996; Brissett-Chapman, 1997; Horejsi & Pablo, 1991; Stevenson, Cheung, & Leung,1992; Pecora & English, 1994; Walker & Tabbert; undated).

Is There a Bias in CPS Assessments?

Recent discussion implications of the NIS-3 and NCANDS of the child welfare admissions data by Tom Morton of the National Resource Center for Child Maltreatment in Atlanta, Georgia, (Yegidis & Morton, 1999) suggest a systematic bias in the rates of child abuse substantiation and inclusion of families of color in the child welfare system, particularly for African-American families. This is a crucial issue and one in which there are analyses that contradict those conclusions (see Ards, Chung, & Myers, 1998, 1999.

CONCLUSION

Carrying out the intake and assessment functions in child welfare services in general, and CPS in particular, is very challenging. Although additional research is needed in a wide range of areas to support these important functions, intervention technology and the availability of treatment protocols have grown tremendously, providing caseworkers with some of the practice frameworks and technical support not available previously. The availability of new risk assessment systems should certainly not be viewed as a cure-all for coping with large caseloads and difficult client situations. Much more developmental research and field testing of these instruments must be conducted, along with a refinement in the approaches taken to prepare child welfare staff members for CPS practice. Prevention and treatment approaches in CPS are rapidly evolving despite the problems in funding. Among the service innovations being employed are family support and family-based services, the subjects of Chapters 8 and 9.

NOTES

1. See Doueck, Bronson, and Levine (1992), English, Marshall, Brummel, and Orme (1999), Starr (1982), Monahan (1981), and Rodwell and Chambers (1989).

2. Children's Research Center (1999), Johnson and L'Esperance (1984), Schuerman, Stagner, Johnson, and Mullen (1989), and Weedon, Rotri, and Zunder (1988).

3. For information on risk factors, see Children's Research Center (1999), Finkelhor and Baron (1984), Hegar et al. (1991), Miller et al. (1987), Pecora and Martin (1989), Starr (1982), and Zuravin, Orme, and Hegar (1995).

4. For validation studies see, for example, Children's Research Center (1999), DePanfilis and Scannapieco (1994), English, Brummel, and Marshall (1997), Tatara (1987, 1988, 1989), and Zuravin and DePanfilis (1997).

5. See Baird, Wagner, Healy, and Johnson (1999), Baird, Wagner, and Nuenfeldt (1995), and Children's Research Center (1999).

6. For example, see Berrick et al. (1998), and Thomas (1990).

REFERENCES

126 Congressional Record 6942, June 13, 1980.

Abel, G. (1978). Treatment of sexual aggressives. *Criminal Justice and Behavior, 5,* 291–293.

Abel, G.G., Becker, J.V., & Skinner, L.J. (1987). Behavioral approaches to treatment of the violent sex offender. In L.H. Roth (Ed.), *Clinical treatment of the violent person.* New York: Guilford.

Abidin, R.R., (1983). *Parenting Stress Index: Manual.* Charlottesville, VA: Pediatric Psychology Press.

Abney, V.D., (1996). Cultural competency in the field of child maltreatment. In *The APSAC handbook on child maltreatment* (pp. 409–419). American Professional Society on the Abuse of Children. Thousand Oaks, CA: Sage.

Abrahams, N., Casey, K., & Daro, D. (1989). *Teachers confront child abuse: A national survey of teacher's knowledge, attitudes, and beliefs.* Chicago, IL: The National Committee for Prevention of Child Abuse, The National Neglect Research Center on Child Abuse Prevention Research (revised edition, October 1989).

Abramczyk, L.W. (1983). *Training for human services supervisors.* Columbia, SC: University of South Carolina, College of Social Work.

Abramovitz, M. (1991). Putting an end to doublespeak about race, gender, and poverty: An annotated glossary for social workers. *Social Work, 36*(5), 369–464.

Achenbach, T. (1982). A normative-descriptive approach to assessment of youth behavior. In A.J. McSweeney, W.J. Fremouw, & R.P. Hawkins (Eds.), *Practical program evaluation in youth treatment* (pp. 24–49). Springfield, IL: Charles C Thomas.

Achenbach, T.M. (1991). *Manual for the Child Behavior Checklist 4-18 and 1991 profile.* Burlington, VT: University of Vermont, Department of Psychiatry.

Achenbach, T., & McConaughy, S. (1987). *Empirically based assessment of child and adolescent psychopathology: Practical applications.* Newbury Park, CA: Sage.

Achenbach, T.M., McConaughy, S., & Howell, C. (1987). Child/adolescent behavioral and emotional problems: Implications of cross-informant correlations for situational specificity. *Psychological Bulletin, 101*(2), 213–232.

Ackerman, P.T., Newton, J.E.O., McPherson, W.B., Jones, J.G., & Dykman, R.A. (1998). Prevalence of post traumatic stress disorder and other psychiatric diagnoses in three groups of abused children (sexual, physical and both). *Child Abuse and Neglect 22*(8), 759–774.

Adams, P., & Nelson, K. (Eds.). (1995). *Reinventing human services: Community- and-family-centered practice.* Hawthorne, NY: Aldine de Gruyter.

Administration for Children and Families. (August 20, 1998). *Program Instruction: The transition rules for implementing the IV-E Termination of Parental Rights Provision in the Adoption and Safe Families Act of 1997* (www.acf.dhs.gov/programs/cb/policy/pi9814.htm).

Agnew, V. (1998). *In search of a safe place: Abused women and culturally sensitive services.* Toronto, Ontario, Canada: University of Toronto Press.

Ainsworth, F. (1996). Group care workers as parent educators. *Child and Youth Care Forum, 25,* 17–28.

Ainsworth, F. (1997). *Family centered group care: Model building.* Brookfield, VT: Ashgate.

Ainsworth, F., & Small, R.W. (1994). Family centered group care: Concept and implementation. *Children Australia, 19,* 22–24.

Ainsworth, F., Maluccio, A.N., & Small, R.W. (1996). A framework for family centered group care practice: Guiding principles and practice implications. In D. Braziel (Ed.), *Family-focused practice in out-of-home care* (pp. 35–43). Washington, DC: Child Welfare League of America.

Ainsworth, M.D.S., Blehar, M.C., Waters, E., & Wall, S. (1978). *Patterns of attachment: A psychological study of the strange situation.* Hillsdale, NJ: Erlbaum.

Akers, A.K., Krohn, M.D., Lanza-Kaduce, L., & Radosevich, M. (1979). Social learning and deviant behavior: A specific test of a general theory. *American Sociological Review,* 636–655.

Albers, E., Rittner, B., & Reilly, T. (1993). Children in foster care: Possible factors affecting permanency planning. *Child and Adolescent Social Work Journal, 10*(4), 329–341.

Aldgate, J. (1980). Identification of factors influencing children's length of stay in care. In J. Triseliotis (Ed.), *New developments in foster care and adoption* (pp. 22–40). London and Boston: Routledge and Kegan Paul.

Aldgate, J. (1990). Foster children at school: Success or failure? *Adoption and Fostering, 14*(4), 38–49.

Aldgate, J. (1991). Partnership with parents: Fantasy or reality? *Adoption and Fostering, 15*(2), 5–10.

Aldgate, J., & Hawley, D. (1986). *Recollections of disruptions: A study of foster care breakdowns.* London: National Foster Care Association.

Aldgate, J., Maluccio, A.N., & Reeves, C. (1989). *Adolescents in foster families.* London: B.T. Batsford, and Chicago: Lyceum Books.

Alexander, J.F., & Parsons, B.V. (1982). *Functional family therapy.* Monterey, CA: Brooks/Cole.

Alfaro, J.D. (1987). *Studying child maltreatment fatalities: A synthesis of nine projects.* New York City: Human Resources Division (mimeograph).

Allen, M. (1991). Crafting a federal legislative framework for child welfare reform. *American Journal of Orthopsychiatry, 61*(4), 610–623.

Allen, M., Brown, P., & Finlay, B. (1993). *Helping children by strengthening families: A look at family support programs.* Washington, DC: Children's Defense Fund.

Allen, M.L., Golubock, G., & Olson, L. (1983). A Guide to the Adoption Assistance and Child Welfare Act of 1980. In M. Hardin (Ed.), *Foster children in the courts* (pp. 575–609). Butterworth Legal Publishers.

Allen, M.L., & Knitzer, J. (1978) *Children without homes.* Washington, DC: The Children's Defense Fund.

Allen, M., & Knitzer, J. (1983). Child welfare: Examining the policy framework. In B. McGowan, & W. Meezan (Eds.), *Child welfare: Current dilemmas, future directions.* Itasca, IL: F.E. Peacock.

Allen, M., Brown, P., & Finlay, B. (1993). *Helping children by strengthening families: A look at family support programs.* Washington, DC: Children's Defense Fund.

Allen, R.I., & Petr, C.G. (1998). Rethinking family-centered practice. *American Journal of Orthopsychiatry, 68,* 4–15.

Allen, T.C. (1988). *Field testing of the child-at-risk field system.* (Presentation for the American Public Welfare Association, Second National Roundtable on CPS Risk Assessment, July 20–21, 1988, San Francisco.) Denver, CO: Action for Child Protection.

Allerhand, M.E., Weber, R., & Haug, M. (1966). *Adaptation and adaptability: The Bellefaire follow-up study.* New York: Child Welfare League of America.

Allerhand, M.E., Weber, R., & Polansky, N.A. (1961, September). The Bellefaire follow-up study: Research objectives and method. *Child Welfare, XL*(7), 7–13.

Allphin, S., Barth, R.P., & Simmons, B. (In press-a). A comparative study of the public cost of raising a foster child in California: Adoption versus long-term foster care. *Children and Youth Services Review.*

Allphin, S., Simmons, B., & Barth, R.P. (In press-b). Adoption of foster children: How much does it cost public agencies? *Children and Youth Services Review.*

Altemeier, W.A., O'Connor, S., Vietze, P.M., Sandler, H.M., & Sherrod, K.B. (1982). Antecedents of child abuse. *Journal of Pediatrics, 100,* 823–829.

Altschuler, D.M., & Armstrong, T.L. (1990). *Intensive community-based aftercare programs: Assessment report.* Washington DC: U.S. Office of Juvenile Justice and Delinquency Prevention.

Altschuler, D.M., & Armstrong, T.L. (1991). Intensive aftercare for the high-risk juvenile parolee: Issues and approaches in reintegration and community supervision. In T.L. Armstrong (Ed.), *Intensive interventions with high-risk youth: Promising approaches in juvenile probation and parole.* Monsey, NY: Willow Tree Press.

Amadio, C., & Stuart, L.D. (1983–84). Open adoption: Allowing adopted children to stay in touch with blood relatives. *Journal of Family Law, 22,* 59–93.

American Association for Protecting Children. (1986). *Professionalism: Take a stand #3.* (Policy Statement). Denver, CO: American Humane Association.

American Association for Protecting Children. (1987). *Highlights of official child abuse and neglect Reporting—1986.* Denver, CO: Author.

American Association for Protecting Children. (1988). *Highlights of official child abuse and neglect Reporting—1987.* Denver, CO: Author.

American Association for Protecting Children. (1989). *Highlights of official child abuse and neglect Reporting—1988.* Denver, CO: Author.

American Association for Protecting Children, a Division of American Humane Association. (June, 1991). *National policy leadership institute.* Englewood, CO: American Humane Association.

American Bar Association Center on Children and the Law, and American Association for Protecting Children. (1989). *Screening in child protective services: Executive summary.* Washington, DC: American Bar Association.

American Civil Liberties Union. (1977). *Children's Rights Report, 1*(7), 4. New York: Juvenile Rights Project of the American Civil Liberties Union.

American Humane Association. (1951). *Standards for child protective agencies.* Albany, NY: Author.

American Humane Association. (1996). *Ethical standards for the implementation of managed care in child welfare.* Englewood, CO: Author.

American Humane Association, Children's Division. (May 15, 1994). Policy Statement on *Cultural competence of child protective services agencies.* Englewood, CO: Author.

American Humane Association, Children's Division, American Bar Association, Center on Children and the Law, Annie E. Casey Foundation, Casey Family Services, Institute for Human Services Management, and The Casey Family Programs. (1998). *Assessing outcomes in child welfare services: Key philosophical principles, concepts for measuring results, and core outcome indicators.* Englewood, CO: Author.

American Humane Association and National Association of Public Child Welfare Administrators, an affiliate of the American Public Welfare Association. (1996). Matrices of indicators prepared for the fourth annual roundtable on outcome measures in child welfare. In American Humane Association. *Fourth national roundtable on outcome measures in child welfare: Summary of proceedings.* Englewood, CO: Author.

American Indian Lawyer Training Program, Inc. (1979). *Indian child welfare act of 1978: A law for our children.* Oakland, CA: Author.

American Psychiatric Association. (1994) *Diagnostic and statistical manual of mental disorders* (4th ed.). Washington, DC: Author.

American Public Human Services Association Financing Work Group. (1999). *Performance measures for child welfare services: APHSA Finance Work Group recommendations.* Washington, DC: Author.

American Public Welfare Association. (1985). *Voluntary cooperation information systems.* Washington, DC: Author.

American Public Welfare Association. (1988). *Risk assessment in child protection: A review of the literature.* (Occasional Monograph Series of APWA's R&D Department.) Washington, DC: Author.

America's Children: Key National Indicators of Well-Being. (1997). Report issued by the Federal Interagency Forum on Child and Family Statistics. In New federal report tracks child and family well-being. *Population Today, 25* (7/8), 8–17.

Anderson, G., Ryan, C., Taylor-Brown, S., & White-Gray, M. (1998, March/April). HIV/AIDS and children, youths, and families: Lessons learned [Special issue]. *Child Welfare, 77*(2).

Anderson, G.R., Ryan, A.S., & Leashore, B.R. (Eds.). (1997). *The challenge of permanency planning in a multicultural society.* New York: The Haworth Press.

Anderson, J.L., & Simonitch, B. (1981). Reactive depression in youth experiencing emancipation. *Child Welfare, 60*(6), 383–390.

Anderson, P.G. (1989). The origin, emergence, and professional recognition of child protection. *Social Service Review, 63*(2), 222–244.

Anderson, R., Ambrosino, R., Valentine, D., & Lauerdale, M. (1983). Child deaths attributed to abuse and neglect: An empirical study. *Children and Youth Services Review 1,* 75–89.

Anderson, S.C., Bach, C.M. & Griffith, S. (1981). *Psychosocial sequelae in intrafamilial victims of sexual assault and abuse.* Paper presented at the Third International Conference on Child Abuse and Neglect, Amsterdam, the Netherlands.

Andrews, A.B. (1997). Assessing neighborhood and community factors that influence children's well-being. In A. Ben-Arieh & H. Winterberger (Eds.), *Monitoring and measuring the state of children—Beyond survival* (pp. 127–141). Vienna, Austria: European Centre.

Annie E. Casey Foundation. (1996). *Getting smart, getting real. Using research and evaluation information to improve programs and policies.* Report of the Annie E. Casey Foundation's September 1995 research and evaluation conference. Baltimore, MD: Author.

Annie E. Casey Foundation. (1999). *Neighborhood Transformation and Family Development (NTFD): The Annie E. Casey Foundation's blueprint for investing in children's, families', and communities' futures over the next decade.* Baltimore, MD: Author

Anthony, E.J., & Cohler, B.J. (Eds.). (1987). *The invulnerable child.* New York: Guilford.

Appelbaum, M., & Sweet, M.A. (1999). *Is home visiting an effective strategy? Results of a meta-analysis of home visiting programs for families with young children.* University of California, San Diego, 1–7. Presented at the Board on Children, Youth and Families. National Research Council, Institute of Medicine workshop on revisiting home visitors, March 8, 1999, Washington, DC.

Apsler, R., & Bassuk, E. (1983). Differences among clinicians in the decision to admit. *Archives of General Psychiatry, 40,* 1133–1137.

Ards, S., Chung, C., & Myers, S.L., Jr. (1998). The effects of sample selection bias on racial differences in child abuse reporting. *Child Abuse and Neglect, 22*(2), 103–115.

Areen, J. (1975). Intervention between parent and child: A reappraisal of the state's role in child neglect and abuse cases. *The Georgetown Law Journal, 63*(4), 887–937.

Armstrong, T.L. (Ed.). (1991). *Intensive interventions with high risk youth: Promising approaches in juvenile probation and parole.* Monsey, NY: Willow Tree Press.

Ascione, F.R., & Arkow, P. (Eds.). (1999). *Child abuse, domestic violence, and animal abuse: Linking the circles of compassion for prevention and intervention.* West Lafayette, IN: Purdue Research Foundation, Purdue University Press.

AuClaire, P., & Schwartz, I.M. (1986). *An evaluation of the effectiveness of intensive home-based services as an alternative to placement for adolescents and their families.* Minneapolis, MN: Hennepin County Community Services Department, and the University of Minnesota, Hubert H. Humphrey Institute of Public Affairs.

Austin, C.D. (1990). Case management: Myths and realities. *Families in Society, 71,* 398–405.

Austin, M. J. (1981). *Supervisory management for the human services.* Englewood Cliffs, NJ: Prentice-Hall.

Austin, M.J., Brannon, D., & Pecora, P.J. (1984). *Managing staff development programs in human service agencies.* Chicago: Nelson-Hall.

Austin, M.J., Cox, G., Gottlieb, N., Hawkins, J.D., Kruzich, J.M., & Rauch, R. (1982). *Evaluating your agency's programs.* Newbury Park, CA: Sage.

Avery R. (1998). *Public agency adoption in New York State: Phase I report. Foster care histories of children freed for adoption in New York State: 1980–1993.* Ithaca, NY: Cornell University.

Axinn, J., & Levin, H. (1982). *Social welfare—A history of the American response to need* (2nd ed.). New York: Harper & Row.

Bachman R. (1991). An analysis of American-Indian homicide—A test of social disorganization and economic deprivation at the reservation county level. *Journal of Research in Crime and Delinquency, 28*(4), 456–471.

Backer, T.E., Liberman, R.P., & Kuehnel, T.G. (1986). Dissemination and adoption of innovative psychosocial interventions. *Journal of Consulting and Clinical Psychology, 54*(1), 111–118.

Bagley, C., & Ramsay, R. (1986). Disrupted childhood and vulnerability to sexual assault: Long-term sequelae with implications for counseling. *Social Work and Human Sexuality, 4,* 33–48.

Bagley, C., & Young, L. (1987). Juvenile prostitution and child sexual abuse: A controlled study. *Canadian Journal of Community Mental Health, 6,* 5–26.

Bailey, J.M., Bobrow, D., Wolfe, M., & Mikach, S. (1995). Sexual orientation of adult sons of gay fathers. *Developmental Psychology, 31*(1), 124–129.

Baily, T.F., & Baily, W.H. (1986). *Operational definitions of child emotional maltreatment: Final report.* Augusta, ME: Bureau of Social Services, Maine Department of Human Services.

Baird, C. (1988). Development of risk assessment indices for the Alaska Department of Health and Social Services. In T. Tatara (Ed.), *Validation research in CPS risk assessment: Three recent studies.* Washington, DC: American Public Welfare Association.

Baird, C., Wagner, D., Caskey, R., & Neuenfeldt, D. (1995). *The Michigan department of social services structured decision making system: An evaluation of its impact on child protection services.* Madison, WI: Children's Research Center.

Baird, C., Wagner, D., Healy, T., & Johnson, K. (1999). *Reliability and validity of risk assessment in child protective services: A comparison of three systems.* Madison, WI: Children's Research Center.

Baird, C., Wagner, D., & Neuenfeldt, D. (1992). Using risk assessment to structure decisions about services, protecting children: The Michigan model. *The National Council on Crime and Delinquency,* March, 1–7.

Bakan, D. (1971). *Slaughter of the innocents: A study of the battered child phenomenon.* San Francisco: Jossey-Bass.

Bakeis, C.D. (1996). The Indian Child Welfare Act of 1978: Violating personal rights for the sake of the tribe. *Notre Dame Law Journal, 10,* 543–586.

Banach, M. (1998). The best interests of the child: Decision-making factors. *Families in Society—The Journal of Contemporary Human Services, 79,* 331–340.

Bandura, A. (1973). *Aggression: A social learning analysis.* Englewood Cliffs, NJ: Prentice-Hall.

Bane, M., & Ellwood, D. (1989). One-fifth of the nation's children: Why are they poor? *Science, 245*(4922), 1047–1053.

Banks, L., Hicks Marlowe, J., Reid, J.B., Patterson, G.R., & Weinrott, M.R. (1991). A comparative evaluation of parent training interventions for families of chronic delinquents. *Journal of Abnormal Child Psychology, 19,* 15–33.

Banks, R. (1998). The color of desire: Fulfilling adoptive parents racial preference through discriminatory state action. *Yale Law Journal, 107,* 875–1025.

Banyard, V.L. (1997). The impact of childhood sexual abuse and family functioning on four dimensions of women's later parenting. *Child Abuse and Neglect, 21*(11), 1095–1107.

Bardach, E. (1977). *The implementation game: What happens after a bill becomes law.* Cambridge, MA: MIT Press.

Barker, P. (1988). The future of residential treatment for children. In C.E. Schaefer & A.J. Swanson (Eds.), *Children in residential care.* New York: Van Nostrand Reinhold.

Baker, B.L., Blacher, J., & Pfeiffer, S.I. (1993). Family involvement in residential treatment of children with psychiatric disorder and mental retardation. *Hospital and Community Psychiatry, 44*(6), 561–566.

Barlow, D.H. (1981). Empirical practice and realistic research: New opportunities for clinicians. *Journal of Consulting and Clinical Psychology, 49*(2), 147–155.

Barnard, K.E. (1983). *Child health assessment: A literature review.* Seattle, WA: University of Washington, School of Nursing.

Barnard, K.E. (1998). Developing, implementing, and documenting interventions with parents and young children. *Zero to Three, 18*(4), 23–29.

Barnett, D., Manly, J.T., & Cicchetti, D. (1993). Defining child maltreatment: The interface between policy and research. In D. Cicchetti & S. Toth (Eds.), *Child abuse, child development and social policy. Journal in Applied Developmental Psychology, 8.* Norwood, NJ: Ablex.

Barrera, M., & Ainlay, S.L. (1983). The structure of social support: A conceptual and empirical analysis. *Journal of Community Psychology, 11,* 133–142.

Barsh, R.L. (1980). Indian Child Welfare Act of 1978: A critical analysis. *Hastings Law Journal, 31,* 101.

Barth, R.P. (1986a). Emancipation services for adolescents in foster care. *Social Work, 31,* 165–171.

Barth, R.P. (1986b). *Social and cognitive treatment of children and adolescents.* San Francisco: Jossey-Bass.

Barth, R.P. (1988a). Older child adoption and disruption. *Public Welfare, 46*(1), 23–29.

Barth, R.P. (1988b). Theories guiding home-based intensive family preservation services. In J.K. Whittaker, J.M. Kinney, E. Tracy, & C. Booth (Eds.), *Improving practice technology for work with high risk families: Homebuilders™—Social Work Education Project.* Seattle, WA: University of Washington, School of Social Work, Center for Social Welfare Research.

Barth, R.P. (1990a). On their own: The experiences of youth after foster care. *Child and Adolescent Social Work, 7,* 419–446.

Barth, R.P. (1990b). Theories guiding home-based intensive family preservation services. In J.K. Whittaker, J.M. Kinney, E. Tracy, & C. Booth (Eds.), *Reaching high risk families: Intensive family preservation services* (pp. 91–114). Hawthorne, NY: Aldine de Gruyter.

Barth, R.P. (1991a). Adoption preservation services. In E.M. Tracy, D.A. Haapala, J. Kinney, & P.J. Pecora (Eds.), *Intensive family preservation services: An instructional sourcebook.* Cleveland, OH: Case Western Reserve.

Barth, R.P. (1991b). An experimental evaluation of in-home child abuse prevention services. *Child Abuse and Neglect, 15,* 363–375.

Barth, R.P. (1991c). Sweden's contact family program: Informal help bolsters vulnerable families. *Public Welfare, 49,* 36–42.

Barth, R.P. (1993). Long-term in-home services. In D. Besharov (Ed.), *When drug addicts have children: Reorienting child welfare's response.* Washington, DC: Child Welfare League of America.

Barth, R.P. (1994). Shared family care: Child protection and family preservation. *Social Work, 39,* 515–524.

Barth, R.P. (1995). *After child protection, what is the guiding principle of child welfare services: Permanency, family continuity or productive development.* The Fedele F. and Iris M. Fauri Memorial Lecture Series on Child Welfare. Ann Arbor, MI: University of Michigan, School of Social Work.

Barth, R.P. (1997a). Effects of age and race on the odds of adoption versus remaining in long-term out-of-home care. *Child Welfare, 76,* 285–308.

Barth, R.P. (1997b). The costs and benefits of adoption. In R. Avery (Ed.), *Public adoption policy.* New York: Auburn House.

Barth, R.P. (1999a). Setting performance goals for adoption services: Estimating the need for adoption of children in foster care. *Adoption Quarterly, 2,* 29–38.

Barth, R.P. (1999b). After safety, what is the goal of child welfare services: Permanency, family continuity, or social benefit? *International Journal of Social Welfare, 8,* 249–252.

Barth, R.P., & Berry, M. (1987). Outcomes of child welfare services since permanency planning. *Social Services Review, 61,* 71–90.

Barth, R.P., & Berry, M. (1988). *Adoption and disruption: Risks, rates, and responses.* New York: Aldine.

Barth, R.P., & Berry, M. (1990). A decade later: Outcomes of permanency planning. In North American Council on Adoptable Children (Ed.), *The Adoption Assistance and Child Welfare Act of 1980: The first ten years* (pp. 7–39). St. Paul, MN: The North American Council on Adoptable Children.

Barth, R.P., & Berry, M. (1994). Implications of research on the welfare of children under permanency planning. In R. Barth, J.D. Berrick, & N. Gilbert (Eds.), *Child welfare research review* (Vol. 1, pp. 323–369). New York: Columbia University Press.

Barth, R.P., & Blackwell, D.L. (1998). Death rates among California's foster care and former foster care populations. *Children and Youth Services Review, 20,* 577–604.

Barth, R.P., & Blyth, B.J. (1983). The contribution of stress to child abuse. *Social Service Review, 57,* 477–489.

Barth, R., Brodzinsky, D., & Freundlich, M. (Eds.). (2000). *Adoption and prenatal drug exposure: The research, policy and practice challenges.* Washington, DC: Child Welfare League of America.

Barth, R.P., & Brooks, D. (1997). A longitudinal study of family structure and size and adoption outcomes. *Adoption Quarterly, 1*(1), 29–55.

Barth, R.P. and Brooks, R.P. (2000). Adoption of drug-exposed children: Outcomes at eight years. In R. Barth, D. Brodzinsky, & M. Freundlich. (Eds.), *Adoption and prenatal drug exposure* (pp. 23–98). Washington, DC: Child Welfare League of America.

Barth, R.P., Brooks, D., & Iyer, S. (1996). *Adoption demographics in California.* Berkeley, CA: University of California at Berkeley, School of Social Welfare, Child Welfare Research Center.

Barth, R.P., Courtney, M., Berrick, J.D., & Albert, V. (1994). *From child abuse to permanency planning: Child welfare services pathways and placements.* Hawthorne, NY: Aldine de Gruyter.

Barth, R.P., Courtney, M.E., Needell, B., & Johnson-Reid, M. (1994). *Performance indicators for child welfare services in California.* Berkeley, CA: University of California at Berkeley, School of Social Welfare, Child Welfare Research Center.

Barth, R.P., & Jonson-Reid, M. (In press). Outcomes after child welfare services. *Children and Youth Services Review.*

Barth, R.P., & Miller, J. (In press). Post-adoption services: What are the empirical foundations? *Family Relations.*

Barth, R.P., Needell, B., Berrick, J.D., Albert, V., & Jonson-Reid, M. (1995). *Child welfare services to young children.* Paper presented at the Third Annual National Child Welfare Conference, Washington, DC, February 23, 1995.

Barth, R.P., & Price, A. (1999). Shared family care: Providing services to parents and children placed together in out-of-home care. *Child Welfare, 78*(1), 99–107.

Barth, R.P., Webster, D., & Lee, S. (1998). *Characteristics of adoptions of American/Indian and Native Alaskan children in California.* Paper presented to the National Association of Welfare Researchers and Statisticians, Chicago, IL, August, 5.

Basch, C.E., Sliepcevich, E.M., Gold, R.S., Duncan, D.F., & Kolbe, L.J. (1985). Avoiding Type III errors in health education program evaluations: A case study. *Health Education Quarterly, 12*(4), 315–551.

Bass, M., Kravath, R., & Glass, L. (1986). Vaccine investigations in sudden infant death. *New England Journal of Medicine, 315,* 100–105.

Bath, H.I., & Haapala, D.A. (1994). Family preservation services: What does the outcome research really tell us. *Social Services Review 68*(3), 386–404.

Bath, H.I., Richey, C.A., & Haapala, D.A. (1992). Child age and outcome correlates in intensive family preservation services. *Children and Youth Services Review, 14*(5), 389–406.

Battistelli, E.S. (1998). *The health care of children in out-of-home care—A survey of state child welfare commissioners.* Washington, DC: CWLA Press.

Beals, J., Piasecki, J., Nelson, S., Jones, M., Keane, E., Dauphinais, P., Shirt, R.R., Sack, W.H., & Manson, S.M.. (1997). Psychiatric disorder among American Indian adolescents: Prevalence in Northern Plains youth. *Journal of the American Academy of Child and Adolescent Psychiatry, 36,* 1252–1259.

Beatty, C. (1997). *Parents in prison: Children in crisis.* Washington, DC: Child Welfare League of America.

Beck, A.T., & Emory, G., with Greenberg, M. (1985). *Anxiety disorders and phobias: A cognitive perspective.* New York: Basic Books.

Beck, B.M. (1979). *The Lower East Side Family Union: A social invention.* New York: Foundation for Child Development.

Belknap, J. (1996). Access to programs and health care for incarcerated women. *Federal Probation, 60*(4), 34–39

Bell, C.J. (1986). Adoptive pregnancy: Legal and social work issues. *Child Welfare, 65,* 421–436.

Belsky, J. (1978). Three theoretical models of child abuse: A critical review. *International Journal of Child Abuse and Neglect, 2,* 37–49.

Belsky, J. (1980). Child maltreatment: An ecological integration. *American Psychologist, 35,* 320–335.

Belsky, J., & Vondra, J. (1989). Lessons from child abuse: The determinants of parenting. In D. Cicchetti & V. Carlson (Eds.), *Child maltreatment: Theory and research on the causes and consequences of child abuse and neglect* (pp. 153–202). New York: Cambridge University Press.

Benard, B. (1989). "Towards Family . . . " *Prevention Forum, 9*(2), 125–134

Bending, R.L. (1997). Training child welfare workers to meet the requirements of the Indian Child Welfare Act. In G.R. Anderson, A.S. Ryan, & B.R. Leashore (Eds.), *The challenge of permanency planning in a multicultural society* (pp. 151–164). New York: Haworth Press.

Benedict, M., & White, R. (1991). Factors associated with foster care length of stay. *Child Welfare, 70*(1), 45–48.

Benedict, M.I., White, R.B., Stallings, R., & Cornely, D.A. (1989). Racial differences in health care utilization among children in foster care. *Children and Youth Services Review, 11,* 285–297.

Benedict, M., Zuravin, S., Brandt, D., & Abbey, H. (1994). Types and frequency of child maltreatment by family foster care providers in an urban population. *Child Abuse and Neglect, 18,* 577–585.

Benedict, M.I., Zuravin, S., & Stallings, R.Y. (1996). Adult functioning of children who lived in kin versus nonrelative family foster homes. *Child Welfare, 75,* 529–549.

Berg, W.E. (1979). The evaluation of treatment in therapeutic communities: Problems of design and implementation. *Evaluation and Program Planning, 2,* 41–48.

Bergan, H., (1996). *Where the information is: A guide to electronic research for nonprofit organizations.* Alexandria, VA: BioGuide Press.

Bergman, A.B., Larsen, R.M., & Mueller, B.A. (1986). Changing spectrum of serious child abuse. *Pediatrics, 77,* 113–116.

Bergmann, B. (1996). Child care: The key to ending child poverty. In I. Garfinkel, J. Hochschild, & S. McLanahan (Eds.), *Social policies for children* (pp. 112–35). Washington, DC: Brookings Institution.

Berlin, F., & Meinecke, C.F. (1981). Treatment of sex offenders with antiadrogenic medication: Conceptualization, review of treatment modalities and preliminary findings. *American Journal of Psychiatry, 138,* 601–667.

Berliner, L. (1993a). Is family preservation in the best interest of children? *Journal of Interpersonal Violence, 8,* 556–557.

Berliner, L. (1993b). Opinion home visitation: Let's be careful out there. *The APSAC Advisor, 6*(4), 13–15.

Berliner, L., & Conte, J.R. (1990). The process of victimization: The victims' perspective. *Child Abuse and Neglect, 14,* 29–40.

Berliner, L., & Ernst, E. (1984). Group work with preadolescent sexual assault victims. In I.R. Stuart & J.G. Greer (Eds.), *Victims of sexual aggression: Treatment of children, women, and men.* New York: Van Nostrand Reinhold.

Bernfeld, G. (March 1994). *Saint Lawrence Youth Association Community Support Services: Annual report.* Kingston, Ontario, Canada: Saint Lawrence Youth Association Community Support Services.

Berrick, J.D. (1997). Assessing quality of care in kinship and foster family care. *Family Relations, 46,* 273–280.

Berrick, J.D., Barth, R.P., & Needell, B. (1994). A comparison of kinship foster homes and foster family homes: Implications for kinship foster care as family preservation. *Children and Youth Services Review, 16,* 33–63.

Berrick, J.D., Barth, R.P., Needell, B., & Jonson-Reid, M. (1997). Group care and young children. *Social Services Review, 71,* 257–274.

Berrick, J., Needell, B., Barth, R.P., & Jonson-Reid, M. (1998). *The tender years—Toward developmentally sensitive child welfare services for very young children.* New York: Oxford University Press.

Berridge, D., & Cleaver, D. (1987). *Foster home breakdown.* Oxford, England: Basil Blackwell.

Berrueta-Clement, J.R., Schweinhart, L.J., Barnett, W.S., Epstein, A.S., & Weikart, D.P. (1984). *Changed lives: The effects of the Perry preschool program on youths through age 19.* (Monographs of the High/Scope Educational Research Foundation, No. 8). Ypsilanti, MI: High/Scope Press.

Berry, M. (1988). A review of parent training programs in child welfare. *Social Services Review, 62*(3), 303–323.

Berry, M. (1991). Open adoption practices among 1396 families. *Children and Youth Services Review, 13,* 282–291.

Berry, M. (1992). An evaluation of family preservation services: Fitting agency services to family needs. *Social Work, 37,* 314–321.

Berry, M. (1993). The relative effectiveness of family preservation services with neglectful families. In E.S. Morton & R.K. Grigsby (Eds.), *Advancing family preservation practice* (pp. 70–98). Newbury Park, CA: Sage.

Berry, M. (1997). *The family at risk—Issues and trends in family preservation services.* Columbia, SC: University of South Carolina Press.

Berry, M., & Cash, J.S. (1998). Creating community through psychoeducational groups in family preservation work. *Families in Society: The Journal of Contemporary Human Services, 79,* 15–23.

Berry, M., Dylla, D.J., Barth, R.P., & Needell, B. (1998). The role of open adoption in the adjustment of adopted children and their families. *Children and Youth Services Review, 20*(1/2), 151–171.

Besharov, D.J. (1984). Malpractice in child placement: Civil liability for inadequate foster care services. *Child Welfare, 63*(3), 195–204.

Besharov, D.J. (1985a). Right versus rights: The dilemma of child protection. *Public Welfare, 43*(2), 19–27, 46.

Besharov, D.J. (1985b). *The vulnerable social worker: Liability for serving children and families.* Silver Springs, MD: National Association of Social Workers.

Besharov, D.J. (1986). Unfounded allegations—A new child abuse problem. *The Public Interest, 83*(Spring), 18–33.

Besharov, D.J. (1987). *Child abuse and neglect reporting and investigation: Policy guidelines for decision making.* Washington, DC: American Bar Association.

Besharov, D.J. (1989). The children of crack: Will we protect them? *Public Welfare, 47*(4), 6–11.

Besharov, D.J. (1990). *Recognizing child abuse.* New York: The Free Press.

Besharov, D.J. (1994). Looking beyond 30, 60, 90 days. *Children and Youth Services Review, 16,* 445–452.

Besharov, D.J., & Germanis, P. (1999). Is WIC as good as they say? *The Public Interest, 134,* 21–36.

Besharov, D.J., & Hanson, K.W. (1994). *When drug addicts have children: Reorienting child welfare's response.* Washington, DC: Child Welfare League of America, Inc.

Bettelheim, B., & Sylvester, E. (1949). A therapeutic milieu. *American Journal of Orthopsychiatry, 18,* 191–206.

Bianchi, S. (1993). Children of poverty: Why are they poor? In J. Chafel (Ed.), *Child poverty and public policy* (pp. 91–125). Washington, DC: The Urban Institute Press

Bickman, L. (1990). Study design. In Y.T. Yuan & M. Rivest (Eds.), *Preserving families: Evaluation resources for practitioners and policy makers.* Newbury Park, CA: Sage.

Biegel, D.E., Farkas, K.J., Abell, N., Goodin, J., & Friedman, B. (1988). *Social support networks and bibliography 1983–1987.* New York: Greenwood.

Biehal, N., Clayden, J., Stein, M., & Wade, J. (1995). *Moving on—Young people and leaving care schemes.* London: HMSO.

Biehal, N., & Wade, J. (1996). Looking back, looking forward: Care leavers, families and change. *Children and Youth Services Review, 18,* 425–446.

Bielawski, B., & Epstein, I. (1984). Assessing program stabilization: An extension of the "differential evaluation" model. *Administration in Social Work, 8*(4), 13–23.

Bilaver, L.A., Jaudes, P.K., Koepke, D., & Goerge, R.M. (1999). The health of children in foster care. *Social Service Review, 73,* 401–417.

Billingsley, A., & Giovannoni, J. (1972). *Children of the storm—Black children and American child welfare.* New York: John Wiley & Sons.

Birt, C.J. (1956). Family-Centered Project of St. Paul. *Social Work, 1,* 41–47.

Bishop, D.M., & Frazier, C. (1997). The transfer of juveniles to criminal court: Does it make a difference. *Crime & Delinquency, 42,* 111–143.

Blair, D.M. (1992). Getting the whole truth and nothing but the truth: The limits of liability in wrongful adoption. *Notre Dame Law Review, 67,* 850–869.

Blanchard, E.L., & Barsh, R.L. (1980). What is best for tribal children? A response to Fischler. *Social Work, 25,* 350–357.

Blank, R. (1994). The employment strategy. In S. Danziger, G. Sandefur, & D. Weinberg (Eds.), *Confronting poverty: Prescriptions for change* (pp. 168–204). Cambridge, MA: Harvard University Press.

Blank, R. (1995). Outlook for the U.S. labor market and prospects for low-wage entry jobs. In D. Nightingale & R. Haveman (Eds.), *The work alternative: Welfare reform and the realities of the job market* (pp. 33–69). Washington, DC: The Urban Institute Press.

Blick, L.C., & Porter, F.S. (1982). Group treatment with female adolescent incest victims. In S.M. Sgroi (Ed.), *Handbook of clinical intervention in child sexual abuse.* Lexington, MA: Lexington Books.

Blome, W.W. (1997). What happens to foster kids: Educational experiences of a random sample of foster care youth and a matched group of non-foster care youth. *Child and Adolescent Social Work Journal, 14,* 41–53.

Bloom, B. (1977). Evaluating achievable objectives for primary prevention. In D.G. Klein & S.E. Goldston (Eds.), *Primary prevention: An idea whose time has come* (p. 51). Rockville, MD: National Institute of Mental Health.

Bloom, M. (1982). *Primary prevention: The possible science.* Englewood Cliffs, NJ: Prentice-Hall.

Bloom, M. (1985). *Life span development—Bases for preventive and interventive helping* (2nd ed.). New York: Macmillan Publishing Co.

Blum, H. (1974). *Planning for health: Development and application of social change theory.* New York: Human Sciences Press.

Blumenthal, K. (1983). Making foster family care responsive. In B. McGowan & W. Meezan (Eds.), *Child welfare: Current dilemmas—future directions* (pp. 299–344). Itasca, IL: Peacock.

Blumenthal, K., & Weinberg, A. (Eds.). (1983). *Establishing parental involvement in foster care agencies.* New York: Child Welfare League of America.

Boersdorfer, R.K., Kaser, J.S., & Tremitiere, W.C. (1986). *Guide to local TEAM programs.* York, PA: Tressler-Lutheran Services Associates.

Bolton, F., Laner, R., & Gai, D. (1981). For better or worse? Foster parents and children in an officially reported child maltreatment population. *Children and Youth Services Review, 3*(1), 37–53.

Bonecutter, F.J., & Gleeson, J.P. (1997a). *Achieving permanency for children in kinship foster care: A training manual.* Chicago: University of Illinois at Chicago, Jane Addams College of Social Work.

Bonecutter, F.J., & Gleeson, J.P. (1997b). Broadening the view: Lessons from kinship foster care. *Journal of Multicultural Social Work, 5,* 99–119.

Booz-Allen & Hamilton. (1987). *The Maryland social work services job analysis and personnel qualifications study.* Baltimore, MD: Maryland Department of Human Resources.

Borders, L.D., Black, L.K., & Pasley, B.K. (1998). Are adopted children and their parents at greater risk for negative outcomes. *Family Relations, 47,* 237–241.

Borgman, R. (1982). The consequences of open and closed adoption for older children. *Child Welfare, 61,* 217–226.

Borgman, R. (1984). Problems of sexually abused girls and their treatment. *Social Casework: The Journal of Contemporary Social Work, 65,* 182–186.

Borrego, J., Uquiza, A.J., Rasmussen, R.A., & Zebell, N. (1999). Parent-child interaction therapy with a family at high risk for physical abuse. *Child Maltreatment: Journal of the American Professional Society on the Abuse of Children, (4)*4, 331–342.

Bowlby, J. (1969). *Attachment and loss, Vol. 1: Attachment.* New York: Basic Books.

Bowlby, J. (1980). *Attachment and loss, Vol. 3: Loss.* New York: Basic Books.

Bowlby, J. (1982). *Attachment and loss.* New York: Basic Books.

Bowlby, J. (1988). *A secure base: Parent-child attachment and healthy human development.* New York: Basic Books.

Boyd-Franklin, N. (1989). *Black families in therapy: A multisystems approach.* New York: Guilford.

Boyne, J., Denby, L., Kettering, J.R., & Wheeler, W. (1984). *The shadow of success: A statistical analysis of outcomes of adoption of hard-to-place children.* Westfield, NJ: Spaulding for Children.

Brace, C.L. (1859). *The best method of disposing of our pauper and vagrant children.* New York: Wynkoop, Hallenbeck & Thomas.

Brace, C.L. (1872). *The dangerous classes of New York.* New York: Wynkoop & Hallenback.

Bradbury, B., & Jantti, M. (1998). *Child poverty across industrialized nations.* Paper presented at the 25th General Conference of the International Conference for Research on Income and Wealth, Cambridge, England, August 1998.

Bradford, J., & McLean, D. (1984). Sexual offenders, violence and testosterone: A clinical study. *Canadian Journal of Psychiatry, 29,* 335–343.

Branham, E. (1970). One parent adoptions. *Children, 17*(3), 103–107.

Brassard, M.R., Germain, R., & Hart, S.N. (Eds.). (1987). *Psychological maltreatment of children.* New York: Pergamon Press.

Brawley, E.A. (1983). *Mass media and the human services: Getting the message across.* Newbury Park, CA: Sage.

Braziel, D. J. (1996). *Family-focused practice in out-of-home care.* Washington, DC: Child Welfare League of America.

Breakey, G., & Pratt, B. (1991). Healthy growth for Hawaii's "healthy start": Toward a systematic statewide approach to the prevention of child abuse and neglect. *Zero to Three, 9*(4), 16–22.

Breakey, G.F., & Pratt, B., & Elliot, L.K. (1994). *Health start training manual.* Honolulu, HI: Department of Health Center for the Future of Children.

Breckenridge, S.P. (1934). *The family and the state.* Chicago, IL: University of Chicago.

Breitmeyer, R.G., Bottum, G., & Wagner, B.R. (1974). Issues in evaluative follow-up for a residential program. *Hospital and Community Psychiatry, 25*(12), 804–806.

Bremner, R.H. (Ed.). (1970–71). *Children and youth in America* (Vol. 1, 1600–1865, Vol. II, 1865–1965). Cambridge, MA: Harvard University Press.

Bremner, R.H. (Ed.). (1970). *Children and youth in America: A documentary history, 1600–1865* (Vol. 1). Cambridge, MA: Harvard University Press.

Bremner, R.H. (Ed.). (1971). *Children and youth in America: A documentary history, 1865–1965* (Vol. 2). Cambridge, MA: Harvard University Press.

Bremner, R.H. (Ed.). (1974). *Children and youth in America: A documentary history* (Vol. 3). Cambridge, MA: Harvard University Press.

Bretherton, I. (1992). The origins of attachment theory: John Bowlby and Mary Ainsworth. *Developmental Psychology, 28*(5), 759–775.

Briar, K. (1990). Transforming human services with family support principles. *Family Resource Coalition Report, 9* (2), 6–7.

Briar, S. (1987). School of social work role. In A. Lieberman & H. Hornby (Eds.), *Professional social work practice in public child welfare: An agenda for action.* Portland, ME: University of Southern Maine, National Child Welfare Resource Center for Management and Administration.

Briar-Lawson, K. (1998). Capacity building for integrated family-centered practice. *Social Work, 43,* 539–550.

Bricker-Jenkins, M., Hooyman, N.R., & Gottlieb, N. (1991). *Feminist social work practice in clinical settings.* Newbury Park, CA: Sage.

Brieland, D. (1987). History and evolution of social work practice. In *Encyclopedia of social work* (18th ed., Vol. 1, pp. 739–754). Silver Springs, MD: National Association of Social Workers.

Briere, J. (1984). The effects of childhood sexual abuse on later psychological functioning: Defining a post-sexual abuse syndrome. *Sexual victimization of children: Conference Report.* Washington, DC.

Briere, J. (1992a). *Child abuse trauma theory and treatment of the lasting effects.* Newbury Park, CA: Sage.

Briere, J. (1992b). Methodological issues in the study of sexual abuse effects. *Journal of Consulting and Clinical Psychology, 60,* 196–203.

Briere, J., Berliner, L., Bulkley, J.A., Jenny, C., & Reid, T. (Eds.). (1996). *The APSAC handbook on child maltreatment.* American Professional Society on the Abuse of Children. Newbury Park, CA: Sage.

Briere, J., & Conte, J. (1993). Self-reported amnesia for abuse in adults molested as children. *Journal of Traumatic Stress, 6*(1), 21–31.

Briere, J., Cotman, A., Harris, K., & Smiljanich, K. (1992). *The trauma symptom inventory: Preliminary data on reliability and validity.* Paper presented at the annual meeting of the American Psychological Association, Washington, DC.

Briere, J., & Runtz, M. (1990b). Differential adult symptomatology associated with three types of child abuse histories. *Child Abuse and Neglect, 14,* 357–364.

Briggs, F., & Hawkins, R.M.F. (1993). Follow-up data on the effectiveness of New Zealand's national school based child protection program. *Child Abuse and Neglect, 18*(8), 635–643.

Brisset-Chapman, S. (1997). *The culture factor in CPS: Essential or elusive? Decision making in children's protective services.* Atlanta, GA: Child Welfare Institute and ACTION for Child Protection.

Brisset-Chapman, S., & Isaacs-Shockley, M. (1996). *Children in social peril: A community vision for preserving family care of African American children and youths.* Report of the First African American Child Welfare Summit convened by the Black Administrators in Child Welfare, Inc. Washington, DC: CWLA Press.

Brisset-Chapman, S., & Issacs-Shockley, M. (1997). *Children in social peril: A community vision for preserving family care of African American children and youths.* Report of the First African American Child Welfare Summit. Washington, DC: CWLA Press.

Broek, E. (1964). California's dual system of family law: Its origin, development and present status, Part I. *Stanford Law Review, 16,* 250–258.

Bronfenbrenner, U. (1979). *The ecology of human development.* Cambridge, MA: Harvard University Press.

Bronfenbrenner, U. (1986). Ecology of the family as a context to human development: Research perspectives. *Developmental Psychology, 22,* 723–742.

Brooks, D., & Barth, R.P. (1998a). Characteristics and outcomes of drug-exposed and non drug-exposed children in kinship and non-relative foster care. *Children & Youth Services Review, 20,* 475–501.

Brooks, D., & Barth, R.P. (1998b). *Parental preferences for adoptable children and agency responses to those preferences.* Unpublished manuscript available from the authors.

Brooks, D., & Barth, R.P. (1999). Adjustment outcomes of adult transracial and inracial adoptees: Effects of race, gender, adoptive family structure, and placement history. *American Journal of Orthopsychiatry, 69*(1), 87–99.

Brooks, D., Barth, R.P., Bussiere, A., & Jackson, G. (1999). Adoption and race: Implementing the Multi-ethnic Placement Act. *Social Work, 44,* 167–178.

Brown, G. (Ed.). (1968). *The multi-problem dilemma.* Metuchen, NJ: Scarecrow Press.

Brown, J., Cohen, P., Johnson, J.G., & Salzinger, S. (1998). A longitudinal analysis of risk factors for child maltreatment: Findings of a 17-year prospective study of official recorded and self-reported child abuse and neglect. *Child Abuse and Neglect, 22*(11), 1065–1078.

Brown, J.H., Finch, W.A., Northen, H., Taylor, S.H., & Weil, M. (1982). *Child, family, neighborhood: A master plan for social service delivery.* Washington, DC: Child Welfare League of America.

Brown, J.H., & Weil, M. (Eds.). (1992). *Family, practice: A curriculum plan for social service.* Washington, DC: Child Welfare League of America.

Brown, S.E. (1984). Social class, child maltreatment, and delinquent behavior. *Criminology, 22,* 259–278.

Brown, S.E., Whitehead, K.R., & Braswell, M.C. (1981). Child maltreatment: An empirical examination of selected conventional hypotheses. *Youth and Society, 13,* 77–90.

Brownmiller, S. (1975). *Against our will: Men, women and rape.* New York: Simon & Schuster.

Bruner, C. (1991). *Thinking collaboratively: Ten questions and answers to help policy makers improve children's services.* Washington, DC: Education and Human Services Consortium.

Bruner, C., & Scott, S. (1995). *Targeting family preservation services—Strategies and guidelines for the field.* Des Moines, IA: The Child and Family Policy Center.

Brunk, M., Henggeler, S.W., & Whelan, J.B. (1987). Comparison of multi-systemic therapy and parent training in the brief treatment of child abuse and neglect. *Journal of Consulting and Clinical Psychology, 55,* 171–178.

Bryant, S.L., Range, L.M. (1997). Type and severity of child abuse and college students' lifetime suicidality. *Child Abuse and Neglect, 21*(12), 1169–1176.

Bryce, M. (1979). Home-based care: Development and rationale. In S. Maybanks & M. Bryce (Eds.), *Home-based services for children and families: Policy, practice, and research.* Springfield, IL: Charles C Thomas.

Bryce, M.E., & Ehlert, R.C. (1971). 144 Foster children. *Child Welfare, 50,* 499–503.

Bryce, M., & Lloyd, J.C. (Eds.). (1981). *Treating families in the home: An alternative to placement.* Springfield, IL: Charles C Thomas.

Bullock, R., Gooch, D., & Little, M. (1998). *Children going home—the re-unification of families.* Aldershot, England: Ashgate.

Bullock, R., Little, M., & Millham, S. (1993). *Residential care of children: A review of the research.* London: HMSO.

Bumpass, L. (1990, November). What's happening to the family? *Demography, 27,* 483–498.

Burchard, J.D., & Clarke, R.T. (1990). The role of individualized care in a service delivery system for children and adolescents with severely maladjusted behavior. *Journal of Mental Health Administration, 17,* 48–60.

Bureau of Justice Statistics (1994a). *Special Report: Women in prison* (NCJ 145321). Washington, DC: U.S. Department of Justice.

Bureau of Justice Statistics (1994b). *Bulletin: Prisoners in 1993* (NCJ 147036). Washington, DC: U.S. Department of Justice.

Bureau of Justice Statistics (1997). *Prisoners in 1996* (NCJ 164619). Washington, DC: U.S. Department of Justice.

Burford, G., & Pennell, J. (1995). Family group decision-making: An innovation in child and family welfare. In B. Galaway & J. Hudson (Eds.), *Child welfare systems: Canadian research and policy implications* (pp. 140–153). Toronto: Thompson Educational Publications.

Burford, G. & Hudson, J. (Eds.). (2000). *Family group conferences: Perspectives on policy, practice, and research.* Hawthorne, NY: Aldine de Gruyter.

Burgess, A., Groth, A.N., Holstrom, L., & Sgroi, S. (1978). *Sexual assault of children and adolescents.* Lexington, MA: Lexington Books.

Burgess, R.L., & Conger, R.D. (1978). Family interaction in abusive, neglectful, and normal families. *Child Development, 49*(4), 1163–1173.

Burkhauser, R.V., Couch, K.A. & Wittenburg, D.C. (1996). "Who gets what" from minimum wage hikes: A re-estimation of Card and Kreuger's distributional analysis in *Myth and measurement: The new economics of the minimum wage. Industrial and Labor Relations Review, 49,* 547–552.

Burnette, D. (1997a). Grandmother caregivers in inner-city Latino families: A descriptive profile and informal social supports. In G.R. Anderson, A.S. Ryan, & B.R. Leashore (Eds.), *The challenge of permanency planning in a multicultural society* (pp. 121–138). New York: Haworth Press.

Burnette, D. (1997b). Grandparents raising grandchildren in the inner city. *Families in Society—The Journal of Contemporary Human Services, 78,* 489–501.

Burns, B.J., & Friedman, R.M. (1990). Examining the research base for children's mental health services and policy. *The Journal of Mental Health Administration, 17,* 87–99.

Burt, M.R., & Balyeat, R. (1974). A new system for improving the care of neglected and abused children. *Child Welfare, 53*(3), 167–197.

Burt, M., & Pittman, K. (1985). *Testing the social safety net.* Washington, DC: Urban Institute.

Burtless, G., & Friedlander, D. (1995). *Five years after: The long-term effects of welfare-to- work programs.* New York: Russell Sage Foundation.

Byler, W. (1977). The destruction of American Indian families. In S. Unger (Ed.), *The destruction of American Indian families* (pp. 2–5). New York: Association on American Indian Affairs.

Byrne, J.M. (1990). The future of intensive probation supervision and the new intermediate sanctions. *Crime & Delinquency,* (1), 6–41.

Cabral, R.J., & Callard, E.D. (1982). A home-based program to serve high-risk families. *Journal of Home Economics, 74*(3), 14–19.

Cadoret, R.J., & Riggins-Caspers, K. (2000). Fetal alcohol exposure and adult psychopathology: Evidence from an adoption study. In R. Barth, D. Brodzinsky, & M. Freundlich (Eds.), *Adoption and prenatal drug exposure* (123–147). Washington, DC: Child Welfare League of America.

Cadoret, R.J., Yates, W.R., Troughton, E., Woodworth, G., & Stewart, M.A. (1995). Genetic-environmental interaction in the genesis of agressivity and conduct disorders. *Archives of General Psychiatry, 52,* 916–924.

Caffey, J. (1946). Multiple fractures in the long bones suffering chronic subdural hematoma. *American Journal of Roentgenology, 56,* 163–173.

Callard, E.D., & Morin, P. (1979). *Parents and children together: An alternative to foster care.* Detroit, MI: Wayne State University, Department of Family and Consumer Studies.

Cameron, G., & Vanderwoerd, J. (1997). *Protecting children and supporting families—Promising programs and organizational realities.* Hawthorne, NY: Aldine de Gruyter.

Carbino, R. (1981). Developing a parent organization: New roles for parents of children in substitute care. In A.N. Maluccio & P.A. Sinanoglu (Eds.), *The challenge of partnership: Working with parents of children in foster care* (pp. 165–186). New York: Child Welfare League of America.

Carbino, R. (1991). Advocacy for foster families in the United States facing child abuse allegations: How social agencies and foster parent organizations are responding to the problem. *Child Welfare, 70,* 131–149.

Card, D., & Krueger, A. (1995). *Myth and measurement: The new economics of the minimum wage.* Princeton, NJ: Princeton University Press.

Carlo, P. (1993). Family reunification practice in residential treatment for children. In B.A. Pine, R. Warsh, & A.N. Maluccio (Eds.), *Together again: Family reunification in foster care* (pp. 93–117). Washington, DC: Child Welfare League of America.

Carnes, P. (1983). *The sexual addiction.* Minneapolis, MN: Compcare.

Carrilio, T.E. (1998). *California safe and healthy families model program: A family support home visiting model.* Sacramento: The California Department of Social Services, Office of Child Abuse Prevention.

Carroccio, D.F. (1982). *Intensive crisis counseling programs.* Tallahassee, FL: Florida Department of Health and Rehabilitative Services, Office of the Inspector General, Office of Evaluation.

Carten, A.J. (1990). Building on the strengths of black foster families. In A.N. Maluccio, R. Krieger,

& B.A. Pine (Eds.), *Preparing adolescents for life after foster care—The central role of foster parents* (pp. 127–141). Washington, DC: Child Welfare League of America.

Carter, B., & McGoldrick, M. (Eds.). (1999). *The expanded family life cycle—Individual, family, and social perspectives* (3rd ed.). Boston: Allyn & Bacon.

Carter, E.A., & McGoldrick, M. (Eds.). (1980). *The family life cycle: A framework for family therapy.* New York: Gardner Press.

Carter, R.K. (1988). Measuring client outcomes: The experience of the states. In R.J. Patti, J. Poertner, & C.A. Rapp (Eds.), *Managing for service effectiveness in social welfare organizations.* [A special issue of *Administration in Social Work, 11*(3–4)]. New York: Haworth Press.

Catalano, R., & Hawkins, J.D. (1985). Project skills: Preliminary results from a theoretically based aftercare experiment. In R.S. Ashery (Ed.), *Progress in the development of cost effective treatment for drug abusers* (NIDA Publication No. ADM 85-1401, pp. 157–181). Washington, DC: U.S. Government Printing Office.

Catalano, R.F., & Hawkins, J.D. (1996). The social developmental model: A theory of antisocial behavior. In J.D. Hawkins (Ed.), *Delinquency and crime: Current theories.* New York: Cambridge University Press.

Caulkins, J.P., & Reuter, P. (1997). Setting goals for drug policy: Harm reduction or use reduction? *Addiction, 92*(9), 1143–1150.

Cautley, P.W. (1979). *The home and community treatment process: Helping families change.* Madison, WI: Mendota Mental Health Institute, Home and Community Treatment.

Cautley, P.W., & Plane, M.B. (1983). *Facilitating family change: A look at four groups providing intensive in-home services.* Unpublished manuscript. Madison, WI: Wisconsin Department of Health and Social Services.

Center for Family Life. (1997). *Center for Family Life annual progress report.* New York: Author.

Center for the Future of Children Staff. (1993). Overview and major recommendations. *The Future of Children, 3,* 4–16.

Center for the Study of Social Policy. (December, 1994). *Results based decision making and budgeting.* Washington, DC: Fiscal Policy Studies Institute, Center for the Study of Social Policy (mimeograph).

Centers for Disease Control and Prevention HIV/AIDS Surveillance Report. (1998). *Year-end edition.* Atlanta, GA: Author.

Chafel, J.A. (1992). Funding Head Start: What are the issues? *American Journal of Orthopsychiatry, 62,* 9–21.

Chaffin, M., Kelleher, K., & Hollenberg, J. (1996). Onset of physical abuse and neglect: Psychiatric, substance abuse and social risk factors from prospective community data. *Child Abuse and Neglect, 20,* 191–200.

Chambers, C.A. (1963). *Seedtime of reform: American social service and social action, 1918–1933.* Minneapolis, MN: University of Minnesota Press.

Chambers, D.E., Wedel, K.R., & Rodwell, M.K. (1992). *Evaluating social programs.* Needham Heights, MA: Allyn & Bacon.

Chan, R.W., Raboy, B., & Patterson C.J. (1998). Psychosocial adjustment among children conceived via donor insemination by lesbian and heterosexual mothers. *Child Development, 69,* 443–457.

Chapin Hall Center for Children. (1997). *An update from the multi-state foster care data archive: Foster care dynamics 1983–1994.* Chicago, IL: Author.

Chasnoff, I.J. (1998). Silent violence: Is prevention a moral obligation? *Pediatrics, 102,* 145–148.

Chasnoff, I.J., Anson A., & Iaukea, K.M. (1998). *Understanding the drug-exposed child: Approaches to behavior and learning.* Chicago, IL: Imprint Publications.

Chasnoff, I.J., Anson, A., Stenson, H., Hatcher, R., DiCara, J., Iaukea, K., & Randolph, L.A. (1998). Prenatal exposure to cocaine and other drugs: Outcome at four to six years. *Annals of the New York Academy of Science, 846,* 314–328.

Chasnoff, I.J., Griffith, D.R., MacGregor, S., Dirkes, K., & Burns, K.A. (1989). Temporal patterns of cocaine use in pregnancy. *JAMA, 161,* 1741–1744.

Chernick, H., & Reschovsky, A. (1996). State responses to block grants: Will the safety net hold? *The LaFollette Policy Report,* (Spring/Summer) *7*(1–4), 12–15.

Chernoff, R., Combs-Orme, T., Risley-Curtiss, G., & Heisler, A. (1994). Assessing the health status of children entering foster care. *Pediatrics, 93,* 594–601.

Cherry, T. (1976). The Oregon child study and treatment centers. *Child Care Quarterly, 5,* 146–155.

Chestang, L.W. (1978). The delivery of child welfare services to minority group children and their families. In *Child welfare strategy in the coming years* (pp. 169–194). Washington, DC: U.S. Department of Health, Education, and Welfare. DHEW Publication No. (OHDS) 78-30158.

Child abuse and neglect in residential institutions. (1978). NCCAN, DHEW Publication No. (OHDS) 78-30160. Washington, DC: U.S. Government Printing Office.

Child Protection Report. (1991). Briefs. *Child Protection Report, 17*(13), 2 (newsletter published by Business Publishers, Inc, Washington, DC).

Child Welfare League of America. (1973). *Standards for adoption services.* New York: Author.

Child Welfare League of America. (1978). *Adoption guidelines.* New York: Author.

Child Welfare League of America. (1982). *CWLA standards for residential centers for children.* New York: Author.

Child Welfare League of America. (1984a). *Directory of member agencies.* New York: Author.

Child Welfare League of America. (1984b). *Standards for organization and administration for all child welfare services.* Washington DC: Author.

Child Welfare League of America. (1987). *Standards for child protective organizations.* New York: Author.

Child Welfare League of America. (1989a). *Standards for service for abused or neglected children and their families.* Washington, DC: Author.

Child Welfare League of America. (1989b). *Standards for services to strengthen and preserve families with children.* Washington, DC: Author.

Child Welfare League of America. (1990). *Out-of-home care: An agenda for the nineties.* Washington, DC: Author.

Child Welfare League of America. (1991a). Another win for CWLA/NOSAC Family Unification Program Initiative. *Children's Voice, 7*(1), 9 (newsletter of CWLA).

Child Welfare League of America. (1991b). *Serving the needs of gay and lesbian youths: The role of child welfare agencies.* Recommendations of a Colloquium—January 25–26, 1991. Washington, DC: Author.

Child Welfare League of America. (1994). *Kinship care: A natural bridge.* Washington, DC: Author.

Child Welfare League of America (1995). *Standards of Excellence for family foster care.* Washington, DC: Author.

Child Welfare League of America. (1996a). Appropriations for selected child welfare programs (in millions). *Children's Monitor, 9*(6).

Child Welfare League of America. (1996b). *CWLA standards of excellence for management and governance of child welfare organizations.* Washington, DC: Author.

Child Welfare League of America. Public policy department. (November 25, 1997). *Summary of the adoption and safe families act of 1997* (P.L. 105-89). Washington, DC: Author (mimeograph).

Child Welfare League of America. (1998a). Funding for selected children's programs. *Children's Monitor, 4*–5.

Child Welfare League of America. (1998b) *Standards for adoption services.* Washington, DC: Author.

Child Welfare League of America. (1998c). *CWLA standards for organization and administration for all child welfare services.* Washington, DC: Author.

Child Welfare League of America. (1999). Funding for selected children's programs. *Children's Monitor, 12*(9), 2–3.

Children's Defense Fund. (1988). *A children's defense budget, FY 1989: An analysis of our nation's investment in children.* Silver Springs, MD: Business Publishers, Inc.

Children's Defense Fund. (1990). *S.O.S. America! A children's defense budget.* Washington, DC: Author.

Children's Defense Fund. (1991a). *Federal budget summary.* Washington, DC: Author (mimeograph).

Children's Defense Fund. (1991b). *The State of America's Children 1991.* Washington, DC: Author.

Children's Defense Fund. (1997). *The state of America's children: Yearbook 1997.* Washington, DC: Author.

Children's Defense Fund. (1998). *The state of America's children: Yearbook 1998.* Washington, DC: Author.

Chobar, J.S., & Wallin, J.A. (1984). A field study of the effect of feedback frequency on performance. *Journal of Applied Psychology, 69*(3), 524–530.

Christoffel, K., & Lui, K. (1983). Homicide death rates in childhood in 23 developed countries: U.S. rates atypically high. *Child Abuse and Neglect, 7,* 339–345.

Chu, J.A., & Dill, D.L. (1990). Dissociative symptoms in relation to childhood physical and sexual abuse. *American Journal of Psychiatry, 147,* 887–892.

Cicchetti, D. (1989). How research on child maltreatment has informed the study of child development: Perspectives from developmental psychopathology. In D. Cicchetti & V. Carlson (Eds.), *Child maltreatment: Theory and research on the causes and consequences of child abuse and neglect* (pp. 377–431). Cambridge, England: Cambridge University Press.

Cicchetti, D. (Ed.). (1994). Development and psychopathology: Advances and challenges in the study of the sequelae of child maltreatment, *Special Issue, 6*(1). New York: Cambridge University Press.

Cicchetti, D., & Lynch, M. (1993). Toward an ecological/transactional model of community violence and child maltreatment: Consequences for children's development. *Psychiatry 56,* 96–118.

Ciliberti, P. (1998). An innovative family preservation program in an African American community: Longitudinal analysis. *Family Preservation Journal, 3*(2), 45–72.

Citro, C., & Michael, R. (Eds.). (1995). *Measuring poverty: A new approach.* Washington, DC: National Academy Press.

Clark, H.B., Prange, M.E., Lee, B., Boyd, L.A., McDonald, B.A., & Stewart, E.S. (1994). Improving adjustment outcomes for foster children with emotional and behavioral disorders: Early findings from a controlled study on individualized services. *Journal of Emotional and Behavioral Disorders, 2,* 207–218.

Clarke-Stewart, K.A. (1998). Parents' effects on children's development: A decade of progress? *Journal of Applied Developmental Psychology, 9,* 41–84.

Clausen, J.M., Landsverk, J., Ganger, W., Chadwick, D., & Lifrownik, A. (1998). Mental health problems of children in foster care. *Journal of Child and Family Studies, 7,* 283–296.

Clear, T.R., & Hardyman, P.L. (1990). The new intensive supervision movement. *Crime & Delinquency, 36*(1), 42–60.

Clement, P.F. (1979). Families and foster care: Philadelphia in the late nineteenth century. *Social Service Review, 53,* 407–420.

Cloward, R.A., & Ohlin, L.E. (1960). *Delinquency and opportunity: A theory of delinquent gangs.* New York: Free Press.

Coates, R.B., Miller, A.D., & Ohlin, L.E. (1978). *Diversity in a youth correctional system.* Cambridge, MA: Ballinger.

Cohen, A.K. (1955). *Delinquent boys: The culture of the gang.* New York: Free Press.

Cohen, J.S., & Westhues, A. (1990). *Well-functioning families for adoptive and foster children.* Toronto, Canada: University of Toronto Press.

Cohen, L.H., Sargent, M.M., & Sechrest, L.B. (1986). Use of psychotherapy research by professional psychologists. *American Psychologist, 41*(2), 198–206.

Cohen, N.A. (Ed.). (1992). *Child welfare—A multicultural focus.* Boston, MA: Allyn & Bacon.

Cohn, A. (1983). *An approach to preventing child abuse.* Chicago: National Committee for Prevention of Child Abuse.

Cohn, A.H. (1979). Effective treatment of child abuse and neglect. *Social Work, 24,* 513–519.

Cohn, A.H. (1987). How do we deal with research findings? *Journal of Interpersonal Violence, 2*(2), 228–232.

Coie, J.D., & Jacobs, M.R. (1993). The role of social context in the prevention of conduct disorder. *Development and Psychopathology, 5,* 263–275.

Coie, J.D., Lochman, J.E., Terry, R., & Hyman, C. (1992). Predicting early adolescent disorder from childhood aggression and peer rejection. *Journal of Consulting and Clinical Psychology, 60,* 783–792.

Cole, C.B. (1986). *Differential long-term effects of child sexual and physical abuse.* Presented at the Fourth National Conference on Sexual Victimization of Children, New Orleans.

Cole, E. (1987). Keynote speech. Institute for Child Advocacy Conference, March 13–14, 1987. (As reported in *Update,* Spring, 1987, pp. 1–2). Cleveland, OH: Institute for Child Advocacy.

Cole, E., & Duva, J. (1990). *Family preservation: An orientation for administrators & practitioners.* Washington, DC: Child Welfare League of America.

Cole, E.S. (1984). Societal influences on adoption. In P. Sachdev (Ed.), *Adoption: Current issues and trends.* Toronto: Butterworths.

Cole, E.S. (1995). Becoming family-centered: Child welfare's challenge. *Families in Society: The Journal of Contemporary Human Services, 76,* 163–172.

Cole, G. (1985). The challenge. *Frontline,* National Child Protective Workers Association, Inc., 1(1).

Coll, C.G., Lamberty, G., Jenkins, R., McAdoo, H.P., Crnic, K., Wasik, B.H., & Garcia, H.V. (1996). An integrative model for the study of developmental competencies in minority children. *Child Development, 67,* 1891–1914.

Comer, E.W., & Fraser, M.W. (1998). Evaluation of six family-support programs: Are they effective? *Families in Society: The Journal of Contemporary Human Services, 79*(2), 134–148.

Committee on Ways and Means, U.S. House of Representatives. (1985). *Children in poverty.* Washington, DC: U.S. Government Printing Office.

Committee on Ways and Means, U.S. House of Representatives. (1991). *1991 Green book: Background material and data on programs within the jurisdiction of the Committee on Ways and Means.* Washington, DC: U.S. Government Printing Office.

Committee on Ways and Means, U.S. House of Representatives. (1996). *1996 Green Book.* Washington, DC: U.S. Government Printing Office.

Committee on Ways and Means, U.S. House of Representatives. (1998). *1998 Green book: Background material and data on programs within the jurisdiction of the Committee on Ways and Means.* Washington, DC: U.S. Government Printing Office.

Compher, J.V. (1983). Home services to families to prevent child placement. *Social Work, 28*(5), 360–364.

Connolly, M. (with McKenzie, M.). (1999). *Effective participatory practice—Family group conferencing in child protection.* Hawthorne, NY: Aldine de Gruyter.

Conte, J.R. (1985). An evaluation of a program to prevent the sexual victimization of young children. *Child Abuse and Neglect, 9,* 319–328.

Conte, J.R. (1986a). *A look at child sexual abuse.* Chicago, IL: National Committee for Prevention of Child Abuse.

Conte, J.R. (1986b). *Sexual abuse and the family: A critical analysis.* Portions of this paper were delivered at the Second National Conference on the Sexual Victimization of Children, Washington, DC, May 6–8, 1982.

Conte, J.R. (1991). The nature of sexual offense against children. In C.R. Hollin & K. Howells (Eds.), *Clinical approaches to sex offenders and their victims.* New York: John Wiley & Sons.

Conte, J.R., & Fogarty, L.A. (1990). Sexual abuse prevention programs for children. *Education and Urban Society, 22*(3), 270–284.

Conte, J.R., Rosen, C., & Saperstein, L. (September 1984). *An analysis of programs to prevent the sexual victimization of children.* Paper presented at the Fifth International Congress on Child Abuse and Neglect, Montreal, Canada.

Conte, J.R., Wolf, S., & Smith, T. (1989). What sexual offenders tell us about prevention strategies. *Child Abuse and Neglect, 13,* 293–301.

Cook, R., McLean, J.L., & Ansell, D.I. (1989). *A national evaluation of Title IV-E foster care independent living programs for youth* (Contract No. 105-87-1608). Rockville, MD: Westat, Inc.

Cook, R.J. (1997). Are we helping foster care youth preparing for their future? In J.D. Berrick, R. Barth, & N. Gilbert (Eds.), *Child welfare research review* (Vol. 2, pp. 201–218). New York: Columbia University Press.

Cook, T.D., & Campbell, D.T. (1979). *Quasi-experimentation: Design and analysis issues for field settings.* Chicago, IL: Rand McNally.

Costello E.J., Farmer, E.M.Z., Angold, A., Burns, B.J., & Erkanli, A. (1997). Psychiatric disorders among American Indian and white youth in Appalachia: The Great Smoky Mountains Study. *American Journal of Public Health, 87*(5), 827–832.

Costin, L.B., Bell, C.J., & Downs, S.W. (1991). *Child welfare: Policies and practices.* New York: Longman.

Costin, L.B., Karger, H.J., & Stoesz, D. (1996). *The politics of child abuse in America.* New York: Oxford University Press.

County Welfare Directors Association of California, Chief Probation Officers Association of California, and California Mental Health Directors Association. (1990). *Ten reasons to invest in the families of California.* Sacramento, CA: Author (mimeograph).

Courtney, M. (1994). Factors associated with the reunification of foster children with their families. *Social Service Review, 68*(1), 81–108.

Courtney, M.E. (1998). The politics and realities of transracial adoption. *Youth Law News,* Jan–Feb, 17–22.

Courtney, M.E., Barth, R.P., Berrick, J.D., Brooks, D., Needell, B., & Park, L. (1996). Race and child welfare services: Past research and future directions. *Child Welfare, 75,* 99–137.

Courtney, M.E., & Collins, R.C. (1994). New challenges and opportunities in child welfare outcomes and information systems. *Child Welfare, 73*(5), 359–378.

Courtney, M.E., Piliavin, I., Grogan-Kaylor, A., & Nesmith, A. (1998). *Foster youth transitions to adulthood: Outcomes of 12–18 months after leaving out-of-home care.* Madison, WI: University of Wisconsin-Madison, School of Social Work and Institute for Research on Poverty.

Courtney, M.E., & Wong, Y.L.I. (1996). Comparing the timing of exits from substitute care. *Children and Youth Services Review, 18,* 307–334.

Courtois, C.A. (1979). The incest experience and its aftermath. *Victimology: An International Journal, 4,* 337–347.

Courtois, C.A. (1988). *Healing the incest wound: Adult survivors in therapy.* New York: W.W. Norton.

Covington, S. (1997). Women in prison: Approaches in the treatment of our most invisible population. *Women & Therapy, 20*(4), 57–73.

Cowan, P.A., Cowan, C.P., Pape, C., & Schulz, M.S. (1996). Thinking about risk and resilience in families. In E.A. Hetherington (Ed.), *Stress, coping, and resiliency in children and families* (pp. 1–38). Mahway, NJ: Erlbaum.

Cox, M.J., & Cox, R.D. (Eds.). (1985). *Foster care: Current issues, policies, and practices.* Norwood, NJ: Ablex.

Coyne, A., & Brown, M.E. (1986). Agency practices in successful adoption of developmentally disabled children. *Child Welfare, 65,* 45–62.

Cross, T.L. (1989). Cultural competence continuum. *Focal Point, 3*(1), 1.

Cross, T.L., Bazron, B.J., Dennis, K.W., & Issacs, M.R. (1989*). Towards a culturally competent system of care: A monograph on effective services for minority children who are severely emotionally disturbed.* Washington, DC: Georgetown University Child Development Center.

Crumbley, J., & Little, R.L. (Eds.). (1997). *Relatives raising children—An overview of kinship care.* Washington, DC: CWLA Press.

Crumpler, A., & Casper, M. (1986). Child protective services intensive services unit. *Frontline, 2*(1), 4 (newsletter of the National Child Protective Workers Association).

Cunningham, J., Pearce, T., & Pearce, P. (1988). Childhood sexual abuse and medical complaints in adult women. *Journal of Interpersonal Violence, 3,* 131–144.

Curry, J. (1991). Outcome research on residential treatment: Implications and suggested directions. *American Journal of Orthopsychiatry, 61*(3), 348–358.

Curry, J. (1993). *The current status of research in residential treatment.* Unpublished Paper. Presented at the American Association of Children's Residential Centers, Boston, MA, October 22, 1993.

Curtis, C.M., & Alexander, R.A. (1996). The Multiethnic Placement Act: Implications for social work practice. *Child and Adolescent Social Work Journal, 13,* 401–410.

Curtis, P.A. (Ed.) (1994). *Child welfare: A research agenda for child welfare* [LXXIII(5)]. Washington, DC: Child Welfare League of America, Inc.

Curtis, P.A., & Feagans, L. (1999). *1999 salary study.* Washington, DC: CWLA Press.

Cutrona, C.E., Cadoret, R.J., Suhr, S.J., Richards, C.C., Troughton, E., Shutte, K., & Woodworth. (1994). Interpersonal variables in the prediction of alcoholism among adoptees: Evidence for gene-environment interactions. *Comprehensive Psychiatry, 35,* 171–179.

Daly, D.L. (1989). Ensuring quality child care and treatment through the program-specific skill training and supervision of personnel. In R.P. Hawkins & J. Breiling (Eds.), *Therapeutic foster care: Critical issues* (pp. 131–159). Washington, DC: Child Welfare League of America.

Daly, M., & Wilson, M. (1987). Children as homicide victims. In R.J. Gelles & J.B. Lancaster (Eds.), *Child abuse and neglect: Biosocial dimensions* (pp. 201–214). Hawthorne, NY: Aldine de Gruyter.

Danish, S.J., D'Angell, A.R., & Hauer, A.L. (1980). *Helping skills.* (2nd ed.). New York: Human Sciences Press.

Danziger, S., & Gottschalk, P. (1995). *America unequal.* New York: Russell Sage Foundation.

Danziger, S., Haveman, R., & Plotnick, R. (1986). Antipoverty policy: Effects on the poor and non-poor. In S. Danziger & D. Weinberg (Eds.), *Fighting poverty: What works and what doesn't* (pp. 50–77). Cambridge, MA: Harvard University Press.

Danzy, J., & Jackson, S.M. (1997). Family preservation and support services: A missed opportunity for kinship care. *Child Welfare, 76,* 31–44.

Daro, D. (1988). *Confronting child abuse: Research for effective program design.* New York: The Free Press.

Daro, D. (1993). Home visitation and preventing child abuse. *The APSAC Advisor, 6*(4), 1, 4.

Daro, D. (1996). Preventing child abuse and neglect. In J. Briere, L. Berliner, J.A. Bulkley, C. Jenny, & T. Reid (Eds.), *The APSAC Handbook on child maltreatment* (pp. 343–358). Newbury Park, CA: Sage.

Daro, D., & McCurdy, K. (1994). Preventing child abuse and neglect: Programmatic interventions. *Child Welfare: A Research Agenda for Child Welfare, LXXIII*(5), 405–430.

Daro, D., & Mitchel, L.B. (1989). *Child abuse fatalities continue to increase: The results of the 1988 annual fifty-state survey.* Chicago: National Committee for Prevention of Child Abuse.

David and Lucille Packard Foundation (1993). Home visiting. *The Future of Children, 3*(3), 23–38.

David and Lucille Packard Foundation (1999). *The future of children home visiting: Recent program evaluations.* Los Altos, CA: Author.

Davids, A., Ryan, R., & Salvatore, P. (1978). Effectiveness of residential treatment. *American Journal of Orthopsychiatry, 38,* 469–475.

Davids, A., & Salvatore, P. (1976). Residential treatment of disturbed children and adequacy of their subsequent adjustment: A follow-up study. *American Journal of Orthopsychiatry, 46*(1), 62–73.

Davies, L., & Bland, D. (1978). The use of foster parents as role models for parents. *Child Welfare, 57,* 380–386.

Davis, I.P., Landsverk, J., Newton, R., & Ganger, W. (1996). Parental visiting and foster care reunification. *Children and Youth Services Review, 18,* 363–382.

Dawes, R. (Undated). *A new approach to child protective services: Structured decision making.* Madison, WI: National Council on Crime and Delinquency.

Dawes, R., Faust, D., & Meehl, P. (1989). Clinical versus actuarial judgment. *Science, 243,* 1668–1674.

Day, P., & Cahn, K. (1988). *Supervising family-centered practice: Using family systems tools to create a supportive work environment.* Presented at the Second National Family-Based Services Conference, Boise, Idaho, October 17, 1988.

Dear, R.B. (1989). What's right with welfare? The other face of AFDC. *Journal of Sociology and Social Welfare, 16*(2), 5–44.

DeFrancis, V. (1955). *The fundamentals of child protection.* Denver: American Humane Association

Deighton, J., & McPeek, P. (1985). Group treatment: Adult victims of child sexual abuse. *Social Casework: The Journal of Contemporary Social Work,* September, 403–410.

deMause, L. (1974). *The history of childhood.* New York: The Psychohistory Press.

deMause, L. (Ed.). (1988). *The history of childhood: The untold story of child abuse.* New York: Peter Bedrick Books.

Denby, R., & Rindfleisch, N. (1996). African Americans' foster parenting experiences: Research findings and implications for policy and practice. *Children and Youth Services Review, 18*(6), 523–552.

Denby, R.W., Curtis, C.M., & Alford, K.A. (1998). Family preservation services and special populations: The invisible target. *Families in Society: The Journal of Contemporary Human Services, 79,* 3–14.

DePanfilis, D. (1988). *Final report: Determining safety in child protective services and child placement decisions.* Charlotte, NC: Action for Child Protection.

DePanfilis, D. (1996). Implementing child maltreatment risk assessment systems: Lessons from theory. *Administration in Social Work, 20*(2), 41–59.

DePanfilis, D. (1997). Intervening with families when children are neglected. In H. Dubowitz (Ed.), *Neglected children: Research, practice and policy.* Thousand Oaks, CA: Sage.

DePanfilis, D., & Scannapieco, M. (1994). Assessing the safety of children at risk of maltreatment: Decision-making models. *Child Welfare League of America, 73*(2), 229–245.

DePanfilis, D., & Wilson, C. (1996). Applying the strengths perspective with maltreating families. *The APSAC Advisor, 9*(3), 15–20.

Department of Health, Social Care Group. (1999). *Framework for the assessment of children in need and their families.* London: Author.

Derezotes, P., & Barth, R.P. (1990). *Preventing adolescent abuse.* Lexington, MA: D.C. Heath.

Desetta, A. (Ed.). (1996). *The heart knows something different—Teenage voices from the foster care system.* New York: Persea Books.

DeVita, C.J., & O'Hare, W.P. (1990). *America in the 21st century and economic support systems.* Washington, DC: Population Reference Bureau Inc.

Devore, W., & Schlesinger, E.G. (1996). *Ethnic–sensitive social work practice* (4th ed.). Boston: Allyn & Bacon.

DeWoody, M. (1994). *Health care reform and child welfare—Meeting the needs of neglected children.* Washington, DC: Child Welfare League of America.

Dhooper, S.S., Royse, D.D., & Wolfe, L.C. (1990). Does social work education make a difference. *Social Work, 35*(1), 57–61.

Diamond, L.J., & Jaudes, P.K. (1983). Child abuse in a cerebral palsied population. *Developmental Medicine and Child Neurology, 35,* 169–174.

Dickinson, N.S., & Perry, R. (1998). *Do MSW graduates stay in public child welfare? Factors influencing the burnout and retention rates of specially educated child welfare workers.* Berkeley, CA: University of California at Berkeley, School of Social Welfare (mimeograph).

Digre, P. (1992). Testimony before the U.S. Senate Financing Committee, Washington, DC.

Dikeou, G.D. (1986). Risk management from the perspective of agency counsel. In L. Freeman (Ed.), *Managing risks while protecting children.* Denver, CO: National Association of Counsel for Children, and American Association for Protecting Children.

Dillman, D.A. (1978). *Mail and telephone surveys: The total design method.* New York: John Wiley & Sons.

Dimock, E.T. (1977). Youth crisis services: Short-term community-based residential treatment. *Child Welfare, 56,* 187–196.

DiNitto, D., & Dye, T. (1987). *Social welfare: Politics and public policy.* Englewood Cliffs, NJ: Prentice-Hall.

Dinnage, R., & Pringle, M.K. (1967). *Residential care: Facts and fallacies.* London: Longman.

Doelling, J.L., & Johnson, J.H. (1989). Foster placement evaluation scale: Preliminary findings. *Social Casework, 70,* 96–100.

Dore, M.M. (1993). Family preservation and poor families: When "Homebuilding" is not enough. *Families in Society, 74,* 545–556.

Dore, M.M. (1999). Emotionally and behaviorally disturbed children in the child welfare system: Points of preventive intervention. *Children and Youth Services Review, 21,* 7–29.

Dore, M., & Alexander, L. (1996). Preserving families at risk of child abuse and neglect: The role of the helping alliance. *Child Abuse and Neglect, 20,* 349–361.

Dore, M.M., Young, T.M., & Pappenfort, D.M. (1984). Comparison of basic data for national survey of residential group care facilities: 1966–1982. *Child Welfare, 63,* 485–495.

Doueck, H.J., Bronson, D.E., & Levine, M. (1992). Evaluating risk assessment implementation in child protection: Issues for consideration. *Child Abuse and Neglect, 16,* 637–646.

Doueck, H.J., English, D.J., DePanfilis, D., & Moote, G.T. (1993). Decision-making in child protective services: A comparison of selected risk-assessment systems. *Child Welfare, LXXII*(5), 441–452.

Doueck, H.J., Ishisaka, A.H., Sweany, S.L., & Gilchrist, L.D. (1987). Adolescent maltreatment: Themes from the empirical literature. *Journal of Interpersonal Violence, 2*(2), 139–153.

Downs, A.C., & Pecora, P.J. (1997). *Application of Erikson's developmental theory to youth foster care research: A working paper.* Seattle, WA: The Casey Family Programs, and University of Washington, School of Social Work.

Downs, S.W., Costin, L.B., & McFadden, E.J. (1996). *Child welfare and family services: Policies and practice* (5th ed.). White Plains, NY: Longman.

Downs, S.W., & Hirayama, K. (1988). Reliability study of the Family Assessment Scales. In *Wayne County Children and Youth Services Field Test of the Family Assessment Scales* (Chapter 6). Detroit, MI: Wayne County Department of Social Services.

Downs, S.W., & Sherraden, M. (1983). The orphan asylum in the nineteenth century. *Social Service Review, 57,* 272–290.

Drews, K., Salus, M.K., & Dodge, D. (1981). *Child protective services: In-service training for supervisors.* Washington, DC: U.S. Department of Health and Human Services, National Center on Child Abuse and Neglect.

Dubowitz, H., et al. (1994). Children in kinship care: How do they fare? *Children and Youth Services Review, 16*(1–2), 85–106.

Dubowitz, H., & DePanfilis, D. (Eds.). (2000). *Handbook for child protection practice.* Newbury Park, CA: Sage.

Duchnowski, A.J., & Friedman, R.M. (1990). Children's mental health: Challenges for the nineties. *The Journal of Mental Health Administration, 17*(1), 3–12.

Duerbeck, N.B. (1997). Fetal alcohol syndrome. *Comprehensive Therapy, 23,* 179–183.

Duggan, A.K., et al. (1999). Evaluation of Hawaii's Healthy Start program. *The Future of Children, 9*(1), 66–90.

Dumas, J.E., & Wahler, R.G. (1983). Predictors of treatment outcome in parenting training: Mother insularity and socioeconomic disadvantage. *Behavioral Assessment, 5,* 301–313.

Duncan, G., Yeung, W., Brooks-Gunn, J., & Smith, J. (1998). How much does childhood poverty affect the life chances of children? *American Sociological Review, 63,* 406–423.

Dunst, C.J., Trivette, C.M., & Deal, A.G. (1988). *Enabling and empowering families: Principles and guidelines for practice.* Cambridge, MA: Brookline Books.

Dunu, M. (1979). The Lower East Side Family Union: Assuring community services for minority families. In S. Maybanks & M. Bryce (Eds.), *Home-based services for children and families: Policy, practice and research* (pp. 211–224). Springfield, IL: Charles C Thomas.

Durkin, R.P., & Durkin, A.B. (1975). Evaluating residential treatment programs for disturbed children. In M. Guttentag & E. Struening (Eds.), *Handbook of evaluative research* (pp. 275–339). London: Sage.

Dziech, B.W., & Schudson, C.B. (1991). *On trial: America's courts and their treatment of sexually abused children* (2nd ed.). Boston: Beacon Press.

Earle, R. (1995) *Helping to prevent child abuse and future criminal consequences: Hawaii Healthy Start.* National Institute of Justice Program Focus Brief. Washington, DC: U.S. Department of Justice.

Eastman, K.S. (1985). Foster families: A comprehensive bibliography. *Child Welfare, 64,* 565–585.

Edelman, M. (1987). *Families in peril: An agenda for social change.* Cambridge, MA: Harvard University Press.

Edleson, J.L. (1999). The overlap between child maltreatment and women battering. *Violence Against Women, 5*(2), 294–298.

Edna McConnell Clark Foundation. (1985). *Keeping families together: The case for family preservation.* New York: Author.

Egeland, B., & Erickson, M. (1987). Psychologically unavailable caregiving. In M.R. Brassard, R. Germain, & S.N. Hart (Eds.), *Psychological maltreatment of children and youth* (pp. 110–120). New York: Pergamon.

Egeland, B., & Jacobvitz, D. (1984). *Intergenerational continuity of parental abuse: Causes and consequences.* Presented at the Conference on Biosocial Perspectives in Abuse and Neglect, York, Maine.

Eisen, L.N., Field, T.M., Bandstra E.S., Roberts, J.P., Morrow, C., Larson, S.K., & Steele, B.M. (1991). Perinatal cocaine effects on neonatal stress behavior and performance on the Brazelton Scale. *Pediatrics, 88,* 477–480.

Ekstein, R. (Ed.). (1983). *Children of time and space, of action and impulse.* Englewood Cliffs, NJ: Appleton Century Crofts.

Ellett, A.J. (1999). *I quit! Can higher education diminish turnover in child welfare?* Paper presented at the Annual Program Meeting of the Council on Social Work Education, March 13, 1999, San Francisco (mimeograph).

Ellett, C.D., & Ellett, A.J. (1999). A statewide study of child welfare personnel needs: Who stays? Who leaves? Who cares? In M. Tracy & M. Miah (Eds.), *A national child welfare challenge: Creating partnerships to strengthen families and children: Proceedings of the National Conference on Child Welfare, Memphis, Tennessee, September 26–29, 1996* (pp. 61–72). Carbondale, IL: School of Social Work, Southern Illinois University.

Ellett, A., Kelley, B., & Noble, D. (1995, October). *Personnel needs and professionalization issues in child welfare.* Paper presented at the National Association of Social Workers Conference, Philadelphia, PA.

Elliott, D.M., & Edwards, K.J. (1991). *Individuals raised by alcoholic versus mentally ill parents: A comparison study.* Paper presented at the annual meeting of the American Psychological Association, San Francisco.

Elliott, D.M., & Gabrielson-Cabush, D.L. (1990, August). *Impaired object relations in professional women molested as children.* Paper presented at the annual meeting of the American Psychological Association, Los Angeles.

Elliott, D.S., & Voss, H. (1974). *Delinquency and dropout.* Lexington, MA: Heath.

Ellwood, D. (1986). *Targeting the would-be long-term recipients of AFDC: Who should be served?* Princeton, NJ: Mathematica Policy Research.

Ellwood, D. (1988). *Poor support: Poverty in the American family.* New York: Basic Books.

Emlen, A., Lahti, J., Downs, G., McKay, A., & Downs, S. (1978). *Overcoming barriers to planning for children in foster care.* Washington, DC: U.S. Department of Health and Human Services, U.S. Children's Bureau, DHEW Publication No. (OHDS) 78-30138.

English, D.J. (1997). *Current knowledge about CPS decision-making.* Atlanta, GA: Child Welfare Institute and ACTION for Child Protection.

English, D.J. (1998). The extent and consequences of child maltreatment. *The Future of Children, 8*(1), 39–53.

English, D.J., Brummel, S., & Marshall, D. (1997). *CPS decision-making: Factors associated with re-referral and substantiation.* Paper presented at the Eleventh National Roundtable on Risk Assessment, San Francisco, July 1997.

English, D.J., Marshall, D.B., Brummel, S.C., & Coghlan, L.K. (1998). *Decision-making in child protective services: A study of effectiveness.* Final Report Phase I: Quantitative Analysis. Federal Grant #90-CA-1563, Office of Child Abuse and Neglect, Washington, DC.

English, D.J., Marshall, D.B., Brummel, S., & Orme, M. (1999). Characteristics of repeated referrals to child protective services in Washington State. *Child Maltreatment: Journal of the American Professional Society on the Abuse of Children, 4*(4), 297–307

English, K., Pullen, S., & Jones, L. (1997). Managing adult sex offenders in the community—A containment approach. (National Institute of Justice Research in Brief.) Washington, DC: U.S. Department of Justice.

English, P.C. (1978). Failure to thrive without organic reason. *Pediatric Annals, 7*(11), 774–781.

Enos, S. (1997). Managing motherhood in prison: The impact of race and ethnicity on child placement. *Women & Therapy, 20*(4), 57–73.

Epstein, M.H., Nelson, C.M., Polsgrove, L., Coutinho, M., Cumblad, C., & Quinn, K. (1993). A comprehensive community-based approach to serving students with emotional and behavioral disorders. *Journal of Emotional and Behavioral Disorders, 1*(2), 127–133.

Erera, P.I. (1997). Foster parents' attitudes toward birth parents and caseworkers: Implications for visitation. *Families in Society: The Journal of Contemporary Human Services, 78,* 511–519.

Ereth, J., Wagner, D., Baird, S.C., Caskey, R. McHoskey, T., Freitag, R. Gramling, S., Quigley, P., Weibush, R., & Paulus, D. (Eds.). (1999). *A new approach to child protective services: Structured decision making.* Madison, WI: Children's Research Center.

Erikson, E.H. (1956). The problem of ego identity. *Journal of the American Psychoanalytic Association, 4*(1), 56–121.

Erikson, E.H. (1959). Growth and crises of the healthy personality. *Psychological Issues, 1,* 50–100.

Erikson, E.H. (1963). *Childhood and society* (2nd ed.). New York: Norton.

Erikson, E.H. (1964). *Insight and responsibility.* New York: Norton.

Erikson, E.H. (1968). *Identity: Youth and crisis.* New York: Norton.

Erikson, E.H. (1974). *Dimensions of a new identity.* New York: Norton

Erikson, E.H. (1975). *Life history and the historical moment.* New York: Norton.

Erikson, E.H. (1985). *The life cycle completed.* New York: Norton.

Erikson, M.F., & Egeland, B. (1996). Child neglect. In J. Briere, L. Berliner, J.A. Bulkley, C. Jenny, & T. Reid (Eds.), *The APSAC handbook on child maltreatment* (pp. 4–20). Newbury Park, CA: Sage.

Esposito, G., & Fine, M. (1985). The field of child welfare as a world of work. In J. Laird & A. Hartman (Eds.), *A handbook of child welfare: Context, knowledge, and practice.* New York: Free Press.

Evans, M.E., Boothroyd, R.A., Armstrong, M.I., Kuppinger, A.D., Brown, E.C., & Greenbaum, P.E. (1997). *Comparisons of three models of intensive in-home services for children experiencing a psychiatric crisis: Outcomes from a three-year study.* Presented at the 10th Annual Research conference: A System of Care for Children's Mental Health, February 23–26, 1997, Tampa, FL.

Evans, S., Reinhart, J., & Succop, R. (1983). Failure to thrive: A study of 45 children and their families. *Journal of American Academy of Child Psychiatry, 11,* 440.

Everett, J.E. (1995). Relative foster care: An emerging trend in foster care placement policy and practice. *Smith College Studies in Social Work, 65,* 239–253.

Everett, J.E., Chipungu, S.S., & Leashore, B.R. (Eds.). (1991). *Child welfare: An Africentric perspective.* New Brunswick, NJ: Rutgers University Press.

Eyler, F.D., Behnke, M., Conlon, M., Woods, N.S., & Wobie, K. (1998). Birth outcome from a prospective, matched study of prenatal crack/cocaine use: I. Interactive and dose effects on health and growth. *Pediatrics, 101,* 229–237.

Fagan, J., & Jones, S.J. (1984). Toward a theoretical model for intervention with violent juvenile offenders. In R.A. Mathias et al. (Eds.), *Violent juvenile offenders: An anthology.* San Francisco: National Council on Crime and Delinquency.

Fahlberg, V. (1978). *Attachment and separation.* Lansing, MI: Michigan Department of Social Services.

Fales, M.J. (1985). Adoption assistance—How well is it working? *Permanency Report, 3,* 3.

Falicov, C.J. (Ed.). (1988). *Family transitions: Continuity and change over the life cycle.* New York: Guilford

Faller, K.C. (1988). *Child sexual abuse: An interdisciplinary manual for diagnosis, case management, and treatment.* New York: Columbia University Press.

Family Resource Coalition of America. (2000). *Guidelines for family support practice.* Chicago, IL: Author.

Fanshel, D. (1982). *On the road to permanency: An expanded data base for children in foster care.* New York: Child Welfare League of America.

Fanshel, D. (1992). Foster care as a two-tiered system. *Children and Youth Services Review, 14,* 49–60.

Fanshel, D., Finch, S.J., & Grundy, J.F. (1990). *Foster children in a life course perspective.* New York: Columbia University Press.

Fanshel, D., & Shinn, E. (1978). *Children in foster care: A longitudinal investigation.* New York: Columbia University Press.

Farley, J.E. (1990). Family developmental task assessment: A prerequisite to family treatment. *Clinical Social Work Journal, 18,* 85–98.

Farmer, E. (1996). Family reunification with high risk children: Lessons from research. *Children and Youth Services Review, 18,* 403–424.

Farrington, D.P. (1985). Predicting self–reported and official delinquency. In D.P. Farrington & R. Taring (Eds.), *Prediction in criminology.* Albany, NY: State University of New York Press.

Farrington, D.P., Loeber, R., Elliott, D.S., Hawkins, J.D., Kandel, D.B., Klien, M.W., McCord, J., Rowe, D.C., & Tremblay, R.E. (1993). Advancing knowledge about the onset of delinquency and crime. In B.B. Lahey & A.E. Kazdin (Eds.), *Advances in clinical child psychology* (Vol. 13, pp. 283–342). New York: Plenum Press.

Farrington, D.P., Loeber, R., & Van Kammen, W.B. (1990). Long-term criminal outcomes of hyperactivity-impulsivity-attention deficit and conduct problems in childhood. In L.N. Robins & M. Rutter (Eds.), *Straight and devious pathways from childhood to adulthood* (pp. 62–81). New York: Cambridge University Press.

Farrow, F. (1991). Services to families: The view from the states. *Families in Society: The Journal of Contemporary Human Services, 72*(5), 268–275.

Farrow, F. (1997). *Child protection: Building community partnerships, Getting from here to there.* Boston, MA: John F. Kennedy School of Government, Harvard University.

Fay, M. (Ed.). (1989). *Speak out: An anthology of stories by youth in care.* Toronto: Pape Adolescent Resource Centre.

Federal Register. (1979a). Part IV Department of the Interior, Bureau of Indian Affairs, Indian Child Welfare Provisions. *Federal Register,* July 31, 1979, 45091–45108.

Federal Register. (1979b). Part III Department of the Interior, Bureau of Indian Affairs, Guidelines for State Courts, Indian Child Custody Proceedings. *Federal Register,* November 26, 1979, 67583–67595.

Federal Register. (1990). Title IV B and Title IV E of the Social Security Act: Data collection for foster care and adoption. *Federal Register, 55* (188), (September 27, 1990), 39540.

Feigelman, W., & Silverman, A.R. (1983). *Chosen children: New patterns of adoptive relationships.* New York: Praeger.

Feild, T. (1996). Managed care and child welfare: Will it work? *Public Welfare, 54*(3) 4–10.

Fein, E., & Maluccio, A.N. (1991). Foster family care: Solution or Problem? In W.A. Rhodes & W.K. Brown (Eds.), *Why some children succeed despite the odds.* New York: Praeger.

Fein, E., & Maluccio, A.N. (1992). Permanency planning: Another remedy in jeopardy. *Social Service Review, 66,* 335–348.

Fein, E., Maluccio, A.N., Hamilton, V.J., & Ward, D. (1983). After foster care: Outcomes of permanency planning for children. *Child Welfare, 62,* 485–560.

Fein, E., Maluccio, A.N., & Kluger, M. (1990). *No more partings: An examination of long-term foster family care.* Washington, DC: Child Welfare League of America.

Fein, E., & Staff, I. (1991). Implementing reunification services. *Families in Society: The Journal of Contemporary Human Services, 72*(6), 335–343.

Fein, E. B. (October 25, 1998). Secrecy and stigma no longer clouding adoptions. *The New York Times, 1,* 18–19.

Fein, L.G. (1979). Can child fatalities, end product of child abuse, be prevented? *Children and Youth Services Review, 1,* 75–89.

Feldman, L. (1990). *Evaluating the impact of family preservation services in New Jersey.* Trenton, NJ: New Jersey Division of Youth and Family Services, Bureau of Research, Evaluation and Quality Assurance.

Feldman, L.H. (1991). Evaluating the impact of intensive family preservation services in New Jersey. In K. Wells & D.A. Biegel (Eds.), *Family preservation services: Research and evaluation* (pp. 47–71). Newbury Park, CA: Sage.

Felker, E. (1974). *Foster parenting young children—Guidelines from a foster parent.* New York: Child Welfare League of America.

Ferguson, S.K., & Kaplan, M.S. (1994). Women and drug policy: Implications of normalization. *AFFILIA, 9*(2), 129–144.

Fergusson, D.M., & Lynskey, M.T. (1997). Physical punishment/maltreatment during childhood and adjustment in young adulthood. *Child Abuse and Neglect, 21*(7), 617–630.

Fernandez, E. (1996). *Significant harm—Unraveling child protection decisions and substitute care careers of children.* Aldershot, England: Avebury.

Fernandez, E. (1999). Pathways in substitute care: Representation of placement careers of children using event history analysis. *Children and Youth Services Review, 21,* 177–216.

Festinger, T. (1983). *No one ever asked us. A postscript to foster care.* New York: Columbia University Press.

Festinger, T. (1996). Going home and returning to foster care. *Children and Youth Services Review, 18,* 383–402.

Festinger, T. (1998). *New York City adoptions.* New York: New York University (mimeograph).

Fine, P. (1995). *A developmental network approach to therapeutic foster care.* Washington, DC: Child Welfare League of America.

Finkelhor, D. (1979). *Sexually victimized children.* New York: Free Press.

Finkelhor, D. (1984). *Child sexual abuse.* New York: Free Press.

Finkelhor, D. (1986a). Abusers: Special topics. In D. Finkelhor et al. (Eds.), *A sourcebook on child sexual abuse.* Beverly Hills, CA: Sage.

Finkelhor, D. (1986b). Prevention: A review of programs and research. In D. Finkelhor et al. (Eds.), *A sourcebook on child sexual abuse* (pp. 224–254). Beverly Hills, CA: Sage.

Finkelhor, D., & Baron, L. (1986a). High-risk children. In D. Finkelhor et al. (Eds.), *A sourcebook on child sexual abuse.* Beverly Hills, CA: Sage.

Finkelhor, D., & Baron, L. (1986b). Risk factors for child sexual abuse. *Journal of Interpersonal Violence, 1*(2), 43–71.

Finkelhor, D., & Browne, A. (1986). Initial and long–term effects: A conceptual framework. In D. Finkelhor et al. (Eds.), *A sourcebook on child sexual abuse.* Beverly Hills, CA: Sage.

Finkelhor, D., & Dziuba-Leatherman, J. (1995). Victimization prevention programs: A national survey of children's exposure and reactions. *Child Abuse and Neglect, 19*(2), 129–139.

Finkelhor, D., Hotaling, G., Lewis, I.A., & Smith, C. (1989). Sexual abuse and its relationship to later sexual satisfaction, marital status, religion, and attitudes. *Journal of Interpersonal Violence, 4,* 279–399.

Finkelhor, D., & Yllo, K. (1982). Forced sex in marriage: A preliminary report. *Crime and Delinquency, 28,* 459–478.

Fiscella, K., Kitzman H.J., Cole, R.E., et al. (1998). Does child abuse predict adolescent pregnancy? *Pediatrics, 101*(4), 620–624.

Fischler, R. (1985). Child abuse and neglect in American Indian communities. *Child Abuse and Neglect, 9*(1), 95–106.

Fischler, R.S. (1980). Protecting American Indian children. *Social Work, 25,* 341–349.

Fitzgerald, J., Murcer, B., & Murcer, B. (1982). *Building new families through adoption and fostering.* Oxford: Basil Blackwell.

Fitzharris, T. (1985). *The foster children of California.* Sacramento, CA: Children's Services Foundation.

Fixsen, D.L., Collings, L.B., Phillips, E.L., & Thomas, D.L. (1982). Institutional indicators in evaluation: An example from Boys Town. In A.J. McSweeney, W.J. Fremouw, & R.P. Hawkins (Eds.), *Practical program evaluation in youth treatment* (pp. 203–230). Springfield, IL: Charles C Thomas.

Flango, V.E., & Flango, C.R. (1995). How many children were adopted in 1992? *Child Welfare, 74*(5) 1018–1032.

Florida Department of Health and Rehabilitative Services. (1982). *Intensive crisis counseling programs.* Unpublished manuscript.

Fluke, J.D. (1995). *The Children's Services Simulation Model: Ingredients for development and decision support.* Unpublished doctoral dissertation, The Union Graduate School, Cincinnati, OH.

Fluke, J.D., Edwards, M.E., Johnson, W., & Wells, S.J. (1997). *Outcome evaluation of the Illinois child endangerment risk assessment protocol.* Englewood, CO: The American Humane Association.

Fluke, J.D., Yuan, Y.T., & Edwards, M. (1999). Recurrence of maltreatment: An application of the national child abuse and neglect data system (NCANDS). *Child Abuse and Neglect, 23* (7), 633–649.

Folaron, G. (1993). Preparing children for reunification. In B.A. Pine, R. Warsh, & A.N. Maluccio (Eds.), *Together again: Family reunification in foster care* (pp. 141–154). Washington, DC: Child Welfare League of America.

Folaron, G., & Hess, P.Mc. (1993). Placement considerations for children of mixed African American and Caucasian parentage. *Child Welfare, 72,* 113–125.

Folks, H. ([1903]1978). *The care of destitute, neglected, and delinquent children* (classic ed.). New York: National Association of Social Workers.

Folman, R.D. (1998). "I was tooken." How children experience removal from their parents preliminary to placement into foster care. *Adoption Quarterly, 2,* 7–35.

Fong, R. (1994). Family preservation: Making it work for Asians. *Child Welfare, 73,* 331–341.

Fontana, V.J. (1971). *The maltreated child.* Springfield, IL: Charles C Thomas.

Fontana, V.J. (1973). *Somewhere a child is crying: Maltreatment—causes and prevention.* New York: Macmillan.

Fontana, V.J., & Alfaro, J.D. (1987). *High risk factors associated with child maltreatment fatalities.* New York: Mayor's Task Force on Child Abuse and Neglect.

Fontes, L. (1993). Considering culture and oppression: Steps toward an ecology of sexual child abuse. *Journal of Feminist Family Therapy, 5*(1), 25–54.

Forsythe, P.W. (1992). Homebuilders™ and family preservation. *Children and Youth Services Review, 14,* 37–47.

Foster Family-based Treatment Association. (1995). *Program standards for treatment foster care.* Teaneck, NJ: Author.

FRAC. (1998). Federal Food Program, National School Lunch Program. Washington, DC: Department of Agriculture.

Fraiberg, S., Adelson, E., & Shapiro, V. (1975). Ghosts in the nursery: A psychoanalytic approach to the problems of impaired infant-mother relationships. *Journal of the American Academy of Child Psychiatry, 14,* 387–421.

Frank, D.A., Bauchner, H., Parker, S., Huber A.M., Kyei-Aboagye, K., Cabral, H., & Zuckerman, B. (1990). Neonatal body proportionality and body composition after in-utero exposure to cocaine and marijuana. *Journal of Pediatrics, 117,* 622–626.

Frankel, H. (1988). Family-centered, home-based services in child protection: A review of the research. *Social Service Review, 62*(1), 137–157.

Frasch, K., Brooks, D., & Barth, R.P. (In press). Openness and contact in foster care adoptions: An eight year follow-up. *Family Relations.*

Fraser, M., Nelson, K., & Rivard, J. (1997). Effectiveness of family preservation services. *Social Work Research, 21*(2), 138–153.

Fraser, M.W. (1996). Cognitive problem solving and aggressive behavior among children. *Families in Society: The Journal of Contemporary Human Services, 58,* 23.

Fraser, M.W. (Ed.). (1997). *Risk and resilience in childhood—An ecological perspective.* Washington, DC: NASW Press.

Fraser, M.W., Pecora P.J., & Haapala, D.A. (1991a). *Families in crisis: The impact of intensive family preservation services.* Hawthorne, NY: Aldine de Gruyter.

Fraser, M.W., Pecora, P.J., & Haapala, D.A. (1991b). *Families in crisis: Finding from the family-based Intensive Treatment Project* (pp. 17–47). Hawthorne, NY: Aldine de Gruyter.

Fraser, M.W., Pecora, P.J., Popuang, C., & Haapala, D.A. (1992). Event history analysis: A proportional hazards perspective on modeling outcomes in intensive family preservation services. *Journal of Social Service Research, 16*(1/2), 123–158.

Fraser, M.W., Walton, E., Lewis, R.E., Pecora, P.J., & Walton, W.K. (1996). An experiment in family reunification: Correlates of outcome at one-year follow-up. *Children and Youth Services Review, 18*(4–5), 335–362.

Frede, E. (1994). *The role of teacher practices and curriculum in early childhood programs.* Paper presented at the Seventh Annual Rutgers Symposium on Early Childhood Education and Care, New Brunswick, NJ, October.

Freed, A.O. (1985). Linking developmental, family and life cycle theories. *Smith College Studies in Social Work, 65,* 169–182.

Freud, S. (1935). *A general introduction to psychoanalysis.* New York: Simon & Schuster.

Freud, S. (1960). *The ego and the id.* New York: Norton.

Freud, S. (1988). Cybernetic epistemology. In R.A. Dorfman (Ed.). *Paradigms of clinical social work* (pp. 356–387). New York: Brunner/Mazel.

Freundlich, M., & Peterson, L. (1998). *Wrongful adoption: Law, policy and practice.* Washington, DC: Child Welfare League of America.

Frey, J.H. (1983). *Survey research by telephone.* Beverly Hills, CA: Sage.

Friedman, M. (1997). *A guide to developing and using performance measures in results-based budgeting.* Washington, DC: The Finance Project.

Friedrich, W.N. (Ed.). (1991). *Casebook of sexual abuse treatment.* New York: Norton.

Friedrich, W.N., & Einbender, A.J. (1983). The abused child: A psychological review. *Journal of Clinical Child Psychology, 12*(3), 244–256.

Friman, P.C., Osgood, D.W., Smith, G., Shanahan, D., Thompson, R.W., Larzelere, R., & Daly, D.L. (1996). A longitudinal evaluation of prevalent negative beliefs about residential placement for troubled adolescents. *Journal of Abnormal Child Psychology, 24,* 299–324.

Fryer, G., & Miyoshi, T. (1994). A survival analysis of the revictimization of children: The case of Colorado. *Child Abuse and Neglect, 18,* 1063–1071.

Gabel, K., & Johnston, D. (1995). *Children of incarcerated parents.* New York: Lexington.

Gabinet, L. (1983). Shared parenting: A new paradigm for the treatment of child abuse. *Child Abuse and Neglect, 7,* 403–411.

Gabor, P., & Grinnell, R.M. (1993). *Evaluation and quality improvement in the social services.* Needham Heights, MA: Allyn & Bacon.

Galinsky, M., & Schopler, J.H. (1994). Negative experiences in support groups. *Social Work in Health Care, 20,* 77–95.

Gallagher, L., Gallagher, M., Perese, K., Schreiber, S., & Watson, K. (1998). *One year after federal welfare reform: A description of state Temporary Assistance for Needy Families (TANF) decisions as of October 1997.* Occasional Paper Number 6. Washington, DC: The Urban Institute.

Gamble, D.N., & Weil, M.O. (1995). Citizen participation. In R.L. Edwards & J.G. Hopps (Eds.), *Encyclopedia of social work* (19th ed., Vol. 1, pp. 483–494). Washington, DC: NASW.

Gambrill E. (1990). *Critical thinking in clinical practice.* San Francisco: Jossey-Bass.

Gambrill, E. (1997). *Social work practice—A critical thinker's guide.* New York: Oxford University Press.

Gannon. (1987). Martin Wolins: An appreciation. *The Child Care Worker, 5*(8), 16.

GAO. (1990). *Foster care: Incomplete implementation of the reforms and unknown effectiveness* (GAO/PEMD-89-17). Gaithersburg, MD: U.S. General Accounting Office.

GAO. (1994). *Foster care: Parental drug abuse has alarming impact on young children* (GAO/HEH-94-89, Report of the Chairman, Subcommittee on Human Resources). Washington, DC: Committee on Ways and Means, U.S. House of Representatives.

GAO. (1995a). *Foster care—Health needs of many young children are unknown and unmet* (GAO/HEHS-95-114, p. 4). Washington, DC: U.S. General Accounting Office.

GAO. (1995b). *Child welfare: Complex needs strain capacity to provide services* (GAO/HEHS-95-208). Washington, DC: U.S. General Accounting Office.

GAO. (1997). *Child welfare: States' progress in implementing family preservation and support services* (GAO/HEHS-97-34). Washington, DC: U.S. General Accounting Office.

GAO. (1998). *Foster care: Implementation of the multiethnic placement act poses difficult challenges* (GAO/HEHS-98-204, PL. 103-382). Washington, DC: U.S. General Accounting Office.

Garbarino, J. (1976). A preliminary study of some ecological correlates of child abuse: The impact of socioeconomic stress on mothers. *Child Development, 47,* 178–185.

Garbarino, J. (1977a). The human ecology of child maltreatment: A conceptual model for research. *Journal of Marriage and the Family, 43*(4), 721–731.

Garbarino, J. (1977b). The price of privacy in the social dynamics of child abuse. *Child Welfare, 56,* 565–575.

Garbarino, J. (1980). Preventing child maltreatment. In R.H. Price, R.F. Ketterer, B.C. Bader, & J. Monahan (Eds.), *Prevention in mental health: Research, policy and practice.* Beverly Hills, CA: Sage.

Garbarino, J. (1982). *Children and families in the social environment.* Hawthorne, NY: Aldine de Gruyter.

Garbarino, J. (1992). *Children and families in the social environment* (2nd ed.). Hawthorne, NY: Aldine de Gruyter.

Garbarino, J., & Ebata, A. (1983). The significance of ethnic and cultural differences in child maltreatment. *Journal of Marriage and the Family, 45* (November), 773–783.

Garbarino, J., Guttmann, E., & Seeley, J.W. (1986). *The psychologically battered child: Strategies for identification, assessment and intervention.* San Francisco, CA: Jossey-Bass.

Garbarino, J., & Hershberger, J.K. (1981). The perspective of evil in understanding and treating child abuse. *Journal of Religion and Health, 20*(3), 208–217.

Garbarino, J., & Kostelny, K. (1992). Child maltreatment as a community problem. *Child Abuse and Neglect, 16,* 455–464.

Garbarino, J., Schellenbach, C.J., Sebes, J., & Associates. (1986). *Troubled youth, troubled families: Understanding families at risk for adolescent maltreatment.* Hawthorne, NY: Aldine de Gruyter.

Garbarino, J., Stott, F.M., & Faculty of the Erikson Institute. (1989). *What children can tell us.* San Francisco: Jossey-Bass.

Garfinkel, I. (1992). *Assuring child support: An extension of Social Security.* New York: Russell Sage Foundation.

Garfinkel, I. (1996). Economic security for children: From means testing and bifurcation to universality. In I. Garfinkel, J. Hochschild, & S. McLanahan (Eds.), *Social policies for children.* Washington, DC: Brookings Institution.

Garfinkel, I., McLanahan, S., & Robins, P. (Eds.). (1994). *Child support and child well-being.* Washington, DC: Urban Institute Press.

Garfinkel, I., McLanahan, S., & Wong, P. (1988). Child support and dependency. In H. Rodgers (Ed.), *Beyond welfare: New approaches to the problem of poverty in America.* Armonk, NY: M.E. Sharpe.

Garfinkel, I., Meyer, D., & Sandefur, G. (1992). The effects of alternative child support systems on blacks, Hispanics, and non-Hispanic whites. *Social Service Review, 66,* 505–523.

Garmezy, N. (1983). Stressors of childhood. In N. Garmezy & M. Rutter (Eds.), *Stress, coping and development in children* (pp. 43–84). New York: McGraw-Hill.

Garmezy, N. (1985). Stress resistant children: The search for protective factors. In J.E. Stevenson (Ed.), *Recent research in developmental psychopathology.* Oxford: Pergamon Press.

Gaudin, J.M. (1993a). Effective interventions with neglectful families. *Criminal Justice and Behavior, 20*(1), 66–89.

Gaudin, J.M. (1993b). *Child neglect: A guide for intervention.* U.S. Department of Health and Human Services, Administration for Children and Families, Administration on Children, Youth and Families National Center on Child Abuse and Neglect.

Gaudin, J.M., Jr., & Polansky, N.A. (1986). Social distancing of the neglectful family: Sex, race, and social class influences. *Children and Youth Services Review, 8,* 1–12.

Gaudin, J.M., Polanksy, N.A., Kilpatrick, A.C., & Shilton, P. (1996). Family functioning in neglectful families. *Child Abuse and Neglect, 20*(4) 363–377.

Gaudin, J.M., Wodarski, J.S., Arkinson, M.K., & Avery, L.S. (1989). *Outcomes of social network interventions with neglectful families.* Research report from Grant No. 90CA1189 from U.S. Department of Health and Human Services, Office of Human Development, National Center on Child Abuse and Neglect with the cooperation of the Georgia Department of Human Resources, Division of Family and Children Services.

Gauld, J. (1993). *Character first: The Hyde School challenge.* San Francisco: Institute for Contemporary Studies.

Geen, R., & Tumlin, K.C. (1999). *State efforts to remake child welfare: Responses to new challenges and increased scrutiny.* (Occasional Urban Institute paper No. 29). Washington, DC: The Urban Institute.

Geismar, L. (1979). Home-based care to children: Harmonizing the approaches of research and practice. In S. Maybanks & M. Bryce (Eds.), *Home-based services for children and families* (pp. 325–332). Springfield, IL: Charles C Thomas.

Geismar, L., & Ayers, B. (1958). *Families in trouble.* St. Paul, MN: Family-Centered Project.

Geismar, L., & Krisberg, J. (1966). The family life improvement project: An experiment in preventive intervention. *Social Casework, 47*(6), 563–570.

Gelles, R. (1975). The social construction of child abuse. *American Journal of Psychiatry, 132,* 363–371.

Gelles, R.A., & Lancaster, J.B. (Eds.). (1987). *Child abuse and neglect: Biosocial dimensions.* Hawthorne, NY: Aldine de Gruyter.

Gelles, R.A., & Straus, M.A. (1987). Is violence toward children increasing? *Journal of Interpersonal Violence, 2*(2), 212–222.

Gelles, R.J. (1987). What to learn from cross-cultural and historical research on child abuse and neglect: An overview. In R.J. Gelles, & J.B. Lancaster (Eds.), *Child abuse and neglect: Biosocial dimensions* (pp. 15–30). Hawthorne, NY: Aldine de Gruyter.

Gelles, R.J. (1996). *The book of David—How preserving families can cost children's lives.* New York: Basic Books.

Gelles, R.J., & Cornell, C.P. (1985). *Intimate violence in families.* Beverly Hills, CA: Sage.

Gelles, R.J., & Straus, M.A. (1979). Determinants of violence in the family: Toward a theoretical integration. In W.R. Burr et al. (Eds.), *Contemporary theories about the family* (Vol. 1). New York: John Wiley & Sons.

General Accounting Office. (1995). *Child welfare: Complex needs strain capacity to provide services.* Report to Congressional Committees, GAO/HEHS-95-208.

General Accounting Office . (1997). *Child welfare: States' progress in implementing family preservation.* Report to the Chairman Subcommittee on Human Resources, Committee on Ways and Means, House of Representatives, GAO/HEHS-97-34.

George, L.J. (1997). Why the need for the Indian Child Welfare Act? In G.R. Anderson, A.S. Ryan, & B.R. Leashore (Eds.), *The challenge of permanency planning in a multicultural society* (pp. 165– 175). New York: Haworth Press.

Germain, C., & Gitterman, A. (1980). *The life model of social work practice.* New York: Columbia University Press.

Germain, C.B. (1979). Ecology and social work. In C.B. Germain (Ed.), *Social work practice: People and environments* (pp. 1–22). New York: Columbia University Press.

Germain, C.G. (1991). *Human behavior in the social environment: An ecological view.* New York: Columbia University Press.

Germain, C.G., & Bloom, M. (1999). *Human behavior in the social environment: An ecological view* (2nd ed.). New York: Columbia University Press.

Germain, C.G., & Gitterman, A. (1996). *The life model of social work practice—Advances in theory & practice* (2nd ed.). New York: Columbia University Press.

Gershenson, C.P. (1956). Residential treatment of children: Research problems and possibilities. *Social Service Review, 30*(3), 268–275.

Gershenson, C.P. (1990). *Preparing for the future backwards: Characteristics of the ecology for children and youth in long term out of home care.* Unpublished manuscript. Prepared for the Casey Family Programs Symposium on Long Term Care, Seattle, WA.

Gershenson, C.P. (1993). The child well-being conundrum. *Readings: A Journal of Reviews and Commentary in Mental Health, 8*(2), 8–11.

Giarretto, H.A. (1981). A comprehensive child sexual abuse treatment program. In P.B. Mrazek & C.H. Kempe (Eds.), *Sexually abused children and their families.* Elmsford, NY: Pergamon Press.

Gil, D. (1970, 1973). *Violence against children: Physical child abuse in the U.S.* Cambridge, MA: Harvard University Press.

Gil, D. (1971). Violence against children. *Journal of Marriage and the Family, 33,* 637–648.

Gil, D.G. (1987). Maltreatment as a function of the structure of social systems. In M.R. Brassard, R. Germain, & S.N. Hart (Eds.), *Psychological maltreatment of children and youth* (pp. 159–170.). New York: Pergamon Press.

Gilbert, N., Berrick, J.D., Le Prohn, N., & Nyman, N. (1989). *Protecting young children form sexual abuse: Does preschool training work?* Lexington, MA: Lexington Books.

Giles-Sims, J. (1983). *Wife battering: A systems theory approach.* New York: Guilford Press.

Gill, M.M., & Amadio, C.M. (1983). Social work and law in a foster care/adoption program. *Child Welfare, 62,* 455–467.

Gilligan, C. (1982). *In a different voice: Psychological theory and women's development.* Cambridge, MA: Harvard University Press.

Gilligan, R. (1997). Beyond permanence? The importance of resilience in child placement practice and planning. *Adoption & Fostering, 21,* 12–20.

Giovannoni, J.M. (1982). Prevention of child abuse and neglect: Research and policy issues. *Social Work Research and Abstracts, 18*(3), 23–31.

Giovannoni, J.M. (1985). Child abuse and neglect: An overview. In J. Laird & A. Hartman (Eds.), *A handbook of child welfare: Context, knowledge, and practice* (pp. 193–212). New York: Free Press.

Giovannoni, J. (1989). Definitional issues in child maltreatment. In D. Cicchetti & V. Carlson (Eds.), *Child maltreatment: Theory and research on the causes and consequences of child abuse and neglect* (pp. 3–37). Cambridge: Cambridge University Press.

Giovannoni, J.M., & Becerra, R.M. (1979). *Defining child abuse.* New York: The Free Press.

Giovannoni, J.M., & Billingsley, A. (1970). Child neglect among the poor: A study of parental adequacy in families of three ethnic groups. *Child Welfare, 49*(4), 196–204.

Gitterman, A. (1996). Ecological perspective: Response to Professor Jerry Wakefield. *Social Service Review, 70,* 472–476.

Gitterman, A., & Shulman, L. (Eds.). (1994). *Mutual aid groups, vulnerable populations, and the life cycle* (2nd ed.). New York: Columbia University Press.

Glaser, B. (1978). *Theoretical sensitivity: Advances in the methodology of grounded theory.* Mill Valley, CA: The Sociology Press.

Glaser, H., Heagarty, M.C., Bullard, D.M., Jr., & Pivchik, E.C. (1968). Physical and psychological development of children with early failure to thrive. *Journal of Pediatrics, 73,* 690–698.

Gleeson, J.P., & Craig, L.C. (1994). Kinship care in child welfare: An analysis of States' policies. *Children and Youth Services Review, 16,* 7–32.

Gleeson, J.P., & Hairston C.F. (Eds.). (1999). *Kinship care—Improving practice through research.* Washington, DC: CWLA Press.

Gleeson, J.P., O'Donnell, J., & Bonecutter, F.J. (1997). Understanding the complexity of practice in kinship foster care. *Child Welfare, 76,* 801–826.

Glisson, C., & Hemmelgarn, A. (1998). The Effects of organizational climate and interorganizational coordination on the quality and outcomes of children's service systems. *Child Abuse and Neglect, 22*(5), 401–421.

Goerge, R.M. (1990). The reunification process in substitute care. *Social Service Review, 64,* 422–457.

Goerge, R.M., Howard, E.C., & Wu, D. (1996). *Adoption, disruption, and dissolution in the Illinois child welfare system, 1976–94 .* Chicago: Chapin Hall Center for Children.

Goerge, R.M., Wulczyn, F., & Fanshel, D. (1994). A foster care research agenda for the '90s. *Child Welfare: A Research Agenda for Child Welfare, LXXIII*(5), 525–549.

Goerge, R.M., Wulczyn, F.H., & Harden, A.W. (1994). *A report from the multistate data archive: Foster care dynamics 1983–1992.* Chicago: Chapin Hall Center for Children, University of Chicago.

Goerge, R.M., Wulczyn, F.H., & Harden, A. (1996). New comparative insights into states and their foster children. *Public Welfare, 54*(3), 12–25, 52.

Gold, E.R. (1986). Long-term effects of sexual victimization in childhood: An attributional approach. *Journal of Consulting and Clinical Psychology, 54,* 471–475.

Goldberg-Glen, R., Sands, R.G., Cole, R.D., & Cristofalo, C. (1998). Multigenerational patterns and internal structures in families in which grandparents raise children. *Families in Society: The Journal of Contemporary Human Services, 79,* 477–489.

Golding, J.M. (1999). Sexual-assault history and long-term physical health problems: Evidence from clinical and population epidemiology. *Current Directions in Psychological Science, 8*(6), 191–194.

Goldstein A.P., Keller, H., & Erné, D. (1985). *Changing the abusive parent.* Champaign, IL: Research Press.

Goldstein, A.P., & Kanfer, F. (Eds.). (1979). *Maximizing treatment gains.* New York: Academic Press.

Goldstein, A.P., & Keller, H. (1987). *Aggressive behavior: Assessment and intervention.* Elmsford, NY: Pergamon Press.

Goldstein, H. (1979). The effective use of volunteers in home-based care. In S. Maybanks & M. Bryce (Eds.), *Home-based services for children and families* (pp. 237–247). Springfield, IL: Charles C Thomas.

Goldstein, J., Freud, A., & Solnit, A.J. (1973). *Beyond the best interests of the child.* New York: Free Press.

Goldstein, J., Solnit, A., Goldstein, S., & Freud, A. (1996). *The best interest of the child: The least detrimental alternative.* New York: Free Press.

Gollub, S.L. (1974). A critical look at religious movements in adoption. *Public Welfare, 32,* 23–28.

Golombok S., Tasker F., & Murray C. (1997). Children raised in fatherless families from infancy: Family relationships and the socioemotional development of children of lesbian and single heterosexual mothers. *Journal of Child Psychology and Psychiatry and Allied Disciplines, 38,* 783–791.

Golub, E.S. (1994). *The limits of medicine.* New York: Times Books-Random House.

Gomby, D.S., Culross, P.L., & Behrman, R.E. (1999). Home visiting recent program evaluations: Analysis and recommendations. *The Future of Children, 9*(1), 4–43.

Gomby, D., Larson, C.S., Lewit, E.M., & Behrman, R.E. (1993). Home visiting: Analysis and recommendations. *The Future of Children, 3,* 6–22.

Goode, W.J. (1961). Force and violence in the family. *Journal of Marriage and the Family, 33,* 624–636.

Goodwin, J., & Flanagan, M. (1983). Incest: Treating child and family. *Physician and Patient, 2,* 59–68.

Goolsby, L. (1991). 1991 Food stamp legislation. *W-Memo, 3*(5), 3–7.

Gordon, A.H., & Jameson, J.C. (1979). Infant-mother attachment in patients with non-organic failure to thrive syndrome. *Journal of American Academy of Child Psychiatry, 18*(2), 251–259.

Gordon, D.A., Arbuthnot, J., Gustafson, K.E., & McGreen, P. (1988). Home-based behavioral-systems family therapy with disadvantaged juvenile delinquents. *American Journal of Family Therapy, 16*(3), 243–255.

Gordon, M. (1979/80). Child maltreatment: An overview of current approaches. *Journal of Family Law, 18,* 115–145.

Gottlieb, B. (1988). *Marshaling social support.* Beverly Hills, CA: Sage.

Grasso, A.J., & Epstein, I. (1992). *Research utilization in the social services innovations for practice and administration.* Binghamton, NY: Haworth Press.

Gray, C. (1978). *Empathy and stress: Their role in child abuse.* Doctoral dissertation, University of Maryland.

Gray, E. (Undated). *What have we learned about preventing child abuse? An overview of the "community and minority group action to prevent child abuse and neglect" program.* Chicago, IL: National Committee for Prevention of Child Abuse.

Gray, E., & Cosgrove, J. (1985). Ethnocentric perception of childrearing practices in protective services. *Child Abuse and Neglect, 9*(3), 389–396.

Gray, J., Cutler, C.A., Dean, J.G., & Kempe, C.H. (1979). Prediction and prevention of child abuse and neglect. *Journal of Social Issues, 35*(2), 127–139.

Grazio, T. (1981). New perspectives on child abuse/neglect community education. *Child Welfare, 60*(5), 679–707.

Green, A.H., Power, E., Steinbook, B., & Gaines, R.W. (1981). Factors associated with successful and unsuccessful intervention with child abusing families. *Child Abuse and Neglect, 5,* 45–52.

Green, B.L., McAllister, C., & Mulvey, L. (1997). *Evaluating family support programs: Issues and benefits in a theory-driven perspective.* Paper presented at the Biennial Meeting of the Society for Research in Child Development, Washington, DC.

Greenberg, M.T., Domitrovich, C., & Bumbarger, B. (1999). *Preventing mental disorders in school-age children: A review of the effectiveness of prevention programs.* Report submitted to the Center for Mental Health Services, Substance Abuse Mental Health Services Administration, U.S. Department of Health and Human Services by the Prevention Research Center for the Promotion of Human Development, College of Health and Human Development, Pennsylvania State University.

Greene, R.B., & Watkins, M. (Eds.). (1998). *Serving constituencies—Applying the ecological perspective.* Hawthorne, NY: Aldine de Gruyter.

Greene, R.R. (1999). *Human behavior theory and social work practice.* Hawthorne, NY: Aldine de Gruyter.

Greenwood, P., & Zimring, F. (1985). *One more chance: The pursuit of promising intervention strategies for chronic juvenile offenders.* Santa Monica, CA: Rand.

Grigsby, R.K. (1994). Maintaining attachment relationships among children in foster care. *Families in Society: The Journal of Contemporary Human Services, 75*(5), 269–277.

Groeneveld, L.G., & Giovannoni, J.M. (1977). Variations in child abuse reporting: The influence of state and county characteristics. *Social Work Research and Abstracts, 13,* 36–47.

Groginsky, L., & Freeman, C. (1995). Domestic violence in Native American Indian and Alaskan native communities. *Protecting Children* [American Humane Association], *11*(3), 13–16.

Grohoski, L. (1990). *Family-based services in Minnesota: A statewide view and case study* (mimeograph). Unpublished manuscript, Minnesota Department of Human Services, Research and Planning Unit, Community Social Services, St. Paul, MN.

Gross, E. (1989). *Contemporary federal policy towards American Indians.* New York: Greenwood Press.

Groth, A.N. (1983). Treatment of the sexual offender in a correctional institution. In J.G. Greer & I.R. Stuart (Eds.), *The sexual aggressor, current perspective on treatment.* New York: Van Nostrand Reinhold.

Grow, L.J., & Shapiro, D. (1972). *Black children, white parents: A study of transracial adoption.* New York: Child Welfare League of America.

Gruber, A.R. (1973). *Foster home care in Massachusetts: A study of children—Their biological and foster parents.* Boston, MA: Governor's Commission on Adoption and Foster Care.

Gruber, A.R. (1978). *Children in foster care: Destitute, neglected, betrayed.* New York: Human Sciences Press.

Gutiérrez, L.M. (1990). Working with women of color: An empowerment perspective. *Social Work, 35*(2), 149–153.

Gutiérrez, L., & Nagda, B.A. (1996). The multicultural imperative in human services organizations: Issues for the twenty-first century. In P. Raffoul & C.A. McNeece (Eds.), *Future issues for social work practice* (pp. 203–213). Needham Heights, MA: Allyn & Bacon.

Guyer, J., & Mann, C. (1998). *Taking the next step: States can now expand health coverage to low-income working parents through Medicaid.* Washington, DC: Center on Policy and Budget Priorities, July 2.

Haapala, D.A. (1983). *Perceived helpfulness, attributed critical incident responsibility, and a discrimination of home-based family therapy treatment outcomes: Homebuilders™ model.* Report prepared for the Department of Health and Human Services, Administration for Children, Youth and Families (Grant 90-CW-626 OHDS). Federal Way, WA: Behavioral Sciences Institute.

Haapala, D.A., & Fraser, M.W. (1987). *Keeping families together: The Homebuilders™ model revisited.* Federal Way, WA: Behavioral Sciences Institute.

Haapala, D.A., & Kinney, J. (1979). Homebuilders™ approach to the training of in-home therapists. In S. Maybanks & M. Bryce (Eds.), *Home-based services for children and families* (pp. 248–259). Springfield, IL: Charles C Thomas.

Haapala, D.A., & Kinney, J.M. (1988). Avoiding the out-of-home placement of high risk status offenders through the use of intensive home-based family preservation services. *Criminal Justice and Behavior, 15*(3), 334–348.

Haapala, D.A., McDade, K., & Johnston, B. (1988). *Preventing the dissolution of special needs adoption families through the use of intensive home-based family preservation services: The Homebuilders™ Model.* (Clinical Services Final Report from the Homebuilders™ Adoption Services Continuum Project.) Federal Way, WA: Behavioral Sciences Institute.

Hackman, J.R., & Lawler, E.E., III. (1971). Employee reactions to job characteristics. *Journal of Applied Psychology, 55,* 259–286.

Hacsi, T. (1995). From indenture to family foster care: A brief history of child placing. *Child Welfare, 74,* 162–180.

Hacsi, T.A. (1997). *Second home: Orphan asylums and poor families in America.* Cambridge, MA: Harvard University Press.

Haeuser, A.A. (1989). *Let's stop physical punishment of children: How Sweden's success can be applied to the U.S.* Presentation for the NASW Annual Conference, San Francisco, CA (mimeograph).

Hage, D. (1987). Love those subsidies. *OURS,* March–April, 18–19.

Haggerty, R.J., Sherrod, L.R., Garmezy, N., & Rutter, M. (1994). *Stress, risk, and resilience in children and adolescents—Processes, mechanisms, and interventions.* Cambridge, UK: Cambridge University Press.

Halfon, N., English, A., Allen, M., & DeWoody, M. (1994). National health care reform, Medicaid, and children in foster care. *Child Welfare, 73,* 99–115.

Hall, D.K., Mathews, F., & Pearce, J. (1998). Factors associated with sexual behavior problems in young sexually abused children. *Child Abuse and Neglect, 22*(10), 1045–1063.

Halper, G., & Jones, M.A. (1981). *Serving families at risk of dissolution: Public preventive services in New York City.* New York: Human Resources Administration.

Halpern, E.S. (1990). *Auditing naturalistic inquiries: The development and application of a model.* Unpublished doctoral dissertation, Indiana University.

Halpern, R. (1984). Lack of effects for home-based early interventions? Some possible explanations. *American Journal of Orthopsychiatry, 54*(1), 33–42.

Halpern, R. (1990). Fragile families, fragile solutions: An essay review. *Social Service Review, 64,* 637–648.

Halpern, R. (1991). Supportive services for families in poverty: Dilemmas of reform. *Social Service Review, 65,* 343–364.

Halpern, R. (1999). *Fragile families, fragile solutions: A history of supportive services for families in poverty.* New York: Columbia University Press.

Hampson, R. (1985). Foster parent training: Assessing its role in upgrading foster home care. In M.J. Cox & R.D. Cox (Eds.), *Foster care: Current issues, policies, and practices* (pp. 167–205.). Norwood, NJ: Ablex.

Hanson, R. (Ed.). (1982). *Institutional abuse of children and youth.* New York: Haworth Press.

Harari, T. (1980). *Teenagers exiting from foster family care: A retrospective look.* Unpublished doctoral dissertation. Berkeley CA: University of California at Berkeley.

Hardin, M. (Ed.). (1983). *Foster children in the courts.* Boston: Butterworth Legal Publishers.

Hardin, M. (1992). *Establishing a core of services for families subject to state intervention,* Washington, DC: American Bar Association.

Hardin, M. (1996). *Family group conferences in child abuse and neglect cases: Learning from the experience of New Zealand.* Washington, DC: ABA Center on Children and the Law.

Harm, N.J. (1992). Social policy on women prisoners: A historical analysis. *AFFILIA, 7*(1), 90–108.

Harris, J.R. (1995). Where is the Child's environment? A group socialization theory of development. *Psychological Review, 102*(3), 458–489.

Harris, N., & Warner, T.W. (1988). Turning CPS philosophy into action: The NAPCWA guidelines offer a concise, generic approach to CPS reform. *Public Welfare, 46*(3), 11–17, 44, 46.

Harrison, L.L. (1976). Nursing intervention with the failure to thrive family. *Maternal Child Nursing, 1*(2), 111–116.

Hart, S.N., & Brassard, M.R. (1987). A major threat to children's mental health: Psychological maltreatment. *American Psychologist, 42,* 160–165.

Hart, S.N., Brassard, M.R., & Karlson, H.C. (1996). In J. Briere, L. Berliner, J.A. Bulkley, C. Jenny, & T. Reid (Eds.), *The APSAC handbook on child maltreatment* (pp. 72–89). Newbury Park, CA: Sage.

Hart, S.N., Germain, R.B., & Brassard, M.R. (1987). The challenge: To better understand and combat psychological maltreatment of youth. In M.R. Brassard, R. Germain, & S.N. Hart (Eds.), *Psychological maltreatment of children and youth* (pp. 3–24). New York: Pergamon Press.

Hartman, A., & Laird, J. (1983). *Family-centered social work practice.* New York: Free Press.

Hartman, M., Finn, S.E., & Leon, G.R. (1987). Sexual abuse experiences in a clinical population: Comparisons of familial abuse. *Psychotherapy, 24,* 154–159.

Haskins, R., & Gallagher, J. (1981). *Models for analysis of social policy.* Norwood, NJ: Ablex.

Haugaard, J., Hokanson, B., & National Resource Center on Family-Based Services. (1983). *Measuring the cost-effectiveness of family-based services and out-of-home care.* Oakdale, IA: University of Iowa, School of Social Work, National Clearinghouse for Family-centered Programs.

Haugaard, J.J. (1998). Is adoption a risk factor for the development of adjustment problems? *Clinical Psychology Review, 18,* 47–69.

Haugaard, J.J., & Reppucci, N.D. (1988). *The sexual abuse of children.* San Francisco, CA: Jossey-Bass.

Hauswald, L. (1987). External pressure/internal change: Child neglect on the Navajo reservation. In N. Scheper-Hughes (Ed.), *Child survival* (pp. 145–164). Norwell, MA: Kluwer Academic Publications.

Haveman, R., & Scholz, J. (1994). Taxes, transfers and welfare reform. *National Tax Journal* (June), *47,* 417–434.

Hawkins, J.D., Catalano, R.S., Jr., & Assoc. (1992). *Communities that care.* San Francisco: Jossey-Bass.

Hawkins, J.D., & Lishner, D.M. (1987). Schooling and delinquency. In E.H. Johnson (Ed.)., *Handbook on crime and delinquency prevention.* Westport, CT: Greenwood Press.

Hawkins, J.D., & Weis, J.G. (1985). The social development model: An integrated approach to delinquency prevention. *Journal of Primary Prevention, 6*(2), 73–97.

Hawkins, R.P., Peterson, R.F., Schweid, E., & Bijou, S.W. (1966). Behavior therapy in the home: Amelioration of problem parent-child relations with the parent in a therapeutic role. *Journal of Experimental Child Psychology, 4,* 99–107.

Hayes, J.R., & Joseph, J.A. (1985). *Home based family centered project evaluation.* Columbus, OH: Metropolitan Human Services Commission.

Hazan, C., & Shaver, P. (1987). Romantic love conceptualized as an attachment process. *Journal of Personality & Social Psychology, 52*(3), 511–524.

Hazel, N. (1989). Adolescent fostering as a community resource. *Community Alternative-International Journal of Community Care,* (1), 1–10.

Heath, A.F., Colton, M.J., & Aldgate, J. (1994). Failure to escape: A longitudinal study of foster children's educational attainment. *British Journal of Social Work, 24*(3), 241–260.

Heclo, H. (1994). Poverty politics. In S. Danziger, G. Sandefur, & D. Weinberg (Eds.), *Confronting poverty: Prescriptions for change* (pp. 396–437). Cambridge, MA: Harvard University Press.

Hefferman, J., Shuttlesworth, J., & Ambroseno, R. (1988). The levels of the ecological system. In J. Garbarino (Ed.), *Children and families in the social environment.* New York: Aldine Publishing Company.

Hegar, R.L. (1988). Legal and social work approaches to sibling separation in foster care. *Child Welfare, 67*(2), 113–121.

Hegar, R.L. (1989). Empowerment-based practice with children. *Social Service Review, 63,* 372–383.

Hegar, R.L. (1999). Kinship foster care. In R.L. Hegar & M. Scannapieco (Eds.), *Kinship foster care— Policy, practice, and research* (pp. 225–240). New York: Oxford University Press.

Hegar, R.L., & Hunzeker, J.M. (1988). Moving towards empowerment-based practice in public child welfare. *Social Work, 33,* 499–502.

Hegar, R.L., & Scannapieco, M. (Eds.). (1999). *Kinship foster care–policy, practice, and research.* New York: Oxford University Press.

Hegar, R.L., Zuravin, S.J., & Orme, J.G. (1991). *Factors prediction severity of child abuse injury: A review of the literature.* Unpublished manuscript, School of Social Work, University of Maryland at Baltimore.

Heisterman, C.A. (1935). A summary of legislation on adoption. *Social Service Review, 9,* 269–293.

Helfer, R.E. (1982). A review of the literature on the prevention of child abuse and neglect. *Child Abuse and Neglect, 6,* 251–261.

Helfgott, K.W. (1991). *Staffing the child welfare agency: Recruitment and retention.* Washington, DC: Child Welfare League of America.

Heller, K., Price, R.H., & Sher, K.J. (1980). Research and evaluation in primary prevention. In R.H. Price, R.F. Ketterer, B.C. Bader, & J. Monahan (Eds.), *Prevention in mental health: Research, policy, and practice* (pp. 285–313). Beverly Hills, CA: Sage.

Henggler, S.W., Pickrel, S.G., & Brondino, M.J. (1999). Multisystemic treatment of substance-abusing and -dependent delinquents: Outcomes, treatment, fidelity, and transportability. *Mental Health Services Research, 1*(3), 171–184.

Henggler, S.W., Schoenwald, S.K., Borduin, C.M., Rowland, M., & Cunningham, P.B. (1998). *Multisystemic treatment of antisocial behavior in children and adolescents.* New York: Guilford.

Hennepin County Community Services Department. (1980). *Family study project: Demonstration and research in intensive services to families.* Minneapolis, MN: Author.

Henschel, D., Briere, J., Magallanes, M., & Smiljanich, K. (1990). *Sexual abuse related attributions: Probing the role of "traumagenic factors."* Paper presented at the annual meeting of the Western Psychological Association, Los Angeles.

Hepworth, D.H., & Larsen, J. (1990). *Direct social work practice* (3rd ed.). Belmont, CA: Wadsworth.

Herman, J.L. (1981). *Father-daughter incest.* Cambridge, MA: Harvard University Press.

Herrenkohl, R.C., & Herrenkohl, E.C. (1981). Some antecedents and developmental consequences of child maltreatment. In R. Rizley & D. Cicchetti (Eds.), *Developmental perspectives on child maltreatment: New direction for child development, No. 11.* San Francisco: Jossey-Bass.

Herrenkohl, R.C., Herrenkohl, E.C., Egolf, B., & Seech, M. (1979). The repetition of child abuse: How frequently does it occur? *Child Abuse and Neglect, 3,* 67–72.

Herrera, E.G., Lifson, B.G., Hartmann, E., & Solomon, M.H. (1974). A 10-year follow-up study of 55 hospitalized adolescents. *Journal of Psychiatry, 131,* 769–774.

Hersen, M., & Barlow, D.H. (1976). *Single case experimental designs.* New York: Pergamon.

Hershorn, M., & Rosenbaum, A. (1985). Children of marital violence: A closer look at the unintended victims. *American Journal of Interpersonal Violence, 7*(1), 77–86.

Herzberger, S.D. (1996). *Violence within the family: Social psychological perspectives.* Boulder, CO: Westview Press.

Hess, P.M., McGowan, B., & Botsko, M. (1997). *Final report of a study of the Center for Family Life in Sunset Park: Greater than the sum of its parts.* New York: Authors.

Hess, P.M., McGowan, B., & Botsko, M. (In press). Preserving and supporting families over time: A preventive services program model. *Child Welfare.*

Hess, P.M., & Proch, K.O. (1988). *Family visiting in out-of-home care: A guide to practice.* Washington, DC: Child Welfare League of America.

Hess, P.M., & Proch, K.O. (1993). Visiting: The heart of family reunification. In B.A. Pine, R. Warsh, & A.N. Maluccio (Eds.), *Together again: Family reunification in foster care* (pp. 119–139). Washington, DC: Child Welfare League of America.

Heying, K.R. (1985). Family-based, in-home services for the severely emotionally disturbed child. *Child Welfare, 64*(5), 519–527.

Hill, M. (Ed.). (1999). *Effective ways of working with children and their families.* London: Jessica Kingsley.

Hill, M., & Aldgate, J. (Eds.). (1996). *Child welfare services—Developments in law, policy, practice, and research.* London: Jessica Kingsley.

Hill, R.B. (1972). *The strengths of black families.* New York: Emerson Hall.

Hill, R.B. (1997). *The strengths of African American families: Twenty-five years later.* Washington, DC: R & B.

Hinckley, E.C., & Ellis, W.F. (1985). An effective alternative to residential placement: Home-based services. *Journal of Clinical Child Psychology, 14*(3), 209–213.

Hirsch, J.S., Gailey, J., & Schmerl, E. (1976). A child welfare agency's program of service to children in their own homes. *Child Welfare, 55*(3), 193–204.

Hirschi, T. (1969). *Causes of delinquency.* Berkeley, CA: University of California Press.

Hobbs, N. (1966). Helping disturbed children: Psychological and ecological strategies. *American Psychologist, 21,* 1105–1151.

Hobbs, N. (1982). *The troubled and troubling child.* San Francisco: Jossey-Bass.

Hodges, V. (1994). Assessing for strengths and protective factors in child abuse and neglect: Risk assessment with families of color. In P.J. Pecora & D.J. English (Eds.), *Multi-cultural guidelines for assessing family strengths and risk factors in child protective services.* Seattle, WA: School of Social Work, University of Washington and Washington State Department of Social Services.

Hodges, V.G. (1991). *Protective factors and children at risk.* Seattle, WA: University of Washington, School of Social Work (mimeograph).

Hodges, V.G., Guterman, N.B., Blythe, B.J., & Bronson, D.E. (1989). Intensive aftercare services for children. *Social Casework, 70*(7), 397–404.

Hodges, V.G., & Pecora, P.J. (2000). What is strengths-based service planning? In H. Dubowitz & D. DePanfilis (Eds.), *The handbook for child protection practice* (pp. 379–383). Newbury Park, CA: Sage.

Hoenack, S.A. (1983). *Economic behavior within organizations.* Cambridge: Cambridge University Press.

Hogan, P.T., & Siu, S-F. (1988). Minority children and the child welfare system: An historical perspective. *Social Work, 33,* 493–498.

Holden, G.W., & Ritchie, K.L. (1991). Linking extreme marital discord, child rearing, and child behavior problems: Evidence from battered women. *Child Development, 62,* 311–327.

Holder, W.M., & Corey, M. (1986). *Child protective services risk management: A decision making handbook.* Charlotte, NC: ACTION for Child Protection.

Holder, W., & Corey, M. (1987). *Child protective services risk management: A decision making handbook.* Charlotte, NC: ACTION for Child Protection.

Holder, W., & Costello, T.E. (1987). *Supervisory assessment methods.* Aurora, CO: ACTION for Child Protection.

Holder, W., & Hayes, K. (Eds.). (1984). *Malpractice and liability in child protective services.* Denver, CO: The American Humane Association.

Holder, W.M., & Mohr, C. (1980). *Helping in child protective services—A casework handbook.* Englewood, CO: American Humane Association, American Association for Protecting Children.

Holliday, M., & Cronin, R. (1990). Families first: A significant step toward family preservation. *Families in Society, 71,* 303–306.

Hollinger, J. (Ed.). (1988). *Adoption, law, and practice.* New York: Mathew Bender.

Holohan, C.J., Wilcox, B.L., Spearly, J.L., & Campbell, M.D. (1979). The ecological perspective in community mental health. *Community Mental Health Review, 4,* 1–9.

Holzer, H. (1994). Black employment problems: New evidence, old questions. *Journal of Policy Analysis and Management, 13,* 699–722.

Hong, G.K., & Hong, L.K. (1991). Comparative perspectives on child abuse and neglect: Chinese versus Hispanics and whites. *Child Welfare, 70*(4), 463–475.

Horejsi, C. (1987). *Child welfare practice and the Native American family in Montana: A handbook for social workers.* Missoula, MT: University of Montana, School of Social Work.

Horejsi, C., & Pablo, J. (1991). *CPS risk assessment and the Native American family.* Missoula, MT: University of Montana, School of Social Work.

Horejsi, C.R. (1982). *Values and attitudes in child welfare: A training manual.* Missoula, MT: University of Montana, School of Social Work

Horejsi, C.R., Bertsche, A.V., & Clark, F.W. (1981). *Social work practice with parents of children in foster care—A handbook.* Springfield, IL: Charles C Thomas.

Hornby, H., Zeller, D., & Karraker, D. (1996). Kinship care in America: What outcomes should policy seek? *Child Welfare, 75,* 397–418.

Hornby, H.C., & Collins, M.I. (1981). Teenagers in foster care: The forgotten majority. *Children and Youth Services Review, 3,* 7–20.

Houlgate, L.D. (1988). *Family and state: The philosophy of family law.* Totowa, NJ: Rowman & Littlefield.

Howard, A., Royse, D., & Skerl, J. (1977). Transracial adoption: The black community perspective. *Social Work, 22,* 184–189.

Howard, J.A., & Smith, S.L. (1995). *Adoption preservation in Illinois: Results of a four year study.* Normal, IL: Illinois State University, School of Social Work.

Howard, J.R. (1982). Consumer evaluations of programs for disturbing youth. In A.J. McSweeney, W.J. Fremouw, & R.P. Hawkins (Eds.), *Practical program evaluation in youth treatment* (pp. 292–313). Springfield, IL: Charles C Thomas.

Howell, J.C. (1998). NCCD's survey of juvenile detention and correctional facilities. *Crime & Delinquency, 44,* 102–109.

Howing, P.T., Wodarski, J.S., Gauding, J.M., Jr., & Kurtz, P.D. (1989). Effective interventions to ameliorate the incidence of child maltreatment: The empirical base. *Social Work, 34*(4), 330–338.

Howing, P.T., Wodarski, J.S., Jurtz, P.D., & Gaudin, J.M., Jr. (1989). Methodological issues in child maltreatment research. *Social Work Research and Abstracts, 25*(3), 3–7.

Hoynes, H. (1995). Welfare transfers in two parent families: The case of AFDC-UP, *Econometrica, 64,* 295–332.

Hoynes, H. (1996). *Work, welfare and family structure: A review of the evidence.* Institute for Research on Poverty Discussion Paper, 1103-96.

Hudson, J., & Galaway, B. (Eds.). (1989). *Specialist foster care: A normalizing experience.* New York: Haworth Press.

Hudson, J., & Galaway, B. (Eds.). (1995). *Child welfare in Canada—Research and policy implications.* Toronto: Thompson Educational Publishing.

Hudson, W. (1982). *The clinical measurement package: A field manual.* Homewood, IL: The Dorsey Press.

Hughes, D.M. (1987). When cultural rights conflict with the "best interests of the child": A view from inside the child welfare system. In N. Scheper-Hughes (Ed.), *Child survival: Anthropological perspectives on the treatment and maltreatment of children* (pp. 377–398). Boston: D. Reidel.

Hughes, R.C., & Rykus, J.S. (1989). *Target: Competent staff—Competency-based in-service training for child welfare.* Washington, DC: Child Welfare League of America, and Columbus, OH: The Institute for Human Services.

Humphreys, K. (1993). From the community mental health movement to the War on Drugs. *American Psychologist, 48*(8), 892–901.

Hunter, R.S., & Kilstrom, N. (1979). Breaking the cycle in abusive families. *American Journal of Psychiatry, 136,* 1320–1322.

Hunter, R.S., Kilstrom, N., Kraybill, E.N., & Loda, F. (1978). Antecedents of child abuse and neglect in premature infants: A prospective study in a newborn intensive care unit. *Pediatrics, 61*(4), 629–635.

Hutchinson, J.R., & Nelson, K.E. (1985). How public agencies can provide family-centered services. *Social Casework, 66*(6), 367–371.

Hyman, I.A. (1987). Psychological correlates of corporal punishment. In S.R. Brassard, R. Germain, & S.N. Hart (Eds.), *Psychological maltreatment of children and youth* (pp. 45–58). New York: Pergamon Press.

IJA/ABA. (1981). Juvenile Justice Standards Project, Standards Relating to Abuse and Neglect, Standard 1.1.

Illinois Department of Children and Family Services, Office of the Inspector General. (1997). *Recommendations for improving the state's child welfare response to families affected by parental substance abuse.* Springfield, IL: Illinois Department of Children and Family Services.

Imhof, A.E. (1985). From the old mortality pattern to the new: Implications of a radical [change] from the sixteenth to the twentieth century. *Bulletin of the History of Medicine, 59,* 1–29.

Immigration and Naturalization Service, Statistical Analysis Branch. (1987). *Statistical year books.* Washington, DC: U.S. Government Printing Office.

Immigration and Naturalization Services. (1998). *Legal immigration, FY 1996.* Washington, DC: Department of Justice.

Ingoldsby, B.B., & Smith, S. (Eds.). (1995). *Families in multicultural perspective.* New York: Guilford.

Ingram, C. (1996). Kinship care: From last resort to first choice. *Child Welfare, 75,* 550–566.

Institute of Medicine. (1989). *Research on children and adolescents with mental, behavioral, and developmental disorders.* Washington, DC: National Academy of Sciences.

Institute for Social Research, The University of Michigan. Tables 2-3-12, 3-3-12, 5-3-12, 9-3-12 through 1996, Table 8 through 1995, and Table 4-7 for 1996. Data for 1997: *The Monitoring the Future Study.* The University of Michigan. Ann Arbor, MI: Author.

Invisible Children: National Association for Mental Health. (1989). *Invisible children project: Final report.* Alexandria, VA: Author.

Iowa Department of Social Services. (1988). *Increasing the effectiveness of foster care through the use of service contracts with children, natural parents, foster parents, and workers.* Des Moines, IA: Iowa Department of Social Services, Division of Community Services.

Isaacs, C.D. (1982). Treatment of child abuse: A review of the behavioral interventions. *Journal of Applied Behavior Analysis, 15,* 273–294.

Isaacs-Shockley, M. (Date TBD). Prevention and early intervention. In *The state of the states: Responses to cultural competence and diversity in child mental health.* Washington, DC: National Technical Assistance Center for Children's Mental Health, Georgetown University Child Development Center.

Jackson, A.D., & Dunne, M.J. (1981). Permanency planning in foster care with the ambivalent parent. In A.N. Maluccio & P.A. Sinanoglu (Eds.), *The challenge of partnership–Working with parents of children in foster care* (pp. 151–164). New York: Child Welfare League of America.

Jackson, S. (1988). The education of children in care. *Adoption and Fostering, 12*(4), 6–10.

Jackson, S., & Brissett-Chapman, S. (Eds.). (1997). Perspectives on serving African American children, youths and families. Special issue of *Child Welfare, 76*(1) (January–February 1997).

Jackson, S., Mathews, J., & Zuskin, R. (1998). *Supporting the kinship triad—A training curriculum.* Washington, DC: CWLA Press.

Jacobs, F.H. (1988). The five-tiered approach to evaluation: Context and implementation. In H.B. Weiss & F.H. Jacobs (Eds.), *Evaluating family programs* (pp. 37–68). Hawthorne, NY: Aldine de Gruyter.

Jacobs, F.H. (1990). Child mental health: Service system and policy issues. *Social Policy Report: Society for Research in Child Development, 4*(2), 1–19.

Jacoby, S. (1985). Emotional child abuse: The invisible plague. *Readers Digest,* February, 86–90.

James, B. (1989). *Treating traumatized children: New insights and creative interventions.* Lexington, MA: Lexington.

Janchill, M.P. (1981). *Guidelines to decision making in child welfare.* New York: Human Services Workshop.

Jansson, B.S. (1994). *Social welfare policy—From theory to practice.* Pacific Grove, CA: Brooks/Cole.

Jason, J., & Andereck, N.D. (1983). Fatal child abuse in Georgia: The epidemiology of severe physical child abuse. *Child Abuse and Neglect, 7*(1), 1–9.

Jason, J., Andereck, N., Marks, J., & Tyler, C. (1982). Child abuse in Georgia: A method to evaluate risk factors and reporting bias. *American Journal of Public Health, 72*(12), 1353–1358.

Jayaratne, S., & Chess, W.A. (1985). Factors associated with job satisfaction and turnover among child welfare workers. In J. Laird & A. Hartman (Eds.), *A handbook of child welfare: Context, knowledge, and practice.* New York: Free Press.

Jayaratne, S., & Levy, R.L. (1979). *Empirical clinical practice.* New York: Columbia University Press.

Jehu, D. (1988). *Beyond sexual abuse: Therapy with women who were childhood victims.* Chichester, UK: John Wiley & Sons.

Jehu, D., Gazan, M., & Klassen, C. (1984–1985). Common therapeutic targets among women who were sexually abused in childhood. *Journal of Social Work and Human Sexuality, 167,* 74–78.

Jencks, C., & Mayer, S. (1996). *Do official poverty rates provide useful information about trends in children's economic welfare?* Evanston IL: Northwestern University, Center for Urban Affairs and Policy Research.

Jencks, C., & Peterson, P. (Eds.). (1991). *The urban underclass.* Washington, DC: The Brookings Institution.

Jenewicz, W.J. (1983). A protective posture toward emotional neglect and abuse. *Child Welfare, 62,* 243–252.

Jenkins, S., & Norman, E. (1975). *Beyond placement: Mothers view foster care.* New York: Columbia University Press.

Jenkins, S., & Sauber, M. (1966). *Paths to child placement: Family situations prior to foster care.* New York: Community Council of Greater New York.

Jenkins, S., & Schroeder, A.G. (1980). *Intake: The discriminant function—A report on the national study on social services intake for children and their families.* Washington, DC: U.S. Department of Health and Human Services, Office of Human Development Services (OHDS No. 80-30259).

Jenkins, S., Schroeder, A.G., & Burgdorf, K. (1981). *Beyond intake: The first ninety days.* Washington, DC: U.S. Department of Health and Human Services, Office of Human Development Services (OHDS No. 81-30313).

Jenson, J.M., & Whittaker, J.K. (1987). Parental involvement in children's residential treatment: From preplacement to aftercare. *Children and Youth Services Review, 9*(2), 81–100.

Jessor, R., Van Den Bos, J., Vanderryn, J., Costa, F.M., & Turbin, M.S. (1995). Protective factors in adolescent problem behavior: Moderator effects and developmental change. *Developmental Psychology, 31*(6), 923–933.

Jewett, C. (1978). *Adopting the older child.* Harvard, MA: Harvard Common Press.

Jewett, C. (1982). *Helping children cope with separation and loss.* Harvard, MA: Harvard Common Press.

Johnson, H.L., Nutter, C., Callan, L., & Ramsey, R. (1976). Program evaluation in residential treatment. *Child Welfare, 55,* 279–291.

Johnson, L., & Reid, J. (1947). *An evaluation of ten years' work with emotionally disturbed children.* Seattle: Ryther Child Center.

Johnson, P.R., Yoken, C., & Voss, R. (1995). Family foster care placement: The child's perspective. *Child Welfare, 74,* 959–974.

Johnson, W., & L'Esperance, J. (1984). Predicting the recurrence of child abuse. *Social Work Research and Abstracts, 20*(2), 21–26.

Johnston, E., & Gabor, P. (1981). Parent counselors: A foster care program with new roles for major participants. In A.N. Maluccio & P.A. Sinanoglu (Eds.), *The challenge of partnership: Working with parents of children in foster care* (pp. 200–208). New York: Child Welfare League of America.

Johnston, L.D., O'Malley, P.M., & Bachman, J.G. (1998). *National survey results on drug use from the monitoring the future study, 1975–1995.* Rockville, MD: National Institutes of Health.

Joint Legislative Commission on Governmental Operations Commission on the Family. (1996). *Family Preservation Services annual report 1996.* Raleigh, NC: Division of Social Services, NC Department of Human Resources.

Jones, C. (1983). *How to speak TV: A self-defense manual when you're in the news.* Marathon, FL: Video Consultants, Inc.

Jones, D. (1969). Child welfare problems in an Alaskan native village. *Social Service Review, 43*(2), 207–309.

Jones, D.P.H., & Krugman, R.D. (1986). Can a 3-year-old child bear witness to her sexual assault and attempted murder? *Child Abuse and Neglect, 10,* 253–258.

Jones, L. (1998). The social and family correlates of successful reunification of children in foster care. *Children and Youth Services Review, 20,* 305–323.

Jones, M.A. (1985). *A second chance for families five years later: Follow-up of a program to prevent foster care.* New York: Child Welfare League of America.

Jones, M.A. (1987). *Parental lack of supervision: Nature and consequence of a major child neglect problem.* Washington, DC: Child Welfare League of America.

Jones, M.A. (1991). Measuring outcomes. In K. Wells & D.E. Biegel (Eds.), *Family preservation services: Research and evaluation* (pp. 159–186). Newbury Park, CA: Sage.

Jones, M.A., & Moses, B. (1984). *West Virginia's former foster children: Their experience in care and their lives as young adults.* New York: Child Welfare League of America.

Jones, M.A., Neuman, R., & Shyne, A.W. (1976). *A second chance for families: Evaluation of a program to reduce foster care.* New York: Child Welfare League of America.

Jones, R.R., Weinrott, M.R., & Howard, J.R. (1981). *Impact of the Teaching Family Model on troublesome youth: Findings from the National Evaluation.* Rockville, MD: NIMH (reproduced by National Technical Information Service, U.S. Department of Commerce, Springfield, VA 22191, PB82-224353).

Jonson-Reid, M., & Barth, R.P. (2000). From maltreatment report to juvenile incarceration. *Child Abuse and Neglect, 24,* 505–520.

Jonson-Reid, M., & Barth, R.P. (In press). From placement to prison: The path to adolescent incarceration from child welfare supervised foster or group care. *Social Work.*

Justice, B., & Justice, R. (1979). *The broken taboo: Sex in the family.* New York: Human Sciences Press.

Kadushin, A. (1971). Child welfare. In H.S. Maas (Ed.), *Research in the social services* (pp. 46–69). Washington, DC: National Association of Social Workers.

Kadushin, A. (1978). Child welfare strategy in the coming years: An overview. In *Child welfare strategy in the coming years.* Washington, DC: U.S. Department of Health, Education, and Welfare (DHEW Publication No. OHDS 78-30158).

Kadushin, A. (1980). *Child welfare services* (3rd ed., pp. 583–631). New York: Macmillan.

Kadushin, A. (1985). *Supervision in social work* (2nd ed.). New York: Columbia University Press.

Kadushin, A., & Martin, J. (1981). *Child abuse: An interactional event.* New York: Columbia University Press.

Kadushin, A., & Martin, J.K. (1988). *Child welfare services* (4th ed.). New York: Macmillan.

Kagan, J. (1984). *The nature of the child.* New York: Basic Books.

Kagan, R., & Schlosberg, S. (1989). *Families in perpetual crisis.* New York: Norton.

Kagan, S., Powell, D., Weissbourd, B., & Zigler, E. (Eds.). (1987). *America's family support programs: Perspectives and prospects.* New Haven, CT: Yale University Press.

Kagan, S.L. (1993). *Integrating services for children and families—Understanding the past to shape the future.* New Haven, CT: Yale University Press.

Kagan, S.L., & Weissbourd, B. (Eds.). (1994). *Putting families first—America's family support movement and the challenge of change.* San Francisco: Jossey-Bass.

Kahn, A., & Kamerman, S.B. (Eds.). (1988). *Child support: From debt collection to social policy.* Newbury Park, CA: Sage.

Kamerman, S.B. (1999). Child welfare and the under-threes: An overview. *Zero to Three: National Center for Infants, Toddlers, and Families, 19*(3), 1–7.

Kamerman, S.B., & Kahn, A. (1989). *Social services for children, youth and families in the U.S.* New York: Columbia University School of Social Work (The Annie E. Casey Foundation).

Kamerman, S.B., & Kahn, A.J. (1990). Social services for children, youth and families in the U.S. *Children and Youth Services Review, 12,* 1–185.

Kamerman, S.B., & Kahn, A.J. (1995). *Starting right: How America neglects its youngest children and what we can do about it.* New York: Oxford University Press.

Kane, R.P., & Chambers, G.S. (1961). Seven year follow-up of children hospitalized and discharged from a residential setting. *American Journal of Psychiatry, 117,* 1023–1027.

Kaplan, L. (1986). *Working with multiproblem families.* Lexington, MA: D.C. Heath.

Kaplan, L., & Girard, J.L. (1994). *Strengthening high-risk families—A handbook for practitioners.* New York: Lexington Books.

Kaplan, M.S., & Sasser, J.E. (1996). Women behind bars: Trends and policy issues. *Journal of Sociology and Social Welfare, XXIII*(4), 43–56

Kaplun, D., & Reich, R. (1976). The murdered child and his killers. *American Journal of Psychiatry, 133*(7), 809–813.

Karger, H.J. (1983). Reclassification: Is there a future in public welfare for the trained social worker? *Social Work, 28*(6), 427–433.

Karger, H.J. (1988). Social workers and labor relations in the public sector: The Missouri Department of Social Services and the Communications Workers of American. *Administration in Social Work, 12*(1), 41–54.

Karger, H.J. (1989). The common and conflicting goals of labor and social work. *Administration in Social Work, 13*(1), 1–17.

Karoly, L.A., Greenwood, P.W., Everingham, S.S., Houbé, J., Kilburn, M.R., Rydell, C.P., Sanders, M., & Chiesa, J. (1998). *Investing in our children: What we know and don't know about the costs and benefits of early childhood interventions.* Santa Monica, CA: Rand.

Karp, C.L., & Butler, T.L., (1996a). *Treatment strategies for abused children: From victim to survivor.* Newbury Park, CA: Sage.

Karp, C.L., & Butler, T.L., (1996b). *Activity book for treatment strategies for abused children: From victim to survivor.* Newbury Park, CA: Sage.

Katz, L. (1998). Wage subsidies for the disadvantaged. In R. Freeman & P. Gottschalk (Eds.), *Generating jobs: How to increase demand for less-skilled workers.* New York: Russell Sage Foundation.

Katz, L. (1999). Concurrent planning: Benefits and pitfalls. *Child Welfare, 78,* 71–87.

Katz, L., & Robinson, C. (1991). Foster-care drift—A risk-assessment matrix. *Child Welfare, 70*(3), 347–358.

Katz, L., Spoonemore, N., & Robinson, C. (1994). *Concurrent planning: From permanency planning to permanency action.* Seattle, WA: Lutheran Social Services of Washington and Idaho.

Katz, S., Ambrosino, L., McGrath, M., & Sawitsky, K. (1977). Legal research in child abuse and neglect: Past and future. *Family Law Quarterly, 11*(2), 151–184.

Kavaler, F., & Swire, M. (1983). *Foster-child health care.* Lexington, MA: D.C. Heath.

Keller, A., Huz, S., Marek, D., & Rejino, E. (1997). *Keeping children at home: New York's home and community based services waiver.* Paper presented at the Tenth Annual Research Conference, A System of Care for Children's Mental Health: Expanding the Research Base.

Kelley, S.J. (1992). Parenting stress and child maltreatment in drug-exposed children. *Child Abuse and Neglect, 16,* 317–328.

Kelley, S.J., Walsh, J.H., & Thompson, K. (1991). Prenatal exposure to cocaine: birth outcomes, health problems and child neglect. *Pediatric Nursing, 17,* 130–135.

Kemp, S.P., & Farrar, A.M. (1996). *The status of African American children in the child welfare system in Washington State.* Report prepared for the African American Initiative, a joint project of the Black Child Development Institute and Washington State Families for Kids, Seattle, WA.

Kemp, S.P., Whittaker, J.K., & Tracy, E.M. (1997). *Person-environment practice.* Hawthorne, NY: Aldine de Gruyter.

Kempe, C.H., Silverman, F.N., Steele, B.F., et al. (1962). The battered child syndrome. *Journal of the American Medical Association, 18*(1), 17–24.

Kempe, R.J. (1982). Behavioral re-orientation of pedophiliacs; Can it be done? *Clinical Psychology Review, 2,* 387–408.

Kendall, P.C., & Grove, W.M. (1988). Normative comparisons in therapy outcome. *Behavioral Assessment, 10,* 147–158.

Kennell, J.H., Jerauld, R., Wolfe, H., Chesler, D., Kreger, N.D., McAlpine, W., Steffa, M., & Klaus, M.H. (1974). Maternal behavior one year after early and extended post-partum contact. *Developmental Medicine and Child Neurology, 16,* 172–179.

Kercher, G. (1990). *Responding to child sexual abuse.* Huntsville, TX: Sam Houston State University, Criminal Justice Center.

Kerlinger, F. (1973). *Foundations of behavioral research* (2nd ed.). New York: Holt, Rinehart & Winston.

Kerr, M.A.D., Bogues, J.L., & Kerr, D.S. (1978). Psychosocial functioning of mothers of malnourished children. *Pediatrics, 62*(5), 778–784.

Kessler, R.C., Davis, C.G., & Kendler, K.S. (1977), Childhood adversity and adult psychiatric disorder in the U.S. national comorbidity survey. *Psychological Medicine,* 1101–1119.

Kettner, P.M., Moroney, R.M., & Martin, L.L. (1990). *Designing and managing programs: An effectiveness-based approach* (pp. 94–129). Newbury Park, CA: Sage.

Kinard, E.M. (1980) Emotional development in physically abused children. *American Journal of Orthopsychiatry, 50,* 686–696.

Kinard, E.M. (1987). Child abuse and neglect. In J. Atkins & K. Greenhall (Eds.), *The encyclopedia of social work* (18th ed., pp. 223–231). Washington, DC: National Association of Social Workers.

King, J.A., Morris, L.L., & Fitz-Gibbon, C.T. (1987). *How to assess program implementation.* Newbury Park, CA: Sage.

Kinney, J., & Haapala, D.A. (1984). *First year Homebuilders™ mental health project report.* Federal Way, WA: Behavioral Sciences Institute.

Kinney, J.M. (1978). Homebuilders™: An in-home crisis intervention program. *Children Today, 7*(1), 15–17, 35.

Kinney, J.M., & Haapala, D.A. (1974). *First year Homebuilders™ mental health project report.* Federal Way, WA: Behavioral Sciences Institute.

Kinney, J.M., & Haapala, D. (1995). *Developing new approaches to helping drug affected families—A proposal for process, materials and training.* Tacoma, WA: Author.

Kinney, J.M., Haapala, D.A., & Booth, C. (1991) *Keeping families together: The Homebuilders™ model.* Hawthorne, NY: Aldine de Gruyter.

Kinney, J.M., Haapala, D.A., Booth, C., & Leavitt, S. (1991). Family-based practice: The evolution of the Homebuilders™ model. In J.K. Whittaker, J.M. Kinney, E. Tracy, & C. Booth (Eds.), *Reaching high risk families: Intensive family preservation services in human services.* Hawthorne, NY: Aldine de Gruyter.

Kinney, J.M., Haapala, D.A., & Gast, J.E. (1981). Assessment of families in crisis. In M. Bryce & J. Lloyd (Eds.), *Treating families in the home: An alternative to placement* (pp. 50–67). Springfield, IL: Charles C Thomas.

Kinney, J.M., Madsen, B., Fleming, T., & Haapala, D.A. (1977). Homebuilders™: Keeping families together. *Journal of Consulting and Clinical Psychology, 45*(4), 667–673.

Kinney, J.M., Haapala, D.A., Booth, C., & Leavitt, S. (1990). The Homebuilders™ model. In J.K. Whittaker, J.M. Kinney, E. Tracy, & C. Booth (Eds.), *Reaching high risk families: Intensive family preservation services in human services* (pp. 31–64). Hawthorne, NY: Aldine de Gruyter.

Kinsey, A.C., Pomeroy, W.B., Martin, C.E., et al. (1953). *Sexual behavior in the human female.* Philadelphia: W.B. Saunders.

Kiresuk, T.J. (1973). Goal attainment scaling at a county mental health service. *Evaluation Monograph,* 1.

Kirigin, K.A., Wolf, M.M., Braukmann, C.J., Fixsen, D.L., & Phillips, E.L. (1979). Achievement place: A preliminary outcome evaluation. In J.S. Stumphauzer (Ed.), *Progress in behavior therapy with delinquents* (pp. 118–155). Springfield, IL: Charles C Thomas.

Kirk, H.D. (1981). *Adoptive kinship: A modern institution in need of reform.* Toronto: Butterworths.

Kirsh, S., & Maidman, F. (1984). Child welfare problems and practice: An ecological approach. In F. Maidman (Ed.), *Child welfare: A source book of knowledge and practice* (pp. 1–14). New York: Child Welfare League of America.

Klein, M., & Stern, L. (1971). Low birth weight and the battered child syndrome. *American Journal of the Disabled Child, 122,* 15–18.

Kluger, M., Alexander, G., & Curtis, P. (Eds.). (2000). *What works in child welfare.* Washington, DC: Child Welfare League of America.

Kluger, M.P., Baker, W.A., & Garval, H.S. (1998). *Strategic business planning: Securing a future for non-profit organizations.* Washington, DC: Child Welfare League of America Press.

Knipe, J., & Warren, J. (1999). *Foster youth share their ideas for change.* Washington, DC: CWLA Press and San Francisco, CA: California Youth Connection.

Knitzer, J. (1982). *Unclaimed children: The failure of public responsibility to children and adolescents in need of mental health services.* Washington, DC: Children's Defense Fund.

Knitzer, J. (1984). Mental health services to children and youth: A national view of public policies. *American Psychologist, 39,* 905–911.

Knitzer, J. (1999). Speech to the Starting Early Starting Smart Steering Committee, January 14, 1999, Bethesda, MD.

Knitzer, J., Allen, M.L., & McGowan, B. (1978). *Children without homes: An examination of public responsibility to children in out-of-home care.* Washington, DC: Children's Defense Fund.

Knox, J. (1996). Home-based services for Southeast Asian refugee children: A process and formative evaluation. *Children and Youth Services Review, 18*(6), 553–578.

Knudsen, D.D., & Miller, J.L. (Eds.). (1991). *Abused and battered: Social and legal responses to family violence.* Hawthorne, NY: Walter de Gruyter.

Kohlberg, L. (1973). Contributions of developmental psychology to education: Examples from moral education. *Educational Psychologist, 10,* 2–14.

Kolko, D.J. (1996). Child physical abuse. In J. Briere, L. Berliner, J.A. Bulkley, C. Jenny, & T. Reid (Eds.), *The APSAC handbook on child maltreatment* (pp. 21–50). Newbury Park, CA: Sage.

Korbin, J. (1981). *Child abuse and neglect: Cross-cultural perspectives.* Berkeley, CA: University of California Press.

Korbin, J. (1986). Childhood histories of women imprisoned for fatal child maltreatment. *Child Abuse and Neglect, 10,* 331–338.

Korbin, J. (1987). Child sexual abuse: Implications from the cross-cultural record. In N. Scheper-Hughes (Ed.), *Child survival: Anthropological perspectives on the treatment and maltreatment of children* (pp. 247–265). Boston: D Reidel with Kluwer Academic Publishers Group.

Kosterman, R., Hawkins, D.J., Spath, R., Haggerty, K.P., & Zhu, K. (1997). Effects of a preventive parent-training intervention on observed family interactions: Proximal outcomes from preparing for the drug free years. *Journal of Community Psychology, 25*(4), 338–352.

Kotch, J.B., Browne, D.C., Ringwalt, C.L., Dufort, V., & Ruina, E. (1997). Stress, social support, and substantiated maltreatment in the second and third years of life. *Child Abuse and Neglect, 21*(11), 1025–1037.

Kraft, A.D., Palombo, J., Woods, P.K., Mitchell, D., & Schmidt, A.W. (1985). Some theoretical considerations on confidential adoptions. Part I: The birth mother. Part II: The adoptive parent. *Child and Adolescent Social Work, 2,* 13–21, 69–82.

Kreilkamp, T. (1989). *Time-limited, intermittent therapy with children and families.* New York: Brunner/Mazel.

Krisberg, B., Schwartz, I.M., Litsky, P., & Austin, J. (1986). The watershed of juvenile justice reform. *Crime & Delinquency, 32,* 5–38.

Kroll, J. (1999). U.S. adoptions from foster care projected to exceed 36,000. *Adoptalk, 1*–2.

Kufeldt, K. (1994). Inclusive foster care: Implementation of the model. In B. McKenzie (Ed.), *Current perspectives on foster family care for children and youth* (pp. 84–111). Toronto: Wall & Emerson.

Kumpfer, K. L., Molgaard, V., & Spoth, R. (1996). The Strengthening Families Program for the prevention of delinquency and drug use. In R. DeV. Peters & R.J. McMahon (Eds.), *Preventing childhood disorders, substance abuse, and delinquency* (pp. 241–267). Thousand Oaks, CA: Sage.

Kunitz, S.J., Levy, J.E., McCloskey, J., & Gabriel, K.R. (1998). Alcohol dependence and domestic violence as sequelae of abuse and conduct disorder in childhood. *Child Abuse and Neglect, 22*(11), 1079–1091.

Kupsin, M.M., & Dubsky, D.D. (1999). Behaviorally impaired children in out-of-home care. *Child Welfare, 78,* 297–310.

Lahti, J. (1982). A follow-up study of foster children in permanent placements. *Social Service Review, 56,* 556–571.

Laird, J. (1995). Family-centered practice in the postmodern era. *Families in Society: The Journal of Contemporary Human Services, 76,* 150–162.

Laird, J., & Hartman, A. (Eds.). (1985). *A handbook of child welfare.* New York: Free Press.

Lamb, M.E., Gaenshauer, T.J., Malkin, C.M., & Schultz, L.A. (1985). The effects of child maltreatment on security of infant-adult attachment. *Infant Behavior and Development, 8,* 35–45.

Lamb, M.E., Sternberg, K.J., & Esplin, P.W. (1994). Factors influencing the reliability and validity of the statements made by young victims of sexual maltreatment. *Journal of Applied Developmental Psychology, 15,* 255–280.

Lamb, M.E., Sternberg, K.J., & Esplin, P.W. (1998). Conducting investigative interviews of alleged sexual abuse victims. *Child Abuse and Neglect, 22*(8), 813–823.

Lamphear, V.S. (1985). The impact of maltreatment on children's psychosocial adjustment: A review of the research. *Child Abuse and Neglect, 9,* 251–263.

Lander, J., & Schulman, R. (1960). The impact of the therapeutic milieu on the disturbed personality. *Social Casework, 41*(5), 227–234.

Landis, J. (1956). Experience of 500 children with adult sexual deviation. *Psychiatric Quarterly Supplement, 30,* 90–109.

Landsverk, J., Davis, I., Ganger, W., Newton, R., & Johnson, I. (1996). Impact of child psychosocial functioning on reunification from out-of-home placement. *Children and Youth Services Review, 18,* 447–462.

Langer, S. (1925). Reply. *Survey, 54,* 624.

Larner, M.B., Stevenson, C.S., & Behrman, R.E. (1998). Protecting children from abuse and neglect. *The Future of Children, 8*(1), 4–22.

Larson, C.P. (1980). Efficacy of prenatal and postpartum home visits on child health and development. *Pediatrics, 66*(2), 191–197.

Lasch, C. (1977). *Haven in a heartless world: the family besieged.* New York: Basic Books.

Lav, I.J., & Lazere, E.B. (1996). *A hand up: How state earned income credits help working families escape poverty.* Washington, DC: Center on Budget and Policy Priorities.

Lawder, E.A., Poulin, J.E., & Andrews, R.G. (1984). *Helping the multi-problem family: A study of services to children in their own homes* (SCOH). Philadelphia, PA: Children's Aid Society of Pennsylvania.

Laws, D.R., & O'Neil, J.A. (1979). *Variations of masturbatory conditioning.* Paper presented at the 2nd National Conference on Evaluation and Treatment of Sexual Aggressives, New York.

Lazar, I., & Darlington, R. (1982). *Lasting effects of early intervention.* Chicago: Society for Research in Child Development.

Lee, J.A.B., & Nisivoccia, D. (1989). *Walk a mile in my shoes: A book about biological parents for foster parents and social workers.* Washington, DC: Child Welfare League of America.

Lee, R.E., & Hull, R.K. (1983). Legal, casework, and ethical issues in risk adoption. *Child Welfare, 62,* 450–454.

Leeds, S.J. (1984). *Evaluation of Nebraska's intensive services project.* Unpublished manuscript. University of Iowa, National Resource Center on Family-Based Services, Iowa City, IA.

Lehman, J. (1994). Updating urban policy. In S. Danziger, G. Sandefur, & D. Weinberg (Eds.), *Confronting poverty: Prescriptions for change* (pp. 226–252). Cambridge, MA: Harvard University Press.

Leigh, D. (1995). Can a voluntary workfare program change the behavior of welfare recipients? New evidence from Washington state's Family Independence Program (FIP). *Journal of Policy Analysis and Management, 14,* 567–589.

Leon, A.M. (1999). Family support model: Integrating service delivery in the twenty-first century. *Families in Society—The Journal of Contemporary Human Services, 80,* 14–24.

Leon, A.M., Mazur, R., Montalvo, E., & Rodrieguez, M. (1984). Self-help support groups for Hispanic mothers. *Child Welfare, 63,* 261–268.

Lerman, P. (1968). Evaluating studies in institutions for delinquents: Implications for research on social policies. *Social Work, 3,* 55–64.

Lerman, P. (1980). Trends and issues in the deinstitutionalization of youths in trouble. *Crime and Delinquency, 26,* 281–298.

Lerman, R. (1996). The impact of the changing U.S. family structure on child poverty and income inequality. *Economica, 63* (May), S119–139.

Lester, B.M., Corwin, M.J., Sepkoski, C., Seifer, R., Peucher, M., McLaughlin, S., & Golum, H.L. (1991). Neurobehavioral syndromes in cocaine-exposed newborn infants. *Child Development, 62,* 694–705.

Leventhal, J.M. (1982). Research strategies and methodologic standards in studies of risk factors for child abuse. *Child Abuse and Neglect, 6*(2), 113–123.

Leventhal, J.M. (1988). Have there been changes in the epidemiology of sexual abuse of childing during the 20th century? *Pediatrics, 82* (5), 766–773.

Leventhal, J.M. (1996). Twenty years later: We do know how to prevent child abuse and neglect. *Child Abuse and Neglect, 20*(8), 647–653.

Levin, H.M. (1983). *Cost-effectiveness: A primer.* Newbury Park, CA: Sage.

Levine, C., & Beck, I. (Eds.). (1988). *Programs to strengthen families: A resource guide.* Chicago, IL: Family Resource Coalition.

Levine, C., Brandt, A.M., & Whittaker, J.K. (1998). *Staying together, living apart: The AIDS epidemic and new perspectives on group living for youth and families.* Final report of the Orphan Project. [Available from Carol Levine, United Hospital Fund, 350 Fifth Ave. 23rd floor, New York, NY 10118.]

Levine, K.G. (1990). Time to mourn again. In A.N. Maluccio, R. Krieger, & B.A. Pine (Eds.), *Preparing adolescents for life after foster care: The central role of foster parents* (pp. 53–72). Washington, DC: Child Welfare League of America.

Levine, R.A. (1964). Treatment in the home. *Social Work, 9*(1), 19–28.

Levine, T., & McDaid, E. (1979). Services to children in their own homes: A family-based approach. In S. Maybanks & M. Bryce (Eds.), *Home-based services for children and families: Policy, practice, and research* (pp. 260–271). Springfield, IL: Charles C Thomas.

Levitan, S., & Shapiro, I. (1987). *Working but poor: America's contradictions.* Baltimore, MD: The Johns Hopkins University Press.

Levy, H.B., Markovic, J., Chaudhry, U., Ahart, S., & Torres, H. (1995). Reabuse rates in a sample of children followed for 5 years after discharge from a child abuse inpatient assessment program. *Child Abuse and Neglect, 19,* 1363–1377.

Lewin, K. (1935). *A dynamic theory of personality.* New York: McGraw-Hill.

Lewis, R. (1990). *Service-related correlates of treatment success in intensive family preservation services for child welfare.* Unpublished doctoral dissertation, University of Utah, Graduate School of Social Work.

Lewis, R.E. (1991). What are the characteristics of intensive family preservation services? In M.W. Fraser, P.J. Pecora, & D.A. Haapala (Eds.), *Families in crisis: The impact of intensive family preservation services* (pp. 93–109). Hawthorne, NY: Aldine de Gruyter.

Lewis, R.E. (1994). Application and adaptation of intensive family preservation services to use for the reunification of foster children with their biological parents. *Children and Youth Services Review, 16,* 339–361.

Lewis, R.E., Walton, E., & Fraser, M.W. (1995). Examining family reunification services: A process analysis of a successful experiment. *Research on Social Work Practice, 5,* 259–282.

Lewis S.O., Shanok, S., Pincus, J., & Glaser, G. (1979). Violent juvenile delinquents: Psychiatric, neurological, psychological and abuse factors. *Journal of the American Academy of Child Psychiatry, 18,* 307–319.

Lewis, W.W. (1982). Ecological factors in successful residential treatment. *Behavioral Disorders, 7,* 149–156.

Liaw, F.-R., & Brooks-Gunn, J. (1994). Cumulative familial risks and low-birth weight children's cognitive and behavioral development. *Journal of Clinical Child Psychology, 23*(4), 360–372.

Lieberman, A.A., Hornby, H., & Russell, M. (1988). Analyzing the educational backgrounds and work experiences of child welfare personnel: A national study. *Social Work, 33*(6), 485–489.

Lieberson, S., & Waters, M. (1988). *From many strands: Ethnic and racial groups in contemporary America.* New York: Russell Sage Foundation

Light, R. (1973). Abused and neglected children in America: A study of alternative policies. *Harvard Educational Review, 43*(4), 556–598.

Lightburn, A., & Kemp, S. (1994). Family-support programs: Opportunities for community-based practice. *Families in Society, 75,* 16–26.

Lindblad-Goldberg, M., Dore, M.M., & Stern, L. (1998). *Creating competence from chaos: A comprehensive guide to home-based services* (1st ed.). New York: Norton.

Lindblom, C.E. (1990). *Inquiry and change.* New Haven, CT: Yale University Press.

Lindsay, P. (1988). *National study of public child welfare salaries.* Portland, ME: University of Southern Maine, National Child Welfare Resource Center for Management and Administration.

Lindsey, D. (1994). Family preservation and child protection: Striking a balance. *Children and Youth Services Review, 16,* 279–294.

Link, K.M. (1996). Permanency planning options in kinship care: A study of children placed in kinship care in Erie County, New York. *Child Welfare, 75,* 509–528.

Lipner, R., & Goertz, B. (1996). Child welfare priorities and expenditures. *W-Memo, 2*(8), 1. Washington, DC: American Public Human Services Association.

Littell, J.H., Schuerman, J.R., Rzepnicki, T.L., Howard, J., & Nagler, S.F. (1993). Shifting objectives in family preservation programs. In E.S. Morton & R.K. Grigsby (Eds.), *Advancing family preservation practice* (pp. 99–118). Newbury Park, CA: Sage.

Little, M., & Mount, K. (1999). *Prevention and early intervention with children in need.* Cambridge, England: Ashgate.

Littner, N. (1950). *Some traumatic effects of separation and placement.* New York: Child Welfare League of America.

Lloyd, J. (1993). Protecting children. *American Humane Association, 10*(3), 5.

Lloyd, J.C., & Bryce, M.E. (1983). *Placement prevention and family unification: A practitioner's handbook for the home-based family-centered program.* Iowa City, IA: The University of Iowa, School of Social Work, National Resource Center on Family-Based Services.

Lloyd, J.C., Bryce, M.E., & Schultze, L. (1980). *Placement prevention and family reunification: A practitioner's handbook for the home-based family-centered program.* Iowa City: University of Iowa, School of Social Work, National Resource Center on Family-Based Services.

Loprest, P. (1999). *Families who left welfare: Who are they and how are they faring?* The Urban Institute, Assessing the New Federalism Report 99-02.

Lowenstein, L.B. (1995). The resolution scrapbook as an aid in the treatment of traumatized children. *Child Welfare, 74*(4), 889.

Lujan, C., DeBruyn, L.M., May, P.A., & Bird, M.E. (1989). Profile of abused and neglected American Indian children in the southwest. *Child Abuse and Neglect, 13*(4), 449–461.

Lundstrom, M., & Sharpe, R. (1991). Getting away with murder. *Public Welfare, 49*(3), 18–29.

Lupton, C. (1998). User empowerment or family self–reliance? The family group conference model. *British Journal of Social Work, 28,* 107–128.

Lustbader, A.S., Mayes, L.C., McGee, B.A., Jatlow, P., & Roberts, W.L. (1998). Incidence of passive exposure to crack/cocaine and clinical findings in infants seen in an outpatient services. *Pediatrics,* (102), 1. URL: http://www. pediatrics. org/cgi/content/full/102/1/e5.

Lutzker, J.R., & Rice, J.M. (1984). Project 12-ways: Measuring outcome of a large in-home service for treatment and prevention of child abuse and neglect. *Child Abuse and Neglect, 8,* 519–524.

Lyle, C.G., & Nelson, J. (1985). *Home based vs. traditional child protection services: A study of the home based services demonstration project in the Ramsey County Human Services Department.* Unpublished manuscript. Ramsey County Human Services Department, St. Paul, MN.

Lyman, R.D., Prentice-Dunn, S., Wilson, D.R., & Taylor, G.E., Jr. (1989). Issues in residential and inpatient treatment. In R.D. Lyman, S. Prentice-Dunn, & S. Gubel (Eds.), *Residential and inpatient treatment of children & adolescents.* New York: Plenum Press.

Lynch, E.W., & Hanson, M.J. (1992). *Developing cross-cultural competence: A guide for working with young children and their families.* Baltimore: Paul H. Brookes.

Lynch, E.W., & Hanson, M.J. (Eds.). (1998). *Developing cross-cultural competence* (2nd ed.). Baltimore, MD: Paul H. Brookes.

Lynskey, M.T., & Fergusson, D.M. (1997). Factors protecting against the development of adjustment difficulties in young adults exposed to childhood sexual abuse. *Child Abuse and Neglect, 21*(12), 1177–1190.

Maas, H.S. (1971). Children's environments and child welfare. *Child Welfare, 50,* 132–142.

Maas, H.S., & Engler, R.E. (1959). *Children in need of parents.* New York: Columbia University Press.

Mackner, L.M., Starr., R.H., Jr., & Black, M.M. (1997). The cumulative effect of neglect and failure to thrive on cognitive functioning. *Child Abuse and Neglect, 21*(7), 691–700.

MacEachron, A.E., Gustavsson, N.S., Cross, S., & Lewis, A. (1996). The effectiveness of the Indian Child Welfare Act of 1978. *Social Services Review, 70*(3), 451–463.

MacFarlane, K., Waterman, J., & Conerly, S. (Eds.). (1986). *Sexual abuse of young children.* New York: Guilford.

MacRae, D., & Wilde, J.A. (1979). *Policy analysis for public decisions.* Belmont, CA: Wadsworth.

Maddock, J.W., & Larson, N.R. (1995). *Incestuous families: An ecological approach to understanding and treatment.* New York and London: Norton.

Magazino, C.J. (1983). Services to children and families at risk of separation. In B.G. McGowan & W. Meezan (Eds.), *Child welfare: Current dilemmas, future directions* (pp. 211–254). Itasca, IL: F.E. Peacock.

Magen, R.H., Conroy, K., Hess, P.M., Panciera, A., & Simon, B.L. (1995). *Evaluation of a protocol to identify battered women during investigations of child abuse and neglect.* Paper presented at the 4th International Family Violence Research Conference University of New Hampshire Durham, NH, July 22, 1995.

Magen, R.H., & Rose, S.D. (1994). Parents in groups: Problem solving versus behavioral skills training. *Research in Social Work, 4*(2), 172–191.

Magura, S. (1981). Are services to prevent foster care effective? *Children and Youth Services Review, 3*(3), 193–212.

Magura, S., & De Rubcis, R. (1980). *The effectiveness of preventive services for families with abused, neglected and disturbed children: Second year evaluation of Hudson County Project.* Trenton, NJ: Division of Youth and Family Services, Bureau of Research.

Magura, S., & Moses, B.S. (1984). Clients as evaluators in child protective services. *Child Welfare, 63*(2), 99–112.

Magura, S., & Moses, B.S. (1986). *Outcome measures for child welfare services: Theory and application.* Washington, DC: Child Welfare League of America.

Magura, S., Moses, B.S., & Jones, M.A. (1987). *Assessing risk and measuring change in families: The Family Risk Scales.* Washington, DC: Child Welfare League of America.

Mallon, G.P. (1997). Toward a competent child welfare service delivery system for gay and lesbian adolescents and their families. In G.A. Anderson, A.S. Ryan, & B.R. Leashore (Eds.), *The challenge of permanency planning in a multicultural society* (pp. 177–194). New York: Haworth Press.

Mallon, G.P. (1998). *We don't exactly get the welcome wagon—The experience of gay and lesbian adolescents in the child welfare system.* New York: Columbia University Press.

Maluccio, A.N. (1979). *Learning from clients: Interpersonal helping as viewed by clients and social workers.* New York: Free Press.

Maluccio, A.N. (1981a). An ecological perspective on practice with parents of children in foster care. In A.N. Maluccio & P.A. Sinanoglu (Eds.), *The challenge of partnership: Working with parents of children in foster care.* New York: Child Welfare League of America.

Maluccio, A.N. (Ed.) (1981b). *Promoting competence in clients: A new/old approach to social work practice.* New York: Free Press.

Maluccio, A.N. (1985). Education and training for child welfare practice. In J. Laird & A. Hartman (Eds.), *A handbook of child welfare practice: Context, knowledge, and practice* (pp. 741–759). New York: Free Press.

Maluccio, A.N. (1990). Client feedback and creativity. In H.H. Weissman (Ed.), *Serious play—Creativity and innovation in social work* (pp. 223–230). Washington, DC: National Association of Social Workers.

Maluccio, A.N. (1990). Family preservation services and the social work practice sequence. In J.K. Whittaker, J. Kinney, E.M. Tracy, & C. Booth (Eds.), *Reaching high-risk families —Intensive family preservation in human services* (pp. 113–126). Hawthorne, NY: Aldine de Gruyter

Maluccio, A.N. (1991a). The optimism of policy choices in child welfare. *American Journal of Orthopsychiatry, 61*(4), 606–609.

Maluccio, A.N. (1991b). Family preservation: An overview. In A.L. Sallee & J.C. Lloyd (Eds.), *Family preservation: Papers from the Institute for Social Work Editors 1990* (pp. 17–28). Riverdale, IL: National Association for Family-Based Services.

Maluccio, A.N. (1999). Action as a vehicle for promoting competence. In B.R. Compton & B. Galaway (Eds.), *Social work processes* (6th ed., pp. 354–365). Pacific Grove, CA: Brooks/Cole.

Maluccio, A.N. (2000). Foster care and family reunification. In P.A. Curtis, G. Dale, & J.C. Kendall (Eds.), *The foster care crisis: Translating research into policy and practice* (pp. 211–224). Lincoln, NE: The University of Nebraska Press.

Maluccio, A.N., & Fein, E. (1983). Permanency planning: A redefinition. *Child Welfare, 59,* 515–530.

Maluccio, A.N., & Fein, E. (1985). Growing up in foster care. *Children and Youth Services Review, 7,* 123–134.

Maluccio, A.N., & Fein, E. (1987). Effects of permanency planning on foster children: A response. *Social Work, 32*(6), 546–548.

Maluccio, A.N., Fein, E., & Davis, I. (1994). Family reunification: Research findings, issues, and directions. *Child Welfare, 73,* 489–504.

Maluccio, A.N., Fein, E., & Olmstead, K.A. (1986). *Permanency planning for children: Concepts and methods.* London and New York: Routledge, Chapman and Hall.

Maluccio, A.N., Krieger, R., & Pine, B.A. (Eds.). (1990). *Preparing adolescents for life after foster care: The central role of foster parents.* Washington, DC: Child Welfare League of America.

Maluccio, A.N., & Marlow, W.D. (1972). Residential treatment of emotionally disturbed children: A review of the literature. *Social Service Review, 46,* 230–251.

Maluccio, A.N., Pine, B.A., & Warsh, R. (1994). Protecting children by preserving their families. *Children and Youth Services Review, 16,* 295–307.

Maluccio, A.N., & Sinanoglu, P.A. (Eds.). (1981). *The challenge of partnership: Working with parents of children in foster care.* New York: Child Welfare League of America.

Maluccio, A.N., Warsh, R., & Pine, B.A. (1993). Family reunification: An overview. In B.A. Pine, R. Warsh, & A.N. Maluccio (Eds.), *Together again: Family reunification in foster care* (pp. 3–19). Washington, DC: Child Welfare League of America.

Maluccio, A.N., & Whittaker, J.K. (1988). Helping the biological families of children in out-of-home placement. In W.W. Nunnally, C.S. Chilman, & F.M. Cox (Eds.), *Troubled relationships: Families in trouble series* (Vol. 3, pp. 205–217). Newbury Park, CA: Sage.

Manalo, V., & Meezan, W. (2000). Toward building a typology for the evaluation of family support services. *Child Welfare, 79*(4), 405–429.

Mannes, M. (Ed.). (1990). *Family preservation and Indian child welfare.* Albuquerque, NM: American Indian Law Center, Inc.

Mannes, M. (1993). Seeking the balance between child protection and family preservation in Indian child welfare. *Child Welfare, 72,* 141–152.

Marcenko, M., Spence, M., & Samost, L. (1996). Outcomes of a home visitation trial for pregnant and postpartum women at-risk for child placement. *Children and Youth Services Review, 18*(3), 243–259.

Marcia, J.E. (1966). Development and validation of ego identity status. *Journal of Personality and Social Psychology, 3*(5), 551–558.

Marcia, J.E. (1976). Identity six years after: A follow-up study. *Journal of Youth and Adolescence, 5,* 145–160.

Marcia, J.E. (1980). Identity in adolescence. In J. Adelson (Ed.), *Handbook of adolescent psychology* (pp. 158–187). New York: John Wiley & Sons.

Margolin, L. (1990). Fatal child neglect. *Child Welfare, 69*(4), 309–319.

Marks, J., McDonald, T., Bessey, W., & Palmer, M. (1989). *Risk assessment in child protective services: A review of risk factors assessed by existing instrument-based models.* Portland, ME: University of Southern Maine, National Child Welfare Resource Center for Management and Administration.

Marsh, P., & Triseliotis, J. (1993). *Prevention and reunification in child care.* London: B.T. Batsford, in association with British Agencies for Adoption and Fostering.

Marshall, W.L., Earls, C.M., Segal, Z., & Darke, J. (1983). A behavioral program for the assessment and treatment of sexual aggressors. In K.D. Craig & R.J. McMahon (Eds.), *Advances in clinical behavior therapy.* New York: Brunner/Mazel.

Martin, F.E., & Palmer, T. (1997). Transitions to adulthood: A child welfare youth perspective. *Community Alternatives—International Journal of Community Care, 9,* 29–60.

Martin, H., Conway, E., Breezle, P., & Kempe, H.C. (1974). The development of abused children, Part I: A review of the literature. *Advances in Pediatrics, 21,* 43.

Martin, M. (1986). Social distancing of the neglectful family: Sex, race, and social class influences. *Children and Youth Services Review, 8,* 1–12.

Martinez, L. (1989). The family assessment factor worksheet. Springfield, IL: Illinois Department of Children and Family Services (mimeograph).

Martinez, L. (Undated). *Illinois child fatalities: A three year statistical profile (1982–1984).* Springfield, IL: Illinois Department of Children and Family Services.

Maryland Governor's Office for Children and Youth. (1988). *So there's a new baby in your family.* Baltimore, MD: Author.

Massinga, R., & Perry, K. (1994). The Casey Family Programs: Factors in effective management of a long-term foster care organization. In J. Blacker (Ed.), *When there is no place like home: Options for children living apart from their natural families* (pp. 163–180). Baltimore, MD: Paul H. Brookes.

Massinga, R.W., & Cargal, J. (1991). Foundations and family-based services: Support, innovation, and leadership. *Families in Society, 72,* 301–309.

Mauzerall, H.A. (1983). Emancipation from foster care: The independent living project. *Child Welfare, 62*(1), 47–53.

Maximus, Inc. (1984). *Child welfare statistical fact book: 1984: Substitute care and adoption.* Washington, DC: Office of Human Development Series.

Maximus, Inc. (1985). *Child welfare statistical fact book: 1985: Substitute care.* Washington, DC: U.S. Department of Health and Human Services, Administration for Children, Youth and Families, Office of Human Development Services.

Maybanks, S., & Bryce, M. (Eds.). (1979). *Home-based services for children and families: Policy, practice, and research.* Springfield, IL: Charles C Thomas.

Mayer, M.F., & Blum, A. (Eds.). (1971). *Healing through living: A symposium on residential treatment.* Springfield, IL: Charles C Thomas.

Mayer, S. (1997). *What money can't buy: Family income and children's life chances.* Cambridge, MA: Harvard University Press.

Maza, P.L. (1983). *Characteristics of children free for adoption. Child Welfare Research Notes #2.* Washington, DC: Children's Bureau, Administration for Children, Youth and Families.

Maza, P.L. (1984). *Adoption trends: 1944–1975. Child Welfare Research Notes #9.* Washington, DC: Children's Bureau, Administration for Children, Youth and Families.

Maza, P.L. (1996). *Children in foster or group care in the U.S.: 1977 vs. 1994.* Washington, DC: Children's Bureau.

McAdams, P.T. (1972). The parent in the shadows. *Child Welfare, 51,* 51–55.

McCarthy, D. (1979). Recognition of signs of emotional deprivation: A form of child abuse. *Child Abuse and Neglect, 3,* 423–428.

McCroskey, J., & Meezan, W. (1997). *Family preservation and family functioning.* Washington, DC: CWLA Press.

McCroskey, J., Nishinmoto, R., & Subramanian, K. (1991). Assessment in family support programs: Initial reliability and validity testing of the Family assessment Form. *Child Welfare, 70,* 19–33.

McDonald, T.P., Allen, R.I., Westerfelt, A., & Piliavin, I. (1996). *Assessing the long-term effects of foster care—A research synthesis.* Washington, DC: CWLA Press.

McFadden, J.E., & Downs, S.W. (1995). Family continuity: The new paradigm in permanence planning. *Community Alternatives: International Journal of Family Care, 7,* 39–59.

McGowan, B. (1990). Family-based services and public policy: Context and implications. In J. Whittaker, J.M. Kinney, E. Tracy, & C. Booth (Eds.), *Reaching high-risk families* (pp. 65–87). Hawthorne, NY: Aldine de Gruyter.

McGowan, B., & Meezan, W. (Eds.). (1983). *Child welfare: Current dilemmas—Future directions.* Itasca, IL: F.E. Peacock.

McInturf, J.W. (1986). Preparing special needs children for adoption through the use of a life book. *Child Welfare, 65,* 373–386.

McKay, M.M, (1994). The link between domestic violence and child abuse: Assessment and treatment considerations. *Child Welfare, 73*(11), 29–39.

McKenzie, B. (Ed.) (1994). *Current perspectives on foster family care for children and youth.* Toronto: Wall & Emerson.

McKenzie, R.B. (1998). *Rethinking orphanages for the 21st century.* Thousand Oaks, CA: Sage.

McKenzie, W., English, D., & Henderson, J. (1987). *Family-centered case management with sexually aggressive youth.* Olympia, WA: Washington Department of Social and Health Services, Division of Children, Youth, and Family Services.

McLeer, S.V., Deblinger, E., Atkins, M.S., Foa, E.B., & Ralphe, D.L. (1988). Posttraumatic stress disorder in sexually abused children. *Journal of the American Academy of Child and Adolescent Psychiatry, 27,* 650–654.

McMillen, C. (1992). Attachment theory and clinical social work. *Clinical Social Work Journal, 2,* 205–218.

McMillen, J.C., Rideout, G.B., Fisher, R.H., & Tucker, J. (1997). Independent living services: The views of former foster youth. *Families in Society: The Journal of Contemporary Human Services, 78,* 471–479.

McMillen, J.C., & Tucker J. (1999). The status of older adolescents at exit from out of home care. *Child Welfare, 78,* 339–362.

McMurtry, S.L., & Lie, G.W. (1992). Differential exit rates of minority children in foster care. *Social Work Research & Abstracts, 28,* 42–48.

McRoy, R.G. (1996). Racial identity issues for Black children in foster care. In S.L. Logan (Ed.), *The Black family: Strengths, self-help, and positive change* (pp. 131–143). Boulder, CO: Westview Press.

Meadow, R. (1985). Management of munchausen syndrome by proxy. *Archives of Disease in Childhood, 60,* 385–393.

Meadowcroft, P., Thomlison, B., & Chamberlain, P. (1994). Treatment foster care services: A research agenda for child welfare. *Child Welfare, 73,* 565–581.

Meadowcroft, P., & Trout, B.A. (Eds.). (1990). *Troubled youth in treatment homes: A handbook of therapeutic foster care.* Washington, DC: Child Welfare League of America.

Mech E.V. (Ed.). (1988). Independent-living services for at-risk adolescents. *Child Welfare, 67,* 483–634.

Mech, E.V., & Rycraft, J.R. (Eds.). (1995). *Preparing foster youths for adult living: Proceedings of an invitational research conference.* Washington, DC: Child Welfare League of America.

Meezan, W. (1980). *Adoption services in the states.* Washington, DC: U.S. Department of Health and Human Services.

Meezan, W., Katz, S., & Russo, E.M. (1978). *Adoptions without agencies: A study of independent adoptions.* New York: Child Welfare League of America.

Meezan, W., & Shireman, J.F. (1982). Foster parent adoption. A literature review. *Child Welfare, 61,* 525–535.

Meezan, W., & Shireman, J.F. (1985). *Care and commitment: Foster parent adoption decisions.* New York: State University of New York Press.

Melton, G.B., & Barry, F.D. (Eds.). (1994). *Protecting children from abuse and neglect—Foundations for a new national strategy.* New York: Guilford.

Melton, G.B., Lyons, P.M., & Spaulding, W. J. (1998). *No place to go: The civil commitment of minors.* Lincoln: University of Nebraska Press.

Mental Health Law Project. (1990). *Protecting children's and family's rights in Part H programs.* Early Intervention Advocacy Network NOTEBOOK. Issue Paper No. 3 (September, whole issue).

Merkel-Holguin, L. (1996). *Children who lose their parents to HIV/AIDS—Agency guidelines for adoptive and kinship placement.* Washington, DC: CWLA Press.

Merkel-Holguin, L., Winterfeld, A., Harper, C., Coburn, N., & Fluke, J. (1997). *Innovations for children's services for the 21st century: Family group decision making and patch.* Englewood, CO: American Humane Association.

Metcalf, T. (1989). *Presentation on failure to thrive for the Utah Department of Social Services.* Salt Lake City: Utah Department of Social Services (mimeograph).

Meyers, D., Garfinkel, I., Robins, P., & Oellerich, D. (1991). *The costs and effects of a national child support assurance system.* Madison, WI: Institute for Research on Poverty.

Michigan may limit race as factor in adoptions and foster care. (1986). *New York Times,* December 14, A6.

Miedema, B., & Nason-Clark, N. (1997). Foster care redesign: The dilemma contemporary foster families face. *Community Alternatives: The International Journal of Family Care, 9,* 15–28.

Miller, A. (1985). *For your own good.* New York: Farrar, Straus, Giroux.

Miller, D.L., Hoffman, F., & Turner, D. (1980). A perspective on the Indian Child Welfare Act. *Social Casework, 61,* 468–471.

Miller, I., Bishop, D., Epstein, N., & Keitner, G. (1985). The McMaster family assessment device: Reliability and validity. *Journal of Marital and Family Therapy, 11*(4), 345–356.

Miller, J. (1991). Child welfare and the role of women: A feminist perspective. *American Journal of Orthopsychiatry, 61*(4), 592–598.

Miller, J.L., & Whittaker, J.K. (1988). Social services and social support: Blended programs for families at risk of child maltreatment. *Child Welfare, 67*(2), 161–174.

Miller, J.S., Williams, K.M., English, D.J., & Olmstead, J. (1987). *Risk assessment in child protection: A review of the literature.* (Occasional monograph series of APWA Social R&D Department, No. 1.) Washington, DC: American Public Welfare Association.

Miller, K., Fein, E., Howe, G., Gaudio, C., & Bishop, G. (1984). Time-limited goal-focused parent aide services. *Social Casework, 65,* 472–477.

Millham, S., Bullock, R., Hosie, K., & Keane, A. (1986). *Lost in care.* Aldershot, England: Gower.

Minty, B. (1999). Annotation: Outcomes in long-term foster family care. *Journal of Child Psychology and Psychiatry, 40,* 991–999.

Mira, M., & Cairons, G. (1981). Intervention in the interaction of a mother: Child with non-organic failure to thrive. *Pediatric Nursing, 7*(2), 41–45.

Mississippi State Department of Public Welfare. (1986). *Annual report, FY 1985.* Jackson: Author.

Mitchel, L.B. (1987). *Child abuse and neglect fatalities: A review of the problem and strategies for reform.* Chicago, IL: National Committee for Prevention of Child Abuse.

Mitchel, L.B. (1988). *Child abuse fatalities.* Presentation for the 1988 Annual Conference of the National Association of Social Workers, Philadelphia (mimeograph).

Mitchel, L.B. (1989). Report on fatalities from NCPCA. *Protecting Children, 6*(6), 2–5.

Mitchel, L.B., & Savage, C. (1991). *The relationship between substance abuse and child abuse* (working paper #854, p. 1). Chicago: The National Committee for Prevention of Child Abuse.

Mnookin, R.H. (1973). Foster care: In whose best interest? *Harvard Educational Review, 43*(4), 599–638.

Moelis, C.S. (1989). *Abolishing corporal punishment in schools: A call to action.* Chicago: The National Committee for Prevention of Child Abuse, The National Center on Child Abuse Prevention Research.

Moen, P., Elder, G.H., & Luscher, K. (Eds.). (1995). *Examining lives in context: Perspectives on the ecology of human development.* Washington, DC: American Psychological Association.

Moffitt, R. (1992). Incentive effects of the U.S. welfare system: A review. *Journal of Economic Literature, 30,* 1–61.

Moffitt, R. (1998). The effect of welfare on marriage and fertility. In R. Moffitt (Ed.), *Welfare, the family and reproductive behavior* (pp. 50–97). Washington DC: National Academy Press.

Monahan, J., (1981). *Predicting violent behavior: An assessment of clinical techniques.* Newbury Park, CA: Sage.

Montagu, A. (1970). A scientist looks at love. *Phi Delta Kappa Magazine,* May, 463–467.

Moone, J. (1997). *States at a glance: Juveniles in public facilities, 1995.* Washington, DC: U.S. Department of Justice.

Moore, E., Armsden, G., & Gogerty, P.L. (1998). A twelve-year follow-up study of maltreated and at-risk children who received early therapeutic child care. *Child Maltreatment, 3*(1), 3–16.

Moore, J.B. (1982). Project thrive: A supportive treatment approach to the parents of children with nonorganic failure to thrive. *Child Welfare, 61*(6), 389–399.

Moore, K., Moretti, M.M., & Holland, R. (1998). A new perspective on youth care programs: Using attachment theory to guide interventions for troubled youth. *Residential Treatment for Children & Youth, 15*(3), 1–24.

Moos, R.H. (1979). Improving social settings by social climate measurement and feedback. In R.F. Munoz, L.R. Snowden, J.G. Kelly, & Associates (Eds.), *Social and psychological research in community settings.* San Francisco: Jossey-Bass.

Moos, R.H. (1984). Context and coping: Toward a unifying conceptual framework. *American Journal of Community Psychology, 12,* 5–25.

Mora, G., Talmadge, M., Bryant, F.T., & Hayden, B.S. (1969). A residential treatment center moves toward the community mental health model. *Child Welfare, 48*(10), 585–590.

Moroney, R.B. (1991). *Social policy and social work: Critical essays on the welfare state.* Hawthorne, NY: Aldine de Gruyter.

Morton, T.D., & Holder, W. (1999). Supplemental paper: Practice considerations in child protective services. In *Guidelines for a model system of protective services for abused and neglected children and their families* (pp. 43–48). Washington, DC: National Association of Public Child Welfare Administrators.

Mott, P.E. (1976). *Meeting human needs: The social and political history of Title XX.* Columbus, OH: National Conference on Social Welfare.

Moynihan, D.P. (1986). *Family and nation.* New York: Harcourt, Brace Jovanovich.

Mrazek, P.J., & Haggerty, R.J. (Eds.) (1994). *Reducing risks for mental disorders: Frontiers for preventive intervention research.* (Institute of Medicine) Washington, DC: National Academy Press.

Mullen, E.J., & Magnabosco, J.L. (Eds.). (1997). *Outcomes measurement in the human services: Cross-cutting issues and methods.* Washington, DC: NASW Press.

Mullender, A. (1996). *Rethinking domestic violence: The social work and probation response.* London: Routledge.

Munson, C.E. (1993). *An introduction to clinical social work supervision.* New York: Haworth Press.

Murphy, J.M., Jellinek, M., Quinn, D., Smith, G., Poitrast, F.G., & Goshko, M. (1991). Substance abuse and serious child mistreatment: Prevalence, risk, and outcome in a court sample. *Child Abuse and Neglect, 15*(3), 197–211.

Murray, K. (1999). Treatment issues in child sexual abuse. In M. Hill (Ed.), *Effective ways of working with children and their families* (pp. 215–240). London: Jessica Kingsley.

Myers, S. (1967). The child slayer: A 25 year survey of homicides involving pre-adolescent victims. *Archives of General Psychiatry, 1,* 211–213.

Myers, S. (1970). Maternal filicide. *American Journal of Diseases of Children, 120,* 534–536.

Nash, J.K., & Fraser, M.W. (1998). After-school care for children: A resilience-based approached. *Families in Society: The Journal of Contemporary Human Services,* 370–383.

Nash, K.A. (1999). *Cultural Competence–A guide for human service agencies.* Washington, DC: Child Welfare League of America.

Nasuti, J.P. (1990). *A test of internal consistency and interrater reliability of the Utah risk assessment instrument.* Dissertation submitted to the faculty of the University of Utah, Graduate School of Social Work.

National Association of Public Child Welfare Administrators. (1987). *Guidelines for a model system of protective services for abused and neglected children and their families.* Washington, DC: American Public Welfare Association.

National Association of Public Child Welfare Administrators (1999). *Guidelines for a model system of protective services for abused and neglected children and their families.* Washington, DC: American Public Human Services Association.

National Association of Social Workers. (1980). *Education and experience requirements for social work jobs—Draft report of the National Classification Validation Project.* Silver Springs, MD: Author.

National Association of Social Workers. (1981a). *NASW standards for social work practice in child protection.* Washington, DC: Author.

National Association of Social Workers. (1981b). *NASW standards for the classification of social work practice—Policy statement 4.* Silver Springs, MD: Author.

National Center for Comprehensive Emergency Services to Children. (1978). *Comprehensive emergency services: Training guide* (2nd ed.). [OHDS Publication No. 77–30120.] Washington, DC: U.S. Department of Health and Human Services, Office of Human Development Services.

National Center for Health Statistics, Centers for Disease Control and Prevention (1999). *Births: Final data for 1997.* Hyattsville, MD: Author.

National Center for Health Statistics. (1990). Advance report of final divorce statistics, 1987. In *Monthly vital statistics report, 38*(12), Supplement 2. Hyattsville, MD: Public Health Service.

National Center for Social Policy and Practice. (1989). *Social workers in public social services: A review of the literature.* Silver Springs, MD: Author.

National Center on Child Abuse and Neglect. (1988). *Study findings: Study of national incidence and prevalence of child abuse and neglect: 1988.* Washington, DC: U.S. Department of Health and Human Services, Office of Human Development Services, National Center on Child Abuse and Neglect.

National Commission on Children in Need of Parents. (1979). *Final report.* New York: NCCINP.

National Commission on Children. (1991). *Beyond rhetoric: A new American agenda for children and families.* Washington, DC: Author.

National Commission on Family Foster Care. (1991). *A blueprint for fostering infants, children and youth in the 1990's.* Washington, DC: Child Welfare League of America, in collaboration with the National Foster Parent Association.

National Committee for Prevention of Child Abuse. (1989). *Substance abuse and child abuse fact sheet.* Chicago, IL: National Committee for Prevention of Child Abuse.

National Council of Juvenile and Family Court Judges, Child Welfare League of America, Youth Law Center, National Center for Youth Law. (Undated). *Making reasonable efforts: Steps for keeping families together.* New York: Edna McConnell Clark Foundation.

National Humane Review. (1931). *Standards for child protection societies.* (December), 3–5, 13.

National Institute of Justice. (1997). *Child sexual molestation: Research issues.* Washington, DC: U.S. Department of Justice.

National Institute on Drug Abuse. (1994). *National pregnancy and health survey.* Rockville, MD: U.S. Department of Health and Human Services.

National Institute on Drug Abuse. (1997). NIH Publication No. 97-4139.

National Resource Center on Family-Based Services. (1988a). *Annotated directory of selected family-based programs.* Iowa City, IA: University of Iowa-Oakdale Campus, School of Social Work.

National Resources Center on Family Based Services. (1988b). *Family based services: Factors contributing to success and failure in family based child welfare services: Final report.* Iowa City, IA: Author.

Navarre, E. (1987). Psychological maltreatment: The core component of child abuse. In R. Brassard, R. Germain, & S.N. Hart (Eds.), *Psychological maltreatment of children and youth* (pp. 45–58). New York: Pergamon Press.

Needell, B., & Barth, R. (1998). Infants entering foster care compared to other infants using birth status indicators. *Child Abuse and Neglect, 22,* 1179–1187.

Needell, B., & Gilbert, N. (1997). Child welfare and the extended family. In J.D. Berrick, R. Barth, & N. Gilbert (Eds.), *Child welfare research review* (Vol. 2 , pp. 85–99). New York: Columbia University Press.

Needell, B., Webster, D., Barth, R.P., & Armijo, M. (1996). *Performance indicators for child welfare services in California: 1995.* Berkeley, CA: University of California, Center for Social Services Research.

Needell, B., Webster, D., Barth, R.P., Armijo, M., & Fox, A. (1998). *Performance indicators for child welfare services in California: 1997.* Berkeley, CA: University of California, School of Social Welfare, Child Welfare Research Center.

Needell, B., Webster, D., Cuccaro-Alamin, S., & Armijo, M. (1998). *Performance indicators for child welfare services in California: 1997.* Berkeley, CA: University of California, Center for Social Services Research.

Nelson, C.M., & Pearson, C.A. (1991). *Integrating services for children and youth with emotional and behavioral disorders.* Reston, VA: Council for Exceptional Children.

Nelson, D. (1990). Recognizing and realizing the potential of "family preservation." In J.K. Whittaker, J. Kinney, E.M. Tracy, & C. Booth (Eds.), *Reaching high-risk families: Intensive family preservation in human services* (pp. 113–126). Hawthorne, NY: Aldine de Gruyter.

Nelson, J.P. (1984). *An experimental evaluation of a home-based family-centered program model in a public child protection agency.* Unpublished doctoral thesis, University of Minnesota, School of Social Work, Minneapolis.

Nelson, K.A. (1985). *On the frontier of adoption.* New York: Child Welfare League of America.

Nelson, K.E. (1991). Populations and outcomes in five family preservation programs. In K. Wells & D.E. Beigel (Eds.), *Family preservation services: Research and evaluation.* Newbury Park, CA: Sage.

Nelson, K.E. (1997). Family preservation—What is it? *Children and Youth Services Review, 19,* 101–118.

Nelson, K.E., Cross, T., Landsman, M.J., & Tyler, M. (1996). Native American families and child neglect. *Children and Youth Services Review, 18*(6), 505–522.

Nelson, K.E., Emlen, A., Landsman, M., & Hutchinson, J. (1988). *Family based services: Factors contributing to success and failure in family based child welfare services: Final report.* (OHDS Grant # 90-CW-0732.) Iowa City, IA: The University of Iowa, School of Social Work, National Resource Center on Family-Based Services.

Nelson, K.E., & Landsman, M.J. (1992). *Alternative models of family preservation: Family-based services in context.* Springfield, IL: Charles C Thomas.

Nelson, K.E., Landsman, M.J., & Deutelbaum, W. (1990). Three models of family-centered placement prevention services. *Child Welfare, 69,* 3–21.

Nelson, K.E., Saunders, E., Landsman, M., Sites, E., Hutchinson, J., & McDevitt, S. (1989). *A study of chronically neglecting families in a large metropolitan county.* National Resource Center on Family Based Services. Oakdale, IA: The University of Iowa School of Social Work (mimeograph).

Nelson, K.E., Saunders, E.J., & Landsmen, M.J. (1993). Chronic child neglect in perspective. *Social Work, 38*(6), 661–671.

Nelson, K.M. (1992). Fostering homeless children and their parents too: The emergence of whole-family foster care. *Child Welfare, 71,* 575–584.

Nelson, R.H., Singer, M.J., & Johnsen, L.O. (1973). Community considerations in evaluation of a children's residential treatment center. *Proceedings of the 81st Annual Convention of the American Psychological Association* (pp. 951–952). Washington, DC: APA.

Nelson, R.H., Singer, M.J., & Johnsen, L.O. (1978). The application of a residential treatment model. *Child Care Quarterly, 7,* 164–175.

Nelson, S. (1982). *Incest: Fact and myth.* Edinburgh: Stramullion.

Nelson, S.H., McCoy G.F., Stetter, M., & Vanderwagen, W.C. (1992). An overview of mental-health-services for American Indians and Alaska Natives in the 1990s. *Hospital and Community Psychiatry, 43,* 257–261.

New York City Administration for Children's Services. (1998). *Community data profiles.* New York City: Author.

New York State Department of Social Services. (1986). *Annual report, 1984, statistical supplement.* New York: Author.

Newman, B.M., & Newman, P.R. (1987). *Development through life: A psychosocial approach* (4th ed.). Chicago: The Dorsey Press.

Newman, B.M., & Newman, P.R. (1995). *Development through life: A psychosocial approach* (6th ed.). Pacific Grove, CA: Brooks/Cole.

Nisivoccia, D. (1996). Working with kinship foster families: Principles for practice. *Community Alternatives—International Journal of Family Care, 8,* 1–21.

Nittoli, J. (1999). *Neighborhood transformation and family development: Conceptual overview.* Presentation to a joint planning meeting, Annie E. Casey Foundation and The Casey Family Programs, January 28, 1999, Seattle, Washington (mimeograph), p. 4.

Nixon, J., Pearn, J., Wilkey, I., & Petrie, G. (1981). Social class and violent child death: An analysis of fatal nonaccidental injury, murder, and fatal child neglect. *Child Abuse and Neglect, 5,* 111–116.

Nollan, K.A. (1996). *Self-sufficiency skills among youth in long-term foster care* Doctoral dissertation, University of Washington, Seattle, WA.

North American Council on Post-Legal Adoption Committee. (1984). *Model statement on post-legal adoption services.* St. Paul, MN: Author.

Norton, A.J., & Miller, L.F. (1990). Remarriage among women in the U.S.: 1985. In Bureau of the Census *Studies in household and family formation.* Washington, DC: U.S. Department of Commerce, Bureau of the Census (Current Population Reports), Series P-23, No. 169.

Nuehring, E.M., Abrams, H.A., Fike, D.F., & Ostrowsky, E.F. (1983). Evaluating the impact of prevention programs aimed at children. *Social Work Research & Abstracts, 19*(2), 11–18.

Nunnally, E.W., Chilman, C.S., & Cox, F.M. (1988). Introduction to the Series. In E.W. Nunnally, C.S. Chilman, & F.M. Cox (Eds.), *Troubled relationships—Families in trouble series* (Vol. 3, pp. 7–14). Newbury Park, CA: Sage.

Nunno, M.A., & Motz, J.K. (1988). The development of an effective response to the abuse of children in out-of-home care. *Child Abuse and Neglect, 12*(4), 521–528.

Oates, R.K., & Bross, D.C. (1995). What have we learned about treating child physical abuse? A literature review of the last decade. *Child Abuse and Neglect, 19*(4), 463–473.

Oates, R.K., & Saunders, W.B. (Eds.). (1990). *Understanding and managing child sexual abuse.* Philadelphia, PA: Harcourt, Brace Jovanovich.

O'Brien, M.M. (1996). *Financing strategies to support comprehensive community-based services for children and families.* Portland, ME: National Child Welfare Resource Center for Organizational Improvement.

Office of Early Childhood, Substance Abuse and Mental Health Administration. (1998). SAMHSA handout.

Okun, B.F. (1996). *Understanding diverse families—What practitioners need to know.* New York: Guilford.

Okun, L.E. (1986). *Women abuse: Facts replacing myths.* Albany, NY: State University of New York Press.

Olds, D.L. (1988a). Common design and methodological problems encountered in evaluating family support services: Illustrations from the prenatal/early infancy project. In H.B. Weiss & F.H. Jacobs (Eds.), *Evaluating family programs* (pp. 239–266). Hawthorne, NY: Aldine de Gruyter.

Olds, D.L. (1988b). The prenatal/early infancy project. In R.H. Price, E.L. Cowen, R.P. Lorion, & J. Ramos-McKay (Eds.), *14 ounces of prevention: A casebook for practitioners* (pp. 9–23). Washington, DC: American Psychological Association.

Olds, D.L., & Henderson, C.R., Jr. (1989). The prevention of maltreatment. In D. Cicchetti & V. Carlson (Eds.), *Child maltreatment: Theory and research on the causes and consequences of child abuse and neglect.* New York: Cambridge University Press.

Olds, D.L., Henderson, C.R., Chamberlin, R., & Tatelbaum, R. (1986). Preventing child abuse and neglect: A randomized trial of nurse home visitation. *Pediatrics, 78,* 65–78.

Olds, D.L., Henderson, C.R., Cole, R., Eckenrode, J., Kitzman, H., Luckey, D., Pettitt, L., Sidora, K., Morris, P., & Powers, J. (1998a). Long-term effects of nurse home visitation on children's criminal and antisocial behavior—15-year follow-up of a randomized controlled trial. *JAMA–Journal of the American Medical Association, 280*(14), 1238–1244.

Olds, D.L., Henderson, C.R., & Kitzman, H. (1994). Does prenatal and infancy nurse home visitation have enduring effects on qualities of parental caregiving and child health at 25 to 50 months of life? *Pediatrics, 93*(1), 89–98.

Olds, D., Henderson C., Kitzman H., Eckenrode, J., Cole, R., & Tatelbaum, R. (1998). The promise of home visitation: Results of two randomized trials. *Journal of Community Psychology, 26*(1), 5–21.

Olds, D.L., Henderson, C., Tatelbaum, R., & Chamberlin, R. (1988). Improving the life course development of socially disadvantaged mothers: A randomized trial of nurse home visitation. *American Journal of Public Health, 78,* 1436–1445.

Olds, D.L., & Kitzman, H. (1990). Can home visitation improve the health of women and children at environmental risk? *Pediatrics, 86,* 108–116.

Olds, D.L., & Kitzman, H. (1993). Review of research on home visiting for pregnant women and parents of young children. *The Future of Children—Home Visiting, 3*(3), 53–92.

Olds, D.L., & Kitzman, H. (1995). Review of research on home visiting for pregnant women and parents of young children. *The Future of Children, 5*(3), 51–75.

Olds, D., Pettitt, L.M., Robinson, J., et al. (1998). Reducing risks for antisocial behavior with a program of prenatal and early childhood home visitation. *Journal of Community Psychology, 26*(1), 65–83.

Olsen, L. (1982). Services for minority children in out-of-home care. *Social Service Review, 56,* 572–585.

Olsen, L.J., & Holmes, W.M. (1986). Youth at risk. *Children and Youth Services Review, 8,* 13–35.

Organization for United Response, Inc. (1987). *Brochure.* Minneapolis, MN: Author.

Orlofsky, J., Marcia, J., & Lesser, I. (1973). Ego identity status and the intimacy versus isolation crisis of young adulthood. *Journal of Personality and Social Psychology, 27,* 211–219.

Ornoy, A., Michailevskaya, V., Lukashov, I., Bar-Hamburger, R., & Harel, S. (1994). The developmental outcome of children born to heroin-dependent mothers, raised at home or adopted. *Canadian Medical Association Journal, 151,* 1591–1597.

Orr, L.L., & Bell, S.H. (1987). *Valuing the labor market benefits of job training and employment programs: Procedures and findings from the AFDC homemaker-home health aide demonstrations.* Washington, DC: ABT Associates Inc.

Overton, A. (1953). Serving families who don't want help. *Social Casework, 34,* 304–309.

Paget, K.D., Philp, J.D., et al. (1993). Recent developments in child neglect. *Advances in Clinical Child Psychology, 15,* 121–174.

Paige, R., & Clark, E.A. (1977). *Who cares? Young people in care speak out.* London: National Children's Bureau.

Palmer, M. (1990). *Risk assessment models: A comparative analysis.* Portland, ME: University of Southern Maine, National Child Welfare Resource Center for Management and Administration (mimeograph).

Palmer, S.E. (1995). *Maintaining family ties—Inclusive practice in foster care.* Washington, DC: Child Welfare League of America.

Panel on Research on Child Abuse and Neglect, National Research Council. (1993). *Understanding child abuse and neglect.* Washington, DC: National Academy Press.

Pannor, R., & Baran, A. (1984). Open adoption as standard practice. *Child Welfare, 63,* 245–250.

Pappenfort, D.M., Kilpatrick, D.M., & Roberts, R.W. (Eds.). (1973). *Child care: Social policy and the institution.* Chicago: Aldine de Gruyter.

Pappenfort, D.M., Young, T.M., & Marlow, C.R. (1983). *Residential group care: 1981: 1966 and preliminary report of selected findings from the National Survey of Residential Group Care Facilities.* University of Chicago, School of Social Service Administration.

Parke, R.D., & Collmer, C.W. (1976). Child abuse: An interdisciplinary analysis. In E. M. Hetherington (Ed.), *Review of child development research* (Vol. 5, pp. 509–590). Chicago, IL: University of Chicago Press.

Partridge, S., Hornby, H., & McDonald, T. (1986). *Learning from adoption disruption: Insights for practice.* Portland, ME: University of Southern Maine.

Pasztor, E.M., & Wynne, S.F. (1995). *Foster parent retention and recruitment: The state of the art in practice and policy.* Washington, DC: Child Welfare League of America.

Patti, R. (Ed.). (2000). *Handbook on social welfare administration.* Newbury Park, CA: Sage.

Patti, R.J. (1983). *Social welfare administration: Managing social programs in a developmental context.* Englewood Cliffs, NJ: Prentice-Hall.

Patti, R.J. (1985). In search of purpose for social welfare administration. *Administration in Social Work, 9*(3), 1–14.

Patti, R.J. (1987). Managing for service effectiveness in social welfare organizations. *Social Work, 32*(5), 377–381.

Patti, R.J., Poertner, J., & Rapp, C.A. (Eds.). (1987). *Managing for service effectiveness in social welfare organizations.* New York: Haworth Press.

Pecora, P.J. (1989). Evaluating risk assessment systems—Methodological issues and selected research findings. In *Research issues in risk assessment for child protection* (pp. 47–59). Denver, CO: The American Humane Association.

Pecora, P.J. (1990). Designing and managing family preservation services: Implications for human services administration curricula. In J.K. Whittaker, J.M. Kinney, E. Tracy, & C. Booth (Eds.), *Reaching high risk families: Intensive family preservation services in human services.* Hawthorne, NY: Aldine de Gruyter.

Pecora, P.J. (1991a). Investigating allegations of child maltreatment: The strengths and limitations of current risk assessment systems. *Child and Youth Services, 15*(2), 73–92.

Pecora, P.J. (1991b). Using risk assessment technology and other screening methods for determining the need for child placement in family-based services. In J. Lloyd (Ed.), *Conference proceedings for the Fourth Annual Empowering Families Conference, National Association for Family Based Services* (pp. 119–130). National Association for Family Based Services.

Pecora, P.J. (1995). Assessing the impact of family-based services. In B. Galaway & J. Hudson (Eds.), *Canadian child welfare: Research and policy implication* (pp. 100–112). Toronto, Canada: Thompson Educational Publishing.

Pecora, P.J. (1997). Emerging trends in child welfare and challenges related to outcome measurement. In *American Humane Association, Fifth national roundtable on outcome measures in child welfare services: Summary of proceedings.* Englewood, CO: Author.

Pecora, P.J. (2000). What works in family foster care. In M. Kluger, G. Alexander, & P. Curtis (Eds.), *What works in child welfare.* Washington, DC: CWLA Press.

Pecora, P.J., & Austin, M.J. (1983). Declassification of social service jobs: Issues and strategies. *Social Work, 28*(6), 421–426.

Pecora, P.J., & Austin, M.J. (1987). *Managing human services personnel.* Newbury Park, CA: Sage.

Pecora, P.J., Carlson, I., Reese, S., & Bartholomew, G. (1986–87). Developing and implementing risk assessment systems in child protective services. *Protecting Children, 3*(4), 8–10, 15.

Pecora, P.J., Delewski, C.H., Booth, C., Haapala, D.A., & Kinney, J. (1985). Home-based family-centered services: The impact of training on worker attitudes. *Child Welfare, 64*(5), 529–540.

Pecora, P.J., Dodson, A.R., Teather, E.C., & Whittaker, J.K. (1983). Assessing worker training needs: Use of staff surveys and key informant interviews. *Child Welfare, LXII*(5), 395–407.

Pecora, P.J., Downs, A.C., Kessler, R., Pennell, S., Heeringa, S., & English, D. (1999). *Foster care as a protective factor for maltreated youth.* Research proposal submitted to the National Institute of Mental Health. Seattle, WA: The Casey Family Programs and the School of Social Work, University of Washington.

Pecora, P.J., & English, D.J. (Eds.). (1994). *Multi-cultural guidelines for assessing family strengths and risk factors in child protective services.* Seattle, WA: School of Social Work, University of Washington and Washington State Department of Social Services.

Pecora, P.J., Fraser, M., Nelson, K., McCroskey, J., & Meezan, W. (1995). *Evaluating family-based services.* Hawthorne, NY: Aldine de Gruyter.

Pecora, P.J., Fraser, M.W., & Haapala, D.H. (1991). Intensive, home-based family preservation services: Client outcomes and issues for program design. In K. Wells & D.E. Biegel (Eds.), *Family preservation services: Research and evaluation* (pp. 3–32). Newbury Park, CA: Sage.

Pecora, P.J., Fraser, M.W., Haapala, D.A., & Bartlome, J.A. (1987). *Defining family preservation services: Three intensive home-based treatment programs.* Salt Lake City, UT: University of Utah, Graduate School of Social Work, Social Research Institute.

Pecora, P.J., Haapala, D.A., & Fraser, M.W. (1991).Comparing intensive family preservation services with other family-based service programs. In E.M. Tracy, D.A. Haapala, J.M. Kinney, & P.J. Pecora (Eds.), *Intensive family preservation services: An instructional sourcebook* (pp. 117–142). Cleveland, OH: Mandel School of Applied Social Sciences, Case Western Reserve University.

Pecora, P.J., & Hunter J. (1988). Performance appraisal in child welfare: Comparing the MBO and BARS methods. *Administration in Social Work, 12*(1), 55–72.

Pecora, P.J., & Hunter, J. (1988). Performance appraisal in child welfare: Comparing the MBO and BARS methods. *Administration in Social Work, 12*(1), 55–71.

Pecora, P.J., Kinney, J.M., Mitchell, L., & Tolley, G. (1988). *Providing intensive home-based family preservation services through public and private agencies: Organizational and service delivery issues.* Research Report No. 2 from the Family-Based Intensive Treatment Project. Salt Lake City, UT: University of Utah, Graduate School of Social Work, Social Research Institute.

Pecora, P.J., Kinney, J.M., Mitchell, L., & Tolley, G. (1990). Agency auspice and the provision of family preservation services. *Social Service Review, 64,* 288–307.

Pecora, P.J., and Maluccio A.N. (2000). What works in family foster care. In M. Kluger, G. Alexander, & P. Curtis (Eds.), *What works in child welfare.* Washington, DC: CWLA Press.

Pecora, P.J., & Martin, M.B. (1989). Risk factors associated with child sexual abuse: A selected summary of empirical research. In P. Schene & K. Bond (Eds.), *Research issues in risk assessment for child protection.* Denver, CO: The American Humane Association.

Pecora, P.J., & Nollan, K. (1998). *One example of a policy analysis framework.* Seattle, WA: University of Washington, School of Social Work (mimeograph).

Pecora, P.J., Schinke, S.P., & Whittaker, J.K. (1983). Needs assessment for staff training. *Administration in Social Work, 7*(3/4), 101–113.

Pecora, P.J., Seelig, W.R., Zirps, F.A., & Davis, S.M. (1996). *Quality improvement and evaluation in child and family services—Managing into the next century.* Washington, DC: CWLA Press.

Pecora, P.J., & Wagner, M. (2000). Managing personnel. In R. Patti (Ed.), *Handbook on social welfare administration.* Newbury Park, CA: Sage.

Pecora, P.J., Whittaker, J.K., & Maluccio, A.N. (1992). *The child welfare challenge: Policy, practice, and research.* Hawthorne, NY: Aldine de Gruyter.

Pelton, L. (1978). Child abuse and neglect: The myth of classlessness. *American Journal of Orthopsychiatry, 48*(4), 608–616.

Pelton, L.H. (1989). *For reasons of poverty: A critical analysis of the public child welfare system in the U.S.* New York: Praeger.

Pelton, L.H. (1991). Beyond permanency planning: Restructuring the public child welfare system. *Social Work, 36*(4), 337–343.

Pelton, L.H. (1994). The role of material factors in child abuse and neglect. In G.B. Melton & F.D. Barry (Eds.), *Protecting children from abuse and neglect—Foundations for a new national strategy* (pp. 131–181). New York: Guilford.

Pennell, J., & Buzford, G. (2000). Family group decision making: Protecting childen and women. *Child Welfare, 79*(2), 131–138.

Peters, T.J., & Waterman, R.H. (1983). *In search of excellence: Lessons from America's best run companies.* New York: Harper & Row.

Peterson, J.L., Kohrt, P.E., Shadoin, L.M., & Authier, K.J. (1995) *Building skills in high-risk families: Strategies for the home-based practitioner.* Boys Town, NB: The Boys Town Press.

Peterson, P., & Rom, M. (1990). *Welfare magnets: A new case for a national standard.* Washington, DC: The Brookings Institution.

Petr, C., Allen, R., & The Beach Center on Families and Disability. (1995). *Family-centered behavior scale and user's manual.* Lawrence, KS: University of Kansas, The Beach Center on Families and Disability.

Pfeiffer, S.I. (1989). Follow-up of children and adolescents treated in psychiatric facilities: A methodology review. *The Psychiatric Hospital, 20*(1), 15–20.

Pfeiffer, S.I. (1993). *Training professionals in interagency collaboration skills.* Research project funded by the U.S. Department of Education. Washington, DC: OSERS.

Pfeiffer, S.I., & Baker, B.L. (1994). Psychiatric disorders in mentally retarded children and adolescents: Diagnostic and treatment issues. In J. Blacher (Ed.), *When there's no place like home.* Baltimore: Paul H. Brookes.

Pfeiffer, S.I., Burd, S., & Wright, A. (1992). Clinicians and research: Recurring obstacles and some possible solutions. *Journal of Clinical Psychology, 48*(1), 140–145.

Pfeiffer, S.I., & Strzelecki, S.C. (1990). Inpatient psychiatric treatment of children and adolescents: A review of outcome studies. *Journal of the American Academy of Child & Adolescent Psychiatry, 29*, 847–853.

Phillips, E.L., Phillips, E.A., Fixsen, D.L., & Wolf, M.M. (1974). *The teaching family handbook.* Lawrence, KS: Bureau of Child Research, University of Kansas.

Phillips, M.H., Shyne, A.W., & Haring, B.L. (1971). *Factors associated with placement decisions in child welfare.* New York: Child Welfare League of America.

Phillips, S.D., & Harm, N.J. (1997). Women prisoners: A contextual framework. *Women & Therapy, 20*(4), 1–9.

Piaget, J. (1960). *The child's conception of the world.* Totowa, NJ: Littlefield, Adams.

Piaget, J., & Inhelder, B. (1969). *The psychology of the child.* New York: Basic Books.

Piasecki, J.M., Manson, S.M., Biernoff, M.P., Hiat, A.B., Taylor, S.S., & Bechtold, D.W. (1989). Abuse and neglect of American Indian children: Findings from a survey of federal providers. *American Indian and Alaska Native Mental Health Research, 3*(2), 43–62.

Pierce, L., & Geremia, V. (1999). Family reunion services: An examination of a process used to successfully reunite families. *Family Preservation Journal, 4*(1), 13–30.

Pike, V. (1976). Permanent families for foster children: The Oregon Project. *Children Today, 5*, 22–25.

Pike, V., Downs, S., Emlen, A., Downs, G., & Case, D. (1977). *Permanent planning for children in foster care: A handbook for social workers.* Washington, DC: U.S. Department of Health, Education and Welfare, Publication No. (OHDS) 78-30124.

Piliavin, I. (1963). Conflict between cottage parents and caseworkers. *Social Service Review, 37*, 17–25.

Piliavin, I., Sosin, M., & Westerfelt, H. (1987). *Conditions contributing to long-term homelessness: An exploratory study.* IRP Discussion Paper No. 853-887. Madison, WI: Institute for Research on Poverty, University of Wisconsin.

Piliavin, I., Wright, B.R.E., Mare, R.D., & Westerfelt, A.H. (1996). Exits from and returns to homelessness. *Social Service Review, 70*, 33–57.

Pilowsky, D.J. (1995). Psychopathology among children placed in family foster care. *Pediatrics, 46,* 906–910.

Pinderhughes, E. (1989). *Understanding race, ethnicity, and power: The key to efficacy in clinical practice.* New York: Free Press.

Pinderhughes, E. (1995). Empowering diverse populations: Family practice in the 21st century. *Families in Society: The Journal of Contemporary Human Services, 76,* 131–140.

Pinderhughes, E. (1997). Developing diversity competence in child welfare and permanency planning. In G.R. Anderson, A.S. Ryan, & B.R. Leashore (Eds.), *The challenge of permanency planning in a multicultural society* (pp. 19–38). New York: Haworth Press.

Pinderhughes, E.E. (1991). The delivery of child welfare services to African American clients. *American Journal of Orthopsychiatry, 61*(4), 599–605.

Pine, B.A. (1986). Child welfare reform and the political process. *Social Service Review, 60*(3), 339–359.

Pine, B.A., Warsh, R., & Maluccio, A.N. (1993). Training for competence in family reunification practice. In B.A. Pine, R. Warsh, & A.N. Maluccio (Eds.), *Together again: Family reunification in foster care* (pp. 35–50). Washington, DC: Child Welfare League of America.

Pine, B.A., Warsh, R., & Maluccio, A.N. (Eds.). (1993). *Together again: Family reunification in foster care.* Washington, DC: Child Welfare League of America.

Pine, B.A., Warsh, R., & Maluccio, A.N. (1998). Participatory management in a public child welfare agency. *Administration in Social Work, 22,* 19–32.

Pinkerton, J. (1994). *In care at home—Parenting, the state and civil society.* Aldershot, England: Avebury.

Plantz, M.C., Hubbell, R., Barrett, B.J., & Dobrec, A. (1989). Indian Child Welfare Act: A status report. *Children Today, 18,* 24–29.

Plomin, R., DeFries, J.C., & Loehlin, J.C. (1977). Genotype-environment interaction and correlation in the analysis of human behavior. *Psychological Bulletin, 84,* 309–322.

Poertner, J., Bussey, M., & Fluke, J. (1999). How safe are out-of-home placements? *Children and Youth Services Review, 21*(7), 549–563.

Polansky, N.A. (1979). Help for the help-less. *Smith College Studies in Social Work, 439,* 169–191.

Polansky, N.A., Ammons, P.W., & Gaudin, J.M. (1985). Loneliness and isolation in child neglect. *Social Casework: The Journal of Contemporary Social Work, 66*(1), 38–47.

Polansky, N.A., Ammons, P.W., & Weathersby, B.L. (1983). Is there an American standard of child care? *Social Work, 28*(5), 341–346.

Polansky, N.A., Chalmers, M.A., Buttenweiser, E., & Williams, D.P. (1979). The absent father in child neglect. *The Social Service Review, 53*(2), 163–174.

Polansky, N.A., Chalmers, M.A., Buttenweiser, E., & Williams, D.P. (1981). *Damaged parents: An anatomy of child neglect.* Chicago: University of Chicago Press.

Polansky, N.A., & Gaudin, J.M. (1983a). Social distancing of the neglectful family. *Social Service Review, 57*(2), 196–208.

Polansky, N.A., & Gaudin, J.M. (1983b). *Preventing child abuse through public awareness activities* (Working Paper No. 19). Chicago: National Committee for Prevention of Child Abuse.

Polansky, N.A., Gaudin, J.M., Ammons, P.W., & Davis, K.B. (1985). The psychological ecology of the neglectful mother. *Child Abuse and Neglect, 9,* 265–275.

Polansky, N.A., Gaudin, J.M., Jr., & Kilpatrick, A.C. (1992). Family radicals. *Children and Youth Services Review, 14,* 19–26.

Polansky, N.A., Hall C., & Polansky, N.F. (1975). *Profile of neglect.* Washington, DC: Public Services Administration, Department of H.E.W.

Polsky, H. (1962). *Cottage six: The social systems of delinquent boys in residential treatment.* New York: Russell Sage Foundation.

Polsky, H., Claster, D.S., & Goldberg, C. (1968). *The dynamics of residential treatment: A social systems analysis.* Chapel Hill: University of North Carolina Press.

Population Reference Bureau, Inc. (1990). *America in the 21st century: Social and economic support systems.* Washington, DC: Author.

Post-Adoption Center for Education and Research. (1986). *Newsletter.* Walnut Creek, CA: Author.

Potter, C.C. (1998). Intensive family preservation in children's mental health: Predictors of placement. *Family Preservation Journal, 3*(2), 21–44.

Powell, D. (1994). Evaluating family support programs: Are we making progress? In S. Kagan & B. Weissbourd (Eds.), *Putting families first: America's family support movement and the challenge of change* (pp. 441–469). San Francisco, CA: Jossey-Bass.

Price, R.H., Ketterer, R.F., Bader, B.C., & Monahan, J. (Eds.). (1980). *Prevention in mental health: Research, policy, and practice.* Beverly Hills, CA: Sage

Primus, W., Rawlings, L., Larin, K., & Porter, K. (1999). *The initial impacts of welfare reform on the economic well-being of single-mother families.* Washington, DC: Center on Policy and Budget Priorities, August.

Proceedings of the International Conference on Psychological Abuse of Children and Youth. (1983). Indianapolis: Office for the Study of the Psychological Rights of the Child, Indiana University.

Proch, K., & Hess, P.M. (1987). Parent-child visiting policies of voluntary agencies. *Children and Youth Services Review, 9,* 17–28.

Prosser, H. (1976). *Perspective and residential child care: An annotated bibliography.* Atlantic Highlands, NJ: Humanities Press.

Prue, D., & Fairbank, J. (1980). Performance feedback in organizational behavior management: A review. *Journal of Organizational Behavior Management, 3,* 1–16.

Putnam, F.W. (1989). *Diagnosis and treatment of multiple personality disorder.* New York: Guilford.

Quinton, D., & Rutter, M. (1984). Parents with children in care: Intergenerational continuities. *Journal of Child Psychology and Psychiatry, 25,* 21–250.

Rae-Grant, N., Thomas, B.H., Offord, D.R., & Boyle, M.H. (1989). Risk, protective factors, and the prevalence of behavioral and emotional disorders in children and adolescents. *Journal of the American Academy of Child and Adolescent Psychiatry, 28*(2), 262–268

Rainwater, L., & Smeeding, T. (1995). *Doing poorly: The real income of American children in a comparative perspective.* LIS Working paper 127. Maxwell School of Citizenship and Public Affairs, Syracuse University.

Rapp, C.A. (1982). Effect of the availability of family support services on decisions about child placement. *Social Work Research and Abstracts, 18*(1), 21–27.

Rapp, C.A. (1998). *The strengths model—Case management with people suffering from severe and persistent mental illness.* New York: Oxford University Press.

Rapp, C.A., & Poertner, J. (1988). Moving clients center stage through the use of client outcomes. In R.J. Patti, J. Poertner, & C.A. Rapp (Eds.), *Managing for service effectiveness in social welfare organizations* (pp. 23–38). [A special issue of Administration in Social Work, *11*(3–4).] New York: Haworth Press.

Ray, J., & Dietzel, M. (1984). *Teaching child sexual abuse prevention.* Unpublished manuscript available from authors at Rape Crisis Network, N. 1226 Howard St., Spokane, WA 98201.

Rector, F. (1998). *Balancing risk and resiliency in neglecting families: A review of the literature.* Seattle: University of Washington, School of Social Work (mimeograph).

Reddy, A., & Pfeiffer, S.I. (1997). Effectiveness of treatment foster care with children and adolescents: A review of outcome studies. *Journal of the American Academy of Child and Adolescent Psychiatry, 36*(5), 581–588.

Redl, F., & Wineman, D. (1957). *The aggressive child.* New York: Free Press.

Reeder, R.R. (1925). Our orphaned asylums. *Survey, 54,* 283–287.

Reid, J., Taplin, P., & Lorber, R. (1981). A social interactional approach to the treatment of abusive families. In R.A. Stuart (Ed.), *Violent behavior: Social learning approaches to prediction, management, and treatment* (pp. 83–101). New York: Brunner/Mazel.

Reid, W.J., & Hanrahan, P. (1982). Recent evaluations of social work: Grounds for optimism. *Social Work, 27,* 328–340.

Reid, W.J., Kagan, R.M., & Schlosberg, S.B. (1988). Prevention of placement: Critical factors in program success. *Child Welfare, 67*(1), 25–36.

Reidinger, P. (1988). Why did no one protect this child? *ABA Journal,* December, 49–51.

Reppucci, N.D., & Haugaard, J.J. (1989). Prevention of child sexual abuse. *American Psychologist, 44*(10), 1266–1275.

Resnick, P.J. (1969). Child murder by parents. *American Journal of Psychiatry, 126*(3), 375–384.

Reynolds, A.J. (1993). One year of preschool intervention or two: Does it matter? *Early Childhood Research Quarterly, 10,* 1–31.

Reynolds, A.J. (1998). Developing early childhood programs for children and families at Risk: Research-based principles to promote long-term effectiveness. *Children and Youth Services Review, 20,*(6), 504–505.

Reynolds, A.J., & Bezruczko, N. (1993). School adjustment of children at risk through fourth grade. *Merrill-Palmer Quarterly, 39,* 457–480.

Reynolds, A.J., Maurogenes, N.A., Bezruczko, N., & Hagemann, M. (1996). Cognitive and family support mediators of preschool effectiveness: A confirmatory analysis. *Child Development, 28,* 392–422.

Rhodes, S.L. (1977). A developmental approach to the life cycle of the family. *Social Casework, 58,* 301–311.

Rhodes, W.A., & Brown, W.K. (1991). *Why some children succeed despite the odds.* New York: Praeger.

Rhodes, W.C. (1967). The disturbing child: A problem of ecological management. *Exceptional Children, 33,* 449–455.

Richan, W.C. (1978). Personnel issues in child welfare. In U.S. Department of Health and Human Services, *Child welfare strategy in the coming years* (pp. 227–281).Washington, DC: U.S. Children's Bureau [DHEW Publication No. (OHDS) 78–30158].

Ricketts, W. (1991). *Lesbian and gay men as foster parents.* Portland, ME: University of Southern Maine, National Child Welfare Resource Center for Management and Administration.

Ricketts, W., & Achtenberg, R.A. (1990). Adoption and foster parenting for lesbian and gay men: Creating new traditions in family. *Marriage and Family Review, 14,* 83–118.

Rindfleisch, N., Bean, G., & Denby, R. (1998). Why foster parents continue and cease to foster. *Journal of Sociology and Social Welfare, 25,* 5–24.

Rindfleisch, N., & Rabb, J. (1984). How much of a problem is resident mistreatment in child welfare institutions? *Child Abuse and Neglect, 8*(1), 36–38.

Rinsley, D.B. (1980). Principles of therapeutic milieu with children. In P. Sholevar, R. Benson, & B. Binder (Eds.), *Emotional disorders in children and adolescents* (pp. 191–208). New York: Spectrum.

Risley, J.R., & Wolf, M.M. (1966). Experimental manipulation of autistic behaviors and generalization into the home. In R. Ulrich, J. Stachnik, & J. Mabry (Eds.), *Control of human behavior* (Vol. 1, pp. 193–198). Glenview, IL: Scott, Foresman.

Rispens, J., Aleman, A., & Goudena, P.P. (1997). Prevention of child sexual abuse victimization: A meta-analysis of school programs. *Child Abuse and Neglect, 21(*10), 975–987.

Rittner, B., & Wodarski, J. (1999). Differential uses for BSW and MSW educated social workers in child welfare services. *Children and Youth Services Review, 21*(3), 217–238.

Rivara, F.P., & Grossman, D.C. (1996). Prevention of traumatic deaths to children in the United States: How far have we come and where do we need to go? *Pediatrics, 97*(6), 791–797.

Robin, M.H. (Ed.). (1991). *The problem of false allegations.* New York: Haworth Press.

Roditti, M.G. (1995). Child day care: A key building block of family support and family preservation programs. *Child Welfare, LXXIV*(6), 1043–1068.

Rodwell, M.K. (1988). *Policy implications of the multiple meaning of neglect: A naturalistic study of child neglect.* Doctoral dissertation, University of Kansas, School of Social Work, Lawrence.

Rodwell, M.K., & Chambers, D.E. (1989). Promises, promises: Child abuse prevention in the 1980s. *Policy Studies Review, 8*(4), 749–773.

Roff, J.D. (1992). Childhood aggression, peer status, and social class as predictors of delinquency. *Psychological Reports, 70,* 31–34.

Rogers, C.M., & Terry, T. (1984). Clinical intervention with boy victims of sexual abuse. In I.R. Stuart & J.G. Greere (Eds.), *Victims of sexual aggression: Treatment of children, women, and men.* New York: Van Nostrand Reinhold.

Roman, N.P., & Wolfe, P.B. (1997). The relationship between foster care and homelessness. *Public Welfare, 55,* 4–9.

Rome, S.H. (1997). The child welfare choice: An analysis of social work students career plans. *Journal of Baccalaureate Social Work, 3*(1), 31–48.

Rose, S.J. (1999) Reaching consensus on child neglect: African American mothers and child welfare workers. *Child and Youth Services Review, 2*(6), 464–479.

Rosenbaum, J., & Popkin, S. (1991). Employment and earnings of low-income blacks who move to middle-class suburbs. In C. Jencks & P. Peterson (Eds.), *The urban underclass.* Washington, DC: The Brookings Institution.

Rosenberg, M.S. (1983). The techniques of psychological assessment as applied to children in foster care and their families. In M. Hardin (Ed.) *Foster children in the courts* (pp. 550–574). Boston: Butterworth Legal Publishers.

Rosenberg, M.S. (1987). New directions for research on the psychological maltreatment of children. *American Psychologist, 42*(2), 166–171.

Rosenberg, S.A., McTate, G.A., & Robinson, C.C. (1982). *Intensive services to families-at-risk project.* Omaha, NE: Nebraska Department of Public Welfare.

Ross, C.A., Miller, S., Reagor, P., Bjornson, L., Fraser, G.A., & Anderson, G. (1990). Structured interview data on 102 cases of multiple personality disorder from four centers. *Journal of Psychiatry, 147,* 596–601.

Ross, S. (1996). *Helping battered women: New perspectives and remedies.* New York: Oxford University Press.

Rossi, P.H. (1992a). Assessing family preservation programs. *Children and Youth Services Review, 14*(1/2), 77–97.

Rossi, P.H. (1992b). Some critical comments on current evaluations of programs for the amelioration of persistent poverty. *Focus, 14*(1), 22-24. University of Wisconsin-Madison: Institute for Research on Poverty.

Rossi, P.H. (1992c). Strategies for evaluation. *Children and Youth Services Review, 14*(1/2), 167–191.

Rothman, D.J. (1980). *Conscience and convenience: The asylum and its alternatives in progressive America.* Boston: Little-Brown.

Rothman, J. (1980). *Social R & D: Research and development in the human services.* New York: Columbia University Press.

Rothman, J., & Thomas, E.C. (1994). *Intervention research: Design and development for human services.* New York: Haworth Press.

Roundy, L.M., & Horton, A.L. (1990). Professional and treatment issues for clinicians who intervene with incest perpetrators. In A.L. Horton, B.L. Johnson, L.M. Roudy, & D. Williams (Eds.), *The incest perpetrator: A family member no one wants to treat.* Newbury Park, CA: Sage.

Rowe, J., Cain, H., Hundleby, M., & Keane, A. (1984). *Long-term foster care.* London: B.T. Batsford.

Rubenstein, J.S., Armentrout, J.A., Levin, S., & Herald, D. (1978). The parent therapist program: Alternative care for emotionally disturbed children. *American Journal of Orthopsychiatry, 48,* 654–662.

Rubin, A. (1985). Practice effectiveness: More grounds for optimism. *Social Work, 30,* 469–476.

Ruess, C. (1916). Personal correspondence to W.H. Slingerland, October 1911. Quoted in W.H. Slingerland, *Child welfare work in California.* New York: Russell Sage Foundation.

Ruggles, P. (1990). *Drawing the line: Alternative poverty measures and their implications for public policy.* Washington, DC: The Urban Institute Press.

Runtz, M. (1987). *The psychosocial adjustment of women who were sexually and physically abused during childhood and early adulthood: A focus on revictimization.* Unpublished master's thesis, University of Manitoba, Canada.

Rush, F. (1980). *The best kept secret.* New York: McGraw-Hill.

Russell, D.E. (1983). The incidence and prevalence of intrafamilial and extrafamilial sexual abuse of female children. *Child Abuse and Neglect, 7,* 133–146.

Russell, D.E.H. (1984). *Sexual exploitation: Rape, child sexual abuse, and workplace harassment.* Beverly Hills, CA: Sage.

Russell, M. (1987). *1987 national study of public child welfare job requirements.* Portland, ME: University of Southern Maine, National Child Welfare Resource Center for Management and Administration.

Russo, R.J. (1999). Applying a strengths-based approach in working with people with developmental disabilities and their families. *Families in Society: The Journal of Contemporary Human Services, 80,* 25–33.

Rutter, M. (1981a). Stress, coping and development: Some issues and some questions. *Journal of Child Psychology and Psychiatry, 22*(4), 323–356.

Rutter, M. (1981b). Maternal deprivation reassessed. *Child Development,* 179–197.

Rutter, M. (1985). Resilience in the face of adversity: Protective factors and resistance to psychiatric disorder. *British Journal of Psychiatry, 147,* 598–611.

Rutter, M. (1987). Psychosocial resilience and protective mechanisms. *American Journal of Orthopsychiatry, 57*(3), 316–331.

Rutter, M. (1989a). Intergenerational continuities and discontinuities in serious parenting difficulties. In D. Cicchetti & V. Carlson (Eds.), *Child maltreatment: Theory and research on the causes and consequences of child abuse and neglect* (pp. 317–348). Cambridge, England: Cambridge University Press.

Rutter, M. (1989b). Pathways from childhood to adult life. *Journal of Child Psychiatry, 30*(1), 23–51.

Rutter, M. (1990). Psychosocial resilience and protective mechanisms. In J. Rolf (Ed.), *Risk and protective factors in the development of psychopathology.* New York: Cambridge University Press.

Rutter, M., Cox, A., Tupling, C., Berger, M., & Yule, W. (1975). Attainment and adjustment in two geographical areas: I. The prevalence of psychiatric disorders. *British Journal of Psychiatry, 126,* 493–509.

Ryan, A.S. (1997). Lessons learned from programs for unaccompanied refugee minors. In G.R. Anderson, A.S. Ryan, & B.R. Leashore (Eds.), *The challenge of permanency planning in a multicultural society* (pp. 195–205). New York: Haworth Press.

Ryan, C.G., & Futterman, D. (1998). *Lesbian and gay youth—Care and counseling.* New York: Columbia University Press.

Ryan, P., McFadden, E.J., & Warren, B.L. (1981). Foster families: A resource for helping parents. In A.N. Maluccio & P.A. Sinanoglu (Eds.), *The challenge of partnership: Working with parents of children in foster care* (pp. 189–199). New York: Child Welfare League of America.

Ryan, P., McFadden, E., & Wiencek, P. (1987). *Analyzing abuse in family foster care.* Final report to the National Center on Child Abuse and Neglect on Grant #90CA097.

Rycraft, J. (1994). The party isn't over: The Agency role in the retention of child welfare workers. *Social Work, 39*(1), 75–80.

Rykus, J.R., & Hughes, R.C. (1998). *Field guide to child welfare* (Vols. I–IV). Washington, DC: Child Welfare League of America Press and Columbus, OH: Institute for Human Services.

Rykus, J.R., & Hughes, R.C. (1998). *Field guide to child welfare* (Vol. IV): *Placement and permanence.* Washington, DC: CWLA Press and Columbus, OH: Institute for Human Services.

Rzepnicki, T.L. (1987). Recidivism of foster children returned to their own homes: A review and new directions for research. *Social Service Review, 61*(1), 56–70.

Rzepnicki, T.L., Schuerman, J.R., & Johnson, P.R. (1997). Facing uncertainty: Reuniting high-risk families. In J.D. Berrick, R.P. Barth, & N. Gilbert (Eds.), *Child welfare research review* (Vol. II, pp. 229–251). New York: Columbia University Press.

Rzepnicki, T.L., Schuerman, J.R., Littell, J.H., Chak, A., & Lopez, M. (1994). An experimental study of family preservation services: Early findings from a parent study. In R.Barth, J. Duerr-Berrick, & N. Gilbert (Eds.), *Child welfare research review* (Vol. 1, pp. 60–82). New York: Columbia University Press.

Saleebey, D. (1992). The strengths perspective in social work practice: Extensions and cautions. *Social Work, 41,* 296–305.

Saleebey, D. (Ed.). (1997). *The strengths perspective in social work practice* (2nd ed.). New York: Longman.

Salzinger, S., Kaplan, S., & Artemyeff, C. (1983). Mothers' personal social networks and child maltreatment. *Journal of Abnormal Psychology, 92*(1), 68–76

Sanchirico, A., Lau, W.J., Jablonka, K., & Russell, S.J. (1998). Foster parent involvement in service planning: Does it increase job satisfaction? *Children and Youth Services Review, 20,* 325–346.

Sandefur, G.D., & Liebler, C.A. (1997). The demography of American Indian families. *Population Research and Policy Review, 16,* 95–114.

Sander, G.D., & Liebler, C.A. (1997). The demography of American Indian families. *Population Research and Policy Review, 16,* 95–114.

Sanders, B., & Becker-Larsen, E. (1995). The measurement of psychological maltreatment: Early data on the child abuse and trauma scale. *Child Abuse and Neglect, 19*(3), 315–323.

Sanders, B., & Giola, M.H. (1991). Dissociation and childhood trauma in psychologically disturbed adolescents. *American Journal of Psychiatry, 148,* 50–54.

Sanford, L.T. (1980). *The silent children.* New York: Doubleday.

Sapiro, V. (1990). The gender basis of American social policy. In L. Gordon (Ed.), *Women, the state, and welfare* (pp. 36–55). Madison, WI: The University of Wisconsin Press.

Saslawsky, D.A., & Wurtele, S.K. (1986). Educating children about sexual abuse: Implications for pediatric intervention and possible prevention. *Journal of Pediatric Psychology, 11,* 235–245.

Savin-Williams, R.C. (1995). Lesbian, gay male, and bisexual adolescents. In A.R. D'augelli & G.J. Patterson (Eds.), *Lesbian, gay and bisexual identities over the life span: Psychological perspectives* (pp. 165–189). New York: Oxford University Press.

Sawhill, I. (1988). Poverty and the underclass. In I. Sawhill (Ed.), *Challenge to leadership* (pp. 215–252). Washington, DC: The Urban Institute Press.

Saywitz, K., & Camparo, L. (1998). Interviewing child witnesses: A developing perspective. *Child Abuse and Neglect, 22(8),* 825–843.

Scalzo, J.O. (1991). *Beyond survival: Keys to resilience among women who experienced childhood sexual abuse.* Unpublished doctoral dissertation, Simon Fraser University, Burnaby, British Columbia.

Scanlon, J.W., Horst, P., Nay, J.N., Schmidt, R.E., & Waller, J.D. (1977). Evaluability assessment: Avoiding type III and IV errors. In G.R. Gilbert & P.J. Conklin (Eds.), *Evaluation management: A source book of readings.* Charlottesville: U.S. Civil Service Commission.

Scannapieco, M. (1994). Home-based services program: Effectiveness with at risk families. *Children and Youth Services Review, 16,* 363–377.

Scannapieco, M., & Hegar, R.L. (1999). Kinship foster care in context. In R.L. Hegar & M. Scannapieco (Eds.), *Kinship foster care—Policy, practice, and research* (pp. 1–13). New York: Oxford University Press.

Schaaf, K.K., & McCanne, T.R. (1998). Relationship of childhood sexual, physical, and combined sexual and physical abuse to adult victimization and posttraumatic stress disorder. *Child Abuse and Neglect, 22*(11), 1119–1133.

Schecter, S., & Edleson, J.L. (1994). *In the best interest of women and children: A call for collaboration between child welfare and domestic violence constituencies.* Briefing paper prepared for the conference, Domestic Violence and Child Welfare: Integrating Policy and Practice for Families (June 8–10, 1994), Wingspread Racine, Wisconsin.

Schecter, S., & Edleson, J.L. (1995). In the best interest of women and children: A call for collaboration between child welfare and domestic violence constituencies. *Protecting Children [American Humane Association], 11*(3), 6–11.

Schene, P. (1987). Is child abuse decreasing? *Journal of Interpersonal Violence, 2*(2), 225–227.

Schene , P., & Bond, K. (1989). *Research issues in risk assessment for child protection.* Denver, CO: American Association for Protecting Children.

Schene, P.A. (1998). Past, present and future roles of child protective services. *The Future of Children, 8*(1), 23–38.

Scheper-Hughes, N. (1987). The cultural politics of child survival. In N. Scheper-Hughes (Ed.), *Child survival: Anthropological perspectives on the treatment and maltreatment of children* (pp. 1–29). Boston: D. Reidel.

Scheper-Hughes, N., & Stein, H.F. (1987). Child abuse and the unconscious in American popular culture. In N. Scheper-Hughes (Ed.), *Child survival* (pp. 339–358). Boston: D. Reidel.

Schinke, S.P. (1981). Ethics. In R.M. Grinnell (Ed.), *Social work research and evaluation.* Itasca, IL: F.E. Peacock.

Schiraldi, V., & Soler, M. (1998). The will of the people? The public's opinion of the Violent and Repeat Juvenile Offender Act of 1997. *Crime & Delinquency, 44,* 590–601.

Schlosberg, S.B., & Kagan, R.M. (1988). Practice strategies for engaging chronic multiproblem families. *Social Casework, 69,* 3–9.

Schneider, D. (1976). The meaning of incest. *Journal of Polynesian Society, 85*(2), 149–169.

Schneiderman, M., Connors, M.M., Fribourg, L.G., & Gonzalez, M. (1998). Mental health services for children in out-of-home care. *Child Welfare, 77,* 5–27.

Schoech, D., & Schkade, L. (1980). Computers helping caseworkers: Decisions support systems. *Child Welfare, 59,* 566–575.

Schor, E.L. (1982). The foster care system and health status of foster children. *Pediatrics, 69,* 521–528.

Schorr, L.B. (1988). *Within our reach: Breaking the cycle of disadvantage.* New York: Doubleday.

Schorr, L.B. (1997). *Common purpose: Strengthening families and neighborhoods to rebuild America* (1st Anchor ed.). New York: Anchor.

Schorr, L., & Schorr, D. (1988). *Within our reach: Breaking the cycle of disadvantage.* New York: Anchor.

Schriver, J.M. (1995). *Human behavior and the social environment—Shifting paradigms in essential knowledge for social work practice.* Boston: Allyn & Bacon.

Schuerman, J.R., (1987). *Discussion paper: Social work research and abstracts* (pp. 14–18). Chicago, IL: Chapin Hall Center for Children, the University of Chicago.

Schuerman, J.R. (1997) *Discussion paper: Best interests and family preservation in America.* Chicago, IL: Chapin Hall Center for Children, the University of Chicago.

Schuerman, J.R., Rzepnicki, T.L., & Littell, J.H. (1991). From Chicago to Little Egypt: Lessons from an evaluation of a family preservation program. In K. Wells & D.E. Biegel (Eds.), *Family preservation services: Research and evaluation* (pp. 187–206). Newbury Park, CA: Sage.

Schuerman, J.R., Rzepnicki, T.L., & Littell, J.H. (1994*). Putting families first: An experiment in family preservation.* Hawthorne, NY: Aldine de Gruyter.

Schuerman, J.R., Rzepnicki, T.L., Littell, J.H., & Chak, A. (1993). *Evaluation of the Illinois Family First placement prevention program: Final report* (pp. 104-118). Chicago, IL: Chapin Hall Center for Children, the University of Chicago.

Schuerman, J.R., Stagner, M., Johnson, P., & Mullen, E. (1989). *Discussion Paper: Child abuse and neglect decision-making in Cook County.* Chicago, IL: Chapin Hall Center for Children, the University of Chicago.

Schulberg, H.C., & Baker, F. (1968). Program evaluation models and the implementation of research findings. *American Journal of Public Health, 58*(7), 1248–1255.

Schultz, K.G. (1988). *One hundred cases of wrongfully charged child sexual abuse: A survey and recommendations.* Unpublished manuscript, West Virginia University, School of Social Work, Morgantown.

Schwartz, I., Ortega, R., Guo, S., & Fishman, G. (1994). Infants in nonpermanent placement. *Social Service Review, 68,* 405–416.

Schwartz, I.M. (1984). Getting tough with juveniles. *Public Welfare, 42,* 28–31.

Schwartz, I. M. (1989). *Justice for juveniles.* Lexington, MA: Lexington Books.

Schwartz, I.M., & AuClaire, P. (1995). *Home-based services for troubled children.* Lincoln, NE: University of Nebraska Press.

Schwartz, I.M., Jackson-Beelk, M., & Anderson, R. (1983). *Minnesota's "hidden" juvenile control system: Inpatient psychiatric and chemical dependency treatment.* Unpublished Paper, University of Minnesota, Hubert H. Humphrey Institute of Public Affairs.

Scott, S., Bruner, C., Hastings, J., & Perlowski, K. (1995). *Family preservation services or placement: How to decide—The views of front-line workers and supervisors in Iowa.* Des Moines, IA: The Child and Family Policy Center.

Seaberg, J.R. (1981). Foster parents as aides to parents In A.N. Maluccio & P.A.. Sinanoglu (Eds.), *The challenge of partnership: Working with parents of children in foster care* (pp. 209–220). New York: Child Welfare League of America.

Sedlak, A.J. (1991a). *National incidence and prevalence of child abuse and neglect: 1988.* Rockville, MD: Westat, Inc. (Original report published July 1988, U.S. Department of Health and Human Services, under Contract 105-85-1702.)

Sedlak, A.J. (1991b). *Supplementary analyses of data on the national incidence of child abuse and neglect.* Rockville, MD: Westat. (Original report written in May 1989, U. S. Department of Justice under Grant No. 88-VF-GX-0004.)

Sedlak, A.J., & Broadhurst, D.D. (1996). *Executive summary of the third national incidence study of child abuse and neglect.* Washington, DC: National Clearinghouse on Child Abuse and Neglect.

Sedlak, A.J., & Broadhurst, D.D. (1998). *Executive summary of the third national incidence study of child abuse and neglect.* Washington, DC: National Clearinghouse on Child Abuse and Neglect.

See, L.A. (Ed.). (1998). *Human behavior in the social environment from an African American perspective.* Binghamton, NY: Haworth Press.

Segal, E.C. (1985). Adoption assistance and the law. In E.C. Segal (Ed.), *Adoption of children with special needs: Issues in law and policy* (pp. 127–168). Washington, DC: American Bar Association.

Select Committee on Children, Youth, and Families. (1983). *A report.* Washington, DC: U.S. Government Printing Office.

Select Committee on Children, Youth and Families, U.S. House of Representatives. (1989). *No place like home: Discarded children in America.* Washington, DC: U.S. House of Representatives.

Selinske, J. (1981). *A guide to the delivery of child protective services: Analysis of tasks, knowledge and skill requisites, and performance criteria of the child protective functions.* Washington, DC: American Public Welfare Association.

Seltzer, M.M., & Bloksberg, L.M. (1987). Permanency planning and its effects on foster children. *Social Work, 32*(1), 65–68.

Selznick, P. (1984). *Leadership in administration.* Berkeley, CA: University of California Press.

Settles, B.H., Culley, J.D., & Van Name, J.B. (1976). *How to measure the cost of foster family care.* Washington, DC: U.S. Department of Health, Education, and Welfare, Office of Human Development Services (DHEW Publication No. 78-30126).

Sgroi, S.M. (Ed.). (1982). *Handbook of clinical intervention in child sexual abuse.* Lexington, MA: Lexington Books.

Sgroi, S.M. (1988). *Vulnerable populations: Evaluation and treatment of sexually abused children and adult survivors* (Vol. 1). Lexington, MA: Lexington Books.

Sgroi, S.M. (1989). *Vulnerable populations: Sexual abuse treatment for children, adult survivors, offenders, and persons with mental retardation* (Vol. 2). Lexington, MA: Lexington Books.

Shapiro, D. (1976). *Agencies and foster children.* New York: Columbia University Press.

Shealy, C.N. (1995). From *Boys Town* to *Oliver Twist:* Separating fact from fiction in welfare reform and out-of-home placement of children and youth. *American Psychologist, 50*(8), 565–580.

Sherman, E.A., Phillips, M.H., Haring, B.A., & Shyne, A.W. (1973). *Service to children in their own homes: Its nature and outcome.* New York: Child Welfare League of America.

Sherraden, M.W. (1986). Benefit-cost analysis as a net present value problem. *Administration in Social Work, 10*(3), 85–97.

Sherraden, M.S., & Segal, U.A. (1996). Multicultural issues in child welfare. *Children and Youth Services Review, 18*(6), 497–504.

Sherraden, M.W. (1991). *Assets and the poor: A new American welfare policy.* New York: M.E. Sharpe.

Sherrod, K., O'Connor, S., Altemeier, W.A., & Vietz, P. (1986). Toward a semispecific, multidimensional, threshold model of maltreatment. In D. Drotar (Ed.), *New directions in research and practice on failure to thrive.* New York: Plenum.

Shireman, J.F. (1983). Achieving permanence after placement. In B.G. McGowan & W. Meezan (Eds.), *Child welfare: Current dilemmas, future directions* (pp. 377–424). Itasca, IL: F.E. Peacock.

Shireman, J.F., & Johnson, P.R. (1986). A longitudinal study of black adoptions: Single parent, transracial, and traditional. *Social Work, 31,* 172–176.

Shnaps, Y., Frand, M., Rotem, Y., & Trosh, M. (1981). The chemically abused child. *Pediatrics, 68,* 119–121.

Shyne, A.W., & Schroeder, A.G. (1978). *National study of social services to children and their families.* Washington, DC: Department of Health and Human Services, U.S. Children's Bureau (DHEW Publication No. 78-30150).

Sia, C.C.J., & Breakey, G.F. (1985). The role of the medical home in child abuse prevention and positive child development. *Hawaii Medical Journal, 44*(7).

Siefert, K., Schwartz, I.M., & Ortega, R.M. (1994). Infant mortality in Michigan's child welfare system. *Social Work, 39*(5), 574–579.

Siegal, M. (1982). *Fairness in children.* New York: Academic Press.

Siegel, L., & Lane, I.M. (1982). *Personnel and organizational psychology.* Homewood. IL: Richard D. Irwin.

Silver, J.A., Amster, B.J., & Haecker, T.A. (1999). *Young children and foster care—A guide for professionals.* Baltimore, MD: Paul Brookes.

Silverman, A., Reinherz, H., & Giaconia, R. (1996). The long-term sequelae of child and adolescent abuse: A longitudinal community study: *Child Abuse and Neglect, 20*(8), 709–723.

Simmons, B., Allphin, S., & Barth, R.P. (In press). The changing face of public adoption practice. *Adoption Quarterly.*

Simms, M.D., Freundlich, M., Battistelli, E.S., & Kaufman, N.D. (1999). Delivering health care and mental health care services to children in family foster care after welfare and health care reform. *Child Welfare, 78,* 166–183.

Simms, M.D., & Halfon, N. (1994). The health care needs of children in foster care: A research agenda. *Child Welfare, 73,* 505–524.

Simms, M.D., & Kelly, R.W. (1991). Pediatricians and foster children. *Child Welfare, 70,* 451–461.

Simon, R.J., & Alstein, H. (1987). *Transracial adoptees and their families: A study of identity and commitment.* New York: Praeger.

Sims, A.R. (1988). Independent living services for youths in foster care. *Social Work, 33,* 539–545.

Simpson, J.S., Koroloff, N., Friesen, B.J., & Gac, J. (1999). Promising practices in family-provider collaboration. In *Systems of care: Promising practices in children's mental health, 1998 Series, Volume II.* Washington, DC: Center for Effective Collaboration and Practice, American Institutes for Research.

Sinanoglu, P.A., & Maluccio, A.N. (Eds.). (1981). *Parents of children in placement: Perspectives and programs.* New York: Child Welfare League of America.

Singer, J.D., & Butler, J.A. (1987). The education for all handicapped children act: Schools as agents of social reform. *Harvard Educational Review, 57*(2), 125–152.

Singer, L.T., Garber, R., & Kliegman, R. (1991). Neurobehavioral sequelae of fetal cocaine exposure. *Journal of Pediatrics, 119,* 667–672.

Slingerland, W.H. (1916). *Child welfare work in California.* New York: Russell Sage Foundation.

Slingerland, W.H. (1919). *Child-placing in families.* New York: Russell Sage Foundation.

Small, R., Kennedy, K., & Bender, B. (1991). Critical issues for practice in residential treatment: The view from within. *American Journal of Orthopsychiatry, 61*(3), 327–335.

Smeeding, T., & Torrey, B. (1987). *The children of poverty: The evidence from LIS on comparative income support policies.* Prepared for the American Economic Association, December 1987 conference.

Smeeding, T., Torrey, B., & Rein, M. (1988). Patterns of income and poverty: The economic status of children and the elderly in eight countries. In J. Palmer, T. Smeeding, & B. Torrey (Eds.), *The vulnerable* (pp. 89–119). Washington, DC: The Urban Institute Press.

Smith, H., & Israel, E. (1987). Sibling incest: A study of the dynamics of 25 cases. *Child Abuse and Neglect, 11*(1), 101–108.

Smith, L.L. (1986). A crisis intervention model. *Emotional First Aid, 3*(1), 9–17.

Solomon, B. (1976). *Black empowerment: Social work in oppressed communities.* New York: Columbia University Press.

Sorosky, A.D., Baran, A., & Pannor, R. (1978). *The adoption triangle—The effects of the sealed record on adoptees, birth parents, and adoptive parents.* Garden City, NY: Anchor/Doubleday.

Sotomayor, M. (Ed.). (1991). *Empowering families: A critical issue for the '90s.* Milwaukee, WI: Family Service America.

Spaid, W.M. (1987). *An assessment of family variables as they relate to child placement outcomes in family-based services.* Salt Lake City, UT: University of Utah, Graduate School of Social Work, Unpublished Doctoral Dissertation.

Spearly, J.L., & Lauderdale, M. (1983). Community characteristics and ethnicity in the prediction of child maltreatment rates. *Child Abuse and Neglect, 7,* 91–105.

Spencer, J.W., & Knudsen, D.D., (1992). Out-of-home maltreatment: An analysis of risk in various settings for children. *Children and Youth Services Review, 14,* 485–492.

Spencer, M. (1985). Meeting the need for comprehensive post-legal adoption services. *Permanency Report, 3*(4), 5.

Spinetta, J., & Rigler, D. (1972). The child abusing parent: A psychological review. *Psychological Bulletin, 77,* 296–304.

Stack, C. (1974). *All our kin: Strategies for survival in the black community.* New York: Harper & Row.

Staff, E., & Fein, E. (1994). Inside the black box: An exploration of service delivery in a family reunification program. *Child Welfare, 73,* 195–211.

Starfield, B., & Budetti, P. (1985). Child health status and risk factors. *Health Services Research, 19*(6), 817–886.

Stark, D. (1999). *Introduction:* Nittoli, J. (1999). *Neighborhood transformation and family development: Conceptual overview.* Presentation to a joint planning meeting, Annie E. Casey Foundation and The Casey Family Programs, January 28, 1999, Seattle, Washington (mimeograph).

Starling, S.P., Holden, J.S., & Jenny, C. (1995). Abusive head trauma: The relationship of perpetrators to their victims. *Pediatrics, 95,* 259–262.

Starr, R.H. (Ed.). (1982). *Child abuse prediction: Policy implications.* Cambridge, MA: Ballinger.

Starr, R.H., Dietric, K.N., Fischhoff, J., Ceresnie, S., & Zweier, D. (1984). The contribution of handicapping conditions to child abuse. *Topics in Early Childhood Special Education, 4,* 55–69.

State of Alaska. (1985). *Alaska vital statistics annual report, 1983.* Anchorage: Author.

State of California Department of Social Services. (1984a). *Characteristics of relinquishment adoptions in California, July 1981–June 1982.* Sacramento: Author.

State of California Statistical Services Branch. (1987). Unpublished data.

State of Colorado. (1985). *1982 annual report of vital statistics, Colorado.* Denver, CO: Author.

Steele, B.F., & Pollock, C.B. (1974). A psychiatric study of parents who abuse infants and small children. In R.E. Helfer & C.H. Kempe (Eds.), *The battered child.* Chicago, IL: University of Chicago Press.

Stehno, S.M. (1982). Differential treatment of minority children in service systems. *Social Work, 27,* 39–46.

Stehno, S.M. (1990). The elusive continuum of child welfare services: Implications for minority children and youth. *Child Welfare, 69,* 551–562.

Stein, J.A., Golding, J.M., Siegel, J.M., Burnham, M.A., & Sorenson, S.B. (1988). Long–term psychological sequelae of child sexual abuse: The Los Angeles Epidemiologic Catchment Area Study. In G.E. Wyatt & G.J. Powell (Eds.), *Lasting effects of child sexual abuse* (pp. 135–154). Newbury Parks, CA: Sage.

Stein, J.J., & Gambrill, E.D. (1985). Permanency planning for children: The past and present. *Children and Youth Services Review, 7*(2/3), 83–94.

Stein, T. (1981). *Social work practice in child welfare.* Englewood Cliffs, NJ: Prentice-Hall.

Stein, T. (1984). The Child Abuse Prevention and Treatment Act. *Social Service Review, 58*(2), 302–314.

Stein, T. (1991). *Child welfare and the law.* New York and London: Longman.

Stein, T.J. (1985). Projects to prevent out-of-home placement. *Children and Youth Services Review, 7*(2/3), 109–122.

Stein, T.J. (1987). The vulnerability of child welfare agencies to class action suits. *Social Service Review, 61,* 636–654.

Stein, T.J. (1996). Child custody and visitation: The rights of lesbian and gay parents. *Social Service Review, 70,* 435–450.

Stein, T.J. (1998). *Child welfare and the law* (revised edition). Washington, DC: CWLA Press.

Stein, T.J., & Rzepnicki, T.L. (1983). *Decision making at child welfare intake: A handbook for practitioners.* Washington, DC: Child Welfare League of America.

Stein, T.J., & Rzepnicki, T.L. (1984). *Decision making in child welfare services: Intake and planning.* Boston: Kluwer-Nijhoff.

Stein, T.J., Gambrill, E.D., & Wiltse, K.T. (1978). *Children in foster homes: Achieving continuity of care.* New York: Praeger.

Steinberg, L., Catalano, R., & Dooley, D. (1981). Economic antecedents of child abuse and neglect. *Child Development, 52,* 975–985.

Steiner, G. (1976). *The children's cause.* Washington, DC: Brookings Institute.

Steiner, G. (1981). *The futility of family policy.* Washington, DC: Brookings Institute.

Stephens, D. (1979). In-home family support services: An ecological systems approach. In S. Maybanks & M. Bryce (Eds.), *Home-based services for children and families: Policy, practice, and research* (pp. 283–295). Springfield, IL: Charles C Thomas.

Stevenson, K.M., Cheung, K-F.M., & Leung, P. (1992). A new approach to training child protective services workers for ethnically sensitive practice. *Child Welfare, 71*(4), 291–305.

Stone, H.D. (1989). *Ready, set, go—An agency guide to independent living.* Washington, DC: Child Welfare League of America.

Stovall, B.M., & Krieger, R. (1990). Preparing minority foster adolescents for adulthood: The need for ethnic competence. In A.N. Maluccio, R. Krieger, & B.A. Pine (Eds.), *Preparing adolescents for life after foster care—The central role of foster parents* (pp. 147–161). Washington, DC: Child Welfare League of America.

Stratton, C. (1985). Comparison of abusive and nonabusive families with conduct-disordered children. *American Journal of Orthopsychiatry, 55*(1), 59–69.

Straus, M.A. (1986). Domestic violence and homicide antecedents. *Bulletin of the New York Academy of Medicine, 62,* 446–65.

Straus, M.A. (1991). Physical violence in American families: Incidence rates, causes, and trends. In D.D. Knudsen & J.L. Miller (Eds.), *Abused and battered: Social and legal responses to family violence.* Hawthorne, NY: Aldine de Gruyter.

Straus, M.A., & Gelles, R.J. (1986). Societal change and change in family violence from 1975 to 1985 as revealed by two national surveys. *Journal of Marriage and the Family, 48,* 465–479.

Straus, M.A., & Gelles, R.J. (Eds.). (1990). *Physical violence in American families: Risk factors and adaptations to violence in 8,145 families.* New Brunswick, NJ: Transaction Press.

Straus, M.A., & Smith, C. (1990). Family patterns and child abuse. In M.A. Straus & R.J. Gelles (Eds.), *Physical violence in American families: Risk factors and adaptations to violence in 8,145 families* (pp. 245–261). New Brunswick, NJ: Transaction Press.

Stroul, B.A. (Ed.). (1996). *Children's mental health creating systems of care in a changing society.* Baltimore, MD: Paul H. Brookes.

Stroul, B.A., & Friedman, R.M. (1996). The system of care concept and philosophy. In B.A. Stroul (Ed.), *Children's mental health: Creating systems of care in a changing society.* Baltimore: Paul H. Brookes.

Struhsaker Schatz, M., & Bane, W. (1991). Empowering the parents of children in substitute care: A training model. *Child Welfare, 70*(6), 665–678.

Stuart, M. (1999). Barriers and facilitators to use of services following intensive family preservation services. *The Journal of Behavioral Health Services & Research, 26*(1), 39–49.

Stuart, R.D. (1970). *Trick or treatment: How and when psychotherapy fails.* Champaign, IL: Research Press.

Stumphauzer, J.S. (1979). Editorial comments. In J.S. Stumphauzer (Ed.), *Progress in behavior therapy with delinquents* (pp. 118–119). Springfield, IL: Charles C Thomas.

Sturkie, K., & Flanzer, J.P. (1987). Depression and self-esteem in the families of maltreated adolescents. *Social Work, 32*(6), 491–496.

Suffer the Children. *The Atlanta Constitution.* (1989). Atlanta, GA: *The Atlanta Journal.* Reprint of articles from June 4–10.

Sullivan, M., Spasser, M., & Penner, G.L. (1977). *Bowen Center project for abused and neglected children: Report of a demonstration in protective services.* Washington, DC: U.S. Department of Health, Education, and Welfare.

Summer, L., Parrott, S., & Mann, C. (1996). *Millions of uninsured and underinsured children are eligible for Medicaid.* Washington, DC: Center on Budget and Policy Priorities, December.

Sundel, M., & Homan, C.C. (1979). Prevention in child welfare: A framework for management and practice. *Child Welfare, 58,* 510–521.

Super, D., Parrott, S., Steinmetz, S., & Mann, C. (1996). *The new welfare law.* Washington, DC: Center on Budget and Policy Priorities, August 14.

Susser, E., Struening, E.L., & Conover, S. (1987). Childhood experiences of homeless men. *American Journal of Psychiatry, 144,* 1599–1601.

Sussman, A., & Cohen, S. (1975). *Reporting child abuse and neglect: Guidelines for legislation.* Cambridge, MA: Ballinger.

Sutherland, E.H. (1931). Mental deficiency and crime. In K. Young (Ed.), *Social attitudes* (pp. 357–375). New York: Henry Holt.

Sutherland, E. H., & Cressey, D. R. (1978). *Criminology* (10th ed.). New York: Lippincott.

Swan, H.L., Press, A.N., & Briggs, S.L. (1985). Child sexual abuse prevention: Does it work? *Child Welfare, 64,* 395–405.

Sweet, J.J., & Resick, R.A. (1979). The maltreatment of children: A review of theories and research. *Journal of Social Issues, 35,* 40–59.

Swett, C., Surrey, J., & Cohen, C. (1990). Sexual and physical abuse histories and psychiatric symptoms among male psychiatric outpatients. *American Journal of Psychiatry, 147,* 632–636.

Szykula, S.A., & Fleischman, M.J. (1985). Reducing out-of-home placements of abused children: Two controlled field studies. *Child Abuse and Neglect, 9*(2), 277–283.

Tajima, E. (1999). *Understanding connections between two forms of family violence: Wife abuse and violence towards children.* Doctoral Dissertation, University of Chicago.

Takas, M. (1993). *Kinship care and family preservation: A guide for states in legal and policy development.* Unpublished manuscript. Washington, DC: ABA Center on Children and the Law.

Tatara, T. (Ed.). (1987). *National roundtable on CPS risk assessment and family systems assessment: Summary of highlights.* Washington, DC: American Public Welfare Association.

Tatara, T. (1989). Substitute care flow data and national estimates of children in care. *VCIS Research Notes.* Washington, DC: Voluntary Cooperative Information System, American Public Welfare Association.

Tatara, T. (1991a). Parental drug problems and child substitute care: A review of the VCIS data on children who entered care during FY 88. *VCIS Research Notes.* Washington, DC: Voluntary Cooperative Information System, American Public Welfare Association.

Tatara, T. (1991b). Child substitute care flow data for FY 90 and child substitute care population trends since FY 86. Revised estimates. *VICS Research Note.* Washington, DC: Voluntary Cooperative Information System, American Public Welfare Association.

Tatara, T. (1992a). *Characteristics of children in substitute and adoptive care: Based on FY 82 through FY 88 data.* Washington, DC: American Public Welfare Association.

Tatara, T. (1992b). National child substitute care flow data for FY 91 and current trends in the state child substitute care populations. *VCIS Research Notes.* Washington, DC: Voluntary Cooperative Information System, American Public Welfare Association.

Tatara, T. (1993). U.S. child substitute care flow data for FY 92 and current trends in the state child substitute care populations. *VCIS Research Notes.* Washington, DC: American Public Welfare Association.

Tatara, T. (1994). The recent rise in the U.S. child substitute care population data: An analysis of national child substitute care flow data. In R. Barth, J.D. Berrick, & N. Gilbert (Eds.), *Child welfare research review* (Vol. 1). New York: Columbia University Press.

Tatara, T. (1997). U.S. child substitute care flow data and the race/ethnicity of children in care for FY 1995, along with recent trends in the U.S. child substitute care populations. *VCIS Research Notes.* Washington, DC: American Public Welfare Association.

Tatara, T., & Pettiford, E.K. (1985). *Characteristics of children in substitute and adoptive care: A statistical summary of the VICS National Child Welfare Data Base.* Washington, DC: The American Public Welfare Association.

Tatara, T., Morgan, H., & Portner, H. (1986). SCAN: Providing preventive services in an urban setting. *Children Today, 15*(6), 17–22.

Tavantzis, T.N., Tavantzis, M., Brown, L.G., & Rohrbaugh, M. (1985). Home-based structural family therapy for delinquents at risk of placement. In M.P. Mirkin & S.L. Koman (Eds.), *Handbook of adolescents and family therapy* (pp. 69–88). New York: Gardner Press.

Taylor, D.A., & Alpert, S.W. (1973). *Continuity and support following residential treatment.* New York: Child Welfare League of America.

Taylor, D.K., & Beauchamp, C. (1998). Hospital-based prevention strategy in child abuse: A multi-level needs assessment. *Child Abuse and Neglect, 12*(3), 343–354.

Taylor, M.S. (1988). The effects of feedback on the behavior of organizational personnel. In R.J. Patti, J. Poertner, & C.A. Rapp (Eds.), *Managing for service effectiveness in social welfare organizations* (pp. 191–204). [A special issue of *Administration in Social Work, 11*(3–4).] New York: Haworth Press.

Taylor, R.B. (1981). *The kid business.* Boston: Houghton Mifflin.

Teare, R.J. (1983). Reclassification and licensing. In S. Briar, A. Minahan, E. Pinderhughes, & T. Tripodi (Eds*.), 1983–1984 Supplement to the encyclopedia of social work* (17th ed.). Silver Springs, MD: National Association of Social Workers.

Teare, R.J. (1987). *Validating social work credentials for human service jobs: Report of a demonstration.* Silver Springs, MD: National Association of Social Workers.

Testa, M.F. (1992). Conditions of risk for substitute care. *Children and Youth Services Review, 14,* 27–36.

Tharp, R.G., & Wetzel, R.J. (1969). *Behavior modification in the natural environment.* New York: Academic Press.

Thoburn, J., Murdoch, A., & O'Brien, A. (1986). *Permanence in child care.* Oxford, England: Basil Blackwell.

Thomas, E.J. (1984). *Designing interventions for the helping professions.* Newbury Park, CA: Sage.

Thomas, G. (1990). *"Bottomed out" in a "bottom up" society: Social work education and the default and recapture of professional leadership in child welfare.* Paper presented at the 36th Annual Program Meeting of the Council on Social Work Education, Reno, March 3–6.

Thomas, M.P. (1972). Child abuse and neglect: Part 1. Historical overview, legal matrix, and social perspectives. *North Carolina Law Review, 50,* 293–349.

Thomlinson, R.J. (1984). Something works: Evidence from practice effectiveness studies. *Social Work, 29,* 51–56.

Thompson, L., & Wilson, D. (1989). *Report on child fatalities related to child abuse and neglect.* Olympia, WA: Washington Department of Health and Human Services, Division of Children and Family Services.

Thompson, R. (1997). *How to prepare and present outcomes reports to external payers and regulators.* Boystown, NE: Father Flanagan's Boys Home, National Resource and Training Center.

Thompson, R.A. (1995) *Preventing child maltreatment through social support: A critical analysis.* Thousand Oak, CA: Sage.

Three Feather Associates. (1989). Risk level assessment in rural, remote Native Indian communities. *Indian Child Welfare Digest—Model Practice Approaches* (August–September), 20–23. Norman, OK: Author.

Three Feathers Associates. (1990). *American Indian community awareness: A campaign to combat child abuse and neglect.* Norman, OK: Author (mimeograph).

Tiddy, S., Swan, F., & Pecora, P.J. (1998). *A skills based approach to trauma recovery in childhood.* Portland, OR and Seattle, WA: The Casey Family Programs (mimeograph of a working paper).

Tower, C. (1989). *Understanding child abuse and neglect.* Needham Heights, MA: Allyn & Bacon.

Towles, C. (1948). *Common human needs* (reprinted in 1987). Silver Springs, MD: National Association of Social Workers.

Tracy, E.M. (1991). Defining the target population for family preservation services. In K. Wells & D.E. Biegel (Eds.), *Family preservation services: Research and evaluation* (pp. 138–158). Newbury Park, CA: Sage.

Tracy, E.M. (1992). *Substance abuse and child welfare: Protecting the child, preserving the family.* Cleveland, OH: Case Western Reserve University, Mandel School of Applied Social Sciences (mimeograph).

Tracy, E.M. (1995). Family preservation and home-based services. In R.L. Edwards & J.G. Hopps (Eds.), *Encyclopedia of social work* (19th ed., Vol. 2, pp. 973–983). Washington, DC: National Association of Social Workers.

Tracy, E.M., Haapala, D.A., Kinney, J.M., & Pecora, P.J. (Eds.). (1991). *Intensive family preservation services: An instructional sourcebook.* Cleveland, OH: Mandel School of Applied Social Sciences, Case Western Reserve University.

Tracy, E.M., & Pine, B.A. (2000). Child welfare education and training: Future trends and influences. *Child Welfare, 79,* 107–114.

Tracy, E.M., & Whittaker, J.K. (1987). The evidence base for social support interventions in child and family practice: Emerging issues for research and practice. *Children and Youth Services Review, 9,* 249–270.

Tracy, E.M., & Whittaker, J.K. (1990). The social network map: Assessing social support in clinical social work practice. *Families in Society, 71,* 461–470.

Tremitiere, B. (1979). Adoption of children with special needs: The client-centered approach. *Child Welfare, 58,* 681–685.

Trieschman, A.E., Whittaker, J.K., & Brendtro, L.K. (1969). *The other 23 hours: Child care work in a therapeutic milieu.* Hawthorne, NY: Aldine de Gruyter.

Turbett, J.P., & O'Toole, R. (1980). *Physician's recognition of child abuse.* Presented at the Annual Meeting of the American Sociological Association, New York.

Turner, J. (1984). Reuniting children in foster care with their biological parents. *Social Work, 29,* 501–505.

U.S. Advisory Board on Child Abuse and Neglect. (1991). *Creating caring communities.* Washington, DC: U.S. Department of Health and Human Services.

U. S. Bureau of the Census. (1989). *Changes in American family life, Current population reports, Special Studies Series P-23* (No. 163). Washington, DC: U.S. Government Printing Office.

U.S. Bureau of the Census. (1990). *Statistical abstract of the U.S., 1990* (110th ed.). Washington, DC: U.S. Government Printing Office.

U.S. Bureau of the Census. (1991). *Current population reports, Series P-60, No. 171, "Poverty in the U.S.: 1988 and 1989."* Washington, DC: U.S. Government Printing Office.

U.S. Bureau of the Census. (1998). *Statistical abstract of the United States, 1998* (118th ed.). Washington, DC: U.S. Government Printing Office.

U.S. Bureau of the Census. (1999a). *Population Reports, P25-1095, and Population Paper Listings 91.* (*www.census.gov/prod/3/98pubs/98statab/sasec1.pdf*).

U.S. Bureau of the Census. (1999b). *Current population reports, Series P-60, No. 207, "Poverty in the United States: 1998."* Washington, DC: U.S. Government Printing Office.

U.S. Children's Bureau. (1983). *Child welfare research note #1.* Washington, DC: Department of Health and Human Services.

U.S. Code. (1995). *1994 Edition, Title 42, The Public Health and Welfare, Volume 21.* Washington, DC: U.S. Government Printing Office.

U.S. Department of Commerce, U.S. Bureau of the Census. (1989). *Changes in American family life: Current population reports, Special Studies Series P-23, No. 163.* Washington, DC: U.S. Government Printing Office.

U.S. Department of Health and Human Services. (1980). *Broadening adoption opportunities.* Washington, DC: Author.

U.S. Department of Health and Human Services. (1981). *Study findings: National study of the incidence and severity of child abuse and neglect.* DHHS Publication No. (OHDS) 81-30325. Washington, DC: Author.

U.S. Department of Health and Human Services. (1984). *Report to Congress on Public Law 96-272— The Adoption Assistance and Child Welfare Act of 1980.* Washington, DC: Author.

U.S. Department of Health and Human Services. (1994). Children's Bureau. *National study of protective, preventive and reunification services delivered to children and their families.* Washington, DC: U.S. Government Printing Office.

U.S. Department of Health and Human Services. (1995). *Child maltreatment 1993: Reports from the states to the National Conference on Child Abuse and Neglect.* Washington, DC: U.S. Government Printing Office.

U.S. Department of Health and Human Services. (1996). *Child maltreatment 1994: Reports from the states to the National Conference on Child Abuse and Neglect.* Washington, DC: U.S. Government Printing Office.

U.S. Department of Health and Human Services. (1998). *Trends in the well-being of America's children & youth.* Washington, DC: U.S. Government Printing Office 1988-447-239/91074.

U.S. Department of Health and Human Services, Administration for Children and Families, Administration on Children, Youth and Families, Children's Bureau. (1998). *Progress report to the Congress on conducting a study of performance-based financial incentives in child welfare.* Washington, DC: Author.

U.S. Department of Health and Human Services, Administration for Children and Families, Administration on Children, Youth and Families, Children's Bureau. (1999). *The AFCARS report: Current estimates as of January 1999. www.acf.dhhs.gov/programs/cbdata.*

U.S. Department of Health and Human Services, Administration on Children, Youth and Families. (1998). *Child maltreatment 1996: Reports from the states to the National Child Abuse and Neglect Data Systems.* Washington, DC: U.S. Government Printing Office. Web: http://www.calib.com/nccanch

U.S. Department of Health and Human Services, Administration on Children, Youth and Families. (1999). *Child maltreatment 1997: Reports from the states to the National Child Abuse and Neglect Data Systems.* Washington, DC: U.S. Government Printing Office. Web: http://www.calib.com/nccanch

U.S. Department of Health and Human Services, Children's Bureau. (1997). *National study of protec-*

tive, preventive and reunification services delivered to children and their families. Washington, DC: U.S. Government Printing Office.

U.S. Department of Health and Human Services, Children's Bureau, National Center on Child Abuse and Neglect. (1998). *Child maltreatment 1996: Reports from the states to the National Child Abuse and Neglect Data System.* Washington, DC: U.S. Government Printing Office.

U.S. Department of Labor, Office of the Chief Economist. (1995). *What's working and what's not.* Washington, DC: Author.

U.S. General Accounting Office. (1998). *Foster care: Implementation of the Multiethnic Placement Act poses difficult challenges* (September 14). Washington, DC: GAO/HEHS-98-204.

U.S. General Accounting Office. (1995). *Child welfare complex needs strain capacity to provide services* (September). Report to Congressional Committees. Washington, DC: GAO/HEHS-95-208.1.

U.S. General Accounting Office. (1997). *Child welfare: States'progress in implementing family preservation and support services* (February). Report to the Chairman, Subcommittee on Human Resources, Committee on Ways and Means, House of Representatives. Washington, DC: GAO/HEHS-97-34.

Unger, S. (Ed.). (1978). *The destruction of American Indian families.* New York: Association on American Indian Affairs.

Uniform Parentage Act. 9A U.L.A. 579. (1979). New York: Nathan Bender.

Urban Institute. (1996). *Potential effects of Congressional welfare reform legislation on family incomes.* http://www.urban.org/pec72696.htm#r11, August.

Urban Systems Research & Engineering Inc. (1985). *Evaluation of state activities with regard to adoption disruption.* Washington, DC: Office of Human Development Services.

Usher, C.L., Randolph, K.A., & Gogan, H.C. (1999). Placement patterns in foster care. *Social Service Review, 73,* 22–36.

Utah Child Welfare Training Project. (1987). *Utah child protective services risk assessment project—Dissemination manual.* Salt Lake City, UT: University of Utah, Graduate School of Social Work.

VanderMey, B.J., & Neff, R.L. (1986). *Incest as child abuse: Research and applications.* New York: Praeger.

Van Meter, M.J.S. (1986). An alternative to foster care for victims of child abuse/neglect: A university-based program. *Child Abuse and Neglect, 10*(1), 79–84.

Veronico, A. (1983). One church, one child: Placing children with special needs. *Children Today, 12,* 6–10.

Videka-Sherman, L. (1985). *Harriet M. Bartlett practice effectiveness project.* Silver Springs, MD: National Association of Social Workers.

Vogeltanz, N.D., Wilsnack, S.C., et al. (1999). Prevalence and risk factors for childhood sexual abuse in women. *Child Abuse and Neglect, 23*(6), 579–592.

Voluntary Cooperative Information Systems. (September 1997). *Child substitute care—Flow data for FY 96.* Washington, DC: American Public Welfare Association.

Wachs, T.D., & Gruen, G.E. (1982). *Early experience & human development.* New York: Plenum.

Wagner, D., & Squadrito, E. (1994). Family risk assessment study by the Rhode Island Department of Children, Youth and Families and the National Council on Crime & Delinquency/Children's Research Center. In T. Tatara (Ed.), *Seventh national roundtable on CPS risk assessment: Summary of highlights* (pp. 61–83). Washington, DC: American Public Welfare Association.

Wahler, R.G. (1980). The insular mother: Her problems in parent-child treatment. *Journal of Applied Behavioral Analysis, 13,* 207–219.

Wahler, R.G., & Meginnis, K.L. (1997). Strengthening child compliance through positive parenting practices: What works? *Journal of Clinical Child Psychology, 26*(4), 433–440.

Wahler, R.G., Leske, G., & Rogers, E.S. (1979). The insular family: A deviance support system for oppositional children. In L.A. Hammerlynck (Ed.), *Behavioral systems for the developmentally disabled: I. School and family environments* (Vol. 1, pp. 102–127). New York: Brunner/Mazel.

Wakefield, J.C. (1996a). Does social work need the eco-system perspective? Part 1. Is the perspective useful? *Social Service Review, 70,* 1–32.

Wakefield, J.C. (1996b). Does social work need the eco-system perspective? Part 2. Does the perspective save social work from incoherence? *Social Service Review, 70,* 183–213.

Wald, M. (1975a). State intervention on behalf of "neglected" children: A search for realistic standards. *Stanford Law Review, 27,* 985–1000.

Wald, M. (1975b). State intervention on behalf of 'neglected' children: Standards for removal of children from their homes, monitoring the status of children in foster care, and termination of parental rights. *Stanford Law Review, 28,* 623–707.

Wald, M. (1976). State intervention on behalf of 'neglected' children: Standards for removal of children from their homes, monitoring the status of children in foster care, and termination of parental rights. *Stanford Law Review, 28,* 623–645.

Wald, M.S. (1980). Thinking about public policy toward abuse and neglect of children: A review of "Before the best interests of the child." *Michigan Law Review, 78,* 645–693.

Wald, M.S. (1988). Family preservation: Are we moving too fast? *Public Welfare, 46*(3), 33–38, 46.

Wald, M.S., Carlsmith, J.M., & Leiderman, P.H. (1988). *Protecting abused and neglected children.* Stanford, CA: Stanford University Press.

Waldfogel, J. (1997). The new wave of service integration. *Social Service Review, 71*(3), 463–484.

Waldfogel, J. (Spring, 1998). Rethinking the paradigm for child protection. *The Future of Children, 8*(1), 104–119.

Walker, C.E., Bonner, B.L., & Kaufman, K.L. (1988). *The physically and sexually abused child: Evaluation and treatment.* Elmsford, NY: Pergamon Press.

Walker, E., Katon, W., Harrop-Griffiths, J., Holm, L., Russo, J., & Hickok, L.R. (1988). Relationship of chronic pelvic pain to psychiatric diagnosis and childhood sexual abuse. *American Journal of Psychiatry, 145,* 75–80.

Walker, P.J., & Tabbert, W. (Undated). *Culturally sensitive risk assessment: An ethnographic approach.* Berkeley, CA: University of California at Berkeley, California Social Work Education Center, and Fresno State University.

Walsh, B.W., & Rosen, P. (1988). *Self-mutilation: Theory, research, and treatment.* New York: Guilford.

Walsh, J. (1997). *The eye of the storm: Ten years on the front lines of new futures.* Seattle, WA: The Annie E. Casey Foundation.

Walton, J. (1985). Does the workplace work for waiting children? *Permanency Report, 3*(4), 6.

Walton, M. (1986). *The Deming management method.* New York: Perigee Books.

Ward, M. (1981). Parental bonding in older-child adoptions. *Child Welfare, 60,* 24–34.

Ward, M. (1984). Sibling ties in foster care. *Child Welfare, 63,* 321–332.

Warren, S.B. (1992). Lower threshold for referral for psychiatric-treatment for adopted. *Journal of the American Academy of Child and Adolescent Psychiatry, 31*(3), 512–517.

Warsh, R., Maluccio, A.N., & Pine, B.A. (1994). *Teaching family reunification—A sourcebook.* Washington, DC: Child Welfare League of America.

Warsh, R., Pine, B.A., & Maluccio, A.N. (1996). *Reconnecting families—A guide to strengthening family reunification services.* Washington, DC: CWLA Press.

Washington Post. (1990). January 9, p. 1 and following.

Waterman, R.H., Jr. (1987). *The renewal factor: How to best get and keep the competitive edge.* New York: Bantam Books.

Watkins, S.A. (1990). The Mary Ellen Myth: Correcting child welfare history. *Social Work, 35*(6), 500–503.

Watson, K.W. (1982). A bold, new model for foster family care. *Public Welfare, 40,* 14–21.

Wattenberg, E., Brewer, R., & Resnick, M. (1991). *Executive summary of a study of paternity decisions: Perspectives from young mothers and young fathers.* (Highlights from the full report submitted to the Ford Foundation, February 12, 1991.) Minneapolis, MN: Center for Urban and Regional Affairs, University of Minnesota.

Webb, S., & Aldgate, J. (1991). Using respite care to prevent long-term family breakdown. *Adoption and Fostering, 15,* 6–13.

Webster, D. (1999). *California's group care population: A longitudinal analysis of placement dynamics and outcomes.* Berkeley, CA: University of California, doctoral dissertation.

Webster, D., Barth, R.P., & Needell, B. (In press). Group care: Who enters and who leaves? *Child Welfare.*

Webster, D., Barth, R.P., Needell, B., & Berrick, J.D. (1998). *Foster care, treatment foster family care and group care in California: An empirical analysis of lengths of stay and exits.* Presentation made to the California Association for Services to Children. San Diego, CA (May).

Wedeven, T., & Mauzerall, H. (1990). Independent living programs: Avenues to competence. In A.N. Maluccio, R. Krieger, & B.A. Pine (Eds.), *Preparing adolescents for life after foster care—The central role of foster parents* (pp. 91–105). Washington, DC: Child Welfare League of America.

Wedeven, T., Pecora, P.J., Hurwitz, M., Howell, R., & Newell, D. (1997). Examining the perceptions of alumni of long-term family foster care: A follow-up study. *Community Alternatives—International Journal of Family Care, 9,* 88–106.

Weedon, J., Rotri, T.W., & Zunder, P. (1988). Vermont Division of Social Services family risk assessment matrix research and evaluation. In T. Tatara (Ed.), *Validation research in CPS risk assessment: Three recent studies.* (Occasional monograph series of APWA Social R&D Department, No. 2.) Washington, DC: American Public Welfare Association.

Weeks, N.B. (1953). *Adoption for school-age children in institutions.* New York: Child Welfare League of America.

Weil, M., Karls, J.M., & Associates. (1985). *Case management in human service practice.* San Francisco: Jossey-Bass.

Weininger, O., & Brown, D.B. (1972). *The Browndale therapeutic family: An evaluation of treatment results.* Involvement Supplement.

Weinstein, E. (1960). *The self-image of the foster child.* New York: Russell Sage Foundation.

Weiss, H. (1983). *Strengthening families and rebuilding the social infrastructure: A review of family support and education programs.* Paper prepared for the Charles Stewart Mott Foundation, Flint, MI.

Weiss, H. (1993). Home visits: Necessary but not sufficient. *The Future of Children—Home Visiting, 3*(3), 113–128.

Weiss, H., & Jacobs, F. (1988). *Evaluating family programs.* Hawthorne, NY: Aldine de Gruyter.

Weiss, J.G., & Hawkins, J.D. (1981). *Reports of the national juvenile justice assessment centers: Preventing delinquency.* Washington, DC: U.S. National Institute for Juvenile Justice and Delinquency Prevention.

Weissbourd, B. (1987). A brief history of family support programs. In S. Kagan, D. Powell, B. Weissbourd, & E. Zigler (Eds.), *America's family support programs: Perspectives and prospects* (pp. 38–56). New Haven, CT: Yale University Press.

Weissbourd, B., & Kagan, S.L. (1989). Family support programs: Catalysts for change. *American Journal of Orthopsychiatry, 59,* 20–31.

Weissbourd, R. (1996). *The vulnerable child.* Reading, MA: Addison-Wesley.

Weisz, J.R., Weiss, H.B., & Donenberg, G.R. (1992). The lab versus the clinic: Effects of child and adolescent psychotherapy. *American Psychologist, 47*(12), 1578–1585.

Wells, K. (1991). Placement of emotionally disturbed children in residential treatment: A review of placement criteria. *American Journal of Orthopsychiatry, 61*(3), 339–347.

Wells, K., & Biegel, D.E. (1991). *Family preservation services: Research and evaluation.* Newbury Park, CA: Sage.

Wells, K., & Freer, R. (1994). Reading between the lines: The case for qualitative research in intensive family preservation services. *Children and Youth Review, 16*(5), 323–378.

Wells, K., & Whittington, D. (1993a). Child and family functioning after intensive family preservation services. *Social Service Review, 67,* 55–83.

Wells, K., & Whittington, D. (1993b). Characteristics of youth referral to residential treatment. *Children and Youth Services Review, 15,* 195–217.

Wells, K., Wyatt, E., & Hobfoll, S. (1991). Factors associated with adaptation of youths discharged from residential treatment. *Children and Youth Services Review, 13*(3), 199–217.

Wells, K.W. (1991). Long term residential treatment for children: Introduction. *American Journal of Orthopsychiatry,* 324–327.

Wells, K.W., & Whittaker, J.K. (1989). Integrating research and agency based practice: Approaches, problems and possibilities. In E. Balcerzak (Ed.), *Group care of children: Transition toward the year 2000* (pp. 67–92). Washington, DC: Child Welfare League of America.

Wells, S., Stein, T., Fluke, J., & Downing, J. (1989). Screening in child protective services. *Social Work, 34*(1), 45–48.

Wells, S.J. (1994). Child protective services: Research for the future. *Child Welfare: A Research Agenda for Child Welfare, LXXIII*(5), 431–447.

Werner, E.E. (1989). High risk children in young adulthood: A longitudinal study from birth to 32 years. *American Journal of Orthopsychiatry, 59*(1), 72–81.

Wheeler, C.E., Reuter, G., Struckman-Johnson, D., & Yuan, Y.T. (1992). *Evaluation of state of Connecticut intensive family preservation services: Phase V annual report.* Report prepared for Division of Family Support and Community Living, Department of Children and Youth Services, Hartford, CT. Sacramento, CA: Walter R. McDonald & Associates, Inc.

Whitbeck, L.B., Hoyt, D.R., & Ackley, K.A. (1997). Abusive family backgrounds and later victimization among runaway and homeless adolescents. *Journal of Research on Adolescence, 7*(4), 375–392.

White, K.R. (1988). Cost analyses in family support programs. In H.B. Weiss & F.C. Jacobs (Eds.), *Evaluating family programs* (pp. 429–443). Hawthorne, NY: Aldine de Gruyter.

White, R., & Cornely, D. (1981). Navajo child abuse and neglect study: A comparison group examination of abuse and neglect of Navaho children. *Child Abuse and Neglect, 5*(1), 9–17.

Whiteman, M., Fanshel, D., & Grundy, J.F. (1987). Cognitive-behavioral interventions aimed at anger of parents at risk of child abuse. *Social Work, 32,* 469–474.

Whitey, V., Anderson, R., & Lauderdale, M. (1980). Volunteers as mentors for abusing parents: A natural helping relationship. *Child Welfare, 59,* 637–644.

Whitley, D.M., White, K.R., Kelley, S.J., & Yorke, B. (1999). Strengths-based case management: The application to grandparents raising grandchildren. *Social Work, 80,* 110–119.

Whitmore, W.H. (1876). *The law of adoption in the U.S.* Albany, NY: J. Munsell.

Whittaker, J.K. (1971a). Colonial child care institutions: Our heritage of care. *Child Welfare, 50,* 396–400.

Whittaker, J.K. (1971b). Mental hygiene influences in children's institutions: Organization and technology for treatment. *Mental Hygiene, 55,* 444–450.

Whittaker, J.K. (1978). The changing character of residential child care: An ecological perspective. *Social Service Review, 22,* 21–36.

Whittaker, J. K. (1979/1997). *Caring for troubled children: Residential treatment in a community context.* Hawthorne, NY: Aldine de Gruyter.

Whittaker, J.K. (1981). Family involvement in residential treatment: A support system for parents. In A.N. Maluccio & P.A. Sinanoglu (Eds.), *The challenge of partnership: working with parents of children in foster care* (pp. 67–88). New York: Child Welfare League of America.

Whittaker, J.K. (1984). Formal and informal helping in child welfare services: Implications for management and practice. *Child Welfare, 65,* 17–25.

Whittaker, J.K. (1991a). The leadership challenge in family-based practice: Implications for policy, practice, research, and education. In A.L. Sallee & J.C. Lloyd (Eds.), *Family preservation: Papers for the institute for social work educators 1990.* Riverdale, IL: National Association for Family-Based Services.

Whittaker, J.K. (1991b). The leadership challenge in family-based services: Policy, practice, and research. *Families in Society: The Journal of Contemporary Human Services, 72*(5), 294–300.

Whittaker, J. K. (2000). The future of residential group care. *Child Welfare, 79*(1), 59–74.

Whittaker, J. K. (In press). Reinventing residential childcare: An agenda for research and practice. *Residential Treatment for Children and Youth.*

Whittaker, J.K., Fine, D., & Grasso, A. (1989). Characteristics of adolescents and their families in residential treatment intake: An exploratory study. In E. Balcerzak (Ed.), *Group care of children: Transition toward the year 2000* (pp. 67–87). Washington, DC: Child Welfare League of America.

Whittaker, K., Fine, D., Grasso, A., & Mooradian, J. (1990). *Differential patterns of family involvement in residential youth care and treatment: An empirical analysis.* Unpublished manuscript. Clinton, MI: Boysville of Michigan.

Whittaker, J.K., Garbarino, J., & Associates. (1983). *Social support networks: Informal helping in the human services.* Hawthorne, NY: Aldine de Gruyter.

Whittaker, J.K., Kinney, J.M., Tracy, E.M., & Booth, C. (Eds.). (1990). *Reaching high-risk families: Intensive family preservation in human services.* Hawthorne, NY: Aldine de Gruyter.

Whittaker, J.K., & Maluccio, A.N. (1988). Understanding families in trouble in foster and residential care. In F. Cox, C. Chilman, & E. Nunnally (Eds.), *Families in trouble* (Vol. 5): *Variant family forms.* Newbury Park, CA: Sage.

Whittaker, J.K., Overstreet, E.J., Grasso, A., Tripodi, T., & Boylan, F. (1988). Multiple indicators of success in residential youth care and treatment. *American Journal of Orthopsychiatry, 58,* 143–147.

Whittaker, J.K., & Pecora, P.J. (1981). The social "R & D" paradigm in child and youth services. *Children and Youth Services Review, 3,* 305–317.

Whittaker, J.K., & Pecora, P.J. (1984). A research agenda for residential care. In J. Philpot (Ed.), *Group care practice: The challenge of the next decade* (pp. 71–87). Sutton, Surrey, England: Community Care/Business Press International.

Whittaker, J.K., & Pfeiffer, S.I. (1994). Research priorities for residential group child care. *Child Welfare, 73,* 583–601

Whittaker, J.K., Schinke, S.P., & Gilchrist, L.D. (1986). The ecological paradigm in child, youth, and family services: Implications for policy and practice. *Social Service Review, 60,* 483–503.

Whittaker, J.K., & Tracy, E.M. (1989). *Social treatment: An introduction to interpersonal helping in social work practice* (2nd ed.). Hawthorne, NY: Aldine de Gruyter.

Whittaker, J.K., Tracy, E.M., & Marckworth, M. (1989). *Family support project: Identifying informal support resources for high risk families.* University of Washington, School of Social Work, Seattle, Washington and Behavioral Sciences Institute, Federal Way, Washington.

Whittaker, J.K., & Trieschman, A.E. (Eds.). (1972). *Children away from home: A sourcebook of residential treatment.* Hawthorne, NY: Aldine de Gruyter.

Widom, C.S. (1989). The cycle of violence. *Science, 244,* 160–166.

Wiehe, V.R. (1980). Current practices in performance appraisal. *Administration in Social Work, 4*(3), 1–11.

Wiehe, V.R. (1997). Approaching child abuse treatment perspective of empathy. *Child Abuse and Neglect, 21*(12), 1191–1204.

Willems, D.M., & DeRubeis, R. (1981). *The effectiveness of intensive preventive services for families with abused, neglected or disturbed children.* Trenton, NJ: Bureau of Research, New Jersey Division of Youth and Family Services.

Williams, B.K. (Ed.). (1995). *Family centered services: A handbook for practitioners.* Iowa City, IA: The National Resource Center for Family Centered Practice.

Williams, W. (1980). *The implementation perspective: A guide for managing social service delivery programs.* Berkeley: University of California Press.

Williams, W., & Elmore, R.F. (1976). *Social program implementation.* New York: Academic Press.

Williamson, M. (1931). *The social worker in child care and protection.* New York: Harper.

Wilson, D., & Morton, T.D. (1997). *Issues in CPS decision making. Decision making in children's protective services.* Atlanta, GA: Child Welfare Institute and ACTION for Child Protection.

Wilson, D.B., & Chipungu, S.S. (1996). Introduction. Special issue on kinship care. *Child Welfare, 75,* 387–662.

Wiltse, K.T. (1978). Current issues and new directions in foster care. In *Child welfare strategy in the coming years* (pp. 51–89) (Publication No. 78–30158). Washington, DC: U.S. Government Printing Office.

Wiltse, K.T. (1980). *Education and training for child welfare services.* Unpublished manuscript. Berkeley, CA: School of Social Welfare, University of California at Berkeley.

Wischlacz, C., Lane, J., & Kempe, C. (1978). Indian child welfare: A community team approach to protective services. *Child Abuse and Neglect, 2*(1), 29–35.

Wisconsin General Laws 1932. (Ter. Ed., C.210, Sec. 5A). Madison, WI: State of Wisconsin.

Wolfe, D.A. (1993). Prevention of child neglect. *Criminal Justice and Behavior, 20*(1), 90–111.

Wolfe, D.A., & McGee, R. (1994). Dimensions of child maltreatment and their relationship to adolescent adjustment. *Development and Psychopathology, 6,* 165–181.

Wolfensberger, W. (1972a). *The principle of normalization in the human services.* Toronto, Canada: National Institute on Mental Retardation.

Wolfensberger, W. (1972b). *Normalization.* New York: National Institute on Mental Retardation.

Wolin, S., & Wolin, S. (1996). Let childhood adversity challenge rather than defeat you. *The Brown University Family Therapy Letter.* Providence, RI: Manissess Communications Group, Inc.

Wolins, M. (1974a). *Group care: Explorations in the powerful environment.* Hawthorne, NY: Aldine de Gruyter.

Wolins, M. (1974b). *Successful group care: Explorations in the powerful environment.* Chicago: Aldine de Gruyter.

Wolins, M., & Piliavin, I. (1964). *Institution and foster family: A century of debate.* New York: CWLA.

Wood, J.M. (1997). Risk predictors for re-abuse and re-neglect in a predominantly Hispanic population. *Child Abuse and Neglect, 21,* 379–389.

Wooden, K. (1976). *Weeping in the playtime of others.* New York: McGraw-Hill.

Woolf, G.D. (1990). An outlook for foster care in the U.S. *Child Welfare, 69,* 75–81.

Wright, B. (1980). *An overview of the Indian Child Welfare Act of 1978.* State of Washington: Office of the Attorney General.

Wulczyn, F., Brunner, K., & Goerge, R. (1999). *An update from the multistate foster care data archive: Foster care dynamics (1983–1997).* Chicago, IL: Chapin Hall Center for Children at the University of Chicago.

Wulczyn, F.H., & Goerge, R.M. (1992). Foster care in New York and Illinois: The challenge of rapid change. *Social Services Review, 66,* 278–294.

Wulczyn, F.H., Harden, A., & Goerge, R.M. (1997). *Foster care dynamics: 1983—1994: An update from the multistate foster care data archive.* Chicago, IL: The University of Chicago, The Chapin Hall Center for Children.

Wulczyn, F.H., & Zeidman, D. (with A. Svirsky). (1997). HomeRebuilders: A family reunification demonstration project. In J.D. Berrick, R.P. Barth, & N. Gilbert (Eds.), *Child welfare research review* (Vol. II, pp. 252–271). New York: Columbia University Press.

Wurtele, S.K., Marrs, S.R., & Miller-Perrin, C.L. (1987). Practice makes perfect? The role of participant modeling in sexual abuse prevention programs. *Journal of Consulting and Clinical Psychology, 55,* 599–602.

Wyatt, G.E. (1985). The sexual abuse of Afro-American and white American women in childhood. *Child Abuse and Neglect, 9,* 231–240.

Wynn, J., Costello, J., Halpern, R., & Richman, H. (1994). *Children, families, and communities: A new approach to social studies.* Chicago, IL: The Chapin Hall Center for Children at University of Chicago.

Wynn, J.R., Merry, S.M., & Berg, P.G. (1995). *Children, families, and communities: Early lessons from a new approach to social services.* Washington, DC: American Youth Policy Forum.

Yale Bush Center in Child Development and Social Policy, and Family Resource Coalition. (1983). *Programs to strengthen families: A resource guide.* Chicago, IL: The Family Resource Coalition.

Yegidis, B., & Morton, T.D. (1999). Item bias and CPS assessments. *Ideas in Action.* Atlanta: Child Welfare Institute.

Yinger, J. (1995). *Closed doors, opportunities lost: The continuing costs of housing discrimination.* New York: Russell Sage Foundation.

Young, D.W., & Allen, B. (1977). Benefit-cost analysis in the social services: The example of adoption reimbursement. *Social Service Review, 51,* 249–264.

Young, L.R. (1964). *Wednesday's children: A study of child neglect and abuse.* New York: McGraw-Hill

Young, N., Gardner, S., Coley, S., Schorr, L., & Bruner, C. (1994). *Making a difference: Moving to outcome based accountability from comprehensive service reforms.* Des Moines, IA: National Center for Service Integration.

Youssef, R.M., Attia, M.S., & Kamel, M.I. (1998). Children experiencing violence I; parental use of corporal punishment. *Child Abuse and Neglect, 22*(10), 959–973.

Yuan, Y.Y., & Rivest, M. (Eds.). (1990). *Preserving families—Evaluation resources for practitioners and policymakers.* Newbury Park, CA: Sage.

Yuan, Y.Y., McDonald, W.R., Alderson, J., & Struckman-Johnson, D. (1988). *Evaluation of AB1562 demonstration projects: Year two interim report.* Sacramento, CA: Walter R. McDonald and Associates.

Yuan, Y.T., McDonald, W.R., Wheeler, C.E., Stuckman-Johnson, D., & Rivest, M. (1990). *Evaluation of AB1562 in-home care demonstration projects* (Vol. 1): *Final report.* Sacramento, CA: Walter R. McDonald & Associates.

Zainaldin, J.S. (1976). *The origins of modern legal adoption child exchange in Boston, 1951.* Chicago, IL: The University of Chicago Press.

Zastrow, C., & Kirst-Ashman, K. (1997). *Understanding human behavior and the social environment.* Chicago: Nelson-Hall.

Zigler, E. (1979). Controlling child abuse in America: An effort doomed to failure. In R. Bourne & E. Newberger (Eds.), *Critical perspectives on child abuse.* Lexington, MA: D.C. Heath.

Zigler, E., & Black, K. (1989). America's family support movement: Strengths and limitations. *American Journal or Orthopsychiatry, 59,* 6–20.

Zigler, E., & Hall, N.W. (1989). Physical child abuse in America: past, present, and future. In D. Cicchetti & V. Carlson (Eds.), *Child maltreatment: Theory and research on the causes and consequences of child abuse and neglect* (pp. 38–75). Cambridge, England: Cambridge University Press.

Zigler, E., & Styfco, S. (Eds.). (1993). *Head Start and beyond: A national plan for extended childhood intervention.* New Haven, CT: Yale University Press.

Zlotnik, J.L. (1997). *Preparing the workforce for family-centered practice: Social work education and public human services partnerships.* Alexandria, VA: Council on Social Work Education.

Zlotnik, J.L., McCroskey, J., Gardner, S., Gil de Gibaja, M., Taylor, H., Goerge, S., Lind, J., Jordan-Marsh, J., Costa, V., & Taylor-Dinwiddie, S. (1999). *Myths and opportunities: Executive summary,* Alexandria, VA: Council on Social Work Education.

Zlotnik, J.L., Rome, S.H., & DePanfilis, D. (1998). *Educating for child welfare practice—A compendium of exemplary syllabi.* Alexandria, VA: Council on Social Work Education.

Zuravin, S. J. (1987). The ecology of child maltreatment: Identifying and characterizing high-risk neighborhoods. *Child Welfare, 66,* 497–506.

Zuravin, S.J. (1989). *Suggestions for operationally defining child physical abuse and physical neglect.* Paper prepared for meeting on Issues in the Longitudinal Study of Child Maltreatment, Toronto, Ontario. Baltimore, MD: The School of Social Work and Community Planning, University of Maryland at Baltimore.

Zuravin, S.J., McMillen, C., DePanfilis, D., & Risley-Curtiss, C. (1996). The intergenerational cycle of child maltreatment: Continuity versus discontinuity. *Journal of Interpersonal Violence, 11*(3), 315–334.

Zuravin, S.J., Orme, J.G., & Hegar, R.L. (1995). Disposition of child physical abuse reports: review of the literature and test of a predictive model. *Children and Youth Services Review, 17*(4), 559–580.

Zuravin, S.J., & DePanfilis, D. (1997). Factors affecting foster care placement of children receiving child protective services. *Social Work Research, 21(*1), 34–42.

Zuravin, S., & Starr, R., Jr. (1991). Psychosocial characteristics of mothers of physically abused and neglected children: So they differ by race? In R. H. Hampton (Ed.), *Black family violence.* Lexington, MA: Lexington Books.

Zuravin, S., & Taylor, R. (1987). *Family planning behaviors and child care adequacy.* Final report submitted to the U. S. Department of Health and Human Services, Office of Population Affairs (Grant FPR 000028-01-1).

Zwimpfer, D.M. (1983). Indicators of adoption breakdown. *Social Casework, 64,* 169–177.

Author Index

AAPC, 460–461, 463
Abbey, H., 317
Abbott, Grace, 21
Abel, G.G., 186, 191
Abell, N., 275
Abney, V.D., 482
Abrahams, N., 461
Abramovitz, M., 26
Achtenberg, R.A., 310
Adams, P., 236–237
Addams, J., 21
Adelson, E., 243
Administration for Children and Families, 350
Administration of Children, Youth, and Families
    (U.S. Children's Bureau), 1, 19, 269
Adoption and Safe Families Act (ASFA), 16
Ahart, S., 140
Ainsworth, F., 343, 351, 430
Albers, E., 438
Albert, V., 356–357, 424
Alderson, J., 290
Aldgate, J., 80, 306, 321, 324
Alexander, G., 436
Alexander, R.A., 313
Alfaro, J.D., 141
Allen, M., 12, 33–34, 39, 56, 60, 237, 249
Allen, M.L., 267
Allen, R.I., 64, 321
Allen, T.C., 479
Allerhand, M.E., 412, 415
Allphin, S., 402
Alpert, S.W., 412, 415
Ambrosino, L., 458
Ambrosino, R., 156
American Association for Protecting Children,
    135
American Bar Association, 4
American Civil Liberties Union (ACLU), 29
American Humane Association (AHA), 4–6, 8–
    9, 145–146, 165
American Public Human Services Association, 434
American Public Welfare Association, 5, 163

Ammons, P.W., 202, 207
Anderson, G., 74
Anderson, G.R., 314, 350
Anderson, P.G., 29, 161, 460
Anderson, R., 156
Andrews, A.B., 68
Annie E. Casey Foundation, 4, 256–257
Anthony, E.J., 72
APHSA Finance Work Group, 17
Applebaum, M., 242
Apsler, R., 417
Ards, S., 482
Areen, J., 458
Arkinson, M.K., 207
Armijo, M., 324, 350–351, 424
Artemyeff, C., 156
Attia, M.S., 130
Austin, M.J., 438, 443
Authier, K.J., 272
Avery, L.S., 207
Avery, R., 1, 311, 364
Axinn, J., 458
Ayers, B., 266

Bachman, R., 370
Backer, T.E., 416–417
Bailey Developmental Assessment, 213
Bailey, J.M., 389
Bailey, T.F., 216, 218
Bailey, W.H., 216, 218
Baird, C., 140
Bakan, D., 156
Bakeis, C.D., 371
Baker, B.L., 418
Baker, W.A., 435
Balyeat, R., 270
Banach, M., 302
Bane, W., 343
Banks, L., 342
Baran, A., 366, 385
Barker, P., 417
Barlow, D.H., 416

Barnard, K.E., 246, 285

Barnett, D., 134

Barnett, W.S., 404

Barrett, B.J., 38

Barry, F.D., 68

Barsh, R.L., 370–371

Barth, R., 306

Barth, R.P., 41–42, 67, 74, 88, 156, 167, 259, 291, 307–308, 311–312, 317, 319, 323–324, 346, 350–352, 354, 356–359, 372–373, 380–383, 385–392, 394–396, 398–402, 418, 423–424, 450

Bassuk, E., 417

Bath, H.I., 290

Beals, J., 370

Bean, G., 129, 316

Beatty, C., 53

Beauchamp, C., 242

Becerra, R.M., 130, 134, 148, 195

Becker, J.V., 186

Becker-Larsen, E., 217

Behrman, R.E., 166, 240, 258

Belknap, J., 54

Bell, C.J., 473

Belsky, J., 128, 147–151, 221

Benard, B., 200, 213

Bender, B., 421, 426

Bending, R.L., 313–314

Benedict, M., 317, 354

Berg, P.G., 255

Berger, M., 223

Bergman, A.B., 244

Bergmann, B., 108

Berlin, F., 191

Berliner, L., 162, 259

Berrick, J., 41, 67, 306, 308–309, 345–346, 351–352

Berrick, J.D., 13, 317, 356–357, 423–424

Berrueta-Clement, J.R., 404

Berry, M., 74, 85, 88, 319, 342, 380–381, 383, 385–386, 389, 394–396, 398–401

Besharov, D.J., 23, 42, 55, 241, 359, 454–455, 466

Bezruczko, N., 252

Bianchi, S., 102

Biegel, D.E., 275

Biehal, N., 321, 341

Billingsley, A., 156, 312

Black, K., 249

Blackwell, D.L., 312, 346, 450

Blair, D.M., 383

Blanchard, E.L., 371

Blank, R., 102, 106–107

Blome, W.W., 306

Bloom, M., 70–72, 78

Blumenthal, K., 303

Blyth, B.J., 156

Bobrow, D., 389

Boersdorfer, R.K., 397

Bogues, J.L., 214

Bolton, F., 468

Bonecutter, F.J., 353–354

Bonner, B.L., 469

Booth, C., 263, 265, 270

Booz-Allen & Hamilton, 438

Borduin, C.M., 273, 290

Borgman, R., 385

Borrego, J., 158

Botsko, M., 248–249

Boyd, L.A., 347

Boyd-Franklin, N., 83

Boylan, F., 427

Boyne, J., 381

Boystown, 422

Brace, C.L., 297, 300, 367, 409

Bradbury, B., 102

Bradford, J., 156

Brandt, A.M., 430

Brandt, D., 317

Branham, E., 389

Brannon, D., 443

Brassard, M.R., 215–216, 218–219, 222–224

Braswell, M.C., 221

Brawley, E.A., 445

Braziel, D.J., 407, 430

Breakey, G., 231, 233, 243, 245–246

Breakey, G.F., 247

Breckenridge, S.P., 367

Breezle, P., 149, 468

Bremner, R.H., 266, 300, 409

Brewer, R., 28

Briar, K., 455

Briar, K.H., 440

Briar-Lawson, K., 84, 436

Bricker-Jenkins, M., 6

Brieland, D., 275

Briere, J., 162

Brissett-Chapman, S., 6, 482

Broadhurst, D.D., 140, 152, 175, 198, 219, 461, 465

Brondino, M.J., 293

Bronfenbrenner, U., 65, 150, 275

Brooks, D., 354, 385, 388, 390, 392, 400

Brooks-Gunn, J., 103, 200–201
Bross, D.C., 161
Brown, J., 201
Brown, J.H., 81, 436
Brown, M.E., 381, 389
Brown, P., 237
Brown, S.E., 221
Brown, W.K., 72
Browne, A., 184, 186, 469
Bruner, C., 8, 291
Brunner, K., 424
Bryce, M., 264
Bryce, M.E., 273, 276, 279, 291
Budde, S., 131
Budetti, P., 103
Bulkley, J.A., 162
Bullock, R., 418
Bumbarger, B., 258
Bumpass, L., 26
Burd, S., 417
Burford, G., 83
Burgess, R.L., 150, 173
Burkhauser, R.V., 108
Burnette, D., 313, 350
Burns, B.J., 417–418
Burt, M.R., 270
Burtless, G., 106
Bussey, M., 129, 468
Bussiere, A., 388
Butler, T.L., 185
Buttenweiser, E., 199, 205, 469
Byler, W., 372

Cabral, R.J., 271
Cadoret, R.J., 71
Caffey, J., 460
Cahill, B., 25
Cahn, K., 451–452
Cairons, G., 214
Callard, E.D., 271
Cameron, G., 68, 157, 236–237, 258
Campbell, M.D., 67
Carbino, R., 86, 316
Card, D., 107
Carlo, P., 343
Carnes, P., 187
Carrilio, T.E., 242
Carten, A.J., 312
Carter, B., 70
Carter, R.K., 449
Case, D., 73–74

Casey, Annie E., 7
Casey Family Programs, 4, 315, 320–321, 324, 419
Casey Family Services, 4
Cash, J.S., 85
Caulkins, J.P., 53
Cautley, P.W., 270
Center on Children and the Law (American Bar Association), 4
Center for Disease Control, 27
Center for Family Life, 249
Center for the Study of Social Policy, 16
Centers for Disease Control and Prevention, 55
Chafel, J.A., 253
Chak, A., 291
Chalmers, M.A., 199, 205, 469
Chamberlain, P., 319
Chamberlin, R., 243
Chambers, C., 21
Chambers, C.A., 297
Chambers, D.E., 449
Chan, R.W., 389
Chasnoff, I.J., 17, 55, 253–255
Chaudhry, U., 140
Chernick, H., 113
Chess, W.A., 447
Cheung, K-F.M., 7, 482
Child Abuse Prevention and Treatment Act Report, 29, 173
Child Protection Report, 55
Child Protective Services, 200
Child Welfare League of America (CWLA), 9, 36, 47, 56, 233, 262–263, 303, 309, 315, 347, 349, 386, 407, 420, 431, 448
Children Research Center, 475
Children's Defense Fund, 26, 28–30
Children's Division (American Humane Association), 4, 6
Chilman, C.S., 64
Chipungu, S.S., 83, 348, 353
Chobar, J.S., 449
Chung, C., 482
Cicchetti, D., 134
Ciliberti, P., 272
Citro, C., 99
Clark, E.A., 414
Clark, Edna McConnell, 265
Clark, H.B., 347
Clarke-Stewart, K.A., 252
Clausen, J.M., 306
Clement, P.F., 367

Clements, G., 392
Clinton, Bill, 377, 393
Coburn, N., 7
Cohen, S., 460
Cohler, B.J., 72
Cohn, A., 158, 162
Cohn, A.H., 140, 161, 192–193
Coie, J.D., 291
Cole, Betsy, 395
Cole, E., 431
Cole, E.S., 376
Cole, G., 208
Cole, R.D., 350
Coley, S., 8
Collins, L.B., 414
Collmer, C.W., 147, 149
Colorado Revised Statute, 358
Comer, E.W., 250, 253
Committee on Ways and Means (U.S. House of
    Representatives), 13, 27, 98, 111–112, 114,
    119
Conger, R.D., 150
Congressional Record, 373
Connolly, M., 83
Conover, S., 323
Conte, J.R., 171–172, 174, 178–180
Conway, E., 149, 468
Cook, R.J., 307, 323
Corey, M., 15, 451, 475–476, 478
Cornell, C.P., 153–154
Cosgrove, J., 468
Costello, E.J., 370
Costello, J., 260
Costello, T.E., 451
Costin, L.B., 23, 33, 161, 470, 473
Couch, K.A., 108
Courtney, M.E., 42, 321, 323, 339, 424
Covington, S., 54
Cowan, P.A., 200
Cox, A., 223
Cox, F.M., 64
Coyne, A., 381, 389
Craig, L.C., 350
Cranston, A., 373
Cristofalo, C., 350
Cronin, R., 273
Cross, T.L., 6
Crumbley, J., 349–350, 353
Cuccaro-Alamin, S., 424
Culross, P.L., 240, 258
Cunningham, P.B., 273

Curry, J., 412, 415–416, 422
Curtis, C.M., 313
Curtis, P., 436
Curtis, P.A., 436, 442

D'Angell, A.R., 275
Danish, S.J., 275
Danzinger, S., 102, 122
Danzy, J., 83
Darke, J., 186
Daro, D., 157, 244, 258–259, 461–462, 469
Davis, C.T., 348
Davis, I., 339, 341
Davis, I.P., 80, 339, 344
Davis, K.B., 202
Davis, S.M., 448
Dawes, R., 475
Day, P., 451–452
Deal, A.G., 79
Dear, R.B., 28
DeFrancis, V., 142
Deighton, J., 156, 187
deMause, L., 139, 149
Denby, L., 381
Denby, R., 316
Dennis, Karl, 7
DePanfilis, D., 206, 209, 475, 479
Department of Health (Great Britain), 72
Derezotes, P., 167
DeVita, C.J., 27–28, 30
Devore, W., 71
Dhooper, S.S., 440
Diamond, L.J., 156
Dickinson, N.S., 441
DiNitto, D., 32, 222
Dobrec, A., 38
Dodge, D., 451
Domitrovich, C., 258
Donenberg, G.R., 290
Dore, M.M., 291
Doueck, H.J., 167, 475
Downing, J., 462, 474
Downs, G., 73–74, 267
Downs, S., 73–74, 267
Downs, S.W., 23, 33, 73, 473, 478
Drews, K., 451
Drizd, T.A., 211
Duchnowski, A.J., 418
Duggan, A.K., 248
Duncan, G., 103
Dunst, C.J., 79

Durkin, A.B., 414
Durkin, R.P., 414
Dye, T., 32, 222
Dylla, D.J., 385
Dziech, B.W., 160

Earle, R., 248
Earls, C.M., 186
Ebata, A., 217
Edelson, J.L., 154
Edna McConnell Clark Foundation, 268
Edwards, M., 140
Edwards, M.E., 140
Egeland, B., 203, 221
Egolf, B., 140
Einbender, A.J., 149
Ekstein, R., 425–426
Elder, G.H., 65
Ellett, A., 440–441
Ellett, A.J., 441
Ellett, C.D., 441
Elliot, L.K., 243
Ellwood, D., 121, 122
Elmore, R.F., 436
Emlen, A., 73, 267
Eng. Rep., 458
Engler, R.E., 22, 267, 300
English, D., 467
English, D.J., 7, 200–201, 212, 214, 475, 476–
477, 479, 482
Enos, S., 54
Epstein, A.S., 404
Epstein, I., 449
Epstein, M.H., 418
Erera, P.I., 344
Erikson, E.H., 71, 205
Erikson, M.F., 203, 221
Erné, D., 147–148, 158
Esplin, P.W., 192
Esposito, G., 431
Evans, S., 214
Everett, J.E., 83, 351
Everingham, S.S., 258
The Executive Session on Child Protection, Far-
row with, 164, 166

Falicov, C.J., 70
Faller, K.C., 183
Family Resource Coalition, 233, 236
Fanshel, D., 22, 73, 79–80, 267–270, 284, 300,
305, 320–322, 324, 418–419, 468

Farkas, K.J., 275
Farley, J.E., 70
Farmer, E., 341
Farrington, D.P., 291
Farrow, F., 164, 166, 233, 235, 275
Feagans, L., 442
Federal Interagency Forum on Child and Family
Statistics, 27
Feild, T., 450
Fein, F., 12, 156, 305, 311–312, 320–322, 324,
339–340, 346
Ferguson, C., 235
Ferguson, S.K., 54
Fergusson, D.M., 469
Fernandez, E., 306, 344, 466
Festinger, T., 321, 341, 345
Filip, J., 146
Finch, S.J., 284, 320–321, 419, 468
Fine, D., 80, 426
Fine, M., 431
Finkelhor, D., 154, 161, 173–178, 180–184,
186, 187–189, 191, 193, 469
Finlay, B., 237
Fiscella, K., 241
Fischler, R.S., 370–371
Fitzgerald, J., 396
Fitzgerald, R., 273
Fitzharris, T., 426
Fixsen, D.L., 414
Flanagan, M., 185
Flango, C.R., 364
Flango, V.E., 364
Flanzer, J.P., 222
Fleming, T., 270
Fluke, J., 7, 129, 462, 468, 474
Fluke, J.D., 140
Folaron, G., 311, 356
Folks, H., 458
Folman, R.D., 321
Fong, R., 272–273, 311, 314
Fontana, V.J., 141, 149, 221
Fontes, L., 185
Forsythe, P.W., 270
Fox, A., 324, 350–351
FRAC, 49
Fraiberg, S., 243
Frasch, K., 385
Fraser, M., 285, 287, 290–292
Fraser, M.W., 68, 250, 266, 270, 273, 314, 340–
341, 357
Frede, E., 253

Freed, A.O., 70
Freud, A., 11, 23, 470
Freud, S., 71
Freundich, M., 384
Friedlander, D., 106
Friedman, B., 275
Friedman, M., 16
Friedman, R.M., 16, 417–418
Friedrich, W.N., 149
Friman, P.C., 412
Fryer, G., 140

Gabel, K., 53–54
Gabinet, L., 156
Gabriel, K.R., 469
Gai, D., 468
Gailey, J., 270
Gaines, R.W., 140
Galagher, J.J., 59
Galaway, B., 289, 305, 319
Galinsky, M., 421
Gallagher, J., 22
Gamble, D.N., 86
Gambrill, E., 56, 64, 74, 475
Ganger, W., 80, 335, 341
Garbarino, J., 65, 67–68, 72, 86, 135, 148–150,
    156, 216–218, 221–226, 275, 469
Gardner, S., 8
Garfinkel, I., 110, 123–124
Garval, H.S., 435
Gaudin, J.M., 199, 201–203, 207, 209, 221, 284
Gauding, J.M., Jr., 480
Gauld, J., 421
Geismar, L., 266
Gelles, R.J., 23, 130, 136, 153–154, 168
General Accounting Office, 8, 56, 235–237,
    306, 411–412
Geremia, V., 273, 336, 341
Germain, C.G., 65–67, 70–72, 78
Germain, R., 215
Germanis, P., 241
Giaconia, R., 468
Gil, D., 24, 129, 134–135, 148–149
Gil, D.G., 59, 224
Gilbert, N., 354
Gilchrist, L.D., 67–68, 167, 416
Giles-Sims, J., 154
Gilligan, C., 71
Giovanni, J., 312
Giovanni, J.M., 129–130, 134, 148, 156, 195, 460

Girard, J.L., 68, 81
Gitterman, A., 65–68, 86
Glaser, G., 468
Gleeson, J.P., 350, 353–354
Glisson, C., 437
Goerge, R., 424
Goerge, R.M., 1, 13, 269, 271, 308, 310–313,
    325, 339, 346, 354–356, 373, 401
Goertz, B., 13
Gogan, H.C., 323
Goldberg-Glen, R., 350
Golden, O., 386
Golder, S., 54
Golding, J.M., 469
Goldstein, A.P., 147–148, 158–160
Goldstein, J., 11, 23, 302, 470
Goldstein, S., 23
Gollub, S.L., 386
Golombek, S., 389
Gomby, D., 240
Gomby, D.S., 240, 258
Goode, W.J., 156
Goodin, J., 275
Goodwin, J., 185
Gordon, M., 221
Gottlieb, B., 275
Gottlieb, N., 6
Gottschalk, P., 102, 122
Government Accounting Office (GAO), 41–42,
    231, 258, 262, 431
Grasso, A., 80, 426–427
Grasso, A.J., 449
Gray, E., 241, 468
Grazio, T., 245
Green, A.H., 140
Green, B.L., 260
Greenberg, M.T., 258
Greene, R.B., 68
Greenwood, P.W., 258
Grogan-Kaylor, A., 321
Grohoski, L., 273
Gross, E., 37
Grossman, D.C., 140
Groth, A.N., 187, 190
Grow, L.J., 388
Gruber, A.R., 267
Grundy, J.F., 284, 320–321, 419, 468
Gutiérrez, L., 438
Guttman, E., 216, 218, 469
Guyer, J., 123

Haapala, D.A., 270, 280, 290, 292
Haas, P.J., 59
Hackman, J.R., 448
Hacsi, T., 297, 409
Haeuser, A.A., 129
Hage, D., 375
Hagemann, M., 252
Haggerty, K.P., 250
Haggerty, R.J., 230, 239
Hainston, C.F., 353
Halfon, N., 306
Hall, C., 196
Halpern, E.S., 284
Halpern, R., 60–61, 253, 260, 335
Hamill, P.V.V., 211
Hanson, K.W., 52, 55
Harden, A.W., 269, 271, 308, 310–312, 325,
    339, 346, 355–356, 373
Hardin, A., 1, 13
Hardin, M., 8, 12, 83, 450
Harm, N.J., 54
Harper, C., 7
Harris, J.R., 71
Harris, N., 143
Harrison, L.L., 214
Hart, S.N., 215–216, 218–219, 222–224
Hartman, A., 14, 64, 78
Harvard Executive Session on Child Protection, 5
Haskins, R., 22, 59
Hastings, J., 291
Hauer, A.L., 275
Haug, M., 412, 415
Haugaard, J.J., 184–185
Haveman, R., 121
Hawkins, D.J., 250
Hawley, D., 324
Hayes, K., 163, 455
Heclo, H., 105
Hegar, R.L., 85, 347–349, 353, 355, 480
Heisterman, C.A., 367
Helfer, R.E., 258
Hemmelgarn, A., 437
Henderson, C., 242
Henderson, C.R., 243, 260, 290–291
Henderson, J., 467
Henggler, S.W., 273, 279, 293
Herman, J.L., 187–188
Herrenkohl, E.C., 140
Herrenkohl, R.C., 140
Hershberger, J.K., 149

Hershorn, M., 154
Herzberger, S.D., 153
Hess, P.M., 80, 248–249, 311, 343–344
Hicks Marlowe, J., 342
Hill, M., 321
Hill, R.B., 312
Hirayama, K., 478
Hirsch, J.S., 270
Hobbs, N., 411, 421–422
Hobfoll, S., 412, 415
Hodges, V.G., 68, 85, 157
Holden, G.W., 154
Holden, J.S., 244
Holder, W., 162–163, 451, 455, 475–476, 478
Holder, W.M., 15
Holliday, M., 273
Hollinger, J., 371
Holmes, W.M., 222
Holohan, C.J., 67
Holzer, H., 108
Hong, G.K., 468
Hong, L.K., 468
Hooyman, N.R., 6
Horejsi, C.R., 480, 482
Hornby, H., 352
Horton, A.L., 186, 190
Houbé, J., 258
Houlgate, L.D., 80
Howard, A., 392
Howard, E.C., 401
Howard, J.A., 396–397, 400–401
Howell, J.C., 51
Howing, P.T., 151, 480
Hubbell, R., 38
Hudson, J., 83, 289, 305, 319
Hughes, R.C., 316–317, 336
Hull, R.K., 380, 390
Humphreys, K., 53
Hunter, R.S., 156
Hunzeker, J.M., 85
Hutchinson, J.R., 267
Hyman, I.A., 223–224

Immigration and Naturalization Service, 364
Ingram, C., 348
Institute for Human Services Management, 4
International Conference on Psychological
    Abuse of Children and Youth, 216
Invisible Children, 425
IOM, 418

Isaacs-Shockley, M., 6
Ishisaka, A.H., 167
Iyer, S., 390

Jablonka, K., 317
Jackson, G., 388
Jackson, S., 353
Jackson, S.M., 83
Jacobs, F.H., 418
Jacoby, S., 221
Jansson, B.S, 58, 84
Jantti, M., 102
Jaudes, P.K., 156
Jayaratne, S., 447
Jencks, C., 99–100
Jenewicz, W.J., 220
Jenkins, S., 143
Jenny, C., 162, 244
Jenson, J.M., 275
Johnson, C.L., 211
Johnson, I., 341
Johnson, P.R., 357
Johnson, W., 140, 156
Johnston, D., 53–54
Jones, C., 445
Jones, D.P.H., 192
Jones, L., 340
Jones, M.A., 198, 267, 271, 291, 319–320, 478
Jonson-Reid, M., 41, 67, 259, 308, 312, 346,
    356–357, 423–424, 450
Justice, B., 187–189
Justice, R., 187–189

Kadushin, A., 149–150, 156, 297, 306, 313,
    340, 451, 460
Kagan, J., 71
Kagan, R., 81
Kagan, S., 233–234
Kagan, S.L., 79, 236–237, 249, 258, 437
Kahn, A. J., 8, 23–24, 57, 60, 67–68, 258, 260,
    270, 326, 435, 472
Kamel, M.I., 130
Kamerman, S.B., 8, 23–24, 57, 60, 67–68, 253,
    258, 260, 270, 326, 435, 472
Kaplan, L., 68, 81, 270–271, 276, 281
Kaplan, M.S., 54
Kaplan, S., 156
Karger, H.J., 161, 438, 442, 470
Karlson, H.C., 216
Karoly, L.A., 242, 258, 260
Karp, C.L., 185

Karraker, D., 352
Kaser, J.S., 397
Katz, L., 77, 105, 391
Katz, S., 364, 458
Kaufman, K.L., 469
Keller, H., 147–148, 158–160
Kelley, S.J., 191, 350
Kelly, B., 440
Kemp, S.P., 66, 68, 416
Kempe, C.H., 460, 468
Kempe, H.C., 149, 468
Kennedy, K., 421, 426
Kennell, J.H., 242
Kercher, G., 176
Kerr, D.S., 214
Kerr, M.A.D., 214
Kettering, J.R., 381
Kilburn, M.R., 258
Kilpatrick, A.C., 203, 284
Kilstrom, N., 156
Kinard, E.M., 147–148, 150, 468
Kinney, J.M., 263, 265, 270, 276, 279–283,
    291
Kinsey, A.C., 176
Kirsh, S., 66
Kirst-Ashman, K., 70
Kitzman, H., 16, 240, 242–243
Klein, M., 149, 156
Kluger, M., 436
Kluger, M.P., 346, 435
Knipe, J., 88, 267
Knitzer, J., 12, 33–34, 56, 418
Knox, J., 273
Knudsen, D.D., 468
Kohrt, P.E., 272
Korbin, J., 139, 174, 468
Kosterman, R., 250
Kozol, J., 254
Kraft, A.D., 385
Kraybill, E.N., 156
Kreilkamp, T., 71
Kreuger, A., 107
Krieger, R., 88, 314
Krisberg, B., 51
Krisberg, J., 266
Kroll, J., 364
Krugman, R.D., 192
Ku, Inhoe, 125
Kuehnel, T.G., 416
Kufeldt, K., 88, 315
Kumpfer, K.L., 258

Kunitz, S.J., 469
Kurtz, P.D., 480

Lahti, J., 267, 320
Laird, J., 14, 64, 78
Lamb, M.E., 192
Lamphear, V.S., 468
Landis, J., 178–179
Landsverk, J., 80, 335, 341, 346
Lane, I.M., 447
Laner, R., 468
Larner, M.B., 166
Larsen, R.M., 244
Larson, C.P., 242
Larson, C.S., 240
Larson, N.R., 186
Lasch, C., 301
Lathrop, J., 21
Lau, W.J., 317
Lauerdale, M., 156
Lav, I.J., 115
Lawler, E.E., III, 448
Lazere, E.B., 115
Leashore, B.R., 74, 83, 350
Lee, B., 347
Lee, R.E., 380, 390
Lee, S., 372, 387
Lehman, J., 105, 122
Leiblur, C.A., 370
Leigh, D., 107
Leon, A.M., 81–82, 86
Lerman, P., 407
Lerman, R., 102
L'Esperance, J., 156
Leung, P., 7, 482
Leventhal, J.M., 176, 178, 243, 477
Levin, H., 458
Levine, C., 430
Levine, R.A., 281
Levitan, S., 28–29
Levy, H.B., 140
Levy, J.E., 469
Lewin, K., 66
Lewis, R., 279
Lewis, R.E., 340, 357
Lewis, S.O., 468
Lewit, E.M., 240
Liaw, F.-R., 200–201
Liberman, R.P., 416
Lie, G.W., 311
Lieberman, A.A., 438

Lieberson, S., 26
Light, R., 148
Lindblad-Goldberg, M., 291
Lindblom, C.E., 437
Lindsay, P., 442
Lindsey, D., 470
Lipner, R., 13
Littell, J.H., 23, 242, 290, 292
Little, M., 418
Little, R.L., 349–350, 353
Littner, N., 319
Lloyd, J., 149, 232
Lloyd, J.C., 264, 273, 276, 279, 291
Loda, F., 156
Loeber, R., 291
Loprest, P., 113
Lorber, R., 156
Lupton, C., 83
Luscher, K., 65
Lutzkert, J.R., 271
Lyman, R.D., 417
Lynskey, M.T., 469
Lyons, P.M., 407, 412, 424

Maas, H.S., 22, 267, 300
McAllister, C., 260
McCanne, T.R., 469
McCarthy, D., 221
McCloskey, J., 469
McCroskey, J., 23, 249, 266, 285, 290, 478
McDaniel, N., 146
McDonald, B.A., 347
McDonald, T., 448
McDonald, T.P., 321
McDonald, W.R., 290
MacEachron, A.E., 311, 372
McFadden, E., 468
McFadden, E.J., 23, 33, 87
McFadden, J.E., 73
McGoldrick, M., 70
McGowan, B., 33, 248–249, 267
McGrath, M., 458
McKay, A., 267
McKenzie, M., 83
McKenzie, R.B., 315, 325
McKenzie, W., 467, 469
McLean, D., 156
McMillen, J.C., 321
McMurty, S.L., 311
McPeek, P., 156, 187
MacRae, D., 22

Maddock, J.W., 186
Madsen, B., 270
Magen, R.H., 342
Magnabosco, J.L., 448
Magura, S., 449, 478
Maidman, F., 66
Mallon, G.P., 309–310, 313
Maltos, F., 89–91
Maluccio, A.N., 12, 23, 65–66, 68–69, 73, 76,
        80, 85–88, 284, 307, 321–323, 331–336,
        339–340, 343, 346, 360, 415, 420, 444,
        449, 473
Manalo, V., 239
Manly, J.T., 134
Mann, C., 123
Mannes, M., 314
Marcenko, M., 242
Marcia, J.E., 71
Mare, R.D., 323
Margolin, L., 200
Markovic, J., 140
Marlowe, W.D., 420
Marshall, W.L., 186
Martin, H., 149, 468
Martin, J., 150, 156, 297, 306, 313, 340
Martin, J.K., 149
Martin, M.B., 469
Martinez, L., 476
Massinga, R.W., 315
Mathews, J., 353
Maurogenes, N.A., 252
Maximus, Inc., 269, 373
Mayer, M.F., 408
Mayer, S., 99–100
Maza, P.O., 2, 373
Mazur, R., 86
Meadow, R., 152
Meadowcroft, P., 315, 317, 319
Meech, E.V., 307, 323
Meezan, W., 23, 239, 249, 266, 285, 290, 364,
        367, 390
Meinecke, C.F., 191
Melton, G.B., 68, 407, 412, 424–425
Merkel-Holguin, L., 7
Merry, S.M., 255
Michael, R., 99
Mikach, S., 389
Milham, S., 418
Miller, A., 156, 222–223
Miller, J., 23, 26, 400
Miller, J.S., 477

Minty, B., 321
Mira, M., 214
Mitchel, L.B., 52
Mitchell, D., 385
Mitchell, L.B., 462
Miyoshi, T., 140
Mnookin, R.H., 267
Moelis, C.S., 129
Moen, P., 65
Molgaard, V., 258
Montagu, A., 224
Montalvo, E., 86
Moone, J., 51
Mooradian, J., 80
Moore, J.B., 213–214
Moore, W.M., 211
Moote, G.T., 475
Morgan, H., 270
Moroney, R.B., 56
Morton, T.D., 162, 482
Moses, B.S., 449, 478
Mott, P.E., 33
Motz, J.K., 468
Moynihan, D.P., 61
Mrazrek, P.J., 230, 239
Mueller, B.A., 244
Mullen, E.J., 448
Multi-state Data Archive Reports, 269
Murcer, B, 396, 396
Murdoch, A., 75
Murphy, J.M., 52, 269
Murray, C., 389
Murray, K., 183
Myers, J.B., 472
Myers, S.L., Jr., 482

Nagda, B.A., 438
Nash, J.K., 250
Nash, K.A., 314
Nasuti1 J.P., 150
Nasuti, J.P., 478
The National Adoption Center, 392
National Association of Public Child Welfare
        Administrators (NAPCWA), 5, 57, 143,
        473
National Association of Public Child Welfare
        Agency Administration, 142
National Association of Social Workers
        (NASW), 162, 431, 438
National Center on Child Abuse and Neglect
        (NCCAN), 133, 135–136, 219

National Center for Health Statistics (Center for Disease Control), 27
National Commission on Child Welfare and Family Preservation, 60
National Commission on Children, 267
National Commission on Family Foster Care, 352
National Commission for the Prevention of Child Abuse, 172
National Council of Family and Juvenile Court Judges et al., 39
National Research Council, 128–129, 134, 162
National Resource Center on Family-Based Services, 273, 278
Navarre, E., 224
Needell, B., 41, 67, 306, 308, 317, 324, 350–352, 354, 356–357, 385, 418, 423–424
Neff, R.L., 186
Nelson, C.M., 418
Nelson, D., 23
Nelson, K., 236–237, 266, 285, 287, 290
Nelson, K.A., 380, 382
Nelson, K.E., 198–199, 201–202, 267, 272, 275
Nelson, K.M., 88
Nesmith, A., 321, 323
Neuenfeldt, D., 140
Neuman, R., 271
New York City Administration for Children's Services, 136
New York State Preventive Services Demonstration Project, 271
Newman, B.M., 70
Newman, P.R., 70
Newton, R., 80, 335, 341
Nguyen, Q., 174, 480
Nishimoto, R., 249
Nisivoccia, D., 349, 353
Noble, D., 440
Nollan, K., 59
Nollan, K.A., 323
North American Council on Adoptable Children, Post-Legal Adoption Committee), 399
Nunnally, E.W., 64
Nunno, M.A., 468

Oates, R.K., 161
O'Brien, A., 75
O'Brien, M.M., 253
O'Donnell, J., 354
Office of Early Childhood Substance Abuse and Mental Health Administration, 16, 253

O'Hare, W.P., 27–28, 30
Okun, L.E., 71, 154
Olds, D.L., 16, 240–243, 260
Olmstead, K.A., 12
Olsen, L.J., 222, 311
Orme, J.G., 480
Ortega, R.M., 141
O'Toole, R., 136
Overstreet, E.J., 427
Overton, A., 266

Pablo, J., 480, 482
Paget, K.D., 200–201
Paige, R., 414
Palmer, S.E., 80, 344
Palombo, J., 385
Panel on Child Abuse and Neglect (National Research Council), 128–129, 134, 162
Panel on Research on Child Abuse and Neglect, 103, 240
Pannor, R., 366, 385
Pappenfort, D., 411
Pappenfort, D.M., 418, 425
Parke, R.D., 147, 149
Partridge, S., 395, 401
Pasztor, E.M., 316
Patterson, C.J., 389
Patterson, G.R., 342
Patti, R.J., 433, 435, 448, 452
Pearson, C.A., 418
Pecora, P.J., 7–8, 59, 68, 85, 266, 289–292, 294, 340, 357, 415, 420, 438, 440, 443, 448, 456, 469, 476–477, 482
Pelton, L.H., 24, 57, 67–68, 133, 161, 319, 434, 470
Pennell, J., 83
Penner, G.L., 271
Perlowski, K., 291
Perry, K., 315
Perry, R., 441
Peters, T.J., 433
Peterson, J.L., 272
Peterson, L., 384
Petr, C.G., 64
Pfeiffer, S.I., 412, 416–418
Phillips, E.L., 414, 422
Phillips, S.D., 54
Pickrel, S.G., 293
Pierce, L., 273, 339, 341
Pike, V., 12, 73–74, 301
Piliavin, I., 321, 323, 422

Pincus, J., 468
Pinderhughes, E., 85, 312, 314
Pine, B.A., 80, 87–88, 268, 301, 331–332,
    335–336, 340, 360, 434, 444, 473
Pizzini, S., 437
Plantz, M.C., 38, 314, 371–372
Poertner, J., 129, 435, 448–449, 468
Polansky, N.A., 148, 196, 199, 202–203, 205–
    209, 221, 281, 284, 469
Polansky, N.C., 196
Popkin, S., 108
Population Paper Listings (U.S. Bureau of the
    Census), 25
Population Reports (U.S. Bureau of the Census),
    25
Portner, H., 270
Power, E., 140
Prange, M.E., 347
Pratt, B., 231, 233, 243, 245–246
Prentice-Dunn, S., 417
Price, A., 88
Primus, W., 113, 117
Proch, K.O., 80, 343–344
Public Law 93–247, 196

Rabb, J., 468
Raboy, B., 389
Rainwater, L., 120
Randolph, K.A., 323
Rapp, C.A., 68, 435, 448–449
Rasmussen, R.A., 158
Rector, F., 201
Redl, F., 411
Reed, R.B., 211
Reid, J.B., 342
Reid, T., 162
Reid, W.J., 156
Reilly, T., 438
Reinhart, J., 214
Reinherz, H., 468
Reppucci, N.D., 184–185
Reschovsky, A., 113
Resnick, M., 28
Resnick, R.A., 221
Reuter, P., 53
Reynolds, A.J., 250–253
Reynolds, B., 21
Rhodes, W.A., 72
Rice, J.M., 271
Richman, H., 260
Ricketts, W., 310

Rigler, D., 148
Rindfleisch, N., 129, 316, 468
Rinsley, D.B., 417
Ritchie, K.L., 154
Rittner, B., 438
Rivara, F.P., 140
Rivard, J., 285, 287, 290
Rivest, M., 290
Robin, M.H., 161, 192
Robinson, C., 391
Roche, A.F., 211
Roditti, M.G., 250
Rodrieguez, M., 86
Rodwell, M.K., 130, 449, 461
Roff, J.D., 291
Rogers, C.M., 185
Roman, N.P., 323
Rome, S.H., 445
Rose, S.D., 342
Rosenbaum, A., 154
Rosenbaum, J., 108
Rosenberg, M.S., 11
Ross, S., 154
Rothman, D., 410
Rothman, J., 50, 436
Roundy, L.M., 186, 190
Rowland, M., 273
Rowse, D., 392
Rush, F., 173
Russell, D.E., 176–177
Russell, D.E.H., 183
Russell, M., 166, 439, 441–442
Russell, S.J., 317
Russo, E.M., 364
Russo, R.J., 85
Rutter, M., 11, 157, 216, 223
Ryan, A.S., 74, 313, 350
Ryan, P., 86, 468
Rycroft, J.R., 307, 323, 441
Rydell, C.P., 258
Rykus, J.R., 316–317, 336
Rzepnicki, T.L., 10, 23, 143, 145, 242, 268, 270,
    290, 292, 357, 472, 475

Saleebey, D., 68, 85
Salus, M.K., 451
Salzinger, S., 156
Samost, L., 242
Sanchirico, A., 317
Sandefur, G.D., 370
Sanders, B., 217

Sanders, M., 258
Sands, R.G., 350
Sanford, L.T., 173
Sasser, J.E., 54
Savage, C., 52
Savin-Williams, R.C., 309
Sawitsky, K., 458
Scannapieco, M., 347, 349, 353, 355
Schaaf, K.K., 469
Schellenbach, C.J., 275
Schene, P., 146, 458
Schene, P.A., 144
Scheper-Hughes, N., 149
Schinke, S.P., 67–68, 416
Schiraldi, V., 51
Schkade, L., 448
Schlesinger, E.G., 71
Schlosberg, S., 81
Schmerl, E., 270
Schmidt, A.W., 385
Schneider, D., 174
Schoech, D., 448
Schoenwald, S.K., 273
Scholz, J., 121
Schopler, J.H., 421
Schorr, D., 249
Schorr, L., 8, 249
Schorr, L.B., 5, 57, 79, 258, 435
Schriver, J.M., 70
Schroeder, A.D., 300–301, 311, 374
Schroeder, A.G., 143, 166
Schudson, C.B., 160
Schuerman, J.R., 23, 242, 253, 285, 290, 292, 357, 480
Schultz, K.G., 160, 191–192
Schultze, L., 273
Schwartz, I.M., 51, 141, 407, 425
Schweinhart, L.J., 252, 404
Scott, S., 291
Sebes, J., 275
Sedlak, A.J., 140, 151–152, 155–157, 167, 175, 183, 198, 219, 259, 461, 465
Seech, M., 140
Seeley, J.W., 216, 218, 469
Seelig, W.R., 448
Segal, E.C., 376
Segal, Z., 186
Selznick, P., 433
Sgroi, S.M., 184
Shadoin, L.M., 272
Shalala, D.E., 3

Shanok, S., 468
Shapiro, D., 281, 388
Shapiro, I., 28–29
Shapiro, V., 243
Shinn, E., 22, 73, 79–80, 267–268, 270, 300, 320, 322
Shireman, J.F., 390
Shulman, L., 86
Shyne, A.W., 166, 271, 300–301, 311, 374
Sia, C.C.J., 247
Sicfert, K., 141
Siegel, L., 447
Silver, J.A., 309
Silverman, A., 468
Silverman, F.N., 460, 468
Simmons, B., 402
Simms, M.D., 306
Skerl, J., 392
Skinner, L.J., 186
Slingerland, W.H., 297, 373
Small, R., 421, 426
Small, R.W., 343, 351, 430
Smeeding, T., 120
Smith, C., 154
Smith, J., 103
Smith, L.L., 281
Smith, S.L., 396–397, 400–401
Smith, T., 178
Social Care Group (Department of Health), 72
Soler, M., 51
Solnit, A.J., 11, 23, 470
Solomon, B., 86
Sorosky, A.D., 366
Sosin, M., 323
Sourcebook of Criminal Justice Statistics, 53
Spasser, M., 271
Spath, R., 250
Spaulding, W.J., 407, 412, 424
Spearly, J.L., 67
Spence, M., 242
Spencer, J.W., 468
Spencer, M., 397
Spinetta, J., 148
Spoth, R., 258
Springer, J.F., 59
Squadrito, E., 140
Stack, C., 84, 221, 349
Staff, E., 340
Stalling, R.Y., 354
Starfield, B., 103
Stark, D., 257

Starling, S.P., 244
Starr, R., Jr., 480
State of California Department of Social Services, 389
Steele, B.F., 460, 468
Stein, H.F., 149
Stein, T., 29, 227, 454, 462, 473–474
Stein, T.J., 10, 56, 74, 143, 145, 163, 166, 302, 309, 472, 475
Steinbook, B., 140
Steiner, G., 25
Stern, L., 149, 156, 291
Sternberg, K.J., 192
Stevenson, C.S., 166
Stevenson, K.M., 7, 482
Stewart, E.S., 347
Stoesz, D., 161, 470
Stovall, B.M., 314
Stratton, C., 156
Straus, M.A., 136, 152–154
Stroul, B.A., 16
Struckman-Johnson, D., 290
Struening, E.L., 323
Struhsaker Schatz, M., 343
Strzelecki, S.C., 415, 418
Stuart, R.B., 280
Study of the National Incidence and Prevalence of Child Abuse and Neglect, 201
Sturkie, K., 222
Styfco, S., 252
Subramanian, K., 249
Succop, R., 214
Sullivan, M., 271
Summer, L., 122
Susser, E., 323
Sussman, A., 460
Svirsky, A., 272
Sweany, S.L., 167
Sweet, J.J., 221
Sweet, M.A., 242

Tabbert, W., 7, 482
Tajima, E., 154
Takas, M., 350
Taplin, P., 156
Tasker, F., 389
Tatara, T., 1, 52, 55, 269–270, 305
Tatelbaum, R., 243
Taylor, D.A., 412, 415
Taylor, D.K., 242
Taylor, G.E., Jr., 417

Taylor, M.S., 447
Taylor, R., 196–197
Taylor, R.B., 425
Teare, R.J., 438
Temporary Assistance to Needy Families (TANF), 16
Terry, T., 185
Testa, M.F., 269, 350
Thoburn, J., 75
Thomas, D.L., 414
Thomas, E.C., 436
Thomas, G., 435
Thomas, M.P., 459
Thomlison, B., 319
Torres, H., 140
Tower, C., 173
Towles, C., 58
Tracy, E.M., 52, 66–68, 79, 263, 265, 275, 416, 444
Tremitiere, B., 394–395, 397
Tremitiere, W.C., 397
Trieschman, A., 421–422
Tripodi, T., 427
Trivette, C.M., 79
Trout, B.A., 315, 317, 319
Tucker, J., 321
Tupling, C., 223
Turbett, J.P., 136

Uquiza, A.J., 158
The Urban Institute, 117
Urban Systems Research and Engineering, 401
U.S. Advisory Board on Child Abuse and Neglect, 244, 258, 472
U.S. Bureau of the Census, 25–27, 101, 109, 116
U.S. Bureau of Justice Statistics, 54
U.S. Children's Bureau, 1, 19, 168, 269, 425, 435, 463
U.S. Code, 49–50
U.S. Department of Health, Education and Welfare (USDHEW), 175, 197, 461
U.S. Department of Health and Human Services, 1, 131, 136–137, 139, 141, 168, 219, 269, 351, 373, 422–423, 461–464, 466–467
U.S. Department of Labor, 106–107
U.S. General Accounting Office, 8, 56, 235–237, 306, 411–412
U.S. Government Accounting Office (GAO), 41–42, 231, 258, 262, 431

U.S. House of Representatives, 13, 27, 98, 111–112, 114, 119
Usher, C.L., 323

Valentine, D., 156
Van Kammen, W.B., 291
Van Meter, M.J.S., 271, 281
VanderMey, B.J., 186
Vanderwoerd, J., 68, 157, 236–237, 258
Veronico, A., 392
Vogeltanz, N.D., 177
Vondra, J., 147–151

Wade, J., 321, 341
Wagner, D., 140
Wagner, M., 448
Wahler, R.G., 156
Wakefield, J.C., 68
Wald, M., 23, 269, 302–303, 309
Waldfogel, J., 161–164, 434, 470–472
Walker, C.E., 184, 186, 469
Walker, E., 185
Walker, P.J., 7, 482
Wallin, J.A., 449
Walsh, J., 258
Walton, E., 340, 357
Walton, J., 393
Walton, W.K., 340, 357
Ward, M., 390
Warner, T.W., 143
Warren, B.L., 87
Warren, J., 88
Warsh, R., 80, 87, 317, 331–332, 335–336, 340, 344, 360, 473
Waterman, R.H., Jr., 375
Waternan, R.H., 433
Waters, M., 26
Watkins, M., 68
Watkins, S.A., 459
Watson, K.W., 87
Wattenberg, E., 28
Weber, R., 412, 415
Webster, D., 317, 324, 350–351, 372, 387, 418, 424
Wedel, K.R., 449
Wedeven, T., 321
Weeks, N.B., 369
Weikart, D.P., 404
Weil, M., 81, 436
Weil, M.O., 86
Weinrott, M.R., 342

Weiss, H., 236, 284
Weiss, H.B., 290
Weissbourd, B., 72, 79, 236–237, 249, 258, 435
Weisz, J.R., 290
Wells, K., 290, 291, 412, 415, 418, 422, 426–427
Wells, S., 462, 474
Wells, S.J., 140
Westefelt, A.H., 323
Westerfelt, A., 321
Westerfelt, H., 323
Wheeler, W., 381
White, K.R., 350
Whitehead, K.R., 221
Whitley, D.M., 350
Whitmore, W.H., 367
Whittaker, J.K., 66–68, 80, 85–86, 235–236, 263, 265, 275, 410, 412, 415–417, 420–422, 426–427, 429–430
Whittington, D., 290, 426
Wiehe, V.R., 157, 448
Wiencek, P., 468
Wilcox, B.L., 67
Wilde, J.A., 22
Williams, A., 235
Williams, D.P., 199, 205, 469
Williams, W., 436
Williamson, M., 161
Wilson, D., 162
Wilson, D.B., 348, 353
Wilson, D.R., 417
Wiltse, K.T., 74
Winterfeld, A., 7
Wisconsin General Laws, 367
Wittenburg, D.C., 108
Wodarski, J., 438
Wodarski, J.S., 207, 480
Wolf, S., 178
Wolfe, D.A., 199–200
Wolfe, M., 389
Wolfe, P.B., 323
Wolfensberger, W., 275
Wolins, M., 408, 421
Wong, Y.L.I., 339
Wood, J.M., 140
Wooden, K., 425
Woods, P.K., 385
Woolf, G.D., 304
Wozner, Y., 406
Wright, A., 417
Wright, B.R.E., 323

Wu, D., 401
Wulczyn, F., 269, 271, 424
Wulczyn, F.H., 1, 13, 272, 305, 308, 310–312, 325, 339, 346, 355–356, 359, 373
Wyatt, E., 412, 415
Wyatt, G.E., 176–177
Wynn, J., 260
Wynn, J.R., 255
Wynne, S.F., 316

Yegidis, B., 482
Yeung, W., 103
Yinger, J., 108
Yllo, K., 154
Yorke, B., 350
Young, L.R., 460
Young, N., 8

Youssef, R.M., 130
Yuan, Y.T., 140, 290
Yule, W., 223

Zainaldin, J.S., 367
Zastrow, C., 70
Zebell, N., 158
Zeidman, D., 272, 359
Zeller, D., 352
Zhu, K., 250
Zigler, E., 149, 156, 249, 252, 275
Zirps, F.A., 448
Zlotnick, J.L., 437, 440
Zuravin, S., 196–197, 201–202, 227, 317, 354, 480
Zuskin, R., 353
Zwimpfer, D.M., 381

Subject Index

Abecedarian Project, 251
Achievement Place, 411
ACTION for Child Protection, 479
Adoption 2002, 377
Adoption (*see also specific legislation*)
  benefits, 402–403
  black market, 381–382
  challenges, 402–403
  Code of Hammurabi and, 366
  community support and, 403
  cost effectiveness of, 402
  criminal background checks and, 46
  demand for, 389–390
  foster parent, 390–391
  geographic barriers to, 44
  history of, 366–369
  illegal, 381–382
  incentive payments, 35–36, 43
  information sharing, 382–384
  legislation, 369–378
    Adoption 2002, 377
    Adoption Assistance and Child Welfare Act
      of 1980, 364, 373
    Adoption and Safe Families Act of 1997
      and, 377–378
    Indian Child Welfare Act of 1978, 370–
      373
    Inter-Ethnic Adoption Provisions Act of
      1996, 376–377
    Multi-Ethnic Placement Act of 1994, 376–
      377, 386, 388, 392
    overview, 369–370
    Safe and Stable Families Act, 378
    subsidy policy and issues, 374–376
  matching parents and children, 386–389
  nontraditional, 389–390
  numbers, by state, 365–366
  open, 385–386
  overview, 363
  parents, 389–395
  paths to, 378–381
  permanency planning and, 395

planning for child, 395–396
postplacement services, 396–399
preservation services, 400–402
recruitment of adoptive parents, 391–395
types of, 363–364, 366
wrongful, 382–385
Adoption Assistance and Child Welfare Act of
    1980 (PL 96–272) (AACWA)
  adoption and, 364, 373
  Adoption and Safe Families Act of 1997 and,
    42, 45–46
  agency mission and philosophy and, 433
  family reunification and, 330
  Family-Based Services and, 268
  foster care and, 302, 308
  implementation challenges, 56, 61
  judicial case review and, 474
  liability and, 454
  permanence principle and, 11
  permanency planning and, 74–77
  policy context for child welfare and, 38–41
  "reasonable efforts" clause of, 76–77, 273
Adoption and Foster Care Analysis and Report-
    ing System (AFCARS), 47–48, 305–306,
    364
Adoption and Safe Families Act of 1997 (PL
    105–89) (AFSA)
  adoption and, 377–378
    incentive payments and, 35–36
  Adoption Assistance and Child Welfare Act of
    1980 and, 42, 45–46
  aftercare services and, 342
  agency mission and philosophy and, 434
  family reunification and, 360
  Family-Based Services and, 268
  foster care and, 302, 324
  implementation challenges, 61
  judicial review and, 474
  kinship care and, 349–350
  permanence principle and, 11
  permanency planning and, 75
  policy context for child welfare and, 42–48

Adoption and Safe Families Act of 1997(*cont.*)
  Promoting Safe and Stable Families Program
    and, 35–36
  provisions of, 42–48
Adoptive Families of America (AFA), 397
Advocacy, 84
Aftercare services, 340–342
Aid to Families with Dependent Children
    (AFDC), 33, 36, 49–50, 109–113, 117–
    118
AIDS, 53, 55
Alameda Project, 74
American Academy of Pediatrics, 247
American Association for Protecting Children,
    60, 195
American Civil Liberties Union (ACLU), 269,
    455
American Humane Association (AHA), 4, 162,
    459
American Psychological Association, 410–411
American Public Human Services Association,
    17
American Public Welfare Association, 60, 456
Anger management, 158–160
Annie E. Casey Foundation, 256–257, 411
"Apathy-futility" syndrome, 202
Association for Baccalaureate Program Direc-
    tors (BPD), 446
Avance Parent-Child Educators, 250

"Baby Jessica" case, 369
Balanced Budget Act of 1997, 120
Behavioral health care, 230
Behavioral Sciences Institute, 453
Berkeley Planning Associates, 162, 193
Black market adoption, 381–382
Blaming the victim, 148–149
Block grants, 33, 35–36, 49
Bowen Center, 207, 270–271
Boystown, 315, 414, 422
Boysville, 422, 427
"Bracket creep," 116
Breakdown, foster home, 323–324
British National Children's Bureau, 414
Bureau of Indian Affairs (BIA), 38
Burnout, worker, 452–453

California Social Work Education Center (CAL-
    SWEC), 446
California Youth Connection, 88
Carolinas Project, 430

"Carrot and stick" approach, 38–41
Carter administration, 301
Case targeting, 291
Casey Family Programs, 4, 315, 320–321, 324,
    419
Categorical services and benefits, 23–24
Center for Family Life's Preventive Services
    Program, 248–250
Center for the Future of Children (Packard
    Foundation), 240
Centers for Disease Control and Prevention, 53
Chicago Child Parent Center Program, 251
Child Abuse and Neglect Prevention and Treat-
    ment Act (amended), 134, 151
Child Abuse Prevention and Treatment Act of
    1974 (PL 93–247), 29, 33, 460–461
Child at Risk Field (CARF), 479
Child maltreatment (*see* Maltreatment)
Child nutrition programs, 114
Child poverty
  causes of continuing high levels of, 101–102
  comparisons, international, 102–103
  maltreatment as consequence of, 102–104
  measuring, 99
  policy
    child support system for single-parent fam-
      ilies, 119–120
    events related to, 96
    government income support programs and
      taxes, 115–119
    increasing market incomes, 105–109
    lessons from, 120
    overview, 104–105
    supplementing market incomes, 109–115
  race and, 100–101
  tax policies and, 114–119
  trends in, 99–100
  type of family and, 100–101
Child protection, family preservation and, 23
  (*see also* Child Protective Services [CPS])
Child Protective Services (CPS)
  adolescent victims and, 167
  assessments, 482
  case screening and, 474–475
  conflicting roles in, 161
  court involvement in, 473–474
  cultural issues in, 167, 480–482
  decision-making stages and, 146
  focus of, 10
  historical overview of, 458–461
  improvement in programs and, 163–167

intake processes and, 143–145
    challenges, 469–475
intervention research and, lack of, 161–162
judicial case review and, 474
liability and, agency and worker, 163
Little Mary Ellen case and, 459
maltreatment and, 132, 141–146
mission of, 141–142
problems of, major, 471–472
risk assessment and, 474–475
scope of, 141–143
workload standards and, 162–163
Child sexual abuse (CSA), 176–177 (*see also*
    Sexual abuse)
Child Support Enforcement Amendments of
    1984, 119
Child Support Enforcement program, 119
Child Welfare League of America (CWLA), 43,
    60, 162, 303–304, 309, 313–314, 366,
    416, 430, 446, 478
Child welfare services (*see also* Organizational
    requisites for child welfare services; *specif-
    ic types*)
    challenges, 13–14
    child protection versus family preservation,
        23
    demonstration waivers, 3, 47
    expense versus gain in, 25
    goals of, 9–13
        child well-being, 12–13
        family well-being, 13
        permanence, 11–12
        safety, 9–11
    in-home, family-centered versus out-of-home,
        substitute-care approaches, 24
    intake processes, 143
    mission of, 8–9
    philosophical underpinnings, 4–8
        child and family well-being, 4–5
        child safety and family support, 4
        community supports for families, 5
        coordination of system resources, 8
        cultural competence, 6–7
        family-centered services, 5–6
        system accountability and timeliness, 7–8
    practice transformations, 14–19
        accountability, increased, 16
        funding mechanisms, restructured, 17, 47
        overview, 14–15
        partnerships with public health and sub-
            stance abuse treatment providers, 16

safety and permanency planning, reempha-
    sis on, 15
service delivery models, innovative, 15
system of care approaches, 16
prevention versus treatment, 24–25
as resource for families in America, 1–3
risk assessment issues in, 476–480
universal versus categorical and targeted ser-
    vices and benefits, 23–24
waiver states, 18–19
Child Well-Being scale, 478
Childhood Level of Living Scale, 207
Children (*see also specific services for*)
    gay, 309–310
    income support for, 109–110
    interests of, 80–81
    lesbian, 309–310
    psychosocial functioning of, 346–347
    at risk, 157
    roles of, 88
Children in Need of Parents (Maas and Engler),
    22
Children Services Division (CSD), 272
Children's Defense Fund, 26, 60
Children's Health Insurance Program (CHIP), 29
Civil Rights Act of 1964, 313
Clients, roles of, 86–87
Code of Hammurabi, 366
Common human needs, 58
Communal model of family, 80
Community-based services
    in continuum of services, 81–82
    family resource and education services and,
        253–258
Competence-centered perspective, 68–70, 84–
    86
Comprehensive Employment and Training Act,
    122
Concrete services, 208, 279
Concurrent planning, 77–78
Congressional Budget Office, 114
Contingency Fund for State Welfare Programs,
    47
Continuum of services, establishing
    biological and foster parents, roles of, 87–88
    children and youths, roles of, 88
    competence perspective, adopting, 84–86
    family's environment, restructuring, 82–84
    neighborhood- or community-based services,
        emphasizing, 81–82
    practitioners and clients, roles of, 86–87

"Cosby Show" (television show), 26
Council on Social Work Education, 446
County Child Welfare Directors, 446
"Creaming off," 414
Criminal background checks, 46
Cruelty to Children Act, 458
Cultural competence, 6–7, 438–439
Cultural issues, 6–7, 167, 438–439, 480–482
Cunnilingus, 172
"CWLA Standards of Excellence for Family
    Foster Care" (CWLA), 303
CWLA's Kinship Care Policy and Practice Com-
    mittee, 349, 352–353

Dartington Research Group (Great Britain), 418
Daughters and Sons United, 186
Decennial census (1990), 25–26
Demonstration waivers of child welfare, 3, 47
Developmental perspective, 70–72
Diagnostics and Statistical Manual (DSM-IV),
    147–148
Distrust, 408
Drug abuse, 17, 52, 54

Early Head Start, 226
Earned Income Credit (EIC), 107, 109–110,
    114–118, 120, 123
Ecological model of maltreatment, 150
Ecological perspective, 65–68
Economic security for families with children
    "bracket creep" and, 116
    challenges, 121–124
        earnings, improving, 121–122
        nonwelfare income support, improving,
            122–124
    economic status of family, 96–102
        income trends, 96–98
        poverty among children, 98–102
    maltreatment and, 102–104
    overview, 95
    policy to reduce child poverty and, 104–120
        child support system for single-parent fam-
            ilies, 119–120
        events related to, 96
        government income support programs and
            taxes, 115–119
        increasing market incomes, 105–109
        lessons from, 120
        overview, 104–105
        supplementing market incomes, 109–115
Edna McConnell Clark Foundation, 411

"Effect-of-the-child-on-the-caregiver" model of
    maltreatment, 149–150
Effective Participatory Practice (Connolly and
    McKenzie), 83
Elmira PEIP, 241–242
Emotional abuse, 160, 219 (*see also* Psychologi-
    cal abuse)
Emotional neglect, 219–220 (*see also* Neglect)
Empirical-predictors method, 477–478
Exhibitionism, 171

Failure to thrive (FTT)
    defining, 209–211
    diagnosing, 209–211
    family dynamics in nonorganic, 213–214
    impact on children, 214
    organic versus nonorganic, 212–213
    treatment of nonorganic, 214–215
False allegations
    of physical abuse, 160–161
    of sexual abuse, 191–192
Families First, 263
Family (*see also* Economic security for families
    with children)
    assessment scales, 478
    as central unit of attention, 78–79
    communal model of, 80
    environment, restructuring, 82–84
    extended, involving, 83–84
    in family-centered services, 78–81
    individualistic model of, 80
    issues and trends, 26–29
        composition, 26–28
        health care and insurance, 29–30
        income, 28–29, 96–98
        single-parent, 119–120
    ties, preservation of, 79–80
Family Assessment Form, 249
Family Empowerment Training Program, 342–343
Family preservation
    child protection and, 23
    short-term foster care versus, 356–358
Family Preservation and Support Services Pro-
    gram (PL 103–66), 43, 48
Family Resource Centers (FRCs), 235
Family Resource Coalition, 235–236
Family reunification
    Adoption Assistance and Child Welfare Act of
        1980 and, 330
    Adoption and Safe Families Act of 1997 and,
        360

aftercare service and, 340–342
case example, 333–334
challenges, 360–361
child's psychosocial functioning and, 346–347
competencies, 335–338
defining, 330–332
dilemmas, recurring, 359–360
effectiveness of, 338–347
exit from foster care and, 339–340
from foster care, 355–359
    family preservation versus short-term foster care, 356–358
    long-term foster care, 359
    overview, 355–356
    postreunification, 358–359
guidelines, underlying, 332, 334–335
issues, recurring, 359–360
kinship care and, 347–355
    Adoption and Safe Families Act of 1997 and, 349–350
    advisory panel, 44
    defining, 349
    increase in, 350–352
    overview, 347–348
    practice standards, 352–353
    research considerations, 354–355
overview, 330
parental visiting and, 343–345
principles, underlying, 332, 334–335
reentry into foster care and, 345–346
training parents and, 342–343
Family Risk scale, 478
Family Support Act of 1988, 111, 119
Family support model, 82
Family support programs
benefits of, 258–259
defining, 234–239
diverse, 231–234
resource and education services, 239–258
    community-based approaches, 253–258
    needs for, 253
    other innovative programs, 244–253
    overview, 239–240
    perinatal and maternal health derived programs, 240–244
Substitute Care versus, 436
Family Teaching Model at Boystown, 414
Family Unification Program of the Housing and Urban Development (HUD) Department, 56

Family-Based Services (FBS)
Adoption and Safe Families Act of 1997 and, 268
challenges to implementation, 291–294
characteristics of, 263–264
Child Welfare Act of 1980 and, 268
events and projects related to, 274
growth in, 229
history of, 265–275
    current programs, 273–275
    early programs, 265–267
    1960–1980, 267–271
    recent developments, 271–273
Intensive Family Preservation Services versus, 263–264
intervention, 275–290
    clinical, 275–278
    concrete services, 279
    empirical data on, 285–290
    limitations and pitfalls, 284–285
    philosophy shaping, 279–284
    policy, 285
Multi-ethnic Placement Act of 1995 and, 268
outcome criteria, 288–289
overview, 262–263
permanency planning and, 268
target populations, 264–265
term, 265
Family-centered services
applying, 78–81
continuum of, establishing, 81–88
    biological and foster parents, roles of, 87–88
    children and youths, roles of, 88
    competence perspective, adopting, 84–86
    family environment, restructuring, 82–84
    neighborhood- or community-based services, emphasizing, 81–82
    practitioners and clients, roles of, 86–87
family in, focus on, 78–81
foster care and, 89–91
framework, conceptual, 65–78
    competence-centered perspective, 68–70
    developmental perspective, 70–72
    ecological perspective, 65–68
    permanency planning, 72–78
overview, 64
Federal Child Abuse Prevention and Treatment Act of 1974 (PL 93–237), 129–130
Federal Parent Locator Service, 47
Federal Register, 37

Fellatio, 172
Florida Mental Health Institute, 347
Follow Through program, 251
Fondling, 172
Food stamps, 109, 115
Fost-adoption, 390–391
Foster care (*see also specific legislation*)
    adolescents leaving, 322–323
    Adoption Assistance and Child Welfare Act of
        1980 and, 302, 308
    Adoption and Safe Families Act of 1997 and,
        302, 324
    age distribution, 307–309
    breakdown, 323–324
    census, daily, 269
    challenges, 13, 326–327
    criminal background checks and, 46
    defining, 303–304
    disruption, 323–324
    effectiveness of, 319–324
    evolution of, 297–303
        early history, 297, 300
        legal framework, 301–303
        milestones, 298–299
        permanency planning and, 300–301
        policy framework, 301–303
    exit from, 339–340
    family-centered services and, 89–91
    gay and lesbian youths, 309–310
    impact of, 319–322
    Independent Living Initiative and, 302, 307
    Indian Child Welfare Act of 1978 and, 302,
        313–314
    Inter-Ethnic Adoption Provisions Act of 1996
        and, 302
    living arrangements of children in, 408
    long-term, 359
    minority youths, 310–314
    Multi-ethnic Placement Act of 1994 and, 302,
        313, 316
    numbers in care, 305–306
    overview, 297
    parents
        adoption by, 390–391
        roles of, 87–88
        training, 318–319
    permanency planning and, 300–301, 324
    professionalization of foster parents, 314–
        318
    purpose of, 303–305
    reasons for placement, 306
    reentry into, 345–346
    reunification from, 355–359
        family preservation versus short-term fos-
            ter care, 356–358
        long-term foster care, 359
        overview, 355–356
        postreunification, 358–359
    same-race, 6
    short-term, family preservation versus, 356–
        358
    status, current, 324–326
    Title XX Amendments to the Social Security
        Act of 1975 and, 302
    training social workers and foster parents,
        318–319
    in U.S. (1977 vs. 1994), 2
Foster Care Independence Act (H.R. 3443), 50
Foster Family-based Treatment Association, 315
Freeing Children for Permanent Placement pro-
    ject, 73
Funding mechanisms, 17, 47–48, 244–245

Gay parents, 389
Gay youths, 309–310
General Accounting Office, 44, 235–236
Goals of child welfare services
    child well-being, 12–13
    family well-being, 13
    permanence, 11–12
    safety, 9–11
Government Accounting Office (GAO), 42
Group care (*see* Residential group care services)
Group prostheses, 208–209
Guardianship, standby, 44–45

Harm Standard, 465
Hawaii Healthy Start program, 243, 245–248
Head Start, 23, 226, 251, 404
Health care and insurance, 29–30, 123, 230,
    240–244
Healthy Start, 231, 243, 245–248
High/Scope Perry Preschool, 241, 251, 253, 404
HIPPY, 226
HIV and children, 53, 55
Home and Community Treatment Team, 270
Home visitation, 258
HOMEBUILDERS™, 79, 263, 270, 400, 453
Hudson, Achenbach, and Child Well-Being
    scales, 449
Humane Society, 459
Hyde Schools, 421–422

Illegal adoption, 381–382
Imprisonment of women, 52–54
In-home, family-centered approaches, 24
Incest, 187–190
Incidence, prevalence versus, 131–132
Income assistance, 109
Income trends, 28–29, 96–98
Independent Living Initiative (PL 99–272), 48–49, 302, 307
Indian Child Welfare Act of 1978 (PL 95–608) (ICWA)
  adoption and, 370–373
  foster care and, 302, 313–314
  institutional maltreatment and, 129
  policy context for child welfare and, 34, 36–38, 41
Indicated preventive intervention, 231
Individualistic model of family, 80
Infant Health and Development Program, 250
Institutional maltreatment, 129
Insurance, health, 29, 122–123
Intake processes
  Child Protective Services, 143–145
    challenges, 469–475
  child welfare services, 143
Integrative model of maltreatment, 150
Intensive Family Preservation Services (IFPS)
  comparison- and control-group studies, 286–287
  Family-Based Services versus, 263–264
  growth in, 229
Intensive Family Services, 263
Inter-Ethnic Adoption Provisions Act of 1996 (IAP)
  adoption and, 376–377
  foster care and, 302
    same-race, 6
  policy context for child welfare and, 41–42
Intercourse, vaginal or anal, 172
Interdependent living, 307
Interests of children, 80–81
International Conference on Psychological Abuse of Children and Youth (1983), 215–216
Intervention (*see specific child welfare services*)

Job Training Partnership's Act (JTPA), 106–107
John H. Chafee Foster Care Independence Program, 50
Judicial case review, 474
Juvenile Justice and Delinquency Prevention Act of 1974 (PL 93–415) (JJDPA), 50–52

Kinship care
  Adoption and Safe Families Act of 1997 and, 349–350
  advisory panel, 44
  defining, 349
  increase in, 350–352
  overview, 347–348
  practice standards, 352–353
  research considerations, 354–355
Kinship Care Policy and Practice Committee (CWLA), 349, 352–353
Kissing, 172

Learning, Earnings and Parenting (LEAP), 106
"Leave It To Beaver" (television show), 26
Legislation (*see specific types*)
Lesbian parents, 389
Lesbian youths, 309–310
Liability, agency and worker, 163, 454–456
Little Mary Ellen case, 459
Loneliness, alleviating client, 207–208

Maltreatment (*see also* Neglect; Physical abuse; Psychological abuse; Sexual abuse)
  challenges, 160–163
  child poverty and, consequence of, 102–104
  Child Protective Services and, 132, 141–146
  data on, statistical, 134–140
    early studies, 134–136
    recent, 136–139
    recidivism, 139–140
    service responses, 139
  defining, 128–130
  economic security for families with children and, 102–104
  "effective-of-the-child-on-the-caregivers" model of, 149–150
  effects of, 468–469
  factors contributing to, theoretical perspective, 147–157
    integrative or ecological model, 150–151
    overview, 147
    physical abuse contributing factors and, 154–157
    physical abuse reporting and rates, 151–152
    protective factors, 157
    psychiatric or psychological model, 147–148
    social-situational model, 149–150
    sociological model, 148–149
    spousal abuse, 153–154

Maltreatment (*cont.*)
 fatal, 140–141
 incidence of, in U.S., 131–134
 institutional, 129
 integrative model of, 150
 in out-of-home care, 468
 overview, 128
 psychiatric or psychological model of, 149–150
 psychological, 227
 reporting, 132–134, 136–137, 140–141, 461–466
 serious, 140–141
 severity, 140–141
 social-situational model of, 149–150
 sociological model of, 148–149
 special groups and, 467–469
 statistics, 466–467
 types of, 134–135, 137–139
 victims, by state, 138–139
Marginalization, 408–411
Maternal health derived programs, 240–244
Maternal Infant Health Outreach Worker Project, 250
Matrix approaches, 476–477
Medicaid, 109, 113
Medical care coverage, 29, 122–123
Medina Children's Services, 400
Mendota Mental Health Institute, 270
Mental health, 230
Minority youths, 310–314, 467–468
Mission of child welfare services, 8–9
Model Approach to Partnership in Parenting (MAPP), 395
Multi-Ethnic Placement Act of 1994 (PL 103–382) (MEPA)
 adoption and, 376–377, 386, 388, 392
 Family-Based Services and, 268
 foster care and, 302, 313, 316
 policy context for child welfare and, 41–42
 same-race foster care and, 6
Multisystemic Family Preservation Services (MST), 273

National Academy of Sciences Panel on Research on Child Abuse and Neglect, 240
National Association of Black Social Workers, 386
National Association of Deans and Directors of Schools of Social Work (NADD), 446
National Association of Public Child Welfare

Administrators (NAPCWA), 4, 57, 142, 446
National Association of Social Workers (NASW), 60, 313, 446, 456
National Center of Child Abuse and Neglect Data System (NCANDS), 133, 136–137, 219
National Center on Child Abuse and Neglect (NCCAN), 29, 136, 461
National Commission on Family Foster Care, 304
National Conference of Commissioners on Uniform State Laws, 369
National Federation for Child Rescue Agencies, 459
National Foster Parent Association, 314
National Incidence Studies (NIS-1, -2, and -3), 132–133, 152, 155–156, 175, 195, 219, 461, 465–466
National Institute on Drug Abuse, 52
National Institute of Mental Health (NIMH), 411
National Resource Center on Family-Based Services, 273
National School Lunch Program (PL 101–147) (NSLP), 49
Neglect
 case example, 203–205
 causal typologies, 199–203
 challenges, 227–228
 defining, 129–130, 196–199
 emotional, 219–220
 failure to thrive and, 209–215
  defining, 209–211
  diagnosing, 209–211
  family dynamics in nonorganic, 213–214
  impact on children, 214
  organic versus nonorganic, 212–213
  treatment of nonorganic, 214–215
 overview, 196
 policy, 226–227
 reporting, 196–199, 461–466
 risk factors, 199–203
 subtypes, 198
 treatment, 205–209
Neighborhood Centers for Families, 82
Neighborhood-based services, 81–82
New Jobs Tax Credit, 121
Nonplacement services, 24
Nontraditional adoption, 389–390
North American Council on Adoptable Children (NACAC), 397–398

North American Post-Legal Adoption Committee, 397
Nutrition programs, 114

Office of Child Abuse Prevention, 235
Omnibus Reconciliation Act (PL 97–35), 33
One Church, One Child program, 392
Open adoption, 385–386
Oregon Permanency Planning Project, 73–74, 268
Oregon State Department of Human Resources, 73
Organizational requisites for child welfare services
  agency mission and philosophy, establishing clear, 433–435
  appraisal methods, 447–448
  cultural competence, 438–439
  evaluation of services, 448–450
  liability, agency and worker, 454–456
  overview, 431–432
  personnel recruitment, selection, and training, 437–439
  professionalizing staff, challenges, 439–447
    caseloads, high worker, 440–441
    education and training, opportunities for professional, 443–444
    educational reforms, need for, 445–447
    public image, poor or controversial, 444–445
    qualifications, low minimal worker, 439–440
    salaries, low worker, 442–443
    turnover, high worker, 440–441
    working conditions, poor, 441–442
  program names and position titles, 435–436
  supervision, providing quality, 450–453
  technology, selection of effective, 436–437
OURS, Inc., 397
Out-of-home care, 24, 468
Out-of-home, substitute-care approaches, 24
Outcome domains, 9

Packard Foundation's Center for the Future of Children, 240
PACT program, 271
Parental prostheses, 208–209
Parental rights, 45, 80–81
Parental visiting, 343–345
Parenting, minimum standards of, 10–11
Parents

adoptive, 389–395
biological, roles of, 87–88
foster
  adoption by, 390–391
  professionalization of, 314–318
  roles of, 87–88
  training, 318–319
gay, 389
lesbian, 389
as resources, 85
Parents as Teachers, 250
Parents United, 186
"Pariah care," 408
People's Places, 315
Perinatal health derived programs, 240–244
Permanence as goal of child welfare services, 11–12
Permanency hearings, 45
Permanency planning
  adoption and, 395
  Adoption Assistance and Child Welfare Act of 1980 and, 74–77
  Adoption and Safe Families Act of 1997 and, 75
  concurrent, 77–78
  defining, 73
  emergence of, 73–74
  Family-Based Services and, 268
  foster care and, 300–301, 324
  framework for family-centered services and, 72–78
  legislation, federal, 74–76
  Oregon project, 268
  practice transformations and, 15
  status, current, 76–77
  support for, staff, 269
Perry Preschool, 241, 251, 253, 404
Personal Responsibility and Work Opportunity Reconciliation Act of 1996 (PL 104–193) (PRWORA)
  antipoverty impacts of government income support programs and taxes and, 115–119
  block grants and, 35–36, 49
  effect of, 113
  eligibility for Supplemental Security Income and, 114
  funding and, 47, 107, 111
  health care insurance and, 123
  Temporary Assistance to Needy Families and, 49

Philosophical underpinnings of child welfare
      services
   child and family well-being, 4–5
   child safety and family support, 4
   community supports for families, 5
   coordination of system resources, 8
   cultural competence, 6–7
   family-centered services, 5–6
   system accountability and timeliness, 7–8
Physical abuse (*see also* Maltreatment)
   challenges, 160–163
   contributing factors, 154–157
   false allegations of, 160–161
   overview, 145, 147
   reporting, 151–152, 461–466
   treatment, 157–160
Placement services, 24
Placing Out System of the New York Children's
      Aid Society, 297
Policy context for child welfare (*see also* Child
      poverty, policy)
   analysis framework, 58–59
   appropriations and, 35–36
   changes in, continuing, 55–57
   decennial census (1990) and, 25–26
   defined, 22–25
   family issues and trends, 26–29
   HIV and children, 53, 55
   imprisonment of women, 52–54
   legislation shaping, 29–52
      Adoption Assistance and Child Welfare Act
         of 1980, 38–41
      Adoption and Safe Families Act of 1997,
         42–48
      Aid to Families with Dependent Children,
         49–50
      Child Abuse Prevention and Treatment Act
         of 1974, 29, 33
      Family Preservation and Support Services
         Act of 1993, 48
      Foster Care Independence Act of 1999, 50
      Independent Living Initiative, 48–49
      Indian Child Welfare Act of 1978, 34, 36–
         38, 41
      Juvenile Justice and Delinquency Preven-
         tion Act of 1974, 50–52
      list of, 31–32
      Multi-ethnic Placement Act of 1994, 41–42
      Survivor's Insurance, 49–50
      Temporary Assistance to Needy Families,
         48–50

Title XX Amendments to the Social Securi-
      ty Act of 1975, 33–34
   overview, 21–22
   practice and, opportunities for, 57–59
   substance abuse, 52, 54
Pornography, 172
Postplacement services, 396–399
Postreunification services, 358–359
Poverty (*see* Child poverty)
Practitioners, roles of, 86–87
Preservation services, adoption, 400–402
Prevalence, incidence versus, 131–132
Prevention services (*see also* Family support
         program models; Family-Based Services
         [FBS]; Intensive Family Preservation Ser-
         vices [IFPS])
   framework for, 230–231
   indicated, 231
   as moral obligation, 254–255
   multifaceted, 259
   overview, 229
   psychological abuse, 222–224
   resource and education, 239–258
      community-based approaches, 253–258
      needs for, 253
      other innovative programs, 244–253
      overview, 239–240
      perinatal and maternal health derived pro-
         grams, 240–244
   selective, 230–231
   treatment versus, 24–25
   typology of programs, 231–239
      diversity of, 231–234
      family support programs, 234–239
   universal, 230
"Program Standards for Treatment Foster Care"
      (Foster Family-based Treatment Associa-
      tion), 315
Project RE-ED, 411, 422
Promoting Safe and Stable Families Program of
      1997 (PL 105–89), 22, 35–36, 75
Protective factors, 157
Protective Services Act, 458
PRYDE, 315
Psychiatric model of maltreatment, 147–148
Psychological abuse
   challenges, 227–228
   defining, 215–217
   family dynamics of, 220–222
   incidence of, 218–220
   overview, 195

policy, 227
prevention services, 222–224
risk factors, 220–222
treatment, 224–226
types of, 217–218
Psychological model of maltreatment, 147–148
Psychosocial functioning of child, 346–347
Public health treatment providers, 16
Public Law (PL) 83–280, 34
Public Law (PL) 93–237, 129–130
Public Law (PL) 93–247, (*see* Child Abuse Prevention and Treatment Act of 1974)
Public Law (PL) 93–415, 50–52
Public Law (PL) 95–608 (*see* Indian Child Welfare Act of 1978 [ICWA])
Public Law (PL) 96–272 (*see* Adoption Assistance and Child Welfare Act of 1980)
Public Law (PL) 97–35, 33
Public Law (PL) 99–272, 48–49, 302
Public Law (PL) 101–147, 49
Public Law (PL) 103–66, 43, 48
Public Law (PL) 103–382 (*see* Multi-ethnic Placement Act of 1994)
Public Law (PL) 104–193 (*see* Personal Responsibility and Work Opportunity Reconciliation Act of 1996)
Public Law (PL) 105–89 (*see* Adoption and Safe Families Act of 1997)
Purposeful case plans, 12

Race and child poverty, 100–101
Rand Corporation, 241, 259–260
Reagan, Ronald, 111
Recidivism, maltreatment, 139–140
Renewal Factor (Waterman), 375
Residential group care services
  ambivalence toward, 406–411
  challenges, 426–429
  defining, 406–407
  future, 429–430
  highlights of, historical, 409
  marginalization and, 408–411
  placement uses and costs, 424–426
  powerful environment of, 421–424
  research base for, 411–419
    controls, absence of, 413
    future directions, 416–419
    overview, 411–413
    sample selection, 414
    selection of outcome criteria, improper, 413

service units, poorly defined, 413
utility, lack of, 414–416
in U.S. (1977 vs. 1994), 2
varieties of, 419–426
Reunification of family (*see* Family reunification)
Risk assessment concept and issues, 476–482
Rural America Initiative Project, 250

Safe and Stable Families Act, 378
Safety as goal of child welfare services, 9–11
Safety planning for children, 15
Sawyer family case example, 333–334
Second National Conference on Family-Based Services, 451
Select Committee on Children, Youth and Families, 325
Selective preventive intervention, 230–231
Self-control skills, 158–160
Self-help groups, 85–86
Service delivery models, innovative, 15–16
Service responses to maltreatment, 139
Sexual abuse
  challenges, 191–193
  contributing factors, 178–179
  cunnilingus, 172
  defining, 171–173
    cross-cultural, 174–175
    federal versus professional, 173–174
  exhibitionism, 171
  false allegations of, 191–192
  fellatio, 172
  fondling, 172
  incest, 187–190
  incidence of, 175
  intercourse, vaginal or anal, 172
  kissing, 172
  models, explanatory, 179–183
  pornography, 172
  preconditions, 180–183
  prevalence of, 175–178
  risk factors, 178–179
  staff issues and, 193
  treatment, 183–191
    effectiveness of, 192–193
    incest, 187–190
    offenders, 186, 190–191
    victim, 183–186
  voyeurism, 171–172
Single-parent families, 119–120, 389
Small Business Job Protection Act, 377

Social action, 84
Social insurance, 109
Social workers, training of, 318–319 (*see also* Staff issues)
Social-situational model of maltreatment, 149–150
Societal abuse, 129
Society for the Prevention of Cruelty to Animals, 459
Sociological model of maltreatment, 148–149
Special groups and maltreatment, 467–469
Special Supplemental Food Program for Women, Infants and Children (WIC), 114, 241
Spousal abuse, 153–154
Staff issues
  burnout, 452–453
  practitioner-client roles, 86–87
  professional versus informal helpers, 82
  professional versus lay, 24
  professionalizing staff, challenges, 439–447
    caseloads, high worker, 440–441
    education and training, opportunities for, 443–444
    educational reforms, need for, 445–447
    public image, poor or controversial, 444–445
    qualification, low minimal worker, 439–440
    salaries, low worker, 442–443
    turnover, high worker, 440–441
    working conditions, poor, 441–442
  sexual abuse and, 193
  supervision, providing quality, 450–4453
  supervisor-staff ratios, 439
  workload standards, 162–163
"Standards of Excellence for Family Foster Care" (CWLA), 303
"Standard Review Instrument" (Foster Family-based Treatment Association), 315
Standards for Adoption Services (CWLA), 366
Stigmatization, 408–411
Subsidy policy and issues for adoption, 374–376
Substance abuse, 17, 52, 54
  treatment providers, 16
Substitute Care, 436
Supervision, providing quality, 450–453
Supplemental Security Income (SSI), 109, 114
Supportive Child Abuse Network (SCAN), 245, 270
Supreme Court, 114
Survivor's insurance, 49–50, 110

Targeted Jobs Tax Credit (TJTC), 105
Targeted services and benefits, 23–24
Taxpayer Relief Act of 1997, 124
Tax policies, 114–119, 124
Technology, selecting effective service, 436–437
Teenage Parent Demonstration (TPD), 106
Temporary Assistance to Needy Families (TANF), 48–50, 55–56, 109–113, 115, 122–123, 350
Theory-based interventions, 293
Title IV-A of the Social Security Act, 38–39
Title IV-B of the Social Security Act, 38–39, 56
Title IV-E of the Social Security Act, 14, 39, 43, 56, 302, 446
Title XX Amendments to the Social Security Act of 1975, 33–34, 302
Transitional relationships, 208
Treatment
  neglect, 205–209
    nonorganic, 214–215
  physical abuse, 157–160
  prevention services versus, 24–25
  psychological abuse, 224–226
  sexual abuse, 183–191
    effectiveness of, 192–193
    incest, 187–190
    offenders, 186, 190–191
    victim, 183–186
Tressler-Lutheran Agency, 398
Trust Funds, 244–245

Uniform Adoption Act (UAA), 369
United Kingdom, 129, 414, 418
United Way, 16
Universal preventive intervention, 230
Universal services, 23–24
University of California at Berkeley, 446
U.S. Children's Bureau, 407, 411, 478
U.S. Department of Health and Human Services (HHS), 44, 46–47, 393
U.S. Department of Housing and Urban Development (HUD), 56

Voluntary Cooperative Information Systems (VCIS), 2, 305
Voyeurism, 171–172

Waiver states, 18–19
Walker School for Children, 421–422
"Wednesday's Child," 393

Well-being of child as goal of child welfare services, 12–13
White House Conference on Children (1909), 410
"Who Cares" project, 414
Wisconsin Children's Code Commission, 367

"Within Our Reach" (Halpern), 60–61
Work Opportunity Tax Credit, 105
Workload standards, 162–163
Wrongful adoption, 382–385

Yale Child Welfare Research Program, 250